Madison County
Tennessee

COUNTY COURT
MINUTES

VOLUME 1

1821–1825

WPA RECORDS

Heritage Books
2024

HERITAGE BOOKS

AN IMPRINT OF HERITAGE BOOKS, INC.

Books, CDs, and more—Worldwide

For our listing of thousands of titles see our website
at
www.HeritageBooks.com

A Facsimile Reprint
Published 2024 by
HERITAGE BOOKS, INC.
Publishing Division
5810 Ruatan Street
Berwyn Heights, MD 20740

Originally published 1938

— Publisher's Notice —

Pages 136, 243, 275 are blank in this book;
they are not in the original book.

In reprints such as this, it is often not possible to remove
blemishes from the original. We feel the contents of this
book warrant its reissue despite these blemishes and
hope you will agree and read it with pleasure.

International Standard Book Number
Paperbound: 978-0-7884-9079-8

WPA RECORDS

The WPA Records are, for the most part, carbon copies of the original that was typed on onion skin paper during the Depression. Since these records were typed on poor machines by people who did not type well either and read by persons not always sure of the older handwritten material, the results are often less that perfect.

We have made every attempt to make as good a copy as can be made from these older papers. Sometimes there are water stains and burned edges around the paper.. This is the results of a fire at the home of one of the workers, Mrs. Penelope Allen, who was over most of the project.

The WPA Records are now very scattered between the State Archives, various Public and Private Libraries and other collections. Some day, there is a hope that all of these can be collected and stored in one place. In spite of their many mistakes and problems, these are still the most complete collection of Tennessee records found anywhere.

TENNESSEE

RECORDS OF MADISON COUNTY

MINUTE BOOK VOL. I (INDEX)
1821-1825

HISTORICAL RECORDS PROJECT
Official Project No. 165-44-6999

COPIED UNDER WORK'S PROGRESS ADMINISTRATION

MRS. JOHN TROTWOOD MOORE
STATE LIBRARIAN & ARCHIVIST SPONSOR

MRS. ELIZABETH D. COPPEDGE
DIRECTOR OF WOMEN'S & PROFESSIONAL PROJECTS

MRS. PENELOPE JOHNSON ALLEN
STATE SUPERVISOR

MRS. KATHLEEN W. CARADINE
SUPERVISOR THIRD DISTRICT

COPIED BY
ROBBIE ROE ANDERS
MARY W. BEATTY

TYPED BY
RENA A. DAVIS

March 2, 1938

ERRATA FOR INDEX

Pages 9,10,331,332 are missing

" 78,244,245 are blank

" 565 is duplicated

MADISON COUNTY

MINUTE BOOK VOL. I
1821-1825

INDEX

Note: Page numbers in this index refer to those of the original volume
from which this copy was made. These numbers are carried in the body
of the manuscript within parentheses, as (p 124)

A

A (Cont'd)

Anderson, Joseph, 432
Anderson, Joshua, 45,49,58,60,74
Anderson, Levi, 45,132,135,265,289,
    300,346,393
Anderson, Samuel, 337,426,429,430,
       431,432,433,434,435,436,
       437,438,439,440,441,442,
       443,444,445,446,447,448,
       449,450,451,452,453,454,
       459,495
Anderson, William, 86,232,250,308,
       320,467
Andres, 126
Andrew, 126
Andrews, Gutheridge, 461,479,515,516,
    517,518
Andrews, James, 566
Andrews, John, 540
Andrews, Thomas, 249,369,555
Arlin, James, 92
Armour and Lake, 469,564
Armstrong, James, 341
Armstrong, James L., 315
Armstrong, John, 126,163,228,367
Armstrong, M., 308
Armstrong, Martin (heirs of),167
Armstrong, Martin (Rep. of),171,315
Armstrong, Martin Jr., 308
Armstrong, Robert, 176,251
Arnold, (Major),260,564
Arnold & Gibson, 503
Arnold, John, 37,150,251,270,479,480
      499,517,526,540,557,558,564
Arnold, John (Major),540
Arnold, John Jr., 239
Arnold, William, 26,30,31,209,248,262,
    263,290,291,395,396,397,401,405,
    407,419,421,431,434,441,452,472,
    482,483,485,499,503,517,526,542,
    550,561
Asbery, William, 167
Ashe and Strudivick, 315
Askew, William, 269
Astun, William, 54
Atchison, William, 11,13,14,16,17,18,19
    26,32,39,47,53,55,57,80,86,92,112
    115,128,136,137,144,149,161,199,253
    254,258,275,279,280,281,329,330,344
    364,370,372,401,412,465,535,536,562
    565,566
Atchison, William A., 1
Averett, Samuel, 40,42,338
Avery, James, 216,217

B

Baker, 351
Baker, Caleb,525
Baker, Elijah, 25,34,35,36,40
    42,51,54,115,273,374,466
    547,549,550,551
Baker, Elisha Sr., 115
Baker, Henry, 140,162
Baker, Joshua, 465
Baker, William (heirs of) 309
Balding, Thomas, 87
Balding, William, 5
Baldridge, Francis(heirs of)315
Ball, James, 241
Ball, John H.,195,216,217,238,
    240,256,261,277,282,362,
    366,396,401,418,486
Ball, Sarah, 238
Barber, Joseph, 316
Barefield, Frederick, 124
Barker, Elijah, 54
Barncass, Richard, 316
Barncastle, Richard, 495
Barnes, John, 132,133
Barnhardt, John, 282,340,343,
    425,429,430,431,432,433,
    434,435,436,437,438,439,
    440,441,442,443,445,446,
    447,448,449,450,451,452,
    453,454,459,463,474
Barnhart, Adam, 564
Barnhart, John, 501,515,518,
    530,545,558,565(a)
Barren, John, 417
Barren, William, 362,373,376,
    377,378,381,382,383,384,
    389,390,392,417
Barrow, Matthew, 114
Barrow, William, 375
Bartholomew, Jacob, 315
Bass, James Jr., 88
Bathe, Benjamin, 141
Batton, Mooney, 51
Bear Creek, 541
Bearfield, Frederick, 51,52
Bedford, Robert, 102,104,205,
    229,490
Bedford and Wynn, 185
Bell, John, 224
Bell, Samuel, 296
Ben, 473
Bennet, Stephen, 149,209

B (Cont'd)

B (Cont'd)

Bradberry, Jacob Sr., 372
Bradberry, John, 6,13,14,16,18,
   20,115,117,364,524
Bradbury, Edward, 518,548
Bradbury, George, 55 (Marked out)
Braden, Alexander, 25,34,36,42,49,
   101,103,279,280,338,542
Braden, William, 1,5,6,7,11,12,17
   22,24,25,26,28,32,39,44,47,
   48,49,68,75,83,135,138,144,
   153,205,206,209,251,253,256,
   289,291,300,362,370,393,394,
   419,426,429,430,431,432,433,434,
   435,436,437,438,439,440,441,442,
   443,444,446,447,448,449,450,451,
   452,453,454,500
Braden, William, 459 (Marked out)
Bradford, Absolom, 338
Bradford, Alexander, 270
Bradford, Alexander B., 5,39,64,73,81,
   141,151,156,193,205,258,259,268
   295,365,417,421,429,455,456,469
   471,477,503,527,534,541,553,566
Bradford, Harris, 215,272,338,349,362,
   445,517,528
Bradley, John, 308
Bradshaw, James, 284
Bradshaw and Pillow, 318
Bradshaw, Samuel, 275,362
Bradshaw, William, 270
Brahan, John, 167,171,232,270,306,316
Branagam, John, 240
Branch, Joseph, 316
Branch, Stanley, 389
Brandon, Charles, 195,479,492,556
Brannon, 195
Brantz, Lewis, 65
Brattan, William, 456
Bratton, James Jr., 456
Bratton, James Sr., 456
Brevard, Cyrus, 269 (marked out)
Brevard, Cyrus W., 427
Brevard, John, 168,255,315
Brewer, Sterlin, 56
Brian, William H., 333
Bridges, Bennet, 539
Bridgman, Nathan, 95,194,210
Brigance, Stewart, 537
Bright, James, 167,171,270
Brinkley, William, 309
Brit, Thomas, 167,308
Brock, Calep, 398,399
Brook, John Thomas, 96,186,218,219

Brooks, 477
Brooks, Benjamin S., 260,271,
   464,487
Brooks, Jacob, 355
Brooks, Jeremiah, 463,536
Brooks, Oliver, 366
Brooks, Robert, 315
Brooks, Ruben, 366
Brothers, John, 61
Brown, Abner, 6,27,45,115,199,
   275,335,340,362
Brown, Adam, 272,338,419,464,502,
   518
Brown, Charles (heirs of),247
Brown's Ferry, 160,207
Brown, Henry, 38
Brown, James, 4,6,7,8,26,29,31,
   241,242,257,276,294,368,
   383,404,516,518,533,553,
   558,564,565(a)
Brown, Jeremiah, 216,217,333,529
Brown, Jesse, 483,526,565
Brown, John, 112,118,261,316,463
   522
Brown, John (heirs of),495
Brown, John B., 333
Brown, John F., 297,325,380,398,
   399,407,454,468,485,510,
   519,522,529,550,556
Brown, John T., 561
Brown, Joseph, 39
Brown, Nathaniel, 316,495
Brown, Sterling, 45
Brown, Thomas, 113,167,261,308,
   565 (a)
Brown, William, 135
Brown, William L., 232,530
Brown, William T., 421
Brown, Wilson, 40,216,217,220,284
   285,286
Brownsville (town of),464,543,564
Bruce, Anderson, 402
Bruce, John, 49
Bruff, Samuel, 9,276,480,485,504,
   520,521,522,524,527,547,553
Bryan, John, 140,208,308
Bryan, John T., 412,424,503,508,
   510,542,552
Bryan, Joseph, 168,320
Bryan, Joseph H., 269,370,390,391
Bryan, Stephen, 208,254,260,477
Bryan, Stephen Sr., 365
Bryan and Watson, 497

B (Cont'd)

Bryant and Freeman, 316,496
Bryant, Joseph H., 316
Bryant, Stephen, 200
Bryant, William, 299
Brydenbusher, John J., 195
Buchannon, Robert, 316
Buchannn, MaxMillian H., 141,269
Buckhanon, John, 167,168,171,315
Buckley, William, 250,337
Bugg, Joel, 108,367,368,526
Burk, Richard H., 368,564
Burk, Robert H., 362
Burks, Richard H., 417,464,565(a)c.
Burks, Robert H., 495
Burn, William, 374
Burns, Robert, 27,45,52,53,82,84,138
    158,200,271,272,542
Burrough and Mitchell, 43,99
Burrow, Banks, 72,74,262,503
Burrow, John, 156,353,425,462
Burrow, William, 425,524
Burrus, S., 469
Bury, William W., 366
Butler, Bennet R., 123,195,349
Butler's Bridge, 563
Butler, Burwell, 515,516,517,518,537
Butler's Creek, 15,130,161,205,237,
    246,250,338,415,487,541
Butler, David, 57
Butler's Ferry, 239,260
Butler, Henry, 12,57,105,336,505,540
Butler, Obediah, 57
Butler, William E., 6,11,27,37,57,68,
    105,116,121,123,130,148,155,175,
    201,203,205,238,246,248,249,251,
    253,258,270,290,297,325,329,330
    335,344,346,348,364,373,374,378,
    384,389,390,394,395,397,398,399,
    404,419,423,425,446,458,462,465
    467,468,477,478,486,493,500,510,
    516,517,526,539,550,552,560,562
    565(a),566
Butler, William E., 440 (Marked out)
Butler, William E. (Dr.),57,250,260,
    335
Byan and Watson, 316
Byers, James, 167,171,235,320
Byers, Joseph, 235,320
Byler, William, 410
Byrd, J. H., 318 (marked out)
Byrn, Ransom H., 541
Byrn, Thomas, 512,516,541
Byrne, David, 238

Byrns and Anderson, 135
Byrns and Henderson, 135
Byrns, Robert, 84

C

Cabbin Branch, 565
Cadwell, John G., 251
Cain Creek, 53,82,130,131,135,
    195,201,206,236,337,463,
    477,530
Caison, Larkin, 418,463,540
Calahan, Cornelius, 316
Caldwell, James, 6,13,20,39,48,49
    82,84,135,148,158,362,408,
    422,511,537,542,543
Caldwell, John, 316
Camp, John H., 182,191
Campbell, Arthur, 231,326
Campbell, David, 168,316
Campbell and Goddlett, 317
Campbell, Samuel, 273
Campbell, Thomas, 24,26,29,85,91,
    309,456,457
Campbell, William, 168,171,309
Cannon, C., 168,309
Cannon, Clement, 335
Cannon, Minor, 141,335
Cannon, Robert, 168,309
Cannon, William, 72,73
Cantrell, Stephen, 491,492
Card, James, 396,401
Carithers (Squire),137
Carithers Ferry, 22,43,49,73,368
Carithers, Grandon C., 73 (marked
                        out)
Carithers, James, 126,127,469,478
    495,503,509,513,514,519
Carithers, James D., 77,96,186,
    218,219
Carithers, John G., 24,28,32,42,65
    69,74,75,91,109,115,117,122
    123,137,138,142,144,192,194,
    199,200,204,208,212,215,226
    233,240,253,257,258,386
Carithers, John G., 488 (marked out)
Carl, William, 85
Carloss, Archelans, 256
Carlton, Thomas, 366,539
Carney, Benjamin, 528
Carney, Sanders, 429,430,431,432,433
    434,435,436,437,438,439,440,441,
    442,443,444,445,446,447,448,449
    450,452,453,454

C (Cont'd)

Carney, Sanders, 459 (marked out)
Carney, Sanders R., 141,147
Carpender, Lewis, 272,338,364
Carpenter, Benjamin, 168,171,309,
    495
Carr, Daniel, 560
Carr and Winchester, 97
Carroll, 137
Carroll County, 8,16,27,43,45,46,53,
    73,74,365
Carroll County Circuit Court, 456
Carroll County Court House, 27,83,
    130,131,196
Carroll County Road, 22,158,206,272,
    275,335,337,338,368,417
Carroll County Road, 43 (marked out)
Carroll, Joseph, 473
Carroll line, 49
Carroll, William(Govenor of the State
    of Tennessee),1,2,3,5,246,253,
    413
Carrollville, 464,564
Carrollville Road, 462
Carson, Charles, 309,548
Carson, John, 234,550
Carson, Larkin, 369
Carter, John, 309
Carter, King, 564
Carter, Wilson, 307
Cartmell, Martin, 27,48,57,110,261,
    264,362,528,534
Cartwright, John, 519
Cartwright, William, 207,339,495,513,
    514
Caruthers, Andrew N., 50
Caruthers Ferry, 22,43,73
Caruthers, James, 124,126,127,211,212
    264,514
Caruthers, James D., 50,96
Caruthers, Jefferson, 527
Caruthers, John, 28
Caruthers, John G., 22,24,32,33,42,65
    69,75,81,92,109,115,153
Caruthers, John S., 50
Caruthers, Samuel, 564
Caruthers, Samuel D., 64
Caruthers, William, 102
Caruthers, William A., 50
Casey, 506
Casey, Thomas, 35,36,45,72
Caslin, Henry, 346
Cason, Joshua, 362
Casort, Joshua, 500

Cassels, Henry,50,220,353,414
    536
Cassels, Henry Jr., 355,376,389
Cassels, Henry Sr., 355,420
Cassels, John, 304,305,326,353
    355
Castles, Henry, 30,84,147,175,
    177,180,181,182,183,185
Castles, Henry Sr., 350
Castles, John, 350
Cathey, George, 309
Catron, John,522,531
Cavanar, William, 357
Chaffen, Archibald, 345,373,376
    377,378,381,382,383,384,385
    389,392,395,396,482
Chaffin, Edward H., 482
Chalmers, John, 320
Chalmiss, Green B., 152
Chamberlin, George, 41,58,60
Chambers, Barney, 133,160,200,201
    212
Chambers, Elijah P., 159
Chambers, John, 232
Chambers, Patten, 200
Chambers, William C., 211
Champion, Thomas, 309
Chance, George, 336
Chandler's Bridge, 366,414
Chandler, Eli, 250,337,483,484
Chandler, Gabriel, 6,27,36,38,39
    56,140,152,209,369
Chandler's New Bridge,366,539
Chandler, Parks, 15,36,45,57,77,
    86,130,150,160,161,206,237
    240,250,282,334,337,341,366
Chandler, Pitts, 57,83,150,151,160
    200,206,236,250,338,362,366
    373,375,376,377,378,382,383
    384,385,386,387,390,392,398
    459,495,564
Chandler, Ryland, 6,8,15,26,27,36,
    57,81,82,92,93,95,97,115,
    118,122,124,127,130,150,160
    161,237,250,334,398,459,541
Chapman, Manley, 147
Charlotte, 459,460
Charlton, John, 278,279
Cherry, Daniel, 196,306,321,522
Cherry, Willie, 522
Chester, William, 543
Childress, Edwin H., 114,543
Childress, John (Rep. of),168,171
    508,522

C (Cont'd)

Childress, Stephen L., 389
Childress, William, 545,546,547
    549,550,551
Chisum, Clabourne, 140,162,200
    208,365,369,463,508
Chisum, Jacob, 140
Chisum, James, 309
Christian, Mark, 200,246,253,258,
    275,309,329,330,335,344,
    355,360,361,363,412,462,495,
    507,513,535,536,537,538,563
Claibourn, Thomas, 251
Clanton, Robert, 150,195,197,235,239
    260,271,329,343,347,357,362
    365,424,463,495,508,518,537
    563,565
Clanton, W., 250
Clark, D., 309
Clark, Henry, 159,309
Clark, James W., 306,321
Clark, John, 417,537
Clark, Jonas, 246,306,321
Clark, Michael, 6,275,532,536,545,546
    547,549,550,551
Clark, Nathan, 206,250,275,335,362,463
Clay, Henry M., 559
Cleft, Daniel, 385
Clemm, M., 266
Clendenning, James, 316
Clenny, Samuel, 316
Clift, Thomas, 149,209
Clifton, John, 41,51,58,120
Clihe, Michael, 306,321
Cloud, Joseph F., 166,210,214,228,290
    299,330,389,467,475,500,506
Cloud, Joseph F., 440 (marked out)
Cloud, Nancy, 210,214
Clouston, Edward G.,483,503
Clover Creek, 137,203,239,336,369,463
    508,540,565
Cloverlee, 137
Cobb, Robert L., 295,408
Cobb, Robert L., 270 (marked out)
Cochrane (Mr.),239
Cochrane, Cathalene, 505,520,546
Cochrane, Eli, 480,499
Cock, Joseph, 541,544
Cock, William, 496
Cock, William (heirs of),316,495
Cockrill, James, 25,32,33,38,68,125,127
    130,150,174,235,247,276,347,362
    368,394,464,512
Cockrill, M. R., 309

Cockrill, Mark R., 236
Codwell, J. G., 412
Coffee, John, 359
Cole Creek, 508
Coleman, B., 477
Coleman, Blackman, 63,193,477
Coleman, William, 316
Colley, Cader, 337,424
Collier, Carter C., 95,290,439
Collier, Catser, 6
Collier, Elizabeth A., 562
Collier, John R., 299,396,401,458
    474,475,476,533,541,548,562
    566
Collin, Carter C., 6,181
Collins, Henry D., 66,220,251,408
    422,491
Collins, W., 250
Connell, Hardin, 130
Connell, Jonathan, 130
Conner, Jacob (heirs of),316
Conner, Joseph, 420
Conner, William, 68
Connolly, G. D., 497
Connolly, Henry D., 436
Connelly, Henry G., 195,429,430,
    431,432,435,437,441,442,448,
    501,520,545
Connelly, John T., 175,177,180,181
    182,183,185,217,443
Conrad, John, 316
Cook, Isaac L. W., 18
Cook, John W., 18,44,235,443
Cook, Mark, 316
Coop, Richard, 201,213,562
Coopender, Lewis, 531
Copender, 281
Copender (Doc),282
Corbit, James, 306,321
Corns, James, 150
Corothers, Andrew N., 50
Corothers, J. G., 33
Corothers, James D., 50,64
Corothers, John L., 50
Corothers, William M., 50
Corpender, D.A., 240
Cotner, Solomon, 64,65,66,67,70,71
    72,79,86,103
Cotton, Alexander, 397
Cotton, Soloman, 168,171,256,269,
    320,436
Coulter, Henry, 65,337
Coulter, Henry A., 81

C (Cont'd)

D

D (Cont'd)

Deberry, Mathias, 459 (Marked out)
Deckerd, Benjamin, 548
Deen, Thomas, 138
Deen, William, 33,35,37,44,46,65,75,
    76,94,110,111,123,133,135,138,
    367,415
Deen, William C., 408
Deer Creek, 477
Deer, William C., 546
Delaney, Isaac, 523,548
Dellard, James, 6
Deloach, 565
Delph, Jane, 333
Delph, Philip, 272,333
Dement, Thomas M., 109,153,165,196,
    209,215,216,217,293,345,346
    351
Devereaux and Polk, 269
Devereaux, Thomas P., 168,269,279,320
Devitt, Washington J., 263,379,561
Dial, Pleasant, 337
Dial, W., 462
Dickens, Samuel, 4,6,50,53,56,200,278,
    279,310,333,334,335,342,370,372,
    388,412,424,466,467,484,485,500,
    515,518,520,524,532,536,537,546,
    565(a).
Dickenson, Matthew L., 447
Dickenson, Michael, 40,42,65,66,67
Dicking, Samuel, 370
Dickins, Samuel, 4,6,53,56,168,199,495,
    498,501,536,543,565(a).
Dilland, Isaac, 283
Dillard, 414
Dillard, (Esq.),336,540
Dillard, Allen, 149
Dillard, Isaac, 426
Dillard, Isaac, 268 (marked out).
Dillard, James, 6,24,28,32,115,147
Dillard, John L., 80,144,152,200,329,
    330,339,344,355,364,426
Dillard, Joseph, 217,532
Dillard, Josiah, 536,545,546,547,549,
    550,551,554,555,556,558
Dillon, Allen, 209
Dillon, William F., 116
Dillon, Wilson F., 70,71,72,134
Dixon, Robert, 68,77,86,87,160,255,
    257,261
Dixon, William, 168,171,231,310
Doak (Mrs.),130
Doak, Alanson F., 92,93,95,97
Doak, Martha, 57

Doak, Patsey, 6,7,14,17,38,230,
    278
Doak, Robert, 6,7,14,17,230,278,
    304,420,471
Doak, Thomas, 39,45,77,86,264,339,
    362,368,417
Doak, Thomas M., 86
Doak, William, 148,371,495,513,514
Doak, William H., 4,7,14,25,27,38,
    45,60,83,95,125,198,265,278,
    472,482,504,506
Doak, William R., 38
Dockins, Allen, 200
Dod, William, 138
Dodd, Wiley, 134,196
Dodson, Nimrod, 309,418
Dodson, Obediah, 272,424,525
Dodson, Susannah, 525
Dokes, 226
Donaldson, Robert, 168
Donaldson, William, 168
Donelson, Robert, 496
Donelson, William, 309
Donley, Charles, 425,558
Donley, John, 496
Donnell, Andrew, 270,(Marked out)
Donnell, John, 97,98
Donnell, William, 6,97,98
Dorace, James, 33
Dorris, James, 175,177,180,181,182,
    183,185,229,240,243,282,
    288,301,323,328,346,415
Dorris, William B., 329,343,352
Dotson, Harvy, 126,177,178,179,180
Dougan, James, 310
Dougan, John, 310
Douge, Jacob (heirs of),310
Dougherty, George, 168,171,309,310,
    316,496
Dougherty, Robert E.C.,56,165,467,
    551
Douglas, Donovan, 567
Douglas, Henry L., 309,355,494,498,
    514,545/
Douthel, Enoch, 12
Downing, William, 417
Drake, (heirs of),310
Draper, (Squire), 137
Draper, Benjamin, 509,512
Draper's Company, 465
Draper's Company(Capt.),258,339,509
Draper, John, 61,62,65,68,207,208

D (Cont'd)

Draper, William, 45,50,56,57,64,65,
    68,80,115,117,128,144,147,
    161,165,205,246,248,253,269,304
    329,330,340,344,364,367,412,416,
    422,423,462,463,465,486,497,498,
    507,509,510,530,535,537,538,539,565(a)
    567.
Drummonds, M., 220,224,225,226,228
Dry Creek, 208
Due, William C., 195,479,487,545,547
Duer, Joel, 284
Duffy, Patrick, 37,140,162,356,357,473,477
Duglas, H. L., 168
Dun, John, 496
Duncan, Allen, 57
Duncan, Robert, 563
Dunlap, Hugh W., 162,198,316,350
Dunlap, John, 271,537
Dunlap, Richard G., 197
Dunn, Thomas, 195
Dunn, William, 509
Dupery, Sarah, 469,470
Dupery, Starke, 469,470,563
Dupries, Stark, 197,337,366
Duty, Hiram, 466
Duty, William, 466,565(a).
Dyers,(Col.),197
Dyer County, 525
Dyer, Hannah (Mrs.),541
Dyer, Joel, 28,34,35,36,42,52,61,62,63,
70,74,86,87,107,109,120,134,163,193,194,
196,199,237,242,285,288,484,490,502,503,
525,541,542,543,553,562
Dyer, Joel (Major),272
Dyer, Joel, 29,459,(Marked out).
Dyer, Joel Sr., 24,324,350,384
Dyer, Joel and wife, 29
Dyer, Mariah T., 193
Dyer and Marr, 312
Dyer, Robert H., 1,11,13,15,17,20,21,22,
    28,29,30,31,40,42,43,46,52,55,61,
    73,74,75,97,99,100,111,112,113,
    143,144,155,190,192,242,243,246,
    253,258,262,285,291,344,359,360,
    379,399,450,466,476,487,500,514,
    515,529.
Dyer, Robert H., 43,200,438 (marked out).
Dyer, Sarah J., 542
Dyer, Warehouse, 113
Dyer, Wiley B., 479,484,501,520,545
Dyer, Wilie B., 459 (marked out)
Dyer, William H.,196
Dyol, Pleasant, 366,565
Dyson, Aquila, 342

E

Earbutton, James, 198
Easley, Warham, 160,205,257,
    420,471,487,488,489,490
    491,492,493,494,495,498
    499
Easters, Early, 49
Easters, John, 24,25,48
Eastham, James, 75,79,94
Eastwood, William, 139
Eatheradge, Jeramiah, 87
Eaton, John H., 168,171
Eckols, Richard A., 333,355,
    494,498,514,545
Eddings, Joseph, 45,240,282,284
    285,286,292,299,302,304,
    305,326
Eddins, Sullivan, 49
Eddleman, Francis, 316
Edmison, Robert, 52,86,92,93,
    95,96,97,101,103,104,316
Edmison, Wilmath, 52,96,133
Edmiston, Robert, 104(marked out)
Edmondson, Robert, 39,45,64,77,
    133,388,409,496
Edmondson, Samuel, 231
Edwards, James, 462
Edwards, James A., 334,564
Edwards, Joseph, 537
Edwards, Luceford, 201
Edwards, Sanford, 130,212,367
Edwards, William, 41,65,66
Edwards, William A., 495,513
Eldridge, Thomas Lofton, 335
Elijah, 34
Elliott, Thomas, 67,70,71,72,
    118,254,264,363,408,418
Elliott, William, 168,310
Ellison, Thomas, 111
Elrod and Horton, 535
Elrod and Houston, 535
Emory, Jessee,473
Epperson, Anthony, 501,515,520,
    546
Epps, Ann, 496,508
Epps, Thomas, 369
Epps, Wyatt, 330,362,369,532,534
    562
Espey, 260
Espy, William, 6,20,28,51,66,67,
    72,84,86,87,105,110,115,142,
    197,217,242,259,383,388,417,
    420,495,513,514,518,528.

G

Gaitly, John, 130,132,272
Galloway, James, 317
Galloway, William, 337,366
Gannaway, Banele, 324
Gant, William, 306
Garrett, David, 1,17
Garrison, John, 133,206,210
Garson, Charles, 136,137
Gartly, John, 471,562
Gately, John, 83,372,420
Gather, John, 83
Gatlin, John, 272
Gatlin, Thomas, 45,58,86,87
Gattis, James, 58
Gatty, John, 333
Gatty, Rebecca, 333
Gay, Benjamin, 209
Gay, Bryant, 209
General Assembly of State of
         Tennessee, 20
Gentry, George, 102,220,227
Gentry, Zebider, 100,101,103,104,
         415
Gerrard, Charles, 168,310,317
Gholson, Benjamin, 117,130,150,160,
    161,185,205,239,250,282,322,323,
    328,338,339,340,354,390,396,398,
    410,426,429,430,431,434,437,447,
    456,470,473,474,476,484,493,498,
    503,505,517,520,521,524,526,527,
    529,532,535,543,548,560
Gholson, Benjamin, 423 (marked out)
Gholson, M., 250
Gholson, Samuel, 338,366,386,387,401,548
Gibbins and Wells, 171
Gibson, (Adm.),546
Gibson, Ann, 349,410
Gibson and Arnold, 503
Gibson County, 365,477
Gibson County line, 565
Gibson, John A., 50,51,68,86,163,208,268,
        338,349,360,420,471,520,540
Gibson, John H., 87
Gibsonport, 420,477,507
Gilbreath, 135
Gilchrist, Daniel, 85
Gilchrist, Malcolm, 85,246
Giles, Thomas N., 565 (a)
Gill, George W., 474
Gill, John Jr. and Co., 222
Gillespie, Berry, 162, 478
Gillespie, John C., 173,284,285,286,304,
        305,326,339,368,371,404,408,417,
        510, 565 (a)

Givens, Andrew, 129
Givens, John, 462,563,565
Glisten, Isaac, 40
Glisten, James, 41
Glover, Lancaster, 201,213,355,
        368,418,480,485,504,508,
        509,522,547,553
Goddlett and Campbell, 317
Goff, Andrew, 231,320
Golden, Foster, 345,481,564
Golden, Jesse, 115
Golden, Jesse G., 115,118,121
Golden, Reuben, 541
Golden, Richard, 420,471,487,488
        489,490,491,492,493,499
Goldin, 49
Golding, Foster, 464
Golding, Richard, 498
Goldson (Major),237
Goldson, Benjamin, 237
Colson, Benjamin, 206
Goodlet, A.G.,168
Goodloe, George, 545,546,547,
        549,550,551,552,554,
        555,556
Goodman, (Mr.),238
Goodman, G.,563
Goodman, Tobias, 337,366
Goodrich, Archibald W., 428
Goodrich, Russell,166,168,171,
        257,306,321,366,375
Goodwin, Samuel, 154,205,273
Gordon, Thomas, 148,149,246,249,
        253,258,330,344,367,368,
        372,373,389,390,467,518,
        534,537,539,540
Goslin, Ambrose, 168,171,317
Gossett, Elisha, 160
Grace, John, 17
Graham, Dempsey, 272
Graham, G.R.,227
Graham, Griffith, 228
Graham, Robert, 562
Graham, William, 307
Grand and Grisom, 143
Grant and Grisom, 143
Grant, Spencer, 25,32,33,65,66,
        67,70,71,72,75,92,144,224,
        225,226,275,284,479,502
Graves, 174,508
Graves, John, 25,32,33,65,66,68,
        115,130,141,150,173,193,209,
        368,494,512,532,536
Graves, Philip, 66

G (Cont'd)

Gray, Anthony F., 27,35,41,42,45,
    61,80,140,150,162,220,241,
    290,342,343,370,382,404,422,
    457,458,500
Gray, Anthony F., 440 (marked out)
Gray, George, 338,537
Gray, Henry D., 120
Gray, Henry L., 5,22,28,42,79,86,87,
    88,92,93,94,107,180,134,178,
    196,202,224,227,542
Gray, Robert, 347,361,363,370,460
Gray, Sally F., 107
Gray, Sarah, 80
Gray, Sarah F., 426
Gray, W., 250
Gray, Washington, 366
Gray, William, 126
Gree, Vinson, 462
Green, David H., 372
Green, James, 27,124,137,562
Green, R.W.,231
Green, Robert G., 121
Green, Sherwood, 310
Greer, A., 241
Greer, Alexander, 25, 47,77,92,93,95,
    97,100,101,102,103,110,200,294
    362,364,368,420,463,471,487,488,
    489,490,491,492,493,494,498,499,
    508,530,531.
Greer, J., 117,146,161,241,252,257,268,
    297,303
Greer, James, 27,80X84,112,115,124,136
    142,144,147,155,158,192,200,250,
    253,258,265,286,294,304,330,342,
    344,350,365,368,374,390,394,412,
    457,509,562
Greer, Robert G., 404
Greer and Simmes, 231
Greer, Thomas, 306
Greer, Vincent, 564
Greer, William, 83
Gremmer, Robert, 463
Greyer, Alexander, 39,45
Grider, Tobias, 468
Griffin, John, 45,47
Griffin, Lewis, 140,162,163,173,175,177,
    180,181,182,183,185,420,471,487,
    488,489,490,491,492,493,494,498,
    499,524
Griffin, Owen, 271,362,375,378,381,382,
    383,384,385,389,390,392,
    420,464
Griffith, Sarah An, 55,67

Griffith, Will, 68
Griffith, William, 4,20,55,67,
    86,87,247,565(a)
Grimes, John, 173
Grisom and Grand, 143
Grisom and Grant, 143
Grisom, Grant F., 203
Grisom, Thomas, 92,144,179,217,
    292
Grissom, Grant S., 223
Grissom, Thomas, 106,116,175,
    177,180,181,182,183,185,
    216,217,220,247,276,284,
    346,353
Guin, Owen, 118
Guthrie, James S., 342
Guthrie, John, 210,564
Guy, William, 126,396,407,474

H

Haddon, Philip J., 231
Hail, William, 565
Hailie (Widow),563
Hainey, Elijah, 49,209,224,225
    226,240,282
Hains, James D., 520
Hale, Albert A., 565(a)
Hale, James, 137
Hale, William J., 507
Halefield, Elish, 537
Haley, Isaiah, 12,28,29
Haley, James, 6,12,28,29,35,36,
    83,111,201,356,362,367
Haley, James W., 197,239,356
Haley, Josiah, 339
Haley, Philip R., 463
Haley, Thomas, 12,111,367,540
Haley, William P., 197,356
Halkup, James, 163
Hall, 139
Hall, Archibald C., 26,65
Hall, John, 139,235,238
Hall, Samuel, 272
Hall, William Q., 139,235,238
Hallen, Josiah, 115,118
Hallum, Morris, 495
Haltom, Ebenezer, 130,249,329,
    343,345,350,353,355,464,
    532,536,545,546,547,549,
    550,551,554,555,556,558
Haltom, Thomas, 249,343,345,350,
    353,355,357,464,555

H (Cont'd)

Halton, William, 8,83,138,464
Hamilton, David, 168
Hamilton and Howard, 323
Hamilton, John, 168
Hamilton, John, W., 267
Hamlet, E., 66
Hammel, Andrew, 276,540
Hancock, Benjamin, 404
Hanes, John, 168
Hanna Company (capt.),137,255,258,
        368
Hannah, Jesse M., 42,45,58,70,71,72,
        75,76,83,102,137,140,201,213,
        353,367,408,422,532,557
Happy, Enoch, 347,401,402,411
Haralson, Green L., 92,93,95,97,103,
        115,118,121,130,197,188,189,
        192
Haralson, Green L., 191 (marked out)
Haralson, Herndon, 1,67,7,8,15,17,26
        32,39,47,48,56,57,64,65,70,75,
        77,79,80,85,86,91,92,105,114,
        116,122,143,144,145,147,152,155,
        158,160,161,174,186,187,192,205,
        206,212,215,230,233,237,239,240,
        243,246,248,250,252,253,257,258,
        265,267,268,269,277,278,280,281,
        286,287,290,292,303,304,326,329,
        330,334,337,342,344,346,348,349,
        355,360,361,363,364,371,372,373,
        381,391,394,395,398,404,405,412
        416,419,421,426,428,429,430,433
        440,435,459,460,461,462,465,466,
        473,478,482,483,486,498,502,507,
        513,518,519,522,523,525,526,529,
        530,534,536,537,538,539,541,542,
        544,552,553,557,558,562,566,567
Haralson, Vincent, 6,8,12,20,26,27,39,
        49,82,84,115,118,121,130,143,145
        158,248,277,329,343,352,364,391,
        398,414,419,459,466,468,511,542
        543
Haralson, Vincent, 265 (marked out)
Hardaway, Joseph, 177,178,179,180,188
        189,191,192
Hardeman County, 335
Hardeman County Road, 507
Hardeman, Thomas J., 82,83,200
Hardgraves, John, 6,20,21,30,38,56,86,
        87,113,134,207,210,232,265,277
        329,360,368,439,440,441,442,495
        513,514,523,537

Hardin Court House, 83,130,131,
        132,150,158,197,206,337
Hardin, William, 310,496
Hardridge (Mr.),197
Hardridge, Zachariah, 364,371,563
Hardwick, John, 350,353,355,394
        401,467,490
Hardwick, Robert, 544
Hardy, Humphrey, 232
Hardyman, Thomas J.,152
Harkins, 254
Harkins (Mr.),197
Harkins, Daniel, 149,197,238,249
        337,362
Harkins, Daniel Jr., 238,337,366
        563
Harkins, Daniel Sr., 366,563
Harkins, Hiram, 197,238,377,366
Harles, Elisa, 243
Harper, Henry, 298,354
Harrell, Elisha, 6
Harrington, Fairfax, 496
Harrington, Thomas, 392,420,435,
        471,487,488,489,490,491,
        492,493,494,498,499,516
Harris Bluff, 28,51,73,86,87,109,
        153,202,208,276,464,465
Harris, Jacob, 169
Harris, Jeremiah, 371
Harriw, Jesse S., 528,556
Harris, Newton, 83,130,240,282
        464,532,536
Harris, Robert, 168,317
Harris, Sidon, 148,260,338,339
Harris, Tarlton, 151
Harris, West, 149,209
Harris, Western, 532,536
Harris, William, 6,88,113,132,155
        163,174,226,372,417,419,420
        430,446,454,463,469,473,479
        483,487,495,498,499,500,509
        511,527,530,537,541
Harrison, James, 310
Harrison, John, 24,27,32,140,168,
        188,189,191,192,195,216,217
        220,264,265,362,418,421,424
        479,524
Harrison, Powell, 495
Harrison, Robert, 310
Harry, Elijah, 66,117
Hart, Anthony, 168,310
Hart, James, 169,310

175,177,180,181,182,183,188,189
191,192,329,343,495,513,514,
518
James, Willoughby, 317
Jaman, (Squire),137
Jarman's Bridge, 509
Jarman's Ford, 83,130,131,132,136
    137,196,272
Jarman, Robert (Esq.),80,327
Jarman, Stephen, 45,50,56,57,65,69
    80,85,86,115,117,128,142,144,
    146,147,161,192,200,205,212,
    253,258,272,333,344,364,462,465,
    509,510,562
Jarrett (Squire),137,418,508
Jarrett, David, 1,4,6,7,17,26,28,31,
    49,68,74,76,91,92,115,128,140,
    142,144,165,174,186,187,193,229,
    246,249,250,253,264,269,273,275,
    322,329,344,373,387,388,405,407,
    408,416,419,465,467,469,510,518,
    523,532,533,537,557,562
Jarrett, Lavinia, 419
Jarrett, Pleasant, 322
Jarrett, Wade, 71,365,419
Jarrison, John, 132
Jeffers, David, 269,320
Jeffries Creek, 208
Jeffries, David, 43,144
Jelks (Esquire), 486,534
Jelks, Jarrett M., 28,45,77,86,154,156,
    200,205,237,260,281,338,362,405
    413,416,465,477,486,495,507,510,
    561,562
Jelks, Jarrett M., 240 (marked out)
Jenkins, John, 311
Jentry, George, 6
Jeregan, David, 3
Jerigen, David, 6
Jernigan, 111
Jernigan, David, 3,6,160,200,213
Jetton, Robert, 525,526
Johns, John, 27
Johns and Morphis, 255
Johns, Simon (heirs of),489
Johns, William, 27,49,77,86,110,130,150,
    160,250,338,461,473,477,479,515
    516,517,548
Johnson (Col.),198
Johnson, Amos, 311
Johnson, Cave, 241,317
Johnson Creek, 260,365,367,413,416,418,464
    508,533,539,540,564
Johnson, Daniel, 169,171
Johnson, Daniel (Adm.),480,499

Johnson, Duncan, 310
Johnson, George, 317
Johnson, J. M., 132
Johnson, Jacob (heirs of),169,
    311
Johnson, Jacob V., 317
Johnson, James, 57,65,67,153,
    220,237,250,337,426
Johnson, James F., 216,217
Johnson, John, 247
Johnson, John M., 200,238,325,3
    329,337,366,414,495,563
    566
Johnson, Malcolm, 130,177,178,
    179,180,214,254,301,304
    305,346,392,426,528
Johnson, Malone, 260 (marked out)
Johnson, Matthew, 55,107,182,185,
    190,191,194,220,223,256,304
Johnson, Meckham, 326
Johnson, Nathaniel, 342
Johnson, Randal, 310
Johnson, Randle, 169
Johnson, Simon, 55,107,185,194,
    256,358
Johnson, Simon (heirs of),490
Johnson, William H., 345
Johnson, William W., 20,21,22,23
Joiner, Matthew,317
Joiner, Thomas, 209
Jones, 335
Jones, Adeline, 74
Jones, Agness, 5
Jones, Alexander S., 18
Jones, Amey, 74
Jones, Andes, 169,310,496
Jones, Benjamin, 5,6,20,27,115,
    118,122,124,127,362,373,
    375,376,377,378,381,382,
    383,384,385,390
Jones, Beverly, 372
Jones, Calvin, 15,130,161,169,
    234,247,334,387,394
Jones Creek, 8,16,47,48,49,57,
    152,205,209,237,250,539
    564
Jones, Danil, 197
Jones, Edmond, 51,163,333,334,
    375,412,501,515,545,565(a)
Jones, Elijah, 4,5,14,19,22,49,
    68,74,103,104,105,254,264
    272,338,339,371,374,382,
    412,418,502,513,557
Jones, Elijah, 400 (marked out)
Jones, Elijah J., 74

J (Cont'd)

Jones, Elizabeth, 74
Jones, Ferry, 149,209
Jones and Fogg, 311
Jones and Hogg, 232,311,320
Jones, James, 163,211
Jones, Jane T.,398,399
Jones, John, 27,376,389
Jones, John E.,412,565(a)
Jones, Lewis, 5,22,44,68,74,249,
    281
Jones, Lewis, 44 (marked out)
Jones, Lewis S., 338,394,400
Jones, Matthew, 49,255
Jones, Polly, 74
Jones, Robert, 153,474,476
Jones, Robert G., 148,405
Jones, Ridley, 311
Jones, Susan, 5
Jones, Thomas, 20,115,117,224,225,
    226
Jones, Wiley, 209
Jones, Willie (Dr.),149,200,238
Jones, William, 49,110,130,362
Jordan, 254
Jordan, Benjamin, 159,211
Jordan, William, 265,284,285,286,
    293,302,421
Jordan, William C., 346
Jorden, Banister, 337
Justice Company, 465
Justice Company (Capt.),563
Justice, John, 275,417
Justice, John B., 45,58,75,76,275,
    335,362
Justice, William, 201,213,417

K

Kendrick, William, 337,366,564,566
Kennedy, Alfred, 208,212
Kennedy, Ira C., 188,386
Kennedy, Robert C., 169,170,172,270
Kentucky(state of),128
Kerr, Henry, 257
Key Comer, 81
Key, James M., 414
Key, Jefferson, 392
Key, William, 471
Killingsworth, William B.G.,163,211,466
    Kincaid, James, 474,475,476
King, Austin A., 195,251,257,350,365,478,488,553
    485,553
King, Daniel,92,93,95,97,101,103,175,177
    180,181,182,183,185

King and Hoard, 317
King, Isabela, 311
King, Rufus F., 28,29,195
King, Samuel, 269
King, Thomas, 169,172,317
King, William G., 420,486
Kirby, William, 344
Kirk, Jesse L., 367,369,413,
    418,455,458,460,461,462,
    495,539,557
Kirk, John, 149,209
Kirk, Thomas, 356,357
Kirkpatrick, John, 246
Kirkpatrick, Thomas J., 246
Kiser, James, 524,527,479,543
Knight, William, 536
Knoulton, John, 169,172
Knowlet, Joshua, 317
Knox, James, 438
Knuckles, John, 353,479
Koonts, Wright, 277,237,366

L

Lackpam, Archibald S., 278,282
    340,462,474,548,554
Lacy's Company, 339,465
Lacy's Company (Capt.),258
Lacy, Hugh Company, 365
Lacy, Hugh R., 208,239,299,343,
    365,474,475,476,495,533
Lacy, Stephen, 6,45,80,83,130,150
    200,201,208,213,230,239,
    343,365,369,412,415,463,
    467,495,532,537,562
Lacy,Thomas, 12,30,140,150,151,
    162,273,353,396,537
Lacy, William, 539
Lafton, Thomas, 246,260,271,
    333,336,339,364,367,388,
    416,462,495,523,540,564
    566
Lake and Armour, 469,564
Lake, Henry, 368
Lake, Robert, 471,518
Lambert, Jordan, 414
Lambert, Judy, 414
Landers, Richard, 115
Landford, John P., 469
Langston, Mark, 49,115,118,121
    196
Lanier, R. H., 59
Lannon, Samuel H., 62
Laremour, Hance, 213,353,356,
    357
Laremour, Pleasant,338

L (Cont'd)

M (Cont'd)

Madins, Daniel, 38
Mahan, Archibald, 169,318,462,496
Main, Obian, 112,132
Major, Benjamin, 557
Malin, James, 93,95
Mallery, James, 85
Mallory (Doctor),535
Manley, Chapman W., 158
Manley, John, 384
Mannis, John B., 464
Mariah, 61,62,473
Marian, Phillip, 169
Marion, Phillip, 317 (marked out)
Marlin, James, 40,92,93,95,103
Marr and Dyer, 312
Marr, George W. L., 311
Marsh, E., 238
Marsh, Elijah, 337,366
Marsh, Elisha, 539
Marsh, Henry, 537,563
Marsh, Minor, 249,337,366,471,539
Marshall, Charles, 311
Martha, 68
Martin, 336
Martin, A. G., 195
Martin, A. L., 205,213,334,541
Martin, Alexander, 68
Martin, Andrew L., 276,278,322,390
        542,543,553,556,562
Martin, Armstrong, 167
Martin, Ascrius G., 265,303,423
Martin, James, 40,97,98,311
Martin, Lemuel, 83
Martin, Lewis, 367
Martin, Samuel, 83,198,337
Martin, Samuel B., 151,531,541
Martin, Soloman, 292,345,353
Martin, Solomon S., 265
Martin, Thomas, 380
Martin, William, 198,206,525,526
Martin, William H., 132
Mason, Daniel, 390,391
Massey, Absolem, 292,302,483,484,
        485
Massey, Joel, 564
Massia, Absalom, 286
Massie, Absolom, 284,285,518
Mathews, Carlton, 198
Mathews, Charles, 487
Mathews, Elisha, 198
Mathews, Thomas, 66,198
Mathis, Elisha, 414
Mathis, William, 224,225,226

Matlock, William, 562
Matthews, 254
Matthews, Carlton, 337
Matthews, Charles, 483,484,479
Matthews, Elijah, 337
Matthews, Elisha, 366
Matthews, James, 366,539
Matthews, John, 370
Matthews, Thomas, 65,337
Maulding, Richard, 129,206
Maury, Alfred, 118
Maury, Daniel W., 11,48,56
Maury, John, 111
Maury, Robert, 175,180
Maxey, Bennett, 207,329,563
Maxwell and Alexander, 508
May, John, 362,364
May, Obediah, 209
May, William, 277
Mayer, Charles Frederick, 65
Mayer, Christian, 65
Mayers, Charles F., 318
Mayfield, William, 203
Mayho, William, 125,127
Mayo, William, 57,237,250,337,345
McAfee, Ann, 15
McAfee, Elijah, 72,93,94,95,97,98,
        118,119,122,163,176,178,
        179,180,189,191,198,202
McAlister, James, 5
McAlister, John, 23
McBath, Polly, 33,44,46,75,76,94
McBoyde, William, 50
McBride, Archibald, 252
McBride, John, 224,225,226,299
McCabe, Alexander, 311,496,565
McCallister, John, 231
McCampbell, Andrew, 162
McCampbell, W., 168
McCarroll, James A., 252,515,516,
        517,518
McCaslin, William, 18,271,275,518,
        548
McClary, Andrew, 251
McClary, James A., 150,206,278,364
        408,422,495,510,534,537
McClelland, John, 358,420,471,487
        488,489,490,491,492,493,494,
        498,499,537,541
McClelland, John, 413 (marked out)
McClelland, William, 109,153
McClenlen, William B., 271
McClennan, Wilson, 371

Mc(Cont'd)

Mc(Cont'd)

McLennan's Creek, 208
McLennon, John, 278,413
McMahan, Martin, 385
McMahan, Matthew B., 88,142,385
McMillan, Dickson, 130,330,372
McMillan, Hannah, 11,16,26,69,
    330,372
McMillan, Robert, 11,16,26,69,130,
    258,284,330,372
McMillan, William, 563,565
McMinn, Joseph, 15,169,384
McNab, Baptist, 14,149,565
McNairy, John, 121,169,172,297,325,
    344,390,398,443,444,446,450,
    453,468,478,552,563,565.
McNeal, Thomas, 81,83,147,200
McNeil (Capt.),209
McNight, James, 329,336,343,367,563
    564
McPeak, 114
McPeak, Henry M.C.,192
McPeak, Matthew, 116,143,146
McPeak, Nathan, 196
McPike, John, 169,172,318
McReynolds, James, 347
McReynolds, Thomas, 459(marked out)
McReynolds, Thomas J., 330,333,429,
    431,432,433,434,435,436,437,
    438,439,440,441,442,443,444,
    445,446,447,448,449,450,451,
    452,453.
McReynolds, Wilson O., 330,450,552,
    567
McRunolds, 195
McTier, Robert, 311
McVey, Allen, 364,372,431,462,474,476,
    481
McVey, Ruben, 505,520,546,564
McWilbran, William, 311
Meazles, George, 28,140,162,299,302
Medearis, Benjamin H., 413
Medearis, Benjamin W., 404
Medearis, Benjamin W. H., 371,537
Mendinghall, Mordeca, 169,172,317
Meridian Creek, 16,197,201,203,336,367
    540,541,565
Meridian line, 563
Mexico, Abraham (heirs of),169
Midgett, Asa, 77,237,552
Midgett, Asa B., 80,176,178,179,180,240,
    282,477,502
Midgett, Micajah, 157,200
Midyett, 73

Midyett Company (Capt.),207,258
Midyett, Isiah, 537
Midyett, M., 483,486,504
Midyett, Micajah, 86,87,253,258
    269,271,273,276,329,344,355,
    364,368,416,420,465,477,486,
    507,531,537,541.
Miere, John, 495
Miggitt, Micajah, 279,281
Miles, George L., 490,492,503,506
Miller, Austin, 26
Miller, Frederick, 209,369
Miller, Isaac, 365,371
Miller, Jacob, 229,369,463,566
Miller, John, 311
Miller, Joseph, 71
Miller, William H., 358
Milton (Mr.),238
Milton, William, 337
Mimms, Duguid, 388,407,409
Minire, 416
Minire, John, 413,533,539
Mississippi, 112,132
Mississippi (State of),557,559
Mississippi river, 115
Mitchell, 367
Mitchell and son (Mr.),198
Mitchell and Burrough, 43,99
Mitchell, John, 329,343,352,367,
    509,541,564,566
Mitchell, Marmaduke, 72,74
Mitchell, Moody, 541
Mitchell and Moody, 336
Mitchell, W. C., 240,276
Mitchell, W. L., 43
Mitchell, William, 109,201
Mitchell, William C., 66,68,153,
    208,209,212,263,266,273,281
    373,408,465,545,546,547
Mitchell, William L., 18,45,99,112
    113,116,132,135,143,146,196
    263,266,267,381
Mitchell, William S., 58
Mizell, George, 190,215,226,347,
    350,353,356,357,377,386,387
    389,392,426,521
Mizells, George J., 324
Montgomery County, 241
Montgomery, James, 530,565(a)
Montgomery, John, 6,20,28,377,488
    530
Moody, Isaac, 86,87,462,509
Moody, John, 87
Moody and Mitchell, 336

M(Cont'd)

Moody, Phillip, 115,364,367,540
Moore, Alfred,333,334
Moore's Company, 465
Moore's Company (Capt.),418,420
Moore, David, 115
Moore, James, 65,242,311,374,383
    389,420,477
Moore, John, 45
Moore, Lemuel W., 42,65,66
 Moore, M., 170,172
Moore, Morris, 312
Moore, Robert, 311,565 (a)
Moore, Robert (heirs of),419,464
Moore, Samuel, 278,279
Moore, Samuel M., 40
Moore, Travis, 317
Moore, William B., 14,467
Moore, William H., 562
Morgan, John, 169,172,270
Morgan, Presly, 199
Morphis and Johns, 255
Morphis and Johnson, 317
Morrison, Thomas, 386
Moseley, Shadrock, 512
Moss, James L., 272
Moss, Joseph, 398,459
Mosshale, Dixon, 58,59
Mount Pinson, 132,200,206,249,
    534,537,563
Mount Pinson road, 366,539,540,564
Mulden, Richard, 413
Mulherron, James, 496
Mulherron and Overton, 317,321,496
Murchison, Daniel, 137,138
Murchison, Murdock, 4,24,27,32,33,53,
    64,97,206,273,275,276,335,364,
    408,422.
Murfree, Hardy, 317
Murfree, John, 304
Murphreesboro, 1,88
Murphy, A. D., 318
Murphy, Archibald, 159,311
Murphy, Archibald D., 243, 510
Murphy, Enoch, 515
Murphy, John, 239,292,305,326
Murray, Alfred, 151,195,258,322,389,
    394,401,424,506
Murray's Bluff, 365
Murray, John, 111,133,156,160,208,349
    353,354,386,408,445,519,528,
    553,554,565
Murray, R., 390
Murray, Robert, 159,175,177,181,182,183,
    185,249,250,280,288,311,329,337,340,
    341,343,345,350,353,355,372,404,423,

424,432,433,434,435,436,437,438
439,440,441,442,443,444,445,446,
447,448,449,450,451,452,453,454,
461,486,488,493,505,542,543.
Murray, Robert, 459(marked out)
Murray and Rutherford, 267,381
Musgrove, A., 271
Musgrove, Abner, 537
Musgrove, E., 271

N

Nail, Gilbreath, 240,462,537
Nash's Bluff,112,113,132,154,202
    272,464
Nash's Bluff road, 237,338
Nash, Redmond B., 311,318
Nash, Thomas, 113
Nash, William, 112,155,200,311,
    565
Nash, William Junior, 113,132
Nash, William Senr., 132
Nashville Bank, 447
Natchez, 111
Natchez Trace, 38
Neal, Hetty, 257
Needham, Bailey, 55,341
Needham, J.W., 85,91
Needham, Jasper, 562
Needham, Lewis, 6,20,24,26,29,84,
    85,91,140,162,163,166,173
    565 a.
Neely, James L., 327
Neill, Gilbreath, 126,282
Neill, Jacob, 325
Neill, W. M., 518
Neill, Zaphanial, 86,87
Nelson, E., 496
Nelson, Elizabeth, 169,172,231,320
Nelson, Robert, 38,311,496
Nemo, A. C., 195,409
Nemo, Allen C., 122,357
Nesbitt, William, 557,560
Newhouse, Wm., 240,282
Newman, Wm., 196
Newsom _____,210
Newsom, Edward, 156
Newsom, Eldridge, 84,335,336,423,
    462,564
Newsom, Ethelred, 329
Newsom, Ethelridge, 420
Newsom, Harbert, 156,201
Newsom, Herbert, 115,335,408,416
    422,461,462,540,542,563,564

N (Cont'd)

Newsom, James, 214,386,387,507, 524
Newsom, James M., 564
Newsom and Knockley, 507
Newsom, Mill, 540,563,564
Newsom, Newell, 479
Newsom, Newit, 564
Newsom, Rbt., 213
Newsom, Sally, 210,214
Newsom, William, 40
Newton, Edward, 170,311
Nichols, Willis, 45,58,75,76,272, 333,537
Nicholson, O. P., 496
Nickoll, John, 554,556
Nill's, Mr., 563
Nimmo, Allen C., 558
Nix, Obediah, 57,152
Nixon, Thos. (hrs. of),169,311
Nixon, Thomas G., 543
Noody, John, 86
Norrell, Nathan'l., 45
North Carolina (State of),48,112, 135,136,159
North Carolina, University of, 388,424, 537,543
Norvel, Thomas, 195
Norville, N., 49
Norvill, Thomas G., 346
Norville, _____,336
Norwood, William, 69,89,370,496
Novell, Thomas, 483,484
Nuckles, John, 542

O

Oakley, Alexander, 275
Obion, 112,132
Odle, Anderson, 87,277
Oldham, Ebenezer, 367
Oldham, John, 367
Oldham, Moses, 6,13,20,22,140,162,197, 271,278,408,417,422,495,513, 514
O'Neal, Robert, 463,530
O'Neil, Benjamin, 120
Orgain, Sterling, 163,285
Osteen, William, 54
Overton, Jno., 170,306,321,371,496
Overton and Mulherrin, 306,317,321
Owens, John, 318

P

Pace, 174
Pace, Alsey, 214,351,426,528
Pace's Creek, 260
Pace, Henning, 45,77,86,173,177, 178,179,180,193,201,212, 214,276,350,353,368,426 427,528
Pace, William, 118,214,229,298, 304,305,326,346,349,351, 352,415,426,528
Padget, Sarah, 170
Page, Absolem, 58,59
Page, Jno. 187,189,243,425
Page, Jno. 191(marked out)
Palmer, Thos., 40,42
Palmer, Thos. W., 28,51,99,103
Palmer, William, 51,99
Parker, Daniel, 366
Parker, David, 197,337,563
Parker, Jehue,333
Parks, _____ 366,540
Parks, Elizabeth, 424
Parks, Thomas, 337,424
Parks, Thomas L.D.,12,20,40,49 435
Parks, William L., 6
Parr, Moses H., 448
Parsons, Enoch. 172
Partee, John L., 4,5,7
Pate, Matthew, 87
Patrick, Jno., 170,172,318
Patrick, John M., 469
Patten, Alexander, 264
Patten and Irwin, 246
Patterson, _____,271
Patterson, Alexander, 420
Patterson, John T., 314
Patterson, Reuben, 424
Patterson, Samuel, 170,312
Patterson, William, 314
Patterson, Wm., 170,172
Patton, A., 335
Patton, Alexander, 468,476,512
Paulding (Mr.),239
Paulding, Washington, 260,367
Payton, William, 68,119,141,172
Pearce, Allen, 241,261
Pearcy, Cader, 148,270,321
Pelch, John M., 97
Pender, Lewis C., 404

P (Cont'd)

Q (Cont'd)

Quinley, Owen, 115,118,121
Quisinberry, Anderson, 312

R

Rachel, 371
Ragan, Henry, 20,64,271
Ragsdale, 49
Ragsdale, Claiburn J., 107,109,
    115,117,141,190,220,223,284,
    285,286,292,304
Ragsdale, Francis, 45,109,141,217,350,
    353,357
Rainey, Abel, 369
Rainey, Homer, 381,429,430,494,512
Rains, Abel, 271
Rains, William (hrs.),255
Ramsay, John, 252
Ramsey, Wm., 149,170,209
Randal, Jno., 172
Randolph, Beverly, 330
Rasberry, John, 369
Raser, John B., 557,559
Ray, Anderson, 312
Ray, Samuel, 130,312
Ray, Wiley, 458
Rayder, John, 362,378,381,382,383,384,
    385,389,390,425,468,474,476,487,
    508,511,527,528,552
Rayford, Philip, 170,172,312
Raygan, Henry, 6,20,70,71,72,390
Read, Connealy, 247
Ready, Charles, 425
Reagan, Henry, 338,362,373,374,375,376,
    377,378,382,383,384,385,389,392
Roan, Henry Jr., 58
Reaves, _____ 541
Reaves Company, 465
Reaves, (Captain) Co., 254,258
Reaves, John, 402
Reaves, Thomas, 81,83,197,200,329,337,345,
    350,353,356,357,362,366,370,390,534
    537,563
Redens, John, 70
Redfield, Frederick, 52
Redford, Walter, 130
Reed, David, 225
Reed, John, 247,366
Reed, Mary, 29,247
Reener, Thomas, 81
Reid, Archibald, 564
Reid, David, 102,121
Reid, Hugh, 86,87

Reid, John, 337,519,563
Reid, Mary, 26,29,38
Reid, Reuben, 50
Reid, Robert, 50,103,108,111
Reims, Able, 269
Reprogle, Frederick, 86,87
Revira, Edmond,487
Reynolds, Benjamin, 525,526
Reynolds, Bowen, 354
Reynolds, George,269
Reynolds, Joseph, 313
Reynolds, Thomas W., 430
Reynolds, William, 83,121,
    278,313,461
Reynoldsburg, 111,207,275
Reynoldsbury Road, 272,418
    463,530
Reynoldsville, 111
Rhea, John, 172,231,319
Rhodes, 135
Rhodes, Tyree, 270,319
Rhodes, William, 260,312
Rice, John, 313
Richmond, Elizabeth, 26,67
Richmond, Jesse, 26,67
Richy, Robt.(Hs of),312
Ridens, John, 30,50,58,64,65
    70,162,166,240,335
    345,338,403,411,524,563
Ridens, Solomon, 345
Ridings, John, 45, 67,140,227
    233,295,402
Right, Jas., 76
Right, John Sr., 462
Right, John W., 462,507,563
    564
Right, William, 462,507,518
    564
Ring, Daniel, 92
Roach, James C., 450
Roach, James C. (marked out)
    438
Roads, William C., 83,170
    248,336
Roady, Charles, 404
Roain, Henry, 58
Roak, John, 57,65
Roan, Henry, 58,75,76,115,207
Roan, Henry Jr., 45,58
Roan, John, 130
Roan, Woodard, 207
Robb, Joseph, 319
Robb, William, 26,29,85,91

R(Cont'd)

Roberson, James, 319
Roberson, Rutherford, 293
Roberts, Cyrus, 134
Roberts, Moses F., 387,407
Roberts, W., 196
Robertson, _____,195,495
Robertson, Benj., 170,172,312
Robertson, Charles, 513,514
Robertson, Davis and hands, 564
Robertson, Elijah, 313
Robertson, Jas., 170
Robertson, Levi, 347
Robertson, Walter, 229
Robertson, William, 365
Robeson, Asa, 209
Robinson, John, 86,87
Robinson, William, 365,471
Robison, Rutherford, 554,555,556
        564
Robson, Robert, 362,367
Roddy's Causeway, 563
Rodgers, James, 532
Rodgers, Sam'l.,48
Rodgers, Sarah, 135
Roe, James, 368
Rogers, Ephriam, 269
Rogers, James, 536
Rogers, Robert, 375
Rogers, Samuel, 48,135
Rogers, Sarah, 48
Rollman, William, 347
Rook, Benj., 66
Rook, Jno. 57
Rosan, Henry, 64
Rosannah, 16
Rosbury, John, 537
Roses, road, 566
Ross, (Capt.),366
Ross's Cart way, 337
Ross, Daniel, 81,83,197,199,200,238,
      246,264,277,377,371,375,414
        557,563
Ross, Daniel, 240 (marked out)
Ross, Daniel Sr., 566
Ross, David, 313
Ross old cartway, 414
Roswell, Solomon, 359,523,531,549
Rowland, Robert, 463,511
Roy, _____,195
Roy, Wiley, 354,406,425
Royal, (Doct.),486
Royal, Joseph, 150,205,528
Royal, Rich. R.,150

Rudisel, John, 251,264,336,353,421
Ruleman, William, 49,115,118,122,124
        127,240,272,282,495,513,514,
        539
Russell, Anselem, 25,34,35,36,42,140
        162,283,299
Russell, Anselem, 268(marked out)
Russell, Austin, 25,34,35
Russell, Jesse D., 304,305,326,334,
        345,355,520,521,557
Russell, John, 13,334
Rust, George C., 30,31,38,51,114,207
        243,326,359,367,384
Rust, Jeremiah, 207,374,414,420,565
Rutherford, (Squire),137
Rutherford, Dudley,152
Rutherford, Griffith, 124,176,211,
        233,379,400
Rutherford, Griffith Sr.,159
Rutherford, Henry, 81,112,136,159,176
        200,211,234,269,313,321,379,400
Rutherford, Jas., 152
Rutherford, John, 88,144,176,200,217,
        280,313,318,319,325,345,435
        502,520,521,527,546,547,549
        550,551,554,555
Rutherford, Jno.,556(marked out)
Rutherford, John (Trustee),436
Rutherford, John Sr., 159
Rutherford and Murray, 267,381
Rutland, Isaac, 319,502
Rutledge, Henry M., 121,297,325,344,390
        398,443,444,446,450,458,469
        478,510,552,560,565 a.

S

Sanders, 49,344,465,510
Sanders, (Esq.),418,508
Sanders, Aaron, 474,475,476,477
Sanders, Briton, 45,235
Sanders, David, 140,173,176,178,179,
        180,183,185,187,371,413,532,536
Sanders, George, 489
Sanders, Hallan, 49
Sanders, Richard, 115,118,121,362,373,
        375,376,377,381,382,383,384,
        385,386,389,390,392,495,513,531
        532,549
Sanders, Theophilis, 246,253,258,329,
        330,365,371,532,534,537,540
Sanders, Thomas, 141
Sanders, William, 208,371

Senderson and McIver, 169,172
Sandeys Old Place, 272
Sandford, John, 462,564
Sands, Thomas, 141
Sarah, 48,135
Savage, (Capt.),564
Scarborough, _____,366,540
Scarborough, Edmond, 198,337
Scarbrough, John, 85
Scearcy, Robert, 170,172
Scott, Jno., 246
Scruggs, James, 170,173,231,232,
      315,320
Scruggs, Jno., 170,173
Scudder, Philip J., 173
Searcy, William, 337
Seat (Esquire),413
Seat, William P., 81,518
Seaton, William, 271
Sellers, Isaac, 183
Semion, 49
Severe, Charles, 121,157,161,240,
      243,298
Severe, Robert, 121,166,170,180,181,
      182,183,185
Severe, Valentine, 224,225,226
Sevier, Charles, 109,121,140,156,281,
      415,474,476,486
Sevier, Rbt., 175,243
Sevier, Volentine, 524,527
Sewell, Jacob, 164
Shafer, George, 557
Shankle, Abraham, 420
Shankle, George, 115,118,120,121,279,
      462,471,487,488,490,491,492,
      493,494,498,499
Shanklin, John, 313
Shannon, (Sheriff),50
Shannon, Archibald, 57,250
Shannon, Finis W., 193,205,213
Shannon, G., 215
Shannon, George, 193,205,213
Shannon, John D., 31,37,45,73,114,143,
      155,195,201,204,240,290,328,
      329,339,361,363,372,409,415
      417,420,429,430,431,432,433,
      435,436,437,438,439,440,441
      442,443,444,445,446,447,448,
      449,450,451,452,453,454,465,471
      483,503,528,537,544,554,555,556
      557,558
Shannon, John D., 459 (marked out)
Shannongs Landing, 150,153,155,194,195,
      201,208,235,236,239,260,340,363,
      369,463,508

Shannon, Samuel H., 3,4,6,13,20
      20,27,61,73,81,83,92,
      126,134,140,141,144,150,
      174,193,195,199,205,206,
      213,289,239,251,270,276
      299,302,322,368,370,372
      396,407,412,425,434,472
      472,474,486,495,504,506
      513,514,529,534
Shannon, Thomas, 1,3,5,6,25,30,
      31,62,75,81,126,146,153,
      154,167,171,174,176,188,
      193,205,225,230,232,235,239
      241,242,247,251,253,256,259
      264,268,287,288,290,291,296
      308,315,333,334,339,354,382
      385,409,417,419,421,423,434
      435,441,442,447,448,453,455
      456,458,462,471,483,485,487
      495,502,503,506,507,513,519,523
      526,529,565 a
Shannon, Thos., 423(marked out)
Sharp, Alfred, 532, 536
Sharp, Anthony, 266,313
Sharp, E., 266
Sharp, John, 265,346
Sharp, William, 313
Shaw, John, 463,530
Shaw, Timothy, 462
Shaw, Wm., 231,321
Shelby County, 160,526
Shelby County Court, 149,207,209
Shelly, Elis Wm., 198
Shelly, Joseph, 539
Shelly, Thomas, 337,356,357,366,
      539
Shepherd, Abraham, 174,319
Shepherd, William, 84,319,509,511
Sherley, Paul, 163,410
Sherwood, Wm., 170,172,313,314
Shinault, Walter, 160,313
Shinault, Wm., 149,160,209
Shinault and Yeary,313
Shockler, B., 368
Shropshire, David, 366,413,539,
      543
Shute, Asa, 319,496
Shute, Thomas, 313,319
Sikes, Cyrus, 375
Simmes and Greer, 231
Simmons, Samuel, 25,34
Simms, Higgin J., 390
Simms, Thos., 184
Simpson, 142
Simpson, Alfred, 540

S (Cont'd)

Simpson, Nathan, 6,20,64,66,
     125,126m127,153,163,173
     256,384,385,386,362,375
     376,378,381,382,383,384
     385,389,390,392,420,471
Simson, Golden, 49
Sitter, James W., 447
Sitters, Isaac, 447
Skinner, Evans, 173,496
Sloan, John, 170,306,319
Smith, ____,195
Smith, (Capt.),76
Smith, (Squire),137
Smith, Abraham, 271,323,329,351
     358,395
Smith, Andrew, 70
Smith, Benjamin, 124,211,299,313,
     314,399,463
Smith, Bennett, 186,218
Smith, Burd B., 153,196,201,208,209,
     213,329,368,369,396,401,408
     422,519
Smiths Company, 465
Smith, Co. (Captain),76,137,258,271
Smith, Francis, 128,472,482,504,506
Smith, Guy,22,24,28,32,33,92,102,109
     115,144,147,196,199,200,222,
     233,239,240,241,253,258,281,
     329,348,364,369,378,412,418,
     422,529,534,537
Smith, Guy, 241 (marked out)
Smith, John J., 45,73,88,109,120,134,
     153,196,209,217,221,229,255,
     271,281,329,333,340,342,343
     347,369,372,423,475,519
Smith, Oliver B., 263
Smith, Richard, 43,124,211,212,496
Smith, Ruben, 338
Smith, Stephen, 260,367
Smith, Thomas J., 42,76,109,114,138
     162,196,230,235,240,263,267,290
     350,351,424,426,451,456,459,503
     505,506,508,541,543,563
Smith, Thos. J., 266,423(marked out)
Smith, Thomas J. Co. (Captain),281,534
Smith, William, 121,170,172,173,176,178
     196,313
South Fork ferry, 81
Sowell, Jacob, 350
Sparks, Daniel, 337
Spencer, 50,70,132
Spencer, Clark, 35,36,82,115,118,121,150
     181,182,183,185,188,189,191,192,
     217,313,372,512

Spencer's Creek, 414
Spencer, Hiram, 564
Spencer, Isaac, 184,203
Spencer, John, 83,183,319,364
     371,386,387,392,408,422,
     425,434,444,458,463,470,
     477,505,510,545,546,547,
     549,550,551,554,555,556
     558
Spencer, John Jr., 564
Spencer, Jordan, 48,57
Spencer, Seymour, 563
Spencer, William J., 83,158,179
     240,246,249,252,253,326,
     329,344,368,397,462,465,
     467,469,486,497,498,510
     511,532,536
Spencer, William Sen., 83,564
Spraggins, Samuel, 319
Spring Branch, 206
Spring Creek, 275,335,369,462
Springer, Jesse, 564
Spruce, Joseph, 70,407,425,509
Stalcup, George, 41,125
Stalkup, James, 6,22,41,42,50
     60,99,100,101,127,217,228
     369,537
Stalkup, John, 41,86,89
Stalkup, John, 62,(marked out)
Stalings, Thomas, 562
Stamps, Thomas, 525
Standley, James, 145
Stanley, B., 464
Stanley's branch, 156,195,335
Stanley, James, 444
Stanley, Widow, 564
Stanlkeen, James, 22
Starnes, John, 20,21,57,130,237
     240,250,282
Starnes, Moses, 21,22,57,115,118
     237,250,337,392,486,515,
     516,517,541
Stays, Wm., 154
Steed, Callier A., 420,464,471,
     487,488,489,490,491,492,493
     494,498,499
Steed, Moses, 130,420,464,473,479,
     487
Steel, Nathaniel, 149,207
Steel, William, 464,537
Step, John, 567
Step, William F., 567
Stephens, Josiah, 404
Stephens, Levin, 338

S (Cont'd)

Stephens, Lewis, 313
Stephens, William, 271
Stephenson, William, 510
Stewart, (Col.), 368
Stewart, (Squire), 137
Stewart, Andrew, 534,537
Stewart, Bartholomew G., 1,4,8,11,
    13,16,17,18,20,26,27,30,31,32,
    39,41,42,51,52,53,56,57,70,75,
    83,86,91,92,96,97,102,112,113,
    124,128,129,133,134,136,142,143
    144,165,192,203,214,222,223,227
    232,243,248,258,265,269,284,287
    292,295,297,304,322,327,329,330
    340,344,350,358,360,369,374,376
    385,388,389,405,407,409,419,429
    430,439,440,441,442,451,453,454,462
    470,500,506,521,526,535,538,557
    565 a.
Stewart County, 85
Stewart, James, 41,534
Stewart, John, 278,350,476,481,487,
    490,522
Stewart and Wilson, 322,406,408
Still, George W., 82,282,554
Stobaugh, John, 50,61,62,187,190,367,
    386,387,392,501,520
Stockton, _____,195
Stockton, Daniel D., 522
Stockton, John C., 156,356,357,386,387
    396,401,408,430,431,432,433,434
    435,536,437,438,439,440,441,442,
    443,444,445,446,447,448,449,450
    451,452,453,454,476,481,522,564
Stockton, Jno. C., 459,(marked out).
Stoddert, William, 26,73,151,205,258,265
    268,295,409,455,456,458,503,519,
    535,543
Stokes, John, 319
Stokes, Jordan G., 28,45,50,58,75,76,77,84,
    88,101,111,114,120,142,192,200,207,
    221,256,281,367,475,483,484,489,520
    521.
Stone, E. P. T., 195
Stone, Reuben P. T., 14,39,42,45,46,58,69,
    70,75,76,94,101,105,106,118,122,126
    127,216,217,292,396,425,429,430,431
    470,479,507,527,558.
Stotharto Robert, 406
Stotts, William, 541
Stoven, Jno., 214
Stranes, John, 20
Strong, Christopher, 222

Strother, Henry, 468,469,518
Stroud, Wm., 170,242,418
Strudwick and Ashe, 315
Stubblefield, Clement, 170,173
    313
Stubblefield and Swindle, 313
Stubblefield, Thomas, 107
Stump, Christopher, 232,320
Stubblefield, A., 496
Sulliman, Thos. N., 497
Sullivan, 49
Sullivan, Daniel, 36,45,335,
    357
Sullivan, George, 275,335
Sullivan, Lee, 229,230,313,469
    497,542
Sullivan, Levy, 49
Sullivan, Smith, 6
Sullivan, Turner, 404,435,454
    491
Summer, Jethro, 319
Sutton, Harriet, 230
Sutton, John, 85,279,346
Sutton, Moses, 229,230
Sutton, Wm., 230
Swan, Isaac, 277,363,462,463
    516,550
Swan, Samuel, 77,86,121,195,
    225,284,285,286,363,406
    421,425,429,430,431,432
    433,434,435,436,437,438
    439,440,441,442,443,444
    445,446,447,448,449,450
    451,452,453,454,473,479
    527,530
Swancy, John, 50
Swandies, Frederick, 402,403
Swann, Sam'l. H., 459(marked
    out).
Swanson, Edmond, 235,320
Swanson, James, 242,320
Swanson, Peter, 170,173
Swaver, John, 69
Swindle, Isaac, 496
Swindle and Stubblefield, 313
Synne, Deveraux, 86
Sypert, Stephen, 195,207,304
    305,326,362,373,375,
    375,376,377,378,381
    382,383,384,389,390
    474,475,476,479,486
    519
Sypress Creek, 508

T

Talbot, Joseph H., 11,350,354,543,561
Tallieferro, Benj., 171,173,319
Tally, (Mr.), 198,238
Tally, John, 337,366,546
Tally, Sterling, 337,366,540,563
Tally, William, 197
Tally, Wisdom, 563
Tantrum, Euberry, 473,479
Tapley, James, 537
Tarbutton, James, 366,464,540
Tarbutton, Joseph, 420,474,475,476,479
        481,483,484,487
Tate, Larke, 130
Tate, Turner, 181,200,369,408,422,515,
        516,517,518
Taylor (Squire),137,537
Taylor, Drury, 314
Taylor, Francis, 6,8,13,16,20,81,173,199
    201,213,214,215,271,277,304,305,314
    326,330,364,408,471,473,479,495,514
    518,534,537,548
Taylor, Francis, 11 (marked out).
Taylor, Gamaliel, 13
Taylor, George, 82,96
Taylor, George M., 93,96
Taylor, George W., 42,45,92,93,95,96,97
    115,228,330,368,464,564
Taylor, Hugh P., 28,29
Taylor, Jesse, 557,559
Taylor, Nathaniel, 319
Taylor, Samuel, 1,5,7,8,11,13,14,16,17,18,
    19,20,21,22,24,31,32,39,42,44,47,
    58,59,64,65,69,76,80,86,91,92,97,
    102,111,112,114,117,122,128,136,144
    147,186,187,192,204,205,212,215,222,
    239,253,256,267,269,277,284,286,288,
    290,303,304,344,354,378,394,395,411,
    412,416,419,428,439,461,473,482,486
    513,519,529,538,565 a.
Taylor, Thos., 26
Tayo, William, 249,337
Tedford, Jas., 212
Tedford, John, 130
Tedford, Joseph, 45,69,115,121,124,130
Tedford, Jothias, 130
Tedford, Prudence, 367,389
Tedford, Simon, 130
Tedford, Walter, 45,275
Tedford, William, 25,34,36,130
Telfapaugh, Daniel, 342
Tedford and Little, 222
Tennessee, 21,22,23,26,34,35,41,58,59,60,
        61,63,64,65,66,67,69,89,90,97,
        100,102,104,105,108,125,126,127,
        157,166,174,175,176,177,178,227,
        228,229,298,299,301,302,307,
        321,322,350,351,352,353,392,394
        395,401,402,403,411,415,428,
        470,478,479,552,553,558,559,560
Tennessee, State of, 62,362
        (marked out).
Tennessee River, 1,5,160,207
Tepit, James, 77,86
Terrell, John, 314
Terrell, Wm., 170
Terry, 50,209
Tharp, Wm., 497
Thedford, Jothias, 130
Thedford, John, 130
Thedford, Joseph, 45,115,118,121
        129,322,333,335,406
Thedford, Prudence, 322,376
Thedford, Simon, 130
Thedford, Walter, 45,129,333,521
        526
Thedford, William, 34,35,36,130
        370
Theobald, James, 129
Theobald, James F., 45,65,68,83
    119,129,156,195,305,329,342
    343,345,350,353,365,417,419
    423,446,460,471,474,517,526
Thetford, James, 201
Thetford, Joseph, 220
Thetford, William, 25,518,565
Thomas, (Squire),137&367
Thomas, Andrew, 80
Thomas,Brother, 344
Thomas Company (Captain),419
Thomas, David, 11,44,73,121,122
        195,279,280,287,407,429
Thomas, James, 462
Thomas, John, 1,6,7,11,17,18,68
        80,83,97,105,111,115,116
        133,135,138,144,146,192
        197,201,204,205,258,303,
        304,329,330,335,339,344,
        362,364,367,462,465,495,
        534,535,537,564
Thomas, John Jr., 564
Thomas, John P., 13,14,18,19,23
        24,25,34,115,183,201,213
        239,377,429
Thomas, John Sen., 564
Thomas, Micajah, 170,314
Thomas;s Mill, 336,540
Thomas, Nathan, 303,541
Thomas, Sam'l., 80,197,255,476
Thomas, William, 122,124
Thomas, Zachariah, 6

T (Cont'd)

V Cont'd)

Vaulx, James, 124,163,173,177,178,179
        180,200,208,211,212,224,225
        226,239,329,364,466,468,469
        495,498,508,549
Vaulx, James, 270,532 (marked out)
Vinsant, Thomas, 417,422,532,536
Vinsons, Thomas, 408

W

Waddell's Bridge, 367,413,420
Waddell's Creek, 477,565
Waddell, Samuel D., 217,220,227,334,340
      374,420,477,536,537,555,565
Waddell, Samuel D., 548 (marked out).
Waddle's Ford, 50
Waddle, Samuel D., 6,50,102,108,115
Wade's Creek, 201
Wade, James, 205
Waggoner, David, 238
Waggoner, John, 238
Waggoner, John Jr., 238
Waggoner, William, 271
Wain County, 464
Walker Company (Capt.),137
Walker, Jacob, 171
Walker, James, 49,171,319,467,468
Walker, John, 314
Walker, John M., 122,163,173,187
      188,189,191,192,195,217
Wallace, Francis, 463
Waller, Jonathan, 86,87
Wallin, James, 566
Walsh, John M., 200
Walsh, Jonathan, 201,216,217,220,225
      226,228,304,305,326,377,532,
      537,562
Walton, Isaac, 217
Warlick (Mr.),250
Warlick's Mill, 84,161,250,338,415
Warlick, Phillip, 252,268,338,362,397,
      408,415,422,537
Warner, Amos, 521,547
Warner, S. A., 407
Warner, Samuel A., 276,499
Warner, Samuel M., 193
Warren, Green, 112,132,155
Warren, John, 132,200,202
Watkins, Achabod, 1,271,329,337,340,
      343,352
Watkins, W., 250
Watson and Bowers, 495
Watson and Bryan, 316,497

Watson, George H., 358,480,481
Watson, Jacob, 371
Watson, Jason, 144
Watson, Jeremiah, 314
Watson, John, 314
Watson, Richard C., 497
Watson, Robert C., 320,370,391
Watson, William L., 70
Watt, James H., 272
Watt, John, 272
Watt, Samuel, 333
Watts, James, 333
Watts, John, 333
Watts, Thomas, 333
Watts, Thomas T., 272
Wayne, 564
Weakly, Polly, 270
Weakly, Robert, 497
Weaks, Abraham, 194
Wear, John, 47,49,87,115
Weatherspoon (Mr.),461
Weatherspoon, William, 365,408
      557,559
Weaver, 534,537
Weaver, Asa, 507
Weaver, John, 11,13,16,18,65,66,
      67,69,70,71,72,130
Weaver, Joshua, 239,260,329,338,
      342,343,352,367,369,421,463
      486,508,518,537
Weaver, William, 532, 536
Webb, Able, 364
Webb, Cyrus, 96
Webb, Handley, 515,516,517,518
Webb, Henly, 366
Webb, Henry, 337
Webb, John, 494
Webb, Josiah, 57
Webb, Robert, 57,200,515,516,517
      518
Webb, Sandy (heirs of), 497
Webb, W., 250
Webber, Philip (heirs of), 469
Weger, John, 33
Weir, Hugh, 87
Weir, John, 25,51,86,118,165,184
      200,223,289,314,329,368,408
      421,422,495,501,520,537,545
      564
Welburn, William, 43,76,77,380
Welch, John M., 45,49,52,77,92,93
      95,97,100,101,103,116,272
      283,338,362,368

W Cont'd)

Welch, Jonathan, 83,163,213,356,
        357.
Welche, John M., 338
Wells, Abel, 462
Wells and Gibbins, 171
Wells, Harden, 173
Welsh, Jonathan, 130,131,224
Wharton, John, 279,280,465,508
Wheaton, D., 314
Wheaton, Dal (dec.of),231
Wheaton, Sterling, 178
Wheaton and Tisdale, 319,320
Whitaker, John, 232
White, Benjamin, 6,70,71,72,73,85,91
White, Charles, 543
White, David, 386,387
White, Drew, 272
White, Greenup, 4,14,347,362,408,422,
        518,521,526
White, Greenup, 11 (marked out).
White, Robert, 466
White, William, 319
Whitesides, Jenkins, 171,319
Whitfield, Henry, 412
Whitt, Benjamin, 70
Whitworth, 49
Whitworth, Fendull, 51,141
Whitworth, Samuel, 298,302
Wiatt, H.C.,502
Wiggins, 314
Wiggs, Martin, 466
Wilbourn, William, 27,43,45,65,67,68,74
        76,77,82,85,140,162,201,203,213
        260,336,339,382,421,465,495,507,
        534,536,537,539,562,563,564,565
Wilbourn, William, 33(marked out)
Wilkerson, William, 471
William, S. H., 320
Williams, 195
Williams, (Mr.),413
Williams, Adon,539
Williams, Allen F., 560
Williams, Allen T.,348
Williams, Allen T., 56,(marked out).
Williams, Amos, 45,140,162,179,329
        509
Williams, Calvin J., 49
Williams, Christopher, 557,559
Williams Company (Capt.),61,62,68,137,208
Williams, Drury,362,373,375,376,377,386
        387,390
Williams, Edward, 344,369,377
Williams, Elijah, 338

Williams, Elisha, 49
Williams, Iredell, 532,536
Williams, Joseph, 15,171,173,
        319_
Williams, Lewis, 103,127
Williams and McGovock, 231,320
Williams, Patrick, 195
Williams, Rice, 48,551
Williams, Riding S., 348
Williams, Robert W., 171,314
Williams, William, 85,284
Williams, Willoughby,280,314,
        319,320
Williamson (Col.),532
Williamson's Company, 465
Williamson's Company (Capt.),535
Williamson, George, 208
Williamson, James, 208,562
Williamson, James Company(Capt)
        365
Williamson, James D., 539,566
Williamson's Mill, 532,539
Williamson, Thomas, 68,233,234,
        257,458,562
Williamson, Thomas (Col.),539
Williamson, William, 156
Willbourn, 266
Willbourn, N. (Dr.),195
Willbourn, Nicholas, 556
Williford, Britain, 171,270
Willis (Col.),272
Willis, A., 495
Willis, Abel,200,329,338,343,345
        355,368,565
Willison, William, 25
Wilson, 336
Wilson,(Widow),272,338
Wilson and Bowers, 336
Wilson, Caldwell G., 493,514,520
        546
Wilson, Francis, 229
Wilson, George, 314
Wilson, J., 261
Wilson, J.C.,433
Wilson, J.H., 234,365,474,476,481
Wilson, James, 26,95,125,314
Wilson, James H., 264,424,487,488
        490,515,516,517,518,520,521
        522,528,550,551,554,556
Wilson, James H., 543(marked out)
Wilson, Jason, 83,115,136,137,143,
        144,201,213,242,243,264,302
        347,365,395
Wilson, Jason H., 443,483,488,510

W (Cont'd)

520,521,528,543,550,554,556
        565(a).
Wilson, Jessee,198,337,366,540
Wilson, John, 171,173,314,448
Wilson, John C., 479,520,521,556
Wilson, Joseph, 33,34
Wilson, Lewis D., 314
Wilson, Maths,198
Wilson, Matthew,95,125
Wilson, Moses, 27,565
Wilson, Robert,232,357,409,412
Wilson, Robert,362(marked out).
Wilson, Samuel, 87,110,201
Wilson, Samuel D., 130,131,132,212,254
        264,365,424,432,473,488,529,532
        553,554,556
Wilson and Stewart, 322,328,406,408
Wilson, W., 106
Wilson, William, 25,27,41,52,65,66,86,
        87,115,116,118,121,179,217,229
        233,237,250,261,292,356,357,379
        399,400,424,425,435,516,520,521
        532,536,545,546,547,549,550,551
        554,555,556,558,565(a).
Wilson, William(son of Moses),27
Wilson, William M., 399,433,449,471,476
        514,553,556
Wilson, Young E., 177,178,179,180,213
        565 (a).
Wincer, John, 202
Winchester and Carr, 97
Wingate, William, 299
Winn, Richard A. G.,178
Winstead, Felicia Charles, 510
Winter, 79
Winters, James, 40,41,45,53,54,70,71,72,
        79,101,103,329,342,343,509,510
Winters, Lane, 337
Witherspoon, William, 553
Witwo, Fendull, 51
Witworth, 49
Womble, John, 269
Wood, Joseph, 548
Wood, Robert, 548
Wood, William, 269
Woodcock, John H. and Co., 262
Woodfin, M., 211,212
Woodfin, Moses, 525
Woodfolk, William W., 6,7
Woodfork, William W., 16,438
Woods, Samuel, 431
Word, John, 109
Work, John, 109

Wortham, Charles, 420,473,479
        483,484
Wortham, James L., 19,34,35,36
        40,65,70,153,196,208,209
Wortham, James L., 240(marked out)
Wortham, James S., 40,66
Wright, James, 24,33,38,64,75,195
        323,328
Wright, Roderick, 38,64,67,77,119
        163
Wright, William, 540
Wyatt, John F., 478,485
Wyatt, John H., 276
Wyman, Tiffany and Co., 433
Wynn and Bedford, 185
Wynn, Deveraux, 47
Wynn, Duncan, 57
Wynn, George, 49
Wynn, Robert H., 189,309,517
Wynn, Robert H., 300 (marked out)
Wynn, Thomas L., 191
Wynne, Albert H., 355
Wynne, Bedford S., 489
Wynne, Debrair, 45
Wynne, Deveraux, 45,57,77,81,84,86
        237,250,270,333,338,414
        415,432,495,513,514
Wynne, George,115,122,125,127
Wynne, George L., 554
Wynne, James, 545,546,547,549,550
        551,554,556
Wynne, R. H., 506
Wynne, Robert H.,6,31,96,104,241
        272,294,330,405,419,485
        490,526,544,550,561,563
Wynne, Robert W., 506
Wynne, Thomas, 474,476,515,516,517
Wynne, Thomas L., 187,188,189,192
        256,528.

Y

Yarbrough, Henry, 235
Yeary, Isaac, 314
Yeary and Shinault,313
Yoes, Deborah,171
Yoke, George,431
Young's Branch, 49,86,87,209,369
Young's Company,465
Young's Company (Capt.),137,254
        258,275
Young's Creek, 152,154
Young, James,38,49,57,115,118,121

121,150,160,201,
212,250,338,366
Young, James,33 (marked out)
Young, James Sr.,25
Young, John, 57,187,366,392
Young, Milton, 537
Young, Robert,49,57,115,118,121
Young, Samuel,95,115
Yount, John, 198,337,563
Yues, Deborah,14

Z

Zenis, Allen, 497

END March 3, 1938

TENNESSEE

MADISON COUNTY
RECORDS
MINUTE BOOK #I
1821 - 1825

HISTORICAL RECORDS PROJECT

OFFICIAL PROJECT NO. 165-44-6999

COPIED UNDER WORKS PROGRESS ADMINISTRATION

MRS. JOHN TROTWOOD MOORE

STATE LIBRARIAN & ARCHIVIST SPONSOR

MRS. ELIZABETH D. COPPEDGE

STATE DIRECTOR OF WOMEN'S & PROFESSIONAL PROJECTS

MRS. PENELOPE JOHNSON ALLEN

STATE SUPERVISOR

MRS. KATHLEEN W. CARADINE

SUPERVISOR FIFTH DISTRICT

JOHN H. MCMILLAN

COPYIST

CLARA ALLEN

TYPIST

MAY 1936

MADISON COUNTY
MINUTE BOOK COUNTY COURT
VOL. 1   1821-1825

PREFACE

A List of Attorneys:

  Mr. McKinzie

  Mr. Garner

  Mr. King

  Mr. Wyatt

  Mr. King

  Mr. Talbot

  Mr. Murry

  Mr. Thomas

  Mr. McCampbell

  Mr. Gillespie

  Mr. Stoddert

  Mr. Huntsman

  Mr. Hays

  Mr. Hughes

  Mr. Allen

  Mr. Bradford

  Mr. Arnold

  Mr. Dunlap

  Mr. Hess

  Mr. Martin

  Mr. Haslet

  Mr. Taylor

Pg. Alexanders Office Monday December 17th 1821

1   Be it remembered that on Monday the 17th day of December in the year of our Lord one thousand eight hundred and twenty one in pursuance of the act of the General Assembly establishing new counties West of the Tennessee River pass= ed at the last session held at Murfrusboro the following persons to wit Bartholomew G. Stewart David Jawitt William Atcheson Robert H Dyer John Thomas Adam R. Alexander Duncan McIver Joseph Lynn James Trousdale Hurndon Haralson William Bradin Samuel Taylor and William W Woodfork, gentlemen justices of the peace by virtue of a commission from his excellency William Carroll Governor of the State of Tennessee appeared at the house of Adam R Alexander Esp. in the county of Madison as directed by the before recited act and took the sev- eral oaths prescribed by the constitution and laws of the state whereupon.

       At a Court of Pleas and Quarter Sessions began and held for the county of Madison on Monday 17th. day of December 1821 and in the 46th. year of Ameri- can Independence.

       Present the Worshipful Bartholomew G. Stewart David Garrett, William Atchison Robert H Dyer, John Thomas Adam R Alexander Duncan McIver Joseph Lynn James Trousdale Hurndon Haralson William Bradin Samuel Taylor and William W Woodfork, gentlemen.

       Ordered that Robert Hughes be appointed Clerk protempore of this court.

       The Court then proceeded the ballot for a clerk and after counting the votes Roderick McIver was declared duly and constitutionally elected Clerk of this Court who thereupon took the several oaths prescribed by law.

       The court then proceeded to ballot for a sheriff and upon counting the votes Thomas Shannon Esq. was duly and constitutionally elected Sheriff of the County of Madison for the ensuing two years.

P.2 Alexanders Office Madison County Monday Dec. 17,1821

       Who thereupon took the several oaths prescribed by the constitution and laws of the state.

       Ordered that Hurndon Haralson Esquire be appointed chairman of this court.

       County then adjourned until tomorrow morning ten o'clock.

                                   Attest

Tuesday Morning 18th December 1821

       Court met agreeable to adjournment. Present the same Justices that were yesterday. Roderick McIver who was on yesterday appointed Clerk of this court appeared in open court and with Duncan McIver Joseph Lynn and George Todd his securities entered into and acknowledged their bond in the penal sum of Five Thousand Dollars conditioned as the law directs for the faithful discharge of duties of his office which bond was ordered to be entered of record and is in words and figures following to wit. Know all men by these presents that we Roderick McIver Duncan McIver Joseph Lynn and George Todd and held and firmly bound unto William Carroll Esquire Governor of the State of Tennessee and his successors in office in the just and full sum of Five Thousand dollars the payment of which well and truly to be made and each of us bind ourselves our heirs. Exs. and Adms. jointly and severally firmly by these present sealed with our seals and dated this 18th. day of December 1821

       The condition of above oblication is such that whereas the above bound Roderick McIver has been appointed Clerk of the County Court of Pleas and Quarter Sessions in and for the County of Madison, now if the said Roderick McIver shall safely keep all the records of said Court of Pleas and Quarter Sessions and in all things faith fully discharge the duties of the said office then the above obligation to be void else to be and remain in full force and virtue. Attest

                 R McIver (seal)   Joseph Lynn (seal)
                 Duncan McIver (seal) George Todd (seal)

Alexander Office Madison County Tuesday December 18,1821

Pg.
3
     Thomas Shannon who was on yesterday appointed Sheriff in and for the county of Madison appeared in open court and with Adam R Alexander David Jeregan and Samuel H Shannon his securities entered into and acknowledge their bond in the penal sum of Five Thousand Pounds conditioned as the law directs for the faithful discharge of the duties of his office which Bond was ordered to be entered of record and is in words and figures following (to wit).

     Know all men by these presents that we Thomas Shannon Adam R Alexander David Jernegan and Samuel H Shannon are held and firmly bound unto William Carroll Esquire Governor of the State of Tennessee and his successors in office in the just and full sum of Five Thousand Pounds the payment of which will and truly to be made and we and each of us bind ourselves our heirs exe's and Admr's jointly and severally firmly by these presents. Sealed with our seals and dated this 18th. day of December 1821.

     The conditions of above obligations is such that wheras the above bound Thomas Shannon has been constituted and appointed Sheriff of Madison County by an election held on yesterday by the Court of Pleas and Quarter Sessions of said county if therefore the said Thomas Shannon shall will and truly execute and truly do return make of the Process and precepts to him directed and pay and satisfy all fees and sums of money by him received or levied by virtue of any process into the proper office by which the same by the tenor thereof ought to be paid or to the person or persons to whom the same may be due his, her or their excr's Admi's Attorneys or Agents and in all other things will and truly and faithfully execute the duties of said office of sheriff during his continuance therein the the above obligation to be void otherwise to remain in full force and virtue.

     Attest   Thomas Shannon (seal)   David Jeregan   (seal)
R McIver Clerk   Adam R Alexander   (seal) Samuel H Shannon   (seal)

P.4 Alexanders Office Madison County Tuesday Dec 18,1821

     The Court then proceded to elect a Register for this County and on counting our the votes it was found that John T Porter was duly and constitutionally elected Register for the County of Madison.

     The Court then proceded to ballot for a Rainger for the County of Madison and to that office do appoint James Brown.

     The court then proceeded to ballot for a County Trustee for the County of Madison and a counting of votes it was found that William Atchison Squire was duly elected to that office and who thereupon came into open court and took the several oaths prescribed by law and Bartholomew G Stewart and Samuel Dickens his securities entered into and acknowledged their bond in the penal sum of Two Thousand Dollars conditioned as the law directs for the faithful discharge of the duties of his office which bond was ordered to be recorded.

     The Court then proceded to ballot for a Coroner and found that William Griffeth on counting the votes duly elected to that office who thereupon came into open court and took the several oaths prescribed by law and with Murdock Murchison and Duncan McIver his securities entered into and acknowledged their bond in the penal sum of Five Thousand dollars conditioned as the law directs for the faithful discharge of his office which bond was ordered to be recorded.

     The court then proceeded to ballot for constables and upon counting the votes Greenup White John Fare Elijah Jones William H Doak were declared duly and constitutionally elected constables of Madison County who thereupon took the several oaths prescribed by the constitution and laws of the State and entered into bonds the said Greenup White and Bartholomew G Stewart and William Atchison his securities John Fair with James Trousdale and Elijah Jones his securities. Elijah Jones with Duncan McIver and David Jarrett his securities and the said William H Doak with Samuel H Shannon and John L Partee his securities several in the penal sum of two hundred fifty pounds conditioned agreeable to law which Bonds are ordered recorded.

P.5 Alexanders Office Madison CountyTuesday December 18,1821

The Court then proceeded to levy a tax in persuance of the act entitled An act to direct the manner of collecting taxes West of the Tennessee river and for all other purposes for the purpose of defraying the expenses of the County whereupon it was ordered that the collectors of the State and country revenues do collect from each person from whom it should be collected and amount equal with that collected for the State revenue.

Ordered by the court that the following justices be appointed commissioners to take list of taxable property in this county (to wit) Samuel Taylor Squire in the 10th & 11th sections in the first and second rainges and the Ninth District Duncan McIver Esquire South of Samuel Taylor district and Southern boundary of said county James Trousdale Esq. in the 10th & 11th sections in the 10th. district and the Western and Northern boundary of said county and William Braden Esq. in the boundary of South and West of Maj. Trousdales district in said county and make returns at the next term of court.

An indenture of mortgage from James McAlister to William Bolding was produced in open court and proven by the oath of William Bolding (senior) a subscribing witness thereto to be act and deed of the said James McAlister for the purpose therein mentioned and ordered to be so certified.

The last will and testament of Lewis Jones deceased was produced in open court and proven by the oath of Elijah Jones Benjamin Jones and Agness Jones agreeable to the act of Assembly in the case made and provided and ordered to berecorded and on motion of Elijah Jones and Susan Jones who took the several oaths prescribed by law and wit John L Partee and Thomas Shannon their securities entered into and acknowledged their bond in the penal sum of Five Thousand Dollars that letters of Administration with the will annexed issued to the said Elijah Jones accordingly.

Henry L Gray Alexander B Bradford and Robert Hughes took the several oaths prescribed by law as attorneys at law in this county.

Alexander B Bradford produced in Court a commission from his Excellency William Carroll Esquire Goernor of the State of Tennessee appointing him Solicitor General of the 14th. Solicitoreal District and took thereupon the several oaths prescribed by the constitution and laws of the state.

P.6 Alexanders Office Madison County Tuesday December 18th. 1821

The last will and testament of Robert Doak deceased was produced in open court and provento be the last will and testament of the deceased by the oaths ofThomas Shannon and Robert H Wynne subscribing witnesses thereto and ordered to be recorded and Patsey Doak an executrix therein named came into court and agreed to take the burden and execution and entered into and acknowledged bond with Adam R Alexander and Thomas Shannon her securities in the penalty of Five Thousand Dollars conditioned agreeable to law whereupon it is ordered that letters testimentary do issue to the said Patsey Doak accordingly.

A Power of Attorney from Patsey Doak to William Donnel was produced in court and acknowledged by the said Patsey Doak to be her act and deed and ordered to be certified.

Ordered that the following persons be summoned by the Sheriff as Grand and Petite Jurors to the next term of the court (to wit) John Montgomery Martin Lorence Lewis Needham Henry N Coulter John Hardgraves Smith Sullivan James Dillard Moses Oldham Francis Taylor Zachariah Thomas William Davis Samuel ShannonJohn Bradberry Thomas James William L Parks Benjamin Jones David Jernigan William Espry Vincent Heralson James Caldwell James Baily Henry Raggin Francis Herrin Nathan Simpson James Brown Carter C Colleen.

Ordered that the Sheriff summons the following persons as Grand and Petite Jurors to the Circuit Court (to wit) Elisha Herrell Drury Bettis Benjamin White James Stalkeep Ezekial B McCoy, Gabriel Chandler Samuel D Waddle George Jentry Michael Clark Samuel Dichens William Harris John SPorter Jacob Bradberry Abner Brown George Todd Duncan McIver William E Buttes

P.6 William Bradin Ryland Chandler Henderson Haralson Stephen Lacy John Thomas Adam con-R Alexander Aquela Davis William W Woodfork and David Jarrett. The court then tin-adjourned until tomorrow morning 10 o'clock.
uedAlesanders Office Madison County Tuesday Dec. 18, 1821
Attest

P.7   Wednesday morning 19th. December 1821 Court met agreeable to adjournment present the Worshipful Herndon Haralson, Adam R Alexander Samuel Taylor, John Thomas David Jarrett, William Braden and William W Woodfolk. Gentlemen.

Ordered that David Jarrett Equire be appointed commissioner to take in the lists of taxable property in the territory attached to the western part of this county and that the territory attached to the Southern part of said county be attached to the district of which William Braden, Squire is commissioner and John Thomas Esquire do as a commissioner assist the said William Braden Esquire.

Ordered that the sheriff summons William H Doak a constable of this county to attend on the Grand Jury at the next term of this court.

An inventory of the estate of Robert Doak deceased was returned to Court by Patsey Doak the Executrix and ordered to be recorded.

John L Partee who was appointed Register of the County on yesterday this day came into open court took the several oaths prescribed by law and entered into and acknowledged bond with Adam R Alexander David Jarrett William W Woodfolk, James Brown, and Herdon Haralson in the penalty of Five Thousand pounds conditioned according to law.

Benjamin Blythe who was appointed a constable of this county on yesterday came into open court and took the several oaths prescribed by law and entered into and acknowledged bond with William Braden and David Jarrett his recurities in the penalty of two hundred fifty opounds conditioned according to law.

Present the Worshipful Duncan McIver.

P.8 Alexanders Office Madison County Wednesday Dec. 19th. 1821

James Brown who was appointed Rainger of this county on yesterday this day came into open court and took the several oaths prescribed by law.

On motion and petition filed ordered that Bartholomew G Stewart, Francis Taylor Jacob Bradberry Jr. Samuel Taylor and Thomas James be appointed a jury of view to view a way for a foad to run as follows, to wit beginning at the Court house thence to the nearest and best way by the Forked Deer Post Office and Francis Taylor Will as nearly as may be a direct course to the center of Carroll County to the Northern boundary of Madison County and make returns three off to the next term of court.

On motion and petition filed ordered that Duncan McIver Herndon Haralson, William Halton, George Todd, Ryland Chandler, Vencent Haralson, and Roderick McIver or any five of them be a jury appointed to view and lay off a road the nearest and best way from the present court house of Madison County to meet a road contimplated to be opened from the office of the 9th. district on the lines of this county near the North East corner of the 8th. section in the 2nd. raing, running by or so near Duncan McIvers mill on Jones Creek as the situation of the county there will admit so as to meet the road to be layed out from Henderson Court House near the above corner of the 8th. section and that the Sheriff of this county summons them for that purpose and that they report their proceedings to the next court.

Ordered that it be certified to the Bugadier General of the 11th. Bregade that this court was organized on Monday the 17th. day of December 1821.

Court then adjourned until Court in Course
Attest

P.   Alexanders Office Madison County Monday March 18, 1822
11   At a court began and held for the County of Madison at the house of Adam R Alexander on Monday the 18th. day of March 1822 and forty sixth year of American Independence.

Present the Worshipful William Braden Samuel Taylor, John Thomas, James

P.11   Trousdale, Duncan McIver Joseph Lynne, Robert H Dyer, Bartholomew G. Stewart,
cont.   William Atchison and Adam R. Alexander, Gentlemen. Ordered that Adam R. Alexander Esquire be appointed Chairman of this court in the absence of the chairman.

Daniel W Maury and David Thomas produced in court their license and it
appearing to the satisfaction of the court that they have heretofore taken the
several oaths prescribed by law as attorney at law they are permitted to
practice in this court.

A deed of bargain and sale from William E. Butter to George Todd was
this day produced in open court and acknowledged by said William E Butter to
be his act and deed for the purposes therein mentioned and ordered to be certified.

Joseph H. Talbot produced in court his license and thereupon took the
several oaths prescribed by law as an attorney at law in this court.

On motion of John Weaver and Hannah McMillan ordered that they be appointed Administrator and Administratrix of all and singular the goods chattles
right and credits of Robert McMillan deceased who thereupon entered into and
acknowledged bond with Jacob Frank and Daniel Crane their securities in the
penalty of sixteen hundred dollars conditioned agreeable to law and took the
oath of Admisstration.

P.12 Alexander Office Madison County Monday Mar. 18, 1822

Ordered that it be certified that Thomas Lacy is entitled to three wolf
scalps over the age of six months which he killed in the bounds of this county.

Ordered that it be certified that Thomas Lacy is entitled to three wolf
scalps over the age of six months which he killed in the bounds of this county.

Ordered that it be certified that Enoch Douthel is entitled to one wolf
scalf over the age of six months which he killed in the bounds of this county.

On motion of James Haley Administrator of all and singular the goods
chattles rights and credits of Isiah Haley deceased is granted him who thereupon took the oath of Administrator and entered into and acknowledged bond
with Thomas Hailey and Henry Butter, his securities in the penal sum of Eight
hundred dollars conditioned agreeable to law.

On motion of Duncan McIver, Administration of all and singular, the goods
chattels, rights and credits of James L Price deceased, is granted him who
thereupon took the oath of an administrator entered and acknowledged bond with
Thomas L. D. Parks and William Braden his securities in the penalty of Twelve
hundred dollars conditioned according to law.

James Foer came into court and records his stock mark as follows (towit)
a half crop over the right ear and a half crop under the left.

Vincent Harelson comes into court and records his stock mark as follows,
to wit. A half crop off the underside of each ear.

P.13 Alexanders Office Madison County March 18th. 1822

Bartholomew G. Stewart comes into court and records his stock mark, as
follows (to wit) a crop and slit in left ear and a hole in the right.

Joseph Lynn comes into court and records his stock mark as follows
(to wit) a crop of each ear and underbit out of the right ear.

Robert H Dyer comes into court and records his mark as follows (to wit) a smooth crop
a crop off the left ear.

and two slits in each ear. his stock mark as follows (to wit) a swollow
John Bradberry records his stock mark as follows (to wit)
James Caldwell records his stock mark as follows (to wit) a crop
fork in the right and an underbit in the left ear.
Samuel H Shannon records his stock mark as follows (to wit) a crop
and an underbit in the left and a half crop in the right ear.
Ordered that William McCauslin be appointed constable in the neighfor-
hood of William Atchison who thereupon took the several oaths prescribed by
a swollow fork in each ear and an overbit in the left.   Duncan McIver came
into court and records his stock mark as follows (to wit)

P.13 law and entered into and acknowledged bond with Moses Oldham and Francis
cont.Taylor his securities in the penalty of Twelve hundred & fifty dollars
conditioned agreeable to law.

On motion and petition of John P Thomas ordered that Thomas J ames
John Russell, John Bradberry William McCauslin and John Weaver be appointed
a Jury to view and mark out a way for a private road from the house of John
P. Thomas through the inclosure of Gamaliel Taylor into the premises of
said Thomas and make report to the present term of this court so as to do to
the least trouble.

P.14 Alexander Office Madison County Monday Mar. 18 1822

Ordered that Elijah Jones as constable be directed to attend the Grand
Jury at the present term of this court.

A deed of bargain and sales from Patsy Doak as administrator of Robert
Doak deceased to William H Doak was this day produced in open court and
acknowledged by the said Patsy Doak to be her act and deed for the purpose
named therein and ordered to be certified.

A deed of Bargain and Sale from Baptist McNab to Deborah Yues was this
day produced in open court and proven by the oaths of John P Thomas and Ruben
Stone subscribing witnesses thereto and ordered to be certified. A Deed of
Bargain & Sale from Jacob Bradberry to John Bradbury was this day produced
in open court and proven by the oaths of Samuel Taylor and William Atchison
subscribing witnesses thereto and ordered to be certified.

A deed of bargain and sale from Deborah Yues to William B Moore was this
day produced in open court and proven by the oaths of Samuel Taylor and John
Bradberuy subscribing witnesses thereto and ordered to be certified.

A deed of Bargain and Sale from Baptist McNab to William Atchison was
this day produced in open court and proven by the oaths of Samuel Taylor and
Greenup White subscribing witnesses thereto and ordered to be certified.

A deed of Bargain & Sale from Deborah Yues to William Atchison was this
day produced in open court and proven by the oaths of John P. Thomas and Reube
Stove subscribing witnesses thereto and order to be certified.

P.15 Alexanders Office Madison County Monday Mar. 18, 1822

A deed of bargain and sale from Joseph Williams to Adam R. Alexander
was this day produced in open court and proven by the oaths of Robert H Dyer
a subscribing witness thereto and ordered to be certified.

A deed of Bargain and Sale from Joseph McMinn to Adam R. Alexander wa s
this day produced in open court and proven by the oath of Robert H Dyer a
subscribing witness thereto and ordered to be certified.

Ordered that a Dedimus Postestatum issue to be directed to Robert H
Dyer and James Trousdale Esquire, to take the Relinquishment of Dower of
Margaret McGuire to two deeds of Bargain & Sale one from Laurence McGuire and
wife to Simson Vannorydale and the other from Laurence McGuire and wife to
Ann McAfee.

It appearing to the satisfaction of the court that at the December term
last of this court Calvin Jones presented a petition praying for leave to wit
erect a mill on Butlers Creed in the first range and eigth section and ninth
serveyors district on a track of one thousand acres of land of which the
said Calvin Jones was the owner and proprietor the prayer of said petition was
granted and it further appearing to the court that the Clerk neglected to
enter the order granting the same on the minutes it is therefore ordered by
the court that the said order be now made to have the same effect that it
should have had had it been entered on the minutes on the last term.

On Motion and petition filed it is ordered that Herndon Heralson, Ryland
Chandler and Park Chandler, have leave to erect a water grist mill and saw mill
on their land on Butlers Creek in this County.

P.16 Alexanders Office Madison County Monday March 18, 1822

On motion and petition filed ordered that Adam R. Alexander have leave
to erect a grist & saw mill on his land on Meridian Creek in the first range

P.16   eith section and in the 10th district of this county.
cont.   On motion and petition filed ordered that Duncan McIver have leave to
erect a mill and dam on his land across Jones Creek in the first range and ninth section of the ninth District in the county of Madison.

         On motion and petition filed ordered that Ezekiel B McCoy have leave to
erect a mill and dam across Trace Creek on his own land in the 2nd. range, ninth section of the Ninth district in the county of Madison.

         John T. Porter records his stock mark as follows (to wit) a swallow fork
in each ear and underbit in the left.

         Ordered that Bartholomew G. Stewart, Francis Taylor, Jacob Bradbury Jr.
Samuel Taylor and Thomas James the jury appointed to view and lay off a road
from the Court House in this county the nearest and best way by the Forked Deer
Post Office. Francis Taylors mills and thence on a direct course to the center
of Carroll County as far as the North boundary of this county have further
time till the next term of court to make report.

         An inventory of the estate of Robert McMillan was returned by John Weaver
administrator and Hannah McMillan Administratrix of Robert McMillan, deceased,
and ordered to be recorded.

         A bill of sale from William Atchison to John Bradbury for a negro woman
named Rosannah was this day produced in open court and acknowledge to be his
act and deed and ordered to be certified.

P.17 Alexander Office Madison County Monday Mar. 18, 1822
         Patsey Doak Executris of Robert Doak deceased, returned an inventory of
the sale of property of the estate of Robert Doak and ordered to be recorded.

Record-   The court then proceeded to class the justices of this county (to wit)
ed Book William Atchison, Robert H Dyer, Duncan McIver, Adam R Alexander Bartholomew G.
Ap. 5 Stewart and Joseph Lynn, Esquires in the first class to serve the terms of
June and December and John Thomas, William Braden, David Jarrett, James Throus-
dale, Herdon Haralson and Samuel Taylor, Esquires in the second class the
terms of September and March in each year.

              John Grace   )
                  Vs.   ) Debt
              Drury & John Bettes   )

         This day came the parties aforesaid by their attorneys and the defendant
says he cannot gainsay the plaintiffs action against him for the sum of One
hundred and ninety-eight dollars. It is therefore considered by the court that
the plaintiff recover of the defendant the aforesaid sum of one hundred ninety-
eight in form aforesaid confessed also his cost by him about his suit in this
behalf expended and the defendant in mercy & etc. and by consent of the parties
execution in this case is to be staid until fifteen days before the next September term of this court.

         Court Adjourned until tomorrow morning nine o'clock.
                                       Joseph Linn   JP.
                                       William Atchison JP.
                                       B. G. Stewart   JP.

P.18 Alexanders Office Madison County Tuesday March 19, 1822
     Tuesday March 19, 1822
     Court met agreeable to adjournment.
     Present the worshipful Joseph Lynn William Atchison, Bartholomew G. Stewart,
Samuel Taylor Adam R. Alexander, Esqrs.

              William L. Mitchell   )
                  Vs.   ) Debt
              John Thomas   )

         This day came the parties aforesaid by their attorneys and the defendant
says he cannot gainsay the plaintiffs action against him for the sum of Three
hundred and nine dollars. It is therefore considered by the court that the
plaintiff recover of the defendant the aforesaid sum of Three hundred nine
dollars in the form aforesaid confessed also his costs by him about his suit in
this behalf expended and the defendant in mercy & etc. and by the consent of

P.18 of the parties execution in this case is to be staid until September County
cont. Court unless required by the plaintiff.

John W. Cook Richard C. Allen, Isaac S. W. Cook and Alexander S. Jones
produced in open court their license and thereupon took the several oaths
as attorneys at law in this court.

Present the worshipful Duncan McIver, Thomas James, John Fussell,
John Bradbury, John Weaver and William McCaslin who were appointed yesterday
by this court to view and mark out a private road leading from John P.
Thomas's house though the premises of Samuel Taylor & etc. return here
into court the following report (to wit)

P.19 Alexanders Office Madison County Tuesday March 19th. 1822

We have reviewed and layed off a way from John P. Thomas's house
to his enclosure out at his gate thence along Samuel Taylor's fence, Eastward to a cherry tree and hickory marked near the fence thence with said
marked to said Thomas inclosure if said Thomas makes the lain from his inclosure outside of Taylors fence the damage seventy five cents if Taylor
makes the loin the damage to be two dollars and seventy-five cents which
was ordered by the court and received accordingly.

Elijah Jones as constable appeared in open court and took the necessary
oaths to attend on the Grand Jury.

William Atchison comes into court and records his stock mark as fellows
(to wit) a swallow fork in both ears and an underbitout of the right ear.

Ordered that the county tax be equal to the state tax for the years
1821 and 1822 and the commissioners appointed by the last term of this court
to receive lists of taxable property are appointed to receive lists for the
years aforesaid and make return to the next term of this court
and ordered that the sheriff summons them for that purpose.

```
J. Fussell        )
     Vs.          )        Certeorari
James L. Wartham  )
```

This day came the parties aforesaid by their attorneys and the plain-
till moved to the court to dismiss the certiorari herein and the court being
sufficiently advised of and concerning the matters of law arising in the
motion to dismiss are of the opinion that the motion be overruled.

P.20 Alexanders Office Madison County Tuesday Mar. 19th. 1822

William Griffith this day came into open court and resigned the coro-
ners appointment of this county.

Henry N. Coulter was ordered to be exhonorated from attending as a
juryman at this term of court.

Ordered that Joseph Lynn, Bartholomew G. Stewart and James Trousdale
be appointed commissioners in pursuance of an act of the General Assembly of
the State of Tennessee to fix upon the site of the seat of justice of the
county of Madison and that in case of absence of one of the commissioners appointed by said act Joseph Lynn do act with the other two, that in case of
absence of any two of said commissioners the said Joseph Lynn and Bartholomew
G. Stewart do act with the remaining one and in case of absence of all of the
said commissioners then the said Joseph Lynn Bartholomew G. Stewart and James
Trousdale do act and it is further ordered that Bartholomew G. Stewart, Joseph
Lynn, James Trousdale Adam R. Alexander and John Hardgraves be appointed commissioners in pursuance of the before recited act to superintend the laying of
town at said cite when it may be fixed upon and also wuperintend the public
buildings and etc.

The Sheriff of this county this day made return of the venire's faceas
to him directed from the last term of this court, that he had summoned the
following persons who were attending in pursuance of said venire facias(to wit)

P. 20Moses Oldham, Nathaniel Simpson, James Caldwell, John Hardgraves, John Bradbury
Cont.Henry Ragan, Vincent Haralson, Francis Taylor, Benjamen Jones, Thomas L. D.
Park, John Montgomery, William L. Davis, Samuel H. Shannon, Thos. Jones, Wile
Espey, Lewis Needham, Francis Hearn, and thereupon the following persons, to
wit John Hardgraves, Moses Oldham, Nathaniel Simpson, James Caldwell John
Bradbury, Henry Ragan, Vincent Haralson, Fraenis Taylor, Benjamin Jones,
Thomas L. D. Parks, John Montgomery, William L. Davis and Samuel H Shannon
were elected.
P.21 Alexander Office Madison County Tuesday Mar. 191822

Charged and sworn as a Grand Jury to inquire in and for the body of this
county with John Hardgraves their foreman who thereupon retired to consider
of presentments.

    State   )
     Vs.   ) Indictment for an Affray
   John Starnes and)
   William W. Johnson)

This day came the solicitor general on the part of the State as the
defendants in their proper persons and the defendants were then and there
arraigned and upon their arraignment plead that they were genlty in manner and
form as charged in the indictment. It is therefore considered by the court that
the State recover of the defendants the sum of Five dollars each and the damage
which she has sustained by reason of the affray aforesaid also her costs by
her about her prosecution in this behalf expended and the defendant may be taken
& etc.

This day the Grand Jury returned a bill of indictment against John Starnes
and William W. Johnson for an affray in a tree bill. Ordered that capias issued
& etc.

This day the Grand Jury returned a bill of indictment against William H.
Johnson and moses Starnes an affray a true bill ordered that a capias issue & etc.
   Court then adjourned until tomorrow 9 o'clock
          Sam Taylor JP.
          Duncan McIver JP.
          R. H. Dyer
P.22 Alexanders Office Madison County Wednesday Mar. 20th. 1822

Wednesday the 20th of March 1822

Court met agreeable to adjournment, present the worshipful James Trousdale
Robert H. Dyer, Duncan McIver, William Braden Adam R. Alexander and Samuel
Taylor, Esquire.

On motion and petition filed, ordered that Guy Smith H. L. Gray, John G.
Caruthers, James Stanlkeep, John Boor, D. Furguson, John B. Hogg, Moses Oldham,
and James Trousdale, or any five of them be appointed a jury to view and lay off
a road, beginning where Carroll County road will stop on the Madison line,
leading on by Robert H. Dyers and Caruther's Ferry on the South fork of Forked
Deer river thence the nearest and best way to McGuires ferry on Big Hatchie river
and that the Sheriff of this county summons them for that purpose and that they
report these proceedings to the next court.

Elijah Jones, administrator of Lewis Jones, deceased this day returned
into court an inventory of the estate of the deceased which was ordered recorded.

    State   )
     Vs.   ) An indictment for an effray
   Moses Starnes)

This day came as well the solicitor general on the part of the state
as the defendant in his proper person and the defendant being arraigned on his
arrangment plead that he was quilty in the manner and form charged in the indict-

P.22 ment. It is therefore considered by the sum of Five dollars, the damages which
Cont. she has sustained by reason of the affray aforesaid also her costs by her about
her prosecution in this behalf expended and the defendant may be taken & etc.
It is further considered by the court that the defendant remain in custody of
the sheriff

P.23 Alexanders Office, Madison County Wednesday 20, 1822
untill the sum aforesaid together with all costs be fully satisfied and paid.
Then came John Farr into open court and acknowledged himself the defendants
security for the payment of the aforesaid sum together with all costs. The
defendant is thereupon discharged out of custody.

State	)	
Vs.	)	Indictment for an affray.
William W. Johnson	)	

This day came the defendant and John P. Thomas into open court and acknowledged themselves held and firmly bound unto the State of Tennessee in the
just and full sum of Three hundred seventy-five dollars the said defendant in
the sum of Two hundred fifty dollars and the said John P. Thomas in the sum of
One hundred twenty five dollars to be leved of their goods and chattels,
lands and tenements to be void never the less on the following condition that
the defendant do make his personal appearence at the next term of the court of
Pleas and Quarter Sessions to be held for the County of Madison at the house
of Adam R Alexander on the third Monday of June next then and there to answer
the state in an indictment for an affray and that he do not depart hence without leave and this cause to be continued until next term.

John McAllister	)	
Vs.	)	Case
William Bolding Jr.	)	

This day came the defendant by his attorney and the plaintiff being solemnl
called came not but made default, it is therefore considered by the court that
the plaintiff be non-suited and the defendant go thereof hence without day and
recover of the plaintiff his costs by him about this suit in this behalf expended and the plaintiff for his false clamor may be in mercy & etc.

P.24 Alexanders Office Madison County Wednesday Mar.20, 1822
A deed of bargain and sale from Thomas Campbell to Lewis Needham was this
day produced in open court and acknowledged by the said Thomas Campbell to be
his act and deed and ordered to be recorded.
Ordered that it be certified that James Adams is entitled to one wolf
scalp over the age of six months which he killed within the bounds of this county.
Ordered that John P. Thomas have leave to open a private way from his
house to his inclosure out at his gate thence along Samuel Taylor fence Eastward
to a cherry tree and a hickory marked near the fence thence with inside of Taylor
fence in pursuance of the report returned here by the Jury of view appointed on
a former day of this court.
Court then adjourned until nine o'clock tomorrow morning.

Jas. Trousdale   JP.
Adam R. Alexander JP.
William Braden   JP.

Thursday morning March 25, 1822
Court met agreeable to adjournment. Present the worshipful Adam R. Alexander, James Trousdale, William Braden, Esquires. Ordered that the following
persons be summoned by the sheriff as Grand and Petit Jurors to attend at the

P.24 term of this court (to sit) James Wright, John Harrison, Jacob Hill, Hazael
Cont.Hewitt, Andrew Hays, James Dillard, John G. Caruthers, Joel Dyer, Sen. Guy Smith
Josiah Pullin, Thomas James, Murdoch Murchison.

P.25 Alexander Office Madison County Thursday Mar. 21, 1822

John Easters, James Young Sen, John P. Thomas, William Wilson, John Wier,
John Graves, James Cockeral, William Thedford, Austin Russell, Spencer Grant,
Martin Lorance, Samuel Simmons.

Adam R. Alexander comes into court and records his stock mark as follows,
to wit, a half crop under each ear and an overbit out of each ear.

Thomas Shannon comes into open court and records his stock mark as follows,
to wit, a crop off the right ear and underbit out of the left ear.

William H. Doak comes into open court and records his stock mark as
follows, to wit a crop off the left ear and an underbit out of the same and split
in the right ear.

William Braden comes into open court and records Alexander Bradens stock
mark as follows to wit, a half crop off the right ear underside.

William Braden comes into open court and records his stock mark as follows,
to wit, a half crop in the underside of right ear and a split and underbit in
the left ear.

Court then adjourned until court in course.

>   Adam R. Alexander   JP.
>   William Braden   JP.
>   Jes. Trousdale   JP.

P.26 Alexander Office Madison County Monday June 17,1822
State of Tennessee

At a court of pleas and quarter sessions began and held for the
county of Madison at the house of Adam R. Alexander on Monday
the 17th. day of June 1822 and the 46th. year of American Independence.

Present the worshipful Herndon Haralson Duncan McIver, William Braden, Joseph
Linn Adam R. Alexander and Bartholomew G. Stewart.

On motion of Elizabeth Richmond Administration of all and singular the
goods, chattels rights and credits of Jesse Richmond, deceased, was granted her
who thereupon took the oath of an administratrix and entered into and acknowledged
bond with Herdon Haralson and Vincent Haralson her securities in the penalty of
one thousand dollars conditioned agreeable to law and the administratrix then
returned an inventory of the estate of the deceased which is ordered to be recorded.

Present the worshipful James Trousdale, David Jerret and William Atchison.

A deed of bargain and sale from Thomas Campbell, William Rolle, Joseph B.
Porter and Lewis Needham to Mary Reid for two thousand acres of land was this
day produced in open court and proven by the oaths of James Brown and Adam R.
Alexander, subscribing witnesses thereto and ordered to ne certified.

Hannah McMillan Administratrix of all and singular the goods and chattels,
rights and credits of Robert McMillan, deceased appeared in court and took the
oath of an administratrix.

Stokely D. Hays, Thomas Taylor, Austin Miller, William Stoddert, William
Arnold, Archibald C. Hall, and James Wilson, Esquires, produced their licenses
in open court and took the several oaths prescribed by laws as attorneys at
law in this court.

P27 Alexanders Office Madison County Monday June 17th. 1822
On motion and petition filed.

Ordered that Ezekial B. McCoy Duncan McIver, William E. Butler, Vincent
Haralson, Gabriel Chandler, Moses Wilson, William Wilson (son of Moses) Martin
Cartmell, John Johns, Hazael Hewitt and Ryland Chandler or any five of them
being first duly sworn be and they are are hereby appointed a Jury to view and

P.27 lay off a road of the first class the nearest and best way from the seat of
cont. Justice of this county on a cirection to the county seat of Henderson as far as
the county line and that they make a report of their proceedings to the next
term of this court.

On motion and petition filed , Ordered that Bartholomew G. Stewart, William E. Butler, Samuel Shannon, Abner Brown, James Greer, Robert Burns, Benjamin
Jones, William C. Love, William Bilvorn, Martin Lorance, and Murdock Murchison,
or any five of them being first duly sworn, benad they are hereby appointed a
jury to view and lay off a road of the first class the nearest and best way from
the county seat in this county to meet a road directed to be layed off from the
Court House of Carroll County on a direction to the center of this county and
that they make a report to the next term of this court.

On motion an petition filed:
Ordered that Daniel Harton, Samuel H. Shannon, Stokely D. Hays, William H.
Doak William M. Butter, John Harrison, and Anthony F. Gray or any five of them,
being first duly sworn be and theyare hereby appointed a Jury to view and lay off
a road of the first class the nearest and best way from the public square of hte
town of Alexandria to the most convenient landing on the South fork of Forked
Deer river and that they make a report thereof to the next term of this court

P28 Alexanders Office Madison County Monday June 18, 1822
On motion and petition filed:
Ordered that James Trousdale, N. 1. Hess, Wilbam Huston, Andrew Hays,
William Espy, James Tidwell, James Door, and George Measles, or any five of them
being first duly sworn, be a jury to view and lay off a road of the first class
from the town of Alexandria the nearest and best way to the house of Robert H.
Dyer to the middle fork of the Forked Deer River and that they make a report
to the next term of this court.

On motion and petition filed:-
Ordered that John B. Cross, Robert H. Dyer, Josiah Puttin, Thomas W.
Palmer, Jordan G. Stokes, Jarrett M. Jelks, James Dillard and John Montgomery
or any five of them being first duly sworn, be and they are hereby appointed ro
view and lay off a road in the second class the nearest and best way from the
home of Robert H. Dyer to Harris Bluff on the Forked Deer River.

On motion and petition filed:-
Ordered that William Braden, Adam R. Alexander, John Caruthers, Joel
Dyer, John T. Porter, David Jarrett, Henry I. Gray, Thomas Boling, Sen. and
Guy Smith, or any five of them being first duly sworn, be and are hereby appointed a jury of a view to lay off a road of the second class, from Alexandria the
nearest and best way to Harris's Bluff and that they make a report thereof to
the next term of this court.

Ordered that the order made at the December term of this court laying county taxes for the years 1821 and 1822 so far as regard the tax for the year 1821
ne and the same is hereby recinded and the taxes be collected in lien thereof be
twelve and one half cents in each hundred acres of land and twelve and one half
cents on each pole for the year 1821.

P29 Alexanders Office Madison County Monday June 17, 1822
Ordered that the clerk of this court be allowed the sumof Fifty-six Dollars
and fifty cents for books and county seal furnished for the use of the county
and that the trustee pay the same out of any money not otherwise appropriated.

Ordered that it be certified that Rufus F. King who intends making application for license to practice law is a man of honesty, probity and good demeanor, and that he is over twenty-one years of age.

Ordered that it be certified that Hugh P. Taylor intends making application
for license to practice law is a man of honesty probity and good demeanor and
that he is over twenty one years of age.

James Haley, Administrator of the estate of Jarah Haley, deceased, return-
edthe amount of the sales and an additional inventory of an additional amount of

P 29 of sales of the estate of the deceased.

Cont.   A deed of bargain and sale from Mary Reid to Thomas Campbell W. Robb, Lewis Needham and I. B. Porter for 3000 acres of land was this day produced in open court and proven by the oaths of James Brown and R. H. Dyer subscribing witnesses thereto and ordered to be certified for registration.

P.30 Alexanders Office Madison County Monday June 17 1822

Bartholomew G. Stewart, Joseph Linn, John Hardgraves, Adam R. Alexander and James Trousdale the commissioners appointed at the last term of this court this day came into open court and acknowledged bonds in the penalty of and with the conditions required by law.

Thomas Lacy this day came into open court and made oath to the killing one wolf over the age of four months within the bounds of this county which is ordered to be certified.

Jacob Bradberry this day came into open court and made oath of the killing one wolf court and made oath of the killing one wolf over the age of four month within the bounds of this county which is ordered to be certified.

On motion and petition of Thomas Shannon it is ordered that he have leave to keep an ordinary at his house in this county who thereupon entered into and acknowledged bond with Stokely D. Hays and William Arnold his securities in the penalty and with the conditions prescribed by law.

On motion and petition of John Riding it was ordered that he have leave to keep an ordinary at his house in this county who thereupon entered into and acknowledged bond with Henry Castles, and James Trousdale his securities in the penalty and with the conditions prescribed by law.

Ordered that George C. Rust be appointed constable in Capt. Hays company who thereupon entered into and acknowledged bond in the penalty and with the conditions prescribed by law with Josiah Pullen and Robert H. Dyer his securities and took the several oaths prescribed by law.

P.31 Alexanders Office Madison County Monday June 17, 1822

Ordered that John D. Shannon be appointed constable for the town of Alexandria who thereupon entered into and acknowledged bond with Thomas Shannon and William Arnold his securities in the penalty and with the conditions prescribed by law.

Ordered that the sheriff summons George C. Rust and John Shannon as constables to attend on the Grand and Petite Jurors during the present term of this court.

A deed of bargain and sale from Robert and Thomas Love to John Love for 3416 acres of land was this day produced in open court and acknowledged by Thomas Love one of the grantors therein named to be his act and deed for the purpose therein mentioned and ordered to be certified.

On motion and petition of Robert H. Dyer it is ordered that Robert H. Dyer have leave to keep an ordinary at this house in this county and thereupon entered into and acknowledged bond with Duncan McIver Joseph Lynn, B. G. Stewart Samuel Taylor, his securities in the penalty and with the conditions prescribed by law.

James Brown Ranger of this County entered into and acknowledged bond in the penalty and with the conditions prescribed by law with his securities Robert H. Wynne and David Jarrett which bond was ordered to be recorded.

P.32 Alexanders Office Madison County Monday June 17, 1822

Roderick McIver Clerk of this court this day entered into and acknowledged bond with Adam R. Alexander and William L. Davis his securities in the penalty of five hundred dollars conditioned for the collection and payment over to the proper arthorities of the fives forfeitures and taxes which bond is ordered to be recorded.

Ordered that court be adjourned intil tomorrow morning 9 o'clock.

Ordered that Tuesday the 21st. day of this court be set apart for the transaction of the business for the state.

P.32
Cont.

H. Haralson Chairman
B. G. Stewart JP.
William Atchison JP.

Tuesday morning the 18th. June 1822

Court met agreeable to adjournment, Present the worshipful Herndon Haralson Adam R. Alexander, Bartholomew G. Stewart, Samuel Taylor, William Atchison and William Braden.

The sheriff this day made returns on the writ of venire facias to him directed from the last term and returnable to the present term of this court and in pursuance thereof had summons the persons named in said writ except James Dillard who was not found of whom the following persons were attending (to wit) John G. Caruthers, James Cockril, Murdock Murchison, Martin Lorance Josiah Pullen, Hazael Hewitt, John Harrison, Spencer Grant, John Graves, Guy Smith, there not being a sufficient number attending it was commanded the Sheriff to summons a sufficient number of the by standers to complete the panel.

P.33 Alexanders Office Madison County Tuesday June 18, 1822

and thereupon the following persons (to wit) John Graves, Martin Lorance, John Howard John G. Caruthers, James Dorace, James G. Heskill, James Cockrell Hazel Hewit, Spencer Grant Murdock Murchison, William C. Love, GuySmith with John Graves their foreman was elected impanelled, sworn and charged a Grand Jury to inquire into and for the body of the county of Madison and thereupon retired to consider presentments.

Ordered that John Esters, James Wright and John Weger attend at the next term of this court to show cause if any who they should not be find $2.50, each for failing to appear at the present term.

The Grand Jury returned into court an indictment against William Dean for an assault and battery upon the body of Polly McBeth indorsed a true bill John Graves, Foreman.

The Grand Jury returned into open court an indictment against Bejamin Blythe for an assault and battery upon the body of Francis Herrin indorsed a true bill John Graves, foreman.

The Grand Jury returned into open court an indictment against Joseph Wilson for an assault and battery committed upon the body of Joseph Allen indorsed a true bill John Graves, foreman

State)
Vs.) Indictment for an affray
William W. Johnston)

This day came as well the solicitor general on the part of the state as the defendant in his proper person who being arraigned upon his arraignment plead not guilty and for his tryal put himself upon God and his country whereupon it was commanded the sheriff,

P.34 Alexanders Office Madison County Tuesday June 18, 1822,

caused a jury to come here, whereupon came a jury (to wit)

Joel Dyer	Alexander Braden	Francis Herrin
Andrew Hays	William Thedford	Elijah Baker
Thomas James	James L. Worthen	Jacob Hill
John P. Thomas	Samuel Simmons	Austin Russell

Who being elected tried and sworn the truth to speak upon the issues joined to say they found the defendant guilty in the manner and form as charged in the bill of indictment. It is therefore ordered that the defendant make his peace with the state for the payment of two dollars and forty cents and that the plaintiff go hence without day and recover of the defendant her costs by her about the suit in this behalf expended and the defendant may be taken &etc.

F.34
cont.

State)
Vs.) Indictment for Assault & Battery
Joseph Wilson)

This day came the solicitor general on the part of the state as the defendant in his proper person and the defendant being arraigned upon his arraignment plead that he was guilty in the manner and form as charged in the indictment. It is therefore considered by the court that he defendant make his peace with the state by the payment of two dollars and fifty cents and that the plaintiff go thereof hence without day and recover of the defendant her costs by her about her suit in this behalf expended and the defendant may be taken &etc.

State)
Vs.) Indictment for an assault and battery
Benjamin Blythe)

This day came as well the solicitor general on the part of the state as the defendant in his proper person and the defendant being arraigned upon his arraigment plead not guilty and for his trial put himself upon God and his country whereupon it was commanded that he cause a jury to come here and whereupon came a jury (to wit) Joel Dyer, Andrew Hays, Thomas James, William Tedford, Samuel Simmons, Elijah

P.35 Alexanders Office Madison County June 18, 1822

Baker, Austin Russell, James Hailey, Thomas Caisey, Clark Spencer, James L. Worthem, Jacob Hill who being elected tried and sworn the truth to speak upon the issues joined do say we of the jury find the defendant guilty in manner and form as charged in the indictment. It is therefore considered by the court that the defendant make his peace with the state by the payment of One dollar and that the plaintiff go thereof hence without day and recover of the defendant her costs by her about her suit in this behalf expended and the defendant may be taken, & etc. and the defendant prays an appeal from the judgment of this court to the next term of the Circuit Court for the County of Madison which is granted him whereupon he entered into bond with Duncan McIver his security in the penalty of three hundred dollars conditioned for the prosecution & etc. of said appeal.

State)
Vs.) Assault and Battery
William Deems)

The defendant and James Trousdale and James Hailey acknowledged themselves held and firmly bound unto the State of Tennessee for the sum of Four hundred dollars the defendant in the sum of Two hundred dollars and the said Trousdale and Hailey in the sum of one hundred dollars each to be levied of their good and chattels lands and tenements to be void on condition that the defendant go make his personal appearance at the September term of this court to answer the state on charge by indictment for an assault and battery and that he do not depart hence without leave of court. It is ordered that this case be continued until next term.

Anthony F. Grey)
Vs.) Debt
Joel Dyer)

This day came the parties aforesaid by their attorneys and thereupon came a jury (to wit) Andrew Hays.

P.36 Alexanders Office Madison County Tuesday June 18, 1822

Thomas James, William Thedford, Alexander Bradin, Samuel Lemon, Elijah Baker, Anselem Russell, James Haley, Thomas Casey Clark Spencer, James L. Worthem and Jacob Hill who being sworn well and truly to try the issue joined upon their oaths do say we of the Jury find for the plaintiff One hundred

P.36 Eighty five dollars the debt in the declaration mentioned and do assesshis
Cont. damages by reason of the detention thereof to seventeen dollars and fifty
seven and one half cents, it is therefore considered by the court that the
plaintiff recover of the defendant the aforesaid sum of One hundred eithty five
dollars the debt in the declaration mentioned together with the damages aforesaid in form aforesaid assessed also his costs by him about his suit in this
behalf expended and the defendant in mercy & etc.

      Daniel Sullivan)
          Vs.   )   Case
      Gabriel Chandler)

    This day came the parties aforesaid by their attorneys and thereupon came
a jury (to wit) Joel Dyer, Andrew Hays, Thomas James, William Tedford, Samuel
Lemon, Elijah Baker, Anselem Russel, William Altun, Alexander Braden, James L.
Wortham, Francis Herrin, and Jacob Hill, who being sworn well and truly to try
the issue upon their oaths do say they find for the plaintiff and do assess his
damages by reason the trespass in the declaration suppose to forty seven dollars
and fifty cents. It is therefore considered by the court that the plaintiff
recover of the defendant the sum of forty seven dollars and fifty cents the
damages aforesaid in form aforesaid assessed also his costs by him about his
suit in this behalf expended and the defendant in mercy & etc, and the defendant
prayed an appeal from the judgment of this court to the next term of circuit
Court which was granted him upon his entering into bond with Ryland Chandler
and Parke Chandler his securities in the penalty of one hundred dollars & etc.
which was done accordingly.

P.37 Alexanders Office Madison County Tuesday 18th. 1822

      William Beeh__)
         Vs.   )   Debt
      William Butler)

    This day came the defendant by his attorney and the plaintiff called
came not but made default. It is therefore considered by the court that the
plaintiff be non suit and that the defendant go thereof henve without day and
recover of the plaintiff his costs by him about his defense in this behalf expended and the plaintiff for his false clamor may be in mercy & etc.

    Ordered that Patrick Duffy and William Bolding be fined two dollars each
for contempt offered this court.

      Joseph Linn
         Vs.
      James Alexander & etc.

    On motion of plaintiff by his attorney by attorney leave is given to a-
mend his writ herein which is done accordingly by paying the cost of this amendment.

    John B Cross one of the justices of the peace named in the commission from
his Excellency the Governor of the state came into open court and took the
several oaths prescribed by the law and constitution of the state and thereupon
took his seat upon the bench.

    John Arnold came into open court and took the several oaths prescribed by
law and constitution of this state as deputy clerk of this court.

    John D. Shannon was ordered by the court to be sworn as a constable to at-
tend the Grand Jury this term which was done accordingly.

P.38 Alexanders Office Madison County Tuesday June 18, 1822

    A power of attorney from Mary Reid to James Wright was produced in open
court and proven by the oaths of Roderick Wright and Samuel S. Craften, subscribing witnesses thereto and ordered to be certified.

    A deed of bargain and sale from John C. McLemore to James Cockeral was
produced in open court for five hundred and thirty-five acres (535) which was

P.38   ordered to be certified for registration.
Cont.   A deed of Bargain and sale from William H. Doake to Patsy Doke for fifty
acres of land (50) was this day produced in open court and acknowledged by the
grantor to be his act and deed which was ordered to be registered.

          Ordered that George C. Rust be appointed constable to attend the petite
jury who was sworn to attend accordingly.

          A deed of bargain and sale from Robert Nellson to John Love for three
thousand one hundred thirty three acres (3133) was this day produced in open
court and proven by the oath of William Love, the probate of the other witnesses
being made on a former day, which was ordered to be registered.

          A deed of bargain and sale from Robert and Thomas Love for three thousand
and four hundred sixteen acres (3416) to John Love was this day produced in open
court and proven by the oaths of William C. Love one of the subscribing witnesses
thereto, the probate of the other witnesses being taken on a former day of this
court, which is ordered to be registered.

          On motion andpetition filed it is ordered that the following persons be
appointed a jury of view to lay off to mark and lay out a road from the town of
Alexandria to interest a road at a point leyed out and marked by authority of the
worshipful court of Henderson County from Henry Browns on the Natchez Grace to
the Eastern boundary of Madison County (to wit) John Hardgroves, James Young,
Gabriel Chandler, Daniel Madins,

P.39 Alexanders Office Madison County Tuesday June 18, 1822
Alexander Greyer, James Coldwell, Vincent Haralson, Thomas Doak and Robert
Edmondson or any five of them and that the Sheriff summons them for that pur-
pose.

          On motion of A. B. Bradford Esquire, it is ordered that an order of sale
issue commanding the sheriff to depose of a certain tract of land of Ninty-five
acres (95) lying in Madison County 10th. Surveyors district entered in the name
of Relso Porter by entry No. 698 which tracts of land was levied on under an
execution issued by Adam R. Alexander Justice of the Peace of said County against
said Well Porter in favor of Joseph Brown for the sum of thirty five dollars
debt and costs of suit dated 9th. day of May 1822 Court adjourned until tomorrow
morning 9'ocKock.

                                        H. Haralson Chairman
                                        B. G. Stewart JP.
                                        Duncan McIver JP.

Wednesday morning 12th June 1822
          Court met agreeable to adjournment.
          Present the worshipful Herndon Haralson Duncan McIver, Bartholomew G.
Stewart, William Braden, Joseph Linn, William Atchison and Samuel Taylor.

          R. P. T. Stone)
               Vs.   )   Covenant
          W. D. Lewis)

          This day came the parties aforesaid by their attorneys and the demuror
to the plaintiff declaration came on and was argued and the court being sufficient
ly advised thereof it seems to the court that the low is for the plaintiff
It is therefore considered by the court that the demurer be over ruled and it
further considered by the court.

P.40 Alexanders Office Madison County Wednesday 19th June 1822.
that the plaintiff recover of the defendant such damages as he as sustained by
reason of the breach of covenant in the declaration mentioned but because those
damages are unknown it is commended ShatSheriff to secure a Jury to come here
the next term to inquire of damages until which time this cause is continued.

          John Fussell   )
               Vs.   )   Surtiorari
          James S. Wortham)

P.40   An affidavit filed
Cont. Ordered that this cause be continued until next term.

      William Newsom)
          Vs.   )   Debt
      John B. Hogg)
      Robert H. Dyer)

This day came the parties aforesaid by their attorneys and whereupon the defendant by his attorney ask leave of the court to file additional pleas which motion was overruled and thereupon came a jury (to wit) Thomas L. D. Parks, Thomas Palmer, James Winters, Samuel M. Moore, Samuel Averett, James Merlin Nelson Brown, Isaac Glister, Michael Dickinson, Robert Lumpkin, James Poor, Elijah Baker, who being sworn welland truly to try the issue joined on their oaths do say we the jury do find for the plaintiff the debt in the ceclaration mentioned and do assess his damages by reason and detention thereof to Eight Dollars four and one half cents it is therefore considered by the court,

P.41 Alexanders Office Madison County Wednesday 19th. June 1822
that the plaintiff recover of the defendant the sum of Two hundred and seventy dollars the Debt in the declaration mention together with the damage aforesaid in the form aforesaid assessed also his costs by him about his suit in this behalf expended and the defendant in mercy & etc.

The Grand Jury this day returned into court an indictment against Francis Herron for an assault and battery on the body of Benjamin Blyth and made the following presentment to wit.

A presentment against John Stalkeep and Robert Houston for an effray: a presentment against James Stewart and William Edwards; a presentment against George Stalkeep and John Houston for an effray; a presentment against John Clifton and George Chamberlin for an effray; a presentment against James Stalkeep and William Houston for an effray; a presenument against John Russell for an assault and battery upon the body of William Wilson, ordered that Copias issue.

        State
          Vs.
        Stokely D. Hays

This day came as well the solicitor general on the part of the state as the defendant in his proper person and the defendant being arraigned upon his arraignment plead not guilty and for his trial put himself on his God and his country whereupon it was commended the sheriff that he cause a jury to come here and whereupon came a jury (to wit) James Glisten, James Winters, Alesa

P.42 Alexanders Office Madison County Wednesday 19th. June 1822
Robert Lumpkin, Thomas Palmer Samuel Averett, Alexander Braden, Elijah Baker, Micheil Dickerson, Anselom Russell, Ruben F. T. Stone, Lemnel W. Moore, who being elected tried and sworn the truth to speak upon the issue joined do say we of the Jury find the defendant not gently in the manner and form as charged in the indictment it is therefore considered by the court that the defendant go thereof hence without day and recover of the plaintiff his costs by him about his suit in this behalf expended and the plaintiff for his false clamor may be in mercy & etc.

      Anthony F. Gray   )
          Vs.   )
      Henry L. Gray &)
      Joel Dyer   )

This day the defendant by their attorneys prayed an appeal to the next term of the circuit court for Madison County for a Judgment rendered herein on a former day of this term which is granted him on their entiring into bond with Bartholomew G. Stewart Adam R. Alexander, Samuel Taylor, Robt. H. Dyer,
  * A presentment against Stokely D. Hays and Anthony F. Grays;

P.42 their securities in the penalty of five hundred dollars cinditioned agreeable to
cont.to law which was done accordingly.

Ordered that the following persons (to wit) Guy Smith, John C. Caruthers,
James Stalkeep, Thomas J. Smith, Andrew Hays, Jacob Bradberry Jr. George W. Taylor
Jesse Hannah Elijah Baker, or any five of them being first sworn be and are
hereby appointed a jury of view.

P.43 Alexanders Office Madison County Wednesday June 19,
to lay off a road beginning at the place where the road from the county seat in
Carroll County to the county seat in Madison will interest the line between the
two counties thence the nearest and best way to Caruthers Ferry on the South
fork of Forked Deer river and that they make report of their proceedings to
the term of this court.

David Jefferies one of the Justice of the Peace named in the commission
from the Governor of this State of Madison County came into open court and took
the several oaths prescribed by the constitution and laws of this state who
thereupon took his seat upon the bench.

Ordered that the Grand Jury be discharged from further service during the
present term of this court.

Mitchell & Burrow   )
Vs.   )
W. L. Mitchell   )

Ordered that this case be continued until the next term.

A deed of bargain and sale from Richard Smith to William Welburn for three
hundred twenty & ¼ (320¼) acres of land was this day produced in open court
and proven by the oaths of Robert H. Dyer one of the subscribing witnesses thereto and ordered to be so certified.

P.44 Alexanders Office Madison County Wednesday June 19th. 1822
An inventory of the estate of Lewis Jones deceased was this day returned
into open court by the administration and ordered to be recorded.

An inventory of the Sales of the Estate of James L. Price deceased was
this day returned into open court by the administration and ordered to be recorded.

Polly McBeth   )
Vs.   )   Assault and battery
William Deen   )

The plaintiff in this action having made oath in pursuance of the act
of the assembly that in consequence of his proverty that she is unable to bear
the expenses of the law suit & etc.

It is therefore ordered that David Thomas and John W. Cook be assigned her
as counsel.

Court then adjourned until tomorrow morning 9 o'clock.

Duncan McIver   JP.
Joseph Linn   JP
Sam Taylor   JP.

Thursday Morning 20th. of June 1822
Court met agreeable to adjournment Present the worshipful Joseph Linn,
Duncan McIver, Adam R. Alexander, and Samuel Taylor.

William Braden came into open court and made oath that he killed a wolf
over the age of four months within the limits of this county.

P.45 Alexanders Office Madison County Thursday June 20, 1822
Ordered by the court that the following persons be appointed Jurors to
serve the next circuit court to be holden on the 3 Monday of October (to wit)

P.45
Cont.

Daniel Hading	James McCutchen
John M. Welch	Daniel Lutwan
Francis Ragsdale	Abner Brown
Nathaniel Norrell	Eriton Sanders
Alexander Greyer	Henning Pace
Thomas Cayce	Robert Burns
James F. Theobold	Robert Edmondson
John Smith	Thomas Dake
Stephen Lucy Jr.	James Winters
Jerott M. Jelks	William Wilborn
Parks Chandler	Daniel Horton
James Henderson	Anthony F. Gray
Debrair Wynne	Levi Anderson

Ordered by the court that the following persons be appointed Jurors and
that the sheriff summons them for that purpose as grand and petite jurors to
serve the next term of this court which is to be holden on the 3 Monday of
September next (to wit)

Joshua Anderson	Geo. W. Taylor
Joseph Edings	Stephen Jarman
Bevery B. Acree	Willie Nichols
John Griffin	Walter Thedford
William Draper	Joseph Thedford
Ames Williams	John Tidwell
John Moore	Jesse M. Hannah
John Evans	Ruben B. T. Stone
Thomas Catlin	William L. Mitchell
John B Justice	Allen Forchand
Joshua Tera	Francis B. McCoy
Henry Roan Jr.	Jordan G. Stokes
William Freer	John Ridings

Ordered that William H. Doak and John D. Channon be and are hereby appointed to attend at the next County Court as constables, to attend the grand and
petite Juries.

James Kenriss and Sterling Brown two of the commissioners appointed by
an act of the Assembly of the last session to locate the seats of Justice of the
counties of Henry Carroll Henderson and Madison this day made report that they
had proceeded on the discharge of their duties in this county and had fixed upon
the seat of justice and,

P.46 Alexanders Office Madison County Thursday June 20, 1822
purchased the fifty five 91/160 acres of land directed by the act of assembly
which report together with deed accompanying the same is ordered to be recorded.

Polly McBath)
Vs.) Assault & Battery
William Dean)

This day came the plaintiff by her attorney and the defendant the solemly
called came not but made default, it is therefore considered by the court that
the plaintiff recover of the defendant such damages as she has sustained by
reason of the assault and battery in the declaration mentioned byt because
those damages are not known it is commanded the sheriff that he cause a jury
to come here at the next term to inquire of damages until which time the cause
is continued

R. F. T. Stone)
Vs.) Covenant
N. D. Lewis)

This day came the parties aforesaid by their attorneys and whereupon
it was agreed by their parties that the plaintiff should have leave to file
a new declaration and the defendant new pleas and go to trial at next term and

P.46 that the defendant should pay all costs which have accrued up to this time and
Cont.this cause is continued until next term.

Ordered the Court be adjourned until Court in course to meet at the place
fixed upon by the commissioners appointed by the act of Assembly in such case
made and provided to fix upon the seat of justice of the Counties of Henry,
Carroll, Henderson and Madison.

Duncan McIver   JP.
R. H. Dyer
Joseph Lynn   JP.

P.47 Jackson Madison County Monday September 16, 1822
State of Tennessee

At a Court of Pleas and Quarter Sessions began and held in
the town of Jackson, Madison County, on Monday the 16th.
day of September 1822 and the 47th year of American
Independence.

Present the Worshipful Herndon Haralson , Joseph Lynn, William Atchison, Adam
R. Alexander William Braden, Duncan McIver and Samuel Taylor Esquire.

Randolph Phelps)
        Vs.   )   In case
John Wear   )

This day came the parties aforesaid and the plaintiff by his attorney
dismisses his suit and the defendant assumes all costs in the aforesaid action.

On Motion of Stokely D. Hays it is ordered by the court that all motions
be made to the Court from the Bar.

On application of John Griffin and good cause shown it is ordered by the
Court that he be released from serving as a juror at this term.

On motion of Stokeley D. Hays it is ordered that the report of the Jury
of view appointed at the last term of this court to mark out a road the nearest
and best way from Jackson on a direction to the county seat of Henderson as
far as the county line be received and the road opened and established in
the first class and that Devereux Wynn, Esquire be appointed oversur to open
and keep in repair that part of said road commencing at the Northeast corner of
the town of Jackson and ending at the East Bank of Jones Creek below McIver Mill.

P.48 Jackson Madison County

and that Jordan Spencer be appointed overseer of that part of said road commencing at the East Bank of Jones Creek below McIvers Mill, and ending at the house
of Ezekial B. McCoy as marked by said Jury of view and that Martin Cartmell be
appointed overseer of that part of said road commencing at Ezekiel B. McCoy
house and ending at the Eastern boundary of this county and marked out by the
aforesaid Jury of view. And it is further ordered by this court that Herndon
Haralson and Duncan McIver Esquires be appointed to assign to each overseer of
the road aforesaid the hands to open and keep in repair the respective parts
of said road of which they are appointed overseer as aforesaid.

On motion of Daniel W. Maury it is ordered that John Easters Exum for
non attendance as a Juror at the last term be received and that he stand discharged from all fines in that behalf.

The resignation of William Braden one of the acting justices of the peace
for the county of Madison was offered and accepted by the Court.

On motion and petition filed it is ordered that the prayer of Thomas
Davidson, Gilbreath Falks, Davidson, Samuel Rogers, and Sarah his wife,
John Edwin Davidson, Louisa Davidson, and Emmaline Davidson for the division of
twenty five hundred acres of land laying in the Western District granted by the
State of North Carolina to George Davidson Senior dated the 18th. day of July
1788 be granted them and that the division be made according to the prayer of
said petitioners.

P.49 Monday Sept 16th. 1822

On motion of Stokely D. Hays it is ordered by the court that the report
of the jury of view to mark out a road commencing at the public square and ending

P.49 at the Eastern boundary of this county where the road marked out by the worship-
Cont. ful court of Henderson County striker the Eastern boundary be received by the
court and that said road be opened and kept in repair which is ordered to be of
the first class and that George Todd be appointed overseer of that part of said
road lying between Jackson and the foot of the hill on the Eastern side of Jones
Creek and Elijah Hainey be appointed overseer from the last named point to the
head of Youngs branch and that John Wear be appointed overseer from thence to
the Eastern boundary of this county and that the following hands be called and
put under the command of said George Todd, Alexander Greer, Alexander Braden,
John Bruce, James Caldwell, H. Booth, M. Norvile, V. Haralson, Thomas L. D. Parks
and William Jone and Elijah Hainey allowed the following hands to work on that
part of said road of which he is overseer o(to wit) McCaskle, Wm Ruleman, ich
Ragsdale, Whitworth, Vantrees, Hollan Senders, Mading, McIver, Langston, Quinly
Golden Simson, Sullivan, Levy, Sullivan, Addins Joshua Anderson, Early Easters, J
Joseph Linn, James & Robert Young, Elisha Williams, John Frazer, Calbin I. Wil-
liams, George Wynn, John Welch, Elijah Jones, Matthew Jones.

William Braden and Daniel Mading came into court and took the oath of
deputy Sheriff of the county of Madison.

A power of attorney from James Walker to David Jarrett was proven in
open court by the oaths of Adam R. Alexander and John H. Bills subscribing
witnesses thereto and ordered to be registered.

Order the the report of the commissioners of the road directed to be laid
off and marked by an order of the last court commencing at the Carroll line
and ending at Caruthers ferry or Forked Deer river be received by the court.

P.50 Records of September Term 1822

On motion and petition filed ordered that William McBoyde, Samuel D.
Waddle, Henry Cassels James Stalkeep, Jordan Stokes, Andrew Hays, John Houston
Josiah Pullen, John Trousdale, Robert Reid, John Ridens and John A Gibson,
or any five of them, being first duly sworn, be a jury of new to lay out a
road the nearest and best way from the town of Jackson to a bridge in the North
or middle fork of Forked Deer river at a place known by Waddles ford thence
to the county line on a direction to Thomas Fights Mill on the little North fork
of said river and that the Sheriff summons them for that purpose.

A bill of sale from John Stobough to Reubin Reid was this day produced
in open court and proven by the oaths of William R. Hess a subscribingwitness
thereto and ordered to be certified for registration.

A deed of bargain and sale from Samuel Dickens to John McFarland for one
hundred sixty acres was this day produced in open court and acknowledged by the
grantor thereof to be his act and ordered to be certified for registration.

A deed of gift from John Swancy to John S. Caruthers, James D. Caruthers
Andrew N. Caruthers and William ". Caruthers for a negro girl named Terry was
this day produced in open court and ordered to be certified for registration.

Sephen Jarman and William Draper two of the justices of the peace named in
the commission from the governor of this state for Madison County bearing the
date the 23re. day of August 1822 came into open court and took the several
oaths prescribed by the constitution and laws of their state who thereupon took
their seats upon the bench.

P.51 September 16th, 1822

Ordered that John Tidwell be permitted to keep an ordinary at this house
in this county who thereupon entered into and acknowledged with George C. Rust
and John B. Cross his securities in the penalty and with the conditions prescribed by law who obtained license at June term for the same.

Present the worshipful B. G. Stewart and John B. Cross, Ordered the order
granted at the last term of this court directing a road to be layed out and
marked from the plan to Harries Bluffs be renewed with the addition of John
H. Gibson and William Espy as jurors of view after being first sworn agreeable
to law.

Ordered that Fendull Witworth be released from standing baill for John Clifton

P.51 and the said John Clifton is ordered into the custody of the sheriff.
Cont.   William Palmer
          Vs.
     Thomas. W. Palmer

     Ordered that a Dedemus Prostaten Debone Epic issues to take the deposstion of Thomas W. Palmer in favor of the plaintiff upon ten days notice being given the defendant.

     Ordered that John Weir be liberated from paying his fine for non attendance at June term.

     A deed of trust from Frederick Bearfield to Edmon Jones Henry M. Houston and Mooney Batton was this day produced in open court and proven by the oath of Jeslius Heskell one of the subscribed witnesses thereto and acknowledged by the grantor thereof to be his act and deed and ordered to be certified for registration.

P.52   A deed of Bargain & sale from John McIver to Frederick Redfield and Ingram Blanks for 2486 acres was this day produced in open court and proven by the oaths of Robert H. Dyer and Joel Dyer to subscribing witnesses thereto and ordered to be certified for registration.

     A motion of Welmoth Edmison and Bartholomew G. Stewart, administration of all and singular the goods, chattels, right and credits of Robert Edmison, deceased was granted them who thereupon took the oath of Administratrix and administrator and entered into and acknowledged bond with Thomas James their security in the penalty of thirty two hundred dollars conditioned agreeable to law and that letters of adminstration issue accordingly. On motion and petition filed ordered that the road leading from Robert Burns by the way of Benon Cruffon to William Wilson be established in the 2nd. class and straightened and kept in repair and that John M. Welch be appointed overseer thereof and that the hands living on the said road and to the North thereof within a convenient distance be assigned to work thereon from the house of Robert Burns to said William Wilson and be exempt from working on any other road except in opening new roads.

P.53   A bond for the conveyance of two hundred forty acres of land from James Alexander to Bartholomew G. Stewart was this day produced in open court and proven by the oath of Duncan McIver a subscribing witness thereto to be his act registration which obligation was assigned over to Joseph Linn by said Stewart for value received.

     A deed of bargain and sale from William Atchison to Samuel Dickens for thirty acres was this day produced in open court and acknowledged by the grantor thereof to be his act and deed and ordered to be certified for registration.

     Ordered the report of the Jury of View appointed last term to mark and lay off a road from the town of Jackson in a direction to Carroll County be received and that Robert Burns be appointed overseer to open and keep in repair that part of said road commencing at town and ending at the home of James Winters and William Love overseer to keep in repair that part of said road commencing at Winters and ending at Cain Creek and that Murdock Murchison be appointed ourseer as above commencing at the last named point and ending at the county line and that all the hands within the limits of three miles on each side of said road be assigned to them for opening & keeping up said road except those assigned for opening other roads.

P.54   Ordered that William Osteen a minor of the age of eleven years be bound to Elijah Barker until he is twenty one years of age to learn the art and trade of making hats and the said Elijah Baker entered into and acknowledged bond with James Winters his security in the penal sum of five hundred dollars to be void on condition that if he the said Baker will give said minor eighteen months schooling six months between this time and the year eighteen hundred twenty eight and will furnish said minor with good living and comfortable wearing apparel and at the experation of his said apprenticeship or when arriving at

P.54 the age of twenty one will furnish him with a horse saddle and bridle to be
Cont.woxth eighty dollars.

Ordered that John Houston be allowed the sum of one hundred and thirty-
five dollars for building the present court house and that the trustee of this
county pay the same out of any money not otherwise appropreated.

Ordered that Roderick McIver the clerk of this court be allowed the sum
of fifty dollars for making out the tax list for the year Eight hundred and
twenty one and 1822 and that the trustee pay the same out of any monies not
otherwise appreceted.

P.55 On motion of Sarah An Groffith & Duncan McIver Administration of all
and singular the goods and chattels, right and credits of William Griffith,
deceased was granted them who thereupon took the oath of administratrix and
administrator and entered into and acknowledged bond with Aquilla Davis and
Danil Mading their securities in the penalty of three thousand dollars conditioned agreeable to law.

Bailey Needham came into open court and proved by his own oath the Killing of two wolves within the bounds of Madison County over the age of four
months and produced to the court the scalps of said wolves.

On motion of Matthew Johnson Administrator of all and singular the good
and chattels, rights and credits of Simon Johnson, deceased was granted him
who thereupon took the oath of administrator and entered into and acknowledged
bond with Robert H. Dyer his security in the penalty of two hundred dollars
conditioned agreeable to law.

A deed of Bargain and Sale from Jacob Bradberry to William Atchison for
Eighty acres was this day produced in open court and proven by the oaths of
Thomas James and William McCauslin two of the subscribing witnesses thereto
and ordered to be certified for registration.

P.56 A deed of Bargain and Sale from Sterlin Brewer and James Fentress two
of the commissioners appointed by an act of the Legestature to procure a
site for a town at the Seat of Justice of Madison County to the commissioners
appointed by the court of said county to superintend the laying off and selling
the lots in said town and the public building of said town towit, Bartholomew
G. Stewart, Joseph Linn, John Hardgraves, Adam R. Alexander and James Trousdale
was this day produced in open court and proven by Danil W. Maury one of the
subscribing Witnesses thereto and ordered to be filed for further probate.

A deed of Bargain and Sale from Samuel Dickens to Thomas James for 160
acres was this day produced in open court and acknowledged by the grantor thereof to be his act and deed and ordered to certified for registration.

A deed of Bargain and sale from Joseph Linn R. E. C. Doherty and Bartholomew G. Stewart to Gavriel Chandler for 119 acres was this day produced in open
court and acknowledged by the grantor thereof to be their lawful act and deed
for the purposes therein named and ordered to be certified for registration.

Ordered that the clerk record the plan of this town and that he preserve
the original as filed in his office.

H. Haralson JP
William Draper
Stephen Jarman

P.57 Tuesday morning the 17th. day of September 1822

Court met agreeable to adjournment, present the worshipful Herdon, Haralson
Duncan McIver, Stephen Jerman. William Draper, William Atchison and Bartholomew
G. Stewart.

On motion and sufficient cause shown ordered that Beverly D. Acres be
discharged from serving as a grand juror at the present term.

Herndon Haralson and Duncan McIver esquires who we appointed on a former
day of this court to assign and apportion the hands to work on that part of the
road ordered to be opened and kept in repair from the Northeast corner of the
public square to Jones Creek returned to court the following report (to wit)

P.57 Duncan McIver and Herndon Harelson, pursuant to an order of this court report
Cont. that the following hands be appointed to work on the new road from the North-
east corner of the public square to Jones Creek where Duncan Wynn, is overseer
(to wit) the hands of said Wynne James Henderson, Doctor Williams E. Buttter,
Martha Doak William Butler, Herndon Harelson, James Johnson, William Mayo,
John Starnes, Moses Starnes, Ryland Chandler, Parks Chandler, Josiah Webb,
Hazeal Hawitt, Pitts Chandler, Robert Webb and his sons in law James Young,
John Young Archibold Shannon, John Rock, Obediah Mix, Allen Duncan, Obutiah
Butler, David Butler, and Henry Butler and their hands to work thereon, and
they further report that all the hands beyond Jones Creek, living South of
said McCoys hands work on the road where Jordan Spencer is overseer and that
all the hands living South of said road and South of Trau Creek work on and
open the road where Martin Cortmell is overseer to the East Boundary of this
county.

P.58   The sheriff this day made return of the writ of veniri facias to him
directed from the last term and returnable to the present term of this court
and in pusuance thereof have summoned all the persons named in said veniri except William S. Mitchell who was not found of whom the following persons were
attending (to wit)

Jordan G. Stokes	Ruben P. T. Stone	Joshua Penn
Joshua Anderson	John Tidwell	Jesse M Hanna
John B. Justice	John Evens	William Freer
Tjomas Gathie	Willis Nichols	Henry Rosin
Allen Forehand	Francis D. McCoy	John Ridens

and thereupon the following persons (to wit)

Jordan G. Stokes	Joshua Anderson	John B. Justice
Thomas Gatten	Ruben P. T. Stone	John Tidwell
John Evens	Willis Nichols	Joshua Penn
Jesse M Hanna	Allen Forehand William Freer	Henry Dean Jr.

with Jordan G. Stokes their foreman were elected empannelled sworn and charged
as a Grand Jury to inquire into and for the body of the county of Madison and
thereupon retired to consider presentments.

State   )
     Vs.   )   Indictment for an affray
John Clifton   )
George Chamberlain)

This day came as well the solicitor general on the part of the state
as the defendant in their proper persons and the defendant being arraigned
upon their arraignment plead that they were guilty in manner and form as charged
in the indictment, it is therefore considered by the court that the defendants
make their peace with the state by the payment of one dollar each and that the
plaintiff go thereof hence without day and recover of the defendants her
costs by her about her suit in this behalf expended and that the defendants
may be taken &tc. who were thereupon ordered into coustody of the sheriff
until the fine and costs aforesaid be settled or sufficient security for the
same be given.

On motion of Stokely D. Hays, Attorney it is ordered by the court that
a _____ ___ ____to the sheriff of Madison County commanding him to expose to sale a 640 track of land lying on the South side of Hatchie river,
entered in the name of Dixon Moschele by Entry No. 853 in the 10th. surveyors
district in the 3rd. Range and 2nd. Section on warrent No. 3357 to satisfy two
executions issued by Adam R. Alexander in a acting justice of the peace in
and for the county of Madison one in favor of R. M. Lanier against said Dixon
one for the sum of $10.00 and 50 cents Debt and costs of such the other for
11.38¾ cents and costs of such in favor of absolom Page on which said execution
said Sheriff made the following indorsement (to wit) No personal property

P.58 found and levied on the tract of land above discribed.
Cont.

State	
Vs.	) An indictment for assault & battery
Francis Herron	)

This day came as well the solicitor general on the part of the state as the defendant in his proper person and the defendant being arraigned upon his arraignment plead that he was guilty in manner and form as charged in the indictment, it is therefore considered by the court that the defendant make his peace with the state by the payment of one dollar and that the plaintiff go thereof hence without day and redover of the defendant her costs by her about their suit in this behalf expended and the defendant may be taken in mercy etc.

Present the worshipful Adam R. Alexander, Samuel Taylor, John B. Cross and Joseph Lynn.

P.60 This day came Joshua Anderson into open court and acknowledged himself as security for George Chamberlain for the payment of the fine and costs of a suit the state against said Chamberlain to be levied of his goods and chattels, lands and tenements which was received by the court.

This day came Aquilla Davis into open court and acknowledged himself as security for Francis Herrin for the payment of fine and costs a suit of the state against said Herrin to be levid of his goods and chattels, lands and tenements which security was rec(d by the court.

Ordered that William H. Doak a constable be sworn to attend on the Grand Jury during the present term who was sworn accordingly.

State	
Vs.	) Indictment for an affray
James Stalkeep	)

This day came as well the solicitor general on the part of the state as the defendant in his proper person and the defendant being arraigned upon his arraignment plead he was guilty in manner and form as charged in the indictment it is therefore considered by the court that the defendant make his peace with the state by the payment of one dollar and that the plaintiff go thereof hence without day and recover of the defendant her costs by her about her suit in this behalf expended and that the defendant may be taken etc.

P.61

State	
Vs.	) An indictment for an affray
Anthony F. Gray	)

This day came as well the solicitor general on the part of the state as the defendant in his proper person and the defendant on being arraigned upon his arraignment plead he was guilty in the mahner and form as charged in the indictment, it is therefore consideredjby the court that the defendant make his peace with the state by the payment of one dollar and that the plaintiff go hence without day and recover of the defendant her costs by her about her suit in this behalf expended and that the defendant may be in mercy etc.

A deed of bargain and sale from Robert H. Dyer and wife to John Bothers for 100 acres was produced in open court at the last term of this court and acknowledged by Robert H. Dyer and Joel Dyer two of the grantors thereof which is ordered to stand as if the same had been entered on the minutes of last term and continued for further probate in acknowledgment.

State	
Vs.	) Indictment for an affray
Robert Houston	)

This day came as well the solicitor general on the part of the state as the defendant in his proper person and the defendant being arraigned upon his arraignment plead that he was guilty in the manner and form as charged in the indictment, it is therefore consideredjby the court that the defendant make his peace with the state by the payment of fifty cents and the plaintiff go

P.61
Cont.
thereof hence without day and recover of the defendant her cost by her about
her suit in this behalf expended and the defendant may be taken etc.

P.62 John Draper was this day duly and constitutionally elected constable in
Captain Williams Company for the county of madison.

Samuel H. Shannon was this day duly and constitutionally elected corner
for the county of Madison.

Ordered that Thomas Shannon be appointed collector of the public taxes
in the county of Madison and that he enter into bond in the penal sum of Five
Thousand Dollars conditioned for the faithful discharge of the duties of said
appointment.

The Grand Jury this day returned into court an indictment against Squire
Dawson for petite larceny, and also a bill of indictment against Jonathan
Houston for an assault on which indictment was indorsed By the foreman of
the Grand Jury a tree bill.

A bill of sale from John Stobough to Joel Dyer for a negro girl named
Mariah was this day produced in open court and proven by the oath of John B.
Hogg a subscribing witness thereto and ordered to be certified for registra-
tion.

P.63
A deed of bargain and sale from Joel Dyer to Blackmon Coleman for one
thousand acres of land was this day produced in open court and acknowledged
by the grantor thereof to be his act and deed and ordered to be certified for
registration

State   )
Vs.   )   Indictment for petite larceny
Squire Dawson   )

Squire Dawson, late of the County of Madison who stands indicted for
petete larceny was led to the bar in custody of the sheriff of said county
who being arraigned plead not quilty to the indictment and for his trial put
himself upon God and his country whereupon came a jury of good and lawful men
who being elected tried and sworn the truth of and upon the premises to speak
and having heard the evidence to say that the said Squire Dawson is guilty as
charged in the bill of indictment and whereupon he is remanded to Jail.

State   )
Vs.   )   Indictment ffrr petete larceny
Squire Dawson   )

The defendant by his counsel moved to the court to grant him a new trial.
P.64 The court then adjourned until tomorrow morning 9 o'clock.

State   )
Vs.   )   Indictment for petete larceny
Squire Dawson   )

This day came the solicitor general Alexander B. Bradford on the part of
the state as well as the said Squire Dawson in his own proper person who be-
arraigned at the bar upon an indictment for petete larceny pleads not guilty
and puts himself upon God and his country whereupon came a jury of good and
lawful men (to wit) Stephen Booth, John Ridens, Nathan Simpson, James Wright
Henry Rosan, Robert Edmonson, Roderick Wright, Murdock Murchison, Henry Booth,
Samuel A. Tyson, Sam D. Caruthers, and Solomon Cotner, who being elected tried
and sworn the truth of and upon the premises to speak and having heard the ev-
dence upon their oaths do say that the said Squire Dawson is guilty as charged
in the bill of endictment whereupon he is remanded to jail.

State   )
Vs.   )   An indictment for petate larceny
Squire Dawson   )

The defendant in this case by his counsel moved to the court to grant
him a new trial whereupon and rule is entered that the defendant and approved
by the court to theow cause why a new trial should be granted.

Court then adjourned until tomorrow morning 8 o'clock.

H. Haralson Jp.
Sam G. Taylor JP.
William Draper

P,65 Wednesday morning the 18th. day Sept. 1822 Court met agreeable to adjournment, Present the worshipful Hernden Haralson, Samuel Taylor, William Draper,
Stephen Jarman, Adam R. Alexander and John B. Cross.

John G. Caruthers one of the justices named in the commissiones from
the Governor of the State for Madison County bearing date of 23rd. day of
August 1822 came into open court and took the several oaths prescribed by
the constitution and laws of this state who thereupon took his seat upon the
bench.

On motion and petition filed it is ordered that James F. Thebald have
license to keep an ordinary at this house in the vicinety of the town of
Jackson and who thereupon entered into bound with John Houstons and Archebald
C. Hall his securities in the penalty and condition prescribed by the laws
of this state.

A deed of bargain and sale from Christian Mayer and Lewis Brantz to
Charles Frederic Mayer for five thousand acres of land was produced in open
court and ordered to be certified for registration with the certificates indorsed thereon entitling it to the same.

```
        State       )
              Vs.   )    Indictment for Assault and Battery
        William Deen )
```

This came came as well the solicitor general on the part of the state
and the defendant in his proper person and the defendant in this case plead
not guilty but for his trial put himself uponGod and his country and thereupon
came a jury of good and lawful men (to wit) William Gilborne, Solomon Cotner,
John Ridens, James Johnson, John Weaver, Robert Lowther, Michael Dickerson,
Henry Coalter, and James Moore who being elected tried and sworn the truth
to speak upon their oaths do say that We of the Jury do find for the defendant Guilty in manner and form as charged in the indictment, it is therefore
P.66 considered by the court that the defendant make his peace with the state by
the payment of two dollars and the plaintiff go thereof hence without day
and recover of the defendant her costs by her about her suit in this behalf
expended and that the defendant be in mercy etc.

```
        State          )
              Vs.      )    An indictment for an affray
        William Edwards )
```

This day came as well the solicitor general on the part of the state
as the defendant in his proper person and the defendant being arraigned upon
his arraignment plead not guilty and for his trial put himself upon God and
his country whereupon it was commanded the sheriff that he cause a jury to
come here and whereupon came a jury (to wit) John Graves, John Weaver,Gabriel
Anderson, Solomon Cotner, William Wilson, Andrew Hays, Grancis B. McCoy, Philips
Graves, James L. Wortham, Thomas Matthews, Lemuel W. Moore, and John Fussell
who being elected tried and sworn the truth to speak upon the issue joined
do say, We of the jury do find the defendant not guilty in manner and form
as charged in the indictment, it is therefore considered by the court that the
defendant go thereof hence without day and recover of the plaintiff costs by
him about his suit in this behalf expended and the plaintiff for her false
clamor may be in mercy etd.

```
        State          )
              Vs.      )    Indictment for an affray
        William Houston )
```

This day came as well the solicitor general on the part of the state as
the defendant in his proper person and the defendant being arraigned upon his
arraignment plead not guilty and for his trial put himself upon God and his

P.66 country, wherefore it was commanded of the sheriff that he cause a jury to
Cont. come here etc. whereupon came a jury (to wit) Elijah Harry, Henry D. Collins,
Nathan Simpson, Benjamin Roak, William Espey, Samuel Lemnions, William C.
Mitchell, Abner Fentress, Michael Dickinson, E Hamlet, James Flock and Spencer
Grant, Who being elected, tried and sworn the truth to speak upon the issue
joined, do say We of the jury do find the defendant not guilty in manner
and form as charged in the indictment. It is therefore considered by the court
that the defendant go thereof hence without day and recover of the plaintifg
his costs by him about his suit in this behalf expended and the plaintiff for
false clamor may be in mercy etc.

P.67
                    State   )
                    Vs.   )   Indictment for an affray
               John Houston   )

This day came as well the solicitor general on the part of the state
as the defendant in his proper person and the defendant being arraigned upon
his arraignment plead not guilty but put himself upon God and his country
wherefore it was commanded the sheriff that he cause a jury come here etc.
whereupon came a jury (to wit) William Wilbourne, Solomon Cotner, John
Fussell, Spencer Grant, Samuel A. Lyon, John Ridens, James Johnson, John
Weaver, Robert Lowther, Michael Dickenson Henry N. Coulter, and Andrew Hays
who being elected tried and sworn the truth to speak upon the issue joined do
say We of the jury do find the defendant not guilty in the manner and form
as charged in the indictment. It is therefore considered by the court that
the defendant go thereof hence without day and recover of the defendant his
costs by him about this suit in this behalf expended and that the plaintiff
for his false clamor be in mercy etc.

               William T. C. Thompson)
                    Vs.   )   Trespass with force and arms
               Michael Dickinson   )

This day came the parties aforesaid by their attorneys and thereupon
came a jury of good and lawful men (to wit) Solomon Cotner John Fussel,
Spencer Grant, Samuel A. Lyon, John Ridens, William Espy, Andrew Hays, John
Weaver, Henry L. Coulter, John Houston Thomas Elliot, Roderick Wright who
being elected tried and sworn the truth to speak upon the issue joined do
say We of the jury do find for the plaintiff and do assess his damages by
reason of the ptesepess in the declaration supposed to twenty five cents.
It is therefore considered by the court here that the said plaintiff do recover of the said defendant the damages aforesaid in manner and form aforesaid
in manner and form aforesaid assessed and his costs of suit in this behalf expended and the defendant in mercy etc.

Ordered that Francis H. McCoy be discharged from serving as a juror
during the present term.

Sarah Ann Griffith administratrix of the estate of William Griffith
deceased returned an inventory of the estate so deceased.

Elizabeth Richmond administratrix of the estate of Jesse Richmond deceased returned an inventory of the amount of sales of the estate of the de-
P.68 ceased.

A deed of conveyance from Elijah Jones Administrator of Lewis Jones, deceased and Susan Fentress adminstratrix of said deceased and Abner Fentress
in right of his wife Susan Fentress to Alexander Martin for one hundred ninety
acres of land was this day produced and proven by the oaths of Will Wilborne
and Samuel A. Lion two subscribing witness is thereto and ordered to be certified for regestration.

A deed of conveyance from William Payton to Benjamin Bythe for seventy
one and half acres was this day produced in open court and proven by the oath
of Aquilla Davis one of the subscribing witnesses thereto and ordered to be
filed for further probate.

A deed of conveyance from Andrew McCorkle and his wife Martha, Joseph

P.68 Blyth, James Blyth and William Corner to Benjamin Blyth for one hundred and
Cont.fifty acres of land was this day produced in open court and acknowledged
by Joseph Blyth one of the grantors thereof and ordered to be continued for
further acknowledgment.

Ordered that Joseph Lynn, Robert Dickson and Daniel Mading be appointed
to allow a siffocoemt postion of present crop, stock and money out of the estate of Will Griffith, dec. for the support of his family for one year and that
they make a return thereof to the next term of this court.

William Braden having resigned on a former day of this court as justice
of the peace do this day return the papers of his office to the clerk of this
court.

On motion and petition filed, ordered that the following persons be
appointed a jury of view to mark and lay off a road commencing at the public
square in the town of Jackson and running to the western boundary of the county
the nearest and best way to the center of the county next West of this yet
to be organized (to wit) Adam R. Alexander, Daniel Huston William El Butler,
John Graves, David Jarret, James Cockrill, John H. Gibson, James F. Theobold,
Thomas Williamson, John Thomas and William C. Michhell or any five of them
being first duly sworn and that they make a report thereof to the next term
of this court.

John T. Draper who was appointed constable for the County of Madison
in Captain Williams, Miletee Company on a former day of this court, this day
came into open court and entered into bond with William Draper and Duncan
McIver his securities in the penalty and condition prescribed by law and con-
stition prescribed by law and constitution of this state and took the several
oaths prescribed by law.

P.69   Grand Jury returned this day into open court the following presentments
(to wit) a presentment against William Norwood for an assault, a presentment
against Jacob Breadbury for selling spuitous liquors without license, a presentment against Jonas Acord, for selling spiritons liquors, a presentment
against Joseph Tedford for an assault upon the body of John Fare and that
capias issue etc.

Court then adjourned until temorrow morning 9 o'clock.

                                        Adam R. Alexander   JP,
                                        Saml Taylor   J .
                                        Jno. G. Caruthers   JP.

Thursday morning the 19th Sept. 1822
        Court met agreeable to adjournment present, the worshipful Adam R.
Alexander Samuel Taylor, and John G. Carithers.
½   John Weaver and Hannah McMillan Administrator and Administratrix of the
estate of Robert McMillan deceased, this day returned an inventory of the
amount of sales of said estate.

Present the worshipful Joseph Linn andStephen Jarman.

        State   )
                Vs.   )   An indictment for an assault and battery.
        John Fussell   )

        This day came as well the solicitor general as the defendant in his
proper person and the defendant being arraigned upon his arreignment plead
that he was guilty in the manner and form as charged in the bill of indictment and it is therefore considered by the court here that the defendant make
his peace with the state by the payment of one dollar and the plaintiff go
thereof hence without day and recover against the defendant her costs by her
about her suit in this behalf expended and the defendant may be taken etc.

Rubern P. T. Stone)
        Vs.   )   In casr
William D. Lewis   )

        An affidavit of the plaintiff this cause is continued until nest term
                                                                        ..

P.70   Present the worshipgul Bartholomew G. Stewart and Herndon Haralson

Andrew Smith)
         Vs.   )   An appeal
Spence   )

This day came the defendant by his attorneys and the plaintiff being solomnly called came not but made default it is therefore considered by the court on motion here that the plaintiff be nonsuited and that the defendant go thereof hence without day and recover of the plaintiff his costs by him about his suit in this behalf expended and that the plaintiff for his false clamor may be in mercy etc.

John Fussell   )
         Vs.   )   Certerrori Debt
James L. Wortham)

This day came the parties aforesaid by their attorneys and whereupon came a jury of good and lawful men (to wit) John Weaver, John Houston, John Redens, James Winters, Josiah Pullin, Spencer Grant, Solomon Cotner, Samuel A. Lyon, Henry Raygan, Martin Lorance, Wilson F. Dillon, Joseph Spruce, Who being elected tried and sworn the truth to speak upon the matters in dispute do say We of the jury do find for he plaintiff and that he recover of the defendant the sum of thirteen dollars and seventy-five cents also his cost vy him about this suit in thai behalf expended and that the defendant may be in mercy by-the--curt-that-the It is therefore considered by the court tha t the plaintiff recover of the defendant the sum aforesaid in the form aforesaid assessed together with his costs about his suit in this behalf expended.

         Ruben P. T. Stone)
                 Vs.   )   Covenant
         William D. Lewis)

An affidavit of the Plaintiff this cause is continued until nest term.

Ordered that a dedimus protestatem debenesse issue to take the deposition of James M. Lewis in favor of the defendant to be read in evidence in this suit of said Stone against William D. Lewis upon twenty days notice being given the plaintiff.

         William L. Watson etc.)
                 Vs.   )   In debt
         Joel Dyer   )

This day came the parties aforesaid by their attorneys and thereupon came a jury of good and lawful men, to wit, Henry Raygan Solomon Cotner, Spencer Grant, Wilson F. Dillon, Thomas Elliot, John Weaver, Benjamin Whitt, Samuel A. Lyon, Jesse M. Hanna, Martin Lorance, Samuel S. Crafton, and James Winters, who being elected tried and sworn well and truly to try the issue joined upon their oaths do say, We the jury doo find tt-- --- --- --- --- ---

P.71   --- --- --- --- of the detention thereof to Eight Dollars and fifty cents and the plaintiff go thereof hence without day and recover of the defendant the debt aforesaid with the damages aforesaid in form afore said his suit in this behalf expended and that the defendant be in mercy --- --- ---- ----
----

         Joseph Miller   )
            nVs.   )   In debt
         Wade Jarrett   )

Thid day came the parties aforesaid by their attorneys and thereupon came a jury of good and lawful men (to wit) Henry Raygan, Solomon Cotner, Spencer Grant, Wilson F. Dillon, Thomas Elliott, John Weaver, Bejamin White, Samuel A. Lyon, Jesse M. Hanna, Martin Lorance, Samuel S. Crafton, and James Winters who being elected tried and sworn upon their oaths do say We of the jury do find ofr the plaintiff the sum of one hundred dollars the debt in the declaration mentioned and do assess his damages by reason of the detention

P.71 thereof to four dollars and thirty seven and one half cents and it is therefore
Cont. considered by the court that the plaintiff go thereof hence without day and
recover of the defendant the devt aforesaid with the damages aforesaid in
manner and form aforesaid assessed together with his costs by him about his
suit in this behalf expended and that the defendant be in mercy etc.

             Joseph Linn Assignee etc.)
                    Vs.   )   Balance in Debt
             James Alexander &   )
             Henry N Coulter   )   )

     This day came the parties aforesaid by their attorneys and thereupon
came a jury of good and lawful men (to wit) Henry Raygan Solomon Cotner,
Spencer Grant, Wilson F. Dillon, Thomas Elliott, John Weaver, Benjamin White,
Samuel A. Lyon, Jesse M. Hanna Martin Lorance, Samuel S. Crafton and James
Winters, who being elected tried and sworn, upon their oaths do say We of the
jury do find for the plaintiff the two hundred and eighty two dollars the
balance of debt in the declaration mentioned and do assess his damages by
reason of the detention thereof to six dollars and thirty one cents and that
the plaintiff go thereof hence without day and recover of the defendance the
debt aforesaid and the damages aforesaid in form aforesaid assessed also his
cost by him about his suit in this behalf expended and that the defendant be
in mercy etc.

P.72 Marmaduke Mitchell &   )
     Vs.   )   In debt
   John B. Hogg   )

     This day came the parties aforesaid by their attorneys and thereupon
came a jury of good and lawful men (to wit) Wilson F. Dillon, Solomon Cotner,
Spencer Grant, Henry Raygan, Thomas Elliott, John Weaver, Benjamin White, Samuel
A. Lyon, Jesse M. Hanna, Martin Lorance, Samuel S. Crafton, James Winters who
being elected tried and sworn the truth to speak upon the issues joined to say
We of the jury do find for the plaintiff the debt in the declaration mentioned
of six hundred and fifty three dollars & 15 cents and do assess the damages
by reason and detention thereof to twenty six dollars and eighty eight cents
and it is therefore considered by the court here that the plaintiff go thereof
hence without day and recover of the defendant the debt aforesaid with the
damages aforesaid in manner and form aforesaid assessed and their costs
by them about their suit in this behalf expended and that the defendant in
mercy.

             William Espy   )
               Vs.   )   In case
             James G. Haskill)

     This day came the parties aforesaid by their attorneys and the plaintiff
desmisses his suit aforesaid and the defendant paying all costs in this suit
expended and that the defendant be taken etc.

             Elijah McAfee   )
                vs   )   Case
             Joseph B. Porter)

     On affidavit of the plaintiff the cause is continued until next term.

     Thomas Cayse came into open court a quorum being on the bench and prived
by his own oath the killing of one wolf in the bounds of Madison County over
the age of four months.

     A deed of conveyance from Andrew McKarkle and his wife, Joseph Blythe
James Blyth Benjamin Blyth and William Cannon was this day produced in open
court and after the private examination of said Martha McKarkle apart from
her husband by said court as to her free will and voluntary act was thereupon
acknowledged by said Andrew McKarkle and Martha his wife to be their act and
deed, the acknowledgement of Joseph Blyth being made on a former day of this
court and ordered to be continued for further acknowledgement.

P.73   Ordered by the court that Alexander B. Bradford, David Thomas, William Stotdert, S. D. Hays and William R. Hess be appointed a committee to adopt rules for pleadings and other purposes for the govenment of the practice of this court and that they make report thereof to the next term of this court.

Samuel H. Shannon who was appointed on former day of this court Coroner for the county of Madison this day came into open court and with Daniel Horton and John D. Shannon his securities entered into bond in the penalty of and in conditions prescribed by law which bond is ordered to be recorded and took the several oaths prescribed by the constitution and laws of this state.

The Grand Jury this day returned into Court an indictment against Benony Crowford for an assault.

Ordered that John Smith be appointed and ordered overseer on the road directed to be opened from Carithers Ferry on the South fork of Forked Deer river to Carroll County commencing at Carithers Ferry and ending at Midyets and that all the hands living South of the road leading from Robert H. Dyers to Harris's Bluff North of the South fork and West of said Midyets are assigned to said overseer to open and keep in repair part of said road and Benjamin White is appointed overseer on that part of said road commencing at Midyets and ending where said road crosses Crooked Creek and be allowed all the hands South of the middle fork and North of the dividing ridge between the North and South forks of said river and west of said creek as fares Midyets and that Benjamin White be appointed overseer of that part of said road commencing at Crooked Creek and ending where said road intersects the road,

P.74 Jackson Madison County Thursday September 19th. 1822
leading from Jackson to Carroll County and be allowed all the hands on the waters of the North fork Westward from where said Roads intersect to Crooked Creek to open and keep in repair said road.

Elijah Jones Administrator and Abner Fentress in right of his wife this day returned an additional inventory of the sales of the estate of Lewis Jones, deceased.

Ordered that Elijah Jones and David Jarrett, Esquire, be appointed gaurdian for Elijah J. Jones, Elizabeth Jones, Amey Jones Adeline Jones, and Rolly Jones, minors and Elijah Jones one of the Guardians entered into bond with William Wilbourne and Benjamin Blyth his securities in the penalty of four thousand dollars conditioned as by law directed.

Ordered that the Grand Jury be discharged as grand jurors during the present term but be continued as as petit.

Ordered that Joshua Anderson be discharged from any further service as a juror during the present term.

Ordered that John Evans be discharged from further service as a juror at this term.

Marmaduke Mitchell & Banks Burrow   )
              Vs.   )   In debt
Robert H. Dyer & John G. Carithers   )

This day came the parties aforesaid by their attorneys and the defendants withdrew their plea in the cause and say they cannot gainsay the plaintiffs action thereof against them but that they justly owe the remainder debt in the declaration mentioned whereupon came into open court Joel Dyer andconfessed judgement together with the said defendants for the sum of Nine hundred and twenty three dollar debt and the sum of thirty eight dollars and thirty nine cents interest, it is therefore considered by the court here that the plaintiff

P.74 do recover against the said defendants together with the said Joel Dyer,
the said sum of nine hundred twenty three dollars debt $38.39 cents interest
confessed aforesaid and their costs by them about their suit in this behalf expended, whereupon it is agreed by the plaintiffs that execution in this cause
be stayed twelve months.

P.75 Court then adjourned until tomorrow morning 9 o'clock.

         B. G. Stewart JP.
         Jno G. CaruthersJP.
         H. Harelson   JP.

   Friday morning the 20th. day Sept. 1822
   Court met agreeable to adjournment, Present the worshipful Herndon
Harelson, Bartholomew G. Stewart, John G. Carithers.

   Thomas Shannon who was appointed on a former day of this court Collecter of
the Public Taxes for the county of Madison this day came into open court and
entered into bond with William Braden and Daniel Mading his securities in
the penalty of sum of Five thousand dollars conditioned for the faithful
collestion and payment of said taxes agreeable to law.

   James Eastham, Assignee of Garrand &)
   Nicholas Long   )
       Vs.   )   Debt
   Robert H. Dyer   )

   This day came the parties aforesaid by their attorneys and thereupon
came a jury (to wit) Jordan G. Stokes, Joshua Pin, Henry Roan, Jesse M. Hanna
Ruben P. T. Stone, Allen Farehand, John Tidwell, Willis Nichols, John B.
Justice, William Freer, John Fussell and John Houston, who being elected
tried and sworn the truth to speak upon their oaths do say that the defendant
doth owe the plaintiff $140.00 the balance of the debt in the declaration
mentioned as the plaintiff in replying hath alleded and they do assess the
plaintiff damages sustained by reason of the said defendants mon performance
of a certain promise and assumption to $4.55 four dollars and 55 cents besides
his costs therefore it is considered by the court that the plaintiff recover
against said defendant the debt aforesaid with his damages aforesaid in form
aforesaid confessed and his costs by him in this behalf expended and the defendant in mercy etc.

   Baratholomew G. Stewart, Adm etc.
       Vs.
   Spencer Grant etc.

   On motion of the plaintiff by his attorney this cause is continued on
affidavit until next term.

P.76 Jackson Madison County Friday September 20, 1822
      Polly McBath)
        Vs.   )   Trespass
     William Deen)
   This day came the parties aforesaid by their attorneys and thereupon
came a jury of good and lawful men (to wit) Jordan G. Stokes Joshua Penn, Henry
Ryan, Jesse M. Hanna Ruben P. T.Stone, Allen Farehand, John Tidwell Willis
Nichols, John B. Justice, William Freer, John Fussell, James Wright, who being
elected tried and sworn the truth to speak upon the writ of inquiry went out
of court to consult their verdict and sometime returned into court and declared
they could not agree in their verdict therefore by consent of the parties and
with the assent of the court Jordan G. Stokes, one of the jurors are withdrawn

P.76   and the rest of said jurors from rendering verdict are discharged and
Cont. the cause to be continued until next term for a new trial to be had thereon.

        Squire Dawson late of County of Madison, laborer, who stands convicted
of petet larceny was again led to the bar in custody of the Sheriff of said
county and thereupon being demanded of him if any thing for himself he had to
or knew to say why the court here to judgment and execution of upon the premises
not prodede, he said he had nothing but what he had before said therefore it
is considered by the court that he be publicly whipped in the court house yard
there to receive twenty lashes on his bare back and the said prisoner by his
counsel prays an appeal to the nest Circuit Court of Madison County which is
granted him and ordered to be remanded to the custody of the sheriff.

        Ordered that the Grand Jury who were continued on yesterday as petit be
this day discharged from further service during this term.

        Thomas I Smith was this day duly and constitutionly elected constable
for the county of Madison in Captain Smith company who thereupon took the
several oaths prescribed by the constitution and laws of the state and entered into bond with Samuel Taylor and M. McLaurine his securities in the
penalty and conditions as by law directed.

        A deed of conveyance from David Jarett to William Wilbourne for forty
five and three fourth acres of land was this day produced in open court and
P.77acknowledged by the grantor thereof to be his act and deed and ordered to be
certified for registration. Court then adjourned until tomorrow morning
9 o'clock.

                                        H. Haralson JP.
                                        Joseph Linn JP.
                                        Adam R. Alexander JP.

Saturday Morning 21st. Sept. 1822

        Court met agreeable to adjournment, present the worshipful Herndon
Haralson, Adam R. Alexander and Joseph Linn.

William Welbourne	Robert Edmonson	Thos Deak
Hazael Hewett	Park Chandler	Ales Greer
Devereus Wynnet	Jas. Henderson	Jarett M Jilke
John Houston	Hemning Pace	Henry Booth
Stephen Booth	George Todd	Henry M Caulter
Robert Dixon	John M Welch	James McCutchen
James Tepit	Aquilla Davis	Roderick Wright
William Johns	Asa Midyet	James D. Carithers
Samuel Swan	Danil Horton	

Jordan G. Stokes)
     Vs.   )   Case
John J.Smith   )

        This day came the defendant by his attorney and the plaintiff being
solemly called came not but made default now is his suit further prosecuted,
therefore on the prayer of said defendant it is considered by the court that
he recover against the plaintiff his costs by him about his defense in this
* Ordered that the following persons be appointed to attend the next term
 of this court as jurors, to wit.

P. 77 behalf expended and be taken etc.
Cont.

J. G. Stokes)
    Vs.   )   Covenant
Jno J. Smith)

This day came the defendant by this attorney and the plaintiff being solemnly called came not but made default. Nor is his suit further presecuted therefore on prayer of said defendant it is considered by the court that he recover against said plaintiff his costs by him about his defense in this behalf expended and that he be taken etc.

P.79 Winters   )
       Vs.   )   Certeoraia
Solomon Cotner   )

This day came the said parties by their attorneys and whereupon the saidSolomon Cotner by his attorney moved the court to dismiss the certeoraia in this case and an argument being had thereon it is ordered by the court that the said petition for certioraia be dismissed and that the said Cotner have judment against the said Winters and his securities for the devt in the court below recovered with twelve and half per cent interest from the date of said judgement with costs of suit in this behalf expended and maybe taken etc.

Eastham Etc.   )   This day came the parties aforesaid by their attorneys
    Vs.   )   and the defendant demurred against the plaintiffs
H. L. Gray etc.   )   declaration being argued and overruled it is considered by the court it is considered by the court that the defendant taken nothing by his bill but for his false clamor be in mercy and that the plaingiff
go thereof hence without day and recover a gainst the defendant his costs by
him about his defense in this behalf expended and may be taken etc.

James Winters)   This day James Winters in this case comes by his at-
   Adsenture   )   torney and prays and appeal to the neat term of cir-
Solomon Cotner)   cuit court to be held for the county of Madison in
 the nature of a writ of error who entered into bond with William R. Hess and
Martin Lorance conditioned for the prosecution of said appeal with effect.
Court then adjourned until Court in course.
                                    H. Haralson   JP.
                                    Adam R. Alexander JP.
                                    Joseph Linn   JP.

P.80   At a court of pleas and quarter sessions began and held for the county
of Madison at the court house in the town of Jackson on Monday the 16th. day
of December in the year 1822 and forty seventh of American Independence.

        Present, the worshipful Herndon Haralson, William Atchison, Duncan McIver
Samuel Taylor, William Draper, Joseph Lynn, John Thomas and Stephen Jarman.
                        Court proclaimed
        A bill of sale from Anthony F. Gray to Sarah Gray for a negro girl was
exhibited in open court and duly acknowledged by the barganor and ordered to
be registered.

P80
Cont.

It is ordered by the court that Daniel Horton be released from serving as a juror during the present term.

A grant from the State of Tennessee to Sanl Taylor for 160 acres was produced in court and ordered to be registered.

Asa B Midyet is released from further attendance as a juror at the present term.

On motion, it is ordered by the court that all lands liable to double taxation in the county of Madison for the years 1821 & 1822 be released therefrom upon the owners paying the single tax and costs accruing and the sheriff is here by ordered to receive the single tax.

Stephen Lacy appeared in court and made oath to killing 2 wolves in the county of Madison over the age of 4 months which is ordered to be certified.

James Greer & John L. Dillard appeared in court and took the oaths of qualification as justices of the peace for Madison County.

Robert Jarman, Esq. appeared in open court and took the oaths as an attorney and counsellor at law and thereupon admitted to practice in said court.

Sam'l Thomas made oath to the killing one wolf over the age of four months which is ordered to be certified, also Andrew Thomas one of the same age.

Records of December Term 1822

P.81

It is ordered by the court that Hazel Hewitt be appointed overseer of the road in the room of Diveraux Wynne resigned and that the hands heretofore alloted to attend Hewitt to keep the same in repair.

Thomas Reener appeared in open court and made oath to the killing of one wolf over the age of four months which is ordered to be certified.

In motion it is ordered by the court that Sanuel Shannon be allowed the sum of ninty five dollars for building a jail in Madison County as per account filed and that the county trustee pay the same upon copy of this order.

I t is ordered by the court that Thos. Shannon, sheriff be allowed the sum of fifty dollars for his ex-officers services for the year 1822 and that the county trustee pay the same upon copy of this order.

It is ordered that Alexander B. Bradford Solicitor be allowed the sum of fifty dollars for ex-officers services for the year 1822 and that the county trustee pay the same upon a copy of this order.

It is ordered that Roderick McIver be allowed the sum of forty dollars for ex-officers servies for the year 1822 and that the county trustee pay the same upon copy of this order Henry A Coulter is exempted from serving as juror at this term.

Aquilla Davis is exempted from serving as a juror at this term.

It is ordered by the court that the following places be established for holding elections to elect members to congress and the state legislature and

P.81   all other elections necessary to be held (to wit) Francis Taylor on the
Cont.middle fork; William P. Seats on the middle fork; Henry Rutherford's ,near
the Key corner; John G. Caruthers, South, Fork ferry; Danil Ross and Thomas
McNeals on the South side of Big Hatchie in the territorial county South of
Madison.

P.82   William Wilbourne exempts from serving as a juror the present term.

George Taylor released from paying his fine as delinquent juror at last
term.

Ordered that Ryland Chandler who came into court and made oath that he
has served two days as a juror of view be allowed the sum of one dollar per
day and that the county trustee pay the same upon a copy of this order.
Vincent Haralson served four days which was ordered as above. James Caldwell
served two days and ordered as above. Robert Burns two days and ordered as
above.

Ordered that Thursday of this court be set apart for transacting State
business to take effect from and after the present term of this court.

On motion that Friday next be set apart for transacting county business
from the hours of ten o'clock until twelve.

On motion and petition filed it is ordered that George W. Still, be
allowed to build a grist and saw mill on Trace creek in the ninth district,
2nd. range and ninth section on 40 acres of land entered in the name of said
Still.

On motion and petition filed ordered that the petition of Clark Spencer
to build a grist mill on his own land lying in the 10th. district 1st. range
and 9th. section on a creek known by name of Cain Creek be granted him.

On motion and petition filed it is ordered that Thomas J. Hardeman be
allowed to build a mill across the Pleasant--- on his own land.

P83   On motion and petition filed ordered that the following persons be appointed a jury of view or any five of them to mark out a road the nearest and
best way from the town of Jackson to the county line of this county on a direction to Hardin Court House (to wit) Hazael Hewitt, Thomas Reaves, Danil Ross,
Lemuel Martin, John Gather, Pitts Chandler, Ezekeal McCoy, William Alexander,
Sen. William Spencer, William Haltom and N. Harris and the applicants agree to
open said roads.

On motion and petition filed order ed the following persons, to wit
Thomas J. Hardeman, James Haley, Stephen Lacy John Thomas, John Spencer,
Jacob Hill, John H. Bills, William Road, Samuel H.Shennon. Daniel Horton
William Reynold, William Breden, William H. Doak, James F. Theobold, and
Thomas McNeal, or any five of them after first being duly sworn to be a jury
of view to mark out and lay off a road the nearest and best way from the
town of Jackson on a direction to Polk's ferry on Big Hatchie river as fares
the Southern boundary of this county and that they make a report of this county
proceedings to the next term of this court.

On motion and petition filed ordered that the following persons (to wit)
William Greer, Jason Wilson, Jonathan Welch, Bartholomew G. Stewart, John Gately,
James Greer, Jesse M Hannah Andrew Hays and James Tidwell or any five of them
after first being duly sworn be a jury of view to mark and lay off a road com-

P83
Cont. mencing at Jarmans Ford on the middle fork of the Forked Deer river to extend up said fork to intersect the road leading to Carroll Court House and also a road from the ford above mentioned the nearest and best way to the town of Jackson and that they make report to the next term of this court.

P84
On motion and petition filed ordered that the following persons, towit Devereaux Wynne, James Henderson, Vincent Haralson Gabriel Anderson, Robert Burns James Caldwell and William Shepherd be granted them a road of the 3rd. class from Warlick's Mill to Robert Byrns.

On motion, it is ordered that the following persons, to wit, James Greer John B. Hogg, Lewis Needham, N. I. Hess, after first being duly sworn to be a jury of view to mark and lay of a road from the house of William Love to the house of William R. Hess and that they make report to the next term of this court.

Ordered that the report of the jury of view appointed at the last term of this court to view a road from the town of Jackson to the county line in a direction toThomas Fights Mill on the little North fork of Forked Deer river be received and that William Espy be appointed overseer of said road from town to the section line dividing 9 and 10 sections and that Jordan G. Stokes be appointed overseer from hence to a bridge on the North or middle fork of Forked Deer river and Henry Castler's from thence to the county line.

On motion and petition filed it is ordered by the court that the petition of Eldridge Newson for the erection of a mill be laid over until Friday next.

P85
A deed of bargain and sale from Malcolm Gilchrist to Duncan McIver, for Eighty Acres of land was this day produced in open court and proven by Daniel Gilchrist one of the subscribing witnesses thereto and ordered to be continued for further probate.

A deed of Bargain and sale from William Wilbourn to John Sutton for 100 acres of land was this day produced in open court and acknowledged by the grantor to be his act and deed and ordered to be registered.

A deed of bargain and sale from Thomas Campbell, Joseph B. Portes & Lewis Needham to William Robb for 876 acres was this day produced in open court and proven by the oaths of I. W. Needham and Benjamin White two of the subscribing witnesses thereto and ordered to be registered.

A deed of bargain and sale from Thomas Campbell to William Robb for one third part of a 5000 acres of land was this day produced in open court and proven by the oath of Lewis Needham and I. W. Needham two subscribing witnesses thereto and ordered to be regestered.

The following deeds of bargain and sale were this day produced in open court and ordered to be regestered (to wit).

A deed from John C. McLemore to Drury Pulliam for four hundred forty three and one half acres of land. A deed from John Allen to John Scarbrough for 200 acres land. A deed from William Cuilt, to John Scarbrough for 200 acres of land. A deed from John Scarbrough to John Henderson for 600 acres of land, and one deed from James Mallery sheriff of stewart county to Ephriam, B. Davidson, William Carl, John Scarbrough, William Williams, and John Allen for one thousand acres of land . Court then adjourned until tomorrow morning nine o'clock.

H. Haralson JP.   W. B. Cross   Jp.

Joseph Linn JP'   Stephen Jarman

P86   Tuesday morning 17th. December 1822

Court met agreeable to adjournment; present the worshipful Herndon Haralson, Joseph Linn, John B. Cross, Stephen Jarman, Samuel Taylor, William Atchison, Bartholomew G. Stewart.

William Anderson Esq. appeared in open court and took the oath of qualification as an attorney and counsellor at law and was thereupon admitted to practice in saidcourt.

This day the sheriff made returns of the writ of veniri focias to him directed from the last term and returnable to the present term of this court and in pursuance these of have summoned the persons named in said veniri of whom the following persons were attending (to wit),

Robert Edmisson	Deveraux Wynne
Hazael Hewitt	Parks Chandler
Henning pace	Henry Booth
Stephen Booth	James Tepit
William Johns	Samuel Swan
Thomas M. Doak	Jarett M. Jelks

then not being a sufficient number attending it was considered the sheriff to summon a sufficient number of the by standers to complete the panel.

Thereupon the following persons (to wit) Hazael Hewitt, Jarret M. Jelks, Solomon Colner, Samuel Swan, James Tipit, John Stalkeep, John Fisher, Thomas Doak, Henry Booth Devoreaux Wynne, Henning Pace, William Johns, Parks Chandler, with Hazel Hewitt their foreman were elected, empanelled, sworn and charged as a Grand Jury to inquire into and for the body of thecounty of Madison and thereupon retired to comsider presentments.

Joseph Linn and Robert Dixon two of the commissioners appointed at last term of this court to make allowance for the support of the family of William Griffith deceased for one year, returned into court the following report, We the undersigned are of the opinion that three cows and calves and one hundred four dollars will be sufficient for the support of said family.

Joel Dyer, John H. Gibson, Thomas Bolding William Espy and Henry L. Gray a jury of view appointed at the last term of this court to view and mark out a road from the town of Jackson to Harris's Bluff on the South fork of the Forked Deer river made the following report from town to the house of William Espy from thence to Micajoh Midyete thence to Joel Dyers thence to Harris Bluff.

Ordered by the court that the following persons be assigned to John Wear who was appointed at the last term of this court overseer of that part of the road leading from Jackson by the house of Joseph Linn Esq. and thence by the house of said Wear to thecounty line to open and keep in repair that part of said road commenceing at the head of Younge branch and ending at the county line (to wit) William Wilson, William Howard James Howard Squire Dawson, Hiram Dawson George Thompson, John Hardgraves & hands John Moody, Isaac Moody, Alvin Cross, John Fawbuck Andrew Fawbuck Thomas Gethin, Anderson Odle, Jiremiah Etheridge John Robinson, John Philps, John Weirs hands, Matthew Pate, Hugh Reid, George James, Zaphaniel Neill, Bevery B. Acre, Jonathan Waller, John Howard Federick Repogle.

P88   A deed of Bargain and sale from William Harris to James Bass Junior and William Ledbetter for an undivided third part of two lots of ground on the South side of the town of Murfreesborough No. 64 & 65 was this day produced in

P88 open court and the execution thereof proven by the oaths of Henry L. Gray a subscribing witness thereto and ordered to be certified.

George Todd exempted from serving as juror at the present term.

John Rutherford appeared in Court this day and took the several oaths of qualification as a justice of the peace for Madison County who thereupon took his seat upon the bench

Jordan G. Stokes   )
        Vs.   )   Covenant
John J. Smith   )

On motion it is ordered that the parties have leave to take depositions generally upon their giving 10 days notice to state and 20 days notice out of the state.

Jordan G. Stokes   )
        Vs.   )   Case
John J. Smith   )

Ordered that the parties be allowed to take depositions generally by giving 10 days notice in the state and 20 days if out of the state.

        M Bell McMahan   )   Devt Same rule allowed as above
             Vs.   )
        Jordan G. Stokes)

P.89 State   )
        Vs.   )   Indictment for an affray
John Stalkeep   )

This day came as well the solicitor general on the part of the state as the defendant in his own proper person and the defendant being arraigned upon his arraignment plead that he was guilty in the manner and form as charged in the indictment, it is therefore considered by the court that the defendant make his peace with the state by the payment of one dollar and that the plaintiff go thereof hence without day and recover of the defendant her costs by her about her suit in this behalf expended and that the defendant bein mercy etc.

State   )
        Vs.   )   Indictment for an assault
William Norwood)

This day came as well the solicitor general on the part of the state as the defendant in his proper person and the defendant being arraigned upon his arraignment plead that he was guilty in the manner and form as charged in the indictment, it is therefore considered by the court that the defendant make his peace with the state by the payment of one dollar and that the plaintiff go thereof hence with out day and recover of the defendant her costs by her about her suit in this behalf expended and that the defendant be in mercy etc.

State   )
        Vs.   )   Indictment for an assault
Benoni Crawford)

This day came as well the solicitor general on the part of the state as the defendant in his own proper person and the defendant on being arraigned upon his arraignment plead that he was guilty in the manner and form as charged in the indictment, It is therefore considered by the court that the defendant make his peace with the state by the payment of one dollar and that the

P.90 plaintiff go thereof hence without day and recover of the defendant her costs
by her about her suit in this behalf expended and that the defendant be in
mercy etc.

State   )
      Vs.   )   Indictment for an assult.
Jonathan Houston   )

    This day came as well the solicitor general on the part of the state
as the defendant in his own proper person and the defendant on being arraigned upon his arraignment plead that he was guilty in the manner and form as
charged in the indictment, it is therefore considered by the court that the
defendant make his peace with the state by the payment of one dollar and that
the plaintiff go thereof hence and recover of the defendant her costs by her
about her suit in this behalf ex ended and the defendant be in mercy etc.

State   )
      Vs.   )   Indicement for tipling
Jacob Bradbury)

    This day came as well the solicitor general on the part of the state
as the defendant in his own proper person and the defendant being arraigned
upon his arraignment plead that he was guilty in the manner and form as charg-
edin the indictment it is therefore considered by the court that the defendant make his peace with the state by the payment of one cent and that the
plaintiff go thereof hence without day and recover of the defendant her costs
by her about her suit in this behalf expended and the defendant in mercy etc.

P.91 William B. McLeland)
            Vs.   )   Trespass on the case
James McCutchen   )

    This day came the parties aforesaid by their attorneys and it being
agreed on by said parties the plaintiff dismiss his suit and the defendant
assumes the payment of one half the costs of said suit.

    A deed of bargain and sale from Thomas Campbell to Joseph B. Porter
for five hundred and eighty one acres of land was this day produced in open
court and proven by the oaths of J. W. Needham and Benjamin White two subscribing witnesses thereto and ordered to be registered.

    A deed of bargain and sale from William Robb to Joseph B. Porter for
315 acres of land was this day produced in open court and the execution thereof proven by the oaths of Lewis Needham and J. W. Needham two subscribing
witnesses thereto and ordered to be regestered.

    A deed of bargain and sale from Thomas Campbell William Robb and Joseph
B. Porter to Lewis Needham for 876 acres of land was this day produced in
open court and the execution thereof proven by the oaths of J. W. Needham
and Benjamin White two suscribing witnesses thereto and ordered to be registered.

    Court then adjourned until tomorrow morning 9 O'clock
                        B. J. Stewart   JP
                        Jno. G. Carithers JP
                        H. Haralson   JP

Wednesday morning the 18th. day of December 1822 Court met agreeable to adjournment present: the worshipful Herndon Haralson Jno. G. Caruthers,
Bartholomew G. Stewart David Jarrett Samuel Taylor.

P.92   Ordered by the Court that all Captains of Militia companies in the county of Madison do make a true list of all such persons on their roll as are qualified to serve as jurors and return the same to the Clerk of this court on his furnishing them with a copy of this order.

       Guy Smith appeared in open court and took the oaths of qualification as a justice of peace for Madison County who thereupon took his seat upon the bench.

Bartholomew G. Stewart, Adm.   )
            Vs.   )   Case
Spencer Grant & Thomas Grisom   )

       By consent of the parties by their attorneys all matters in difference between them in this suit is referred to the final determination of Herndon Haralson Samuel H. Shannon, and Samuel Taylor and William Atchison and their award or award of such persons as they shall choose for an umpire is to be thereupon made the judgment of the court and the same is ordered accordingly.

Gerrard W. Long)
       Vs.   )   Case
H. L. Gray   )

       This day came the parties aforesaid by their attorneys and thereupon came a jury of good and lawful men (to wit) Alexander Greer, Robert Edmison James McCutchen George W. Taylor Stephen Booth Alanson F. Doak, Ryland Chandler, John M. Welch, Green L. Haralson, Daniel Ring James Marlin and Elijah

P93 McAfee, who being elected tried and sworn on the issue joined upon their oaths do say that the defendant did assume upon himself in manner and form as the plaintiff in declaring against him hath alleged and they do assess the plaindamages by reason there of to Eighty seven dollars and twenty five cents besides their costs therefore it is considered by the court that the plaintiff recover of the defendant this damage aforesaid in manner and form aforesaid assessed and their costs by them about their suit in this behalf expended and the said defendant may be taken etc.

Gerrard Long   )
     Vs.   )   Case
Henry L. Gray)

       This day came the parties aforesaid by their attorneys and thereupon came a jury of good and lawful men (to sit) Alexander Greer, Robert Edmison James McCutchen George M. Taylor, Stephen Booth, Alanson F. Doak Ryland Chandler, John M. Welch, Green L. Haralson, Daniel King James Malin and Elijah McAfee, who being elected, tried and sworn on the issue joined upon their oaths do say that the defendant did assume upon himself in the manner and form as the plaintiff in declaration hath alleged and they do assess the plaintiff damages by reason thereof to two hundred and eighty one dollars besides his costs therefore it is considered by the court that the plaintiff go hence and recover of the defendant his damages aforesaid in manner and form aforesaid assessed and this behalf expended and the defendant may be taken etc.

P94 Reuben P. T. Stone)
        Vs.   0   Case
William D. Lewis)

       On affidavit of the defendant filed this cause is ordered to be continued until the next term.

P94   Elijah McAfee   )
Cont.   Vs.   )   Case
       Joseph B. Porter .)
       On motion of the plaintiff by his attorney leave is granted him to
amend his declaration by paying the defendant his costs by such amendment and
this case is continued until next term and it ordered by the court that the
parties have leave to take depositions generally, by giving 10 days notice in
the state and 20 out.

       James Eastham assn)
             Vs.   )   Case
       Henry L. Grey   )
       This day came the parties aforesaid by their attorneys and the defend-
ant relinguished his farmer plea, saith he cannot gainsay the plaintiff
action as the plaintiff in declaration hath alleged, therefore it is considered by the court that the plaintiff recover against the said defendant the sum
of one hundred twenty seven dollars sixty two and one half cents and his costs
by him in this behalf expended and the defendant be in mercy etc.

       Polly McBath   )
             Vs.   )   Trespass
       William Deen   )
       The plaintiff by her council comes into court and dismisses her suit
and the defendant assumes the payment of the costs of said suit.

P95 Matthew Wilson Exr.)
     of James Wilson etc.)
             Vs.   )   Case
       William H. Doak   )
       On affidavit of the defendant this cause is continued until the next
term.

       James Love   )
             Vs.   )   Debt
       Carter C. Collier)
       This day came the parties aforesaid and thereupon came a jury of good
and lawful men to wit Alexander Greer, Robert Edmison, James McCutchen George
W. Taylor, Stephen Booth Alanson F. Doak Ryland Chandler John M Welch
Green L. Haralson Danil King James Marlin and Elijah McAfee who being elected
tried and sworn will and truly to try the issue joined on the oaths do say
that the defendant hath not paid the debt of two hundred dollars in the ceclaration mentioned and that they assess the plaintiff damages by reasonthere-
to thirty eight dollars and thirty cents. It is therefore considered by
the court that the plaintiff recover against the defendant the debt and demages aforesaid in manner and form aforesaid and also his costs about his suit
in this behalf expended and the defendant in mercy etc.

       Samuel Young   )
             Vs.   )   Case
       Nathan Bridgman   )
       On affedivit filed this case is continued until next term.

       James McCutchen   )
             Vs.   )   Case
       Madison McLaurine)
       This case is continued until next term as of an affidavit of the de-
fense.

P.96 John Thomas Book   )
      Vs.   )   Debt
James D. Caruthers   )

     It is ordered by the court that commissions issue to take deposition generally to be read in evidince by giving 20 days notice of the time and place of taking the same John Stewart Book

John Thomas Brook   )
      Vs.   )   Debt
James D. Caruthers   )

     It is ordered by the court that commissions issue to take the depositions generally to be read in evidence the parties giving twenty days notice of the time and place of taking the same.

John Thomas Brook   )
      Vs.   )   Debt
James D. Carithers   )

     It is ordered by the court that commissions to take depositions generally to be read in evidence the parties giving 20 days notice of the time and place of taking of same.

     Bartholomew G. Stewart and Wilmoth Edmison this day returned into court an inventory of the estate of Robert Edmison deceased.

     The last will and testament of George Taylor was this day produced in open court and the execution thereof duly proven by the oath of George W. Taylor a subscribing witness thereto and ordered to be recorded.

     The Grand Jury this day returned into court the following bills of indictment (to wito) two against Robert H. Wynne for an assault indorsed on the back a true bill Hazael Hewett foreman of the Grand Jury and also a presentment against Robert Edmiston and Cyrus Webb for an effray.

P97   Mudock Murchison came into open court and proven his attendance three days as a juror of view and it was thereupon ordered by the court that he be allowed the sum of one dollar per day to be paid by the county trustee one copy of this order.

     Court then adjourned until tomorrow morning 9 o'clock.

                           B. G. Stewart   JP.
                           John Thomas   JP.
                           Sam'l Taylor   JP.

     Thursday morning 19th. December 1822 court met according to adjournment present; the worshipful B. G. Stewart, John Thomas and Sam'l Taylor who took their seats and proceeded to business.

The State Plff   )
      Vs.   )   Affray
Robert Edmison, Deft.   )

     This day came the state by the Solicitor who prosecuted in behalf of the state, and the defendant in proper person who submits to the mercy of the court.

P97   It is therefore considered by the court that said defendant make his
Cont.fine to the state by the payment of one dollar and that he pay the costs of
the prosecution.

Winchester & Carr Plff.)
        Vs.   )   In Debt
Robert H. Dyer, Deft.   )
        This day came the parties by their attorneys thereupon came a jury of
good and lawful men (to wit) Alexander Greer Robert Edmison James McCuthhen,
George W. Taylor Stephen Booth Alanson F. Doak Ryland Chandler John M Welch
Green L. Haralson, Daniel King James Martin and E. McAfee who being elected
tried and sworn the truth to speak upon the issue joined upon their oaths
do say the defendant hath not paid the balance of the debt in the declaration
mentioned of two hundred dollars and seventy seven cents and assess the damages
by reason of the detention thereof to twenty one dollars. It is therefore consid
ered by the court that theplaintiff recover of the defendant the debt aforesaid
in form aforesaid assessed, and also their costs by them about their suit in
this behalf expended and the defendant in mercy.

Wm. & John Donnell Assers, Plff.)
        Vs.   )   Debt
John B. Hogg Dft.   )
        This day came the parties by their attorneys and thereupon came a jury of
good and lawful men viz the same in above cause who being elected tried and
sworn the truth to speak upon the issue joined on their oaths do say they
find the defendant has not paid the debt in the declaration mentioned of one
hundred forty four dollars twenty eight cents and assess the plaintiff damages
by reason of the detention thereof to sixteen dollars and forty cents. It is
therefore considered by the court that said plaintiff recover of the defendant
the debt aforesaid together with the damages aforesaid assessed and also their
costs by them about their suit in this behalf expended etc.

P99 Records at Dec. term 1822

Mitchell & Burrough Assers Plff.)
        Vs.   )   In Debt.
William L. Mitchell, Deft.   )
        This day came the parties by their attorneys and thereupon came a jury
of good and lawful men (to wit) the same as in foregoing cause who being elected,
tried and sworn the truth to speak upon the issue joined upon their oaths do
say they find the defendant has not paid the debt in the declaration mentioned
of sixty eight dollars and thirty seven and one half cents and assess the plaintiff damages by reason thereof to five dollars and fifty five cents. It is
therefore considered by the court that the said palintiff recover of the defendant the aforesaid together with the damages aforesaid in form aforesaid assessed
and also their costs by them about their suit in this behalf expended etc.

William Palmer Plff   ◊
        Vs.   )   Case
Thomas W. Palmer Deft.   )
        This day came the defendant by his attorneys and their plaintiff being
solemnly called to come in and prosecute his suit in this behalf came not.
It is therefore considered by the court the said plaintiff be non properd and
that defendant recover of the plaintiff his costs by him about his suit in
this behalf expended.   Motion to set aside.

P1COJames Stalkeep Pliff)
      Vs.)   Appeal
Robert H Dyer Deft)

      This day came the defendant by his attorney and the plaintiff being
solomnly called to come in to prosecute his appeal came not. It is therefore
considered by the court that the said plaintiff be non proped and that the defendant recover of him the costs by him about his defense in htis behalf appended

James Stalkeep Plff.)
      Vs.)   Appeal
Robert Dyer Deft.)

      This day came the defendant by his attorney and the plaintiff being
solomnly called to come into court and prosecute his appeal came not. It is
therefore considered by the court that said plaintiff be non propd. and that
the deft. recover of the pla utiff his costs by him about his defense in this
behalf expended etc.

John H. Lockert, Plff)
      Vs.)   Appeal
Begnial Crook, Deft.)

      This day came the defendant by his attorney and the plaintiff being
solemnly called to come in and prosecute his appeal came not . It is therfore
considered by the court that the plaintiff be non propd. and that the defendant
recover of the plff his costs by him about his defence in this behalf expended.

The State)
      Vs.) $100
Zebider Gentry)

      This day came the state by the solicitor and the defendant in proper person
who pleads quilty and submits to the mercy of the court. lt is therefore considered by the court that said defendant make his fine to the state by the paymant
of one dollar and pay the costs of his prosecution the said defendant in mercy etc.

P101 Records of Dec'r. Term 1822
James Stalkeep, Plff)
      Vs.)   Appeal
Jordan G. Stokes, Deft.)

      This day came the parties by their attorneys and thereupon came a jury
of good and lawful men to wit Alexander Greer Robert Edminson James McCutchen.
J Booth John M Welch, Zebider Gentry James Winters Marlin Lorence Daniel King
R. P. T. Stone and Alexander Braden who being elected tried and sworn to try
the matter in deapute between the parties upon their oath do say they find the
deft is indebted to the plaintiff in the sum of ten dollars and fifty cents.

      It is therefore considered by the court that the plaintiff recover of the
defendant the said sum of ten dollars and fifty cents and also hi costs by him
about his suit in this behalf expended etc.

James Stalkeep Plff)
      Vs.)   Appeal
Jordan G. Stokes, Def.)   (The same Jury)

      This day came the parties by their allorneys and thereupon came a jury
of good and lawful men (to wit) Alexander Greer, Robert Edmiston James McCutchen
Stephen Booth John M Welch, Zebider Gentry James Winters Martin Lorence Daniel
King Reuben P. T. Stone and Alexander Braden who being elected tried and sworn
to try the matters in deapute between the parties upon their oaths do say they
find the defendant indebted to the plaintiff in the sum of minteen dollars

P101 and fifty cents, debt. It is therefore considered by the court that the plain-
Cont. tiff recover of the defendant the said sum of ninteen dollars and fifty cents
and also his costs by him about his suit in this behalf expended etc.

P102 Records at Dec'r. Term 1822

The State   )
    Vs.   )   Indictment
Robert Bedford   )

This day came the state by the solicitor and the defendant by his attorney
and because he cannot gainsay the charged contained in the indictment, pleads
guilty and submits to the mercy of the court.

It is therefore considered by the court that the said defendant make his
fine to the state by the payment of one dollar and that he pay the costs of
this prosecution.

Samuel D. Waddle Plff)
    Vs.   )   Appeal
George Gentry, Debt.)

It is ordered by the court with the consent of the parties that the matter
in despute in the cause between the parties be referred to the arbitration of
B. C. Stewart, Guy Smith Sam'l Taylor Esq. McIver and Alexander Greer, and
that their award be made the judgement of the court.

Wilham Caruthers Plff)
    Vs.   )   Certiorari
Jesse m Hanna, Deft.   )

This day came the deft. by his attorney and the plaintiff being solemnly
called to come in and prosecute his certoraeri aforesaid came not. It is therefore considered by the court that the said plaintiff be non prop'd and that
the defendant recover of the plaintiff his costs by him about his defense on
this behalf expended.

A deed of bargain and sale from R. C. Thompson to David Reid for 260
acres of land was exhibited in open court and the execution thereof proved
by the oaths of Duncan McIver R. McIver the subscribing witnesses thereto
and ordered to be registered.

P103 Records at December term 1822
Solomon Cotner, Plff)
    Vs.   )   Certiorari
James Winters, Deft)

This day came the parties by their attorneys and therupon came a jury
of good and lawful men (to wit) Green L. Haralson James Marlin, Robert Reid
Alexander Greer Robert Edminson James McCutches, Stephen Booth John M Welch
Zebider Gentry Thomas W. Palmer, Daniel King R. P. T. Stone and Alexander
Braden who being elected tried and sworn to try the matters in dispute between
the parties upon their oath do say they find for the plaintiff twenty one dollars
the amount of the judgment in the court below.

It is therefore considered by the court that the plaintiff recover of the
defendant and his securities Joseph H. Adams and Robert Edminston the amount

P103 of the judgment afore said with six per cent interest from the rendition of the
Cont. judgment below and his costs by him about his suit in this behalf expended.

John B. Cross   )
        Vs.   )   Viat Annis
Lewis Williams   )

This day came the parties aforesiad and it being agreed on the plaintiff
dismisses his suit and the defendant assumes the payment of all costs accrued
by reason of said suit, it is therefore considered by the court that the plaintiff go thereof hence without day and recover of said defendant his costs by
him about his suit in this behalf expended.

P104 Records of December Term. 1822

The Grand Jury this day returned into court the following indictments,
to wit, one against Elijah Jones for an assault and one against Zebider Gentry
for an assault and one against Robert Bedford for an assault.

State   )
        Vs.   )   An assault
Robert H. Wynne)

This day came the solicitor general on the part of the State and the dependant in his proper person who plead guilty and put himself on the grace and
mercy of the court that the defendant make his peace with the state by the payment of one dollar and costs of this prosecution and the said defendant may be
taken etc.

State   )
        Vs.   )   Assault
Robert Haynes   )

This day came as well the solicitor general on the part of the state as
the defendant in his proper person who pleads guilty and puts himself upon the
mercy of the court. It is therefore considered by the court that the defendant make his peace with this state by the payment of one dollar and the costs
of this prosecution and the said defendant may be taken etc.

State   )
        Vs.   )   Affray
Robert Edmiston)

This day came as well the solicitor general on the part of the state as the
defendant in his proper person who plead guilty and put himself upon the grace
and mercy of the court. It is therefore considered by the court that the defendant make his peace with the state by the payment of one dollar and the costs
of this prosecution and be in mercy.

P105 Records of December Term 1822
State   )
        Vs.   )   Assault
Elijah Jones   )

This day came as well the solicitor general on the part of the state as
the defendant in his proper person who pleads guilty and submits to the mercy
of the court. It is therefore considered by the court that the defendant make
his peace with the state by the payment of one dollar and costs of this prosecution
and the defendant in mercy.   Court then adjourned until tomorrow morning 9 o8clock

                                    H. Harrison
                          John Thomas   JP
                          Jas. Trousdale JP.

P105   Friday morning 20th Dec. 1822, court met according to adjournment. Present
Cont.the Worshipful H. Haralson John Thomas and James Trousdale who took their seats
    and proceeded to business.

            Dean   )
            Vs.   )
            Butler)
            On motion it is ordered by the court that Henry Butler appearance bail
for the defendant be released there from and the defendant thereupon offend
William Espy as his security who is accepted by the court.

            Archibald B. Daindridge   )
                    Vs.   )   Debt
            Stokely D. Hays   )
            It is agreed by the parties with the assent of the court that depositions
be taken generally in this cause by the parties giving ten days notice within
the state and 20 days if without of time and place of taking the same.

P106 Records of December Term 1822
            W. Wilson, Plff.   )
            Vs.   )   Case
            Thomas Grissom, Deft.   )
            This day came the plaintiff by his attorney and the defendant being solem-
nly called to come and plead to the suit against him came not. It is therefore
considered by the court that a writ of inquiry of damage be awarded against the
said defendant returnable to the next term of this court.

            Reuben P. T. Stone, Plff.)
            Vs.   )   In covenant
            William D. Lewis, Deft.   )
            This day came the parties aforesaid by their attorneys and the matters of
law arising on the defendant demurer to the plaintiffs declaration being fully
argued and the court being sufficiently informed thereon it seems to the court
that the law is for the plaintiff. It is therefore ordered by the cour that
the plaintiff recover of the defendant such damages as he has sutained by reason
of the breach of covenant in the declaration supposia but because those damages
are unknown it is connanded the sheriff that he cause a jury come here etc. at
the next term to inquire of damages until which time this case is continued.

P. 107   Records of December Term 1822.
            A bill of sale from Henry L. Gray to Joel Dyer for a negro girl named
Flora was this day produced in open court and the execution there of was proven
by the oath of William R. Hess a subscribing witness thereto and ordered to be
registered.

            A bill of sale from Thomas Stubble field to Sally F. Grey was this day
produced in open court and the execution thereof duly proven by the oath of John
H. Hyde a subscribing witness thereto andordered to be recorded.

            Matthew Johnson Administrator of the estate of Simon Johnson, Deceased
returned this day into court an inventory of said estate and also an account of
sales which was ordered to be recorded.

            Stephen Booth   )
                 Vs.   )   Debt
            C. J. Ragsdale &Matthew Johnson)

P1O7   This day came the parties aforesaid by heir attorneys and the plaintiff
Cont. dismisses his suit and assumes the payment of all costs of said suit; it is
therefore considered by the court that the defendant go thereof hence without
day and recover of the plaintiff their costs by them about their suit in this
behalf expended and may be taken etc.

P108 Records of December Term 1822
      Benjamin Purtle this day appeared in court and proved the killing of one
wold in the county of Madison over the age of four months which is ordered to
be certified accordingly.

          State)
Vs.   )   Assault and Battery
Joel Bugg)
      This day came as well the solicitor general on the part of the state as
the defendant in his proper person and the defendant being arraigned upon his
arraignment plead guilty. It is therefore considered by the court that the defendant make his peace with the state by the payment of one dollar that the plff.
recover of the deft. her cost by her about her prosecution in this behalf expended and the defendant may be taken etc.

      Andrew Hays appeared in open court and proved his attendance as a juror
of view three days and is entitled to one dollar per day for the same.

      Samuel D. Waddle appeared in open court and proved his attendance as a
juror of view three days and is entitled to one dollar per day for the same.

      Robert Reid came into open court and proved his services for three days
as a juror of view and entitled to the same for the same.

P109   Record of December Term 1822
      On motion ordered by the court the confirmation of the report of the jury
of view appointed at the last term of this court to mark and lay off a road from
Jackson to Harris Bluff be resended and that the following persons (to wit)
Thomas M Dement Charles Sevier John G. Caruthers, Guy Smith Thomas and John J.
Smith William McClellen, Joel Dyer, Aquilla Davis John T. Porter and William
Mitchell or any five of them after first being duly sworn to mark and lay off
a road the nearest and best way from Jackson to Harris Bluff on the South fork
of the Forked Deer river and make a report to the next term of this court.

John Word   )
Vs.   )   in debt
C. J. Ragsdale Etc.)
      This day came the parties aforesaid by their attorneys and the defendants
withdrawing their former pleas say they cannot gainsay the plaintiffs action for
one hundred dollars as he hath in his declaration alleged. Therefore it is considered by the court that the plaintiff recover of the defendant the said sum
of one hundred dollars and damages four dollars and alson that he recover against
said defendant his costs about his suit in this behalf expended.

P 110   Records of December Term 1822
      Ordered that William Deen be appointed as an additional juror of view on
the road directed to be viewed and marked out from this to Polks ferry on Hatchie river.

      Ordered that Allen Fuller be appointed overseer of the road in the place
Martin Cartmell resigned commencing at Ezekial B. McCoy's and ending at the
Eastern boundary of Madison County

F110   Ordered that Ezekiel B. McCoy be released from paying any tax on the
Cont. following tracts of land (to wit) one containing 640 acres of land and one
containing 25 acres, said tracts of land appearing to the satisfaction of this
court by a certificate of Samuel Wilson, Surveyor of the ninth district to have
been entered in the year 1821.

     Ordered by the court that William Expy be allowed the sum of one dollar
per day for serving as a juror of view who came into court and proved by his
own oath of having served five days as juror as aforesaid.

     Alexander Greer proved his serving two days which was ordered as above.

     William Johns proved his serving two days and ordered as above.

     Ordered that all persons having heretofore served as jurors of new to mark
and lay off roads in the county of Madison on coming into court and proving the
same be allowed one dollar per day .

P111 Records of December Term 1822
     Andrew Hays comes into court and proves his attendance six days as a
juror of view view

     Robert Reid comes into court and proves his attendance three days as a
juror of view

     Jordon G. Stokes comes into court and proves his attendance three days as a
juror of view .

     On motion and petition filed ordered that John Murray have leave to extab-
lish a ferry your petitioner having entered the land on both sides of the river
binds himself to keep the same in good repair and it is further ordered that the
following rates of feriage be allowed him (to wit) for each loaded wagon and
four horse team one dollar, for each two wheel carriage fifty cents and for each
four wheel carriage and two horse tema, fifty cents and for each four whill
Carriage and three horse team seventy five cents and for each man horse, twelve
one half cents and for each footman six and one fourth cents, for each loose
house the same. for each head of cattle two and one half cents and for each head
of Hogs or sheep two cents.

     On motions and petition filed it is ordered that the following persons
(to wit) David Jernigan, Thomas Bogot Thomas Ellison, John Thomas James Haley
John Maury William Deen, Stephen Booth and Jacov Hill or any five of them, being
first duly sworn be a jury of view to mark and lay off a road from the town of
Jackson to a place known as Fowler's ferry on Big Hatchie river from thence
Southwardly the nearest and best route to the South boundary of the state to
intersect the road leading from Reynoldsville to Natchiz and make a report to
the next term of this court.

P112   Records of December Term 1822
     On application of Benjamin McCulloch by his attorney. It is ordered by the
court that R. H. Dyer Samuel Taylor, John B. Cross, Bartholomew G. Stewart
William Atchison, Adam R. Alexander and James Greer be appointed commissioner
them or and two of them to attend Benjamin McCulloch at his beginning corner
(being) the Southeast of a tract of 5000 acres granted by the state of North
Carolina to the said Benjamin McCulloch by Grant No. 78 then and there to attend
said Benjamin McCulloch in taking the deposition of Henry Rutherford and others

P112 teaching his and their knowledge of said begining corner and then to proceed to
Cont. second or Northeast corner of said tract calling for a sycamore and box elder
on the bank of a creek and then and there to take the deposition of said Rutherford and others respecting his and their knowledge of said corner and to do
and perform such matters and things as they may seem proper and legal to perpetuate and make notorious the beginning corner and that special places called
for in said grant No. for five thousand acres and such depositions and proceedings make return to our ensuing county court.

On motion and petition filed, ordered that the following persons (to wit)
William L. Mitchell John Drown, William Nash, Green Warren, Henry Herly, Jeremiah Pierce and William Bowen or any five of them after being first duly sworn
be a jury of view to mark and lay off a road from the town of Jackson to Nash's
Bluff on the North fork of Forked Deer river thence crossing the main Obian at
the old Indian crossing place in the 5th. section and 8th. Range in the 13th
District and continued in a direction to point Pleasent on the Mississippi so
far as the
P113 Records of December Term 1822
attached county extends and make report to the next term of this court.

On motion and petition filed, ordered that the following persons to
wit William Harris William L. Mitchell, William Nash Junior, Earl Fitzhugh,
David Udsley and R. H. Dyer, or any five of them being first duly sworn be a
jury of view to mark out a road from Nash'sBluff on the North fork of Forked
Deer river to Dyers Warehouse on the Mississippi river and make a report to
the next term of this court.

J. A. Hightower)
Vs.   )
John B. Hogg &)   On motion
J. C. McLemore)
This day came the plaintiff aforesaid by his attorneys and in persuance
to notice given by the plaintiff by his attorney moved the court for a judgment
against John B. Hogg and John C. McLemore one of his securities given to keep
the prison bouds for a breach of the condition of their bond given for the
purpose, Whereupon it is considered by the court that the plff recover of the
defendant the sum of one hundred and two dollars the amount of the original
debt together with interest and costs also his costs by him about his motion in
this behalf expended and the defendant in mercy and etc. and the defendant prays
an appeal in the nature of a writ of error to the next circuit court to be held
for the county of Madison which was granted them on condition they enter into
bond with Bartholomew G. Stewart their security in the penalty of five hundred
dollars conditioned agreeable to law which was done accordingly.

P114 Court then adjourned until tomorros morning 9 o'clock
                                        H. Haralson   JP.
                                        Jas. Trousdale JP.
                                        Sam Taylor   JP
Court met agreeable to adjournment. Present the Worshipful H. Haralson, Samuel
Taylor Adam R. Alexander and Jas Trousdale.

McPeak   )
Vs.   )   In debt.
Jordan G. Stokes)
This day came the parties aforesaid by their attorneys and on motion of the
plaintiff by his attorney affidavit being filed ordered that the plaintiff have
until next term to file his declaration to which time this cause is continued

P114   A deed of bargain and sale from Matthew Barrow to Edwin H Childress for
Cont. three hundred forty-five acres of land was this day exhibited in open court and
the execution thereof was duly acknowledged by the grantor to be his act and
deed for the purpose there in named and ordered to be registered.

     Ordered by the court that Thomas Smith and John D. Shannon be appointed
constables to attend the court and Jury at the next term of this court and that
the Sheriff summons them for that purpose.

     Ordered that Benjamin Blythe and George E. Rust be appointed as constables
to attend on the Circuit Court at the April term 1823 and that the sheriff summons them for that purpose.

P115 Records of December Term 1822
     Ordered that the following persons (to wit) Claiburn J. Ragsdale, Josiah
Hollan William Ruleman Benjamin Jones Thomas Jones Venoni Crawford William
Wilson, James Young Robert Young John Wear Clerk Spencer George Wynne John
Frazer George Shankle Elijah Haney Owen Quinly Jesse Golden Mark Langston
Richard Landers Vincent Haralson Moses Starns Green L. Haralson Ryland Chandler
Jacob Bradbury John Bradbury and Joseph Thedfor jurors to serve at the next
term of this court and that the sheriff summons them for that purpose.

     Ordered by the court that the following persons (to wit) William Draper,
John G. Caruthers Guy Smith William Atchison James Greer John B. Cross David
Jarrett Stephen Jarman John Pardgraves Ezidial B. McCoy John Thomas John Houston
James L. Dillard Abner Brown Samuel D. Waddle James Trousdale Herbert Newson Will-
iam Espy Geo W. Taylor John P. Thomas Henry Roan Jason Wilson Elisha Baker Phillip
Moody Aqila Davis and John Graves be appointed a jury to attend at the Circuit
Court at the April term 1823 and that the sheriff summons them for that purpose.

     David Moore comes into court and records his stock mark as follows (to wit)
a crop and two splits in the right ear and a half crop in the left ear.

P116 Record of December Term 1822
     Ordered that Stephen Booth and John M Welch two of the original veniri at-
tending in pursuance of said veniri be this day discharged from any further
service at the present term.

Matthew McPeak   )
    Vs.   )   Certeorari
William L. Mitchell)
     This day came the parties by their attorneys and thereupon the said plain-
tiffs attorney moved the court for motion to dismiss the petition for a certiorari
in this case and an argument being had and heard. It is ordered by the court
that the said plaintiff have a rule entered to dismiss said certiorari and that
the cause be continued until next term for arguement.

William Wilson)
     Vs   )   Case
Thomas Grissom)
     On motion a rule is entered to shew cause why the judgement by non suit
taken in this case should be set aside and a good cause shown it is done
accordingly. On leave of the court the defendant has leave to plead at thenest
term of this court in chief or in barr or demurer so as not to delay tim.

P116 William E. Butler)
Cont.   Vs.   )   Notion for an order of sale of a lot of ground in the
   William F. Dillon)   town of Jackson levied on No. 38 and motion overruled to
which opinion of the court the plaintiff by his council files his bill of exception which is signed and sealed by the court and made part of the record.

                                        H. Haralson   JP.
                                        John Thomas   JP.
                                        Adem R. Alexander JP.

P117 Records of March Term 1823
        At a Court of Pleas and Quarter Sessions began and held for the county of
Madison at the court house in the town of Jackson on Monday the 17th. day of
March in the year 1823 and forty seventh of American Independence.

        Present, the Worshipful Samuel Taylor John B. Cross, Stephen Jarman, Wil-
liam Draper.

        Ordered that Thomas Jones be released from serving as a juror at the pre-
sent term.

        Benjamin Gholson comes into court and records his stock mark as follows,
to wit a split in each ear.

        Elijah Haney exempted from serving on the jury at the present term.

        Ordered that Friday next be set apart for transacting of County business.

        Court then adjourned until tomorrow morning 9 o'clock.
                                        Sam Taylor   JP.
                                        J. Greer   JP.
                                        Jno. G. Carithers JP.

Tuesday morning 18th March 1823
        Court met agreeable to adjournment present the Worshipful Samuel Taylor
James Greer and John G. Carithers.

        Claburn I Ragsdale exempted from serving as a juror at the present term.
        John Bradbury exempted from serving as a juror at the present term.

P118Records of March Term 1823
        Alfred Maury and John Brown appeared in court and took oath of qualification
as attorneys and counsellors at law and was thereupon admitted to practice on
said court.

        John Weir exempted from any further service as a juror at the present
term.

        The sheriff this day made return of the writ of veniri issued from the
last term of this court and returnable to the present term, who summons all
persons named in said veniri of whom the following persons were attending
(to wit) Owen Quinly George Shankle Clark Spencer Richard Sanders Jesse Golden
Green L. Haralson, Mark Langston John Frazer William Wilson Vincent Haralson
Joseph Thedford Robert Young James Young Benjamin Jones Josiah Holland, Benoni
Crawford, Jacov Bradbury Moses Starnes, Ryland Chandler and William Ruleman and
there upon (to wit) Vincent Haralson, Owen Quinly George Shankle, Clark Spencer
Richard Sanders Jesse Golden, Green L. Haralson, Mark Langston, John Frazer
William Wilson, Joseph Tedford Robert Young James Young, with Vincent Haralson
their foreman were elected empanelled, sworn and charged as a Grand Jury to

P118 inquire into and for the body of the county of Madison and thereupon retired to
Cont. consider of presentment.

R. P. T. Stone)
   Vs.) Covenant
William D. Lewis)
     This day came the parties aforesaid by their attorneys and thereupon came
a jury to wit Benj. Jones Josiah Holland Benoni Crawford Ryland Chandler, Thomas Elliott Elijah McAfee Francis Herron James McCutchen, William Pace John
McClish, William RRoulman and Redding Lewis who being sworn will and truly
to inquire of damages returned into court the following verdict (to wit) We
of the jury assess the damages sustained by the plaintiff by reason of the defendants breach of covenant to Thirty five Dollars. It is there fore considered
by the
P119 Record of March Term 1823
     Court that the plaintiff recover of the defendant the damages aforesaid
in form aforesaid assessed also his costs by him about his suit in this behalf
expended and the defendant in mercy etc.

William Peyton)
   against) Debt
Benjamin Blythe)
     This day came the parties aforesaid by their attorneys and thereupon by
consent of parties the suit is dismissed at the cost of the defendant. It is
therefore considered by the court that the plaintiff reciver of the defendant
his costs by him about his suit in this behalf expended and the defendant in
mercy etc.

Elijah McAfee)
Against) Case
Joseph B. Porter)
     Ordered that this case be continued until next term.

Jonathan Houston)
   against) Trespass vi et armis
William Love)
     This day came the parties aforesaid by their attorneys and by consent
of parties this cause is dismissed at the costs of the plaintiff, It is thereupon considered by the court that the defendant recover of the plaintiff his
costs by him about his defense in this behalf expended and the plaintiff may be
taken etc.

James F. Theobald)
   against) Case
Roderick Wright)
     This day came the parties aforesaid by their attorneys and by the consent
of the parties this cause is dismissed at the cost of the defendant.

P120 Records of March Term 1823
     It is therefore considered by the court that plaintiff recover of the de-
fendant his cost by him about his suit in this behalf expended and the defendant
may be taken in mercy.

John Clifton)
   against) Case
Benjamin O'Neil)
     This day came the parties aforesaid by their attorneys and thereupon by

P120 consent of parties this cause is dismissed at the cost of the plaintiff.
Cont. It is thereupon considered by the court that the cefendant recover his cost
by him about his defense in this behalf expended and the plaintiff for his false
clamour may be in mercy etc.

Jordan C. Stokes)
against   )   Covenant
John J. Smith)

same   )
against)   Case
same   )

    This day came the parties aforesaid by their attorneys and thereupon the
parties agree each to pay the proportionable part of the cost accruing up to the
present time and by consent of the parties by their attorndys it is ordered
that the matters in dispute in this case between the parties be referred to
arbitration and award of Joel Dyer and Henry L. Gray and in case of their not
agreeing and in that case they should chose an unpire to decide between them
and the award when made and returned to the next term of court shall be made
the final determination and judgment of the court in this suit and ordered to be
continued until the next term of this court.

P121 Records of March Term 1823
    The Grand Jury who were elected empanelled sworn and charged to inquire
into and for the Body of the county of Madison returned into court the following
presentments (to wit) Two against William Smith for an assault one against Robert Sivier for an assult and one against Charles Sivier and ----- Binkley for
an affray which presentment were indorsed by the Grand Jury Vincent Haralson
foreman, Owen Quinley George Shankle Clark Spencer, Richard Sanders Jesse Golden
Greer L. Haralson John Frazer Mark Langston Robert Young James Young Joseph
Thedford and William Wilson.

    An indenture of bargain and sale from Robert C Thompson to John C. McLe-
more 614¼ acres of land was this day produced in court and the execution thereof
duly proven by the oath of David Thomas and Roderick McIver subscribing witnesses
thereto and ordered to be certified for registration.

    An indenture of Bargain and sale from David Reid to Robert C. Thompson for
614 acres of land was this day produced in court and its execution proven by
Duncan McIver and Roderick McIver subscribing witnesses thereto and ordered to
certified for registration.

    An indenture of bargain and sale from William B. Buttler for himself and
as attorney in fact for John McNairy and Henry M. Rutledge to Robert G. Green
for four acres of land was this day produced in open court and the execution
thereof duly proven by the oath of Richard C. Allen and Samuel H. Swan subscribing witnesses thereto and ordered to be certified for registration.

    A deed of trust from Robert G. Green to William B. Butler for himself and
as attorney in fact for John McNairy and Henry M Rutledge for four acres of
land was produced in open court and the execution thereof duly proven by the
oaths of Richard Allen and Samuel H. Swan subscribing witnesses thereto and
ordered to be certified for registration.

P122 Records for March Term 1823
    An indenture for bargain and sale from John C. McLemore to Robert C. Thomps

P122 son for 1020½ acres of land was produced in court and the execution thereof
Cont. proven by the oaths of David Thomas and Roderick McIver subscribing witnesses t
thereto and ordered to be certified for registration.

Ordered that Adam R. Alexander be appointed chairman pro tem of this court
in the adsence of Herndon Haralson Chairman.

Ordered that Joshua Haskill be appointed Guardian for Charles Ready Haskill the minor son of said Joshua Haskill.
Court then adjourned until tomorrow morning 9 O'clock.

Jno. G. Carithers   JP.
Adam R. Alexander   JP.
Sam Taylor   JP.

Wednesday morning the 19th of March 1823.
Court met agreeable to adjournment present the Worshipful Adam R. Alexander John G. Carithers and Samuel Taylor.

Reuben P. T. Stone   )
Vs.   )   Case
William D. Lewis   )
This day came the parties aforesaid by their attorneys and thereupon
came a jury of good and lawful men, to wit Benjamin Jones, Josiah Holland
Benoni Crawford Ryland Chandler William Ruleman George Wynne John K. Houston
Elijah McAfee and William Thomas who being elected, tried and sworn the truth
to speak upon the issues joined upon their oaths do say that they find the issues
joined in favor of the plaintiff and they do assess the plaintiff damages by
reason.

P123 Records of March Term 1823
thereof to one hundred and fifty dollars, therefore it is considered by the
court that the plaintiff recover against the defendant his damages aforesaid
in manner and form aforesaid assessed besides his costs by him about his suit
in this behalf expended and that said defendant be in mercy etc.

William Deen   0
Vs.   )   Case
William Butler   )
By consent of the parties by their attorneys all matters in difference
between them in this suit is referred to the final determination of Hazael
Hewitt and William E. Butler and in case they cannot agree in that they shall
chose an umpire whose award thereupon shall be made the judgment of this
court. The plaintiff agrees to pay all costs of said suit up to the present
time. It is therefore considered by the court that the defendant recover of
the plaintiff his costs by him about his defense up to the present time
expended. The arbitration aforesaid thereupon returned into court their award
in favor of the defendant that the plaintiff suit be dismissed and that he
pay costs of the suit. It is therefore considered by the court that this suit
be dismissed and that the defendant recover of the plaintiff his costs by him
about his suit in this behalf expended and the plaintiff for his false clamor
may be in mercy.
The Grand Jury returned into court a presentment against Bennet R. Butler
for an assault etc.

P124 Records of March Term 1823
A power of attorney from Elizabeth Crenshaw to Griffith Rutherford was
this day produced in open court and the execution thereof duly proven by the

P124 oaths of Frederick Barefield and William Thomas subscribing witness thereto
Cont. and ordered to be certified for registration.

A deed fo conveyance from Richard Smith to John C. McLemore James Vaux and
James Caruthers for one fouth the part a 428 acre tract of land was this day
produced in court and proven by the oath of John B. Hogg a subscribing witness
thereto and filed for further probate.

An indenture of bargain and sale from Richard Smith deceased to John C.
McLemore James Vaulx and James Caruthers for one-sixth part of a 1500 acre
survey of land was produced in court and the execution thereof proven by the
oath of John B. Hogg a subscribing witness thereto and filed for further probat.
Court then adjourned until tomorrow morning nine o'clock.

Adam R. Alexander   JP.
James Greer   JP
B. G. Stewart   JP

Thursday morning 20th of March 1823
Court met agreeable to adjournment present Batholomew G. Stewart,
James Green and Adam R. Alexander.

State   )
vs.   )   Pled not guilty
Joseph Tedford   )

This day came as well the solicitor general on the part of the state as
the defendant by this attorney and thereupon came a jury of good and lawful
men to wit, Benjamin Jones, Benoni Crawford Josiah Hollan Ryland Chandler,
William Ruleman,

P125 Records of March Term 1823

George Wynne Nathan Simpson James Cockrill Francis Herron Samuel Fitzhugh
William Mayho andThomas Bolin who being elected, tried and sworn will and truly
to try the issue joined upon their oaths do say that the defendant is guilty in
manner and form as charged in the Bill of Indictment It is therefore considered
by the court that the defendant make his peace with the state by the payment
of one dollar and the plaintiff go hence without dayand recover of said defendant her costs by her about her suit in this behalf expended and the defendant
may be taken etc.

The State   )
Vs.   )   An affray
George Stalkeep)

This day comes as well the solicitor general on the part of the state as
the defendant in his own proper person and the defendant being arraigned upon
his arraignment plead guilty in manner and form as charged in the indictment.
It is therefore considered by the court that the defendant make his peace with
the state by the payment of one dollar and that the plaintiff recover against
the defendant her costs by her about her prosecution in this behalf expended
and the defendant be in mercy.

Matthew Wilson Ex'r. of James Wilson deceased)
            Vs.   )   Case
William H. Dock   )

This day came the defendant by his attorney and the plaintiff being called
came not and made default nor is his suit any further prosecuted. Therefore
on prayer of the said defendant, ti is considered by the court that the defendant recover against said plaintiff his costs by him about his defense in this
behalf expended.

P.   Records of March Term 1823
126   John Armstrong   )
Cont. Vs.   )   Case
       Harry Dotson   )

    This day came the parties aforesaid by their attorneys and thereupon by consent of the parties this case is dismissed at the cost of the plaintiff. It is therefore considered by the court that the defendant recover of the plaintiff his costs by him about his defense in this behalf expended and that the plaintiff for his false clamor may be in mercy etc.

    An indenture of bargain and sale from John Fendy to Gilbreath Neill for two hundred acres of land was this day produced in court and the execution thereof acknowledged by the grantor thereof to be his act and deed and ordered to be certified for registration.

    A bill of sale from William Guy to Samuel H. Shannon for a negro named Andrew was this day produced in open court and the execution thereof duly proven by the oath of Wilbam R. Hess and Richard C. Allen subscribing witnesses thereto and ordered to be certified for registration.

State   )
Vs.   )   An assault
Thomas Shannon   )

    This day the Grand Jury returned into court a presentment against Thomas Shannon for an assault.

Reuben P. T. Stone)
Vs.   )   Covenant
William D. Lewis   )

    This day came the defendant by his attorney prayed an appeal to the next term of Circuit court for Madison County for a judgement rendered on a former day of this term which is granted him on his entiring into bond with Stokeley D. Hays and James Caruthers his securities in the penalty of seventy dollars, conditioned agreeable to law which was done accordingly.

P.   Records of March Term 1823
127   Reuben P. T. Stone)
       Vs.   )   Slander
       William D. Lesis)

    This day came the defendant by his attorney prayed an appeal to the next term of Circuit Court for Madison County for a judgment rendered herein on a former day of this term which is granted him on his entiring into bond with Stokely D. Hays and James Caruthers his securities in the penalty of three hundred dollars conditioned agreeable to law which is done accordingly.

    Benjamin Jones this day came into court and proved his attendance three days as a juror of view to the order of December term last.

State   )
Vs.   )Peace Warrent, This day came as well the solicitor general prose-
James Poor   )   cuting in behalf of the state as the defendant in his own proper person and the matters in dispute being fully heard by the court that the said defendant be discharged from any further prosecution in this case and the defendant pay the costs of this prosecution.

James McCutchen   )
Vs.   )   Case
Madison McLaurine)

    This day came the parties aforesaid by their attorneys and thereupon came a jury of good and l... ... ...

P.   a jury of good and lawful men (to wit) Lewis Williams Benjamin Jones Benoni
127   Crawford, Joseah Holland Ryland Chandler, William Huleman George Wynne Nathan
Cont. Simpson James Cockrill James Stalkeep Thomas Bolin and William Mayho
      Records of March Term 1823
P.   who being elected, tried and sworn the truth to speak upon the issue joined
128   retired out of court to consider of their verdict and after some time returned
      into court and not agreeing in their verdict, it was therefore considered by
      the court that the jury be discharged from rendering this verdict until tomorrow.
          The Grand Jury was this day discharged from any further services at the
      present time.
          Court then adjourned until tomorrow morning 9 o'clock.
                                        B. G. Stewart   JP.
                                        W. B. Cross   JP.
                                        Sam Taylor   JP.

Friday Morning March 25th 1823
          Court met agreeable to adjournment present the Worshipful B. G. Stewart
      Samuel Taylor William Draper David Jarrett, Stephen Jarman John C Carithers,
      William Atchison and Joseph Linn Justices.

James McCutchen   )
      Agt.   )   Case
Madison McLaurine   )
          The jury empanelled on yesterday not being able to agree upon a verdict
      by consent of parties a juror is withdrawn and the cause continued until next
      term on motion of the defendant by his attorney. Leave is given him to take
      the deposition of Francis Smith of the State of Kentucky thirty days notice of
      the time and place of the taking of same being given to be read fibine esse
      in this case.

          John Hopkins   )
              agt.   )   Appeal
          Thomas Bowling   )
P.   This day came the defendant aforesaid by his attorney and the plff though
129   solemnly called came not but made default neither does he prosecute his suit.
      It is therefore considered by the court that the plaintiff be non suited and
      that the defendant go thereof hence without day and recover of the plaintiff
      his costs by him about his defense in this behalf expended and the plaintiff
      for his false clamor may be in mercy erc.
          Robert Hughes came into open court and qualified as deputy register of this
      county.
          Ordered that the petet jury be discharged from further service at the
      present term.
          Bartholomew G. Stewart this day came into open court and made oath to the
      by Richard Maulding of one wolf over four months old within the bounds of this
      county.

Benjamin Blythe   )
Vs.   )   Case
Francis Herron   )
          This day came the parties aforesaid by their attorneys and by consent of
      parties leave is granted the defendant to take the depositions de bene ipsi of
      Andrew Herron Sen'r. Andrew Herron Jr. and Andrew Givens, The deposition of
      Andrew Herron Sen. to be taken at the house of James F. Theobold in the town of
      Jackson between the hours of one and three in the evening and twenty days notice
      to be given of the time and place of taking the others to the plaintiff, ordered
      that this case be continued until the next 'term.

P.   Ordered that the following persons to wit Joseph Thedford John Foley
130 Walter Redford Leggie Fisher, Daniel Crouse John Weaver Sandford Edwards
Jothias Thedford John Tedford, John McFarlin, Simon Tedford Thomas James John
Roan, John Tidwell Robert Tidwell Samuel Ray, Dickson Mc Millan Rovert McMillan
Richard Tisdale Larke Tate William Thedford Hardin Cornell and Jonathan Cornell
be assigned to William C. Love to keep in repair the road of which he as heretofore been appointed overseer and that they assist in keeping said road in repair
exclusively except when called upon to open new roads.

          On motion and petitioned filed, Ordered that William E. Butler Hazael
Hewitt Benjamin Gholson Ryland Chandler, Parks Chandler, John Stames, Vincent
Haralson William Johnis and Green L. Haralson or any five of them be and they are
hereby appointed a jury who being first duly sworn shall view lay off and mark
a road. Beginning at the Northeast corner of the public square in the town of
Jackson thence East to Mrs. Doek's Northwest corner thence with her line to her
northease corner bearing a little South to a point on Butters Creek where the
section line crosses said creek thence with said section line to near the North
east corner of Calvin Jones one thousand acre tract thence bearing a little
North to Hazael Hewitts North boundary line thence East to a point a little
North of Benjamin Golsons spring thence centemuing East to intersect the old
road to McIvers Mill and that they made a report to the next term of this court.

          On motion and petition filed ordered that John Graves Stephen Lacey
James Cockrill Malcolm Johnson James Crook Lawrince McGuire and Benjamin Blythe
or any five of them be and they are hereby appointed a jury who first being
duly sworn shall view lay out and mark a road the nearest and best way from
the point where the road running South from the town of Jackson crosses the
South fork of the Forked Deer river to McGuir's ferry on Big Hatchie river
and that they make report to the next term of this court.

          On motion and petition filed ordered that Henry N. Coulter, Ebanezer Haltom
Newton Harris William Alexander Ezekeal B. McCoy and Moses Steed or any five
of them be and they are hereby appointed a jury being first sworn to mark and
lay off a road commencing at the town of Jackson thence the nearest and best
way to the county line at a point in the center on said line between the roads
leading to Lexington and Hardin C. H. and that they make report to the next
term of this court.

          This day the jury of view appointed at the last term of this court to
mark a lay off a road commencing at Jarmens ford on the middle fork of Forked
Deer river, and extending up said fork to intersect the road leading to Carroll
Court House and also a road from the fork above mentioned the nearest and best
way to the town of Jackson, reported that in pursuance of said order that they
have viewed and marked a road as contemplated whereupon ordered said road be
established and that William Pen be appointed overseer of that part of the road
above mentioned that is to say from Jackson to said Penn's and that all the
hands living within two miles of said road be assigned said Penn to open and
keepin repair that part of said road and that Jonathan Welsh be appointed overseer of that part of said road commencing at said Penn to Crooked Creek and
allowed all the hands East and West of said road from the distance of three
miles to open said road and that Samuel D. Wilson shall be overseer of the road
from Crooked Creek to Jarman's ford and that all the hands North of Crooked
Creek within three miles of said creek excluding the hands on Cain Creek and the
waters of said creek and including all the hands living within three miles East
and West of where said road crosses Crooked Creek leading to Jarman's ford
shall be assigned to said Samuel D. Wilson to open said road and that John
Caitly be appointed overseer from Jarman's ford to the North boundary of Madison

P
132
County and that all the hands above said ford within three miles of said road as not to interfere with the hands allowed Samuel D. Wilson be allowed said Caitly to open said road.

Ordered that the reviewers heretofore appointed, to wit William L Mitchell John Bowen William Nash Senr. Green Warren Henry Herley Jeremaih Pierce and William Bowen with the addition of William Nash Junior and John Warren after being first duly sworn or any five of them be and they are hereby appointed to mark and lay off a road from the town of Jackson to Nash's Bluff on the North fork of Forked Deer river thence to the main Obion at the old Indian crossing place in the 5th section and 8th range of the 13th district and thence in a dirition to point Pleasant on the Mississippi so far as the attached county extends and make report to the next term of this court.

On motion and petition filed. Ordered that the following persons to wit William Harris Levi B. Anderson William G. Love, Nathaniel Henderson J. M. Johnson William H. Martin or any five of them after first being duly sworn be and they are hereby appointed a jury of view to mark and lay off a road commencing at or near Spencers and the road leading South from Jackson to Polk's ferry running thence by Mount Pinson so as to intersect the new road lately marked from Jackson to Hardin Court House and that they make report to the next term of this court.

Ordered the road heretofore ordered to be marked out from the town of Jackson to a place known as Fowler's ferry on Big Hatchie river from thence South the nearest and best route to the South boundary of the state be renewed

P
133
and that the following persons to wit John Jarrison John Barnes, Joseph Fowler Barney Chambers, William Deen, Thomas Allison John Thomas John Murry and Robert Box or any five of them after first being duly sworn be and they are hereby appointed to mark and lay off said road and make report to the next term of this court.

On motion and petition filed ordered that the sheriff summons twelve good and lawful men free holders of the county to go on the lands of Thomas Brown adjoining the town of Jackson to inquire if any and any what damage has b been sustained by the said Thomas Brown by reason of the road from the town of Jackson, Runing Northwardly to the county line having been cut out through the land of said Thomas Brown whether the said road should be altered in its course and if so in what manner and make a report of their proceedings immediately to the court which was done accordingly and thereupon the jury returned into court and said the said Brown had sustained fifty dollars damages by reason thereof. It is therefore ordered that the trustee pay the said Brown the said sum of fifty dollars out of any monies not otherwise appropriated.

Wilmouth Edmonson and Bartholomew G. Stewart Administratrix and Administrator of the estate of Robert Edmonson deceased returned into court and inventory of the amount of sales with additional inventory of property of siad deceased.

P
134
On motion and petition filed. Ordered that the commissioners heretofore appointed by court to lay off and sell the lots in the town of Jackson be allowed the sum of four dollars per day each for the same who served the following number of days, Bartholomew G. Stewart served eithteen days Joseph Linn served eighteen days John Hartgrave served eleven days Adam R. Alexander served eleven days James Trousdale served seven days and it is further ordered that Joseph Linn be allowed the sum of twenty dollars for spirits etc. furnished at the sale of said lots and that Samuel H. Shannon and Wilson F. Dilton who served six days each be allowed the sum of one dollar and fifty cents per day each and that said commissioners be allowed the sum of six dollars for stakes.

On motion and petition filed. Ordered that the following persons (to wit) Charles Howard Wiley Dodd Will Trusty Cyrus Roberts, Henry L. Gray Joel Dyer and John Smith or any five of them after first being duly sworn be and they are hereby appointed a jury of view to mark and lay off a road from the house of

P. Howard to Joel Dyer and make a report to the next term of this court.
134 ½   Ordered that the following rates and no higher shall be allowed to
Contkeepers of ordinaries in the county of Madison (to wit)

For each diet, twenty five cents.
For each lodging (12½ cents) Twelve and one half cents.
For each horse per night 37½ cents, thirty seven and one half cents.
For each horse feed eighteen and three fourth cents.
For each half pint of domistic spirits twelve and one half cents.
For each half pint of foreign spirits or wine twenty five cents.

P.   This day the jury of view returned into court the following report which
135 was rec'd and ordered accordingly (to wit) we the undersigned having been
appoiited and sworn to lay off a road agreeable to within order report and that
it shall run as follows (to wit) to leave Jackson at the South east end of the
street leading South from the Southwest corner of the public square as marked
to the South fork of the Forked Deer river near a South Course from thence to
a point on Cain Creek thence as marked to Rhodes on the county line. John
Thomas William Bradin William Deen Jacov Hill John H. Bills and thereupon the
following persons were appointed oversee; thereof with the hands living in the
following bounds to open said road to wi' Levi B. Anderson overseer from town
to 8th. section line with all the hands in town and within two miles round with
all the hands living in the 8th. section first and second ranges. John Thomas
overseer from thence to the county line with all the hands living on the 6th.
and 7th. sections first and 2nd ranges.

On motion, Ordered that the petition and prayer of Thomas Davidson
James Caldwell Ephriam Davidson Gilbreath, Falls Davidson Samuel Rogers and
Sarah his wife John Elwin Davidson, George Davidson, Isabella Davidson, and
Emmaline Davidson, which was granted at the last September term of this court
be renewed to wit For the division of twenty five hundred acres of land granted
by the state of North Carolina to George Davidson Senior, on the 10th day of
July 988 lying in the Western district and now on the Northfork of Forked Deer
River and that William L Mitchell John Bowers William Brown Henderson & Byrns
be and they are hereby appointed commissioners for the running of and division o
of said land and that the same be done accordingly.

P.   On application Benjamin McCullock by his attorney at December term last,
136 it was ordered by the court that Robert H. Dyer Samuel Taylor John B. Cross
Batholomew C. Stewart, William atchison, Adam R. Alexander and James Creer, Be
appointed commissioners them or any two of them to attend Benjamin McCullock
at his beginning corner being the Southeast of a tract of 5000 acres granted
by the State of North Carolina to said Benjamin McCullock by grant No 78 then
and there to attend said Benjamin McCullock in taking the deposition of Henry
Rutherford and mothers touching his and their knowledge of said beginning corner
and then to proceed to the second or Northeast corner of said tract calling
for a sycamore tree and box elder on the banks of a creek and then and there to
take the deposition of said Rutherford and others respecting his and their
knowledge of said corner and to do and perform such matters and things as they
may deem proper and legal to perpetuate and make notorious the beginning corner
and that special places called for in said grant No. 78 for five thousand acres
and such dispositions and proceedings and make return to our insuing county
court. It is therefore ordered by the court that the same be renewed and stand
in the same way of if the same had been granted at this term.

Ordered on motion that the road leading from the Poplar corner to Jarman's
ford be altered so as to intersect the road layed off Jackson to Jarman's ford
at or near Crooked Creek leaving the present road from the poplar corner to

P. Jarman's ford East of John B. Hog's and the part East of where said road is to
137 commence will be done away on the applicants Jason H. Wilson and Charles
Carson opening said road.

Ordered by the court that the tax for the year 1823 be equal to the state
tax and that each stud horse and jack be taxed equal to that of the price of the
season of one mare.

Ordered that the following persons be appointed for taking in the lists
of taxable property for the present year in the captain companies etc. (to wit)
William Atchison in Captain Freer's company, James Green in Captain Hanna's
company, Squire Jarman in Capt Hays company Squire Taylor in Capt Walkers company, Major Linn in Capt Young's Company Sq. Carithers in Capt Smiths company
Squires Thomas and Janett all South of Forked Deer river except the attached
county West of Madison. Squire Rutherford in the attached county West of Carroll
Squire, Smith in the attached county West of Madison.

Ordered that John C. Carithers be allowed to keep a ferry on the South
fork of Forked Deer River at or near his own house and that he may be allowed
the following rates and no more and that this operate as a general order in the
county for regulating ferriage.

For each Wabon and term   75¢
For each deerbourn   50¢
For each two wheel carriage 37½¢
For each two wheel pleasure carriage 75¢
For each man and horse   12½¢

Ordered that precint elections be held at the following places to wit, at the
house of John Bowen in the Thirteenth district at the house of James Hale on
cloverlea in the 10th. district and at the house of Fowler on Big Hatchie river
in the 10th district.

P.   Thom I Smith came into court and proved his attendance on the court and
138 jury five days.

William Dod comes into court and proves by his own oath the killing of
of two wolves over the age of four months and that the same was killed in the
bounds of Madison County.

Joseph Allen appeared in court and proved by his own oath the killing of
one wolf in the bounds of Madison County over the age of four months.

Daniel Murchison came into court and proved by his own oath the killing of
one wolf over the age of four months and the same was killed in the bounds of
Madison Co.

Robert Burns came into open court and proved by his own oath the killing
of one wolf within the bounds of Madison over the age of four months.

William C. Love came into court and proved the serving three days as a
juror of view previous to December term last.

William Braden John Thomas and William Deen proved three days attendance
each as a juror of view and allowed by the court one dollar per day for same.

Ordered that William Haltom and Hazael Hewitt who came into court and proved by their own oaths of serving two days each as jurors of view in the county
of Madison be allowed one dollar per day each for the same.

Ordered that John G. Carithers who came into court and proved by his
own oath of serving two days as a juror of view be allowed the sum of one
dollar per day for the same.

P.   On motion of James Alexander senior letters of administration of all and
139 singular the goods and chattels, of rights and credits of William S. Alexander
deceased is granted him who thereupon took the oath of administrator and entered
into bond with Henry N Colter his security in the penalty of two hundred dollars
and thereupon returned into court an inventory of the property of said decedant.

On motion of John Hall Administrator de bonis with the will annexed is
granted him on the estate of William Hall deceased who thereupon took the oath
of administrator and entered into bond with Ezekial B. McCoy his security in

Fine the penalty of four hundred dollars and returned into court an inventory of
Cont. the estate of said Hall, deceased.

The last will and testament of William Q. Hall was this day exhibited in
open court and proven by the oaths of William Eastwood and Ezekial B. McCoy
two of the subscribing witnesses thereto and who also proved that the said Hall
was of sound and disposing mind and memory at the time of the execution of
said will. Ordered that said will be recorded.

P.   Ordered that the following persons (to witd

140
Lewis Griffin	Lemuel S. Hunter
Amos Williams	William B. McLelland
Patrick Duffy	Daniel Beville
Thomas James	Lewis Needham
Ansolons Russell	Jesse M. Henna
George Meazles	Henry Baker
David Sanders	John Bryan
William Wilbourne	Thomas Lacy
Clabourne Chisham	William Freer
Jno T. Porter	Champineé Mading
Green Hill	Anthony F. Gray
Charles Sevier	John Harrison
Moses Oldham	John Ridings

be appointed a jury to the next county court to be held for the county of Madison

A bill of sale from Jacob Chisum to Samuel H. Shannon for a negro girl was
this day produced in court and the execution thereof duly proven by the oath of
David Crocket a subscribing witness thereto and ordered to be certified for
registration.

An indenture of bargain and sale from Duncan McIver to Champines Mading
171 152/160 acres of land was this day produced in court and the execution thereof to be his act and deed for the purpose therein mentioned and ordered to be
registered.

An indenture of bargain and sale from Gabriel Chandler to Ezekial B. McCoy
for 119 acres of land was this day produced in court and the execution thereof
duly acknowledged by the said Chandler to be his act and deed for the purpose
therein contained and ordered to be registered.

P.   A bill of sale from Samuel H. Shannon to the firm of Herton & Hicks for
141 four negroes was this day produced in court and the execution thereof proven
by D A C Hays a subscribing witness thereto and ordered to be certified for
registration.

An indenture of bargain and sale from Alexander B. Bradford to Sanders
R. Carney for one hundred acres of land was this day produced in open court and
the grantor there of to be his act and deed for the purpose therein contained
and ordered to be registered.

An indenture of bargain and sale from Max Million H. Buchanan to Duncan
McIver for 178 152/160 acres of land was this day produced in open court and
the execution thereof proven by the oaths of Fendull Whitworth and Adam R.
Alexander two subscribing witnesses thereto and ordered to be registered.

An indenture of bargain and sale from William Payton to Benjamin Blythe
for 71½ acres of land was this day produced in open court and the execution
thereof proven by the oath of John Graves one of the subscribing witnesses,
the probat of the other being taken on a former day of this court and ordered
to be registered.

A deed of gift from Thomas Sanders to the heirs of C. I Ragsdale deceased

P141 was this day produced in open court and the execution duly proven by the oath
Cont.of F. H. Ragsdale and Henry Booth two subscribing witnesses thereto, and ordered to be registered.

A bill of sale fom Minos Cannon to Thomas Sands was this day produced in
court and proven by the oath of Benjamin Bathe and F. H. Ragsdale to be his act
and deed for the purposes therein named and ordered to be registered.

P.   Records of March Term 1823
 142On motion: Ordered that the hands living within the following bounds to wit
West from the town of Jackson with the river including Simpsons and Alexanders
thence North to the sectional line between the 9th & 10th. sections thence
East so as to include Mr. Houstons thence South to town by the old Indian path
be assigned to William Espy to keep in repair that part of the road of which
he is overseer.

Court then adjourned until tomorrow morning nine o'clock.

Stephen Jarman   JP
David Jarrett   JP
Jno G. Carithers   JP

Saturday morning 22nd March 1823.

Court met agreeable to adjournment Present, The worshipful B. G. Stewart
James Greer, Stephen Jarman David Jarrett Justices, James Greer Jason H Wilson
and Bartholomew G. Stewart came into court and proved two days each as jurors
of view in the county of Madison and allowed at the rate of one dollar per day.

James Greer came into court and made oath of serving three days as a
juror of view previous to the last December term.

Matthew B. McMahan   )
Vs.   )   Debt
Jordan G. Stokes   )

This day came the defendant by his attorney and withdrew his plea and
demurer in above cause and says he cannot gainsay the plaintiff's action but he
justly owes said plaintiff the debt in the declaration mentioned. It is therefore considered by the court here that the plaintiff recover against the defend-
P.143ant the sum of five hundred dollars the amount of the debt in the declaration
mentioned and the further sum of eighty-five dollars damages and also his costs
by him about his suit in this behalf expended and the defendant in mercy etc..

Matthew McPeake   )
Vs.   )   Certiorari
William L Mitchell   )

This day came the parties aforesaid by their attorneys and the motion
heretofore entered to dismiss came to be argued and the court being sufficiently
advised of and concerning the permises. It is considered that the same be
dismissed and that the plaintiff recover of the defendant and Nelson J Hays
and Robert H. Dyer his securities in the certiorari the sum of forty-eight
dollars sixty two and one half cents the amount of the judgment below together
with six per centum per annum on the whole amount thereof from the date of the
rendition of the judgment below until payment also his costs by him about his
suit in this behalf expended and the defendant may be in mercy etc.

An indenture of bargain and sale from Bartholomew G. Stewart to Jason H.
Wilson for fity acres of land was this day produced in open court and acknowledged by the said Stewart to be his act and deed for the purposes therein contained
and ordered to be registered.

John D. Shannon came into courtCareved his services as a constable attend-
on the jury at the September term five days and at the March term three days.

Bartholomew G. Stewart Adm etc.)
Vs.   )
Grand and Grisom   )   Case

P143
Cont.   The arbitrators to whom the determination of the matters in difference between the parties were submitted by a rule of the court the third day of March 1823 this day returned their award in the words and figures following, to wit, This day in persuance of an order of our Court of Pleas and Quarter sessions at December term 1822 the referees to wit Vincent Haralson} by the consent of parties in the place of Herndon Haralson absent,

P144 Records of March Term 1823
      Samuel H. Shannon Samuel Taylor William Atchison and William Braden chosen by said referees as umpire met and after being duly sworn went into the examination of testimony both on the part of the plaintiff as well as the defendants and after such examination and due deliberation ont the matters in controversy between Bartholomew G. Stewart, Administrator etc. Vs. Spencer Grant and Thomas Grisom do decide and say and this is their judgment that the plaintiff on the case pay the costs incident and accruing on his behalf and that the defendant pay the costs incident and accruing on their behalf severally and jointly given under our hands this day and date above written (signed) Samuel Taylor William Atchison and Wm. Braden In conformation whereof it is considered by the court that the plaintiff in this case pay the cost incident and accruing on his behalf and that the defendants pay the costs incident and accruing on their behalf severally and thereupon the plaintiff by his attorney prayed for and obtained an appeal in the nature of a writ of error to the next term of the Circuit Court which was granted him on his entering into bond with Jason Wilson his securities for the prosecution of said appeal which was done accordingly.
      Ordered that the following justices of the peace for Madison County be classed to wit that Duncan McIver David Jeffries William Draper David Jarett and Herndon Haralson to attend at the June term and Guy Smith James Greer Stephen Jarman, Bartholomew G. Stewart Joseph Linn, John L. Dillard and John G. Carithers to attend at September term and John Thomas Samuel Taylor William Atchison, A. R. Alexander Robert H. Dyer and John Rutherford at December term 1823.

P.   Records of March Term 1823
145   William Polk, Plff.   )
      Vs.   )   In debt
      John B. Hogg, Def.   )
      This day came the plaintiff by his attorney and the defendant in proper person who because he cannot gainsay the plaintiff cause of action confesses judgment for one thousand eight hundred and seventy one dollars, wighty four cents the balance of devt in the plaintiff's declaration mentioned and also for one hundred fifty two dollars and eleven cents damages amounting in the whole to $2023,95 cts. It is therefore considered by the court that the plaintiff recover of the defendant the said sum of Two thousand and twenty three dollars, ninety five cents, the debt and damage aforesaid and also his costs by him about his suit in this behalf expended etc.

      James Standley Assce, Plff   )
      Vs.   )   In debt
      Herndon & Vincent Haralson Deft.)
      This day came the parties by their attorneys and upon an argument being had on the defendants demurrer to the plaintiffs declaration it seems to the plaintiffs declaration it seems to the court here that these that there is no error and that the demurrer be overruled. Therefore it is considered by the court that the plaintiff recover of the defendant one hundred forteen dollars and fifty cents for his debt and three dollars and forty cents interest also his costs by him about his suit in this behalf expended etc.

P.   Matthew McPeake   )
146 Vs.   )   On motion to set aside the judgment on cer-
     William L. Mitchell   )   terorari.
     This day came the parties aforesaid by their attorneys and after ar-
gument fully had thereon it is considered by the court here that judgment entered in this cause on this day be set aside by the defindants paying all
cost accruing thereon from the commencement up to the present time. Whereupon
it is considered by the court that the plaintiff recover of the defendant and
his securities his costs by him about his suit in this behalf expended from
the commencement thereof.

                 Matthew McPeake   )
                 Vs.   )   A motion for a certiorari in court.
                 William L. Mitchell   )
     This day came the defendant by his attorney and the defendant filed in
open court his petition for a certiorari and after an argument had thereon,
it is considered by the court that the certiorari be granted whereupon the plaintiff by his attorney excepted to the action of the court and tendered his bill
of exceptions which was signed and sealed by the court and ordered to be made
a part of the recorded.
     A deed fo bargain and sale from Thomas Shannon, sheriff of Madison County
to John Porter was this day produced in open court and acknowledged by the
maker thereof and ordered to be certified for registration.
     Court then adjourned until court in course.
                                          J. Greer   JP.
                                          John Thomas   JP.
                                          Stephen Jarman JP.

P.   Jackson Monday 16th. June 1823
147   At a Court of Pleas and Quarter Sessions began and held for the County
of Madison and the State of Tennessee, in the town of Jackson on Monday the
16th. day of June A. D. 1823 and the 47th year of American Independence.
Present, The worshipful Herndon Haralson, Chairman Joseph Linn, Stephen Jarman,
William Draper, James Greer, Samuel Taylor, and Guy Smith gentlemen justices.
     Ordered that Champniss Mading be discharged from serving as a juror at
the present term same court.
     Henry Castles came into open court and made oath of killing of five
wolves in the county of Madison under the age of four months and that it be
certified accordingly.
                     Same Court
Thomas McNeill came into open court and made oath of the killing of three wolves
in the county of Madison over the age of four months and that it be certified
accordingly.
                     Same Court
     Chapman Manley came into court and made oath of the killing of two wolves
over the age of four months in the county of Madison and that it be certified
accordingly.
                     Same Court
     Ordered that Friday next be set apart for transacting county business.
The worshipful James L. Dillard.   JP.
P.118
     Cader Pearcy comes into cou t and records his stock mark as follows
(to wit) a swallow fork in each ear.
     Thomas Gordon comes into court and records his stock mark as follows
to wit a slit & underbit in each ear.

P148   A deed of Bargain and sale from William E. Butler to Cader Pearcy for one
Cont. hundred acres of land was this day produced in court and the execution thereof
duly acknowledged by the said William E. Tutler, to be his act and deed and
ordered to be certified for registration.

      A deed of trust from Charles Featherston to James Caldwell was this day
produced in open court and the execution thereof duly proven by the oath of
S. Hanna one of the witnesses and ordered to be filed for further probat.

      A deed of bargain and sale from John C. McLemore to Robert G. Jones
for eighty acres of land was this day produced in open court and the execution
thereof acknowledged by the said John C. McLemore to be his act and deed and
ordered to be certified.

      A deed of bargain and sale from Duncan McIver to William Doak for sixty
acres of land and one hundred fifty two poles was this day produced in open
court and the execution thereof duly proven by the oaths of Robert Hughes and
Roderick McIver two subscribing witnesses, thereto and ordered to be certified.

      A deed of bargain and sale from John C. McLemore to James McCutchen for
two hundred twenty-eight acres of land was this day produced in open court and
the execution thereof duly acknowledged by the said John C McLemore to be his
act and deed and ordered to be certified.

P.
149   A deed of bargain and sale from Baptist McNab to Thomas Gordan for seventy
acres of land was this day produced in open court and the execution thereof
proven by William Atchison and Jacob Bradbury Junior two of the subscribing
witnesses thereto and ordered to be certified.
On motion:

      Ordered that Wilie Jones be allowed to keep a ferry on Big Hatchie river
starting on his own land on Hatchie Bluff and landing on the most convenient
point on the North Side directing its course on the best ground toward highland.

      Daniel Harkins records his stock mark as follows to wit a swallow fork
in each ear.

      On motion and petition filed ordered that a road be established commencing
at a point where the jury of view appointed by the court of Madison to lay off
and mark a road in the direction of Polk's ferry on Big Hatchie river, ended
on the county line then on a direction of Jone's ferry and by the way of William
Shinault's so as to intersect a road viewed and marked out by order of Shilby
County Court at which the point where said road ends and that said Jones be
allowed to keep in repair said road and that the following persons be a jury of
view to mark and lay off said road or any five of them after first being duly
sworn to wit Nathaniel Steel, John Hodges William Ramsay, Joseph Haynes,
Thomas Clipt Michael Holshower Allen Dillard, West Harris Stephen Bennett and
Jonah Kirk and make a report to the next court.

P.150   A power of attorney from Joseph Royal to Richard R. Royal was produced
this day in open court and acknowledged by Joseph Royal to be his act and deed
and ordered to be certified.

      James C. McClary comes into court and records his stock mark as follows,
a crop of each ear and a split in the left.

      On motion and petition filed ordered that a road leading from the town
of Jackson to the high land on the South side of Forked Deer river so as to
cross at a point known by the name of Shannons landing from thence to the high
land by the nearest and best way and that the following persons, to wit, Robert
Clanton, Thomas Lacy James Cockrill Samuel Shannon Stephen Lacy, Henry Booth
John Graves, James Corns George Hicks, Clark Spencer John Arnold and Anthony
F. Gray be and they are hereby appointed a jury of view, them or any five of
them after first being duly sworn to mark and lay off said road and make report
to the next term of this court.

      On motion and petition filed ordered that part of the road reported by
a jury of view of last court running from the Court House to Hardin Court House
as was marked out from the town of Jackson to the Forked Deer river near Pitts

Pa.   Chandler's be discontinued and that Benjamin Cholston, Hazael Hewitt, William
150   Johns, Ryland Chandler, Parks Chandlers, James Young Pitts Chandler and Herndon
Cont. Haralson be appointed a jury of view or any five of them to lay off an mark
      a road from the town of Jackson to the Forked Deer river ar or near said Pitts
      Chandler and report their proceedings to this court.

P.   Ordered that the report of the jury of view appointed at the last term
151   of this court to view and mark out a road from the town of Jackson to the South
      boundary of the state by the way of Fowler's ferry on Big Hatchie be received.

              Ordered that the order setting apart Friday for transacting county business
      be rescinded and that Saturday be set apart for that business.

              Ordered that Alexander B. Bradford William Stoddert and Alfred Murray be
      appointed a committee to draw up rules for the government of the Court and Bar
      while in Session and that they make report at the present term of this court.

              Thomas Lacy came into open court and proved by his own oath of the killing
      of one wolf over the age of four months in the county of Madison and that it be
      so certified.

              Tarlton Harris came into open court and proved by his own oath of killing
      one wolf over the age of four months in the county of Madison and that it be so
      certified.

              Samuel B. Martin comes into court and proves fo serving three days as a
      juror of view and that he be allowed one dollar per day for same.

P.   On motion ordered that Green B. Chalmess be released from the payment of
152   four dollars and fifty cents half the appraised value of a stray cow which he
      posted in the county of Madison.

              Administration of all and singular the goods and chattles rights and
      credits of Dudley Rutherford, deceased is granted to James Rutherford who en-
      tered into bond with Jonathan Houston and John L. Dillard his securities in the
      penalty of two thousand dollars and thereupon took the oath of an administrator
      and that letters of administration issue accordingly.

              A transfer of a warrent from Jacob Hill to Thomas J. Hardyman was produced
      in open court and acknowledged by said Hill to be his act for the purposes
      therein mentioned.

              On motion and petition filed ordered that Obediah Nix have leave to build
      a grist mill on his own land on a creek known by the name of Jones Creek in the
      first range and 9th. section of the Ninth district.

              On motion and petition filed ordered that Gavriel Chandler have leave to
      build a saw mill in the second range and 9th. section of the 9th. district on
      his own land on Youngs creek.

              Ordered that Herndon Haralson be released from paying double taxes on sixty
      acres of land and four black polls for the year 1822.

P. 1   Ordered that James Johnson be released from paying double taxes on one
153   white poll and one black poll for the year 1822.

              Ordered that Robert Hughes be released from paying double toxes on one
      acre of land one white poll for the year 1823.

              James Alexander, Administrator of William S. Alexander de'd returned an
      inventory of the amount of sales of the estate of William S. Alexander.

              On motion ordered that the order heretofore granted to lay off a road
      from the town of Jackson to Harris Bluff be renewed and that the following per-
      sons to wit Aquilla Davis William Cl Mitchell William B. McClellan John T. Porter
      John G. Carithers, John I. Smith William Braden Thomas M Dement James L Wortham
      Bird B. Smith Nathan Simpson & Robert Jones be and they are hereby appointed a
      jury of view or any five of them to mark and lay off said road and make an
      return to the next term of this court.

              Ordered that Thomas Shannon be appointed overseer of the road leading
      from town to Shannons landing and that all the hands living in a half mile of
      town be assigned him to open road.

P.
154   Ordered that reports of the jury of view to mark a road leading from the
town of Jackson to Nash's Bluff be received and that William Stays be appointed
overseer of said road and have all the hands subject to work on said road from
Nashs Bluff to where the district line crosses said road on their way to Jackson.

         Administration of all and singular the goods and chattels right and credits
of Samuel Goodwin deceased was this day granted to Jarrett M Jolks, who entered
into bond with Thomas Henderson & Thomas Shannon his securities in the penalty
of one thousand dollars who thereupon took the oath of an administrator and returned an inventory of the estate of sd. deceased. Thereupon it appearing to
the satisfaction of the court that there is not sufficient perishable estate
to discharge the debts of decendant it is ordered that the negro returned in the
inventory by the said adm'r. be the same hereby directed to be sold by the administrator on a credit of twelve months and the proceeds of the sale applied
to payments of the debts.

         Ordered that Lemuel Hunter be appointed overseer of the road in the place
of Allen Fuller resigned and that all the hands living within the following
bounds (to wit) Beginning at McCoys and running up the river to the county
line also up Frace Creek to the mouth of Youngs Creek thence of said Creek
P.   so as to intersect Willis Harriss thence East to the county line.
155   On motion ordered that a bridge be built across the South fork of the
Forked Deer river at a place known by the name of Shannons landing & William E.
Butler Herndon Harelson James Greer Robert H. Dyer & Jno. B. Cross or any therr
of them be appointed commissioners to let out the building of sd. bridge to the
lowest bidder & that the county trustee pay for the building the same out of
county funds not otherwise appropreated and that said bridge be so constructed
as not to materially obstruct the navigation of said river.

         Ordered that John D. Shannon be appointed constable to attend on the
court at the present term.

         John Bowen Green Warren and Henry Hurley came into court and made oath of
serving eight days each as jurors of view in the county of Madison and they be
allowed the sum of one dollar per day for the same.

         William Nash came into court and made oath of serving five days as a juror
of view in the county of Madison and ordered that he be allowed the sum of one
dollar per day for the same.

         Ordered that John Tidwell be appointed overseer of road in the place of
William C. Love resigned.

P.   Ordered that Adam Hunter be released from paying double tax on one thou-
156   sand acres of land entered in the name of Adam Hunter in the 9th. District 8th.
and 9th. sections & 2nd. range and the sheriff is hereby directed to receive
thesingle tax on said land for the years 1821 & 1822.

         John Bowen appeared in open court and took the oath of qualification as
justice of the peace for the county of Madison who thereupon took his seat upon
the bench.

         William Williamson was this day duly and constitutionally elected constable
for the county of Madison and took the several oaths perscribed by the constitution and laws of the state and thereupon entered into bond with Janet M. Jelks
and Alexander B. Bradford his securities in the penalty prescribed by law.

         On motion and petition filed ordered that the road heretofore reported
and ordered to be opened known by the name of Polks ferry road be rescinded
from the town of Jackson so far as a place known by Stanleys branch to the South
of Jacov Hill and that the following persons (to wit) Bird Hill Jacov Hill Herbert
Newsom John Burrow Edward Newsom and John Murrey or any five of them after first
being duly sworn be a jury to mark and lay off a road from the town of Jackson
to said point and make report to the present term of this court.

         On motion and petition filed ordered that John C. Stockton be allowed
to keep an ordinary in the county of Madison and entered into bond with Charles
Sivier and James Theobold his securities in the penalty subscribed by law.

Pa.   Micojah Midgette came into court and records his stock mark as follows
157   to wit a crop off the left ear and a split in the same .
Cont.

    State   )
    Vs.   )   An affrey
    James Benkly)

    This day came as well the solicitor general on the part of the state as
the defendant in his proper person who being arraigned upon his arraignment
plead guilty in manner and form as charged in the Bill of Indictment, it is
therefore considered by the court that he make his peace with the state by the
payment of one dollar fine and that the plaintiff go thereof hence without day
and recover of the defendant her fine aforesaid together with her costs about
her suit in this behalf expended and that the defendant may be taken etc.

    State   )
    Vs.   )   Affray
    Charles Sevier)

    This day came the solicitor general on the part of the state as the de-
fendant in his proper person who being arraigned upon his arraignment plead
guilty in manner and form as charged in the Bill of Indictment. It is therefore
consided by the court that the plaintiff make his peace with the state by the
payment of one dollar fine and the plaintiffto thereof hence without day and
recover of the defendant her costs by her about her prosecution in this behalf
expended and the defendant may be taken etc.

P.   Jacob Hill   )
158   Vs.   )   Debt
    Chapman W. Manley)

    This day came the plaintiff by his attorney and the defendant in his prope
person who because he cannot gainsay the plaintiffs cause of action confesses
judgment for one hundred twenty six dollars 76 cents debt and nineteen dollars
and sixty five cents interest amounting in the whole to One hundred forty six
dollars and forty one cents. It is therefore considered by the court that the
plaintiff recover of the defendant the debt and interest aforesaid together
with his costs by him about his suit in this behalf expended etc.
On motion and petition filed:
    Ordered that the following persons to wit, James Greer Herndon Haralson
Vincent Haralson Jno B. Cross Robert Burns Gabriel Anderson and James Caldwell
or any five of them be and they are therby appointed a jury of view after being
duly sworn for that purpose to view and mark out a road commencing on the Carrol
county Road at or near the Southeast corner of James Veln's tract of land then
in a direction so as to intersect the old road now opened and leading to house
of Joseph Linn at the corner of Vincent Haralson's fence and make report to
the next term of court.
    Ordered that the report of the jury of view appointed at the last term of
this court to mark and lay off a road to the county line in a direction to
Hardin Court House be received and that William Alexander be appointed overseer
of the road from the beginning point East of McCoys to the river and that all
the hands within three miles on either side of the road and that William
Spencer be appointed overseer from the river to the county line with all the
hands withing two miles on either side on his part as boundaries for hands.
P.   On application of Benjamin McCullock by his attorney that John Rutherford,
159   Senior Robert Murrey Benjamin Porter, Elijah P. Chambers, Claiborn Pillow,
Benjamin Jordan and Griffith Rutherford Senior be appointed commissioners them
or any two of them to attend Benjamin McCullock at his North East corner
being the Northeast corner of a 5000 acre tract of land granted to Benjamin
McCullock by Grant No. 78 from the State of North Carolina said corner being
also the corner of a 5000 acre tract in the name of Henry Clark & the corner of

Pa.   a 3210 acre servey in the name of Archibald Murphy on the   North side of the
159   North fork of Forked Deer river in the 13th. district and in the jurisdiction
Cont. of Madison County, then and there to attend said Benjamin McCullock or attorney
      in taking the deposition of Henry Rutherford and others touching his and their
      knowledge of said McCullocks said North East corner calling for a box elder and
      sycamore on the banks of a creek the corner to the three above named tracks or
      any other part of said lines or boundaries of which saiddeponant or deponants
      may have any knowledge and to do and perform such matters and things as they may
      seem proper and legal to perpetuate and make motions the North East corner of
      said McCullocks 5000 acre track and that special places called for in said grant
      No. 78 for five thousand acres and such depositions and proceedings and make
      report to our ensuing county court.

P.   On motion and petition filed ordered that Walter Shenault, David Jerigan
160   Elisha Gossett William Shenault BarneyChambers Joseph Fowler and John Murray
      or any five of them be a jury to mark and lay off a road from where the road
      view and layed of by the county courtof Shelby County strikes the Western
      boundary of the county South of Madison and to run from thence Eastward across
      the county crossing Big Hatchie at a place known by the name of Fowler's ferry
      to the East boundary of said county in a direction to Brown's ferry on on the
      Tennessee river be a jury of view to mark and lay off said road and make return
      to thenext term of court.

              A deed of bargain and sale from Samuel Davis to Robert Dixon for one
      hundred eighty-three acres of land was this day produced in open court and the
      execution thereof duly proven by the oath of Marksm Early and Joseph Linn sub-
      scribing witnesses there to be the act and deed of said Samuel Davis and ordered
      to be certified.

              On motion and petition filed ordered that the following persons (to wit)
      Benjamin Cholson William Johns Hazael Hewitt Ryland Chandler Parks Chandler
      James Young Pitts Chandler and Herndon Haralson or any five of them first being
      duly sworn be appointed a jury of view to lay off and mark out a road from
      the town of Jackson to Warlicks mill leaving the plantation of Herndon Haralson
P161 on the left and to strike the sectional line between Parks Chandlers and Butlers
      Creek from thence East on said sectional line to near Calven Jones Northeast
      corner from thence bearing North so as to strike Hazael Hewitts North boundary
      from thence to run between said Benjamin Cholstons dwelling house and his spring
      and from thence to the bridge below said Warlicks Mill and report there proceed-
      ings to this court and it is further ordered that the road heretofore cut out
      by the house of Herndon Haralson and Ryland Chandler be discontinued.

              Court then adjourned until tomorrow morning 9o'clock.
                                    H. Haralson
                                    J. Greer
                                    Stephen Jarman.

Tuesday Morning the 17th. June 1823.
        Court meet agreeable to adjournment, present, the Worshipful Herndon
Haralson, James Greer Stephen Jarman William Draper and William Atchison,
gentlemen, justices of the peace.
        Ordered that Charles Sevier be discharged from serving as a juror at the
present term.
P. 162   Jackson Tuesday 17th day June 1823.
        The sheriff this day made return of the original veniei to him directed
from the last term of this court and from the return of the said veniri, it
appears the sheriff summonded all the persons named in the veniri except Daniel
Beville and Green Hill and in pursuance thereof the following persons were then
attending (to wit) Patrick Duffy , Lemuel S. Hunter Henry Baker Thomas Lacy
Anselem Russell William Freer, John Ridins Clabourne Chisum Anthony F. Gray
George Meazles William B. McLellan Moses Oldham William Wilbourn Lewis Needham
John T. Porter Thomas James Lewis Griffin David Sanders &8, and thereupon the

P.   following persons to wit Lemuel S. Hunter Patrick Duffy Henry Baker Thomas
182   Lacy Anselem Russell William Freer John Ridins Clabourne Chisum Anthony F. Gray
Cont. George Meazles William B. McLellan Moses Oldham and William Wilbourne with
Samuel S. Hunter their foreman were then empanelled sworn and charged as a Grand
Jury to inquire into and for the body of the county of Madison and thereupon
retired to consider presentments.

Amos Williams released from serving as a juror at the present term.

Ordered that Thomas I. Smith be appointed to attend as a constable on the
Grand Jury at the present term.

Jared S. Allen Berry Gilispie Hugh W. Dunlap and Andrew McCampbell appeared
in open court and took the necessary oaths of qualifications as practicing attorney and it is thereupon ordered that they be admitted to practice in said
court.

P. 163   18th. June 1823

Jonathan Welch appeared in open court and made oath of serving two days
as a juror of view in the county of Madison and ordered that he be allowed the
sum of one dollar per day for same.

A power of attorney from John H. Gibson to Paul Sherley was this day produced in open court and the execution duly proven by the oaths of William Harris
and William R. Hess subscribing witnesses thereto and ordered to be certified.

A deed of bargain and sale from John B. Hogg to Samuel Hogg for four
thousand eight hundred acres of land was this day produced in open court and the
execution thereof duly proven by the oaths of Jeol H. Dyer and William B. G.
Killingsworth subscribing witnesses thereto to be the act and deed of said
John B. Hogg ordered to be certified.

A deed of trust from John B. Hogg to Edmond Jones and Sterling Orgain
was this day produced in open court and the execution thereof duly proven by the
oaths of W. B. G. Killingsworth and James Jones two subscribing witnesses there
to and ordered to be certified.

Elijah McAfee   )
Vs.   )
Joseph B. Porter   )

This day came the parties by their attorneys and thereupon came a jury
of good and lawful men (to wit) Lewis Needham Thomas James Lewis Griffin David
Sanders, Andrew Hays James Vauln James Stalkeep John Armstrong John M. Walker
Nathan Simpson James McCutchen and Roderick Wright who being elected tried and
sworn well and truly to try the issue joined between the parties upon their
oaths

P. 164   17th June 1823

do say the defendant did assume and take on himself in manner and form as the
plaintiff in declaring against him hath alleged and assess the plaintiff damages
for non performance of the promises the declaration mentioned to thirty six dollars. It is therefore considered by the court that he recover of the defendant
the aforesaid damages together with his costs by him about his suit in this
behalf expended and the defendant amy be in mercy etc..

Jacob Sewell   )
Vs.   0   Case
James Tidwell   )

This day came the plaintiff by his attorney and dismissed his suit and
assumes the payment of the costs of said suit. It is therefore considered
by the court that the defendant go thereof hence without day and recover of the
plaintiff his cost by him about his suit in this behalf expended and the plaintiff in mercy etc.

P.   James McCutchen   )
165   Vs.   )   Case
        Madison McLaurine)
        On affidavit of the plaintiff this cause continued until next term.
      L7th. June 1823

        William Love)
        Vs.   )   Case
        John Weir   )
        By consent of parties this cause is continued until next term.
        A deed of bargain and sale from R. E. C. Daugherty and Bartholomew G.
Stewart to Joseph Linn for five hundred twenty one acres of land was this day
produced in open court and acknowledged the grantors thereof to be their act
and deed and ordered to be certified.
        Court then adjourned until tomorrow morning 9o'clock.
                                        David Jarrett   J. Peace
                                        W. B. Cross   JP.
                                        Jas. Trousdale   JP.
Wednesday morning the 18th day of June 1823.
        Court met agreeable to adjournment, present, the Worshipful David Jarrett
John B. Cross James Trousdale and William Draper.

        Thomas M. Dement)
        Vs.   )   Case
        Thomas Boling   )
        The plaintiff in this case has leave to take depositions by giving ten
days notice in the state and twenty dayd notice out of the state and this cause
is continued on affidavit of the plaintiff.

        Thomas M. Dement)
        Vs.   )   Case
        Thomas Boling   )
        Same order as in above.
P.   They gy The Grand Jury this day returned into court the following present-
166 ments to wit one against Thomas Hill and Joseph P. Cloud for an affray one vs.
John Ridens and John Jackson for an affray one vs. John T. Porter for an assault
all indorsed by said Grand Jury with Lemuel S. Hunter their foreman.
        Arthur H. Henley Treasur)
        Unicoy Tum Pike Company   )   Original attachment.
        vs.   )
        Russell Goodrich   )
        On motion of the plaintiff by his attorney and it appearing to the satif-
faction of the court that the defendant is not an inhabitant of this state, where
fore it is ordered by the court that publication be made in the Pioneer for three
weeks successively requiring the defendant to appear at the court of pleas etc.
for Madison County at the court house in Jackson on the third Monday in December
eightteen hundred twenty-three and defend this suit.

        State   )
        vs.   )
        Robert Sevier)
        This day came as well the solicitor General on the part of the state as the
defendant in his proper person who being arraigned upon his arraignment pleaded
guilty in the manner and form charged in the bill of indictment. It is therefore
considered by the court that the defendant make his peace with the state by
the payment one cent fine and that the plaintiff go thereof hence without day
and recover of the defendant her costs by her about her prosecution in this

In. behalf expended and the defendant may be taken etc.

167   Ordered that Lewis Needham be discharged from serving as a juror any longer at this term.

18th. day of June 1823

    Whereas Thomas Shannon Sheriff and collector of the public taxes for the county of Madison reported to court the following tracts of land for the year 1822 and that the taxes thereon remain due and unpaid and that they respective owners or climants thereof have no goods or chattels within his county one which he can distrain for said taxes (to wit) Armstrong Martin heirs of three hundred acres, tenth district second range and seventy section entry No. two hundred and forty six. Armstrong Martin heirs of 500 acres 10th district, ranges 2 & 3 Entry No. 335

	No. Acres	No. dist.	No. Range	No. acct.	No. Ext.	$&¢
Armstrong Martin, Heirs of	400	10	2	7	359	1.50
Asbery William	640	10	1	9	535	240
Allcorn John	240	10	1	8	719	.90
Armstrong Martin, heirs of	160	10	2	6	502	.60
Delto	228	9	12	10	102	.89½
Delto	500	9	1	10	241	1.87½
Academan Francis	274	9	2	10	5	1.02½
Atkinson John	100	9	1	9	55	.37½
Allen Daniel	228	9	1	2	401	.85½
Black Alexander	200	10	2	8.0	74	.75
Booker Peter R.	121	10	4	8	197 233	.45
Bryan James	2000	10	4	8	233	7.50
Black William	322	10	2.3	6	490	1.12½
Buchhanon, John (clerks fee pair)	265	10	2	11	661	1.00
Blount William	228	10	5	10	671	.85½
Bedder, Nathan	1000	10	3.4	7	808	3.75
Benson Gabriel	228	9	1	10	43	48
Bret Thomas	50	9	2	9	735	18½
Brown Thomas	100	9	2	10	763	57½
Bright, James	102	9	2	8	120	38
P168 Braham, John	100	9	1	9	301	37
Boynston, Robert	65	9	1	3	851	.25
Blount John C. & Thos. Grant	5000	11	0	0	342	18.75
Brevard John	640	10	4	3	474	2.60
Bogol Robt.	5000	10	3.4	1	487	18.75
Booker Peter R.	640	10	5	3	659	2.40
Bryan Joseph	274	10	1	4	486	1.02½
Buckhanon, John Clks fee paid Crutcher, Edmond	640	10	4	10.11	104	2.40
Carpenter, Benjamin	428	10	2	10	138	1.60½
Cannon, Robt etc.	327	10	2.3	8.9	764	1.12½
Campbell, William	500	10	6	6	257	1.87½
Cotten Solomon	1000	10	4	8	320	3.75
Craig, John	583	10	6	6	379	2.18¾
Childress John, Representative of	935	9	1	6	453	3.51
Childress John Representatives of	345	9	1	9	3	1.29½
Campbell, David	200	9	2	10	506	.75
Daugherty George	1500	10	2.3	10	26	5.62½
Detto	2000	10	1	11	35	7.50
Daugherty, George	114	10	1	10	242	.43¼
Deveraux Thomas P.	1000	10	1.2	7	283	3.75
Dixon, William	50	10	3	8	454	.18¾

	NO. Acres	NO. Dist.	NO. Range	NO. Sec.	NO. En.	$ & ¢
P168 Donaldson, Robert	1332/3	10	2	9	729	.50
Cont.Douglas, H. L. and others	577¼	10	4	1	470	2.16
Donaldson, William & others	300	10	4	2	705	1.12½
Deckins, Edmond, heirs of	640	10	3	4	743	1.87½
Dixon William	500	10	4	5	791	1.87½
Dixon William	500	104	4	10	190	1.87½
Do Do	500	10	6	9	564	1.87½
Do Do	350	10	5	11	775	1.35
Eaton, John H.	750	10	1	8	18	2.71½
Elliott William	27¼	9	1	9	892	.10
Gerrard Charles	640	10	3	7	483	2.40
Goodlett, A G and Wm. McCampbell	1000	10	2	5	665	3.75
Goslin, Ambrose	640	10	4	10	107	2.40
Goodrich Rupell	1000	9	2	10	2	3.75
Huston, Robert	100	10	3	9	41	.37½
Hart, Antony	326¼	10	3	10	129	1.22
Hays, Robert	147¼	10	3	11	577	.43
Hamilton, John	320	10	1	9	583	1.20
Hanes, John	1000	10	3	9	792	3.75
Harrison, Robt.	1023	10	3	1	465	3.85
Hamilton, David	400	10	4	2	608	1.50
Ferris, Robert	5000	10	5	12	618	18.75
Henry, James	154	10	5	2	619	.51¼
P.169 Henry, James	154	10	5	2	620	.51¼
Harris, Jacob	5000	10	1.2	1	809	18.75
Hart, James	740½	9	2	11	605	2.77½
Hughes, Alexander	1000	9	2	8	762	3.75
Hughlett, William	500	9	2	7	77	1.87½
Hill William	1500	9	2	10	121	5.62½
Hickman, Thomas	74	11	6	6	262	.28
Jones, Calvin	360	11	3	8	322	1.25
Do Do.	640	11	3	6	469	2.40
Do Do	366	11	3	8	481	1.37½
Do Do	640	11	3	4	815	2.40
Do Do	640	9	5	9	514	2.40
Do Do	1000	9	1	8	14	3.75
Jones, Andes	274	11	4	2	609	1.12½
Do Do	1000	11	4	3	401	3.75
Ingram William	99	11	2.3	9	723	.37
Johnson, Daniel	254	11	4	1	212	.95
Johnson, Randall	400	11	4	3	357	1.50
Do Do	640	11	4	2.3	384	2.40
Johnson, Jacob(heirs of)	1140	11	4	2.3	740	4.27½
Johnson, Daniel	14¼	9	2	11	635	.05
Irvin, Robert	2000	10	3	10	127	7.50
Kenady, Robert C.	769	9	2	9	405	2.78¾
Do Do	300	9	1	10	189	1.12½
King, Thomas	640	10	6	6	245	2.40
Knowlton, John	640	9	2	8	258	2.40
Long, Nicholas	923	10	3	10	22	3.46
Long Nicholas	408	10	4	9	331	1.53
Lewis William T. (grant)	1500	10	5	10	2627	5.62½
Lester, William	400	9	2	11	95	1.50
Marian, Phillip	640	10	3	7	657	3.40
Morgan, John	77	9	1	9	355	.28

P.169 Cont.	No. Acres	NO. Dist.	NO. Range	No Sec.	No. En.	$ & ¢
Mendenhall, Mordecai	228	9	1	3	400	.85½
Mexico, Abraham (heirs of)	640	10	3	8	678	2.40
Alahan, Archibald	234	9	1	10	84	.87½
Mac Nary, John & others	2500	10	3	8	193	9.37½
Do Do	500	10	1	9	13	1.87½
Do. Do	500	10	2	10	162	1.87½
McIver & Sanderson	640	10	1	6	165	2.40
Do Do	640	10	2.3	8	4D0	2.40
Do Do	640	10	2	8	410	2.40
Do Do	640	10	3	9	507	2.40
McNairy John & other	500	10	4.5	10	115	1.87½
McDonald, John	450	10	4.5	11	195	1.68½
McPike, John	108	10	4	10	300	.40½
McLay Thomas	425	9	1	8	667	1.60
McMinn, Joseph	250	9	2	8	714	.93¾
Do do	130	9	2	8	715	.60
Nelson, Elizabeth	345	10	5	9	274	1.30
Do do	220	10	6	9	533	.82½
Nelson, Thomas (heirs of)	3840	10	5	8.9	754	14.30
P170 Newton, Edward	640	11	1	9	372	2.40
Overton, John & others	784	10	3	7	621	2.94
Ditto	44½	10	1	10	798	.17½
Pillow William	2452	10	3	10	12	9.19½
Ditto	274	10	4	7	75	1.02½
Ditto	273	10	2	9	92	1.00
Ditto	130½	10	2	9	175	.84
Ditto	274	10	4	7		1.02½
Boston John H.	267	10	4.5	10	73	.95
Pillow, Abner	500	10	4.5	2	437	1.87½
Ditto	400	10	3	2	706	1.50
Ditto	400	10	4	2	707	1.88
Parrick, John	274	10	4	10	631	1.02½
Price, Isaac	1000	10	6	5.6	692	3.75
Polk William (Grant)	200	10	5	10	2525	.75
Powell, Barr	72	9	1	11	42	.27
Padget, Sarah	100	9	2	7	348	.37½
Patterson, Samuel	267¾	9	2	9	556	1.00
Polk, Thomas	200	9	1	10	369	.75
Polk, Thomas, Heirs of	300	10	2	9	732	1.12½
Pinson, Nathan G.	150	9	2	7	662	.56¼
Ditto	62½	9	2	7	703	.23½
Purdy, John	84121/160	9	1	9	738	.28
Phillips Andrew	120	9	1	9	74	.45
Powell Burr	378	9	1	9	211	1.41¾
Purdy, John	200	9	2	8	882	.75
Patterson, William	35¼	9	2	7	898	.13
Robertson, Benjamin	1000	10	2.3	9	85	3.75
Ragford, Phillip	274	10	1	10	158	1.04¼
Ramsey, William	2	10	1	9	800	.00¾
Roads, William, heirs of	37	10	2	4	742	.14
Robertson, James	1000	10	66	6.6	428	3.75
Sloan, John	136	10	1	9	144	.51¾
Sherwood, William	120	10	1	10	181	.45
Stroud, William	268	10	2	7	258	1.02½
Smith, William	1000	10	2	7	284	3.75

P170
Cont.

	No. Acres	No. Dist.	No. Range	No. Sec.	No. En.	$ & ¢
Stubblefield Clement	228	10	5	6	364	.85½
Stoan, John	32	10	1	9	510	.12
Searcy, Robert (&M Moore)	666	10	3.4	3	253	2.49¾
Swanson, Peter	200	10	3	4	280	.75
Ditto	106	10	3	5	606	.39¾
Scruggs, James	250	10	4	6	558	.93½
Stufflefield, Clement	228	10	5	6	364	.85½
Smith William	366	9	1	9	756	1.59½
Scruggs, James	95	11	1	6	595	.35½
Scruggs, John	500	9	1	6	164	1.87½
Thomas Micajah	78	9	1	9	822	.29½
Thompson, James & Odil	6	9	2	11	602	.02½
Terril William	2560	11	2	9	690	9.60
P171 Taliaferro, Benjamin	1000	10	6	6	145	3.75
William Joseph	640	10	3	10	55	2.40
Whitesides, Jenkin	253½	10	4	3	642	.95
Walker, James	640	10	4	3	782	2.40
Do	640	10	2	8	186	2.40
Williford Butian	110	10	4	10.11	121	.40
Walker, Jacob	640	10	5	11	463	2.40
Williams, Robert W.	201	9	1	10	161	.75
Wilson, John	640	9	2	11	29	2.40
Yves, Deborah(occupant)	160	9	2	11		.60

Whereas Thomas Shannon, Sheriff and collector of the public taxes for the county of Madison, Reported to court the following tracts of land for the year 1821 and that taxes thereon remain due and unpaid, that the respective owners or claimants thereof have no goods or charrels within his county on which he can detrain for said taxes (to wit).

Armstrong, Martin represent atives of	300	10	2	9	246	.93¾
Ditto	500	10	2.3	7	335	1.56½
Ditto	400	10	2	9	359	1.25
Ditto	228	9	1.2	10	102	.71½
Ditto	500	9	1	10	241	1.56¼
Academon Frances	274	9	2	1	1	.86
Allen, Daniel	228	9	1	2	401	.52
Black, Alexander	200	10	2	8.9	74	.62½
Byers, James	2000	10	4	8	233	6.25
Benson, Gabriel	128	9	1	10	43	.40
Bright, James	102	9	2	8	120	.32
Brehan, John	100	9	1	9	301	.31¼
Blount John G.	640	9	2	8.9	269	2.02
Buchannan, John Clerks feepaid	640	10	4	10.11	104	2.02
Carpenter, Benjamin	428	10	2	10	138	1.34
Campbell, William	500	10	6	6	257	1.56
Cotton, Solomon	1000	10	4	8	320	3.12½
Craig John	583	10	6	6	379	1.82½
Childess John Representative of	345	9	1	9	3	1.10
Crutchens, Edmond & W. Lytle	87	10	2	10	53	.27½
Darr, Daniel	100	10	2	11	132	.31¼
Dotherty George	2500	9	2	9.10	408	7.81¼
Dixon, William	500	10	4	10	190	1.56¼
Eaton, John H.	450	9	1	8	18	2.34½
Gibbons & Wells	640	9	4	4	179	2.02
Gaslin, Ambrose	640	10	4	10	107	202

P171 Cont.	No. Acres	No. Dist.	No. Range	No. Range	No. Sec.	$ & ¢
Goodrich, Russell	1000	9	2	10	2	3.12½
Hulet, William	500		2	7	77	1.56½
Hill, William	1500	8	210	10	121	4.48¾
Hickman, Thomas	74	6	6	6	262	.23
Johnson, Daniel	254		4	1	212	.80
P. John Randal	400		4	3	357	1.25
172 Ditto	640		4	2.3	384	2.02
Irvin, Robert	2000		3	10	127	6.25
Kennedy, Robert C.	769		2	9	405	2.40½
Knowlton John	640		2	9	258	2.02
King Thomas	640		6	6	245	2.02
Kennedy Robert	300		1	10	189	.93¾
Long Nicholas	923	10	3	10	22	2.88½
Lowe, Robert	500	10	3	9	87	1.56½
Long Nicholas	408	10	4	9	331	1.27½
Lewis, Wm. S. (Grant)	1500	10	5	10	2639	4.68½
Love, Thomas	500	9	2	7	48	1.56½
Lester, William	400	9	2	11	95	1.25
Morgan John	77	9	1	9	355	.24
Mendenhall, Mordecai	228	9	1	3	400	.71½
McNairly John & others	500	10	1	9	13	1.56¼
McGavock, Jacob	80¼	10	1	9	38	.25
McNairy & others	500	10	2	10	160	1.56¼
McIver & Shanderson	640	10	1	6	165	2.02
McNairy, John & others	2500	10	3	8	193	7.81¼
McHatten, Abraham	1000	10	3	7	208	3.12
McGavock, Jacob	40	10	1	9	289	.12½
McIver & Sanderson	640	10	2.3	8	400	2.02
McNairy John & others	500	10	4.5	10	115	1.56¼
McPeke, John	108	10	4	10	300	.33¾
Nelson, Elizabeth	345	10	5	9	278	1.08
Pillow, William	2452	10	3	10	12	7.61¼
Poston, John H.	267	10	4.5	10	73	.83½
Pillow William	274	10	4	7	75	.86
Ditto	273½	10	2	9	92	.86
Payton, William	71½	10	2	8	99	.22½
Parsons, Enoch	100	10	1	10	150	.31¼
Pillow, William	130½	10	2	9	175	140
Pozzer, George	258 78/160	10	1	9	204	.80¾
Patrick, John	640	10	2	10	291	2.02
Parsons, Enoch	240	10	2	11	341	.75
Burr, Powell	636	10	2	8	397	1.48
Pillow Williams	274	10	4	7	75	.86
Patterson Wm. & others	1002½	10	5	10.11	117	3.12½
Polk, Thomas	1434	10	5	6	406	4.48½
Powell Burr	72	9	1	11	42	.22½
Polk William	86	9	1	9	56	.26
Phillips Andrew	121	9	1	9	94	.38
Powell Burr	378	9	1	9	211	1.14
Polk William	86	9	2	8	264	.26¾
Robertson, Benjamin	1000	10	2.3	9	58	3.12
Rayford, Philip	274	10	1	10	158	.86
Rhea, John	640	10	4	11	216	2.02
Sherwood, William	110	10	1	10	181	.37½

Pa.		1000 Acres	NO. Dist.	No. Range	No. Sec.	No.En.	$ & ¢
172	Smith, William	1000	10	2	7	284	3.12½
	Stubblefield Clement	228	10	5	6	364	.71¼
	Searcy, Robert & M Moore	666	10	3.4	3	255	2.68
P173	Swanson, Peter	200	10	4	6	280	.62½
	Scruggs, James	250	10	5	9	294	.78¼
	Scudder, Philip I.	1000	10	5	9	328	3.12½
	Stubblefield, Clement	228	10	5	6	364	.71¼
	Smith, William	366	9	1	9	153	1.14½
	Skinner Evans	193¼	9	1	9	339	.60½
	Scruggs John	500	9	1	6	164	.56¼
	Taylor, Francis	640	10	5	2	141	2.02½
	Trotten Richard	721⅙	10	5	1.2	387	2.34¼
	Taliaferro, Benjamin	1000	10	6	6	145	3.12
	William Joseph	640	10	3	10	55	2.02
	Wells Hardin & John Givens	640		4	11	179	2.02
	Wilson, John	640	9	9	11	29	2.02

Whereupon it is considered by the court that judgment be and is hereby entered against the aforesaid tracts of land in the name of the state for the sums annexed to each being the amount of taxes due severally thereon for the year 1821 and 1822 to gether with the costs and charges due severally thereon for the year aforesaid and it is ordered by the court that the same several tracts of land or so much thereof as shall be sufficient of each of them to satisfy the taxes costs and charge due thereon be sold as the law directs.

Henning Pace   )
Vs.   ) Slander
John Graves   )

This day came the parties aforesaid by their attorneys and thereupon came a jury of good and lawful men, to wit Lewis Needham, Thomas James Lewis Griffin David Sanders, Andrew Hays, James Vaulx, James Staneup, John M Walker, Nathan Simpson, James McCutchen, William C. Love, and John C. Sillespie, Who being elected, tried and sworn well & truly to try the issues joined upon their oaths do say they find the defendant is guilty of falsely and maliciously speaking & publishing they words in the several counts of the plaintiff's declaration mentioned in the manner & form as the plaintiffs against him hath declared and they further say the defendant of his own wrong & without any such cause as in pleading he hath alleged did falsely and maliciously speak and publish with the intent in the declaration ascribed to him the words in the several counts of the declaration mentioned as the plaintiff by replying to the defendants plea in that behalf hath alleged and they further find and say the plaintiffs action is not barred by the statute of limitations as the plaintiff by replying the defendants plea in that behalf hath alleged and assess the plaintiff damages by reason hhereof to one hundred dollars. It is therefore considered by the court that the plaintiff recover of sd. defendant the damages aforesaid in form aforesaid assessed and also his costs by him about his suit in this behalf expended and the defendant in mercy & etc.

A power of attorney was this day produced in open court from William Harris to Abraham Shepherd and acknowledged by the said Harris for the purposes therein and ordered to be certified.

Court then adjourned until tomorrow morning.

H. Haralson   JP.
W. B. Cross   JP.
David Jarrett JP.

P174 Thursday morning 19. day of June 1823
Cont.   Court met agreeable to adjournment, present, the Worshipful Herndon Haralson, John B. Cross & David Jarrett.

Pace   )
vs.   )   Ordered that the plaintiff pay the costs incident and
Graves)   accruing in consequence of James Cockrill and Samuel
H. Shannon being supoened in case and claiming their attendance.

State   )
vs.   )   Assault   Cancelled (a mistake)
Thomas Shannon)

State   )
vs.   )   Plead not guilty assault.
P 175Bennett R. Butler)

     This day came the defendant as well as the solicitor general on the part of the state as the defendant in his proper person and defendant being arraigned upon his arraignment plead not guilty and for his trial put himself upon his country whereupon came a jury, to wit, Thomas James, Lewis Griffin, Daniel King Wilson Hutchings, Rovert Sevier, Madison McLaurine, Rovert Murray, John F. Connolly Daniel Horton, Thomas Grissom, Charles Howard, and Henry Cascels, who being elected tried and sworn the truth to speak upon the issue, joined to say We of the jury find the defendant not guilty. It is therefore considered by the court that the defendant go hence without day and recover of the plaintiff his costs by him about his suit in this behalf expended and the plaintiff etc.

Benjamin Blythe)
vs.   )   Case
Francis Herron)

     This day came the parties aforesaid by their attorneys and thereupon came a jury (to wit) Thomas James, Lewis Griffin, Daniel King Wilson Hutchison, Robert Maury, John T. Connolly James Dorris, Thomas Grisom, Charles Howard and Henry Castles, who being sworn well and truly to the issues joined upon their oaths do say we of the jury find the issuer joined in favor of the plaintiff and do assess his damages by him sustained by reason of the speaking and publishing of the words in the declaration to twenty five dollars. It is therefore considered by the court that the plaintiff recover of the defendant the damages aforesaid by the jury aforesaid in form aforesaid assessed also his costs by him about his suit in this behalf expended.

Robert Armstrong & Thomas Shannon)
vs.   )   Motion
Genry Rutherford, John Rutherford &)
Griffith Rutherford)

     This day came the parties aforesaid by their attorneys, after solemn argument being had and heard, it is considered by the court that the motion be overruled and that plaintiff pay the costs of this motion.

State   )
vs   )   assault & Battery
Thomas Shannon)

     This day came as well the solicitor general on the part of the state as the defendant in his proper person who being arraigned upon his arraignment pleads guilty, whereupon it is considered by the court that the defendant make his peace with the state by the payment of one dollar and also the costs about this

P176 prosecution in this behalf expended and the defendant may be taken etc.
Cont.

State	)	
vs.	)	Assault & Battery
William Smith	)	

     This day came as well the solicitor general on the part of the state as the defendant in his proper person who being arraigned upon his arraignment plead not guilty and for his trial put himself upon God and his country and whereupon it is considered that a jury come here and whereupon came a jury (to wit) David Sanders, Francis Herrin, Asa B. Midyett Elijah McAfee, James Vaulx, John McClish

P177 Joseph Hardaway, James Dorris, ~alcolum, Johnson Henning Pace, Young H. Wilson, Harvey Dotson who being elected tried and sworn the truth to speak upon the issue joined upon their oaths do say we of the jury find the defendant guilty in manner and form as charged in the bill of indictment. It is therefore considered by the court that the defendant make his peace with the state by the payment of one cent, his costs, together with the costs about this prosecution in this behalf expended and the defendant may be taken etc.

State	)	
vs.	◊	Assault & Battery
John T. Porter	)	

     This day came as well the solicitor general on the part of the state as the defendant in his proper person and thereupon the defendant being arraigned upon his arraignment plead not guilty and for his trial put himself upon God and his country and thereupon it was considered that a jury come here and thereupon came a jury (to wit) Thomas James, Lewis Griffin, Daniel King, Wilson Hutchison, Robert Sevier, Madison McLaurine, Robert Maury, John T.Connolly, James Dorris Thomas Grisom, Charles Howard and Henry Castles, who being elected tried and sworn the truth to speak upon the issues joined do say We of the jury find the defendant not guilty. It is therefore considered by the court that the defendant go thereof hence without day and recover of the plaintiff his costs by him about his defence inthis behalf expended and the plaintiff etc.

P178
State	)	
vs.	)	Assault & Battery
William Smith	)	

     This day as well the solicitor general on the part of the state as the defendant in his proper person who being arraigned upon his arraignment plead guilty. It is therefore considered by the court that he make his peace with the state by the payment of fifty cents together with the costs about the prosecution in this behalf expended & the defendant may be taken etc.

State	)	
vs.	)	Assault & Battery
Richard A G Winn	)	

     This day came as well the solicitor general on the part of the state as the defendant in his proper person who being arraigned upon his arraignment, plead guilty. It is therefore considered by the court that he make his peace with the state by the payment of fifty cents together with the costs about his prosecution in this behalf expended & the defendant may be taken etc.

Sterling Wheaton	)	
vs.	)	Debt
Henry L. Gray	)	

     This day came the parties aforesaid by their attorneys and thereupon came a jury (to wit) David Sanders, Francis Herron, Asa B. Midyett Elijah McAfee James Vauls John McClish, Josep Hardaway, Daniel Horton Malcolm Johnson, Hen-

P178 ning Pace, Young E. Wilson, and Harvy Dotson who being sworn well and truly to
Cont. try the issue joined in favor of the plaintiff and assess his damages sustained
by reason of the detention of the debt in the declaration mentioned to Eight
dollars and seventy six cents. It is therefore considered by the court that
the plaintiff recover of the defendant one hundred & twenty dollars the debt
P179 in the declaration mentioned together with the damages aforesaid by the jurors
aforesaid in form aforesaid assessed also his costs by him about his suit in
this behalf expended and the defendant in mercy etc.

William Wilson   )
vs.   )   Case
Thomas Grisom   )

    This day came the parties aforesaid by their attorneys and thereupon
on affidavit of the defendant, this cause is continued until next term.

William Spencer   )
vs.   )   Debt
Amos Williams   )

    This day came the parties aforesaid by their attorneys and thereupon came
a jury, to wit David Sanders, Frances Herron Asa B Midyett, Elijah McAfee,
James Vaulx, John McClish, Joseph Hardaway, Daniel Horton, Malcolm Johnson,
Henning Pace, Young E. Wilson and Harvey Dotson, who being sworn well
and truly to try the issues joined upon their oaths do say the defendant hath
not paid the debt in the declaration mentioned of two hundred and forty dollars
as in replying the plaintiff hath alleged and they futher say the defendant
hath no set off against the devt as in replying to the defendants plea in that
behals the plaintiff hath also alleged and assess the plaintiff damages for the
detention of said debt to fifteen dollars, and forty cents. It is therefore
considered by the court that the plaintiff recover of the defendant the debt afe
foresaid together with the damages aforesaid in form aforesaid assessed by the
said jury and also his costs by him about his suit in this behalf expended and
the defendant in mercy etc.

P180 Joseph McKissick)
vs.   )   Debt
Nelson I Hess   )

    This day came the parties aforesaid by their attorneys and thereupon came
a jury to wit Thomas James, Lewis Griffin David King, Wilson Hutchings,
Robert Sevier, Madison McLaurine Robert Maury, John T. Conley, James Dorris,
Thomas Grissom, Charles Howard, & Henry Castles who being sworn well and truly
to try the issues joined upon their oaths do say We of the jury find for the
plaintiff the debt in the declaration mentioned and do assess the damages sustained by reason of the detention thereof to twenty dollars. It is therefore
considered by the court that the plaitiff recover of the defendant the sum of
one hundred dollars the debt in the declaration mentioned together with the
damages aforesaid by the jury aforesaid in form aforesaid assessed also his
costs by him about his suit in this behalf expended and the defendant in mercy etc.

Archibald B. Dandridge   )
vs.   )   Debt
Stokely D. Hays   )

    This day came the parties aforesaid by their attorneys and thereupon came
a jury David Sanders, Francis Herron, Asa B. Midyett Elijah McAfee James Vaulx
John McClish Joseph Hardaway, Daniel Horton Malcolm Johnson, Henning Pace,
Young E Wilson, and Harvy Dotson who being sworn well and truly to try the
issues joined upon their oaths do say We of the jury find the issues joined on

P180 the first second third and fourth pleas in favor of the plaintiff and the fifth
Cont.find for the plaintiff four hundred dollars the debt in the declaration mentioned
and do assess his damages by reason of the detention thereof to fity-two dollars
and fifty cents. It is therefore considered by the court that the plaintiff recover of the defendent the sum of four hundred dollars and debt in the declaratio
P181 mentioned together with the damages aforesaid by the jurors aforesaid in form
aforesaid assessed also his costs by him about his suit in this behalf expended
and the defendant be in mercy etc.

Samuel Polk   )
vs.   )   Debt
Isaac Curry   )

      This day the parties aforesaid by their attorneys and thereupon came a
jury to wit, Thomas James, Lewis Griffin, Daniel King, Wilson Hutcheson, Robert
Sevier, Robert Murray John T. Conley, Thomas Grissom, Clark Spencer, Henry
Castles, Charles Howard and James Dorris, who being sworn well and truly to
try the issue joined upon their oaths do say We of the jury find for the plaintiff one hundred forty four dollars the debt in the declaration mentioned and do
assess his damages by reason of the detention thereof to eighteen dollars and
seventy-two cents. It is therefore considered by the court that the plaintiff
recover of the defendent the sum of four hundred dollars the debt in the declaration mentioned together with the damages aforesaid by the jurors aforesaid in
form aforesaid assessed also his costs by him about his suit in this behalf
expended and the said defendant be in mercy etc.

Turner Tate   )
vs.   )   Debt
Carter C. Collin   )
      This day came the parties aforesaid by their attorneys and thereupon came
a jury to wit Thomas James, Lewis Griffin, Daniel King, Wilson Hutchens, Robert
Sevier, Robert Murry, John T. Conelly, Thomas Grissom, Clark Spencer, Henry
Castler, Charles Howard and James Dorris who being sworn well and truly to try
the issue joined upon their oaths We of the jury ------- find for the plaintiff
two hundred dollars and do assess his damages by reason of the detention to eighteen dollars. It is therefore considered by the court that the plaintiff recover of the defendant the said sum of two hundred dollars with the damages
aforesaid assessed and also his costs by him about his suit in this behalf expended and the defendant may be in mercy etc.

Linly Box   )
vs.   )   Debt
William Love   )
      This day came the parties aforesaid by their attorneys and thereupon came
a jury to wit Thomas James, Lewis Griffin Daniel King, Wilson Hutchison, Robert
Sevier, Robert Mury, John T. Conelly, Thomas Grissom, Clark Spencer, Henry
Castler, Charles Howard and James Dorris who being sworn will and truly to try
the issues joined upon their oaths do say We of the jury find the issues joined
in favor of the plaintiff, do find one hundred dollars, the debt in the declara -
tion mentioned and assess his damages by reason of the detention thereof to
two dollars and fifty cents. It is therefore considered by the court that the
plaintiff recover of the defindant the said sum of two hundred dollars together w
with the damages aforesaid in form aforesaid assessed and also his costs by him
about his suit in this behalf expended and the said defendant in mercy etc.

John H. Camp &Co.)
vs.   Dabt
Mathew Johnson, Adm &etc.)

P183   On consent of parties this cause is continued until next term.

Isaac Sellers, for the use of Joel Pinson)
vs.   )   Debt
John Spencer   )

This day came the parties aforesaid by their attorneys and thereupon came
a jury to wit, Thomas James, Lewis Griffin Daniel King, Wilson Hutchison, Robert
Sevier Robert Maury, John T. Conolly, Thomas Grissom, Clark Spencer, Henry
Castles, Charles Howard and James Dorris who being sworn well and truly to try
the issue joined do say We of the jury do find for the plaintiff the sum of one
hundred and forty dollars the debt in declaration mentioned and assess his damage
by reason of the detention thereof to twenty one dollars and sixty seven cents.
It is therefore considered by the court that the plaintiff recover of the defendant the said sum of one hundred dollars together with the damages aforesaid
by the jury aforesaid in form aforesaid assessed and also his costs by him about
his suit in this behalf expended.

Elam Purviane   )
vs.   )   Debt
John P. Thomas   )

This day came the parties aforesaid by their attorneys and thereupon came
a jury (to wit) David Sanders, Lewis Griffin Daniel King, Wilson Hutchison,
Robert Sevier, Robert Maury John T. Conelly, Thomas Grissom, Clark Spencer,
Henry Castles, Charles Howard and James Dorris who being sworn well and truly
to try the issue joined do say that the defendant hath not paid the balance
of the debt in the declaration mentioned of one hundred fifteen dollars as the
plaintiff in replying to the defendants plea in that behalf hath alleged and
they further find that the defendant hath no set off as the defendant in his
pleading alleged and assess the plaintiff damages be reason of the detention of
said balance of debt to nineteen dollars. It is therefore considered by the
court that the plaintiff recover of the defendant the balance of the debt the
P184 said sum of one hundred and fifteen dollars the balance of the debt in the
declaration mentioned together with the damages aforesaid by the jury aforesaid
in form aforesaid assessed and also his costs by him about his suit in this
behalf expended and the defendant be in mercy etc.

Thomas Simms   )
vs.   Q   Debt
Daniel Horton   )
James Hicks   )

This day came the parties aforesaid by their attorneys and thereupon be
consent of the parties this cause is dismissed at the cost of the defendant.
It is therefore considered by the court that the plaintiff recover of the defendant his costs by him about his suit in this behalf expended and the defendant be in mercy etc.

William C. Love)
vs.   )   Debt
John Weir   )

This day came the parties aforesaid and thereupon by consent of parties
this cause is dismissed at the cost of the defendant. It is therefore considered by the court that the plaintiff recover of the defendant his costs by him
about his suit in this behalf expended and the defendant be in mercy etc.

The Grand Jury this day returned into court an indictment against Isaac
Spencer for an assault indorsed by the foreman of the Grand Jury a true bill,
ordered.

P185 Bedford & Wynne   )
      vs.   )   Case
Matthew Johnson, Adm. & etc.   )
This day came the parties aforesaid by their attorneys and thereupon came a
jury (to wit) David Sanders, Lewis Griffin, Daniel King, Wilson Hutchison,
Robert Grissom Clark Spencer, Henry Castles, Charles Howard and James Dorris,
who being sworn well and truly to try the issues joined upon their oaths do
say We of the jury do find that the said Simon Johnson, deceased did assume
upon himself in manner and form as the plaintiff hath declared and do assess
the plaintiff damages by reason of the defendants non performance of that assum-
set to Eighty dollars, and further the jurors aforesaid upon their oaths aforesaid do say that the defendant hath fully administered all, singular the goods
and chattels of the decedent in his hands to be administered before the bringing
of this suit and they do further say that these judgments outstanding against
the defendant as administrator of the decedent. It is therefore considered by
the defendant his damages aforesaid in form aforesaid assessed and his costs
by him in this behalf expended to be levied of the goods & chattels of the said
decednt when sufficient shall come to the defendants hands to be administered.

        A bill of sale was this day produced in open court from John B. Cross to
Benjamin Gholston and acknowledged by the said John B. Cross to be his act and
deed and ordered to be certified.

P186 John Thomas Brook   )
      vs.   )   Debt
James D. Carithers   )

John Thomas Brooks   )
      vs.   )   Debt
James   D. Carithers   )

John Thomas Brooks   )
      vs.   )   Debt
James D. Carithers   )

Bennett Smith   )
      vs.   )   Debt
James D. Carithers   )
        This day came the complaintants by their counsels and the defendant came
not and it is suggested to the court here by the said complaintants that the
said James D. Carithers hath departed this life and the same is not demid, and
thereupon it is ordered by the court that they above causes be continued until
next term of this court for the proper parties to appear on the premises to
answer.
        Court then adjourned until tomorrow morning 8 o'clock.

                                        H. Haralson JP.
                                        David Jarrett JP.
                                        Sam Taylor   JP.

P187 Friday morning 20th. June 1823
        Court met agreeable to adjournment, present, the worshipful Herndon Haral-
son David Jarrett, Samuel Taylor and John B. Cross.
        Ordered that David Sanders be discharged from serving any longer as a juror
this term.

p187 George Lyon   )
Cont.vs.   )   Debt
    Willoughby Powell   )
        This day came the plaintiff by his attorney and on motion the plaintiff
has leave to amend his writ and declaration by paying the cost of the amendment.
It is therefore considered by the court that the defendant recover of the plaintiff his cost by him about the amendment in this behalf expended.

John Page   )
vs.   )   Debt
Green L. Haralson & John T. Porter)
        This day came the parties aforesaid and dismisses his suit as to John
T. Porter, one of the defendants in this suit. It is therefore considered by the
said defendant go thereof hence and recover of the plaintiff his costs by him
about his suit in this behalf expended that the plaintiff for his false clamor
be in mercy etc.

James McCutchen)
vs.   )   Debt
John Stobough   )
        This day came the parties aforesaid by their attorneys and there came a
jury to wit, Frances Hearn, John M. Walker, Joshua Hearn, Thomas L Wynne, Willoby
P 188Powell Green L. Haralson, Charles Howard, John Young, Robert Lumpkin, Joseph
Hardaway, John Harrison and Thomas James who being sworn well and truly to try
the issues joined upon their oaths do say, we of the jury do find for the plaintiff two thousand dollars, the debt in the declaration mentioned and assess his
damages by reason of the detention thereof to four hundred ten dollars. It is
therefore considered by the court that the plaintiff recover of the defendant two
thousand dollars the debt aforesaid together with the damages aforesaid by the
jury aforesaid in form aforesaid assessed and also his costs by him about his
suit in this behalf expended and the defendant in mercy etc.

Ira C. Kennedy   )
vs.   )   Case
Thomas Shannon   )
        This day came the parties aforesaid by their attorneys and thereupon came
a jury to wit, Francis Herron, John M Walker Andrew Herron, Thomas L. Wynne,
Willoughby Powell Clark Spencer, Charles Howard, Green L. Haralson, Robert
Lumpkin, Joseph Hardaway, John Harrison, and Thomas James, who being sworn will
and truly to try the issues joined upon their oaths do say We of the jury find
the issues on the first and second pleas in favor of the plaintiff and do assess
his damages by reason of the non-performance of the assumpsit in the declaration
mentioned to fifty dollars, we do further find that the defendant prior to the
P189 commencement of this suit, did tender the plaintiff the said sum of fifty
dollars as in pleading he has alleged. It is therefore considered by the court,
that the plaintiff take nothing but the said fifty dollars and that the defendant
go thereof hence without day and recover of the plaintiff his costs by him
about his suit in this behalf expended etc. Whereupon the plaintiff prayed
and obtained an appeal to the next term of the Circuit Court to be held for the
county of Madison and who thereupon entered into bond with Aquilla Davis and
Robert H. Wynne his securities in the penalty of one hundred dollars conditioned
for the prosecution of said appeal.

John Page   )
vs.   )   Debt
Green L. Haralson, John T. Porter   )

P189   This day came the parties aforesaid by their attorneys and thereupon
Cont. the plaintiff says he will not futher prosecute his suit against the defendant
Porter. It is therefore considered by the court that the said defendant go
thereof hence without day and recover of the plaintiff his cost by him about his
defense in this behalf expended and the plaintiff for his false clamor be in
mercy erc.

John Page   )
vs.   )   Debt On motion
Green L. Haralson   )
       This day came the parties aforesaid by their attorneys and thereupon came
a jury (to wit) Elijah McAfee, Francis Herron, John M Walker, Willoughby Powell
Joseph Hardaway, Thomas James, Andrew Herron, Thomas L. Wynne, Charles Howard,
Clark Spencer, Robert Lumpkin, and John Harrison, who being sworn well and truly
to try upon the issue joined upon their oaths do say, We of the jury do find for
the plaintiff one hundred and forty-three dollars and fifty cents, the debt in
the declaration mentioned and do assess his damages by reason of the detention
thereof to two dollars. It is therefore considered by the court that the plaintiff recover of the defendant the said sum of one hundred forty-three dollars
and fifty cents with the damages aforesaid, in the form aforesaid assessed and
also his costs by him about his suit in this behalf expended and the defendant
in mercy etc.

P190 Benjamin Booth   )
vs.   )   Case
Clarbourn J. Ragsdale & Math. Johnson   )
       This day came the parties aforesaid by their attorneys and because the
defendant cannot gainsay the plaintiffs cause of action against them by leave of
the court and withdraw their pleas filed herein. It is therefore considered by
the court that the plaintiff recover of the defendant such damages as he has
sustained by reason of the non performance of the assumpsit in the declaration
mentioned but because those damages are unknown it is commanded the sheriff that
he cause a jury to come at the next term of this court to inquire of damages
until which time this cause is continued.

James McCutchen   )
vs.   )   Debt
John Stobaugh   )
       Robert H. Dyer and George Mizell the defendant bail in this cause produced
the body of the defendant in open court in discharge of the condition of their
bond heretofore entered into and the defendant having failed to pray him in
custody the said defendant is hence discharged.

P191 John H. Camp, Associates & etc.)
vs.   )   Debt
Matthew Johnson, Adm.   )
       This day came the parties aforesaid by their attorneys and thereupon came
a jury, to wit Francis Herron, John M Walker, Andrew Herron, Thomas L. Wynne,
Willoughby Powell, Elijah McAfee, Charles Howard, Clark Spencer, Robert Lumpkin
Joseph Hardaway, John Harrison, and Thomas James who being sworn well and truly to
try the issues joined upon their oaths do say We of the jury find the issues
joined on the pleas of fline adminstravit and judgments outstanding in favor of
the defendant and we do further say that we do find the issue joined in the plea
of payment in favor of the plaintiff and do assess his damages by reason of the
detention of the debt in the declaration mentioned to two hundred and sixty dollars. It is therefore considered by the court that the plaintiff recover of the

P191 defendant four hundred sixteen dollars the degt in the declaration mentioned
Cont.together with the damages aforesaid by the jury aforesaid in form aforesaid assessed also his costs by him about his suit in this behalf expended to be levied
of the goods and chattels of the decedent when so much thereof shall came into
the hands of the defendant to be administered.

P192 Henry M. C. McPeak for the use of   )
R. H. Dyer & Bartholomew G. Stewart,)
vs.   )   Debt
Jordan C. Stokes   )

    This day came the parties aforesaid by their attorneys and thereupon came
a jury to wit; Francis Herron, John M Walker, Andrew Herron, Thomas L. Wynne,
Willoughby Powell Green L. Harrison, Charles Howard, Clark Spencer, Robert
Lumpkin, Joseph Hardaway, John Harrison, and Thomas James, who being sworn
will and truly to try the issue joined upon their oaths do say We of the jury on
the issues joined do ding for the plaintiff one hundred dollars the debt in the
declaration mentioned and do assess his damages by the detention thereof to
seven dollars and fifty cents. It is therefore considered by the court that the
plaintiff recover of the defendant the said sum of one hundred dollars together
with the damages aforesaid by the jurors aforesaid in form aforesaid assessed
also his costs by him about his suit in this behalf expended and the defendant
in mercy etc.
    Court then adjourned until tomorrow 8 o'clock
                                        H. Haralson   JP.
                                  Jno. G. Carithers JP.
                                  Sam Taylor   JP.

Saturday morning 21st. June 1823.
    Court met agreeable to adjournment, present, the Worshipful Herndon Haralson
Jno. G. Carithers, Jno B.Cross, Stephen Jarman, John Thomas, James Greer, Samuel
Taylor, James Trousdale, and R. H. Dyer.
P193   A deed of trust from Joel Dyer to Blackman Coleman was this day produced
in open court and acknowledged by said Joel Dyer to be his act and deed and
ordered to be certified.
    A deed of gift from Joel Dyer to Maria T. Dyer and others was this day
produced in open court and the execution thereof acknowledged by said Dyer to
be his act and deed.
    A deed of bargain and sale from George Shannon and Finis W. Shannon to
Thomas for eighty five ½ acres of land was this day produced in open court and
proven by the oath of Samuel H. Shannon one of the subscribing witnesses and
ordered to be continued for further probate.

Henning Pace   )
vs.   )   Case
John Graves   )
    This day came the defendant in this case and prayed an appeal to the next
term of circuit court to be held for the county of Madison on a judgment rendered
herein on a former day of this court whereupon it was granted him on his entering
into bond with David Jarret and John T. Porter his secuities in the penalty of
$200.00 conditioned for prosecution of sd. Appeal.
    On motion of Alexander B. Bradford, Esq. and it appearing to the satisfactio
of the court here that Samuel M. Warner, gentleman, hath attained the age of twenty-one years, that he hath resided in the County of Madison three months666 ____
this time and that he is a man of good moral character. It is therefore ordered
by the court that the same be certified by our clerk as preparatory step for the
said Warner to obtain license to practice law in this state.

P194 Abraham Weeks)
vs.)
John B. Cross)

The defendant John B. Cross in this case exhibited his petition for a certiorari which is granted him, it is therefore ordered that writs of certiorari and supercedias issue accordingly.

Charles Howard came into open court and proved by his own oath of the killing of two wolves over the ages of four months in the county of Madison and ordered to be certified accordingly.

Ordered that Matthew Johnson, Adm. of Simon Johnson, deceased be permitted to remark in his inventory returned to this court at December term last of this court, of such debts as are good and such as are bad of the said deceased.

On motion ordered that the road directed to be marked out from Jackson to McGuires ferry on Hatchie be renewed and that the following persons be appointed as additional jurors of view after being sworn, for that purpose to wit, John G. Carithers, Nathan Bridgman & Joshua Haskill and make report to the next term of this court.

Joel Dyer came into open court and made oath of serving four days as a juror of view in the county of Madison and ordered that he be allowed the sum of one dollar per day for the same.

Ordered that the report of the jury of view appointed on a former day of this court to mark a road from town by the way of Shannons landing to the high land on the South side of Forked Deer river be rec'd and that Robert Clanton be
P195 appointed overseer of the road from Shannons landing on the South side of river to the high land to work all the hands West of Cain Creek and that John D. Shannon from town to Shannons landing & work the following hands to wit, William B. Davis, Stephen Lypert, William Due, Robert Hughes, Charley Braden, Henry G. Connelly, Ray, John Beths, Drury Beth, James F. Theobald, John M Walker. Rufus F. King, Austin F. Kind, Alfred Murrey Joseph H. Talbot, David Thomas, Samuel Swan, Stokely D. Hays, & hands, A. Lawhorn, Patrick Williams, ___ Smith ___ Robertson ___ McReynolds A. C. Nemo, Samuel Thrasher,___ Stockton,___ Laurence Williams,___ Brannon, John Harrison, Samuel Shannon & hands, D. Horton & hands James Hicks, Thomas Norvel, P. G. Tucker, James Wright, George Hicks, Jno. J. Brydenbusher, Bennett R. Butler, Doct N. Wilbourne A. G. Martin, Walker Fitz, Jno H. Ball, R. P. T. Stone, Thomas Dunn, John Irons, to open sd. road with all the hands in the town of Jackson.

Ordered that the report of the jury of view appointed ona former day of this court to make and lay off a road from town to Stanleys Branch South of Jacob Hills in end.
P196   Ordered that the road leading from Jarman's ford on the middle fork of Forked Deer river to the town of Jackson opened from said ford as was ordered at March term of this court to the district line with the district line to intersect the road leading from town to Carroll Court House where said road crosses said district line and the overseers and hands heretofore appointed to open said road be ordered to open the same agreeable to this order.

Ordered that the report of the jury of view appointed at the last term of this court to mark and lay off a road from Howards to Joel Duers be received and that Wilie Dodd be appointed overseer of said road and to work the following hands, to wit, Guy Smith & hands, John I. Smith & hands, Thomas I Smith & hands, Bird Smith & hands, Widow Smith's hands, Thomas Bowling & sons. Joseph Bolin, Peter Acre, James L. Wortham, Joel Dyer's hands, Henry L. Gray a nd hands, Hardy Blckwell, Nathan Blackwell, Wm. Roberts, Thomas M. Dement, the hands of Daniel Cherry, Wiett Tweedy & hands W. H. Dyer & hands, Charles Howard, & Mr. Newman.

P197 Matthew McPeake   )
       vs.   )   Certiorari
    William L. Mitchell   )

    This day cam e the parties aforesaid by their attorneys and agree that
above suit be dismissed at the defendants cost. It is therefore considered by
the court that the plaintiff go thereof hence and recover of the defendant his
costs by him about his suit in this behalf expended and the defendant be in mercy.
Ordered tha Mark Langston be released from paying two dollars half the appraised
value of a stray taken up by him in the year 1822. On motion and petition filed
ordered that John Thomas have leave to build a grist mill on Meridian Creek on
his own land.

    Ordered that the order heretofore made to mark a road from Jackson to Cal
Dyers thence to the bridge on the North fork of Forked Deer river be renewed and
that Daniel Mading, Joshua Haskill William Houston, William Espy, Moses Oldham,
Sugars McLemore, John Bl Hogg, or any five of them after being duly sworn for
that purpose be a jury of view to mark and lay off said road and report their
proceedings to next term of this court.

    A power of attorney from William R. Hess to Richard G. Dunlap was this day
produced in court and acknowledged by the said William R. Hess to be his act
and deed and ordered to be so certified.

    Ordered that Matthias Deberry be this day appointed guardian of James W.
Haley and William P. Haley, minor orphans, who thereupon entered into and
acknosledged bond with Joshua Haskill, Robert, Robert Clanton and William Espy h
his securities in the penalty of five thousand dollars conditioned for the discharge of duties as guardian towards said minor orphans.

    Ordered that Daniel Ross be appointed overseer of the road on that part of
the road leading from the town of Jackson toward Hardin Court House, Commencing
at the house of Mr. Talley's to the county line to work the following hands,
to wit, Samuel Thomas, David Parker, Thomas Reaves & hands, Stark Dupries hands,
Mr. Hardridge, Daniel Harkins, Hiram Harkinsk Mr. Harkins hands, Daniel Ross &
hands, Daniel Jones and hands and that Cal Johnson be appointed overseer of
that part of said road commencing at the house of Mr Tally from thence to the
river and that he work the following hands to wit, Cal Henderson's hands, John
Yount & hands, Nathaniel Henderson & hands, Wm. Martin, Henry N Caulter, James
G. Haskill, James Alexander, Edmond Scarbour, James Earbutton Jesse Wilson,
Samuel Martin, Mr. Mitchell & son. Cal Love & hands, Jonathan Houston, Elisha
Matthews, Thomas Matthews Carlton Matthews, Wm Shelly and Cal Johnson hands to
open and keep in repair said road.

Maths Wilson, Exr. etc.)
       vs.   )   Case motion to set aside non suit.
    William H. Dosk   )

    This day came the parties aforesaid by their atto neys and thereupon the
matters of law arising on the pla ntiffs motion herein being fully argued and
understood it is considered that the same be overruled and that the defendant
recover of the plaintiff his costs by him in this behalf expended.

Elijah McAfee   @
       vs.   )   Case
Joseph B. Porter   )

    This day came the defendant by his attorneys and prayed an appeal to the
next circuit court to be held for the county of Madison which was granted him
who thereupon entered into and acknowledged bond with Hugh W. Dunlap and Robert
Hughes his securities in the penalty of one hundred dollars conditioned for the
prosecution of said appeal.

P199 Joel Dyer came into open court and made oath of serving two days as a juror of
view in the county of Madison and ordered that he be allowed the sum of one dollar per day for the same.

Charles Howard proves two days services as a juror of view and ordered
that he be allowed the sum of one dollar per day for the same.

Presly Morgan came into court and made oath of killing of one wolf over
the age of four months in the county of Madison and that it be certified accordingly.

Charles Howard came into court and made oath of killing two wolves in the
county of Madison over the age of four months.

Daniel Ross came into court and proved the serving of two days as a juror
of view in the county of Madison and that he be allowed one dollar per day for
the same.

Ordered that the following persons be appointed judges of the election,
to wit, In the town of Jackson, Samuel H. Shannon, David Horton and Aquilla Davis.

Guy Smith   )
Joel Dyer   )   at John G. Carithers
Bignal Crook   )

William Atchison, Esq   )
Abner Brown &   )   At Francis Taylors
Samuel Dickens   )

P200 William Love   )
Daniel Ross &   )   at Mount Pinson
John M. Johnson   )

John Warren   )
William Bowen   )   at John Bowen's
William Nash   )

John Rutherford Esq.)
Robert Porter &   )   at Henry Rutherford's
Patten Chambers   )

Thomas J. Hardeman   )
William Polk Sen. &   )   at McNeill's
Doct. Wilie Jones   )

David Jernigan   )
Barney Chambers   )   at Joseph Fowlers
Thomas Boyett   )

Stephen Bryant   )
Turner Tate   )   at James Hills
Clarbourn Chisum   )

Ordered that the following persons, towit, Madison McLaurine, Jordan G.
Stokes, Jarett M. Jelks, Micajah Midgett, Petts Chandler, Guy Smith, James Vaulx
John M. Walsh, Robert Webb, Mark Christian, Daniel Ross, Thomas Reaves, Nathaniel
Henderson, Stephen Jarman, Allen Dockins, Alexander Greer, John L. Dilliard, Esq.
John G. Carithers, Henry N Caulter, Abel Willis, Gavriel Anderson, Robert
Burns, George Todd, Samuel Dickins, John Weir and James Greer be and they are
hereby appointed jurors to the next term of circuit court to be held for the
county of Madison and that the following persons to wit, Jonathan Walsh, Samuel
Wilson, Robert Lowery, Harbert Newsom, Jacob Hill, James Haley, Francis Herron

P201 Stephen Lacy Lancaster Glover, Henning Pace, Francis Taylor, John P. Thomas, Richard Coop, Jesse Hanna, Luceford Edwards, James Thetford William Love, Jason H. Wilson, Michael Fisher William Justice, William Mitchell, John T. Porter James Young Bird Smith Halsey Larremore and William Alexander be appointed jurors to the next county court and that John Shannon and Benjamin Blythe be appointed constables to attend at the County court, William Wilbourne and John Far at next circuit court.

Ordered that Jacob Hill be appointed overseer of that part of the road leading from Jackson to Fowler's ferry from Jackson to Meridian Creek and work all the hands living East of Cain Creek and West of Meridian Creek and also all the hands East of the main street East of the public square running North and South and all the hands within one mile of town and with the line above designated to open said road and all the hands East on a direction with said dividing li line shall not be compelled to open the road to Shannon's landing and that Thomas Boyett be appointed overseer from Meridian Creek to Hatchie and work all the hands from the East boundary line of the county lying South of Madison as far West as Porter's creek on the North and South of Hachie including Wades creek and Piney Creek hands and that Barney Chambers be appointed overseer on the South side of Hatchie and that said Boyett & Chambers divide ground and hands Thomas Boyett from Piney to Hatchie instead of beginning at Meridian Creek and Thomas Allison from Meridian Creek to the South bank of Piney and work the following hands, all East of Meridian Creek and West of East boundary of the county as far as Piney Creek so as to include hands of Wm. Butler and John Thomas.

P202   Ordered that John Warren be appointed overseer of the road from Nash's Bluff to where the road crosses Pond Creek to work all the hands North and West of Pond Creek and South of said North fork to Pond Creek and that Charles Howard be overseer of the said road from Pond Creek to a point called the five poplars, and work all the hands North and East of said Pond Creek and that Henry L Gray be overseer of the road from the five poplars, to where said road intersects the Harris Bluff road to work all the hands East and South of the five poplars, said road to be in the second class.

William Love   )
vs.   )   Case
John Wincer   )

On motion of the defendant by his attorney ordered that he have leave to take deposition generally by giving 20 days notice on the state and 30 out of the state to be read as evidence at the next term until which time this cause is continued.

Elijah Mc Afee   )
vs.   )   Case
Joseph B. Porter)

Parties have leave to take deposition generally by giving 20 days notice of time and place of taking the same.

Thomas Allison   )
Vs.   )   Appeal
John T. Porter   )

B. G. Stewart   )
vs.   )   Case
Grant & Grisom   )

Ordered that the foregoing causes be continued until next term.

P203 State   )
     vs.   )   Plead Guilty
     Isaac Spencer)

This day came as well the solicitor general on the part of the state as
the defendant in his proper person who being arraigned upon his arraignment
plead Guilty and put himself upon the grace and mercy of the court. It is therefore considered by the court that he make his peace with the state by the payment of fifty cents and that the plaintiff recover of the defendant the fine
aforesaid together with the costs of this prosecution and that the defendant may
be taken etc.

Ordered that William Bilbourne be appointed overseer of the Polk ferry
road from where the same leaves the Fowler ferry road to the South boundary of
the county to work all the hands from the head of Meridian Creek to the West
of William Butler's and John Thomas's Clover creek and William May fields.

P204   Ordered that John Thomas be allowed six dollars for six days services as
a juror of view in the county of Madison.

John D. Shannon came into open court and proved his attendance on the
court five days at the present term as constable.

Court then adjourned until court in caurse.

                         Sam Taylor   JP.
                         Jno G. Carithers JP.
                         J. B. Cross   JP.

P205 Monday the 15th. day of Sepember 1823

At a court of Pleas and quarter sessions begun and held for the county of
Madison State of Tennessee in the town of Jackson on Monday the 15th. day
of September 1823.
Present, the Worshipful Herndon Haralson, John B. Cross, Stephen Jarman, William
Draper, Samuel Taylor, John Thomas, Joseph Linn gentlemen, justices of the peace.

Ordered that Richard C. Allen be appointed solicitor general pro tem during
the present term of this court in the place of Alexander B. Bradford.

A deed of bargain and sale from Robert Bedford to Samuel Wade for an in-
divided forth part of a certain tract of land was this day produced in open court
and proven by the oath of William Stoddert and Joseph Royal subscribing witnesses thereto and ordered to be registered. A deed of bargain and sale from George
Shannon Finis W. Shannon to Thomas Shannon for eighty-five and a half acres of
land was this day produced in open court and the execution thereof proven by the
oaths of A. L. Martin, one of the witnesses thereto, the probate of Samuel
Shannon, another subscribing thereto, taken on a former day of this court and
ordered to be registered.

Jarett M. Jelks, AdmR. of the estate of Samuel Goodwin, deceased this day
returned an inventory of the amount of sales of said decendent.

A deed of bargain and sale from Samuel Davis to Worsham Easley for 45 acres
of land was this day produced in open court and the execution thereof proven by
the oath of Joseph Lin one of the subscribing witnesses thereto and filed for
further probate.

On petition filed it is ordered that Benjamin Gholston, Hazael Hewitt,
Herndon Harralson, William E. Butler, William Braden, Sam H. Shannon or any
five of them be a jury of view to mark and lay off a road from the court house
to the bridge below McIvers Mill on Jones Creek so as to cross Butler's Creek
below Herndon Haralsons and make report to the present term.

P206   A power of attorney from John B. Cross to Maclin Cross was this day produced in open court and the execution thereof acknowledged by the said John B.
Cross to be his act for the purposes therein mentioned and ordered to be certified

P206
Cont.
    Orderd that Benjamin Gholson Hazael Hewitt, Herdon, Haralson, William Braden & Samuel B. Shannon be a jury to view and mark out a road turning out of the road running by Parks Chandlers at or near his house and running from thence South Eastwardly near Pitts Chandlers so as to strike the Forked Deer river when the jury of view marked out the same for the road leading on a direction to Hardin Court house by Mount Pinson & report immediately to this court. Richard Mauldin comes into court and makes ßoath of killing one wolf in the county of Madison over the age of four months and ordered to be certified accordingly.

    William Martin came into open court and made oath of killing two wolves in the county of Madison over the age of four months and ordered to be certified accordingly.

    Thomas Allison and John Garrison came into court and made oath of serving five days each as jurors of view in the county of Madison who were thereupon allowed one dollar per day each for the same.

    Ordered that James A. McClary be appointed overseer of the road from Cain Creek to the 14 mile tree on the Carroll County road and work all the hands in said bounds and that of Murdock Murchisons spring branch.

    Ordered that Nathan Clark be appointed overseer of the Carroll County road commencing at the 14 mile tree to the county line to work all the hands East of Murchison's Spring Branch.

P207
    On petition filed ordered that the road leading out of the northeast corner of the town of Jackson and running in the direction of Reynoldsburgh be altered agreeable to the plan laid down on said petition that is to say, commencing where said road now leaves the corporation limits of town running east to the Southeast corner of Stephen Lyputs three acre lot, thence with the East boundary of said lot until it intersect said road and that so soon as the same is opened and put in good order by the petitioners as it formerly was that the propritors o of property maybe permitted to inclose the same.

    Jeremiah Rust was this day duly and constitutionally elected constable in Captain Midyett company for the county of Madison who thereupon took the several oaths prescribed by the constitution and laws of this state and entered into bond with George C. Rust and Jordan G. Stokes his securities in the penalty of and condition prescribed by law.

    Allen Fuller, Woodard Roan and Bennett Maxey was this day duly and constitutionally elected constables in the county of Madison who thereupon entered into bond and took the several oaths prescribed by the laws and constitution of the state with their securities, Allen Fuller with John F. Draper & William Cartwright. Woodward Roan with John Bowen & Henry Roan and Bennett Maxy with John Hardgraves & Joseph Lin conditioned for the faithful discharge of their appointments.

    Ordered that the report of the jury of view appointed at June term last to mark a road commencing at a point where the jury of view appointed by Shelby County Court strikes the West boundary of the county South of Madison and thence East wardly across the county, crossing Big Hatchie at a place known by the name of Fowler's ferry to the East boundary of said county on a direction to Browns ferry on Tennessee river be received and that Nathaniel Steel be appointed overseer from the West Boundary of the county on said road to the dividing ridge West of Porters creek to work all the hands South of Hatchie as far East of said ridge and that Joseph Fowler be appointed overseer from said ridge to the county line and work all the hands in said county to South of the fourth Section.

P208
    On petition filed ordered that the following persons towit John Murray, Stephen Bryan, Hugh Lacy, Clabourn Chisum, William Sanders, Joshua Haskell, William Dawing, James Williamson, John Gilliam, John Bryan, Stephen Lacy and George Williamson, or any five of them be a jury of view to mark and lay off a road commencing at a point where the road crossing at Shannon's landing strikes

P208 the high land on the South side of Forked Deer river, from thence to a bluff
Cont. between the mouth of Big Black Creek & Jefferick creek on Big Hatchie thence on
a cirection t the center of a county Southwest of Madison as far as the jurisdiction of Madison County and make report to the next term of court.
On petition filed:
     Ordered that the road lying South of Hatchie leading from Fowlers ferry
to the South boundary of the State be discontinued but with the permission to
John Murray to open and keep the same in repair as a public road.
     Ordered that the report of the jury of view viewing a road from Jackson
to Harris Bluff be received and that William C. Mitchell be appointed overseer
from town to McLennans Creek and Bird B. Smith from said creek to the 2nd.
Creek West of Wortham and Alfred Kennedy from thence to the Bluff and John G.
Carithers divide the hands and furnish the overseer with a list of hands.
     Ordered that William C. Love be appointed overseer of the road in place of
John Tidwell. John F. Draper in Captain William company this day resigned his
appointment as aforesaid.
     Ordered that the order made at the last term of this court appointing
a jury of view to make alteration in the road leading on by George Todds where
it passes through James Vaulx land be renewed and that instead of running said
road as directed by said order they run as follows leaving said road at the North
east corner of James Vaulx land, running thence West on said Vaulx North boundary
line as far as the jury of view may think fit and thence Southweatardly to intersect the old road at the bridge on Dry creek and make report to this term.

P209   Ordered that Champness Mading and Gabriel Chandler be appointed overseers
of the road in the place of Elijah Harmil Champness Mading from Jones Creek to
McIvers branch to the head of young's branch to work all the hands East of McIver
branch.
     Ordered that the report of the jury of view appointed at June term to mark
and lay off a road crossing at Jones ferry be received and that West Harris be
appointed overseer of the road from the county line South to Jone's ferry and
work the following hands, to wit, Stephen Bennett Sherald Tisdale, William Tisdale
James Tisdale, Allen Dillon, Asa Robeson, Obediah May, Thomas Joiner, George
Terry, William McLaughlin and brothers, John Kirk all living within five miles
of said road and that Thomas Clift be appointed overseer of the road from Jone's
ferry to the road laid off by the county court of Shelby below William Shenaults
and work the following hands, to wit, Col. Polks hands, Samuel Polk's hands
Capt. McNeil hands William Ramny, W. Arnold, Benjamin Gay Bryant Gay Wiley Jones
hands, William Shenault and all in five miles of said road to open and keep in
repair said road.
     Ordered that William C. Mitchell be allowed four dollars per day for servin
four days as a juror of view. Ordered that John J. Smith be allowed four dollars
for four days service as a jjuror of view. Ordered that Thomas M Dement be allowed two dollars for two days service as a juror of view. Ordered that Bird B.
Smith be allowed four dollars for four days service as a juror of view. Ordered
that James L. Wortham be allowed four dollars for four days service as a juror
of view . Ordered that William Braden be allowed two dollars for two days service
as a juror of view. Ordered that John Graves be allowed four dollars for four
days service as a juror of view.
     Frederick Miller came into court and made oath of killing one wolf over
four months in the county of Madison.
P210   Ordered that Lawrence McGuire be allowed five dollars for serving five
days as a juror of view.
     Ordered that Joshua Haskill be allowed ten dollars for serving ten days
as a juror of view.
     Ordered that Henry N. Caulter be allowed one dollar for serving one day
as a juror of view.

P210   Ordered that John Guthrie be allowed three dollars for serving three days
Cont. as a juror of view.

Ordered that Nathanel Bridgman be allowed five dollars for serving five
days as a juror of view, on the road leading to MdGuires ferry.

Ordered that John B. Cross and Joseph Linn, Esq. to examine Nancy Cloud
and Sally Newsom whether they do freely and voluntarily and without persuasion
or threats of their husbands relinquish their rights of dower to the land conveyed in a deed of bargain and sale from their husband Joseph Cloud and ___
Newsom and themselves.

Ordered that Thomas Allison be allowed five dollars for serving five days
as a juror of view.

Ordered that John Garrison be allowed five dollars for serving five days
as a juror of view.

Ordered that John Hargrave be allowed ifity two dollars for serving as a
commissioner appointed by the County Court of Madison thirteen days.

Ordered that Joseph Lynn be allowed sixty eight dollars for serving seventeen days a commissioner appointed by the county court of Madisonl

P211   Ordered that Jacob Purtle be released from paying double tax on two black
polls for the year 1823 who now lists the same.

A bond from John McIver to John B. Hogg for the conveyance of seven hundred
and eighty six acres of land was this day produced in open court and the execution thereof duly proven by the oath of James Jones one of the subscribing witnesses thereto the probat of William B. G. Kinblingswor being theretofore taken
was ordered to be so certified.

A deed of bargain and sale from Henry Rutherford for 525 acres of land to
Griffith Rutherford, a deed fo bargain and sale from Henry Rutherford to Elizabeth Crenshaw for five hundred and two acres was this day produced in open court
and the execution of them duly proven by the oath of Benjamin Porter and Benjamin
Jordan to be their acts and deeds and ordered to be so certified. A deed of bargain and sale from James Vaulx to George Todd for twenty three and three eights
acres of land was this day produced in open court and the execution thereof acknowledged by the sames James Vaulx to be his acr and deed and ordered to be so
certified.

A deed of bargain and sale from Richard Smith for himself and as Adm. of
Benjamin Smith to John C. McLemore ames Vaulx and James Carithers was this day
produced in open court and proven by the oath of Woodfin the probat of John
B. Hogg being taken on a former day of court was ordered to be so certified.

P212   A deed of bargain and sale from Richard Smith to John C. McLemore, James
Vaulx and James Carithers was this day produced in open court and proven by the
oath of M. Woodfin the probat of John B. Hogg having been taken on a former day
of court was ordered to be so certified.

Court then adjourned until tomorrow morning nine o'clock.
                                        H. Haralson   JP.
                                        J. B. Cross   JP.
                                        Jno. G. Carithers JP.

P211   A deed of bargain and sale from Henry Rutherford to Benjamin Porter for one
hundred fifty acres of land, Adeed of bargain and sale from Henry Rutherford to
Benjamin Jordon for three hundred five acres of landwere this day produced in
open court and the execution thereof duly proven by the oath of Benjamin Jordon
and William C. Chambers to be their act and deeds and ordered to be so certified.

P212 Tuesday Morning 16th. Sept. 1823
     Court met agreeable to adjournment. Present: Herndon Haralson, John
B. Cross John G. Carithers, Samuel Taylor and Stephen Jarman, Gentlemen, Justices.

P212   Alfred Kennedy came intoccourt and made oath of killing three wolves over
the age of four months and three under the age of four months within the jurisdiction of Madison County and ordered to be so certified.

        Barney Chambers came into open court and made oath of killing one wolf over
the age of four months in the county of Madison and ordered that it be so certified.

        Richard C. Allen who was on yesterday appointed Solicitor General pro tem
during the present term of this court, this day came into open court and took
the necessary oath prescribed by law for the faithful discharge of his appointment.

        Henning Pace, Sanford Edwards, Jacob Jill, James Young, Samuel Wilson,
William C. Mitchell James Tedford and Michael Fisher are all discharged as jurors
at the present term.

        Ordered that John T. Porter and William Alexander, delinquent jurors, be
fined N1 di until they come in & then cause at next term.

P213   David Jernigan this day came into court and made oath of serving three days
as a juror of view in the county of Madison who was thereupona allowed the sum of
one dollar per day for the same.

        The Sheriff this day made return of the writ of veniri facias to him direct-
ed by the last term of the county court, who summoned all the persons name in
said veniri except William Justice in persuance of which the following persons
were then attending: Francis Taylor, Hance Loramore Langster Glover, John P.
Thomas, Jason H. Wilson, Robert Lowery Bird B. Smith, William Love, James Haley
Robert Newsom, Jesse M Hanna Richard Coop, Stephen Lacy and Jonathan Welch and
thereupon the following persons to wit. Francis Taylor, Vance Lorrance Langester
Glover John P. Thomas Jason H. Wilson, Rovert Lowery Bird V. Smith William Love
James Haley, Robert Newsom, Jesse M Hanna Richard Coop & Stephen Lacy with Francis
Taylor their foreman were elected, empanelled and sworn and charged as a Grand
Jury to inquire into and for the body of the county of Madison who thereupon
entered to consider of presentments.

        A deed of bargain and sale from William Willburn to Young E. Wilson for
seventy acres of land was this day produced in open court and acknowledged by the
said William Wilburn to be his act and deed and ordered to be so certified.

        A deed of bargain and sale from George Shannon and Finis W. Shannon to
Samuel H. Shannon for eighty-five and half acres of land was this day produced
in open court and the execution thereof acknowledged by Finis W. Shannon of the
grantors and proven by the oath of A. L. Martin one of the witnesse thereto and
ordered to be certified.

P214   A deed of bargain and sale from Bartholmew C. Stewart to William Liggett
for ninety five acres of land was this day produced in open court and the execution acknowledged by the said Bartholomew C. Stewart to be his act and deed and
ordered to be so certified.

        The Grand Jury returned into court the following presentments, to wit one
against William Pace for an assault, one against Malcolm Johnson for an assault,
and one against, Henning Pace for an assault one against William Pace for an
assault Alsey Pace for an assault, all indorsed by Francis Taylor foreman of the
Grand Jury a true bill and it is thereupon ordered by the court that copias
issues returnable here at next term.

        This day John B. Cross and Joseph Linn Esquires the commissions appointed
by the court returned into court the dedimus protest atum to them directed say
they have under their office as hands pruately examined Nancy Cloud and Sally
Newsom separately and apart from their husbands and that they signed and sealed
a deed of bargain and sale from Joseph F. Cloud, Nancy Cloud, James Newsom and
Sally Newsom to John Stoven for one hundred and seventeen acres by their consent
without coertion from their said husbands and acknowledged in open court by the
said Joseph F. Cloud and James Newsom which is ordered to be certified.

P214   This day the appearance bail of Willoughby Powell came into court and re-
Cont.leased himself as such and thereupon Joseph Linn Esq. came into court and acknowledged himself bound as the appearance bail of said Powell which is ordered accordingly.

      Ordered John C McLemore be released from paying double taxes on the follow-
ing tracts of land for the year 1823 to wit on 80 acres tract granted said Mc#
* Lemore also another 30 acre tract granted to said McLemore and one other tract
of seventy five acres entry No. 687 in the 10th. district which land he now
lists for the year aforesaid.

P215   Court then adjourned until nine o(clock tomorrow morning.

                              H. Haralson JP.
                              Jno G. Carithers   JP.
                              Sam Taylor   JP.

Wednesday morning 17th. Sept 1823
      Court met agreeable to adjournment. Present, The Worshipful Herndon
Haralson, John G. Carithers and Samuel Taylor, gentlemen Justices.
      A deed of bargain and sale from John C. McLemore to Harris Bradford for one
hundred sixty acres of land was this day acknowledged by the said John C. Mc-
Lemore to be his act and deed and ordered to be so certified.

Thomas E. Dement   )
vs.   )   Case
Thomas Bowling   )
      This cause is continued by consent of parties until next term.

Thomas M. Dement)
vs.   )   Case Ordered same as above
Thomas Bowling   )
      George Mizell comes into open court and records his stock mark as follows,
to wit, swallow fork in the right ear and over half crop in the left.
      The Grand Jury this day returned into court and indictment against Sam
Shannon for an assault with the following indorsement A true bill, Francis Taylor
foreman of the Grand Jury, and it is ordered by the court that a capias issue.

P216 Thomas M Dement)
vs.   )   Case
Thomas Bowling   )
      It is ordered by the court that the plaintiff have leave to take the de-
positions of Samuel and Charles Howard by giving ten days notice in the state
and twenty out of the state.

Thomas M Dement)
vs.   )   Case
Thomas Bosling   )
Same rule as above

James McCutchen   )
vs.   )   Case
Madison McLaurine)
      This day came the parties aforesaid by their attorneys and thereupon came
a jury to wit, Jonathan Walsh, John Fassel, Wilson Brown, John H. Ball, Thomas
M Dement, Richard A Akils, John Harrison, Thomas Grissom, James Avery, Jeremiah
Brown, Ruben P. T. Stone and James ohnson who being elected, tried and sworn
the truth to speak upon the issue joined went out of court to consult of their
verdict and some time returned into court and declared they courld not agree on
their verdict, therefore by consent of the parties and with the assent of the court

*by Grant No 15644 dated 20th. Febuary 1822 and the other tract for 35½ acres granted
to said McLemore.

P218 Jonathan Walsh one of the jurors is withdrawn and the rest of said jurors from
Cont. rendering their verdict are discharged and the cause to be continued until next
term of this court for a new trial.

P217 William Wilson   )
       vs.   )   Case
     Thomas Grissom   )

This day the parties aforesaid by their attorneys and thereupon came a jury
of good and lawful men, to wit, William Espy, Samuel D. Waddell, James Stalkeep
Madison McLaurine, John T. Connolly, Francis Ragsdale, Clark Spencer, John
M Walker, Thos. Boling, John I Smith, John Tidwell and Joseph Dillard, who being
elected tried and sworn the truth to speak upon the issue joined this day went
out of court to consult of their verdict and sometime returned into court and
declared they could not agree in their verdict thereupon by consent of the partie
and with the assent of the court William Espy one of the jurors is withdrawn
and the rest of the jury from rendering their verdict are discharged and the
cause to be continued until the next term of this court.

     Isaac Walton   )
       vs.   )   Debt
     John Rutherford   )

This day came the parties aforesaid by their attorneys and thereupon came
a jury to wit, Jonathan Walsh, John Fussell, Wilson Brown, John H. Bell, Thomas
M Dement, Richard A. Akels, John Harrison, Thomas Grisom, James Avery Jeremiah
Brown, Ruben P. T. Stone, and James Johnson, who being elected tried and sworn,
will and truly to try the issue joined upon their oaths do say they find the
defendant hath not paid the debt of one hundred dollars as the plaintiff in his
declaration hath alleged and assess his damages by reason of the detention thereof to nine dollars and twenty-five cents. It is therefore considered by the court that the said plaintiff recover against the defendant the debt aforesaid together with the damages aforesaid by the jurors aforesaid in manner and form aforesaid assessed as also his costs by him about his suit in this behalf expended etc.

     Bennet Smith   )
       vs.   )   Debt
     James D. Carithers   )

This day came the plaintiff by his attorney and the said defendant doth
not come and it appearing to the court that the death of the defendant was suggested at the last term of this court and time given for the proper parties to
appear according to the act of assembly in such case made and provided and the
said cause having been called, no party appearing in place of the defendant it
is ordered by the court that the said suit be dismissed and that the plaintiff
pay the cost theretofore accrued in said cause.

     John Thomas Brook etc.
       vs.
     James D. Carithers

This day came the plaintiff by his attorney and said defendant doth not
come and it appearing to the court that the death of the defendant was suggested
at the last term of this court and time given for the proper parties to appear
according to an act of assembly in such cases made and provided and said cause
having been called no party appearing in place of the defendant, it is ordered
by the court that said suit be dismissed and that the pltff pay the cost heretofore accrued in said cause.

P219 John Thomas Brook & etc.
       vs.
     James D. Carithers   )   Debt.

B219   Same condition and decesions as above .
Cont.

    Benjamin Booth   )
    vs.   )   Case
    C. I. Ragsdale &   )
    Matthew Johnson   )
    John Thomas Brook etc.)
    vs.   )   Debt
P220 James D. Carithers   )
    Same conditions and decesion

        It is ordered by the parties and with the assent of the court that this
cause be continued until next term.

    Samuel D. Waddill   )
    vs.   )   Appeal
    George Gentry   )
        This day came the parties aforesaid by their attorneys and thereupon came
a jury, to wit, John Harrison Thomas Grisom Wilson Brown, Madison McLaurine,
James Johnson Jonathan Walsh William Dean, Anthony F. Gray Thomas Larramore,
John Fussell, M Drummond and Henry D. Collins who being elected tried and sworn
upon their oaths do say we of the jury do find the matter in dispute in favor
of the plaintiff and do assess his damages to twenty eight dollars and 40 cents.
It is therefore considered by the court that the said plaintiff recover of the
defendant the damages aforesaid by the jury aforesaid in form aforesaid assessed
& also his costs etc.

    Joseph Tedford   )
    vs.   )   Appeal
    Henry Cassells   )
        This day came the defendant by his attorney and the plaintiff came not and
it is suggested here to the court that the said plaintiff hath departed this life
and the same is not denied and thereupon it is ordered by the court that this
cause be continued until next term.

P221 Jordan G. Stokes   )
    vs.   )   Case
    J. Smith   )
        It is ordered by the court with the assent of the parties that this cause
be continued until next term.

    Jordon G. Stokes   )
    vs.   )   Case
    John I. Smith   )   Same rule as above

    Daniel C. Tradewell   )
    vs.   )   Debt
    William R. Hess   )
        This day came the parties aforesaid by their attorneys and thereupon came
the defendant in proper person and says he cannot gainsay the plaintiffs action
against him for one hundred and ninety six dollars mentioned and six dollars and
eighty four cents damages the debt in the declaration.. It is therefore considere
by the court that the plaintiff recover of the defendant the debt aforesaid with
the six dollars and eighty four cents damages sustained by reason of the detention thereof together with the costs of said suit by the plaintiff herein expended etc.

P222   A deed of bargain & sale from Laurence McGuire to the firm of John Gill Jr.
& Co. and unto Little & Telford was this day produced in open court and proven
by the oath of John R. McGuire one of the subscribing witnesses thereto and
ordered to be filed for further probate.
       County then adjourned until tomorrow morning nine o'clock.
                                   Sam Taylor JP.
                                   Guy Smith   JP
                                   B. G. Stewart JP

Thursday morning 18th. Sept.
       Court met agreeable to adjournment, Present: Bartholomew G. Stewart Samuel
Taylor Guy Smith.
       Ordered that the list of Christopher Strong for the following tracts of
land listed for taxes for the year 1823, to wit, 640 acres Rangel Section 9
11 district.
309 2/3 Acres in Range 1 Section 10-10the district
219   Acres in Range 3 Section 9-10th district
100   Acres in Range 2 Section 11-10th district
40   Acres in Range 3 Section 11-10th district
20   Acres in Range 5 Section 11010th district
15 acres in Range   5 Section 10-10th district
499½   Acres in Range 1 Section 10-10th district
and--that-in-Range-1-section-19-10th-district
And that the clerk receive the taxes for the county & state for the year aforesaid.

P223 Bartholomew G. Stewart)
     vs.   )   Case
     Grant & Grissom   )
       On affidavit of Grant, one of the defendants, this case is continued until
next term of this court.

     William Love)
     vs   )   Case
     John Weir   )
       By consent of the parties this cause is continued until next term of this
court.

     John T. Porter)
     vs.   )   Appeal
     Thomas Allison)
       This day came the parties aforesaid by their attorneys and the motion to
dismiss the appeal being argued and due debtberation being had thereon, it is con
sidered by the court that said motion be overruled, and that the plaintiff have
leave to amend the bond given for the prosecution of said appeal to which opinion
of the court the defendant by his council except and filed his bill of exceptions
P224 John Bill   )
     vs.   )   Debt
     Henry L. Gray)
       This day came the parties aforesaid by their attorneys and thereupon came a
jury, to wit, Elijah Haynee, Walentine Sevier, Jonathan Welsh, Thomas Jones,
William Dean, Spencer Grant, William Mathis, James Vaulx, Mac Drummond, John
Fussel, John McBride and Benjamin Booth, who being elected, tried and sworn will
and truly to try the issue joined upon their oaths do say We of the jury do find
for the plaintiff the sum of one hundred and thirty dollars, the debt in the
declaration mentioned and do assess his damages by reason of the detention thereof to twenty one dollars 12½ cents. It is therefore considered by the court
that the plaintiff recover against the defendant the debt aforesaid together with

P224 the damages aforesaid in manner and form by the jurors aforesaid in form afore-
Cont.said assessed and also his costs by him about his suit in this behalf expended etc

George Lyne   )
vs.   ) Debt
Willoughby Powell)

     By consent of the parties this cause is contenued until next term of this court.

P225 William Love)
vs.   ) Covenant
John Houston   )

     This day came the parties aforesaid by their attorneys and thereupon came a jury to wit, Elijah Haynes, Valentine Sevier, Jonathan Walsh, Thomas Jones, William Dean, Spencer Grant, William Mathis, James Vaulx Mac Drummond. John Fussel, John McBridge and Benjamin Booth who being elected tried and sworn to will and truly try the issue joined do say We of the jury find that the defendant hath not will and truly kept and performed his covenant as in pleading he hath alleged and we do assess the plaintiff damages by reason thereof to one hundred thirty dollars thirty one and one fourth cents. It is therefore considered by the court that the plaintiff recover of the defendant the said sum of one hundred and thirty dollars thirty one and one fourth cents, the damages aforesaid in form aforesaid assessed together with his costs by him in his suit expended and the defendant in mercy etc.

Robert Box   )
vs.   ) Debt
Samuel H. Swan & Thomas Shannon   )

     This day came the parties aforesaid by their attorneys and thereupon came a jury to wit, Elijah Hayne, Valentine Sevier, Jonathan Walsh, Thomas Jones William Dean, Spencer Grant, William Mathis, James Vaulx Mac Drummond John Fussel John McBride and Benjamin Booth who being elected tried and sworn will and truly to try the issues joined do say We of the Jury do find for the plaintiff-one hundred eleven dollars, the debt in the declaration thereof to four dollars. It is therefore considered by the court that the plaintiff recover of the defend-and the debt aforesaid together with his damages aforesaid in form aforesaid by the jurors aforesaid assessed and also his costs by him about his suit in this behalf expended, etc.

P226 William Harris, for use of)
Dokes Executor   )
vs.   ) Debt
John G. Carithers   )

     This day came the parties aforesaid by their attorneys and thereupon came a jury, to wit Elijah Haynie, Valentine Sevier, Jonathan Walsh, Thomas Jones, William Dean, Spencer Grant, William Mathis, James Vaulx, Mac Drummond John Fussel, John McBride and Benjamin Booth who being elected tried and sworn the truth to speak upon the issue joined do say We of the jury do find for the plaintiff one hundred thirty four dollars & 10cents, the balance of the debt in the declaration mentioned and do further say the defendant has no set off and assess the plaintiff damages sustained by reason of the detention thereof to two dollars 12$\frac{1}{4}$ cents, It is therefore considered by the court that the plaintiff recover against the defendant the balance of debt aforesaid together with the damages aforesaid in form aforesaid by the jury aforesaid assessed and also he's costs by him about his suit in this behalf expended etc.

George Mizell
vs.
Robert Houston) Appeal

P226   By consent of the parties this case is continued until next term of this
Cont. court.

Mathias Deberry   )
vs   )   Debt.
Hays & Haskell   )
         It is ordered by the court that the plaintiff have leave to amend his writ
by paying the cost of the amendment.

P227 Samuel D. Waddill   )
vs.   )   Appeal
George Gentry   )
         This day came the defendant by his attorney and prayed an appeal to the next
term of the circuit court from a judgment rendered herein against him on a former
day of court which was granted him on his entering into bond with Bartholomew
C. Stewart and G. R. Graham his securities in the penalty of two hundred dollars
for the prosecution of said appeal.
         A deed of bargain and sale from Henry L. Gray to Sugars McLemore for sixty
five acres of land was this day produced in open court and the execution thereof
acknowledged by the said Henry L. Gray to be his act and deed and ordered to be
so certified.

State   )
vs.   )   Affray
John Ridings & John Jackson   )
         This day came as well the solicitor general on the part of the state as the
defendant in their proper person who being arraigned upon their arraignment, plead
guilty as charged in the indictment, it is therefore considered by the court
that they make their peace with the state by the payment of one dollar each and
that the plaintiff go thereof hence and recover of the defendant the fine aforesaid
together with the costs about her suit in this behalf expended and the defendants
in mercy etc.

P228 State   )
vs.   )   An affray
Joseph F. Cloud   )
         This day came as well the solicitor general on the part of the state as
the defendant in his proper person, who being arraigned, upon his arraignment
plead not guilty and for his trial put himself upon God and his country and thereupon came a jury of good and lawful men, to wit, Jonathan Walsh, John Armstrong,
John Fussel, George W. Taylor, John Jackson, James Stalkeep, John Tidwell, Mac
Drummond, William Dean, Griffith Graham, Drury Bittis and Samuel A. Lyon who being
elected, tried and sworn well and truly to try the issue, joined on their oath
do say that the defendant is not guilty as charged in the bill of indictment.
It is therefore considered by the court that the dependant go thereof hence without day and recover of the plaintiff his costs by him about his defense in this
costs by him about his defense in this behalf and etc.

State   )
vs.   )   An affray Plead guilty
Thomas Hill   )
         This day came as well the solicitor general on the part of the state as the
defendant in his proper person who being arraigned, upon his arraignment plead
guilty as charged in the bill of indictment. It is therefore considered by the
court that he make his peace with the state by the payment of 50¢ and that the
plaintiff go thereof hence and recover of the defendant her costs by her about

P229 this suit in this behalf expended and that the defendant be in mercy and the said
defendant remain in custody until he discharge the fine and costs aforesaid or
give security.

State   )
vs.   )
Samuel H. Shannon)

By consent of parties this cause is continued until next term of this court.

The last will and testament of James Hill was this day was this produced
in open court and the execution thereof duly proven as the last will and testament of the deceased by the oath of Robert Bedford, Lasus Fenning and Walter
Robertson subscribing witnesses thereto and ordered to be recorded and William
Hill an executor therein named came into court and agreed to take upon himself
the burthen and execution of said will who thereupon took the oath of an executor
and entered into bond with John I Smith and Jacov Miller his securities in the
penalty of three thousand dollars conditioned according to law whereupon it is
ordered that letters testamentary issue to said William Hill accordingly.

The Grand Jury this day returned into court an indictment against William
Pace for an assault and also a presentment against James Dorris for an assault.

A power of attorney from Lee Sullivan to Adam R. Alexander was this day
produced in open court and proven by the oath of David Jarrett one of the subscribing witnesses and filed for further probate.

A power of attorney from William Wilson and Francis Wilson to Benjamin
Thornbury was this day produced by the oath of Davidn Jarrett one of the subscribing witnesses and filed for further probate.

P230   A power of attorney from William Sutton and Harriet Sutton to Benjamin
Thornbury was this day produced in open court and the execution thereof duly
proven by the oath of William Powell and Moses Sutton subscribing witnesses there
to and ordered to be so certified.

A deed of bargain and sale from Lee Sullivan by his attorney in fact Adam
R. Alexander to Gabriel Anderson for one hundred sixty acres of land was this
day produced in open court and acknowledged by the said Adam R. Alexander atty.
as aforesaid to be his act and deed and ordered to be so certified.

Stephen Lacy comes into court and proves four days attendance as a juror of
view in the county of Madison who is allowed the sum of four dollars for the same.

John D. Shannon comes into court and proves three days attendance as a
constable attending on the Grand Jury at the present term.

Ordered that Sheriff Thomas Shannon be fined ten dollars for absenting
himself from this court.

Ordered that Thomas I. Smith constable summoned to attend on this court be
fined ten dollars for non attendance.

Ordered that Adam R. Alexander, Herndon Haralson and Robert Hughes be appointed commissioners to make a settlement with Patsy Doak executor of the last
will and testament of Robert Doak deceased in the estate of the decedent and report to the next term of this court.

P231   On motion it is ordered by the court that the following tracts of land be
listed for the state and county taxes for the year 1823, to wit,
One tract entered in the name of Elizabeth Nelson for 220 Acres No E533, 10th
dist. 6 range 9th. sec.
Ditto 420½ Acres   No. E333   10th. dist 5th. range 9sec.
Ditto 345½ Acres   No. E270   10th. Dist 5th. range 9sec.
John H. Poston 260 Acres E73 R. 4.5 S 10 10th. district
William Shaw 640 A" E"329"R 6 S."o 10th district
Philip Haddon 1000 Acres E. 328 R.5 S. 9 10th. dist.
Anderson Goff 75 Acres E294 R.4 S.9 10th. dist.

P231 James Scruggs   250 Acres E.294 R. 5 S.9   10th. Dist.
Cont.Ditto   250 Acres E556   4 6   10th. Dist.
    William Dixon   100   "   " 557 " 3 " 9   10th. Dist.
    Same   500   "   " 190 " 4 " 10   10th. Dist.
    Same   300   "   " 564 " 6 " 9   10th. Dist.
    Same   500   "   " 791 " 4 " 6   10th. Dist.
    Same   50   "   " 454 " 3 " -   10th. Dist.
    John McCollester
    & others   5000 "   " 624 "6 " 9   10th. Dist.

	Acres	Entry	Range	Section	District	
Simmes & Greer	213½	530	6	9	10	tax pd.
John Rhea	500	701	3.4	10	10	tax pd.
Richard Hightower	18	---	4.	6	10	tax pd.
Heirs of Dal Wheaton	12	---	5	9	10	tax pd.
Richard Hightower	640	---	1	6	11	tax pd.
Same	73¾	---	1	6	11	Tax pd.
O. B. Hays	750	---	1	6	11	
Same	216	---	1	6	11	
Same	268	---	1	6	11	
Same & R. W. Green	1500	---	1	9	11	
Heirs of J. P. McGill	640	---	1	6	11	
Same	180	---	12	9	11	
Same	100	---	1	6	11	
Samuel Edmondson	390	---	2	9	11	tax pd.
Same	640	---	1	6	11	tax pd.
Arthur Campbell	640	---	1	6	11	
P232 Huling & Hightower	640	---	1	6	13th.	paid
James Scruggs	500	---	1	6	10th.	
Same	250	---	1	6	11th.	
Heirs of Tisdale
&Wheaton	640	---	1	9	11th	tax pd.
O. B. Hays	320	799	5	9	11th.	
Same	227½	325	5	9	11th.	
William L. Brown	1000	192	3	11	10th.	tax pd.
William P. Anderson	3119½	534	11	1	13th.	
Thomas Hopkins		~~838~~	~~1-618~~	~~1~~		
	238	1018	1	9	10th.	
Francis McGavock	75	1009	1	8	10	
John Braham	112	962	6	11	10	
Christopher Stump	80	980	3	8	10	
Humphrey Hardy	144	944	1	9	10	
John Whitaker	85	1017	1	9	10	
John Chambers	640	1013	2	8	10	
Blackfan & others	85½	961	6	11	10	
Jones Hogg	113¾	987	1	8	10	

Commissioners of the town of Jackson)
vs.   )   Debt
Robert Wilson & Thomas Shannon   )
        This day came the plaintiffs aforesaid by their attorney and thereupon
came Robert Wilson in his proper person into court and confesses judgment in
favor of Bartholomew G. Stewart, Joseph Linn, John Hardgraves Adam R. Alexander
and James Trousdale for the use of the commissioners of the town of Jackson for
fifty dollars debt & damages for the detention of said debt to this time to
37½ cents and by consent of parties execution is stayed until the next term of

P232 this court and Thomas Shannon in his proper person confesses judgment for the
Cont. above debt as security of said Robert Wilson in consideration of the stay of
execution until next term of this court and cost of suit. It is therefore considered by the court that the plaintiff recover of the defendant aforesaid the
P233 debt aforesaid with damages aforesaid together with the costs of this suit.

Griffith W. Rutherford)
vs.   )   Debt
Benjamin Porter   )

The plaintiff by his attorney comes into court and dismisses his suit
and assumes upon him self the cost of said suit. It is therefore considered by
the court that the defendant recover of the plaintiff his costs by him about
his suit in this behalf expended and the Pltff in mercy etc.

Court then adjourned until tomorrow morning nine o'clock.

W. B. Cross   JP.
Jno. G. Caruthers JP.
Guy Smith   JP.

Friday Morning 17th September 1823.

Court met according to adjournment. Present, the Worshipful Herndon Haralson John G. Carithers, Guy Smith justices.

Joseph Linn   )
vs.   )   Demmurrer
Thos. Williamson   )

This cay came the parties by their attorneys and thereupon the demurrer
to the plaintiffs declaration being solemnly argued & due deliberation being had
thereon it is considered by the (court) that the defendants demurrer to the
plaintiffs declaration be overruled. It is therefore considered by the court
that the plaintiff recover of the defendant in this case the sum of one hundred
dollars the sum in the declaration mentioned together with $4.50 interest besides
his costs by him in this behalf expended and the defendant in mercy etc.

P234 Francis McGavock)
vs.   )   Demurrer
Thomas Williamson   )

This day came the parties by their attorneys and thereupon the dumurer
to the plaintiffs declaration being solemnly argued and due deliberation being
had thereon it is considered by the court here that the defendants demurrer be
overruled and that the plaintiff recover of the defendant the sum of one hundred
thirty dollars the sum in the declaration mentioned together with three dollars
and 57 cents the interest accrued besides the costs by him in this behalf expended and the defendant in mercy etc.

On motion ordered John Carson came into open court and applied for license
to keep an ordinary in the county of Madison which was granted him and he thereupon entered into bond with J. H. Wilson and James Stewart his securities in the
penalty and conditions prescribed by law.

A deed of bargain and sale from Calvin Jones to Emaline Jones Higher for
three hundred sixty six acres of land was this day produced in open court and
acknowledged by the said Jones to be his act and deed ordered to be certified.

Ordered by the court that the deposition of Henry Rutherford & others for
perpetuating testimony which was returned sealed by the commissioners appointed
by first day of the term and opened in the presence of said court be received
ordered to be recorded.

P235   John Hall this day returns an inventory of the amount of sales of the estate of William Q. Hall deceased.

On motion, Ordered that Thomas Shannon, Sheriff, be released from paying
the fine imposed by an order of this court on yesterday. And also that Thomas

P235 I Smith be released from paying the fine imposed by order of this court on
Cont.yesterday.

Henry Yarbrough   )
vs.   )   Case
John W. Cook   )
            This day came the defendant in his proper person and says he cannot gain-
say the plaintiffs action thereof against him for the sum of four hundred twelve
dollars sixty two cents. It is therefore considered by the court that the plaintiff recover of the defendant said sum of four hundred twelve dollars sixty two
cents and also his costs by him about his suit in this expended and the defendant
in mercy etc. and the plaintiff consents that he will stay execution six months.
            Ordered that the following tracts of land be listed for taxes for the year
1823 (to wit) one tract in the name of Joseph Byers for 1500 Acres one tract in
the name of James Byers for 2000 acres, one tract in the name of Edmond Swanson
for 106 acres.
            Ordered that James Cockrill be appointed overseer of the road in place of
Robert Clanton to work and keep in repair the road on the South side of the river
from Shannon landing through the swamp to high land.
P236   Ordered that the sheriff repay Mark R. Cockrill the taxes which he paid on
the following tracts of land for the year 1821 (to wit) one tract of three hundred
twenty acres, One tract of one hundred ten acres, one tract of 117½ acres and one
tract of 640 acres all entered in the name of Mark R. Cockrill which lands were
not liable for the payment of taxes that year as appears from the certificate
of the surveyor of the 10th district for which district those said land were
entered.
            Ordered that the report of the jury of view appointed at the last term of
this court to mark and lay off a road leading from Jackson to McGuires Ferry on
Big Hatchie be received to where same crosses the county line, and that Britain
Sanders be appointed overseer of said road from where the same leaves the road
crossing at Shannon's landing, and that he be allowed to work the hands of
Green Hill the hands of Simon Turnes, to open and keep same in repair with the
addition of all the hands living West of Cain Creek and East of the County line
for the purpose of opening said road. And that Laurence McGuire be permitted to
open and keep up the aforesaid road from the county line to his ferry on Big
Hatchie river as view by the jury and reported and that the same be extablished
as a public road.
            Ordered that the reports of the jury of view appointed by an order of the
present term of this court be received as marked and laid off from the road passing by Pitts Chandlers to Forked Deer river where a former jury marked out the
same and that Pitts Chandler be appointed overseer of the road with all the hands
being living between Jones & Butler's creeks and between the road which runs by
Major Goldson's and the river with the additional hands of Major Colson, Ryland
Chandler, Parks Chandler, John Starns, Moses Starns, William Mayo, and Herndon
Haralson. Haralson to work thereon to open said road.
            Ordered that the report of the jury of view appointed the present term of
this court to view and mark out a road from the public square to the bridge below McIvers Mill be received and that Benjamin Goldson be appointed overseer to
open and keep in repair said road and to work the following hands, James
Johnson, William Mayo Ryland Chandler, John Starnes, James Henderson Doveraux
Wynne, William Wilson, and all the other lawful hands living to the South
of them and al right angle from Tower and McIver's Mill to the river included in
said bounds, shall work on the same and keep it in repair.
            On motion and petition filed, ordered that the following persons(to wit)
Joel Dyer Matthew Robert, Hardy Blackwell, Asa Midyett, Henry H. Horn, Jarett
M Jelks, be a jury to view mark out and lay off a road commencing at Joel Dyers

P238 and running so as to intersect the Nasha Bluff road at the distance of about three miles and report to the next term of this court.

John Hall adm. of the extate of William Q. Hall, deceased, this day returned an inventory of the amount of the extate of the said defendant.

Ordered that the road leaving the road that leads by Ezekiel B. McKays at or near the said McKay's running Southeastwardly to the county line be 6____ ordered that the following hands be taken from the ____ which Daniel Ross is overseer of and added to John M Johnsons hands (to wit) Daniel Harkins and Hiram Harkins and Daniel Harkins Jr. and also the following hands, to wit, John Waggoner and hands, David Waggoner, John Waggoner, Jr. E Marsh and hands, Mr Tally and hands Mr Goodman and hands John Higgins, Mr. Toes and hands and Mr . Milton to keep in repair said road.

A deed of bargain and sale from John H. Ball and Sarah Ball to David Byrne for a certain lot of land was this day produced in open court and acknowledged by the said Sarah Ball she being privately examined separately and apart from her husband and that the same deed was signed by her own free will and voluntary act without threats or persuasion of her husband and ordered to be so certified.

Ordered that the order establishing a ferry on Big Hatchie on the lands of Wilie Jones in the name of William E. Butler, it appearing to the court that the said Wille Jones has sold all his right, title and interest in and to said ferry and premises to the said William E. Butler and that the ferry be established on the land of said Butler from the date of the order to said Wiley Jones to have the same effect as if first granted to W. E. Butler.

On motion ordered by the court that Roderick McIver, the clerk of the court be allowed the sum of twenty-five dollars for recording the list of taxes for the year 1823 and also the sum of twenty dollars for recording the survey on return of the list of lands and that the county trustee pay the same out of any monies not otherwise appropreated.

P239 On motion andpetition filed, ordered that the following persons, to wit Joshua Weaver, Hugh Lacy Stephen Lacy, John Armold Jr. Mr. Paulding, Henry Booth Robert Clanton, William Timms, John Murphy, and Mr. Cochran, or any five of them after being duly sworn, be a jury to view mark out and lay off a road in continuation of that from Shannon landing commencing at the high land on the South side of the river and running in a direction of the center of the county South of this so as to intersect the road leading from Butler's ferry on Hatchie at the county line on the waters of Clover Creek and report to the next term of this court

Ordered that the hands of Samuel Vaulx work on the road where George Todd is overseer.

Ordered that John P. Thomas be allowed one dollar for two days attendance as a juror for which a certificate has been issued, it appearing to the satisfaction of the court that the same has been lost.

Thomas Shannon this day came into court and entered into bond with Herndon Haralson, Guy Smith Samuel Taylor, Benjamin Gholston & Samuel H. Shannon his securities in the penalty of Five thousand dollars conditioned for the collection and payment of the State and county tax for the present year.

Mathias Deberry this day came into open court and entered into bond with Wilson Hutchinson, George Todd and Robert Clanton, his securities in the penal sum of Ten thousand dollars conditioned for the faithful discharge of the duties of Guardian of James W Heley and William P Heley who was by order of the last term of this court appointed guardian of said orphans and then entered into bond of $5,000.00 conditioned as above.

P240 Ordered that the following persons, to wit Gilbreath Naill, Joseph Eddings, Ezekiel B. McCoy, James Alexander, William Spencer Newton Harris, Champness Mading Elijah Haynie, William Ruleman Dock. Carpenter William Newhouse, Asa B. Midyett, W. C. Mitchell Matthias Deberry, Aquila Davis, Daniel Horton John H. Ball James Dorris, Wilson Hutchison Charles Sevier, Bignal Crook, John Redens, John

P240 Starnes, Parks Chandler & John T. Porter be appointed to attend at December term
Cont.of this court and that Thomas I Smith and John Shannon be a pointed toattend on
the court and jury at the same term.

Court then adjourned until tomorrow morning nine o'clock.

H. Haralson   JP.
Guy Smith   JP.
John G. CarithersJP.

Saturday 20th. Sept. 1823
Court met agreeable to adjournment, present, the worshipful Herndon Haralson Guy Smith, John G. Carithers, gentlemen justices.

John Branggan   )
vs.   ) Case
Joshua Haskill   )

This day came the parties aforesaid and agree to dismiss said suit at the
cost of the defendant, It is therefore considered by the court that the plaintiff recover against said defendant his costs by him about his suit in this behalf expended etc.

P241   Thomas J. Smith proves five days attendance on the court at the present
term & ordered to be so certified.

John C Boyd   )
vs.   ) Case
Wilson Hutchison   )

On motion of the plaintiff by his attorney leave is given him to take the
deposition of Cave Johnson of Montgomery County to be read in this case upon
giving the defendant twenty days notice of the time and place of taking the same.

Allen Pierce for the use of James Ball   )
vs.   ) Covenant
John Carvens   )

This day came the plaintiff by his attorney and the defendant being solemnly
called in this case, came not, but made default. It is therefore considered by
the court that a judgment be taken against him which is accordingly done and a
writ of inquiry awarded returnable to next term.

Commissioners of Town of   )
Alexanderie (now Jackson))
vs.   ) Debt
A. & J Greer   )

Same   )
vs   ) Debt
Anthony F. Gray & Thomas Shannon)

Same   )
vs.   ) Debt
Robert H. Wynne & James Brown)

P242 Commissioners of the Town of

Alexandria, now Jackson   )
vs.   ) Debt
James Moore & William Espy)

P242 Same   )
Cont.Vs.   )   Debt
Robert H and Joel Dyer   )

Commissions of the Town
of Alexanderia, now Jackson   )
vs.   )   Debt
James Brown & William Espy   )

This day came the parties in the foregoing cases by their attorneys and the defendants filed their first, second third and fourth pleas herein and the plaintiffs filed his demurrer to defendants third plea and the defendant their joinders thereto and the plaintiffs filed their replication to the fourth pleas and the defendants their joinders thereto and the plaintiffs moved the court not receive byt strike out the first and second pleas which was done by the court to which opindon the court the defendant accepted and prayed their bills of exception to be migned, sealed and enrolled and ordered to be made a part of the record herein which was done accordingly and the causes are continued until next term.

Peter and James Swanson came into court and lists one hundred and forty nine acres & a fraction of land entered in the loth. district, range three, section three of taxes for the year 1823.

William Stroud cames into court and lists $278\frac{1}{2}$ acres of land for taxes for the year 1823 and entered on the 10th section and 10th. district.

A deed of bargain and sale from Thomas Shannon to James H. Wilson for an eighth part of one acre of ground was this day acknowledged by the said Thomas Shannon to be his act and deed and ordered to be certified.

P243   A power of attorney from Archibald D. Murphy to Robert Hughes was produced in open court and proven by the oath of James Vaulx one of the subscribing witnesses thereto and ordered to be filed for further probate.

George C. Rust   )
vs.   )
John B. Cross   )

Ordered that writs of certiorari and supercedss issue in this case returnable to the next term of this court.

It appearing to the satisfaction of the (court) that Robert Sevier departed this life without having made any will or testament on motion of Charles Sevier administration of all and singular the goods and chattels rights and credits of Robert Sevier deceased is granted him who thereupon entered into and acknowledged bond in the penal sum of three hundred dollars, with James Dorris and Elisha Harles, his securities and took the oath of an administrator and it is ordered that letters of administration issue accordingly.

John Page
vs.
John T. Porter

The plaintiff by his attorney in this case moved the court to ament his declaration herein which was granted and done accordingly on the pliff. paying the cost of this term H.

                                H. Haralson   JP
                                Joseph Linn   JP.
                                John B. Cross JP.

P246 Jackson Monday 22nd. December 1823
        Be it remembered that on Monday the 22nd day of December 1823 at a courtof pleas and quarter sessions began and held in the town of Jackson.
Present, The Worshipful Herndon Haralson, William Draper, David Jarrett and

P246 Robert H. Dyer, Gentlemen, justices.
Cont.   James McCutchen, William E. Butler, William Spencer, William C. Love,
Mark Christian, Thomas Gordon, and Teophilis Sanders, seven of the gentlemen
named in the commission from his Excellency William Carroll, Esquire, Governor
of the State of Tennessee appeared in open court and took the several oaths
prescribed by the constitution and laws of the state as justices of the peace for
the county of Madison and thereupon took their seats upon the bench.

On motion and petition filed, it is ordered that Herndon Haralson have leave
to erect a water grist mill and saw mill on Butler's Creek on his own land between twenty and theirty poles above where the eighth section line crosses said
creek in this county.

Daniel Ross came into court and proves by his own rath of killing one wolf
in the dounty of Madison over the age of four months which is ordered to be
certified accordingly.

Ordered that Thomas Lofton be appointed overseer of the road in the place
of James Hill.

Ordered that the double taxes be remitted on the following track of land
for the year 1823 which is hereby listed for the same, to wit,

Those whose name entered	Acres,	District,	Range,	Section		
Joseph Phillips	2500	9	12	10		
Jonas Clark	270	9	2	10		
Stephen Alexander	166	9	1	10		
John Scott	59	9	1	10		
Patton & Irwin	151	9	1	10		
Malcolm Gilchrist	20	9	2	10		
John & Thomas I Kirkpatrick	333	9	2	10		
John Scott	105	9	1	9		
Patton & Irwin	425¼	9	1	9		
Anderson & Mitchell	200	9	2	10	Grant	
Ephrain Davidson	2000	13	6	1	118	
Same	2000	13	6	1	65	
Griffith Rutherford	1960	13	8-9	1	64 part of 2000	
Samuel Wilson	200	9	2	10	Conveyed Hugh Torrand	
P247 John Johnson	5000	10	2	89	Thomas Birdsheirs 640	
Ebenezer Pittygrove	565	13	7	3	John,Mary&Connolly Read	
Charles Browns heir	600	13	6	1		
Same	104	13	7	2		
James McCutchen	500	13	7	2	No warrent	
William McCutchen	120	13	7	2		
Calvin Jones	1000	9	1	8	419	
Ditto	640	10	3	8	557	
Ditto	360	10	3	8	401	
Ditto	366	10	3	8	315	
Ditto	274	10	3	8	476	
Ditto	640	10	3	4	363	
Ditto	640	10	3	6	497	
Ditto	274	10	4	2	595	
Ditto	1168	13	6	1	362 part of 2560 a.	

balance conveyed to Samuel
Polk

On motion and petition filed, it is ordered that double taxes be remitted for
the year 1823 on land owned by William Pillow and subject to taxes in Madison
County on his listing the same on due time and paying the single tax thereon.

Ordered that the board of commissioners for the Town of Jackson allow
Thomas Shannon the sum which the commissioners appointed by the act of Assembly
for fixing on the seat of justice of Madison County agreed to pay him for six
and a fraction acres of land purchased by them for the use of said county.

P247   Ordered that Benjamin Booth be appointed overseer of the road in the place
Cont.of James Cockrill and work all the hands that were assigned to said Cockrill.
        Thomas Crissom comes into court and proves by his own oath the killing of
two wolves in the county over the age of four months and ordered that same be
certified accordingly.
        Ordered that the property remaining unsold of the estate of William Griffith
deceased remain in the possession of the widow during her widowhood.

P248   Ordered that Herndon Haralson, Vincent Haralson, Bartholomew G. Stewart,
William E. Butler, Daniel Horton, Stokely D. Hays, William Arnold, Adam Alexander
James Trousdale & Robert Hughes commissioners of the town of Jackson be allowed
the sum of one dollar per day for serving the following number of days, to wit,

Hearndon Haralson	27 days
Vincent Haralson	24 days
Bartholomew G. Stewart	15 days
William E. Butler	16 days
Daniel Horton	23 days
Stokely D. Hays	11 days
Benjamin Arnold	7 days
Adam R. Alexander	6 days
James Trousdale	10 days
Robert Hughes	15 days

        And that the treasurer of said board pay the same out of any monies not
other wise appropreated.
        Ordered that Herndon Haralson be allowed the sum of two dollars and fifty
cents for a copy of the act of the General Assembly to be paid as aobve.
        Ordered that Joseph Linn, Herndon Haralson andWilliam Draper be appointed
commissioners to settle with the Admr. of James L. Price, deceased and make report thereof to the next term of this court.
        William C. Roads came into court and proved by his own oath the killing of
two wolves in the county of Madison over the age of four months and ordered to be
certified accordingly.

P249   Ordered that Joseph Linn, Dincan McIver and David Jarrett Wsquires be appointed commissioners to settle with the Admr. of Lewis Jones, deceased, and make
report thereof to the next term of this court.
        On motion andpetition filed ordered that Martin Lorance be permitted to
alter the road referred to in said petition according to the prayer of same.
        On motion, it is ordered that the order granting a road to be layed off and
marked from Jackson to Mt. Pinson crossing the river at the ferry kept near W. E.
Butlers be renewed and that the following persons, to wit, Daniel Haskins, Hardin Harkins, Randolph Phelps, William C. Love, William Tayo, John Heggins and
Minor Marsh or any five of them after being duly sworn be a jury to view and
mark out the same and make report to the next term of court.
        Ordered that William E. Butler, Thomas Gordon, and Robert Murray be appoint
ed commissioners to settle with the sheriff and make report to the present term
and also settle with the clerk and county trustee to make report to the next term.
        On motion of Thomas Haltom, Administrator of all and singular the goods
and chattels, rights and credits of Thomas Anderews deceased is granted him
who thereupon entered into and acknowledged bond with William Spencer and
Ebenizer Haltom, his securities, in the penalty of two thousand dollars and took
the oath of an administrator and returned an inventory of the estate.

P250   Ordered that Nathaniel Clark be released from payment of double tax on
one poll.
        Ordered that Devereaux Wynne be appointed overseer of the road from the
bridge on Butlers Creek below Herndon Haralsons to the new bridge on Jones Creek
below Warlicks Mill with the following hands to work thereon Benjamin Gholston
Mr. Warlick and hands, Hazal Hewett and hands, William Wilson, James Henderson
Willoughby Powell Archibald Shannon, William Johns and their hands and the hands

P250 of W. Anderson and John Starnes.
Cont.   Ordered that Moses Starnes be appointed overseer of the road from town of
Jackson to the bridge on ButlersCreek, below Herndon Haralson with the following
hands to work thereon, to wit, Herndon Haralson, W. Watkins, Doct. William
E Butler W. Collins, William Mayo, James Johnson, Adam Huntsman and W. Buckley
and their hands and the hands of Robert Murray.
        Ordered that W. Gray James Young M. Gholson, Parka Chandler, Eli Chandler
Ryland Chandler, Zachariah Bennett, W. Webb and all their hands work on the road
where Pitts Chandler is overseer.
        Ordered that James Greer & David Jarrett be and they are hereby appointed
as surveyors and commissioners for the purpose of running and marking the un-
masked lines which divide this from the adjoining county and that they proceed
in conjunction with any person or persons who may hereafter be appointed for the
same purpose on the part of the adjoining counties.
        Ordered that the report of the jury of view appointed at the last term of
this court to mark a road from the high ground on the South side of the river
by the way of W. Clantons be received.

P251 *   Ordered that John Arnold be excused from paying double taxes on his taxable property for the year 1823 on his paying the single tax and listin g the same
        A deed of conveyance from John C McLemore and William Hill by his attorney
in face John C McLemore to Andrew McClary for six hundred and forty acres of land
was this day produced in open court and the execution thereof duly proven by the
oath of Austin A King and John Rudisel and ordered to be certified for registration.
        A deed of conveyance from Thomas Shannon Sheriff of Madison County to
Robert Armstrong for eleven thousand six hundred acres of land was this day
produced in open court and the execution thereof duly acknowledged by the said
Thomas Shannon to be his act and deed and ordered to be registered.
        A deed of conveyance from Thomas H. Shannon to John G. Caldwell for two
town lots in the town of Jackson was this day produced in open court and the
execution of same duly acknowledged to be his act and deed and ordered to be
registered.
P252   A deed of conveyance from James A. McCarroll to John Tyson for one undivided third part of an undivided seventh part of an Entry of five thousand acres of
land made in the name of John Ramsay was this day produced in open court and
proven by the oath of Duncan McIver one of the witnesses thereto the probat of
Archibald McBride having been heretofore taken is therefore ordered to be
certified for registration.
        A deed of conveyance from Duncan McIver to Phillip Warlick for eighty acres
of land was this day produced in open court and the execution thereof duly acknowledged by the said McIver to be his act and deed and ordered to be certified
for registration.
        A deed of conveyance from Anthany Faster to Duncan McIver for two hundred
seventy four acres of land was this day produced in open court and the execution
thereof duly proven by the oath of William Spencer one of the witnesses thereto
and ordered to be filed for further probate.
        Ordered that Wednesday next be set apart for trainsacting county business.
        Court then adjourned until tomorrow morning nine o'clock.
                                        H. Haralson
                                        J. Greer
                                        D. McIver   JP.

    *   Ordered that Henry D. Collins be exempt from double tas on one white poll.

P253   Tuesday 23rd. December 1823
Cont.Court met agreeable to adjournment.

Present: The worshipful Thomas Gordan James McCutchen, Guy Smith William Atchison, Theophilis Sanders, Mark Christian , Herndon Haralson, Duncan McIver Stephen Jarman, Samuel Taylor, John B. Cross, William Spencer and William Draper.

Samuel Hunter and Micajah Midyett, two of the persons named in the commission from His Exeellency, William Carroll Esquire, governor of the State of Tenn. appeared in open court and took the several oaths of qualification prescribed by the constitution and laws of this state as justices of the peace for the county of Madison and thereupon took their seats upon the bench.

Ordered that the civil causes now for trial be continued until next term of court.

Present David Jarrett, James Greer, Robert H. Dyer, John G. Carithers, John Rutherford, John Bowen William C. Love, James Trousdale, Joseph Linn, Bartholomew G. Stewart, and William E. Butler.

Ordered that a majority of the court present shall elect the sheriff, county trustee and other officers for the next term of two years.

The court proceeded to the election of a sheriff of this county Thomas Shannon, Daniel Mading and William Braden in nomination. After two unsuccessful ballots William Braden withdrew his name from nomination and on a third ballot it was found that Thomas Shannon had furteen andDaniel Mading twelve votes, the said Thomas Shannon having the highest number of votes and a majority of those given in, he was declared duly and constitutionly elected sheriff for the next two years.

P254   The court then proceeded to the election of a county trustee for this county, William Atchison and Samuel Wilson in nomination, after the first ballot it was found that Samuel D. Wilson had twelve votes and William Atchison ten votes the said Samuel D. Wilson having the highest number of votes and a majority of those given in, he was declared duly and constitutionally elected trustee for the next two years.

The court then proceeded to the election of a constable in Captain Reaves company for this county. Harkins, Thomas M Ross Jordan and Matthews in nomination. After the first ballot it was found Thomas M. Ross had fifteen votes, Harkins one Jordan four, Matthews two votes and the said Thomas M Ross having the highest number of votes and majority of those given in he was declared duly and constitutionally elected constable in Captain Reaves Company in this county for the next two years.

The court then proceeded to the election of a constable in Captain Blythes company for this county Thomas Elliot, Stephen Bryan, Malcolm Johnson and Downing it was found that Thomas Elliott had eleven votes, Stephen Bryan four votes Malcolm Johnson one vote and Mr Downing four votes the said Thomas Elliott having the highest number of votes and a majority of those given in, he was declared duly and constitutionally elected constable for the next two years.

The court then proceeded to the election of a constable in Captain Youngs company Elijah Jones in nomination he was declared duly and constitutionally elected for the next two years.

P255   The court then proceeded to the election of a constable in Captain Hannas company. John Fair in nomination he was declared duly and constitutionally elected for the next two years.

Ordered that the taxes on one thousand acres of land entered in the name of John Brevard, No. of Entry 623, also 160 acres in the name of Polk & Porter, Range 1 sect 11 No. Entry 48. 640 acres in the name of Morphis and Johns No Entry 583 Also 276 Acres in the name of William Rains heirs Range five No. Entry 712 be remitted for the year 1823.

Samuel Thomas comes into open court and proves by his own oath the killing of one wolf in the c ounty of Madison over the age of four months and ordered to be certified.

P255   John Smith comes into open court and proves by his own oath of the killing
Cont.of one wolf in the county of Madison over the age of four months and ordered to
be socertified. James Adams comes into court and proves by his own oath the
killing of one wolf in the county of Madison over theage of four months.
            Ordered that the sheriff repay to Matthew Jones the amount of his poll
tax for the year 1822.
            Ordered that the sheriff repay to Robert Dixon the amount of his poll tax
for the year 1822.
            Ordered that double taxes be remitted on two hundred sixty acres of land,
owned by David Reed part of six hundred forty acres of land entered in the name o
of John Grey Bbount on the payment of the single tax.

P256   On motion it is ordered by the court that a venditions exponas issue to the
sheriff of Madison County commanding him to expose to sale the right title, interest and claim that Matthew Johnson, as admr. of Simon Johnson, has in and to
one thousand acres of land entered in the name of John Haynes lying in the 3rd.
range and ninth section of the tenth surveyors district by No. of entry 792 to
satisfy an execution issued by Samuel Taylor an acting Justice of the Peace,
in and for the county of Madison, in favor of Nathaniel Simpson and against said
Matthew Johnson, Administrator as aforesaid for the sum of thirty dollars with
interest from 25th. December 1822 and costs of suit on which the said execution,
the deputy Sheriff William Bradin made the following return, to wit levid on all
the right claim and enterest of Simon Johnson in and to one thousand acres of land
lying in the third range, ninth section, tenth district, No of entry 792 Oct. 17,
1823.
            A power of attorney from Jordan G; Stokes Archelans Carloss was this day
produced in open court and the execution thereof duly acknowledged by the said
Jordan G. Stokes to be his act and died and ordered to be so certified.
            A deed of conveyance from Solomon Cotton to John B. Cross fro seventy-eight
acres of land was this day produced in open court and the execution thereof duly
proven by the oath of Richard C. Allen and Thomas L. Wynne subscribing witnesses
thereto and ordered to be so certified for registration.
            A deed of conveyance from Thomas Shannon to John H. Ball for one acre and
22 poles was this day produced in open court and the execution thereof duly acknowledged by the said Thomas Shannon to be his act and deed and ordered to be
certified for registration.

P257   A deed of conveyance from Samuel Davis to Worsham Easley for forty-five
acres of land was produced in open court and the execution thereof duly proven by
the oath of Robert Dixon the probat of Joseph Linn being here to fore taken.
Marked Out-
            A deed for forth five acres of land was produced in open court and the ex-
ecution thereof duly proven by the oath of Robert Dixon the probat of Joseph Linn
being heretofore taken. (omit) x--
            A deed of conveyance from Josiah Price for himself and as agent for Hetty
Neal, Isaac Price and George Henry, William Price, Henry Kerr to Joseph B. Porter
James Brown, and John Porter for five hundred theirty seven and one half acres
was this day produced in open court and the execution thereof duly proven by the
oath of austin A. King and Thomas Williamson, witnesses thereto and ordered to
be certified for registration

Dec. 1821 to Nov. 1825
Arthur H. Henley
vs.
Russell Goodrich   Arthur H. Henley

)
                 vs.   )   Original attachment
                 Russell Goodrich   )

       This day came the plaintiff by his attorney and dismisses his suit and

P257 assumes the payment of all costs. It is therefore considered by the court that
Cont.the defendant go thereof and recover of the plaintiff his costs about his suit
in this behalf expended and the plaintiff for his false clamor in mercy, etc.
Court then adjourned until tomorrow morning nine o'clock.
H. Haralson
J. Greer
John G. Carithers   J P.

P258 Wednesday 24th. December 1823
Court met agreeable to adjournment
Present: The Worshipful Herndon Haralson, Guy Smith Duncan McIver, John B.
Cross, James Greer, Bartholomew G. Stewart William Atchison, Thomas Gordon and
Robert H. Dyer.
Ordered that Adam Huntsman, Alfred Murray, William Stoddert, William R.
Hess & Alexander B. Bradford be appointed a committee to draw up rules of order
etc. and make report to the next term of court.
Ordered that John B. Cross be excused from paying double taxes on his tax-
able property for the year 1823 on the payment of single taxes.
Ordered that B. G Stewart. Joseph Linn Mark Christian be appointed com-
missioners to settle with the administrator of Robert McMillan deceased and make
report to the next term of this court.
Ordered that the county tax on lands be equal to the state tax for the
year 1824 and that the poll tax be equal to that of the year 1823.
Ordered that the following persons be appointed to take in the list of tax
able property in this country for the year 1824 to wit.
Stephen Jarman, Esquire in Capt. Hannas Company, William E. Butler Esq.
in the town ofcompany, Duncan McIver Esq. in Capt. Youngs Company, James Greer
Esq. in Capt. Hays Company, John G. Carithers in Capt. Smiths Company.
Micajah Midyett in Capt. Midyetts Company, Lemuel I. Hunter in Capt. Drapers
Company Theophilis Sanders in Ca t. Blythe's Company MarkChristian in Capt.
Fishers Company Thomas Gordon in Capt Freers Company John Thomas in Capt. Laeys
Company.
P259   Ordered that the sheriff summons the persons named in the venire issued
from the last term of court to attend as in jurors at the next term of this cour
and they are hereby appointed jurors as aforesaid.
Willie Espy Comes into court and records his stock mark as follows, towit
a slit and an underbit in the right ear and a smooth crop off the left.
Ordered that Alexander B. Bradford be allowed the sum of fifty dollars
for his ex-office services as solicitor general, for the year 1823 and that the
county trustee pay the same out of any monies not otherwise appropriated.
Ordered that Thomas Shannon, Sheriff, Be allowed fifty dollars for ex-
officeio services for the year 1823 and that the county trustee pay the same out
of any monies not otherwise appropriated.
Ordered that Roderick McIver clerk of this court be allowed forty dollars
for his exofficio services for the year 1823 and that the county trustee pay the
same out of any momis not otherwise appropriated.
Ordered that John T. Porter be allowed twenty-two dollars and fifty cents,
price paid for a book for registering deeds etc. and that the county trustee
pay the same out of any monies not otherwise appropriated.
Henry H. Horn comes into court and records his stock mark as follows towit
a swallow fork in each ear.
P260 Jackson Wednesday December 24th. 1823
Green Hill appointed overseer of the McGuire ferry road Johnsons Creek to
the county line to work all the hands South and West of Pons creek within an
half distance of any other road.
Ordered that Stephen Bryan be overseer of the road in continuation of the
road from Shannons landing to Big Black Settlement and work all the hands nemed

P260 in the petition for the purpose of cutting out and keeping the same in repair.
Cont.   Benjamin Booth appointed overseer of the McGuires ferry road from the bridge to Johnsons creek to work all the hands as far Wouth as Sidon Harris's including said Harris and Sons and as far West as Pace's creek including Maj.
Arnold and hands also including Robert Clanton hands.

          Robert Clanton appointed overseer of the road crossing at Buttlers ferry
on Hatchie from the low grounds on the South Side of the river to where the same
intersects the road crossing at Dr. Butlers and work the following hands, to wit
Joshua Weaver, Washington Pauldin, Stephen Smith Thomas Laiton, William Wilbourn
Trousdale William Rhodes and their hands and the hands of said Clanton.
Benjamin Brooks appointed overseer of the road for the first range to Expeys
to work all the hands from river to river.

          Jarett M. Jelks appointed overseer from the 2nd. range line to the 3rd.
P261*range line to the 3rd. having the hands of the second range from river to river.
tax thereon collected for the present year.

James Freeman 228 acres 9th. D. 1st. R & 10th. Sec.
Robert Dixon 188 acres of land
John Brown heirs   1000 acres, No of Grant 168
John Brown   1000 "   "   "   170
Thos. Brown   1000 "   2   "   170
William S. Henderson 400 "   "   "
Same   100 "
Alexander Ewing   620 "
Same   308 "
Same   200 "
Same   900 "
Dec. 1821 to Nov. 1825

Allen Pearce for the use of John H. Ball   )
vs.   )   Debt
John Graves   )
          This day came the plaintiff by his attorney and dismissed his suit and the
defendant assumes the payment of all costs. It is therefore considered by the
court that the plaintiff recover against said defendant his costs by him about
his suit in this behalf expended and the defendant in mercy etc.

Martin Cartmell   )
vs.   )   Case
Wm. & I Wilson   )
          This day came the plaintiff by his attorney and dismisses his suit, the
defendants assuming to themselves the payment of all costs. It is therefore
considered by the court that the plaintiff recover against the defendant his
costs by him about his suit in this behalf expended and the defendant in mercy
etc.

P262The Commissioners of the Town of Jackson   )
vs.   )   Debt
Nelson I. Hays & Robert H. Dyer   )
          This day came the plaintiffs by their attorney and dismisses their suit
and assumes the payment of all costs. It is therefore considered by the court
that the defendant recover against the plaintiffs their costs by them in this
behalf expended and the plaintiff in mercy etc.
     *   Ordered that double taxes on the following lands be remitted and the single

P262 Commissioners of the Town of Jackson)
Cont.vs.   )   Debt
      Isaac Curry & Banks M Burrow   )

     This day came the plaintiff by their attorney and dismissed their suit
the defendants assuming all costs. It is therefore considered by the court that
the plaintiff recover against the defendant their costs by them in this behalf
expended and the defendants in mercy etc.

John H. Woodcock & Co.)
vs.   )   Debt
William Arnold   )

     This day came the plaintiff by his attorney and the defendant in proper
person who because he connot gainsay the plaintiffs action confesses judgment
for ninetyeight dollars sixty eight & three fourth cents the debt in the declaration mentioned and also for five dollars and ninety four cents demages amounting in the whole $104.62¾. It is therefore considered by the court that the plain
tiff recover of the defendant the said sum of one hundred & four dollars sixty
two and three fourth cents the debt and demages aforesaid and also his costs
by him about his suit in this behalf expended etc.

P263 William Arnold   )
      vs.   )   On motion
      Washington I. DeWitt   )

     This day came the plaintiff by his attorney and it appearing to the satis-
facsion of the court that the plaintiff is bound to pay and that there is a
judgment against him for the sum of one hundred and four dollars sixty two and
three fourth cents as the security of the defendant. It is therefore considered
by the court that the plaintiff recover of the defendant said sum of one hundred
four dollars sixty two and three fourth cents by him about his motion in this,
behalf expended and the defendant in mercy etc.

Oliver B. Smith
vs.
Vale

     This day came the defendant by his attorneys and the plaintiff tho solemnly
called came not, thssefore it is considered by the court that the defendant recover of the plaintiff his costs by him about his suit in this behalf expended
and the plaintiff for his false clamor be in mercy etc.
     On motion it is ordered by the court that Venditiones Exponas issue to
Thomas I. Smith one of the constables of Madison County commanding him to expose
to sale the interest which William L Mitchell and William C. Mitchell have in
and to the following described tracts of land, to wit, twenty acres entered in the
name of William L. Mitchell andWilliam C. Mitchell, No Entry 515 No Warrant 1139
in the 3rd. Range Section1, beginning 30 poles East. & 10 poles South of the most
Eastern S. W. Corner of Thomas Love's 500 acre entry No 434 runs then South.

P264   Elijah Jones, Thomas M. RossThomas Elliott & John Fare, who were on yesterday chosen and appointed constables in and for the county of Madison, this day appeared
in open court and took the several oaths of prescribed by the constitution and laws
of the state, entered into and acknowledged the several bonds each in the sum of twelve
hundred fifty dollars with their securities that is to say, the said Elijah Jones with
Duncan McIver and David Jarret, his securities the said Thomas M. Ross with Daniel
Ross, his security, the said Thomas Elliott with John Harrison and Thomas Doak, his
security, and the said John Fair with James Trousdale and Nelson I Hess, his securities.
     Samuel D. Wilson was chosen and appointed County trustee for the county of Madi-
son on yesterday this day appeared in open court and took the several oaths of prescribed by the constitution and laws of the state, entered into and acknowledged
bond in the sum of two thousand dollars conditioned for the faithful discharge of the
duties of his office with James H. Wilson and Jason H. Wilson his securities.

P264   Thomas Shannon who was on yesterday chosen and appointed Sheriff of Madison
Cont.County for the next two years this day came into open court and took the several
oaths prescribed by the constitution and laws of the state.

          A deed of conveyance from James Caruthers to John Rudisell for one acre
of land was this day produced in open court and proven by the oath of Alexander
Patten and Martin Cartmell and ordered to be registered.

P265   A deed of conveyance from Stokely D. Hays, Joseph Linn, Bartholomew G.
Stewart Daniel Horton, James Trousdale, John Hargraves, Herndon Haralson, Robert
Hughes and Adam Huntsman, commissioners for the town of Jackson for eleven lots
of ground in said town to James Greer was this day produced in open court and the
execution thereof duly proven by the oaths of William Stoddert and William H.
Doak and ordered to be certified for registration.

          Administration of all and singular the goods and chattels, rights and
credits of Ascrius Martin is granted to William Jordan who thereupon entered
into bond in the sum of two hundred dollars with John Harrison and Solomon S.
Martin his securities and took the oath of administration. It is therefore o
ordered that letters of administration issue to the said William Jordan.

Levi B. Anderson   )
vs.   )   Original attachment for thirty years.
John Sharp   )
Entry No. 1127 Warrant 18478

          It appearing to the satisfaction of the court that the defendant in this
case is not an inhabitant of this state, it is ordered that publication of three
several times be made in paper printed in the town of Jackson, giving notice to
the said defendant to appear at the June term of our county court of pleas and
quarter sessions to be held for said county of Madison on the 4th. Monday in
June next, give bail to the action to issue or demur otherwise judgment final
will be entered against him and the proceedings are staid herein for six months
next after the present term.

P266   On motion it is ordered by the court that venditioni exponas issue to the
sheriff in and for the county of Madison, commanding him to expose to sale the
interest that William L. Mitchell has in and to the following tracts of land,
to wit, twenty acres of land entered in the name of the said William L. Mitchell
& John C.McLemore, try No. Entry $12 No. Wt. 1132 in the 3rd. Range 1st. section
begins 30 poles East & 10 poles South of the most Eastern So. Wt. corner of Thomas
Love 500 acres Entry No. 434 runs thence South 60 poles and West for compliment
Nov,r 20th. 1821. No. 572 Enters 66 acres, warrant 4761 in Range 2 Section2
begins forty poles North of the Southeast corner of Love and Wellbourn's 1000
acres, runs East fifty South one hundred poles West for compliment, Dec. 11th.1822

          No. 664 Entry one hundred acres Wt. 4728 Range 7 Section 3, begins at
Anthony Sharp's Southwest corner of his 2500 acre grant, East 100 poles, thence
North to the South boundary of M. Clemm's then West With his line to his Southwest
corner, then No. 100 po. then Wo. for compliment so as to join a 5000 acre survey
in the name of E. Sharp on the E & North, Dec. 16th 1822 No. 500 entire 174 acres
Wo. No. 2308 Range 1 Section 1, begins one East corner of his four hundred and
twenty nine acres entry thence So. one hundred poles and Bt. & No. for compliment
Dec. 10th. 1822 which appears to have been levied upon by Thomas I Smith, constable for Madison County by virtue of an execution issued by Samuel Taylor a
justice of the preace for this county, one in favor of James McCutchen against
William L. Mitchell for $12.82½ and make return &c.

          Court then adjourned until tomorrow morning nine o'clock.
                                        H. Haralson   JP.
                                        W. B. Cross   JP.
                                        Sam Taylor   JP.

P266 Thursday Morning 25th. December 1823
Cont.   Court met agreeable to adjournment, present, the Worshipful Herndon Haralson
John B. Cross and SamuelTaylor, gentlemen, justices.

William Huston   )
vs.   )   Trover
John W. Hamilton & Samll P. Howard)
    This day came the plaintiff by his attorney and filed his declaration and
the defendants being solemnly called came not but made default. It is threrfore
considered by the court that the plaintiff recover of the defendant his damages
sustained in this behalf together with his costs by him this behalf expended
but because those damages are not known, it is ordered that a writ of enquiry
issued to the sheriff commanding him to cause a jury to come here at the next
term of this court to inquire there of until which time this cause is continuedetc
    Ordered that Stokely D. Hays Herndon Haralson, John B. Cross and Samuel
Taylor be appointed commissioners to set apart one years provisions out of the
estate of John H. Gipson, deceased, for the support of the widow and make report
to the next court accordingly.

Isaac Dillard)   )
vs.   0 Tresspass etc.   )   Marked out
Anselem Russell)   0
    This day came the defendant by his attorney and the plain.)

    Thomas Shannon who was appointed sheriff on a former day of court this
day came into court and entered into bond with Alexander B. Bradford, William
Stoddert, and Daniel Horton, his securities in the sum of five thousand pounds
conditioned accordingly to law.
    Ordered that Philip Warlick be excused from payment of double taxes on the
folbowing property for the year 1823 on the payment of the single tax, to wit.
220 acres Entered in the 9th. Dist 1st. R & 9th. Sect.
150 acres Entered in the 9th. Dist. 2nd R & 8th. Sect.
Court then adjourned until court in course.
                                H. Haralson   JP.
                                Sam'l Taylor   JP.
                                J Greer

P269 Jackson March Term 1824 (1st. day) State of Tennessee.
    At Court of Plees and Quarter Sessions began and held in the town of Jackson
Madison county on Monday the 22nd. day of March 1824 and 48th. year of American
Independance.
    Present: the Worshipful Herndon Haralson, Bartholomew G. Stewart, David
Jarrett, Samuel Taylor, Joseph Linn, James McCutchen, William Draper, and Micaj-
ah Midyett.
    Ordered that the following list of taxable property be released from
double taxes for the year 1823, to wit,

In whose name listed	Acres	Entry	Dist.	Ran.	TSecs	Taxes	Remarks
William Wood	154					.57¾	
Manimilian H Buckhanna	400		9	1	9	1.50	
George Reynolds	1000		13	6	1&2	3.75	
Ephriam Robers	274	13	13	3	1	1.02½	
James Boon	228		13	11	1	.85½	
William Askew	453	36	10	1	10	1.69⅓	
Solomon Cotton	1000		10	4	9	3.75	
Thomas P. Deveraux	250		9	2	10	193¾	

	Acres	Entry	Dist.	Ran.	Sec.	Taxes	Remarks
P269 Same							
Cont. Same	500		10	5	1	1.87½	
David Jeffers	50	10	10	2	9	.18¾	
Same	640		10	3.4	7.8	2.40	
Some	12		10	1	9	.04½	
Samuel King	167		9	2	11	.62½	
Thomas Polk	200		9	1	10	.75	
Polk & Deveraus	500		9	1	9	1.87½	
Same	500		10	4	1	1.87½	
Joseph H. Bryan	274		10	1	4	1.02½	
John Womble	307		9	1	9	1.12½	
Ephream Davidson	2000		10	6		7.50	
Ephream Davidson	2000					7.50	
Henry Rutherford	5000		12			18.75	
Able Reims						.25	1white poll
P270 Robert L. Cobbs	150			1	9	.56¼	
Deveraux Wynne							
Leach & Polk	500					1.87½	
Ceder Pearcy	100					.37½	
I. & T. Hightower	500	137	10	5	9	1.87½	
Same	400	445	10	5	9	1.50	
Sugar McLemore	196	60	10	1	10	.73¼	part of ent.
Samuel H. Shannon	84	2	10	1	9	.21½	" "
Same one white poll						.25	
William Bradshaw	640		10	4	2	2.40	
Same	50	359	10	1	9	.18¾	
Catherine A McFachin	22	511	10	1	8		
Same	17	512	10	1	8	.06½	
Same	54	616	10	2	8	.24¼	
Same	54	630	10	2	9	.24¼	
Tyree Rhodes	258	40	10	2	89	.96½	
Same	263	790	10	5	9	.98¼	
Same	30	858	10	3	4	.11¼	
John Matthews	50	76	10	1	11	.18¾	
Britain Williford	110	121	10	4	10.11	.41¼	
Alexander Bradford	250		10	1	8	.93¾	
Robert Kennedy	300		9			1.12½	
Robert Kennedy	769		9			2.88¼	
James Bright	102		9			.30¼	
John Breham	100		9			.41	
John Morgen	77		9			.29	
John Arnold	200		10			4.25	7 black polls
William E. Butler	428	96	9	1	9	1.60½	
James	30	589	9	1	9	.11¼	
George Todd						8.10	16 black poll

P271   Ordered that William Powell be appointed overseer in the place of Lemuel S. Hunter.

Abram T. Smith was this day duly and constitutionally elected constable in Captain Smiths Company, who thereupon took the several oaths of office and entered into bond with Moses Oldham, Francis Taylor, his securities in the penalty & condition prescribed by law.

William McCablin was this day duly & constitutionally elected constable in Capt. Freer's company who thereupon took the several oaths of office and entered into bond with Moses Oldham Francis Taylor his securities in penalty & conditions prescribed by law.

Green Hill appeared in court and took the several oaths of qualification as

271 justice of the peace for the county of Madison who thereupon took his seat upon t
Cont the bench.

Ordered that Benjamin S. Brooks be allowed the follosng hands to work and keep up that part of the road which he was heretofore appointed overseer, to wit, A. R. Alexander, Henry Ragin, Owen Griffin, William Seaton, William Waggoner, A Musgrove, E. Musgrove, John Dunlap, Patterson, Robert Lowery, David Jackson, Abel Rains, Micajah Midyett.

Ordered that so much of an order made at the last term of this court as compelled Thomas Lofton to work on that part of the road of which Robert Clanton is overseer be resinded and that said Lofton work all the hands living South of the corporation line and East with said line so as to include Achabud Watkins H. hands to keep in repair that part of the road which Jacob Hilà was overseer of.

Ordered that William Stephens be appointed overseer of the road in the place of Robert Burns.

Ordered that Maj. James Fentress be allowed be the sum. designated by law for seven and one half days services rendered as commissioner in fixing on the site for the seat of justice in this county and that the county trustee pay the same out of any monies not otherwise appropriated.

P272 On motion and petition filed, ordered that the following persons, to wit, Lewis Carpenter, Dock Fenner, Elijah Jones, Adam Brown, Obediah Dodson, Harris Bradford, Col. Willis, John Frazier, and John M. Welch, them or any five of them be a jury to view and lay off a road leaving the Carroll road at Robert Burns plantation to intersect the Reynoldsburgh Road at the widow Wilson's old place and make report to the next term of court.

Ordered that the report of the jury of view to mark and lay off a road from Major Joel Dyer be appointed overseer of the same to work all the hands that is convenient to open and keep the same in repair.

James L. Moss was this day chosen and appointed guardian of Louisa J. H aley a minor orphan and thereupon entered and acknowledged his bond in the sum of five hundred dollars conditioned for the performance of his duties towards said minor with Robert H. Wynne and William Ruleman his securities.

On motion and petition filed , ordered that the order granting a road to be opened from Jarman's ford to Sandey's old place be rescinded and that the road be established as it is now opened from said ford to Fowlers on the North boundary of the county and that John Gaitly be appointed overseer of said road to work the following hands to wit, Samuel Hall Philip Delph, John Watt, James H. Watt, John Gatlin David Bevel Thos. C. Watts, Willis Nichols, Dempsey Graham, Stephen Jarman hands Drew White Richard Lyons, John Hopper, Capt Freer and all the hands in said bounds to keep the same in repair.

P273 Murdoch Murchison comes into court and records his stock mark as follows, to wit, swallow fork and an underbit in the right ear and a swallow fork and a split in the left.

Samuel Campbell comes into court and records his stock mark as follows, to wit, a crop off the left ear and a nich in the underside of the right ear.

Thomas Lacy comes into open court, a quorum being upon the bench and proves by his own oath the killing of two wolves in the county of Madison over the age of four months which is ordered to be so certified.

Elijah Baker comes into open court, a quorum being upon the bench and proves by his county of Madison over the age of four months.

Ordered that Micajah Midyett, William C. Mitchell and David Jarret be appointed commissioners to settle with the admr. of Samuel Goodwin, deceased, and make a report to the present which report is handed in and ordered to be recorded.

Ordered that the following rules of order be received and adopted by the county court of Madison, to wit.

1st. When any attorney shall be addressing the cour or jury the balance of the gentlemen of the bar shall presume silence in the bar, obstain from all talking or even whispering so loud that it may interupt the speaker. 2nd. The gentle-

P273 men of the bar shall keep their seats while any member is speaking and also sit
Cont. with their heads uncovered unless by permission of the court if they bein the
bar. 3rd. If but one allotney shall be employed in any suit, argument, motion etc
he shall state clearly in his introduction his points and when answered he shall
conclude without any further speaking on the subject unless there is new law
introduced, in the conclusion then his adversary may answer the law only. 4th.
If two or more shall be employed, one shall open the point or cause and another
conclude and neither shall speak twice on the same subject unless called upon by
the court for further argument unless new law introduced as above. 5th. No. attor
ney shall interupt the speaker unless in his concluding speech he shall mistake
the testimony then he may be corrected in a polite manner. 6th. No lawyer shall
speak to any cause unless he is employed therein or especially requested by some
attorney who is employed unless it be in the case of an absent friend. 7th.
There shall be no argument upon the first affidavit for the continuance of a cause
but the court shall decide from the reading and inspection. 8th. The clerk shall
make out a list of attorneys regularly practicing in this court, beginning at the
youngest and go on to the oldest and as soon as court meets or the minutes are
read, he shall call them over as they stand on the list in order that they make
motions, present petitions in their proper order. If any attorney is not in
place when his name is called his application shall be post poned for that day
in the same way as it is observed in the supreme court.
9th. In all petitions for roads or other public matter the same if not read by
some member of the bar shall be mentioned by the chairman or some other presiding
justice publicly before it is acted upon.
10th. All causes shall be either tried or continued as they stand and are called
on the docket unless they are continued over by consent of the parties when they
shall be plead at the end of the docket for that term.
11th. No person shall be permitted to go up to the bench to converse with the
justices on the bench during the trial of any cause or while court is sitting
unless they are doing county business.
12th. All motions, applications of whatever sort shall be made from the bar, either
by party or his atty. except it be when county business is before the court.
P275 13th. On Tuesday of every court these rules shall be read to the bench and bar
before entering on the civil docket. Ordered that David Jarret Esquire be
appointed to take list of taxable property in Captain Young's company in place
of Duncan. McIver and return the same to the clerk of this court on or before 15th.
May next.

On motion and petition filed, ordered that the following persons, to wit,
Murdoch Murchison, John Justice, Samuel Bradshaw, Daniel Cruse, William McCaslin,
Walter Tedford, and John Cravens be appointed a jury of view to mark and lay off
a road, beginning on the Carroll road at the corner of Jacob Bradberry's lines
on Spring Cree, thence the nearest and best way so as to intersect the aforesaid
road near where William C. Love formerly lived and make report to the next term
of this court.

On motion and petition filed, ordered that the following persons, to wit,
James McCutchen, William Atchison, Murdoch Murchison, James McClary Mark Christian,
John B. Justice, Nathan Clark, Michael Clark, Abner Brown, George Sullivan, Spencer
Grant, and Alexander Oakley, be appointed a jury to mark and lay off a road from
the county line near Essac Curry's where the road leading from Reynoldsburgh in-
tersects the same to intersect the Carroll road at Murdock Murchison's or William
Atchisons, and make report ot the next term of this court.
P276 John D! Love, James A Haslip, John H. Wyatt, Samuel A Werner, and Andrew
L. Martin appeared in open court and took the oath of qualification as practicing
attorneys in this court.

Ordered that Murdoch Murchison be permitted to turn the road running through
his lands so as to square his fields provided the same is not more than ten poles

P276 from the present road.
Cont.   On motion and petition filed, ordered that the following persons, to wit,
Samuel H. Shannon, James Cockrell Aquilla Davis, Samuel Bruff, James Brown,
John T. Porter, Kenning Pace, Thomas Grissom, Bignal Crook and Andrew Hammel Be
appointed a jury of view to make and lay off a road from the town of Jackson the
nearest and best way to the center of Haywood County as far as the county line so
as to cross the South fork at Davis ferry and make report to the next term of this
court.
        Ordered that John T. Porter be appointed overseer of the road from Jackson
to Harris Bluff to where the same crosses the first range line and that Micajah
Midyett apportion the hands of the said Porter & W; C. Mitchell.
        Ordered that George Todd be exempt as overseer of the road and that James
Vaulx be appointed overseer in the room of said Todd and work all the hands allowed
before for said road.

P277   Ordered that the report of the jury of view returned at September term
last of this court to make an alteration in the road leading from Jackson by the
house of Vincent Haralson be receibed and that the same stand of record as if it
was entered on the minutes at the court to which the same was returnable.
        Administration of all and singular the goods and chattel, rights and credits
of Anderson Odell deceased, is granted to Isaac Swan who entered into ford with
Jno. Hardgroves who his security in the sum of two Hundred Dollars and took the
oath of administration. It is therefore ordered that the letters of administration
issue accordingly.
        A deed of conveyance from Samuel Taylor to William May for 160 acres of
land was this day produced in open court and the execution thereof acknowledged by
said Samuel Taylor to be his act and deed and ordered to be certified for registration.
        A deed of conveyance from Daniel Ross to Right Koonce for seventy five acres
of land was this day produced in open court and the execution of same acknowledged
by the said Daniel Ross to be his act and deed and ordered to be certified for
registration.
        A deed of conveyance from Francis Taylor to William May for eight acres of
land was this day produced in open court and the execution of same acknowledged
by the said Francis Taylor to be his act and deed and ordered to be certified for
registration.
Dec. 1621____ Nov. 1825   Report to the next term of Court.
        A deed of conveyance from Herndon Haralson, Chairman of the Board of
Commissioners for the town of Jackson, by order of said board to Jno. H. Ball
for one third of a lot of ground in the town of Jackson No. 16 was this day pro
duced in open court and acknowledged by the said Herndon Haralson to be his act
and deed and ordered to be registered.

P278   Two deeds of conveyance from Herndon Haralson Chairman of the Board of Commissioners for the town of Jackson, by order of the Board to Jno. McLennan for
two town lots known and designated in the place of said town by No. 41 and No. 70
was this day produced in open court and acknowledged by the said Herndon Haralson
to be his acts and deeds and ordered to certified for Registration.
        A deed of Conveyance from Samuel Dicken's attorney for William Polk to
Moses Oldham for One hundred and fourteen acres of land was this day produced in
open court and the execution thereof acknowledged by the said Samuel Dickin to be
his act and deed and ordered to be registered.
        An indenture of Bargan and Sale from Jno. Charlton to Leegass McLemore for
one Hundred Acres of Land was this day produced in open court and the execution
thereof acknowledged by the Suit Jno. Charlton to be his act and deed and ordered
to be certified for registration.
        A deed of Mortagage from Archibald S. Lakman to William Reynold was this day
produced in open and execution thereof duly proven by the oath of John Stewart.
Andrew Lellerton to be his act and deed or deeds to certified for registration.

P278   A deed of conveyance from Patsy Doak executrix of Robert Doak, Deed to Green
Cont. Hill was this day produced in open court and the execution thereof duly **proven by**
the oath of Robert Hughes and W. H. Doak to be his act and deed and ordered to be
certified for registration.

A deed of Conveyance from Samuel Moon to James A. McLeary for one Hundred
and six acres of land was this day produced in open court and proven by oath of
P279 William McCanslin and William Atcherson to be the act and deed of the said Samuel
Moone and ordered to be certified for registration.

A deed of conveyance from John C. McLemore to John Wharton for two hundred
and seventy four acres of land was this day produced in open court and execution
thereof proven by the oath of David Thomas and Alexander Braden to be the act and
deed, Jno. C. McLemore and ordered to be certified from registration.

A deed of conveyance from John Sutton to George Shankle, for sixty acres of
land was this day produced in open court and the execution threrof acknowledged
and ordered to be certified for registration.

A deed of conveyance from Sugar McLemore to John Chertton for two tracts
each containing one hundred and sixty acres of land was this day produced in open
court and acknowledged and ordered to be certified for registration.

A deed of conveyance from Thomas F. Devercaurix by his attorney in fact
Samuel Dickins to Micajah Miggitt for three hundred and fifty acres of land was
this day produced in open court and acknowledged by said Samuel Dickins and ordered
to be certified for registration.

P280   A deed of conveyance from Willoughby Williams to No. Wharton for five hundred
and fifty nine and two thirds acres of land was this day produced in open court and
the execution thereof acknowledged and ordered to be certified for registration.

A Bill of Sale from John Rutherford to Robert Murray was this day produced
in open court and acknowledged by the Sr. Rutherford and ordered to be certified
for registration.

A deed of conveyance Herndon Haralson Chairman of the Board of Commissioners
for the town of Jackson to Isaac Curry for the onehalf of a lot of ground in the
town of Jackson disignated in the plan of Said Town by No.B was this day produced
in open court and acknowledged by the Sd. Herndon Haralson and ordered to be certified for Registration.

Court then adjourned until tomorrow morning Eight o'clock.

H. Haralson   JP
Jas. McCutcheon
William Atcherson   JP.

P281 Tuesday Morning 23rd. March 1824
Court met agreeable to adjournment, Present Herndon Haralson, William Atcherson and Joseph Lynne, Gentlemen Justices.

Ordered that Champnirs Madding, Copender William C. Mitchell and Charles
Sevier be exempted as Jurrors for the present Term.

Ordered that the order made on yesterday granting License to William Hutcher-
son for keeping an ordinary stand on records as if the same had been entered on
records when made.

Ordered that Guy Smith be appointed to take the list of Taxable Property in
Capt. Thomas I. Smith's Company for 1824 and report the same to the clerk of the
Court by the first day of May next.

The commissioners appointed to Settle with the Admisistrators of the Estate o
of Lewis Jones Deceased the day made report of the same which is ordered to be
recorded.

Stat   Jordan G. Stakes)
Vs.   )   Case
John I. Smith   )
On application of the parties by their attorney.

P281 November 1825--Report to the next Term of Court--Page 281
Cont.   Ordered that the matter in dispute between them in this suit be referred to
the final determination of Jarrett M. Jelks and Micajah Miggitt and their award
when made, be returned to the next term of the court and made the Judgment of the
court theirin.

Jordan C. Stokes)
vs.   )   Covenant
Jno. I. Smith   )
        Same order as above.

P282 George M. Litt)
      vs.   )   Covenant
      Jno. Barnhardt)

      Benjamin Sholson, Acquilla Dairo Archivald S. Lakman and John Barnhardt this
day Personally appeared in open Court and acknowledged themselves bound to the
said George W. Still in the sum of Eight Hundred Dollars as the appearance Bail of
the said Defendant Archibald S. Lakman the condition of the recognision is such
that if the Said Lakman shall well and truly make his personal appearance in
this court from time to time and answer to said action and not a part the court
but by due course of Law then this recognizence to be void otherwise to remain in
force.

      The sheriff this day made return of the writ of venire to him directed from
the last term of this court with the following endorsement theron. Executed onall
but Mathias Deberry in pursuance of which the following persons were attending
Court Acquilla Davis Ezekiel B. McCoy William Ruleman John B. Ball, Asa B. Midyett
Jno. T. Portor, John Starns James Dorris Wilson Hutchison John Ridings Elijah
Haynie, Galbraith Neill, Parks Chandler, Joseph Eddings Charles Severe. Champniss
Mading and Doc. Copender and thereupon the following persons towti Acquilla Davis
Ezekiel B. McCoy William Ruleman, John H. Ball Asa B. Midyett, Jno T. Porter, John
Starnes, James Dorris Wilson Hutchison Jno. Ridings, Elijah Hanyie Galbreath Neill
and Parks Chandler were there, Empanneled sworn and charged as a Grand Jury to
inquire into and for the body of the County of Madison and thereupon retted to
consider of presentments. Ordered that the following persons named in the writ of
venire facia directed to the Sheriff of this County and make returnable to the
present term of court, be fine the sum of two dallars and fifty cents each as
Delinquet Jurrors (to wit) James Alexander Daniel Horton, William Spencer, William
Newhause, Mathias Deberry, Newton Harris, Beginal Crook unless they come in at
the next term of this court and show sufficient cause for said delinguency.

P283 James McCutcheon)
      Vs.   )   Case
      Madison McLawrine)   Marked out-
      This day the Parties by their attorneys and on the cause being called up
for trial the Plaintiff by his attorney filed his affidavit for a continuance
which application for continuance of the cause was over ruled by the court in
over ruling his affidavit (Motion) and matian for a continuence, and the Plaintiff
ordered to go into a trial to which opinion of the court in over Ruling his affidavit and motion for a continuence of the cause. The Plaintiff by his atty. filed
his Bill of Execption which was signed sealed by the court and ordered to be made
part of the record in this case. ----

William Davis)
vs.   )   Case
A. Bostivick)
      This day the Plaintiff came into court and dismissed his suit and assumes
the payment of all cost on said suit. It is therefore considered by the court
that the defendant recover of the Plaintiff this cost aforesaid, by him above
his suit in this behalf expended and this Plff. for his false clamor be in mercy etc.

P283 Isaac Dillard)
Cont.vs.   )   Case
     Andrew Russel)

  This day came the Plft. aforesaid by his attorney and dismisses his suit and
the Defendent assums the payment of all cost in said suit. It is therefore conside
ered by the court that the plaintiff recover against the Said Defendent the cost
incident and accruing then and this Defendant in Mercy etc.

Thomas Bonner)
vs.   )   Debt.
John Welch   )

  This day came the parties aforesaid by their attorney and the Plaintiff in
this case. Dismisses his suit and the Defendant assumesupon hisself the payment
of all cost, of said suit and the Defendant in mercy etc.

P284 The commissioners appointed to settle with the adminstrators of Robert
McMillan Deceased this day reported to court, which report is ordered to be recorde
ed.

Bartholomew G. Stewart   )
Administraton of Jas. Bradshaw, Dec.   )
Vs.   )   Case
Spencer Grant & Thomas Grissom   )

  This day came the parties aforesaid by their attornies and thereupon came a
jury to wit, Joseph Eddings James Henderson, Martin Davis Nathan Simpxon Wilson
Brown Absalom Massie John C. Gillespie Clayborn J. Ragsdale William Jordan,
George Hicks Samuel Swan and James Flack who being elected tried and sworn the truth
to speak on the issues joined upon their oaths do say we of the jury find the
Defendants Guilty in manner and form as they are charged in the plaintiff declaration and do assess the plaintiff Damages sustained by reason of the ____ and
conversion in the declaration mentioned to one hundred and sixty dollars. It is
threrfore considered by the court that the plaintiff recover of the defendants
the damages aforesaid in form aforesaid assessed also his costs by him about his
suit in this behalf upon & the Defendants in mercy etc.

William Williams   )
vs.   )   Debt
Samuel Taylor & Joel Duer)

  This day came the parties aforesaid afforesaid by their attornies and
P285 thereupon came a Jury to wit Joseph Eddings, James Sanderson Martin Davis Nathan
Simpson Wilson Brown, Absolom Massie John C. Gillespie Claiborn J. Ragsdale
William Jordan George Hicks Samuel Swann and James Fleck who being elected tried
and sworn the truth upon the issues joined, do say we of the Jury find the issue
for the plaintiff one hundred and twelve dollars the debt in the declaration
mentioned and do assess his damage by reason of the detention therefof to eight
dollars and forty cents. It is therefore considered by the Court that the plaintiff recover of the Defendants said sum of one hundred and twelve dollars together
with damages aforesaid in form aforesaid assessed also his costs by him about
his suit in this behalf expended and the Defendant in mercy etc.

Sterling Organ   )
Vs.   )   Debt
Robert H. Dyer, Joel H. Dyer)

  This day came parties aforesaid by their attornies and thereupon came a
jury to wit, Joseph Eddings, James Henderson, Martin Davis Nathan Simpson
Wilson Brown Absolom Massie John C. Gillespie Claihorn J. Ragsdale William
Jordan George Hicks Samuel Swan and James Flack who being elected, tried and
sworn the truth to speak upon the issues joined do say we of the Jury find for
the plaintiff the sum of sixty-three dollars the debt in the declaration mentioned

P286 and do assess his damages by reason of the detention. Thereof to eleven dollars
ninety seven cents. It is threrfore considered by the Court that the plaintiff
recover of the defendant said sum of sixty three dollars together with his damages
aforesaid in a form aforesaid assessed also his cost by him about his suit in
this behalf expended and the Defendant in Mercy etc.

James McCutchen   )
vs.   )   Case
Madison McLawrance)

    This day came the parties aforesaid by their attornies and thereupon the
plaintiff filed his affidavit for a contenuance of this cause but the court overruled the motion for a continuance and ordered a Jury to come here & etc. Where
upon came a Jury towit Joseph Eddings James Henderson, Martin Davis, Nathen Simpson Wilson Brown, Absalom Massia, John C. Gillispie Claborn J. Ragsdale William
Jordan, George Hicks, Samuel Swain and James Flock who being elected tried and
sworn the truth to speak upon the issue joined do say we of the Jury for the
Defendant. It is therefore considered by the court that the plaintiff take
nothing by his _____ but for his false clamour be in mercy etc. and that the
Defendant go there of hence without day and recover of the plaintiff his cost
by him about his suit in this behalf expended. To which opinion of the court
overruling the plaintiff application for a continuance the plaintiff by his atty.
before the case was submitted to be _____ filed his bill of exception which was
signed sealed and ordered to be made a part of the record there in. And the
plaintiff by his attorney prays an appeal in the nature of a writ of error to the
next circuit court to be held for the county of Madison which was granted him on
his entering into bond with mark Christian his security in the penalty of two
hundred dollars conditioned according to Law which is done according.
    Court then adjourned until nine o'clock tomorrow morning.
                            H. Haralson   Jp.
                            James Truesdale JP.
                            James Greer   JP.

P287 Wednesday morning 24th. March 1924
    Court met according to adjournment.
Present, the Worshipful Herndon Haralson, B. G. Stewart, James Greer and James
Trousdale, gentlemen justices.
    Administrator of all and Singular the Goods and chattels right and Credits
of August C. Hayes, Deceased is Granted Elijah Bigelow who thereupon took the
oath of Administration and entered into bond in the penalty of twenty-five
hundred Dollars with David Thomas and Thomas Shannon, Joel Dyer this day came
into open court and proved by his own oath the killing two wolves in the county
of Madison over the age of four months which is ordered <u>certified</u>.

Robert Murray)
vs.   )   Order of Sale
James Dorris)

    On motion, It is ordered by the Court that vendition as Exponas issue to
the Sheriff of a Madison County commanding, him to expose the right to take
interest of Claim, that James Dorris has in and to a certain lot of Ground in the
town by No. 62 to satisfy an execution that Robert Murry obtained against Dorris
before Samuel Taylor a Justice of the Peace for said county one for six dollars
and Seventy eight cents & cost of suit the other for twenty four dollars & sixty
nine cents & cost which Execution werehere returned into court with the following
indorsement, No personal property found.Thomas Shannon Shff. levied on one house
and Lot No. 62 in the town plan of Jackson the property of James Dorris 20th.
March 1824.

                                 Thomas Shannon Shff.

P288 Commissioners   )
    vs.   )
Levi B. Anderson William Braden)Debt.
    This day came the parties in the fore going cases by their attornies and
the Defendant filed their pleas in abatement marked A & B. and the said places
being stretchen out on motion of the Plaintiff 's attorney the Defendant then filed their plea in bar marked (E) which on motion of the Plantiff attorney was
also stricken out to which opinion of the court in striking out the court in
strikint out the said pleas the Ddfendent attorney excepted and prayed their
Bill of Exceptions to be signed sealed and enrolled and ordered to be made a
part of the Record herein which was done accordingly.

P289 William Love   )
    vs.   )   Case
John Weir   )
    This day came the parties aforesaid by their attornies and the Plaintiff
being unwilling to prosecut his suit any further dismisses the cases, and the
Deft. assumes all cost . It is therefore considered by the court that the Plaintiff recover against the said Deft. the cost aforesaid and the Defendent in mercy
etc.
Jonathon Huston)
    vs.   )   Case
William Love   )
    This day came the Plaintiff by his attorney and the Defendant to though
solemly called came not but made default. It is then for considered by the court
that the plaintiff take nothing by his bill but for his false clamor be in mercy
P290 etc. and that the Defendant go there of hence without day and recover of the
plaintiff his cost by him about his suit in this behalf expended.

The Board of Commissioners of the Town of Jackson)
Vs.   ) Debt
Samuel Taylor Carter C, Collier and Stokely D. Hays)

The Same   )
    vs.   )   Debt
Thomas I Smith)

The Same   )
    vs.   ) Debt
William R. Hess Nelson, I Hess & Herndon Haralson)

The Same   )
    vs.   ) Debt
Joseph F. Cloud Anthony Gray and William E. Butler)

The Same   )
    vs.   )   Debt
Stokely D. Hays)

The Same)
    vs.   )   Debt.
The Same)

The Same   )
    vs.   )   Debt
William Arnold)

P291 Rhe Same   )
     vs.   )   Debt
     John D. Shannon and Thomas Shannon)

     The Board of commissioner of the town of Jackson)
     vs.   )   Debt
     Robert H. Dyer & John B, Cross   )

     The Board of Commissioners of the town of Jackson)
     vs.   )   Debt
     Thomas Shannon   )

     The Same   )
     vs.   )   Debt
     William Braden & Thomas Shannon   )

     The Same   )
     Vs.   )   Debt
     William Arnold & Stokely L. Hays)

     The Same   )
     vs.   )   Debt
     William R. Hays and Stokely D. Hays)
          This day came the parties aforessid by their attornies and there upon by
     consent of the Defendant by their attornies the plaintiff have leave to amend
     their original writ therein at the next Term as of the present Term so that said
     suit may be commenced in persuance of the act. of assembly in such case made and
     provided upon their paying all cost heretofore accruing _____ and the next term
     is to be considered as the appearance, Term until which these causes are coninued

P292 John C. Boyde   )
     Vs.   )   Case
     Wilbon Hutchison   )
          By consent of the parties by their attornies this cause is ordered to be
     continued until next term.

     B. G. Steward & Others   )
     vs.   )   Debt
     Herndon Haralson   )
          This day came the parties aforesaid in their proper persons and the Defen-
     dant because he cannot gain say the plaintiff causes of action confesses judgement
     for fifty dollars the balance of Debt in the plaintiff Declaration mentioned and
     the Plaintiff assums the judgement of all cost. It is therefore considered by
     the court that the plaintiff go thereof hence and recover against the defendant
     the said sum of fifty Dollars and that the Plaintiff are liable for the payment
     of the Cost aforesaid accruin in t is case.
          Lewis Baling comes into court and Record his Stock Mark to wit, half crop
     off the underside of the left ear and a crop and Slit on the Right ear.
          William B. Boling comes into and records his stock Mark as following towit,
     crop off the under side of the left ear and a smooth crop off of the right ear.

     William Wilson)
     vs.   )   Case
     Thomas Grisome)
          This day the parties afore said by their attornies and thereupon came a jury
     of good and lawful men (to wit) Joseph Eddings Claborn J. Ragsdale, John Murphy.

P293 Absolem Massey, Soloman Martin James Henderson, Philip G. Tucker Andrew Hays Drury
Bittis, Rutherford Roberson William Jordan and Ruben P. T. Stone who being elected tried and sworn the truth to speak upon the issue joined and by the consent
of the parties and with the assent of the court, James Henderson one of the jurors
in this case is withdrawn and this cause by the consent of the parties and the
court is transfered to the next circuit court to be Holden for the county of
Madison to be held on the fourth Monday at May next in the town of Jackson far
trial to be had thereon and it is so ordered by the court accordingly.

P293   This day the grand jury returned into court the following bill of Indictment towit the state against Thomas Dement for an assault and against Joel Madd-
ings and Joseph Linn, for an affray all of which were indorced by the foreman
of the grand Jury a true bill Aquita Davis foreman of the Grand Jury.

P294 The Commission of the Town of Jackson)
      vs.   )   Debt
      James Greer & Alexander Greer   )
         This day came the parties by their attornies and the Defendant saith they
cannot again say the plaintiff action but agrees to with draw their plea and
confess judgement for the sum of twenty two hundred and fifty six dollars Debt.
Also the further sum of seventy seven dollars & 42 cent. Damages and cost and
it is agreed by the plaintiff that Execution be stayed for one third for three
months and the remaining third for nine months and in case it shall not be punct-
ualty paid at the times aforesaid Execution shall issue for the whole amount.
It is therefore considered by the court that the Plaintiff recover against the
Defendant the aforesaid Debt. Damages and cost and that Execution issue according
to the agreement of the parties and the Defendant in mercy etc.

      The Commissioners of the Town of Jackson)
      vs.   )   Debt
      Ribert H. Wynne & James Brown   )
         This day came the parties aforesaid by their attornies and the Defendant
Saith they cannotgain say the Plaintiff cause of Action but agrees to with draw t
their pleas and confesses Judgement for the sum of three hundred & Eighty Six
dollars & 80½ cent Debt and the further sum of twelve dollars and fifty one cent
P295and cost and it is agree by the Plaintiff that Execution in this case be stayed
until the second Monday in December next. It is therefore considered by the court
that the plaintiff recover against the said Defendant that aforesaid sum of
three hundred and Eighty Six dollars. Eighty and half centa _____ Debt.
together with the Damages aforesaid and also the cost by them about their suit
in their cause expended and that the Defendant be in mercy etc.

      Commissions of the town of Jackson   )
      vs.   )
      John Bidings and Bartholomew G. Stewart.)
          This day came the parties aforesaid by their attorneys and the defendants
saith they cannot gainsay the plaintiff cause of action but agrees to withdraw
their pleas and confess judgment for the sum of three hundred and twenty seven
dollars debt and thirteen dollars and twenty five cents damages and the costs
by them about their suit in this behalf expended.

      The commissioners of the town of Jackson   )
      vs   )
      Ribert L. Cobb, Alexander B. Bradford and William Stoddert)
         This day came the parties aforesaid by their attornies and the Defendant
Saith they connot gain say the Plaintiff cause of action but agree to with draw
their plea and confess Judgement for the sum of nine hundred & forty two dollars

P295 Debt and also the sum of thirty seven dollars Damages together with the cost of
Cont.their suit and it is Agreed by the plaintiff that Execution be stayed for two
    hundred and fifty dollars, until the first day of June next and for the balance
P296 until the second Monday in December next. (It is therefore considered by the court
    that Es) and it is agreed by the parties that if it is not punctually payed that
    Execution issue for the whole at time aforesaid. It is therefore considered by the
    court that the Plaintiff recover against the said Defendants the aforesaid sum
    of Debt Damages and cost and that the Defendants be in mercy etc.

    Samuel Bell for the use of Sam Vanlier)
    vs.   )   Case
    Thomas Shannon   )
        This day came the parties by their attornies and by the consent of the
    parties and with the assent of the court this cause is transfered to the next
    cirsuit court to be held for the county of Madison in the town of Jackson and
    the fourth Monday in May next for trial and Judgment to be had there on, and
    that it ordered by the court accordingly.

P297 John McNairy, William E. Butler, Henry M. Rutledg)
    vs.   )   Debt
    John F. Brown   )
        This came the Defendant in proper person and the plaintiff by attorney and
    the Defendant saith that he cannot gain say the Plaintiff cause of action. It
    is therefore considered by the court that the Plaintiff recover against the De-
    fendant the sum of one hundred and forty one dollars debt, and sixty two and one
    half cent damage together with all cost by them about their suit in this behalf.
    Expended and that the Defendant be in mercy etc. and the plaintiff by their at-
    tornies agree to stay Execution Seven month etc.
        Court then adjourned until tomorrow nine o'clock.

                                        B. G. Stewart   JP.
                                        J. Green   JP.
                                        James Trousdale   JP.

    Thursday the 25th March 1824
        Court met agreeable to adjournment, Present B. G. Stewart James Greer
    James Trousdale, Gentleman Justies of the peace.
P298   Charles Severe the Administrator of Robert Severe Deceased this day returned
    into Court an inventory of the amount of Estate deceased which is ordered to be
    entered and recorded.
        The Grand Jury this day returned into Court the following bill of Indict-
    ment to wit one against Joel Madding, Daniel Mading Martin Mading Franklin, Mading
    and Henry Harper for a riot which bill was endorsed by the foreman of the Grand
    Jury a true bill, Aquilla Davis forman of the Grand Jury.
        Also one against Samuel Whitworth and Franklin Mading for an affray, In-
    dorsed same as the above.
        Ordered that Duncan McIver and Lennel S. Hunter be commissioners appointed
    to andit and settle the account of James Alexander Administrator on the Estate
    of William L. Alexander and report to the next term of court.

    State   )
    vs.   )   Assault
    William Pace   )
        This day came as well the solicitor General on the part of the State, as
    the Defendant in proper person and the defendant being arraigned upon his arraign-
    ment, plead guilty in manner and form as charged in the bill of Indictment. It
    is therefore considered by the court that the said defendant make his peace with
    the State by the payment of four dollars five and also his Cost by her about her

P301 ment plead guilty as charged in the bill of indictment. It is therefore consider-
Cont.ed by the court that the defendant make his peace with the state by the payment
of fifty cents fine and the plaintiff go thereof hence and recover against the
defendant her fine aforesaid also her costs by her about her suit in this behalf
expended and the defendant be taken etc.

The State   )
vs.   )   An affray
Joel Madding   )

    This day came as well the solicitor general on the part of the state as the
defendant in his proper person and the defendant being arraigned upon his arraignment plead guilty as charged in the bill of indictment. It is therefore
P302 considered by the court that the defendant make his peace with the state by the
payment of five dollars fine and the plaintiff go thereof hence and recover
against the defendant her fine, costs by her about her suit in this behalf expended and the defendant in mercy etc.

The State   )
vs.   )   An affray
Samuel Whitworth & Franklin Mading   )

    This day came the solicitor general on the part of the state as the defend-
ant in their proper persons and the defendants being arraigned upon their arraignment plead guilty as charged in the bill of indictment. It is therefore considered by the court that the defendants make their peace with the state by the
paymtnt of one dollar fine each and that the plaintiff recover against the said d
defendants her costs by her about her suit in this behalf expended and the defendants may be taken etc.

The State   )
vs.   )   An affray
Joseph Linn   )

    This day came as well the solicitor general on the part of the state as
the defendant in his proper person and the defendand being arraigned, upon his
arraignment plead not guilty as charged in the bill of indictment and for his
trial put himself upon God and his country wherefore came a jury of good and
lawful men, to wit, Joseph Eddings, James Tidwell, William Houston, Robert Houston
Absolem Massey, Jason H. Wilson, Samuel H. Shannon Philip G. Tucker, William
P303 Jordan, Philip Husselbough John Fussel, andGeorge Mezles, who being elected, tried
and sworn the truth to speak upon the issue joined, upon their oaths do say that
the defendant is not guilty of the charge in the aforesaid bill of indictment.
It is therefore considered by the court that the defendant recover against the
plaintiff his costs by him about his suit in this behalf expended.
    The Grand Jury this day returned into court an indictment against Wilson
Curtis for an assault indorsed a true bill also a presentment against Benoni
Crawford and Valentine Vantreese for an affray indorsed by the Grand Jury.
    John Thomas this day came into court and proved that Nathan Thomas killed
one wolf in the county of Madison over the age of four months.
    The administration of the estate of Aserius G. Martin, deceased, this day
returned an inventory of the estate also an inventory of the amount of sales of
* the late decedentadjourned until tomorrow morning nine o'clock.
‡ the late decedent.

                                      H. Haralson   JP.
                                      Sam Taylor   JP.
                                      J. Greer   JP.

P304 Friday 26th. March 1824
Court met according to adjournment-
Present the worshipful Herndon Haralson, James Greer, B. G. Stewart, John Thomas
Samuel Taylor, William C. Love, and William Draper Esq.

John B. Cross comes into court and records his stock mark as follows, to
wit, a crop off the right ear and a half crop off the lower side of the left ear.

The commissioners appointed to audit and settle with the administrators of
Robert Dosk deceased this day returned into court a report of the same which is
ordered to be recorded.

Benjamin Booth   )
vs.   ) Assumsit on writ of inquiry
Claiburn I. Ragsdale & Matthew Johnson)

This day came the parties aforesaid by their attorneys and thereupon came
a jury to wit, Joseph Eddings, Jonathan Walsh, Stephen Lypert, Martin Davis,
William Pace, Francis Taylor, Jesse D. Russell, John Murfree, John Fussell, John
C. Gillespie, John Cassels, and Malcolm Johnson, who being sworn well and truly
to inquire of damages, upon their oaths do say, we of the jury assess the plaintif
damages sustained by reason of the nonperformance of the assumsit in the declaration mentioned to ninety four dollars and eight cents. It is therefore considered
by the court that the plaintiff recover of the defendant the damages aforesaid in
form aforesaid assessed also his costs by him about this suit in this behalf
expended and the defendant in mercy etc.

P305 George Lyne   )
vs   ) Debt
Willoughby Powell)

This day came the partie aforesaid by their attorneys and thereupon came a
jury of good and lawful men, to wit, Joseph Eddings, Jonathan Walsh, Stephen
Lypert, Martin Davis, William Pace, Francis Taylor, Jesse D. Russell, John Murphy
John Fussell John C. Gillispie, John Cassells and Malcolm Johnson who being elected tried and sworn the truth to speak upon the issue joined upon their oaths do
say We of the jury do find for the plaintiff two hundred one dollars and eighty
six cents the debt in the declaration mentioned and do assess his damages by reaso
of the detention thereof to thirteen dollars and six cents, It is therefore considered by the court that the plaintiff recover of the defendant the said sum of
two hundred and one dollar together with his damamges aforesaid in form aforesaid
assessed also his costs by him about his suit in this behalf expended and the defendant in mercy etc.

Samuel McCorkel   )
vs.   ) Debt
James F. Theobald)

This day came the parties aforesaid by their attorneys and thereupon came a
jury of good and lawful men, to wit, Joseph Eddings, Jonathan Walsh, Stephen
Lypert, Martin Davis, William Pace, Francis Taylor Jesse D. Russell, John Murphy
John Fussell, John C. Gillispie John Cassels, and Malcolm Johnson, Who being
elected tried and sworn upon the issue joined & upon their oaths do say we of the
jury do fine both issues for the plaintiff and find for him the sum of one hundred
fifty eight dollars the debt in the declaration mentioned and do assess his damamges by reason of the ditention thereof to eleven dollars and fifty cents. (Marked
out- It is therefore considered by the court to eleven dollars and fifty cents)
It is therefore considered by the court that the plaintiff recover of the defendant the aforesaid sum of two hundred & one dollars together with the damages
aforesaid in form aforesaid assessed also his costs by him about his suit in this
behalf expended and the defendant in mercy etc.

P306 Richard Tisdale)
        vs.   )   Appeal
      William C. Love)

This day came the parties aforesaid and the plaintiff in this case dismisses his suit and the defendant assumes the payment of the costs herein. It is therefore considered by the court that the plaintiff recover of the defendant his costs by him in this behalf expended.

Ordered that the double taxes be remitted on the following tracts of land for the year 1823 to wit,

Owners name	NO. acres	Ent.	D.	R.	S.	Taxes	Remarks
Alexander Mark	1000	157	13	3	3	3.75	
Braham John	112		10	6	9		
Bingham John	442	88	9	2	10		
Clinc, Michael	250	503	13	7	3		
Corbit James	428	26	13	7	2		
Charry Daniel	1000	136	13	6	3.4		
Ditto	640	174	13	6	3		
Grant William	40		10	1	10		
Greer Thomas	1655	804	10	4	8		
Goodrich Russell	1000	2	9	2	10		
Hopkins Thomas	254		10	3	9		
Irvin Robert	2000	127	10	3	10		
Hawes Jacob	5000	809	10	1	12		
Jackson Thomas	5000	13	13	6	2		
Overton & Mulherrin	784	621	10	3	7		
Overton John	46¼	798	10	1	10		
Bigham John	348	326	9	2	10		
Pillow William	2452	12	10	3	10		
Ditto	274						
Ditto	130½	175	10	2	9		
Sloan John	200		9	1	10		
Clark Jonas	750	26	9	2	10		
Clark James W.	500	72	13	6.7	4		
James Poor	210						3 black polls.

P307   This day the Grand Jury returned into court an indictment against Wilson Curtis endorsed a true bill and also a presentment against Thomas Laremore and William Graham for an affray.

The State   )
     vs.   )   An affray
William Graham)

This day came as well the solicitor general on the part of the state as the defendant in this proper person and the defendant being arraigned upon his afraignment plead guilty as charged in the bill of indictment. It is therefore considered by the court that he make his peace with the state by the payment ofe one dollar fine and that the defendant go thereof hence and recover against the said defendant her fine and also her costs defendant-her-fine-and-also-her-cost by her about her suit in this behalf expended and the defendant taken etc.

The State   )
     vs.   )   An affray
Wilson Curtice)

This day came as well the solicitor general on the part of the state as the defendant in his proper person and the defendant being arraigned upon his arraignment plead guilty as charged in the bill of indictment. It is therefore considered by the court that the defendant make his peace with the state by the

P307 payment of twenty-five dollars fine and that the plaintiff go thereof hence and
Cont.recover against the defendant her costs by her about her suit in this behalf
expended and the defendant be taken etc.

P308   The sheriff of this county this day made the following report I Thomas
Shannon Sheriff and Collector of the public taxes for the county of Madison do
hereby report ot the court the following tracts of land as having been omitted
to be given in for the taxes for the year 1823 that the same is liable to double
taxes that the double taxes thereon remain due and unpaid and the respective
owners or claimants thereof have no goods or chattels within my county on which
can distrain for said double taxes to wit,

Owners name or claimant	No. A.	Dis.	Ra.	Sec.	Gr.	En.	Sh. fee	Fee.	Cl. fee	Taxes
Alesander Adam & Porter	640	10	2	9.10		710				4.80
Alexander & Maxwell	300	10	3	7		413				2.25
Alexander Adam R.	30	10	1	8		824				2.22½
Academon Francis	274	9	2	10		5				2.05½
Armstrong M Rep. of	228	10	1.2	10		102				1.71
Alen Daniel	228	9	1	2		401				1.71
Armstrong m Rep. of	500	9	1	10		241				3.75
Armstrong M.	5000	13	6.7	2	162					37.50
Adkinson William	188	10	3	7		1003	100	40	1.40	1.41
Armstrong Martin Jr.	5000	13	6.7	2						37.50
Armstrong Martin Jr.	5000	12	9	2.3	164					37.50
Armstrong Martin Jr.	5000	13	10.11	2.3	38					37.50
Armstrong Martin Jr.	5000	13	10.11	2	96					37.50
Anderson William P.	1000	13	10.11	1		539				7.50
Black William	322	10	2.3	6		490				2.41½
Bradley John	16 16/110	10	2	8.9		615				11½
Blount William	228	10	3	10		671	100	1.50	1.40	1.7.
Bryan John	640	10	1	9.10		756	100	1.50	1.40	4.80
Blount John G.	360	9	1	9		7	100	1.50	1.40	2.70
Britt Thomas	50	9	2	9		735	100	1.50	1.40	.37½
Brown Thomas	100	9	2	10		763	100	1.50	1.40	.75
Bingham John	442	9	2	10		88	100	1.50	1.40	3.31
Blount John G. Thomas	5000	11	-	-	342	-	100	1.50	1.40	37.50
Bledsoe, Anthony	428	10	5.6	9	-	587	100	1.50	1.40	3.21
Brown George	1097	10	2	9.10	-	956	100	1.50	1.40	8.31
Baker William Heirs of	640	10	4	1	-	981	100	1.50	1.40	4.60
Beverly P. R.	640	13	6	34	-	171	100	1.50	1.40	4.8
Blount Riding	793	13	6.7	5	-	541	100	1.50	1.40	5.9
Brinkley William	228	13	7	4	-	467	100	1.50	1.40	17

Owners of Claimants	No. A.	Dist.	Ra.	Sec.	R.	Gr.	En.	Sh. fee	Fee	Cl. fee	Taxes
Carpenter, Benjamin	428	10	2	10	30	-	138	100	1.50	1.40	3.21
Cannon Robert & Co.	327	10	2.5	8.9	31	-	764	100	1.50	.140	2.45
Chisum James	160	10	3	6	32	-	501	100	1.50	1.40	1.20
Campbell William	500	10	6	6	33	-	257	100	1.50	1.40	3.75
Crutcher, Edmond	87	9	2	10	34	-	53	100	1.50	1.40	.65
Champion Thomas	228	9	1.2	10	35	-	106	100	1.50	1.40	1.71
Curren, Hugh	640	10	2	34	36	-	975	100	1.50	1.40	4.80
Curren Francis	46	10	1	8	37	-	995	100	1.50	1.40	.36
Campbell, Thomas	10 100/160										
		9	1	7	38	-	910	100	1.50	1.40	.07
Carson Charles	148¼	9	1	10	39	-	934	100	1.50	1.40	1.11

	Owners name or claimants	NO. A.	Dist.	Ra.	Sec.	R.	Cor.	En.	Sh. fee	Fee fee	Cl. fee	Taxes
09	Christian Drury	20	9	1	8299	40	40	937	100	1.50	1.40	.15
	Cummins Geo D.	1000	9	1.2	6	41	-	987	100	1.50	1.40	7.50
	Cockrill M R.	279½	9	6	1	42	-	310	100	1.50	1.40	2.09¼
	Carter John	1000	13	8	2.3	43	112	-	100	1.50	1.40	7.50
	Crawford David	2000	13	8.9	1		44	379	100	1.50	1.40	15.00
	Henry Clark	5000	13	7.8	4.5	45	95	-	100	1.50	1.40	37.50
	Clark D----	5000	13	8.9	5	46	109	-	100	1.50	1.40	37.50
	Cethey George	613	13	8	5.6	47	-	312	100	1.50	1.40	4.59½
	Dougherty Geo.	2000	10	1	11	48	-	35	100	1.50	1.40	15.00
	Dougherty Geo.	114	10	1	10	49	-	244	100	1.50	1.40	.85½
	Dodson Ninrod	656	10	1	7	50		355	100	1.50	1.40	4.92
	Dougherty Geo.	500	10	3.4	7.8	51	-	704	100	1.50	1.40	4.92
	Davis John	470	9	2	7	52	-	584	100	1.50	1.40	3.52½
	Darr Daniel	100	9	2	11	53	-	132	100	1.50	1.40	.75
	Doughlass H. L. & others	577½	10	4	1	54	-	470	100	1.50	1.40	4.32½
	Donelson William & others	200	10	4	2	55	-	705	100	1.50	1.40	2.25
10	Dickens Edmond Heirs of	640	10	5	11	56	-	743	100	1.50	1.40	4.80
	Dixon William	360	10	5	11	57	-	776	100	1.50	1.40	2.70
	Dawson Ellick Heirs of	1000	10	4	3	58	-	890	100	1.50	1.40	7.50
	Dougherty Geo. deceased	423	10	4	3	59	-	924	100	1.50	1.40	3.17½
	Douge Jacob Hs. of	726	10	1	8	60	-	1148	100	1.50	1.40	5.44½
	Dougan James	3000	13	7	5	61	72	-	100	1.50	1.40	22.50
	Doughan John	2165	13	8	5	62	62	-	100	1.50	1.40	16.23½
	Drake John Hs. of	1600	13	7.8	2	63	-	187	100	1.50	1.40	12.00
	Elliott William	27⅓	9	1	9	64	-	892	100	1.50	1.40	.20
	Everett Matthew Hs. of	640	9	2	9	65	-	984	100	1.50	1.40	4.80
	Fort Elias	428	10	2	6	66	-	465	100	1.50	1.40	3.21
	Fogg Godfrey M.	65	10	3	1	67	-	969	100	1.50	1.40	.48¾
	Gerrard Charles	140	9	2	9	68	-	1048	100	1.50	1.40	1.05
	Green Sherwood	66	13	7	3	69	-	665	100	1.50	1.40	.49½
	Heys Robert	147¼	10	3	11	70	-	577	100	1.50	1.40	1.10¼
	Haynes John	1000	10	3	9	71	-	792	100	1.50	1.40	7.50
	Harrison Robert	1023	10	3	1	72	-	465	100	1.50	1.40	7.67¼
	Howard James	8⅓	9	2	10	73	-	513	100	1.50	1.40	.06¼
	Holmes John	26⅓	9	2	10	74	-	601	1.00	1.50	1.40	.19⅓
	Hart James	7402/3	9	2	11	75	-	606	100	1.50	1.40	5.55
	Hughes Alexander	1000	9	2	8	76	-	762	100	1.50	1.40	7.50
	Hill William	1500	9	2	10	77	-	120	100	1.50	1.40	11.25
	Hart Athony	434	11	2	1	78	-	230	100	1.50	1.40	3.25½
	Harrison James	250	10	2	4	79	831	-	100	1.50	1.40	1.87½
	Hardin William	71	10	1	9	80	-	845	100	1.50	1.40	1.28½
	Hunter Layton	600	10	4	8	81	-	861	100	1.50	1.40	4.50
	Hoard & King	53½	10	2	7	82	-	984	100	1.50	1.40	1.40
	Horton Jonah	88	9	1	7	83	-	1138	100	1.50	1.40	.66
	Henry Robert	100	9	2	8	84	-	964	100	1.50	1.40	.75
	Hughlett William	500	13	6	2.3	85	-	113	100	1.50	1.40	3.75
	Same	500	13	8	1	86	-	23	100	1.50	1.40	3.75
	Hunter I. Hs. of	500	13	8	5.6	87	-	313	100	1.50	1.40	3.75
	Johnson Duncan	100	10	2	10	88	-	548	100	1.50	1.40	.75
	Johnson Randol	640	10	4	2.3	89	-	384	100	1.50	1.40	4.80
	Same	400	10	4	3	90	-	357	100	1.50	1.40	3.00
	Jones Andes	274	10	4	2	91	-	609	100	1.50	1.40	2.05½
	Johnson Jacob Hs. of	1140	10	4	213	92	-	740	100	1.50	1.40	8.55
	Jenkins John	640	10	4	9	93	-	970	100	1.50	1.40	4.80

P311 Owners of claimants	No. A.	Dist.	Ran.	Sec.	R.	Gr.	En.	Sh. fee	Fee	Cl. fee	Taxes
Jones & Fogg	113	10	1	8	94	-	987	100	1.50	1.40	.77½
Jenkins John	2000	10	4	8.9	95	0	1007	-	-	-	7.50
Same	640	10	2	45	96	-	1011	-	-	-	4.80
Jones Ridley	600	13	6	4	97	-	435	-	-	-	4.50
Johnson Amos	358	13	7	3	98	-	538	0	-	-	2.68½
King Isabela	300	10	4	2	99	-	1057	-	-	-	2.25
Long Nicholas	920	10	3	10	100	-	22	-	-	-	6.92
Same	408	10	4	9	101	-	331	-	-	-	3.06
Lewis William F	1500	60	5	10	102	2637	-	-	-	-	11.25
Lester Fountain	267	9	1	9	103	-	16	-	-	-	2.00
Lester, Fountain	150	9	1	10	104	-	57	-	-	-	1.12½
Liddon Benj F.	3362/3	13	6	2	105	-	642	-	-	-	2.52
Leech & Polk	971	13	6.7	3	106	-	106	-	-	-	7.48¼
Lewis Chatte & Wm B	5000	13	6	5	107	-	483	-	-	-	37.50
Lewis Wm. T.	1490	13	8	2	108	-	156	-	-	-	11.17
Same	1000	13	6	1	109	-	60	-	-	-	7.50
Marshall Charles	90	10	1	8	110	-	71	-	-	-	.67½
Moore James	30	9	1	8	111	-	1052	-	-	-	.22½
Moore Robt.	21¼	9	2	9	112	-	1176	-	-	-	.16
McEachern Dan'l	60	10	2	8.9	113	-	96	-	-	-	.45
Same	54½	10	2	8	114	-	101	-	-	-	.41
McKindray Wm.	121	10	1	11	115	-	354	-	-	-	1.00¾
McTier Robt.	640	9	1.2	7	116	-	462	-	-	-	4.80
McFall Sam'l P.	50	10	1	8	117	-	944	-v	-	-	.37½
McWilbean Wm.	526	9	2	6.7	118	-	920	-	-	-	3.94½
McClure Matthew	2136	9	1.2	7	119	-	1013	-	-	-	16.02
McCorkle Alexr.	2411½	13	6	4.5	120	-	50	-	-	-	1808½
McClure James	2158¾	13	7	2	121	541	-	-	-	-	16.29
McCorkel John	640	13	7	4.5	122	-	256	-	-	-	4.80
Martin James	5000	13	7	5.6	123	108	-	-	-	-	37.50
Murrey Robt.	50	13	7	2	124	-	393	-	-	-	.37
Same	50	13	7	2	125	-	394	-	-	-	.37
Miller John	1000	13	7	3	126	-	156	-	-	-	7.50
Marr Geo. W. L.	640	13	8	5.6	127	-	402	-	-	-	4.80
Same	60	13	8	5	128	-	403	-	-	-	.45
P312 Marr & Dyer	34½	13	10&11	2	129	-	559	100	1.50	1.40	.31
Moore Morris	2560	13	10.11	3	130	-	662	100	1.50	1.40	19.20
Murphy Archd.	4350	13	7.8	2	131	339	-		100	1.50	1.40	32.62½
Nixon Thomas Hr. of	3840	10	5	8.9	132	-	754	100	1150	1.40	28.85
Nash William	753	9	2	8.9	133	-	614	100	1.50	1.40	5.64¾
Same	504	9	2	8	134	-	734	100	1.50	1.40	3.75
Newton Edward	640	11	1	9	135	-	572	100	1.50	1.40	4.80
Nelson, Robt	500	10	4.5	1	136	-	492	100	1.50	1.40	3.75
Same	500	10	1	10	137	-	44	100	1.50	1.40	1.87½
Nash Redmond B.	250	13	7	2	138	-	585	100	1.50	1.40	1.87½
Same	502½	13	7	2	139	-	54	100	1.50	1.40	3.77
Nash William	17	13	7	2	140	-	78	100	1.50	1.40	.10¾
Same	50	13	7	2	141	-	644	100	1.50	1.40	37½
Polk, Samuel	57	10	1	8	142	-	251	100	1.50	1.40	.42¾
Poston John H.	267	10	4	7	142	-	73	100	1.50	1.40	2.00¼
Pillow Gideon	500	10	1	7	143	-	416	100	1.50	1.40	3.75
Polk Samuel	1500	10	3	5.6 Pt. of	-	466	100	1.50	1.40	11.25
Poor James	240	10		5000,144							
			1	10.11	145	-	825	100	1.50	1.40	1.80
Pillow Abner	500	10	43	2	146	-	437	100	1.50	1.40	3.75

2 Owners f Claimants	No. A.	Dist.	Ran.	Sec.	R.	Gr.	En.	Sh. fee	Fee fee	Cl.	Taxes
Same	400	10	3	2	147	-	706	100	1.50	1.40	3.00
Same	400	10	4	2	148	-	707	100	1.50	1.40	3.00
Price Isaac	1000	10	6	5.6	149	-	692	100	1.50	1.40	7.50
Powell Burn	72	9	1	11	150	-	42	100	1.50	1.40	.54
Patterson Samuel	267¾	9	2	9	151	-	556	100	1.50	1.40	2.00¼
Phillips Andrew	120	9	1	9	152	-	94	100	1.50	1.40	.90
Powell Burn	378	9	1	9	153	-	211	100	1.50	1.40	2.83½
Purdy John	200	9	2	8	154	-	882	100	1.50	1.40	1.50
Patterson William	35½	9	2	9	155	-	898	100	1.50	1.40	.36½
Polk William	100	10	4	3	156	-	1051	100	1.50	1.40	.75
Patterson John T.	115	10	6	2	157	-	1037	100	1.50	1.40	.86¼
Polk Thos G.	2000	13	7	2	158	-	197	100	1.50	1.40	15.00
Quisinberry Anderson	3019½	13	11	1	159	-	534	100	1.50	1.40	22.64½
Richy Robt. Hs. of	471	13	6	5	160	-	654	100	1.50	1.40	3.53¼
Robertson, Benj.	1000	10	2.3	9	161	-	85	100	1.50	1.40	7.50
Rayford Philip	274	10	1	10	162	-	158	100	1.50	1.40	2.04½
Ray Saml Anderson	200	10	4	6	163	-	601	100	1.50	1.40	1.50
Rhodes Wm. Hs of	37	10	2	7	164	-	74	100	1.50	1.40	.27¾
Rice John	5000	11	-	-	165	291	-	100	1.50	1.40	37.50
Same	5000	11	-	-	166	286	-	100	1.50	1.40	37.50
Same	5000	11	-	-	167	296	-	100	1.50	1.40	37.50
Same	5000	11	-	-	168	282	-	100	1.50	1.40	37.50
Reynolds, Wm.	52	13	1	8	169	-	869	100	1.50	1.40	.39
Robertson Elijah	307½	13	4	7;8	170	-	985	100	1.50	1.40	2.30½
Rutherford John	5000	13	8.9	1	171	109	-	100	1.50	1.40	37.50
Rutherford Henry	2000	13	8.9	1	172	34	-	10	1.50	1.40	15.00
Rutherford John Jr.	50	13	7	2	173	-	215	100	1.50	1.40	.37½
Rutherfored Henry	102	13	8	2	174	-	198	100	1.50	1.40	.76½
Ross David	505	13	11	4	175	-	623	100	1.50	1.40	3.78¾
Rynolds Joseph	640	13	6	1	176	-	261	100	1.50	1.40	4.80
Sherwood Wm.	120	10	1	10	177	-	181	100	1.50	1.40	.90
Stubblefield Clement	228	10	5	6	178	-	364	100	1.50	1.40	1.71
Smith Benjamin	3000	10	5	9.10	179	2408	-	100	1.50	1.40	22.50
Same	2000	10	5	10.11	180	2420	-	100	1.50	1.40	15.00
Same	2000	10	5	11	181	2412	-	100	1.50	1.40	15.00
Stephens Lewis	228	9	2	9	182	-	11o	100	1.50	1.40	1.71
Smith William	366	9	1	9	183	-	155	100	1.50	1.40	2.74½
Sullivan Lee	2000	11	1	6	184	-	375	100	1.50	1.40	15.00
Scruggs James	95	11	1	6	185	-	595	100	1.50	1.40	.71¼
Spencer Clark	274	10	3	4	186	-	841	100	1.50	1.40	2.04½
Swindle & Stubblefield	72	10	4	4	187		914	100	1.50	1.40	.54
Shandlin John	500	10	3	4.5	188	-	969	100	1.50	1.40	3.75
Shineult Walter	51½	10	2	2	189	-	1053	100	1.50	1.40	.38½
Shineult & Yeary	85	10	4	2	190	-	1065	100	1.50	1.40	.63¾
Shute Thomas	68½	9	1	9	191	982		100	1.50	1.40	.51½
Sharp William	5000	13	6.7	5	192	-	-	100	1.50	1.40	37.50
Sharp Anthony	3000	13	6.7	2.3	193	83	-	100	1.50	1.40	22.50
Smith Benjamin	5000	13	9.10	1	194	98	-	100	1.50	1.40	37.50
Same	5000	13	9.10	1	195	84	-	100	1.50	1.40	30.50
Same	4000	13	1.10	1	196	84	-	100	1.50	1.40	30.00
Same	3000	13	8	3	197	122	-	100	1.50	1.40	22.50
Same	5000	13	7.8	1	198	401	-	100	1.50	1.40	37.50
Same	5000	13	7	1	199	402	-	100	1.50	1.40	37.50
Same	5000	13	7	1.2	200	416	-	100	1.50	1.40	37.50

P314 Owners of Claimants	No. A.	Dist.	Ran.	Sec.	R.	Gr.	En.	Sh. fee	Fee	Cl. fee	Taxes
Same	5000	13	9.10	2	201	409	-	100	1.50	1.40	37.50
Same	5000	13	8	2	202	407	-	100	1.50	1.40	37.50
Same	5000	13	7	1	203	411	9	100	1.50	1.40	37.50
Sherwood Wm. Hs.	320	13	10	2	204	-	526	100	1.50	1.40	2.40
Thtmbhe James	499½	10	1	10	205	-	191	100	1.50	1.40	3.74½
Thomas Micajah	78	10	1	9	206	-	822	100	1.50	1.40	.58½
Taylor Francis	160	9	12	11	207	-	12	100	1.50	1.40	1.20
Taylor Samuel	160	9	1.2	11	208	-	13	100	1.50	1.40	1.20
Taulor Srury	23	10	2	7	209	-	1058	100	1.50	1.40	.17¼
Terrell John	640	10	4	8	210	9	968	100	1.50	1.40	4.80
Same	640	10	1	6	211	-	1008	100	1.50	1.40	4.80
Towns Howell & Wdggins	68	9	2	7	212	-	931	100	1.50	1.40	.51
Valk A.	5000	-	-	-	213	305	-	100	1.50	1.40	37.50
Wilson George	188	10	1	9	214	-	713	1000	1.50	1.40	1.41
Weir John	100	10	3	1	215	-	271	100	1.50	1.40	.75
Wilson Lewis D.	640	10	5	1	216	-	516	100	1.50	1.40	4.80
Wilson George	50	9	2	11	217	-	33	100	1.50	1.40	.37
Wilson James	10	9	1	10	218	-	724	-	-	-	.77½
William Robt. W	201	9	1	10	219	-	161	-	-	-	1.50¾
Wheaton D. & I Tisdale	640	11	1	9	220	-	855	-	-	-	4.80
Wilson John	640	9	2	11	221	-	29	-	-	-	4.80
Watson John	120	10	1	7	222	-	829	-	-	-	.90
Walker John	38½	10	1	9	223	-	830	-	-	-	.29
Wilson James	40	10	1	10	224	-	870	-	-	-	.30
Williams Willoughby	510	10	1	9	223	-	830	-	-	-	.27
Wilson James	40	10	1	10	224	-	870	-	-	-	.30
Williams Willoughby	5	10	1	4	225	-	917	0	-	-	-.03¼
Wilson James	40	9	1	10	226	-	914	-	-	-	.30
Same	100	9	1	9	227	-	915	-	-	-	.75
Watson Jeremiah	228	13	6	2	228	-	706	-	-	-	1.71
Yeary Isaac	332½	9	2	7	229	-	1145	-	-	-	2149⅛

P315   Where upon it is considered by the court that judgment be and it is hereby entered against the aforesaid tracts of land in the name of the state for the su? annexed to each being the amount of double taxes cost and charges due severally thereon for the year of eighteen hundred and twenty threr and it is ordered by the court that the said several tracts of land or so much thereof as shall be sufficient of each of them to satisfy the double taxes costs and charges annexed to them severally be sold as the law directs.

    I, Thomas Shannon Sheriff and collector of the public taxes for the county of Madison do report to the court the following tracts of land and having been given in for the taxes for the eighteen hundred and twenty threee that the taxes thereon remain due and unpait and the respective owners or claimants have no good on chattles within my county on which I can distrain for said taxes to wit.

Acin James & Henry	154	10	4	2	830	881	-	100	1.50	1.40	.57¾
Armstrong Martin Rep. of.	300	10	2	9	231	--	246	100	1.50	1.40	1.12½
Ditto	500	10	2	4	232	-	335	100	1.50	1.40	1.87½
Ditto	400	10	2	7	233	-	359	100	1.50	1.40	1.50
Ditto	160	10	2	6	234	-	502	100	1.50	1.40	.60
Ditto	500	10	2	6	235	-	418	100	1.50	1.40	1.87½

Owners name or Claimants	No. A.	Dist.	Ra.	Sec.	R.	Gr.	En	Sh. fee	Fee fee	Cl. fee	Taxes
315 ont.											
Ashe & Strudivick	4350	-	-	-	236	-	-	100	1.50	1.40	16.31½
Alston Alfred	640	10	6	5	237	-	1025	100	1.50	1.40	2.40
Armstrong Jas L.	367	10	-	-	238	-	-	100	1.50	1.40	1.37½
Benson, Gabriel	44	10	1	3	239	-	-	100	1.50	1.40	.16½
Buchannen John	22	10	1	3	240	-	-	100	1.50	1.40	.08½
Brevord John	2560	10	1	8.9	241	-	-	100	1.50	1.40	9.60
Brooks Robert	144	10	2	9	242	-	-	100	1.50	1.40	.54
Same	640	10	6	6	243	-	-	100	1.50	1.40	2.40
Bartholomew Jacob	640	10	4	4	244	-	-	100	1.50	1.40	2.40
Same	640	10	4	3	245	-	-	100	1.50	1.40	2.40
Bowers, George	1097	10	3	3	246	-	-	100	1.50	1.40	4.11½
Baldridge Francis Hs.of	640	10	8	4	247	-	-	100	1.50	1.40	2.40
16 Barncass Richard	182	10	1	9	248	-	-	100	1.50	1.40	.68½
Brown Nathaniel	274	9	8	1	249	-	-	100	1.50	1.40	1.02¾
Bryan & Freeman	1000	11	1	10	250	-	-	100	1.50	1.40	3.75
Barber Joseph	274	13	8	4	251	-	-	100	1.50	1.40	1.02¾
Bledsoe Anthony Hs.of	428	10	5.6	9	252	-	589	100	1.50	1.40	1.60½
Blount, William	1500	10	4	11	253	-	632	100	1.50	1.40	5.62½
Brown John	4000	-	-	-	254	-	-	100	1.50	1.40	15.00
Benson Gabriel	128	-	-	-	255	-	-	100	1.50	1.40	.47½
Bryant Joseph S&	227	10	2	9	256	-	5	100	1.50	1.40	1.02¾
Same	274	10	2	9	257	-	187	100	1.50	1.40	1.02¾
Byan & Watson	640	10	2.3	7	258	-	249	100	1.50	1.40	2.40
Ditto	640	10	2	7	259	-	745	100	1.50	1.40	2.40
Bryant & Freeman	128	10	3	6	260	-	412	100	1.50	1.40	.41¼
Branch Joseph	3989	10	5.6	8	261	-	805	100	1.50	1.40	14.95
Breham John	350	13	6	-	262	-	-	100	1.50	1.40	1.31¼
Bonner John	384½	10	1	8	263	-	-	100	1.50	1.40	1.44
Buchennon Robt	308	-	-	-	264	-	-	100	1.50	1.40	1.15½
Benton Jesse Hs. of	5000	13	8	4	265	-	38	100	1.50	1.40	18.75
Clenny Samuel	521	10	3	9	266	-	-	100	1.50	1.40	1.95½
Craig John	583	10	6	6	267	-	-	100	1.50	1.40	2.18½
Campbell David	200	-	-	-	268	-	-	100	1.50	1.40	.75
Cook Mark	228	-	-	-	269	-	61	100	1.50	1.40	.85½
Calaham Cornelius	294	10	3	10	270	-	62	100	1.50	1.40	1.10¼
Conrod John	226	10	1	1.10	271	-	222	100	1.50	1.40	.84¾
Coleman William	1000	10	6	6.7	272	-	-	100	1.50	1.40	3.75
Conner Jacob Hs. of	640	9	2	7.8	273	-	91	100	1.50	1.40	2.40
Cocke William Hs. of	640	9	2	7	274	-	68	100	1.50	1.40	2.40
Clendenning James	320	10	2	10	275	-	250	100	1.50	1.40	1.20
Coldwell John	146	10	3	5	276	-	-	100	1.50	1.40	.54¾
Dougherty George	260	-	-	-	277	-	-	100	1.50	1.40	.97¼
Dunlap Hugh	5000	-	-	-	278	-	-	100	1.50	1.40	18.75
Ditto	500	-	-	-	279	9	-	100	1.50	1.40	18.75
Edmisson Robt.	590	-	-	-	280	-	-	100	150	1.40	2.21¼
Eddleman Francis	274	9	2	10	281	-	5	100	150	1.40	1.02
Fowler, Tillonus	400	10	4.3	9	282	-	-	100	1.50	1.40	1.50
Freeman James	1000	10	2	10	283	-	-	100	1.50	1.40	3.75
Same	274	10	4	9	284	-	-	100	1.50	1.40	1.02¾
Franklin Ambros Hs. of	228	13	5	285	285	-	354	100	1.50	1.40	.85½
Fairfax Harrington Hiers of	640	10	2	10.11	286	-	-	100	1.50	1.40	2.40
Gerrard Charles	640	10	3	7	287	-	483	100	1.50	1.40	2.40
Goddlett & Campbell	1000	10	2	5	288	-	665	100	1.50	1.40	3.75

P318 Owners name or Claimants	No. A.	Dis.	Ra.	Sec.	R.	Gr.	En.	Sh. fee	Fee	Cl. Fee	Taxes
Goslin Ambrose	640	10	4	10	289	-	107	100	1.50	1.40	2.40
Hollaway James	600	10	-	-	290	-	334	100	1.50	1.40	2.25
Harris Robert	5000	10	5	12	291	-	618	100	1.50	1.40	18.75
Hoard William	2100	10	4	9	292	-	506	100	1.50	1.40	7.87
Same	238¼	10	2	6	293	-	509	100	1.50	1.40	.89
Hoard & King	184	10	2	7	294	-	832	100	1.50	1.40	.69
Same	53¼	10	2	1	395	-	984	100	1.50	1.40	.19
Hays William	35	10	2	4	296	-	1012	100	1.50	1.40	.13
Huddleston Semon	640	10	2	7	297	-	297	100	1.50	1.40	2.40
Hopkins Thomas	40	10	3	4	298	-	-	100	1.50	1.40	.15
Ditto	50	10	5	8	299	-	-	100	1.50	1.40	.18
Hines Levi	161⅓	10	4	5	300	-	-	100	1.50	1.40	.60
Hogg David	100	10	1	9	301	-	154	100	1.50	1.40	.37
Johnson Jacob V.	265¼	9	1	11	302	-	-	100	1.50	1.40	.99½
Johnson George	2500	10	5.6	8	303	-	290	100	1.50	1.40	9.37⅛
James Willoughby	640	10	5	5	304	-	-	100	1.50	1.40	2.40
Johnson Cave	274	10	1	9	305	-	666	100	1.50	1.40	1.02
Same	640	11	1	2.9.10 306	-	685	100	1.50	1.40	2.40
Joiner Matthew	180	10	4	11	307	-	256	100	1.50	1.40	.69
Ingram William	99	10	2	9	308	-	723	100	1.50	1.40	.37
Ingram David	125	10	1	3	309	-	-	100	1.50	1.40	.46
Dittor	33	10	1	3	310	-	-	100	1.50	1.40	.12
Ditto	63	10	1	3	311	-	-	100	1.50	1.40	.23
Knowlet Joshua	640	9	2	8	312	-	-	100	1.50	1.40	2.40
King Thos. Hs. of	640	10	6	8	313	-	-	100	1.50	1.40	2.40
Legit, William	95	9	2	11	314	-	-	100	1.50	1.40	.35
Lester Alexander	300	10	5	3	315	-	934	100	1.50	1.40	1.12
Long Nicholas	640	9	1	8	316	-	-	100	1.50	1.40	2.40
Mendingham Mordacar	228	9	1	3	317	-	401	100	1.50	1.40	.85
Mulherrin & Overton	781	10	3	7	318	-	-	100	1.50	1.40	2.92
Morphis & Johnson	640	10	5	5	319	-	14	100	1.50	1.40	2.40
Murfree Hardy	2581	13	6	5	320	-	519	100	1.50	1.40	9.67
Same	987	13	8	3	321	-	0	100	1.50	1.40	3.50
Moore Travis	2000	-	-	-	322	-	-	100	1.50	1.40	7.50
P318 Mayers Chas. F.	5000	10	1	2	323	-	-	100	1.50	1.40	18.75
Mahan Archibald	234	9	1	10	324	-	-	100	1.50	1.40	.87½
McIver John	140	-	-	-	325	-	-	100	1.50	1.40	.52
Ditto	160	10	1	7.8	326	-	-	100	1.50	1.40	.60
Ditto	293	11	4	10	327	-	-	100	1.50	1.40	1.09
Ditto	198	8	8	3	328	-	-	100	1.50	1.40	.74
Ditto	1000	11	2	10.11	329	-	-	100	1.50	1.40	3.75
Ditto	640	11	8	3	330	-	-	100	1.50	1.40	2.40
Ditto	274	11	4	10	331	-	-	100	1.50	1.40	1.02
Ditto	100	12	2	5	332	-	-	100	1.50	1.40	.37
Ditto	640	12	8	9	333	-	-	100	1.50	1.40	2.40
Ditto	640	12	1	2	334	-	-	100	1.50	1.40	2.40
Ditto	640	12	2.3	6	335	-	-	100	1.50	1.40	2.40
Ditto	2000	13	4	4	336	-	-	100	1.50	1.40	7.50
Ditto	372	13	3	8	337	-	-	100	1.50	1.40	.139
Ditto	1000	13	4	4	338	-	-	100	1.50	1.40	3.75
Ditto	274	13	3	7	339	-	-	100	1.50	1.40	1.02
Ditto	200	10	2	10	340	-	106	100	1.50	1.40	.75
Ditto	160	10	1	7.8	341	-	350	100	1.50	1.40	.60
Ditto	200	10	1	7.8	342	-	351	100	1.50	1.40	.75
Ditto	274	-	-	-	343	-	353	100	1.50	1.40	1.02

18 Owners name or nt.Claimants	No. A.	Dist.	Ra.	Sec.	R.	Cr.	En.	Sh. fee	Fee	Cl. fee	Taxes
McGee John	350	100	2	9	344	-	268	100	1.50	1.40	1.31¼
McCulloch Benj.	5000	3	Forked Deer		354	-	-	100	1.50	1.40	18.75
McIver John	799	10	2	10	346	-	467	100	1.50	1.40	2.99½
Murphy A. D.	2000	13	8.9	4.5	347	-	416	100	1.50	1.40	7.50
McDonley John	274	9	2	8	348	-	-	100	1.50	1.40	1.02¾
McDonald John	450	10	4.5	11	349	-	195	100	1.50	1.40	1.68¾
McPike John	108	10	4	10.11	350	-	300	100	1.50	1.40	.40½
McCulloch Benj.	274	10	2	10	351	-	240	100	1.50	1.40	.99
Same	800	13	8	3	352	-	124	100	1.50	1.40	3.00
McIlhatton Wm.	3880	13	7	4	353	-	46	100	1.50	1.40	14.55
Nash Redmond B.	80	9	1	10	354	-	-	100	1.50	1.40	.30
Owens John	100	9	1	8	355	-	-	100	1.50	1.40	.37½
Ditto	200	9	1	8	356	-	-	100	1.50	1.40	.75
Powers John	50	9	6	3	357	-	-	100	1.50	1.40	.18¾
Poyzer George	258 70/100	12	1	9	358	-	204	100	1.50	1.40	.96¼
Patrick John	640	10	2	10	359	-	291	100	1.50	1.40	2.40
Ditto	274	10	4	10	360	-	631	100	1.50	1.40	1.02½
Porter Recie	95	10	1	10	361	-	-	100	1.50	1.40	.35½
Prustman Lawrence	640	10	4	2	362	-	-	100	1.50	1.40	2.40
Pillow & Bradshaw	500	10	5	3	363	-	-	100	1.50	1.40	1.67½
Polk, Thomas G.	1434	10	5	6	364	-	406	100	1.50	1.40	5.39½
Porter William	95	10	2	10	365	-	698	100	1.50	1.40	.35½
Polk Thos. son of E. Polk	500	10	4	3	366	-	442	100	1.50	1.40	1.87½
Rutherford John	56	13	7	2	367	-	-	100	1.50	1.40	.21
Same	69	13	7	2	368	-	-	100	1.50	1.40	.25¾
Rutherford John	1000	13	8	2	369	-	-	100	1.50	1.40	3.75
Rhodes Tyrea	307	13	4	7	370	-	-	100	1.50	1.40	1.15¾
Rhea John	100	13	3	3	371	-	-	100	1.50	1.40	1.37½
Rutland, Isaac	282½	9	10	9	372	-	-	100	1.50	1.40	1.06
Roberson James	1000	10	6	7	373	-	428	100	1.50	1.40	3.75
Robb, Joseph	320	10	3	8	374	-	644	100	1.50	1.40	1.20
Roberson Jas. Hs. of	716	10	2	11	375	-	1055	100	1.50	1.40	2.68⅛
Shute Thomas	400	9	1	8	376	-	-	100	1.50	1.40	1.50
Same	100	9	1	8	377	-	-	100	1.50	1.40	.37½
Same	640	9	1	8	378	-	-	100	1.50	1.40	2.40
Same	425	9	1	8	379	-	-	100	1.50	1.40	1.59½
Same	40	9	1	8	380	-	-	100	1.50	1.40	.15
Same	200	9	1	8	381	-	-	100	1.50	1.40	.75
Same	153	9	1	8	382	-	-	100	1.50	1.40	.57½
Same	30	9	1	8	383	-	-	100	1.50	1.40	.11½
Spraggins Samuel	88	9	1	8	384	-	-	100	1.50	1.40	.33
Stokes John	2500	13	N. Fork Deer		385	-	-	100	1.50	1.40	9.37½
Sumner Jethro	1880	10	3	10	386	-	7	100	1.50	1.40	6.81¾
Shepherd Abraham	285½	9	1	8	387	-	131	100	1.50	1.40	1.07¾
Sloan John	138	10	1	9	388	-	114	100	1.50	1.40	1.40
											.51¾

P319 Cont.	Owners name or Claimants	No. A.	Dist.	Ra.	Sec.	R.	Cr.	En.	Sh fee	Fee	Cl. fee	Taxes
	Shute Asa	186	10	2	10	389	-	515	100	1.50	1.40	.69¾
	Shepherd F.	2851/310		3	8	390	-	480	100	1.50	1.40	1.07
	Spencer John	731	10	3	7	391	-	338	100	1.50	1.40	2.74½
	Sloan John	32	10	1	9	392	-	210	100	1.50	1.40	.12
	Taylor Nathaniel	300	10	3	4	393	-	963	100	1.50	1.40	1.12½
	Talliaferro, Benj.	1000	10	6	6	394	-	145	100	1.50	1.40	3.75
	Tommer, Henry	2020	13	7	4	395	-	74	100	1.50	1.40	7.57½
	Travis Thomas	5000	10	34	11	396	-	345	100	1.50	1.40	18.75
	Uhle Frederick W.	160	9	1	10	397	-	-	100	1.50	1.40	.60
	Walker John	476	10	1	2	398	-	211	100	1.50	1.40	1.78½
	White William	329	10	1	10	399	-	-	100	1.50	1.40	1.23½
	William Willoughby	88	10	2	9	400	-	-	100	1.50	1.40	.33
	Whitesides Jenkins	243½	10	4	3	401	-	642	100	1.50	1.40	.91½
	Same	1000	10	5	8	402	279	-	100	1.50	1.40	3.75
	William Willoughby	86	10	3	3	403	-	-	100	1.50	1.40	.32½
	Williams Jaseph	640	10	3	10	404	-	-	100	1.50	1.40	2.40
	Wheaton & Tisdale	5000	-	F.	D.	405	400	-	100	1.50	1.40	18.75
	Same	5000	-	-	-	406	403	-	100	1.50	1.40	18.75
	Same	5000	-	-	-	407	407	-	100	1.50	1.40	18.75
	Same	2500 Part of	5000			408	410	-	100	1.50	1.40	9.37½
P320	Wheaton & Tisdale	5000	-	-	-	409	413	-	100	1.50	1.40	18.75
	Watson, Robert C.	640	10	2	9	410	-	20	100	1.50	1.40	2.40
	William S. H.	640	9	4	9	411	-	-	100	1.50	1.40	2.40
	Same	274	-	5	10	412	-	-	100	1.50	1.40	1.02½
	Williams Willoughby	274	10	3	9	413	-	-	100	1.50	1.40	1.02½
	William & McGavock	274	10	3	9	414	-	-	100	1.50	1.40	1.02½
	Elizabeth Nelson	220	10	6	9	415	-	553	100	1.50	1.40	.82½
	Same	420½	10	5	9	416	-	333	100	1.50	1.40	1.57½
	Same	345	10	5	9	417	-	270	100	1.50	1.40	1.29½
	John H. Porter	260	10	6	10	418	-	313	100	1.50	1.40	.97
	Andrew Goff	75	10	6	9	419	-	-	100	1.50	1.40	.28
	James Scruggs	250	10	5	9	420	-	294	100	1.50	1.40	.93¾
	Same	250	10	4	6	421	-	558	100	1.50	1.40	.93¼
	Arthur Campbell	640	11	1	6	422	-	-	100	1.50	1.40	2.40
	Scruggs James	500	10	6	1	423	-	-	100	1.50	1.40	1.87½
	Ditto	250	11	6	1	424	-	-	100	1.50	1.40	.93¾
	Oliver B. Hays	320	11	5	9	425	-	-	100	1.50	1.40	1.20
	William P. Anderson	3119½	13	1	11	426	-	534	100	1.50	1.40	10.95
	Christopher Stump	80	10	1	9	427	-	980	100	1.50	1.40	.30
	Henry Humphreys	144	10	1	9	428	-	974	100	1.50	1.40	.50½
	John Chalmers	640	10	2	8	429	-	113	100	1.50	1.40	2.40
	Jones & Hogg	113½	10	1	8	430	-	987	100	1.50	1.40	.42
	Joseph Byers	1500	-	-	-	413	-	-	100	1.50	1.40	5.62
	James Byers	2000	-	-	-	432	-	-	100	1.50	1.40	7.50
	Edmond Swanson	106	-	-	-	433	-	-	100	1.50	1.40	.40
	Peter & James Swanson	149	10	3	3	434	-	-	100	1.50	1.40	.56

Owners name or Claimants	No. A.	Dist.	Ra.	Sec.	R.	Cr.	Ln.	Sh fee	Fee fee	Ol. fee	Taxes
Rhomas Bonds Heirs	640	-	-	-	435	-	-	100	1.50	1.40	2.40
William S. Henderson	400	-	-	-	436	-	-	100	1.50	1.40	1.50
Ditto	100	-	-	-	434	-	-	100	1.50	1.40	.37½
Alexander Ewing	640	-	-	-	435	-	-	100	1.50	1.40	2.40
Ditto	308	-	-	-	439	-	-	100	1.50	1.40	1.15½
Ditto	200	-	-	-	440	-	-	100	1.50	1.40	.75
Ditto	900	-	-	-	441	-	-	100	1.50	1.40	m3.37½
Solomon Cotton	1000	10	4	9	442	-	-	100	1.50	1.40	3.45
Thomas F Devereaux	250	9	2	10	443	-	-	100	1.50	1.40	.93½
David Jeffers	640	10	3.4	7.8	444	-	-	100	1.50	1.40	2.45
Joseph Bryan	274	10	1	4	445	-	-	100	1.50	1.40	1.02½
Ephrianr Davidson	2000	10	6	-	446	-	-	100	1.50	1.40	7.50
Henry Rutherford	5000	13	-	-	447	-	-	1000	1.50	1.40	18.75
Cader Pearcy	100	-	-	-	448	-	-	100	1.50	1.40	.37½
J. A. T. Hightower	500	10	5	9	449	-	137	100	1.50	1.40	1.87½
Same	400	10	5	9	450	-	445	100	1.50	1.40	1.50
Jonas Clark	750	9	2	10	451	-	26	100	1.50	1.40	2.81½
James W. Clark	5000	13	6.7	4	452	-	72	100	1.50	1.40	18.75
Michael Cline	250	13	7	3	453	-	503	100	1.50	1.40	.93
James Carbit	428	13	7	2	454	-	26	100	1.50	1.40	1.60½
Daniel Cherry	1000	13	8	3.4	455	-	126	100	1.50	1.40	3.75
Same	640	13	6	3	456	-	174	100	1.50	1.40	2.40
John Bingham	462	9	2	10	457	-	88	100	1.50	1.40	1.65¾
Ditto	348	9	2	10	458	-	326	100	1.50	1.40	1.30½
Jacob Hawes	5000	10	1	1.2	459	-	809	100	1.50	1.40	18.75
Thomas Jackson	5000	13	6	2	460	-	13	100	1.50	1.40	18.75
Overton & Mulherron	784	10	3	7	461	-	621	100	1.50	1.40	2.94
John Overton	46¼	10	1	10	462	-	798	100	1.50	1.40	.17½
Mark Alexander	1000	13	3	3	465	-	157	100	1.50	1.40	3.75
William Pillow	2452	10	3	10	464	-	12	100	1.50	1.40	9.19½
Ditto	274	-	-	-	465	-	-	100	1.50	1.40	1.02½
Ditto	130½	10	2	9	466	-	175	100	1.50	1.40	.50
Russell Goodrich	1000	9	2	10	467	-	2	100	1.50	1.40	3.75
William Shaw	640	10	6	10	468	-	329	100	1.50	1.40	2.40

Whereupon it is considered by the court that judgment be and it is hereby
entered against the aforesaid tracts of land in the name of the state for the sum
annexed to each being the amount of the single taxes, costs and charges due severally thereon for the year Eighteen hundred and twenty-three and it is ordered by
the court that said several tracts of land or so much thereof as shall be sufficient of each of them to satisfy the single taxes, cost and charges annexed to them
severally be sold as the law directs.

The State   )
vs.   )   An assault
Samuel H. Shannon)

This day came the defendant in this case and prayed an appeal from a judgment rendered herein on a former day of this court to the next circuit court
to be held for the county of Madison on the fourth Monday in May next which was
granted him on his entering into bond with David Jarrett and Andrew L. Martin his
securities in penalty of one hundred dollars conditioned for the prosecution of
the appeal which was done accordingly.

Administration of all and singular the goods and chattels rights and credits
of Joseph Tedford, deceased was granted to Prudence Tedford and Bartholomew G.

P. 2 Stewart, who thereupon qualified as administratrix and administration to said es-
Cont. tate and entered into and acknowledged their bond in the penalty of five hundred
dollars with Alfred Murray their security. It is therefore ordered by the court
that letters of administration issue accordingly.

An indenture of bargain and sale from James Huggins to Samuel Polk was this
day produced in open court and the execution of the same proven by the oath of
David Jarrett and Pleasant Jarrett to be the act and deed of the said Huggins and
ordered to be certified for registration.

Wilson & Stewart)
vs.) Appeal
Benjamin Gholson)

This day came the plaintiffs by their attorney and the defendant in his
proper person and the said defendant agree to prosecute his appeal no further and
confess judgment of the sum of seventy four dollars eighty-seven and one half cent
debt and also the further sum of one dollar and seventy-five cents damages and als
his costs. It is agreed by the plaintiff that execution be staid three months.
It is threrfore considered by the court that the plaintiff recover against the
defendant the debt damage and cost aforesaid and that the defendant in mercy etc.

P323 William Houston)
vs.) Case
Hamilton & Howard)

This day came the plaintiff by his attorney and the defendants in proper
persons and the plaintiff dismisses his case and assumes all the cost. It is ther
fore considered by the court that the defendant recover of the plaintiff their
cost by them about their suit in this behalf expended and the defendant in mercy
etc.

Abraham T. Smith comes and proves four days attendance as a constable attending on the court and jury at the present term.

Andrew Hays proves two days attendance as juror of vie prior to passage
of an act repealing the act allowing compensation to jurors of view in the Western
district.

Commissioners of the Town of Jackson)
vs.) In debt
James Dorris James Wright & Bing Gholson)

This day came the plaintiffs by their attorney and dismissed their suit as
to James Wright one of the defendants about named. It is therefore considered by
the court that the said James Wright go hence there of without day and recover of
said plaintiff his costs by him about his suit in this behalf expended and the p
plaintiff for their false clamor in mercy etc.

P324 Banele Canneway)
vs.) Debt
Joel Dyer Senr.)

This day came the parties aforesaid by their attorneys and thereupon the defendant withdraws his plea and says he cannot gainsay the plaintiffs action thereo
against him for the sum of one hundred seventeen dollars thirty-three and one
third cents. It is therefore considered by the court that the plaintiff recover
against the defendant said sum of one hundred seventeen dollars thirty-three and o
one third cents also his costs by him about his suit in this behalf expended ent
the defendant in mercy etc.

Robert Huston)
vs.)
George Mizells) Appeal

This day came the parties by their attorneys and on motion of defendant it
..is ordered that the plaintiff be ruled to give secuity in this case for the costs
by Wednesday of next term otherwise on that day suit to be dismissed at his cost.

Thomas Allison)
vs.   )   Appeal
Mc L. Porter   )

This suit is continued on affadavit filed of Porter until the next term of
court.

Joseph Linn & John Rutherford)
vs.   )   Appeal
John M. Johnson   )

This day came the parties by their attorneys ~~and on motion of defendant, it
is ordered~~and the defendant in his proper person and the plaintiffs agrees to
dismiss their suit and assume the cost of this suit, It is therefore considered
by the court that the defendant recover of the plaintiff his costs by him about
his suit in this behalf expended and that the plaintiff for their false clamor
be in mercy etc.

John McNairy William K. Butler & Henry M. Rutledge)
vs.   )   In debt
John F. Brown   )

This day came the defendant in proper person and the plaintiff by their
attorney and the defendant waith that he cannot gainsay the plaintiffs cause of
action. It is therefore considered by the court that the plaintiff recover against
the defendant the sum of one hundred forty-one and sixty-two and one half cents
damages together with all costs by them about their suit in this behalf expended
and the defendant in mercy etc.

George C. Rust)
vs   )   Certeorari
John B. Cross)

This day came the parties aforesaid by their attorneys and thereupon came a
jury to wit, Joseph Eddings, Jonathan Walsh, Stephen Lypert, Martin Davis, William
Pace Francis Taylor, Jesse D. Russell, John Purphy , John Fussell John C. Gillespie
John Cassels and Wickham Johnson who being elected tried and sworn well and truly
to try the matters in dispute between the parties upon their oaths do say, we of
the jury find for the plaintiff the sum of thirteen dollars. It is therefore considered by the court that the plaintiff recover of the defendant said sum of thirteen dollars also his costs by him about his suit in this behalf expended and the
defendant in mercy etc. & the defendant prayed an appeal to the next term of the
circuit court for this county which is granted him.

Andrew Hays theis day came into open court and released to the county the
sum of two dollars on two certificates given him by the clerk of this court for his
services as a juror of view.

Court then adjourned until tomorrow morning nine o'clock.

                                        H. Haralson   JP
                                        J. B. Cross   JP
                                        Wm. Spencer

Saturday morning 27 March 1824
        Court met agreeable to adjournment, present Herndon Haralson, John B. Cross
and William Spencer

P327 James P. Neely---of Robert Jarman)
vs.) Debt on demurrer
Bartholomew G. Stewart)

This day came the parties by their attorneys and thereupon the matters and
things arising upon the defendants demurrer being fully understood and dolemn
argument had thereon before the court and ti appearing to the court that thereis
no error in the plaintiffs declaration. It is therefore considered by the court
that the demurrer to the plaintiffs decleration be overruled and for nothing held,
and that the plaintiff recover against said defendant the sum of eighty seven
dollars and fifty cents the devt in the decleration mentioned together with the
sum of six dollars and seventy cents damages and his costs by him about his costs
by him about his suit in this behalf expended and the said defendant in mercy etc.

John D. Love--of John Haywood O
vs.) Covenant on demurrer
James McCutchen)

This day came the parties aforesaid by their attorneys and thereupon the m
matters and things arising upon the defendants demurrer to the plaintiffs declaration being fully understood and considered and argument had thereon and it appearing to the court that there is no error in the plaintiffs declaration. It is there
fore considered by the court here that the demurrer to the plaintiffs declartion
be overruled and for nothing held in this behalf and that the plaintiff recover of
the defendant such damages as he has sustained by reason of breach of covenant in
the plaintiffs declaration but because those those damages are not known, it is
commanded the sheriff to cause a jury to come here &c.

P328 Wilson & Stewart)
vs.) Debt
James Dorris & Benj. Gholson)

This day came the parties aforesaid by their attorneys and thereupon the defendants withdraw their pleas herein and say they cannot gainsay the plaintiffs
action there of against them for the sum of one hundred fourteen dollars and ten
cents. It is therefore considered by the court that the plaintiff recover of the
defendant said sum of one hundred and fourteen dollars and ten cents and also their
costs by them about their suit in this behalf expended and the defendents in
mercy etc. and it appearing to the satisfaction of the court that the aforesaid
Gholson is the security and indorser of the said Dorris and James Wright one of
the principals in the note on which this judgment is obtained, it is considered
that the said Gholson recover of the said Dorris and Wright said sum of two hundred
and fourteen dollars and ten cents & that execution issue accordingly and the
parties agree that execution in both these judgments be staid unti next term.
Ordered that all causes on the trial docket not otherwise disposed of be
continued until the next term of court.
Ordered that the following persons to wit, Jno B. Cross, Herndon Haralson,
William Spencer, David Jarrett, James Trousdale Guy Smith Micajah Midyett,
William O. Love Joseph Linn, Duncan McIver, Will Draper B. G. Stewart, Theopelis
Sanders, Mark Christian James McCutchen, William E. Buttler, John L. Dillard,
Amos Williams, William Atchison, John Hardgraves, John Weir, John M Johnson,
Ethelred Newsom, James Vaulx & George Todd be appointed jurors to attend the
next Circuit Court to be held on the 4th. Monday in May next and that the follow-
ing persons be summoned as jurors to attend the next county court to be held for
this county, to wit, Thomas Altom, Ebernizer Baltom, Matthias Deberry William
Penn, Henry N. Coulter, James F. -- Theoble, Drury Bettis, Rober Murray, William
B. Dorris Avel Willis, James McKnight, John Mitchell, Robert Clanton, Joshua
Weaver Icabud Watkins, Gabriel Anderson, Martin Lorance James Winters, Michael
Fisher Jacob Bradbury Thomas James, Vincent Haralson, Thomas Reaves, Nathanial
Herndon, John I. Smith & Brid Smith and that John D. Shannon & Abraham Smith be

P328   appointed as constables atattend the Circuit court next and Bennet Maxey and
Cont. John D. Shannon attend at the County Court.

John D. Shannon proves four days attendance on the jury at present term.

Court then adjourned until court in course.

H. Haralson   JP
John Thomas   JP
David Jarrett   JP

P330 June Term Monday 28th. 1824

At a court of pleas and quartersession began and held in the town of Jackson
Madison County on Monday the 28th. day of June 1824 Present, the Worshipful
Herndon Haralson, Duncan McIver James McCutchen, William Draper, William R.
Butler, John Thomas Joseph Linn B. G. Stewart Theophilis Sanders, Samuel S
Hunter, Mark Christian John B. Cross, William Atchison, Thomas Gordon William C.
Lowe James Greer, John L. Dillard, William Draper and Green Hill.

Ordered that Beverly Randolph for the use of Joshua Haskill be allowed the
sum of fifteen dollars and 75 cents for furnishing record books for the circuit
trustee pay the same out of any monies not otherwise appropreated.

On motion, ordered that the list of land as returned by the surveyor to the
clerk of this court be considered as a listing of the same for the the payment
of taxes and that all having failed to list any other taxable property for the
present year can do so and on application to the clerk by paying the taxes thereon.

Deed of conveyance from the commissioners of the town of Jackson to Herndon
Haralson for lot No. 34 in the plan of said town was this day produced in open
court and the execution thereof proven by the oath of Robert H. Wynne & Joseph F.
Cloud & ordered to be certified for registration.

A deed of conveyance from Hannah McMillan Dison McMillan and Robert McMillan
to William Porter for Eighty acres of land was this day produced in open court & pr
proven by the oath of Francis Taylor & George W. Taylor to be their act and deed
and ordered to be so certified.

A deed of mortgage from Nelson O. McReynolds & Thomas I McReynolds to Drury
Bettis & Wyatt Epps was this day produced in open court & the execution proven by
the oath of William R. Hess and ordered to be certified for registration.

P333 (Error in numbering Page)

A deed of conveyance from Jane Delph John Watts, James Watts, Samuel Watt,
John Gatty & wife, Rebecca Tarry Daniel Burl & wife Polly Bevil & Thomas Watts to
John Parker for forty acres of land was this day produced in open court & proven
by the oaths of Stephen Jarman & Philip Delph & ordered to be certified for registration.

A deed of conveyance from Thomas Shannon to Thomas Lofton for 113 acres of
land was produced in open court and acknowledged to be the said Thomas Shannon to
be his act and deed & ordered to be certified for registration.

A deed of conveyance from Samuel Dickens to Joseph & Walter Thedford for 80
acres was produced in open court and proven by the oaths of Willis Nichols & Andrew Tripp and ordered to be certified for registration.

A deed of mortgage from John Smith to Drury Bettis and Thomas J. McReynolds
was this day produced in open court & the execution there of proven by the oath of
William H. Brien and ordered to be certified for registration

A deed of conveyance from James Henderson & Deveraux Wynne to John B. Brown
for Ninety one acres of land was proven by the oaths of Richard A. Echols &
Jeremiah Brown and ordered to be certified for registration.

A deed of conveyance from John McIver to Edmond Jones & Alfred Moore for
1162½ acres of land was produced in open court and proven by the oaths of John
H. Hide & James Tisdale and ordered to be certified for registration.

P334   A deed of conveyance from Fountain Lester to Parks Chandler for 85 acres
was produced in open court & the execution proven by the oaths of Robert Hughes

P354 and H. Haralson & Ordered to be certified.
Cont.   A deed of conveyance from Fountain Lester to Ryland Chandler for 112 1/3 acres was produced in open court & proven by the oath of Robert Hughes & H. Haralson and ordered to be certified for registration.

A deed of conveyance from Samuel Dickesn to Edmond Jones for four tracts of land containing 180¾ was this day produced in open court and proven by the oath of A. L. Martin & James A. Hesslet & ordered to be certified.

A deed of conveyance from Edmond Jones & Alfred Moore to Samuel Dickens for four tracts of land containing 1802⅜ acres was this day oaths of A. L. Martin & James A. Hesslet & ordered to be certified.

A deed of conveyance from John McIver to Edmond Jones & Alfred Moore for six hundred and forty acres of land was this day produced in open court and the execution thereof duly proven by the oath of John H. Hide & James Tisdale & Ordered to be certified.

A power of attorney from Jesse Russell to Robert Russell was this day produced in open court and the execution acknowledged by the said Jesse Russell and ordered to be certified.

A deed of conveyance from the Commissioners of the town of Jackson to George Todd for lot #75 in the plans of said town was this day produced in open court and the execution thereof duly acknowledged by Herndon Haralson, Chairman of the board of commissioners to be their act and deed and ordered to be certified for registration.

A deed of conveyance from Thomas Shannon to James A. Edwards for seventy-five acres was this day produced in open court and the execution duly acknowledged by the said Thomas Shannon & ordered to be certified.

A deed of conveyance from Calins Jones and John C. McLemore to Samuel D. Waddill for two hundred and seventy four acres of land was this day produced in open court and the execution thereof on the part of said Jones was proven by the oaths of John H. Hyde and A. Patton & on the part of John C. McLemore by the oath of John Ridens and ordered to be certified.

A bond for the conveyance fo land from Minos Cannon to Clemant Cannon was th this day rproduced in open court & proven to be executed by Minos Cannon to Clement Cannon & ordered to be so certified.

Duncan McIver and Lemuel S. Hunter commissoners appointed to audit and settle with the administration of the estate of James I. Alexander deceased this day made report which is ordered to be recorded.

An inventory of the estate of Joseph Tedford deceased was this day returned in open court and ordered to be recorded.

Ordered that the report of the Jury marking a road from the county line near Isaac Curries to intersect the Carroll road near Spring Creek be received and that John B. Justice be overseer of the same to work all the hands not subject to work on the Carroll road as named in the following order, to wit.

Ordered that Nathan Clark overseer of the Carroll road work the following hands, to wit, James McCutchen, George Sullivan, Abner Brown Daniel Sullivan Mark Christian Murdock Murchison Samuel Dickens, James Lyon, George Fisher and Mr Hulett

On motion and petition filed it is ordered that the following persons to wit, Thomas Lofton Eldridge Newsom Herbert Newsom, William Butter Jacob Hill John Thomas and Bird Bill be appointed to view and report to the present or next term of court an alteration in the road leading from Jackson to Hardeman County beginning at or near the edge of the bottom South of Dott Butters to Stanleys Branch entersecting with the present road when they shall think best. and it is further ordered that said Jury of View do ascertain the most suitable place on the river & where the said road by them view shall cross the river from erecting a bridge across the same shall be erected with the sums approperated by subscription together with the appropriation of fifty dollars hereby made out of any money in the treasury at any time hereafter not otherwise appropriated and that Thomas Lofton and Eldridge Newsom be commissioners to direct and superintend the building of said bridge

P336 commence building as soon as they may think proper after the jury of new has de-
Cont. signated the place of crossing & before said jury be required to make their report to this court.

Ordered that Thomas Lofton be overseer of the Polk's Ferry Road from the
town of Jackson to the North boundary line of the Bowers & Wilson tract of land and
work the same hands heretofore allowed him except William Dean, James McNight
Moody & Mitchell & hands.

Ordered that William Willbourn be overseer of the Polk Ferry road from the
North boundary line of Bowers & Wilson's tract of land to the county line and work
the following hands, to wit, Norville, William Huston, Trousdale, Evans, Timms
Roads, Rucker McCoy McGill, Martin Wilson, Huston, McGee, George Chance and W. Thompson.

Ordered that James McNight be overseer of the Fowler Ferry road from where it
leaves the Polk's Ferry Road to Meridian Creek and work the following hands,
William Dean Moody Mitchell & Hands.

Ordered that Henry Butler be overseer of the Fowler Ferry road from Meridian
Creek to county line and work all the hands above Thomas's Mill on said creek and
all the hands on Clover Creek a ove Esqr. Dillard.

Ordered that George Hicks be overseer of road from Jackson to the bridge and
work all the hands not included in any other order.

P337 Ordered that Elijah Matthews be overseer of the road leading to Hardin C. H.
from the river to the low gap in the ridge & work the following hands, to wit,
William Higgins, Aden Langhorn & Brothers, William Tags & hands, William C. Love
and hands William Lowery, Robert Phelps, Banister Jorden, John Higgins, William
Milton, Thomas Shelby & hands Carlton Matthews, and Thomas Matthews.

Ordered that Tobias Goodman be overseer of the road from the low gap in the
ridge to where Ross's cart way crosses the new road and work the following hands,
Sterling Tally John Tally, Minor Marsh and hands, Elijah Marsh, Thomas Henderson
and hands, John Yount and hands John Reid, Daniel Harkins, Leege and hands, Hiram
Harkins, Daniel Harkins Jr. John M Johnson and hands, John Criver and Hands, Sam'l
Martin, Henry Coulter, James Alexander, James Alexander r. Jesse Wilson, Edmond
Scarborough Samuel Anderson and Thomas Parks.

Ordered that Daniel Ross be overseer of the road from the low gap to the
county line and work the following hands, Thomas Reaves and hands, William
Gallaway, Vinson Luterel Right Koonce, James Hunter, Daniel Sparks, David Parker,
Joseph Findley, Starks, Dupree and hands, William Kendrick and hands, Nathaniel
Henderson and hands, William Searcy John Hineman & Cader Colley.

Ordered that Morris Hellum be overseer of the Carroll road from Winters Lane
to Cain Creek in the place of William O Love to work the hands heretofore allowed
said Love.

Ordered that Moses Starnes be allowed the following hands to wit, H. Haral-
son Ichabod Watkins, William Mays, James Johnson, Adam Huntsman, Robert Murray
William Buckley Pleasant Deal, Henry Webb James Henderson Tobias Henderson, Eli
Chandler, Parks Chandler, to work on the road from town to the bridge below H.
Haralson and that A Watkins be released from any other road.

P338 Monday 28th day of June 1824
Ordered that John T. Porter be allowed the following hands to work on that
part of the road of which he is overseer, to wit, William Polk, Ruben Smith,
Aquila Davis Samuel Averett, Daniel Tiffapeu, Levin Stephens, Lewis I Jones, Henry
Reagan, A. R. Alexander, E. Alexander Daniel Horton, John Gibson, Mathias Boon
and Pleasant Larcamour.

Ordered that Jarret M Jelks over seer of the Nash's Bluff road to work the
hands that live in the second range of the section that the road leads through
including the hands of John McClellan and the hands living on the South of the
section line.

Ordered that Deveraux Wynne overseer of the road be allowed the following
hands, to wit, Ben Gholson, Philip Warlick H Hewitt, William Johns, Samuel Gholson

MADISON COUNTY
MINUTE BOOK COUNTY COURT
Vol.1

P338
Cont.
James Youn, George Gray and Pitts chandlerand all other hands more over in the bounds to work on the road from the bridge below Warlicks Mill to Butlers Creek.

Ordered that Abel Willis be overseer of the road from Widow Wilson's old place to the West boundary line of John M Welch's tract of land to work the following hands to wit, Adam Browns hands, Capt McDaniels hands Jno M Welch's and all those living on his land, Absolom Bradford, Harris Bradford and hands, abel willis hand Elijah William's hand and those on Widow Wilson old place.

Ordered that Lewis Carpenter be overseer of the road from the West boundary of Welchs tract of land towhere the same entersats the carroll road and work the hands, Alexander Braden Elijah Jones and Doct Fenner.

Joshua Weaver proves the killing of ten wolves over the age of four months in the county of Madison.

Lidon Harris proves the killing of one wold in this county over four months
P339 old.

James Anderson proves the killing of one wold in Madison county over four months old.

Elijah Biglow, administrator of the estate of Augustine C. Hays deceased, returned an inventory of this estate of the decedent.

John Thomas, John L. Dillard, and James McNight, commissioners appointed to settle with the adms. of Iriah Haley, deceased and the administrators returned an additional inventory of the estate.

John C. Gillispie, Miles Fuller, John D. Shannon and Jacob Hill were this day elected constables for the county of Madison and entered into bond with their securities, each in the penal sum of twelve hundred fifty dollars, the said John C. Gillispie with John B. Cross and Thomas Doak, the said Miles Fuller with Willia Cartwright and Allen Fuller thesaid John D. Shannon with Benjamin Gholson and Thomas Fofton and Thomas Shannon who thereupon took the several oaths prescribed by the constitution and laws of the state.

Allen Fuller resigns his office as constable in Caot, Drapers Company.

William Willbourn resigns his office as constable in Capt. Lacy(s company.

Eli Jones proves the killing one wolf in this county over four months old.

Aquila Davis appeared in open court and acknowledged himself bouned as appearance bail of Archibald S. Lackman in place of Benjamin Gholson and John Barnhart who were released.

Samuel D. Waddill comes into court and records his stock mark as follows to wit, a smooth crop off of each ear and split in the right.

Abner Brown proves three days, William Alexander four days, Duncan McIver and Bartholomew C. Stewart two days each as jurors of view previous to the passage of an act repealing the act allowing compensation to jurors of view in the Western District.

Ordered that the order appointing Joseph Linn andWilliam Draper to settle with the administrator of James L. Price, deceased, be renewed and make report to the next term of this court.

Ordered that Josiah Fullen be allowed six hundred and fifty dollars for the building of the bridge across the river at Shannon landing and that the county trustee pay the same out of any monies not other wise approperated.

Ordered that Roderick McIver, Clerk of this Court, be allowed twenty-five dollars for making out the tax list for the present year and that the county trustee pay the same out of any monies not otherwise appropriated on a copy of this order.

Administration of all the goods, rights and credits of John Smith, deceased is this day granted to Robert Murray who thereupon took the oath of an administrator and entered into bond with Joseph Linn and Achabod Watkins in the penalty of fifteen hundred dollars, it is therefore ordered that letters of administration issued to the said Robert Murray accordingly.

James Armstrong   )
vs.   )   In debt
Bailey Needham   )

This day came the defendant in his proper person and says he cannot gainsay

P341   the plaintiffs action hereof against him for the sum of two hu dred fifty three dollars the devt in the declaration mentioned. It is threrfore consider4d by the court that the plaintiff recover of the defendant the said sum of two hundred and fifty three dollars also his costs b y him about his suit in this behalf expended and the defendant in mercy etc. and the plaintiff agrees to stay execution in this case six months.

    Ordered that the jurors who have oattended and served in the circuit and county courts of Madison the first days of January last and who may hereafter serve during the present year be allowed one dollar per day for the same out of any county monies not otherwise appropriated.

    Ordered that the double taxes be remitted on all the lands belonging to county John McIver and liable to taxation in the county of Madison for the year 1823.

    Ordered that the double taxes on the lists marked "B" be remitted for the year 1823.

    An inventory of the estate of James Hill, deceased, was erturned into court which is ordered to be recorded.

P342   Court then adjourned until tomorrow morning nine o'clock.

                    H. Haralson   JP.
                    Joseph Linn   JP.
                    JohnThomas   JP.

Tuesday Morning 29th. June 1824
    Court met agreeable to adjournment, present, Herndon Haralson, Joseph Linn and Duncan McIver.

    Ordered that John Smith, Jacob Bradbury and James Winters be exempt as jurors at the present term and also W. James exempt as above.

    A deed of conveyance from William Polk by his attorney in fact Samuel Dickens to Aquila Dyson for five hundred acres of land was this day rproduced in open court and the execution there of duly proves by the oaths of James Greer and Daniel Teifspaugh and ordered to be certified for registration.

    A power of attorney from James S. Suthrie to Nathaniel Johnson was this day exhibited in open court and the execution of the same was duly acknowledged by the said James S. Guthrie to be his act and deed and ordered to be certified.

    Tge sheriff this day made return of the writ of veniri to him directed by th last term of this court with the following indorsement thereon issued 30th March 1824 came to hand the same day issued A. F. Gray D. S. I have summoned all the persons named in the venire exc8pt Joshua Weaver, who could not be found, who are all freeholders and inhabitants of the county of Madison June 28th. 1824 A F. Gray D. S. In persuance of which the following persons were then attending, Thomas Haltom Ebenezer Haltom, Mathias Deberry, William Penn, Henry N. Caulter, James F. Thaoble, Drury Bettis, Robert Murray, William B. Dorris Abel Willis, James McNight, John Mitchell, Robert Clanton, Achabod Watkins, Gabriel Anderson, Martin Lorance, Michael Fisher, Jacob Bradbury, Thomas James, Vincent Haralson, Thomas Reaves, Nathaniel Henderson, John I. Smith, James Winters, and thereupon the following persons to wit, Vincent Haralson, William B. Dorris, Nathaniel Henderson Michael Fisher, Gabriel Anderson, Martin Lorance, Joshua Weaver Achabod Watkins John Mitchell Mathias Deberry, James McNight, Drury Bettis and James Henderson with Vincent Haralson their foreman were empannelled, sworn and charged as a grand jury to enquire into and for the body of the county of Madison and thereupon retired to consider presentment.

    Stephen Lecy was this day duly and constitutionally elected coroner for the county of Madison for the next two years to come, thereupon entered into bond with Joseph Linn and Hugh Lecy his securities in the penalty and with the condition prescribedby law and took the several oaths prescribed by the constitution and laws of the state.

    M. A. Q. McKnizie appeared in open court and took the oath of qualification as practicing atty. in the court.

344 -   Adeed of conveyance from James Tisdale, deceased to Edward Williams for two

P344 tracts of land containing five hundred acres of land was this day duly acknowledg-
Cont. ed in open court by the said James Tisdale to be his act and deed and ordered to
be certified for registration.

Ordered that the justices of the peace for the county of Madison be classed
after the following manner, to wit, Herndon Haralson, Duncan McIver Mark Christian
Samuel Taylor John B. Cross and The Sanders to hold the court of June term in
each and every year, and that Joseph Linn, James Greer, James McCutchen Thomas
Gordon, William Atchison and William C. Love to hold the courts of September term
in each and every year, and that William E. Butler, B. G. Stewart, John L Dillard,
Lemuel S. Hunter, David Jarrett, Green Hill and Guy Smith to hold the courts of
December term in each and every year, and that Adam R. Alexander, William Spencer,
James Trousdale, John Thomas William Draper, Micajah Midyett and Stephen Jarman
hold the courts of March term in each and every year.

A deed of conveyance from Robert H. Dyer to Thomas Brothers for two hundred
seventy four acres was this day produced in open court and acknowledged by the
Robert H. Dyer to be his act and deed and ordered to be certified.

A deed of conveyance from William E. Butler for himself and also in fact
for John McNairy and Henry M. Rutledge to William Kirby for part of lot No. 1 in
the town of Jackson was this day produced in open court and acknowledged by the
said William E. Butler to be his act and deed and ordered to be certified.

P345   An inventory of the estate of John Smith, deceased, was this day returned
into open court by Rovert Murray the administrator which is ordered to be recorded.

Thomas M Dement   )
vs.   )   Slander
Thomas Boling   )

This day came the parties aforesaid by their attorneys and thereupon came
a jury of good and lawful men, to wit, James F. Theoble, Thomas Reaves, Ebenezer
Haltom, Abel Willis, Jesse Russell, William Mayo, Solomon Ridens, Solomon Martin,
Foster Golden, Archibold Chaffen, John Ridens, and Thomas Haltom, who being elected tried and sworn well and truly to try the issues, joined upon their oaths do
say, We of the jury do find the defendant guilty of falsely and maliciously, speak
ing and publishing the words in the plaintiffs declaration mentioned in the manner
and form as the plaintiff against him hath declared and they further say that the
defendant of his own wrong and without any such cause as in pleading he hath alled
ed did falsely and maliciously speak and publish with the intent in the declaration ascribed to him the words in the declaration mentioned as the plaintiff by
replying to the defendants plea in that behalf hath alleged and do assess the plain
tiff damages by reason thereof to sixty-five dollars. It is therefore considered
by the court that the plaintiff recover of the defendant the damages aforesaid in
manner and form aforesaid assessed and also his cost by him about his suit in this
behalf expended and the defendant in mercy etc.

William H. Johnson   )
vs.   )   Case
John Rutherford.   )

This day came the parties aforesaid by their attorneys and it is agreed by
the parties that their suit in this case be dismissed at the cost of the defendant.
It is therefore considered by the court that the plaintiff go thereof hence and
recover of the defendant his cost by him about his suit in this behalf expended and
the defendant in mercy etc.

P346 Levi B. Anderson
vs.   )   Original attachment
John Sharp   )

This day came the plaintiff by his attorney and dismisses his suit herein
and assumes the cost of said suit. It is therefore considered by the court that

P346 the defendant recover against the plaintiff his cost by him about his defense in
Cont.this behalf expended and the plaintiff for this false clamor be in mercy etc.
        Court then adjourned until tomorrow morning nine o'clock.

                                        H. Haralson   JP.
                                        Joseph Linn   JP.
                                        Duncan McIver   JP.

Wednesday morning 30th. day of June 1824
        Court met agreeable to adjournment, Present, the Worshipful Herndon Haralson
Joseph Linn, Lemuel S. Hunter and Duncan McIver.

Thomas M Dement   0)
vs.   )   Malicious prosecution.
Thomas Boling   )

        This day came the parties aforesaid by their attorneys and thereupon came
a jury of good and lawful men, to wit, James Dorris, Malcolm Johnson William Pace
Henry Caslin, Thomas G. Morvill, John Sutton, James Adams, Bennet R. Butler, Benoni Crawford, Thomas Grissom, William C, Jordan, and Madison McLaurine, who
being elected, tried and sworn well and truly to try the issue joined upon their
oaths do say We of the jury do find the issue joined in favor of the plaintiff and
assess his damages to fifty dollars. It is therefore considered by the court
that the plaintiff recover of the defendant the damages aforesaid in manner and
form aforesaid assessed together with his cost by him about his suit in this behalf and the defendant in mercy.

P347 Greenup White   )
vs.   )
Jason H. Wilson   )

        The plaintiff on motion of his attorney comes and dismisses his suit herein.
It is therefore considered by the court that the defendant recover of said plaintiff his costs by him about his suit in this behalf expended and the plaintiff in
mercy etc.

Robert Gray   )
vs.   )   Certeorari
Andrew Fortrush   )

        On motion of the plaintiff by his attorney, it is ordered that the defendant
be ruled to give security by the last day of the present term for the cost of suit
therein.

        Ordered that the administrator of John Smith be directed to sell the negroes
belonging to the estate of the decedent and the proceeds applied to the payment
of the debts against the estate.

Robert Huston)
vs.   )   Appeal
George Mizel)

        This day came into open courtRobert Huston with his securities, Benjamin
Bolthe and Ellinor Huston in pursuance with a rule of the last court made in this
case and acknowledged themselves to be indebted to the said George Mizel in the su
of one hundred dollars to be void on the payment of the cost that may accrue on
the payme decision of above cause if judgment should be given against said Huston.

        The Grand Jury empannelled sworn and charged to inquire in and for the body
of the county of Madison this day returned into court an indictment against Willia m
Rollman and Enoch Happy for an affray indorsed by the foreman a true bill and
also the following presentments, one against Levi Robertson and James. McReynolds
for an affray and one against Robert Clanton and James, Cockrill for an affray
and it is ordered that capias issued.

P248 Wednesday 30th. day of June 1824

A power of attorney from Allen T. Williams to Riding S. Wulliams was this day produced in open court and the execution of the same proven by the oath of Duncan McIver a subscribing witness and ordered to be so certified.

A deed of conveyance from the commissioners of the town of Jackson to WilliamE. Butler for two lots disignated in the plan of said town by No. 18 & No. 24 was this day produced in open court and the execution of the same acknowledged by Herndon Haralson, Chairman of the board of said commissioners to be their act and deed and ordered to be certified for registration.

A deed of conveyance from William E. Butler to George Todd for partof the lot No. 24 as designated in the plan of the town of Jackson was this day produced in open court and the execution of he same duly acknowledged by the said William E. Butler to be his act and deed and ordered to be certified for registration.

Two deeds of conveyance from th commissioners of the town of Jackson to Duncan McIver for lots number 12 and No 34 as designated in the plan of said town were this day produced in open court and the exection of them acknowledged by Herndon Haralson chairman of the board of said commissioners and ordered to be certified for registration.

A deed of conveyance from Anthony Foster to Duncan McIver for two hundred twentyfour*court and the same proven by the oaths of Michael Fisher the oath of the other witness being heretofore taken, it is ordered to be certified for registration.

Court then adjourned until tomorrow morning eight o'clock.

Lem'l S. Hunter   JP.
D. McIver   JP.
Guy Smith   JP.

P249 Thursday 1st. day of July 1824

Court met agreeable to adjournment. Present, the Worshipful Herndon Haralson, Duncan McIver, Lemuel S. Hunter.

The State)
Vs.) Assault and battery
William Pace)

This day came as well the solicitor general on the part of the state as the defendant in his proper person and the defendant being arraigned upon his arraignment plead guilty as charged in the bill of indictment. It is therefore considered by the court that the defendant go thereof hence and make his place with the state by the payment of ten dollars fine and that the plaintiff recover of the defendant the fine aforesaid together with the cost by her about her suit in this behalf expended and the defendant be taken etc.

Harris Bradford Plff)
vs.) In debt.
John Murray, Deft.)

On motion of the plaintiff by his attorney leave is given the plaintiff to amend his writ herein on the payment of the cost of the amendment.

Ordered that Bennet R. Butler be find two dollars as a delinquent juror.

Administration of all and singular the good and chattels, rights and credits of John M. Gibson, deceased is granted to Ams Gibson who thereupon took the oath of qualification of an administratrix of the estate of said decendant and entered into bond with her securities in the penalty of ---- It is ordered by the court that letters of administration issue accordingly.

*acres of land was this day produced in open

P350 Thursday 1st. day of July 1824

A power of attorney from Benjamin P. Macklin to Hugh W. Dunlap was this day produced in open court and the execution of the same proven by the oaths of Austin a King and Joseph H. Talbot, subscribing witnesses thereto and ordered to be certified.

Thomas I. Smith appeared in open court and took the oath of deputy sheriff for the county of Madison .

Andrew Hays)
vs.) Slander
George Mizell by consent)

The plaintiff in this case is permitted to take the deposition of Jacob Sewell de beno esse at the house of James Creer, Esq. before said Greer and Bartholomew G. Stewart Esq. Between the hours of 10 o'clock A M and 7 O'clock P. R. on Tuesday the sixth day of July.

State)
vs.)
Henning Pace)

This day came the solicitor general on the part of the state as the defendant in his proper person and the defendant being arraigned upon his affaignment pled not guilty as charged in the declaration but for his trial put himself upon his country and thereupon came a jury of good and lawful men, to wit; Thomas Reaves, Robert Murray, James F. Theobold Thomas Haltom, Ebenizer Haltom, Henry James, Francis H. Ragsdale, John Cassels, John Hardwick, Philip Husselbough Henry Cassels, sen'r, and John Stewart, who being elected tried and sworn the truth to speak upon the issue joined upon their oaths do say We of the jury do find the defendant guilty as charged in the bill of indictment. It is therefore considered by the court that the defendant make his peace with the state by the payment of one dollar find and that the plaintiff recover of the said defendant her fine aforesaid together with her cost by her about his suit in this behalf expended and the defendant in mercy and etc.

A power of attorney from Joel Dyer, sen'r, to Robert A. Jackson, was this day produced in open court and acknowledged by the said Joel Dyer to be his act and deed and ordered to be certified.

P351 State)
vs.) An assault
Thomas M Dement)

This day came as well the solicitor general on the part of the state as the defendant in his proper person and the defendant being arraigned upon his arraignment plead guilty as charged in the bill of indictment. It is therefore considered by the court that the defendant make his peace with the state by the payment of five dollars fine and that the plaintiff go thereof and recover of the defendant her fine aforesaid together with her cost about her suit in this behalf expended and the difentant may be taken etc. and the said defendant being ruled to give security in this case came into court Thomas A Smith and Abraham Smith and acknowledged themselves severally bound as securities for the cost of the suit herein. It is therefore soncidered by the court that the plaintiff recover of the said securities the fine and cost after cost of this prosecution.

The State)
vs.) An assault
William Pace)

This day came as well the solicitor general on the part of the state as the defendant in his proper person and the defendant being assaigned upon his arraignment plead quilty as charged in the bill of indictment.

P351   It is therefore considered by the court that the defendant make his peace
Cont. with the state by the payment of ten dollars fine and that the plaintiff recover of the defendant her fine together with her cost by her about her suit
in this behalf expended and the defendant may be taken etc.

          The State   )
          vs.   ) An Assault
          Alocy Pace   )
     This day came as well the solicitor general on the part of the state
as the defendant in his proper person and the defendant being arraigned upon
his arraignment plead not guilty as charged in the bill of indictment and for
his trial put himself upon God and his country and thereupon came a jury of
good and lawful men, to wit, Vincent Haralson, William B. Dorris, Nathaniel
Henderson, Michael Fisher Gavriel Anderson, Martin Lorance, Joshua Weaver,
Achabod Watkins, John Mitchell, Mathias Deberry, James McKnight, Drury Bettis,
who being elected tried and sworn the truth to speak upon the issue joined upon
their oaths do say they find the defendant guilty as charged in the bill of
indictment. It is therefore considered by the court that the defendant make
his peace with the state by the payment of one dollar fine and that the plaintiff recover of the defendant her cost by her about her suit in this behalf
expended and the defendant be taken etc.

          State   )
          vs.   ) An assault
          William Pace   )
          This day came as well the solicitor general on the part of the state
as the defendant in his proper person and the defendant being arraigned upon
his arraignment plead not guilty as charged in the bill of indictment but for
his trial put himself upon God and his country and thereupon came a jury of
P352 good and lawful men, to wit, James Henderson, William B. Dorris, Nathaniel
Henderson, Michael Fisher, Gabriel Anderson, Martin Lorance, Joshua Weaver,
Achabod Watkins John Mitchell, Mathias Deberry, James McNight and Drury Bettis
who being elected tried and sworn the truth to speak upon the issue joined upon
their oaths do say they find the defendant not guilty as charged in the bill of
indictment and on motion of the defendant's counsel the prosecution in this case
is taxed with the cost. It is therefore considered by the court that the plaintiff recover of Francis Herring the said prosecutor her cost by her about her
suit in this behalf expended and be taken etc.

          The State   )
          vs.   ) Assault
          Andrew Herron   )
          This day came as well the solicitor general on the part of the state as
the defendant in his proper person, and the defendant be ng arraigned upon his
arraignment plead not guilty as charged in the bill of indictment but for
P353 his trial put himself upon God and his country and thereupon came a jury of
good and lawful men, to wit, Henry James, James F. Theable, Henry Cassells,
Thomas Haltom, Ebenezer Haltom, Thomas Reaves, George Mizells, John Hardwick,
Francis Ragsdale, John Burrow John Cassels and Solomon Martin, Who being elected
tried and sworn well and truly to try the issue joined upon their oaths do say
that the defendant is not guilty as charged in the bill of indictment but it is
considered by the court that the defendant in this case be taxed with the cost
and that the plaintiff recover of the defendant her cost by her about her suit
in this behalf expended and be taken etc.

          The State
          vs.
          Joel Mading)   Riot

P353   This day came as well the solicitor general on the part of the state as
Cont. the defendant in his proper person and the defendant being arraigned upon his
arraigned plead not guilty as charged in the bill of indictment but for his
trial put himself upon God and his country and thereupon came a jury to wit,
Robert Murray Henning Pace, Thomas Grissom, John Bettis, John Barnhart,
John Rudesel, John Knockals, John Murray Thomas Lacy, Jesse M. Hannah, Norace
Lasemaur and William Hopper who being elected tried and sworn well and truly
to try the issue joined upon their oaths do say the defendant is not guilty
as charged in the bill of indictment and it is considered by the court that
the prosecutor Benoni Crawford be taxed with the cost of this prosecution and
that he be ordered in custody of the sheriff until he gives security for the cost.

P354 The State
vs.   )
Daniel Mading, Martin Mading,   )   Riot
Franklin Mading & Henry Harper   )

        This counsel for the state in this case motioned the court to dismiss
the suit herin which was done. It is therefore considered by the court that
the defendants recover of the state their cost by them in this behalf expended
etc.

Wiley Ray   )
vs.   )   Appeal
Benjamin Gholson   )

        This day came the plaintiff by his attorney and moved the court that the
defendants appeal in this behalf be dismissed and that a procedendo be awarded
directed to the justice of the peace in the court below commanding him to issue
execution in this case. It is therefore considered by the court that the said
appeal be dismissed, a prodedendo issue to Samuel Taylor, Esq. commanding him
to proceed to issue execution on the judgment rendered by him in this cause
to which opinion the defendant by his attorney excepted and filed his bill of
exceptions which is signed, sealed enrolled and made part of the record herein
and from which opinion of the court the defendant prayed an appeal in the nature
of a writ of error to the next Circuit Court for the county of Madison which was
granted and the said defendant came and entered into bond with Bird Hill his
security in the penalty of two hundred dollars conditioned for the prosecution
of said appeal.

        A transfer of a plot and certificate from John C. McLemore to John Murray
to Bowen Reynolds for one hundred acres of land was this day produced in open
court and the execution of the same proven by the oath of Thomas Channon and
Joseph H. Talbot and ordered to be certified.

P355   A schedule of the property received by Micajah Midyett and required by the
last will and testament of Jacob Brooks to be made of the property received
by the said Micajah Midyett of the estate of said Jacob Brooks in his life
time was this day exhibited in open court and proven by the oath of said Mid-
yett-of-the-estate-of-said-Jacob-Brooks-in-his-life-time-was-this-day-exhibit
and ordered to be recorded.

        Court then adjourned until tomorrow morning eight o'clock.

                                        H. Haralson   JP.
                                        Duncan McIver   JP
                                        John L. Dillard JP.

Friday morning 2ne. July 1824
/   Court met agreeable to adjournment. Present the Worshipful Herndon Haralson
Mark Christian, Duncan McIver and John L. Dillard.

P355 Henry L. Douglas   )
Cont. vs.   )

   Richard A. Echols   )

      On motion of the plaintiff by his attorney leave is given him by consent of parties to take the deposition of Albert H. Wynne of Lebanon fifteen day notice being given of the time and place of taking the same.

The State   )
vs.   )   Affray
Thomas Laremour   )

      This day came as well the solicitor general on the part of the state as the defendant in his proper person and the defendant being arraigned upon his arraignment plead not guilty as charged in the bill of indictment but for his t trial himself upon God and his country and there upon came a jury of good and lawful men to wit, Robert Murray, Thomas Haltom, Ebenezer Haltom, Abel Willis Henry Cassels, Senr. Henry Cassels, Jr. John Cassels, John Hardwick, Robert Lowery Langester Glover, Andrew Forbush and Jesse D. Russell, who being elected tried and sworn the truth to speak upon the issue joined do say that they cannot

P356 agree on a verdict in this case and by consent of the parties and with the assent of the court a juror is withdrawn and the rest of the jurors from rendering their verdict and cause continued until next term of court.

The State
vs.
Benoni Crawford

      On motion, it is ordered by the court that the defendant in this case be released out of custody fo the sheriff subject never the less to the cost of this prosecution.

      Mathias Deberry the quardian of James W. Haley and William P. Haley heirs of James Haley deceased, this day returned into court an inventory of the estate belonging to said orphans which is ordered to be recorded.

The State   )
vs.   )   Affray
BenoniCrawford Valentine Vantrease)

      This day came as well the solicitor general on the part of the state as the defendants in their proper persons and the defendants being arraigned, upon their arraignment plead not guilty as charged in the bill of indictment but for their trial put themselves upon God and their country and thereupon came a jury of good and lawful men to wit Thomas Reaves, John C. Stockton, Hence Laramour, Robert Houston, George Mizell, Thomas Shelly, William Wilson, Jonathan Welch, Patrick M Duffy, Thomas Kirk, James Tedwell and George Cowley who being elected tried and sworn the truth to speak upon the issue goined upon their oaths do say that the defendant Benoni Crawford is not guilty and the defendant Valentine Vantrease is guilty as charged in the bill of indictment and that he be fined one cent. It is therefore considered by the court that the defendant V. Vantrease make his peace with the state by the payment of his fine aforesaid also his costs by him about his prosecution in this behalf expended and that the county pay the cost of on the part of Benoni Crawford.

      The Grand Jury empanelled, sworn and charged to inquire into and for the body of the county of Madison this day returned into court an indictment against Jacob Fermaul for petet larceny and one against Joel M ading and Daniel Mading for an affray indorsed by the foreman of the Grand Jury a true bill and that copias issued.

P357

The State
vs.
Robert Clanton   )   An affray

P357   This day came as well the solicitor general on the part of the state as
Cont. the defendant in his proper person and the defendant being arraigned, upon
his arraignment plead not guilty as charged in the bill of indictment and for
his trial put himself upon God and his country and thereupon came jury of
good and lawful men, Thomas Reaves, John C. Stockton, Robert Buston Georbe
Mizell, Thomas Shelby, William Willson Jonathan Welch, Patrick M Duffy, Thomas
Kirk, James Tidwell, George Cawley and George Hicks, who being elected tried
and sworn the truth to speak upon the issue joined do say that the defendant
is guilty as charged in the ill of indictment and the defendants counsel
moved the court in arrest of judgment, whic motion being overruled by the court.
It is therefore considered by the court that the defendant make his peace with
the state by the payment of one dollar fine and that the plaintiff recover of
the defendant her cost by her about her suit in this behalf expended and be in
mercy etc.

The State   )
vs.   ) Indictment for Petit Larceny
Jacob Fermault   )
        This day came as well the solicitor general on the part of the state as
the defendant in his proper person and the defendant, being arraigned, upon his
arraignment plead not guilty as charged in the bill of indictment, but for his
trial put himself upon God and his country and thereupon came a jury of good
and lawful men, to wit, Hance Laremour, John Stockton, George Mizells, Allen
C. Nemo, Robert Wibson, William Wilson, Francis Ragsdale, William Cavenau,
Daniel Sullivan James Priest, Thomas Kirk, and Thomas Haltom, who being elected
tried and sworn well and truly to try the issue, joined upon their oaths do
say We of the jury do find the defendant guilty as charged in the bill of indictment, and on motion of the defendants counsel it is ordered by the court
that judgment in this case be suspended until tomorrow and the prisoner remanded to jail.

P358   Abraham T. Smith proves five days attendance as a counstable on the court
at the present term.
        Ordered that the grand jury be discharged from any further service at the
present term.

Robert C. Thompson   )
vs.   ) Debt
James and William Howard)
        This day came the plaintiff by his attorney and dismisses his suit herein
It is therefore considered by the court that the defendants recover of the plaintiff the cost in this case by him expended and be in mercy etc.

William H. Miller)
vs.   ) Case
Daniel Horton   )
        This day came the partied aforesaid by their attorneys and agree to
dismiss their suit herein each part paying half the cost in said suit. It is
therefore considered by the court that the parties aforesaid bear an equal
proportion of the cost in this case by them expended etc. Adam R. Alexander and
Duncan McIver appointed to settle with the administrator of the estate of
Simon Johnson deceased and report the same to the next term of this court.

George H. Watson)
vs.   ) Case
Jabes Timms   )
        The parties by consent have leave to take depositions generally by giving

MINUTE BOOK COUNTY COURT
Vol.1   165

P358 twenty day notice in the state and thirty days if out of the state.
Cont.   Bartholomew G. Stewart proves two days services as a juror of view in
addition to the No. of days heretofore proven and previous to the passage of
an act repealing an act allowing compensation to jurors of view.

        The Administrator of the estate of William A. Alexander returns an ad-
ditional inventory of the estate of the deceased.

P359 John Coffee   )
     vs.   )   On motion
George C. Rust and Robert H. Dyer and Josiah Pullin)

        This day came the plaintiff aforesaid by his attorney and it appearing
to the satisfaction of the court that defendant Rust as constable of Madison
County has collected the sum of thirteen dollars and fifty cents which of right
belongs to the plaintiff and that he has not paid the same over to the plaintiff as the law directs and that the said Rust has notice of this motion. It
is therefore considered by the court that the plaintiff recover against said
Rust and that the said Robert H. Dyer and Josiah Pullin his securities the
said sum of thirteen dollars and fifty cents also his costs by him about his
suit in this behalf expended and the defendant in mercy etc.

     Solomon Roswell   )
     vs.   )   On motion
Geo C. Rust and Robert H. Dyer and Josiah Pullen)

        This day came the plaintiff aforesaid by his attorney and it appear-
ing to the satisfaction of the court that the defendant George C. Rust and
constable of Madison County has collected the sum of twelve dollars which
of righ belongs to the plaintiff and he has not paid the same over to the
plaintiff as the law directs and that the said Rust has notice of this motion.
It is therefore considered by the court that the plaintiff recover against the
said Rust and the said Robert H. Dyer and Josiah Pullen, his securities, the
said sum of twelve dollars also his cost byy him about his suit in the behalf
expended and the defendant in mercy etc.

P360 G. F. Stewart, Joseph Linn, John Hadgrave, Adam R. Alexander)
     and James Trousdale, Commissioners of The Town of Jackson   )
     vs.   )   Debt
Robert H. Dyer and John B. Cross   )

        This day came the parties aforesaid by their attorneys and the said de-
fendants because they cannot gainsay the plaintiffs cause of action confesses
judgment for the sum of three hundred and four dollars debt together with the
sum of three dollars and sixteen cents balance of interest. It is thereupon
considered by the court that the said plaintiff recover against the said defend-
dants the said sum of three hundred and four dollars debt together with the
interest aforesaid in form aforesaid confessed also their cost by them about
their suit in this behalf expended.

     Adison Gipson , Assignee etc.   )
     vs.   ) On motion Debt
Ann Dibson Admr. of the Estate of John H. Gibson, deceased)

        This day came the parties aforesaid by their attorneys and the defendant
confesses judgment for the sum of one hundred forty nine dollars debt and the
sum of seventy one dollars interest. It is therefore considered by the court
that the plaintiff recover against said defendant the debt and interest aforesaid together with his cost by him about his motion in this behalf expended
and it is ordered byqthe court that scirifacias issue directed to the heirs
of the estate of John / H. Gibson, deceased, commanding them to appear at the
next term of the court and shew cause if any why final judgment should not be
entered.

P361   Court then adjourned until tomorrow morning nine o'clock.

        H. Haralson   JP.
        D. McIver   JP.
        M. Christian   JP.

Saturday 3rd. day of July 1824

Court met agreeable to adjournment. Present, the worshipful Herndon Haralson, Mark Christian and Duncan McIver.

John D. Shannon came into court and proved four days attendance on the Grand Jury at the present term.

The State)
vs.) For Petit Larceny
Jacob Fermault)

This prisoner was this day again brought to the bar and he having nothing to say why sentence should not be passed on him according to same. It is therefore considered by the court that the defendant be taken to the place from whence he came and be imprisoned for and during the term of ten days and that the state recover of the defendant her costs, by her about her prosecution in this behalf expended and the defendant may be taken etc.

Robert Gray)
vs.) Certiorari
Andrew Forbush)

On motion of the defendant Forbush by his attorney --- here on a former day of court that the plaintiff in this case come into court and give security for the costs and having failed to do so it is considered by the court that said cause be dismissed and that the said defendant Forbush recover of the said plaintiff Robert Gray his costs by him about his suit in this behalf expended and the said plaintiff in mercy etc.

Commissioners of the Town of Jackson)
vs.) Motion for Certiorari
Anthony G. Fray and William Braden)

On motion and petition filed and it appearing to the satisfaction that the petitioner has merits, ordered that a writ of certiorari and supercedeas issue according to the prayer of said petitioner.

Ordered that the following persons constitute the venire directed to the sheriff as jurors to the next circuit court, Philip Warlick, John M. Welch, Harris Bradford, Alexander Greer, John Thomas, Lemuel S. Hunter, Jarret M. Jilks William Jones, John May, Morris Hellum, James Trousdale, Abner Brown, Robert Bobson, Greenup White, Richard Thompson, James Cockrell, James Haley, Thomas Doak, John H. Ball, Wyatt Epps, Martin Cartmell, John Fisher, Isaac Swan, Samuel H. Swan, Martin Davis and John Harrison.

Ordered that the following persons constitute the venire of jurymen to attend at the next county court, to wit, Daniel Harkins, James Alexander, John B. Justice, William Barren, Daniel Berryraft, Nathan Clark, James Caldwell Peter G. Reaves, Richard Sanders, Benjamin Jones Drury Williams, Pitts Chandler. Henry Ragan, Burd Hill Samuel Bradhau, Stephen Lypert, John Rayder, Owen Griffin Andrew Hays, Nathaniel Simpson, Aquila Davis, William Polk Robert H. Burk and Joshua Cason.

P363   Ordered that John Shannon as constable attend on the next county of circuit court, next Thomas Elliott to attend at the next co. court and that Jacob Hill be appointed to attend at the next circuit court.

P363 Robert Gray   )
Cont.vs.   )   Certiorari
    Andrew Forbush)

     This day came the plaintiff by his attorney and moved the court to set aside
the judgment rendered herein on the present day which was done and the cause be
reinstate on the docket and she said Robert Gray be ruled to come and give security
for the costs in this case by Tuesday the second day of the next term otherwise
 suit will be dismissed at his cost.
     Court then adjourned until court in course.
                                        H. Haralson   JP.
                                        M. Christian   JP.
                                        D. McIver   JP.

P364   Be it remembered that on Monday the 27th. day of September 1824 at a
court of pleas and quartersessions began and held in the town of Jackson.
     Present, the Worshipful Herndon Haralson, William E. Butler, William Draper,
John L. Dillard, Guy Smith, Samuel S. Hunter, James Trousdale, Stephen Jarman
Micajah Midyett, and John Thomas, gentlemen, Justices of the Peace.
     On affidavit filed ordered that Burd Hill be exempt from serving as a juror
at the present term.
     Zachariah Dandridge came into open court and recorded his stock mark a crop
and two slits in the left ear and a swallow fork in the right.
     John Spencer came into open court and recorded his stock mark as follows, to
wit, a swallow fork in the right ear and half crop in the upper side of the left.
Thomas Lofton comes into court and records his stock mark as follows, to wit, a
smooth crop off the right and a slit in the left ear.
     Ordered that the hands of Adam Huntsman work on that part of the road which
James Vaulx is overseer of and exempt from any other road.
     Ordered that Abel Webb and hands, Philip Moody and hands, and Allen McKey
and hands work on that part of the road on which Thomas Lofton is overseer and be
exempt from any other.
     Ordered that the following persons to wit, Vincent Haralson, George Todd,
James Vaulx, Alexander Greer, Duncan McIver, Adam Huntsman, Lewis Carpenter, and
Herndon Haralson, them or any five of them be a jury of view to view the road
leading from Jackson by the house Squire Linn's at such points as have been selected
for burying places and see if the road will admit of an alteration so as not to
pass immediately near any graveyard that may have been chosen and make report to the
next term of court.
     Ordered that the following persons, to wit, William Atchison, James A.
McClary, Jacob Bradbury, Francis, Taylor, Murdock Murchison and John May be a jury
to alter the road leading by Esq. McCutchen's so as not to interfere with or pass
immediately any ground that may have been used or chosen for burying places and make
report to the next term of court.
P365   Ordered that Austin A. King be appointed solicitor pro tem in the place of
Alexander Bradford for the present term.
     Ordered that Hugh Lacy, Waid Jarrett and Stephen Bryan, Senior, be appointed
overseers of the road leading from Benjamin Booth's to the county line near Murray's
Bluff on Big Hatchie and work all the hands living equidistant from any other road
to wit, Hugh Lacy fromBooths to a bridge on a small creek S. W. of Johnsons Creek.
Waid Jarrett from thence to the sectional line dividing the 7th. and 8th. sections
and Stephen Bryan to the county line.
     Ordered that the resignation of Joseph Linn Esq. as a Justice of the Peace of
this county was received and accepted by the court who thereupon returned to court
all the papers and documents belonging to the office.
     Isaac Miller, William Weatherspoon and William Robertson were this day elected
and chosen constables for the county of Madison, to wit, the said Isaac Miller in
Capt. James Williamson Company, the said William Weatherspoon in Capt. Adcocks Co.

P365
Cont.
and the said William Robertson in Capt. Hugh Lacys' company and thereupon the said
Isaac Miller and William Weatherspoon and William Robinson took the several oaths
of qualification and entered into their several bonds with their securities.   The
said Isaac Miller with Claibourn Chisum and Theopolis Sanders, the said William
Witherspoon with H. Hewett and J. H. Wilson and the said William Robertson with
Stephen Lacy and Robert Clenton.

Ordered that James Greer, Esquire, who was appointed to mark the lines of the
county be allowed the sum of five dollars per day for nine days service in running
and marking the lines dividing this county from Carroll and Gibson County and that
the county trustee pay the same out of any monies not otherwise appropreated.

Ordered that James F. Theoble be permitted to keep an ordinary in the town of
Jackson having given bond with ason H. Wilson andSamuel D. Wilson his securities.

P366
Ordered that David Shropshire be allowed the sum of ten dollars 12½ cents as
jailor's fees in the case of the state Jacob W. Formault and that the county trustee
pay the same out of any monies not otherwise appropreated and that John H. Ball be
allowed the sum of four dollars 37½ cents for making Jail irons etc. to be paid as
above.

Ordered that couble taxes on 808 acres of land entered in the name of Russel
Goodrich be remitted for the year 1823 and 24 and that the sheriff receive the single
tax on the same as by order of the September court which was omitted to be entered.

Ordered that Elisha Matthews be overseer of the Mount Pinson road from
Chandlers new bridge on the middle fork to the deep gap and work the following hands
to wit, Thomas Carlton and James Matthews, Thomas Shelby's hands, Robert Phelps,
William C. Love's hands, William Higgins, Aden, William and Leonard Lawhors, Wil-
liam Toe's hands, Minor and Elish Marsh and hands, John and Stearling Tally's,
John Criner and hands---- Scarborough, James Tabutton, James Alexander, Jesse Wilson
----Parks, Henry N. Coulter and William W. Bury.

Jon M. Johnson, overseer of said road from the deep gap to Capt. Ross's cart
path to work the hands of Thomas Henderson, John Reed, John Yount and hands,
Daniel Harkins, Jr. Daniel Harkens, Sen'r hands, Hiram Harkins, John McKennies hands
Tobias Goodman and Anderson and all the hands of said Johnson.

And that Daniel Ross Senr. overseer of said road from his cart path to the cou
county line and work Oliver and Ruben Brooks, N. Henderson and hands, William
Kendrick and hands, Wright Koonts, ThomasReaves and hands, William Galloway Stark
Dupree's hands, Daniel Parker, Joseph Findly and the ha ds of said Ross.

Ordered that Pitts Chandler be overseer of the road from the forks near
Park Chandler's to Chandler's bridge on the middle fork of the river and work the
following hands, to wit, H. Hewitt and hands, George French, Washington Gray,
James Young, Henly Webb, Pleasant Dyal, Sam'l Gholson and the hands of said Chandler

P367
On motion and petition filed ordered that James Adams, William Deen, John
Mitchel, Phelip Moody and Thomas Haley be a jury to view and mark out a road of the
third class from Love's ford to Esq. Thomas Mill on Meridian Creek and make report
to the next term of court.

On motion and petition filed ordered that Jacob Hill, Thomas Lofton, John
Mitchell, James McNight and James Haley be a jury to mark a road of the second
class from John Thomas's Mill on Meredian Creek to Jackson and make report to the
next term.

On motion and petition filed ordered that Joshua Weaver, Washington Paulding,
Stephen Smith, James Haley and James McNight be a jury to view and mark a road of
the third class from John Thomas's Mill on Meridian Creek to Joshua Weavers on
Johnson's Creek and make report to the next term.   Joseph Linn and William Draper
Esq. Commissioners appointed to settle the accounts of the administrator of James
L. Price, deceased, this day made report which was ordered to be recorded.

Ordered that Thomas Gordon, Sandford Edwards and Jesse M. Hannah be appointed
to lay off the dower right of Prudence Tedford and make report to the next term of
court.

P387   Ordered that Mathias Deberry be appointed overseer of the road leading from
Cont.Jackson on a direction to Fights Mill from town to the sectional line dividing the
    oth. and 10th. sections.

        Ordered that Jesse L. Kirk be overseer of the road from the district line to
Waddills Bridge and work the following hands, Madison McLaurine, J. G. Stokes,
Josiah Pullen, James T. Pullen, Sugars McLemore Lewis Martin Holaand, John B.
Hogg, Joel Bugg, John Stobough, George C. Rust, Gabriel Day, John Armstrong, John
Oldham, Ebenezer Oldhan, Tidwells and Robert Robson and Mitchell.

P368   On motion and petition filed ordered that Thomas Gordon, Duncan McIver,
Abel Willis, Alexander Greer, Joseph Linn, John M. Welch, Eemuel S. Hunter,
William Alexander and Wm. Spruce be a jury to view and mark a road from Alexander's
bridge on the middle fork so as to intersect the Carrol road at or near where it
crosses Spring Creek and make report to the next term of this court.

        On motion and petition filed ordered that Burd Smith, Sugars McLemore, Joel
Bugg Micajah Midyett, James Trousdale, John Herrin, Andrew Hays, John Weir James
Greer, Capt. Hannah and John Hardgraves be a jury to view aroad from Carither's
ferry to intersect the Carroll road near Col. Stewarts and make report to the next
term of court.

        On motion and petition filed ordered that James Brown, Martin Lorance, B.
Shockler, John Gillespie and S. Hatcher be a jury t view and make an alteration in
the Carroll road who have reported the alteration shall be made agreeable to the
prayers of the petition. It is therefore ordered that the same shall be oepened
by the present overseers.

        On motion and petition filed ordered that Thomas Doak, John T. Porter, Aquila
Davis James Cockrill, Henry Lake, James Brown, Samuel Shannon, Lancaster Glover,
Henning Pace, James Roe, William Henry and John Graves be a jury to view a road
from Jackson to the county line in a direction to the center of Haywood County so
as to follow the marks of a former jury until they pass Samuel H. Shannon's land
and upon consent of parties with the assent of the court said road is ordered to be
established and cut out immediately and the hands shall be equally divided between
Benjamin Booth, overseer of the other road and George W. Taylor who is hereby app
pointed overseer of the new road leaving Richard H. Burk and hands on the new road.

        Ordered that John Estes be appointed overseer of the road in place of Gabriel
Chandler from McIvers Branch to the head of Youngs Branch and work all the hands
East of McIvers Branch.

        On motion and petition filed ordered that Jacob Miller, Frederick Miller,
Claibourne Chisum Larkin Carson, Turner Tate, Stephen Lacy, Joshua Weaver, and
John Anderson be a jury to view a road of the 2nd. class from the bridge at
Shannon landing in a direction to the mouth of Clover Creek as far as the county
line and make report to the next term.

        The administrator of Thomas Andrews dec'd, this day returned an inventory
of the amount of sales said estate.

        Administration of all and singular the goods and Chattels, rights and credits
of Joel Mading deceased, was this day grantedto Joseph Linn, who thereupontook the
oath of administration and entered into bond with B. C. Stewart, his security in
the penalty of two thousand dollars and thereupon returned an inventory of the estate of the decedant.

        Administration of all and singular the goods and chattels, rights and credits
of David Jackson, dec'd. was this day granted to Susan Jackson and David Jackson
who thereupon took the oath of administration and entered into bond in the penalty
of six hundred dollars with John Roseberry and Abel Rainey their securities.

        Wyatt Epps was this day chosen and appointed guardian of Thomas Epps who
thereupon entered into bond with Matthias Deberry and Jesse L. Kirk his securities
in the penalty of six hundred and fifty dollars.

        Ordered that Edward William be overseer of the road in the place of Burd

P370 Smith and that Guy Smith divide the -- between him and Jno. J. Smith and that James Stalkeep who is overseer from Hurricane Creek to the county line.

Ordered that Samuel Shannon be released from payment of the amount of money due the county for strays proven to be the property of William Braden.

Thomas Carneyhan proves the killing one wolf over four months old in this county.

William Crook proves the killing one wolf over four months old in theis county

Duncan McIver came into open court and acknowledged himself bound for the cost of the suit Robert Gray vs. Andrew Torbush provided that William Norwood should have the cost to pay.

Thomas Reaves proves the killing one wolf over four months old in this county.

James Crook proves four days attendance as a juror of view in this county p previous to the passage of an act of assembly repealing an act allowing compensation to jurors of view in the Western District.

A deed of conveyance from William Thedford to Samuel Dickens for 160 acres was this day produced in open court and proven by the oath of William Atchison a witness and ordered to be filed for further probate.

A deed of conveyance fwom Joseph H. Bryan, JamesFreeman and Robert C. Watson to Samuel Dicking for 2892 acres was this day produced in open court and acknowledged by the said Joseph H. Bryan, James Freeman and Robert C. Watson to be their act and deed and ordered to be certified for registration.

A deed of conveyance from the commissioners for the town of Jackson to Samuel H. Shannon for lots No. 81-51 and 100 as designated in the plan of said town was this day produced in open court and the execution thereof proven by the oath of Anthony F. Gray and ordered to be filed for futher probate.

P371 A deed of conveyance from John Spencer to Zachariah Hardridge for thirty five and one fourth acres was produced in open court and acknowledged by the said John Spencer to be his act and deed and ordered to be certified for registration.

A bill of sale from Benjamin W. H. Medearez to John G. Gillespie for one negro girl by the name of Fanny was produced in opwn court and acknowledged by the said Benjamin W. H. Medeariz to be his act and deed and ordered to be certified for registration.

A deed of conveyance from Simon Huddliston to Jeremiah Harris for three hundred and twenty acres of land was produced in open court and duly proven by the oath of Isaac Miller and Jacob Watson and ordered to be certified for registration.

A bill of sale from Elijah Jones to William Doak for a negro girl named Rachel was this day produced in open court and acknowledged by the said Elijah Jones to be his act and deed and ordered to be certified for registration.

A power of attorney from DanielRoss to John Overton was this day produced in open court and acknowledged by the said Daniel Ross to be his act and deed and ordered to be so certified.

A deed of conveyance from the commissioners of the town of Jackson to James McKnight and Wilson McClennen for lots No. sixty four and forty-eight as designated in the plan of said town was this day produced in open court and acknowledged by Herndon Haralson Chairman of the board of said commissioners and ordered to be registered.

A deed of conveyance from Theophilis Sanders to David, H. E. and William Sanders for four acres 11 9/11 poles was this day produced in open court and acknowledged by the said Theophilis Sanders to be his act and deed and ordered to

P372   be certified for registration.

A deed of conveyance from William Polk by his attorney in fact Samuel Dickens to John Gately for one hundred fifty acres of land was this day produced in open court and the execution thereof duly proven by the oaths of William Atchison and Beverly Jones subscribing witnesses and ordered to be certified for registration.

A bill of sale from Jacob Bradbury Sen'r to Jacob Bradbury for a negro boy was this day produced in open court and the execution thereof proven by the oath of Beverly Jones and David H. Green, subscribing witnesses thereto, and ordered to be recorded.

A bill of sale from Robert Murray Administrator of John Smith deceased to Samuel H. Shannon for a negro girl was this day produced in open court and proven by the oath of John D. Shannon subscribing witness thereto and ordered to be recorded.

A deed of conveyance from Samuel Dickens to Hannah McMillan, Dixon McMillan and Robert Parks McMillan for Eighty acres of land was this day produced in open court and the execution thereof acknowledged by the said Samuel Dickens to be his act and deed and ordered to be certified.

A transfer of a plat and certificate from Clark Spencer to Allen McVoy for twenty four and a half acres of land was this day produced in open court and the execution of the same duly acknowledged by the said Clark Spencer and ordered to be so certified.

Ordered that William Harris, Joseph Linn and Roderick McIver be appointed to settle with the former trustee and make report to the next term.

Ordered that Saturday next be set apart for argument causes.

Court then adjourned until tomorrow murning nine o'clock.

                                        H. Haralson   JP.
                                        Thos. Gordon   JP.
                                        Adam R. Alexander   JP.

Tuesday 28th. day of September 1824
        Court met agreeable to adjournment. Present, the Worshipful Herndon Haralson William E. Butler, Thomas Gordon and Adam R. Alexander gentlemen justices.

Thomas Allison)
vs.   )   Appeal
John T. Porter)
        This day came the parties aforesaid by their attorneys and thereupon came a jury of good and lawful men, to wit, James Alexander, William Barren, Richard Sanders, Benjamin Jones, Drury Williams, Pitts Chandler, Henry Reagan, Stephen Lypert, Andrew Hays, Nathan Simpson, Mathias Deberry and Archibold Chaffin, who being elected tried and sworn, the truth to speak upon their oath do say they find the matters in dispute in favor of the plaintiff and assess his damages to sixty one dollars. It is therefore considered by the court that the plaintiff go thereof hence and recover of the defendant the damages aforesaid in form aforesaid by the jury aforesaid assessed together with his cost by him about his suit in this behalf expended and the defendant in mercy etc. from which judgment the defendant John T. Porter prayed an appeal to the next Circuit Court to be held for Madison County which was granted him and thereupon entered into bond with William C. Mitchell and David Jarrett his security in the penalty of one hundred fifty dollars conditioned for the prosecution of said appeal.

P374   Order of Sale
        On motion it is ordered by the court that a venditionas exponas issue to the Sheriff of Madison County commanding him to expose to sale the right, title interest and claim that James Moore has in and to one hundred acres of land to satisfy two judgments one in favor of Elijah Baker for the sum of thirty dollars

P374 and cost against Andrew Hays and B. G. Stewart obtained before James Greer on the
Cont.10th. day of January last and the other in favor of John Phillips and against
James Moore, William Penn and Elijah Jones obtained before William E. Butler on
the 31st. day of July 1824 for the sum of fifteen dollars and cost one which judgments executions issued to William McCauslin a constable of Madison County who
has made the following indorsements to wit, no goods or chattels, belonging to
James Moore, the defendant can I find in my county therefore I have levied the
with in execution on one hundred acres of land as the property of said moore
entered by Entry No. 559 in the name of John Gray Blount in Range one and Section
nine of the 10th. district 17th August 1824 W. McCauslin C. M. C.

On motion it is ordered that a venditionas exponas issue to the sheriff of
Madison County commanding him to expose to sale all the right, title interest
and claim and deman that James Moore has in and to fifty acres of land to satisfy
and judgment obtained before James Trousdale for the sum of twenty five dollars
and cost in favor of Samuel D. Waddell and against said Moore before James Trousdale on the 10th day of July 1824 on which judgment execution issued and returned
here into court with the following indorsement theron to wit, No personal property found. Levied on fifty acres of land a part of 274 acres entered in Range
on Sect. 9 district 10 Sept. 18,1824

J. T. Rust C. M. C.

An indenture of bargain and sale from James Howard to Russel Goodrich for
eight and one fourth acres of land was this day produced in open court and the
execution of same duly proven by the oath of Cyrus Sikes andRobert Rogers and sub
scribing witnesses thereto and ordered to be certified.

An indenture of bargain and sale from Edmond Jones to John Trigg for six
hundred and forty acres of land was this day produced and acknowledged by the
said Edmond Jones to be his acr and deed and ordered to be certified.

The sheriff this day made a return of the writ of veniri faceas to him
directed from the last term of this court with the following indorsement thereon
I have summoned all the persons named in the within venire except Daniel Ross
who could not be found all of which are free holders on house holders of my
county in pursuance of which the following persons were then attending to wit,
James Alexander William Barrow, Richard Sanders, Benjamin Jones, Drury Williams,
Pitts Chandler, Henry Reagan, Stephen Eypert, Andrew Hays, Nathan Simpson and
Owen Griffin, there not being a component number of jurors these are discharged
until tomorrow.

P356 Prudence Tedford and B. G. Stewart, Administration etc.   )
vs.   )   Appeal
John Jones and Henry Cassels Jr.   )

This day came the parties aforesaid by their attorneys and thereupon came
a jury of good and lawful men, towit, James Alexander William Barren Richard
Sanders, Benjamin Jones, Drury Williams Pitts Chandler Henry Reagan, Stephen
Lypert, Andrew Hays, Nathan Simpson, Mathias Deberry and Archibold Coffin who
being elected, tried and sworn the truth to speak upon their oaths do say they
find the matter in dispute in favor of the defendants. It is therefore considered by the court that the defendant recover of the plaintiff and their security
Simon Tedford the cost by them about their suit in this behalf expended and the
plaintiff in mercy etc.

William C. Love   )
vs.   )
Jonathan Houston   )

An affidavit filed of the defendant this cause is continued until next
term of this court.

P376 John D. Love   )
Cont. vs.   )   Covenant
James McCutchen   )

This day came the parties aforesaid by their attorneys and thereupon came a jury of good and lawful men, to wit, James Alexander William Barren, Richard Sanders, Benjamin Jones, Drury Williams, Pitts Chandler, Henry Reagan, Stephen Lypert, Andrew Hays, Nathan Simpson, Mathias Deberry and Archibold Chaffin who being elected, tried and sworn well and truly to try the issue joined do say We of the jury find that the defendant has not well and truly kept and performed his covenant as in pleading he hath Alledged and do assess the plaintiff damages by reason thereof to ninety-six dollars and fourteen cents. It is therefore considered by the court that the plaintiff recover of the defendant the said sum of ninety-six dollars and fourteen cents together with his cost by him about his suit in this behalf expended and the def't. in mercy etc.

George Mizell   )
vs.   )   Appeal
Robert Houston   )

This day came the parties aforesaid by their attorneys and thereupon came a jury of good and lawful men to wit James Akexander William Barren, Richard Sanders Benjamin Jones, Drury Williams, Pitts Chandler, Henry Reagan, Stephen Lppert, Matthias Deberry, Archibold Caffin and ------- who being elected tried and sworn the truth to speak upon the issue joined and upon their oaths do say we of the jury do find the matters in dispute in favor of the defendant Robert Huston, and assess his damages to eighty seven and one half cents, confirmation of the judgment of the court below. It is therefore considered by the court here that the said Robert Huston recover of George Mizell the appellant in this case and Jonathan Walsh his security the damages aforesaid in form aforesaid by the jury aforesaid assessed together with his cost by him about his suit in this behalf expended and the plantiff in mercy etc.

Ordered that John Fussell be fined the sum of ten dollars for contemp shown this court by fighting with a certain John Montgomery in the court yard on the 28th day of September 1824 and during the setting of court to their great disturbance.

An indenture of sale from John P. Thomas to Edward Williams for 140 acres of land was this day produced in open court and acknowledged by the said Thomas to be his act and deed and ordered to be so certified.

Elias Fort   )
vs.   )   Certiorari
William R. Hess and Robert H. Dyer)

On motion of the plaintiff by his attorney, he moved the court to dismiss the certeorari in the case which is done accordingly. It is therefore considered by the court that the plaintiff recover of the defendant the sum of thirty two dollars and fifty cents the amount of the judgment rendered in the court below with twelve and one half per cent interest from the rendition of the judgment below together with his costs by him about his suit in this behalf expended and the defendant in mercy etc.

Court then adjourned until tomorrow morning eight o'clock.

                                        Wm. E. Butler   J P.
                                        Guy Smith   JP.
                                        Sam Taylor   JP.

P376   Wednesday morning 29th. September 1824
Cont.   Court met agreeable to adjournment,   Present, the Worshipful William E.
       Butler, Samuel Taylor, Samuel S. Hunter and Guy Smith, gentlemen, justices,

       Elias Fort   )
       vs.   )   Case A &B
       John T. Porter   )
              This day came the parties aforesaid by their attorneys and thereupon came
       a jury of good and lawful men to wit, Stephen Lypert, Archibold Chaffan John
       Rayder, Benjamin Jones, Andrew Hays, James Alexander, Owens Griffin, Nathan Sim-
       pson, William Barren, Pitts Chandler, Richard Sanders and Henry Reagan, who be-
       ing elected tried and sworn, will and truly to try the issue joined upon their
       oaths do say We of the jury do find in favor of the defendant. It is therefore
       considered by the court that the defendant recover of the plaintiff his cost by
       him about his suit in this behalf expended and the plaintiff be in mercy etc.
       From which judgment the plaintiff prayed an appeal which is granted upon his
       coming into court any time during the present term and giving security.

       Matthias Deberry   )
       vs.   )   Debt
       Washington J. Dewet   )
              This day came the parties aforesaid by their attorneys and the defendant
       because of action relinguishes his plea of payment and confesses judgment for the
       sum of one hundred dollars debt and eight dollars interest. It is therefore
       considered by the court that the plaintiff recover of the defendant the said
       sum of one hundred dollars debt and eight dollars interest together with his
       cost by him about his suit in this behalf expended and the defendant be in mercy
       etc.

       William Wilson   )
       vs.   )   Debt
       Henry and Griffith W. Rutherford)
              This day came the parties aforesaid by their attorneys and the defendant
       agrees to withdraw their former plea and confess judgment for the sum of one hun-
       dred and thirty two dollars and fifty cents debt with fifteen dollars and ninety
       cents interest. It is therefore considered by the court that the plaintiff
       recover of the defendant one hundred forty eight dollars and forty cents the debt
       and interest aforesaid together with his cost by him about his suit in this behal
       expended and the defendant in mercy etc.

P380   William Welbourn)
2Pa.   vs.   )   Debt
       John F. Brown   )
              This day came the parties aforesaid by their attorneys and thedefendant
       because he cannot gainsay the plaintiffs cause of action, withdraws his plea and
       confesses judgment for the sum of three hundred and seven dollars debt and
       twenty one dollars interest. It is therefore considered by the court that the
       plaintiff recover of the defendant three hundred and twenty-eight dollars, the
       debt and interest aforesaid together with his cost by him about his suit in this
       behalf expended and the defendant in mercy etc.

       Thomas Martin   )
       vs.   )   In debt
       Stokely D. Hays   )
              This day came the parties aforesaid by their attorneys and the defendant

P381 because he cannot gainsay the plaintiffs cause of adtion with draws his plea
and confesses judgment for the sum of four hundred fifty dollars debt and sixty
seven dollars interest. It is therefore considered by the court that the plaintiff recover of the defendant five hundred seventeen dollars the debt and interest aforesaid toge ther with his cost by him about his suit in this behalf expend
ed and the defendant in mercy etc.

Mathias Deberry   )
vs.   )   In debt
John T. Porter   )

    This day came the parties aforesaid by their attorneys and the defendant
because he cannot gainsay the plaintiffs cause of action withdraws his plea and
confesses judgment for the sum of one hundred and sixty-three dollars debt with
thirteen dollars and four cents interest. It is therefore considered by the court
that the plaintiff recover of the defendant one hundred seventy six dollars and
four cents the dect and interest aforesaid together with his cost by him about
his suit in this behalf expended and the defendant in mercy etc.

Murray and Rutherford   )
vs.   )   Case
William L. Mitchell   )

    This day came the parties aforesaid by their attorneys and thereupon came
a jury of good and lawful men, to wit, Stephen Lypert, Archibold Chaffin, John
Rayder, Benjamin Jones, James Alexander, Andrew Hays Owen Griffin, Nathan Simpson William Barren Pitts Chandler, Richard Sanders, and Henry Raygan who being
elected, tried and sworn the truth to speak upon their oaths do say they find th
issue joined in favor of the plaintiffs and assess his damages to one hundred
and twenty one dollars and fifty two cents. It is therefore considered by the
court that the plaintiffs recover of the defendant the damages aforesaid together with their costs by them about their suit in this behalf expended and the
defendant in mercy etc.

Homer Rainey   )
vs.   )   Debt
Herndon Haralson   )

    On affidavit of the defendant this cause is continued until next term of
court.

Marrhias Deberry   )
vs.   )   In debt
Stokely D. Hays and Joshua Haskill)

    This day came the parties aforesaid by their attorneys and the defendants
because they cannot gainsay the plaintiffs cause of action withdraw their plea
and confess judgment for the sum of one hundred minety six dollars eighty seven
and one half cents debt and sixteen dollars and seventeen cents interest. It
is therefore considered by the court that the plaintiff recover of the defendant
two hundred thirteen dollars four andone half cents, the debt and interest, together with his cost by him about his suit in this behalf expended and the defendant in mercy etc.

Mathias Deberry   )
vs.   )   In debt
Aquila Davis   )

    This day came the parties aforesaid by their attorneys and the defendant
because he cannot gainsay the plaintiff's cause of action withdraws his plea

P382 and confesses judgment for the sum of one hundred five dollars and fifty cents
debt with eight dollars and fifty four cents interest. It is therefore considered by the court that the plaintiff recover of the defendant one hundred fourte
teen dollars and fourteen cents, the debt and interest aforesaid together with h
his cost by him about his suit in this behalf expended and the defendant in mercy
etc.

Commissioners of the town of Jackson   )
vs.   )   In debt
Anthony F. Gray and Thomas Shannon   )
          This day come the parties aforesaid by their attorneys and thereupon came
a jury of good and lawful men, to wit, Stephen Lppert, Archibold Chaffin, John
Rayder, Benjamin Jones, Andrew Hays, James Alexander Owen Griffin, Nathan Simpson William Barren, Pitts Chandler, Richard Sanders, and Henry Reagan, who
being elected tried and sworn will truly to try the issue joined upon their oaths
do say We of the jury do find the issue in favor of the plaintiff, that the
defendant hath not paif the debt in the declaration mentioned as in pleading
they that alleged the sum of two hundred and thirty four dollars debt and assess
their damage by reason of the detention thereof to sixteen dollars. It is therefore considered by the court that the plaintiffs recover of the defendants the
debt and damage aforesaid in manner and form aforesaid by the jury aforesaid in
form aforesaid assessed together with their cost by them about their suit in
this behalf expended and the defendant in mercy etc.

The commissioners of the town of Jackson)
vs.   )   In debt
William Willbourn and Elijah Jones   )
          This day came the parties aforesaid by their attorneys and thereupon came
a jury of good and lawful men, to wit Stephen Lppert, Archibold Chaffin, John
Rayder, Nathan Simpson, Benjamin Jones, Andrew Hays, James Alexander, Owen Griffin
William Barren, Pitts Chandler, Richard Sanders, and Henry Raygan, who being
elected, tried and sworn well and truly to try the issue joined upon their oaths
do say they find the defendants hath not paid the debt in the declaration mentioned of three hundred and seven dollars and assess their damages by reason of the
detention thereof to twenty one dollars damages. It is therefore considered by
the court that the plaintiff recover of the defendant the debt aforesaid with
the damage aforesaid in manner and form by the jury aforesaid assessed together
with their cost by them about their suit in this behalf expended and the defendant in mercy etc.

Commissioners of the town of Jackson   )
vs.   )   In debt
James Moore and William Espy   )
          This day came the parties aforesaid by their attorneys and thereupon came
a jury of good and lawful men, to wit, Stephen Lypert, Archibold Chaffin, John
Rayder, Benjamin Jones, Andrew Hays, James Alexander Owen Griffin, Nathan Simpson
William Barren, Pitts Chandler, Richard Sanders and Henry Reagan, who being elected, tried and sworn the truth to speak upon the issue joined upon their oaths do
say we of the jury do find for the plaintiff the sum of one hundred and seventy
dollars the debt in the declaration mentioned and assess their damages by reason
of the detention thereof to eleven dollars. It is therefore considered by the
court that the plaintiff recover of the defendants the debt and damages aforesaid
by the jury aforesaid assessed together with their cost by them about their suit
in this behalf expended and the defendant in mercy etc.

P382 Commissioners of the town of Jackson)
    vs.)   In debt
William Espy and James Brown)

    This day came the parties aforesaid by their attorneys and thereupon came
a jury of good and lawful men to wit, Stephen Lypert, Archibold Chaffin, John
Rayden, Benjamin Jones, Andrew Hays, James Alexander, Owen Griffin, Nathan
Simpson, William Barren, Pitts Chandler Richard Sanders and Henry Reagan, who
being elected, tried and sworn well and truly to try the issues joined upon their
oaths do say We of the jury do find the issues for the plaintiff one hundred
and five dollars the balance of debt in the declaration mentioned and assess
their damages by reason of the detention thereof to seven dollars. It is therefore considered by the court that judgment be suspended for the determination
of the matters in law arising upon the demurrer in this cause.

P384 John Manley, Plff.)
    vs.)   In debt
Robert Hughes and William E. Butter Defts.)

    This day came the parties aforesaid by their attorneys and thereupon came
a jury of good and lawful men, towit, Stephen Lypert, Archibold Chaffin, John
Rayder, Benjamin Jones, Andrew Hays, James Alexander, Owen Griffin, Nathan
Simpson William Barren Pitts Chandler, Richard Sanders, and Henry Reagan who being elected tried and sworn well and truly to try the issues joined upon their
oaths do say We of the jury do find for the plaintiff Eighty one dollars the
balance of debt in the declaration mentioned and assess his damages by reason
of the detention thereof to seven dollars and twenty nine cents. It is therefore
considered by the court that the plaintiff recoger of the defendants the balance
of debt aforesaid with the damages aforesaid by the jury aforesaid in form aforesaid assessed together with the cost by him about his suit in this behalf expended
and the defendants in mercy etc.

George C. Rust)
    vs.)   A. B.
John B. William C. Cross)

    This day came the parties aforesaid by their attorneys and dismissed their
suit herein each agreeing to pay half the cost. It is therefore considered by
the court that the same be dismissed and the parties pay all the cost accruing
thereon according to the agreement of that parties.

Joseph McMinn)
    vs.)   In debt
Joel Dyer, Senor)

    This day came the parties aforesaid by their attorneys and the defend-
ant, because he cannot gainsay the plaintiffs cause of action withdraws his pleas
and confesses judgment for the sum of one hundred forty seven dollars thirty seven
cents the balance of debt in the declaration mentioned with twenty-three dollars
interest. It is therefore considered by the court that the plaintiff recover of
the defendant the balance fo debt aforesaid with the interest aforesaid together
with his cost by him about his suit in this behalf expended and the defendant in
mercy.

P385

Daniel Cleft)
    vs) Case
Thomas Shannon)

    This day came the parties aforesaid by their attorneys and thereupon came
a jury of good and lawful men, to wit, Stephen Lypert, Archibold Chaffin, John

P385 Rayder, Benjamin Jones,   Andrew Hays, James Alexander, Owen Griffin, Nathan Simp-
Cont. son, William Barren, Pitts Chandler, Richard Sander and Henry Reagan, who being
elected, tried and sworn the truth to speak upon their oaths do say We of the
jury do find the issues joined in favor of the defendant. It is therefore considered by the court that the defendant recover of the plaintiff his cost by him
about his suit in this behalf expended and that the plaintiff in mercy etc.

Josiah Pullen   )
vs.   ) Appeal
Bartholomew G. Stewart)
      By consent of parties this cause is continued until the next term of this
court.

Abraham Smith   )
vs.   ) Appeal
Matthew B. McMahan)
      This day came the defendant by his attorney A. Huntsman and the plaintiff
in the court below being solemnly called to come into court and prosecute his
suit in this behalf but came not. Wherefore it is considered by the court that
he nonsuited and the defendant recover against him his cost by him in this behalf
expended etc.

P386 Ira C. Kennedy   )
vs.   ) Appeal
John G. Carithers   )
      This day came the parties aforesaid by their attorneys and thereupon came
a jury of good and lawful men, to wit, Drury Williams, Mathias Deberry John
Stobough, James Newsom, Henry Booth Thos. Laremour, John C. Stogdon James
Henderson, David White, George Mizel Samuel Tholson and John Spencer, who being
elected, tried and sworn well and truly to try the matters in despute between the
parties upon their oaths do say they find for the plaintiff nineteen dollars
sixty two cents. It is therefore considered by the court that the plaihgiff
recover of the defendant John G. Carithers with Nelson I. Hess and John Murray
his Securities in the appeal the said sum of nineteen dollars and sixty two and
half cents together with the lawful interest and cost by him about his suit in
   this behalf expended and the defendant in mercy etc.

Thomas Merrison   )
vs.   ) Debt
Richard Sanders   )
      This day came the parties aforesaid by their attorneys and thereupon came
a jury of good and lawful men to wit, Drury Williams, Mathias Deberry John Stobough James Newsom, Henry Booth Thomas Laremour, John C. Stockton, James Henderson
David White George Mizell, Samuel Cholson and John Spencer, who being elected,
tried and sworn well and truly to try the issue joined on their oath do say We
of the jury do find for the plaintiff the sum of one hundred twenty eight dollars
and seventeen cents, the balance of the debt in the declaration mentioned and
assess his damage by reason of the detention thereof to eight dollars and twenty
one cents. It is therefore considered by the court that the plaintiff recover
of the defendant the balance of debt aforesaid with the damages aforesaid in form
aforesaid by the jury aforesaid assessed together with his cost by him about his
suit in this behalf expended and the defend in mercy etc. from which judgment
the defendant prayed an appeal to the next term of the circuit court to be
holden for the county of Madison which is granted having entered into bond with
James Trousdale and Duncan McIver, his securities in the penalty of two hundred
and seventy two dollars conditioned for the prosecution of said appeal and signed
his reasons for the appeal.

P387mMoses F. Roberts)
    vs.   )   In debt
David Jarrett   )

     This day came the parties aforesaid by their attorneys and thereupon came
a jury of good and lawful men, to wit, Drury Williams Mathias Deberry, John Stobough, James Newsom, Henry Booth, Thomas Laremour, John C. Stockton, James Henderson, David White, George Mizell, Samuel Gholson and John Spencer who being
elected tried and sworn will and truly to try the issue goined upon their oaths
do say, We of the jury do find for the plaintiff one hundred nine dollars the
balance of the debt in the declaration mentioned and assess his damages by reason
of the detention thereof to eight dollars and seventy-two cents. It is therefor
considered by the court that the plaintiff sworn of the defendant the balance of
debt aforesaid with his damages aforesaid together with his cost by him about his
suit in this behalf expended and the defendant in mercy etc.

Turrence Persons)
    vs.   )   In debt
Calvin Jones   )

     This day came the parties aforesaid by their attorneys and thereupon came
a jury of good and lawful men, to wit, Drury Williams, Mathias Deberry, John
Stobough James Newsom, Henry Boot Thomas Laremour, John Stockton, James Henderson
David White George Mizell, Samuel Gholson and John Spencer who being elected, tried
and sworn well and truly the issues joined upon their oaths do say we of the jury
do find for the plaintiff the sum of three hundred and seventy dollars the debt
in thedeclaration mentioned and assess his damages by reason of the detention thereof to forty seven dollars. It is therefore considered by the court that the plaintiff recover of the defendant the debt and damages aforesaid in manner and form
aforesaid by the jury aforesaid assessed together with his cost by him about his
suit in this behalf expended and the defendant in mercy etc.
     Ordered that James Trousdale and David Jarrett be appointed to settle with
the administration of the estate of Robert Edmondson deceased and make report to
next term of court.
     Administration of the estate of Robert Edmondson, deceased is this day grant-
ed to Duguid Mimms who thereupon entered into bond with David Jarrett and Duncan
McIver his securities in the penalty of thirty two hundred dollars conditioned for
the faithful discharge of said administration. It is therefore ordered that
Bartholomew G. Stewart be released as administrator of said deceased.
     A deed of bargain and sale from the Commissioners of the Town of Jackson to
William Espy for lot No. 83 as designated in the plan of said town, was this day
produced in open court and the execution thereof duly rpoven by the oath of Mathias
Deberry and John Ridins subscribing witnesses and ordered to be certified for registration.
     A deed of conveyance from the trustees of the University of North Carolina
by their agent Samuel Dickens to Thomas Lofton for 274 acres of land was this day
produced in open court and acknowledged by the said Samuel Dickens agent aforesaid
to be his act and deed and ordered to be certified.
     A deed of conveyance from James Moore to Mathias Deberry for 274 acres of
P389 land was this day rpoduced in open court and proved by the oath of Stephen G. C
Childress and Joseph F. Clouds subscribing witnesses and ordered to be certified.

     Ordered that the report of the jury of view viewing the road from near Will-
iam E. Butler to Stanleys Branch be received and that the road be established as
the said jury marked the same by consent of all parties.

Prudence Tedford and B. G. Stewart, Admr. etc.
   vs
John Jones and Henry Cassels Jr.   )   Appeal

P389   The plaintiffs this day came and prayed an appeal to the next circuit c
Cont. court of Madison County from the judgment rendered herein on a former day of
this court which was granted them who entered into bond with Alfred Murray their
security in the penalty of sixty five dollars conditioned for the prosecution
of said appeal

Robert Houston , Andrew Hays   )
vs.   )   Slander
George Mizell   )
       This day came the parties aforesaid by their attorneys and thereupon came
a jury of good and lawful men to wit, Stephen Eypert Archibold Chaffin, John
Rayder, James Alexander, Owen Griffin Nathan Simpson, William Barren, Pitts
Chandler, Richard Sanders Henry Reagan, James Poor and John Irons who being elec
ted tried and sworn the truth to speak upon the issues joined were by consent
of parties with the assent of the court, discharged from rendering their verdict
herein until tomorrow morning.
       Court then adjourned until tomorrow morning 8o'clock.

                                        Tho. Gordon   JP.
                                        Sm. E. Butler   JP
                                        Lemuel S. Hunter   JP.

P390 Thursday morning 30th September 1824
       Court met agreeable to adjournment. Present, the Worshipful William E.
Butler, James Greer, Thomas Gordon and Lemiel S. Hunter.
       Ordered that Double tax be remitted for the year 1823 on two entries made
in the 13th. Dist. Range 7 Sect. 2 by Entry No. 393 No 394 for fifty acres each
(for the benefit) of R. Murray.
       Ordered that taxes one one black poll for the year 1824 be remitted (for
the benefit) of Biggin J. Simms (motion by R. Murray)
       The following persons to wit James Alexander, William Barren, Richard
Sanders, Benjamin Jones, Drury Williams, Pitts Chandler, Stephen Lypert, John
Rayder, Owen Griffin, Andrew Hays Nathan Simpson, Henry Raygan and Peter G.
Reaves were this day empanelled, sworn and charged as a Grand Jury to inquire
into and for the body of the County of Madison and thereupon retired to consider presentments.
       An indenture of sale from Benjamin Sholson to Andrew L. Martin for part
of lot No. 13 as disignated in the plan of the town of Jackson was this day produced in open court and acknowledged by the said Gholson to be his act and deed
and ordered to be certified.
       An indenture of sale from William E. Butler, John McNairy and Henry M.
Rutledge by the said William E. Butler for himself and as attorney for the
said John McNairy and Henry M. Rutledge to Andrew L. Martin for five acres of
land was this day produced in open court and the execution thereof acknowledged to be the act and deed of the said Butler as aforesaid.
       A deed of conveyance from Joseph H. Bryan to Daniel Mason for 640 acres
of land was this day produced in open court and proven by the oath of Matthias
Deberry and John H. Hyde and ordered to be certified for registration.
P391   A deed of conveyance from Robert C. Watson and Joseph H. Bryan to Daniel
Mason for 640 acres of land was this day produced in open court and duly proven
by the oath of Matthias Deberry and John H. Hyde and ordered to be certified
for registration.
       A deed of conveyance from Joseph H. Bryan to Robert C. Watson for 700
acres of land was this day produced in open court and duly proven by the oath
of James Freeman and John H. Hyde and ordered to be certified for registration.
       A deed of conveyance from the commissioners of the Town of Jackson to
Vincent Harelson for lot No. 16 as designated in the plan of said town was this

P391 day produced in open court and acknowledged by Herndon Haralson chairman of the Cont.board of commissioners and ordered to be certified for registration.

A deed of conveyance from James Freeman and Joseph H. Bryan to Daniel Mason for 274 acres of land was this day produced in open court and duly proven by the oath of Matthias Deberry and John H. Hyde and ordered to be so certified.

A deed of conveyance from Joseph H. Bryan and Robert C. Watson to Daniel Mason for 640 acres of land was this day produced in open court and duly proven by the oath of Matthias Deberry and John H. Hyde and ordered to be so certified.

A deed of conveyance from Joseph H. Bryan and Robert C. Watson to Daniel Mason for 640 acres of land was this day produced in open court and duly proven by the oath of Mathias Deberry and John H. Hyde and ordered to be certified.

P392 Andrew Hays, Plff)
vs.) Slander
George Mizell Deft.)

This day came the parties aforesaid by their attorneys and thereupon came a jury of good and lawful men, to wit, Stephen Lypert Archibold Chaffin, James Alexander, Owen Griffin, Nathan Simpson, William Barren, Pitts, Chandler, Richard Sanders, Henry Reagan, James Poor and John Irons who being elected, tried and sworn well and truly to try the issues, joined upon their oaths do say we of the jury do find the defendant is not guilty of the several counts in the plaintiffs declaration mentioned. It is therefore considered by the court that the defendant recover of the plaintiff his cost by him about his suit in this behalf expended and the plaintiff in mercy etc.

The State)
vs.) An affray
Thomas Laremour)

This day came as well the solicitor general on the part of the state as the defendant in proper person and thereupon came a jury of good and lawful men, to wit, John Stobough, James Tidwell, James Henderson, Ruben P. T. Stone Andrew Hamel, Thomas Harrington Jefferson Key, Moses Starnes, John Spencer, Mathias Boon, Malcolm Johnson and John Young who being elected tried and sworn the truth to speak upon the issue joined and upon their oaths do say, we of the jury do find the defendant is not guilty as charged in the bill of indictment. It is therefore considered by the court that the defendant recover of the plaintiff his cost by him about his suit in this behalf expended and the plaintiff f for her false clamor in mercy etc.

The State)
vs.) Peace Warrent
Alexander Bostick)

This day came as well the solicitor general on the part of the state and the prosecutor Williamson Curtis being solemly called, came not therefore it is considered by the court that the defendant be discharged from further recognisance and that the said prosecutor be taxed with the cost.

William Braden)
vs.) In debt
Levi B. Anderson)

On motion of the plaintiff by his attorney and it appearing to the satisfaction of the court that the plaintiff is bound to pay and there is a judgment against him for the sum of two hundred nineteen dollars sixty two and one half cents as the security of the defendant. It is therefore considered by the court that the plaintiff recover of the defendant said sum of two hundred and nineteen dollars sixty two and one half cents, together with his cost by him about his motion in this behalf expended and the defendant in mercy etc.

P392 The State   )
Cont.vs   )   Affray
    Foel Meding & Daniel Mading   )
        On motion of the council for the state, this suit was dismissed and it is
considered by the court that the county be taxed with the cost.

P394 Elias Fort   )
     vs.   )   A & B
     John T. Porter   )
        The plaintiff by his attorney this day came into court and prayed an ap-
peal from a judgment rendered herin on a former day of the court which was granted him who thereupon entered into bond with Mathias Deberry and Alfred Murray
his securities in the penalty of two hundred dollars conditioned for the prosecution of said appeal.

     Turner Persons   )
     vs.   )   In debt
     Calvine Jones   )
        The defendant by his attorney prayed an appeal from a judgment rendered
therein on a former day of this court which was granted him who thereupon entered into bond with Herndon Haralson and James Greer his securities in the
penalty of seven hundred and forty dollars, conditioned for the prosecution of
said appeal.

     The State   )
     vs.   )   An affray
     James Cockril   )
        On motion of the defendants counsel the bill of indictment in this case
is quashed. It is therefore considered by the court that the defendant recover
of the plaintiff his cost by him about his prosecution in this behalf expended.
        The Grand Jury returned into court the following indictments, to wit, one
vs. William Braden and Lewis S. Jones for an affray, one against John Hardwick
for an assault and battery indorsed by the foreman true bills.
        Court then adjourned until tomorrow morning 8 o'clock.

                                        H. Haralson   JP.
                                        Sam Taylor   JP.
                                        Wm. E. Butler JP.

P395 Friday morning 1st. day of October 1824.
     Present the Worshipful Herndon Haralson, W. E. Butler and Samuel Taylor.

     Jason H. Wilson   )
     vs.   )   Debt
     William Arnold and Wm. E. Butler   )
        This day came the parties by the attorneys and the defendants say they can
no longer gainsay the plaintiffs action but withdraw their plea and confess
judgment for the same for the sum of two hundred and fifty dollars debt and the
further sum of sixteen dollars and twenty five cents damages for the detention
 thereof whereupon it is considered by the court that the plaintiff recover
against the defendants his debt and damages aforesaid besides his cost by him
about his suit in this behalf expended but it is agreed by the parties that
execution be issued and collected of W. Arnold alone until further orders by
plaintiff's attorney subject to an agreement between him and the defendants
counsel.

P395 The State   )
Cont.vs   )   An affray
     William Ruleman)

     This day came as well the solicitor general as well on the part of the state as the defendant in his proper person and the defendant being arraigned upon his arraignment plead guilty as charged in the bill of indictment. It is therefore considered by the court that the defendant make his peace with the state by the payment of one dollar as his fine together with the cost of this prosecution and ti is ordered by the court that the defendant in this case be ruled to give security for the cost of the prosecution and thereupon came Archibold Chaffin into open court and acknowledged himself bound with the said William Ruleman for the payment of the cost in this prosecution. It is therefore considered by the court that the said defendant be released from custody.

P396 William Guy   )
     vs.   )   In debt
     William Arnold and Samuel H. Shannon)

     This day came the parties aforesaid by their attorneys and thereupon came a jury of good and lawful men, to wit, Mathias Deberry, Thomas Laremour, John C. Stockton, John R. Collier, Archibold Chaffin, Henry Booth, Drury Betters, John H. Ball, Hazel Hewett, Burd B. Smith, William Adkins and James Card, who being elected tried and sworn well and truly to try the issue joined upon their oaths do say, they find the issue in favor of the plaintiff as to William Arnold, one of the defendants, that he has not paid the debt of two hundred and sixty one dollars and sixty four and ½ cents and assess his damages by reason thereof to twenty seven dollars and forty seven cents. It is therefore considered by the court that the plaintiff recover of the defendant William Arnold two hundred eighty nine dollars eleven and half cents the debt and damages aforesaid together with his cost by him about his suit in this behalf expended and that Samuel H. Shannon the other defendant recover of the plaintiff his cost by him about his suit in this behalf expended and the plff. in mercy etc.

     William Guy   )
     vs.   )   In debt
     William Huston)

     This day came the parties aforesaid by their attorneys and thereupon the defendant withdraws his plea and confesses judgment for the sum of seventy-five dollars debt and the sum of four dollars eighty seven and a half cents interest. It is therefore considered by the court that the plaintiff recover of the defendant the debt and interest aforesaid together with his cost by him about his suit in this behalf expended and the defendant in mercy etc.

     Ruben P. T. Stone)
     vs.   )   Case
     Benjamin Gholson)

     This cause is continued on affidavit of the defendant.

P397 Philip Warlick   )
     vs.   )   In debt
     William Spencern)

     This day came the parties aforesaid by their attorneys and the defendant withdraws his plea and confesses judgment for the sum of two hundred fifty -five dollars debt and thirteen dollars and thirty-eight cents interest. It is there fore considered by the court that the plaintiff recover of the defendant the debt and interest aforesaid together with his cost by him about his suit in this behalf expended and the defendant in mercy etc.

P307 Alexand Cotton   )
Cont.vs.   )   In debt
    Stokely D. Hays, William Arnold,)
    Danil Horton, Wilson Hutchinson   )
       This day came the parties aforesaid by their attorneys and the defendants
because they cannot gainsay the plaintiffs cause of action, withdraw their plea
and confess judgment for the sum of one hundred dollars debt with five dollars
and fifty cents interest. It is therefore considered by the court that the
plaintiff recover of the defendant the debt and interest aforesaid together with
his cost by him about his suit in this behalf expended and the defindant in mercy
etc.

Jesse Blackfan   )
vs.   )   In debt
Stokely D. Hays and William E. Butler)
       This day came the parties aforesaid by their attorneys and the defendants
because they cannot gainsay the plaintiffs cause of action confesses judgment
for the sum of two hundred and thirty seven and nine cents the balance of debt
in the declaration mentioned and eleven dollars and ninety six cents interest.
It is therefore considered by the court that the plaintiff recover of the defendants the balance of the debt aforesaid and interest aforesaid together with his
cost by him about his suit in this behalf expended and the defendants in mercy etc

P398 Isaac Curry   )
vs.   )   Case
Benjamin Cholson   )
       This cause is continued by consent of parties until the next term of this
court.

Calep Brock and Jane T. Jones, Exr. etc.)
vs.   )   In debt
William E. Butler   )
       This day day came the parties aforesaid by their attorneys and the plaintiff
by attorneys dismisses their suit and assums the payment of the cost herein. It
is considered by the court that the defendant recover of the plaintiff his cost
by him about his suit in this behalf expended and the plaintiff in mercy etc.

John McNairy   )
William E. Butler & Henry M Rutledge   )
vs.   )   In debt
John F. Brown   )
       This day came the plaintiffs by their attorneys and dismiss their suit and
assumes the payment of the cost herein. It is therefore considered by the court
that the defendant recover of the plaintiff his cost by him about his suit in
this behalf expended and the plaintiff in mercy etc.

Joseph Moss   )
vs.   ) In debt
Herndon Haralson   )
Ryland Chandler, Titt Chandler & Vincen Haralson)
       This day came the parties aforesaid by their attorneys and the defendants
because they cannot gainsay the plaintiff cause of action, withdraw their plea
& confess judgment for the sum of one hundred four dollars and twenty-five cents
debt with five dollars and forty five cents interest. It is therefore considered by the court that the plaintiff recover of the defendant the devt end interest

P390 aforesaid together with his cost by him about his suit in this behalf expended
and the defendant in mercy etc.

William Nelson)
vs.) In debt
Robert Hughes, William E. Butler)

    This day came the parties by their attorney and the defendants because
they cannot gainsay the plaintiffs cause of action withdraw their plea and confess judgment of one hundred and thirty dollars and seven dollar and eighty cents
interest. It is therefore considered by the court that the plaintiff recover
of the defendants the debt and interest aforesaid together with his cost by him
about his suit in this behalf expended and the defendants in mercy etc.

William M Wilson)
vs.) Case
Robert H. Dyer)

    The plaintiff has leave to amend his declaration by payment of all costs
in filing the demurrer. It is therefore considered by the court that the defendant recover of the plaintiff his cost by him about the amendment in that behalf
expended and the plaintiff in mercy etc.

Caleb Brock and Jane T. Jones)
vs.) Debt
John F. Brown)

    This day came the parties aforesaid by their attorneys and the plaintiffs
by attorney agrees to dismiss their suit and assumes the payment of all cost
accruing herein. It is therefore considered by the court that the defendant recover of the plaintiff his cost by him about his suit in this behalf expended
and the plaintiffs in mercy etc.

James Poor)
vs.) On motion
John Fair & James Trousdale)

    On motion of the plaintiff by his attorney and it appearing to the satis-
faction of the court that the defendant John Fair as constable of Madison county
has collected the sum of forty six dollars and forty three cents which of right
belongs to the plaintiff that he has not paid the same over to the plaintiff
as the law directs and that the said Fair has notice of this motion.

    It is therefore considered by the court that the plaintiff recover against
the said Fair and the said Nelson I Hess and James Trousdale his securities
the said sum of forty six dollars dollars and thirteen cents and also his cost
by him about his motion in this behalf expended and the defendants in mercy etc.

William Wilson)
vs.) In debt
Henry and Griffith Rutherford)

    This day came the parties aforesaid by their attorneys and the defendant
withdraws their demurrer and confess judgment for one hundred thirty one dollars
and forty four cents debt and fifteen dollars and seventy-seven cents interest.
It is therefore considered by the court that the plaintiff recover of the defendant the debt and interest aforesaid together with the cost by him about his
suit in this behalf expended and the defendant in mercy etc.

The State
vs.
Lewis T. Jones) An affray

P399   This day came as well the solicitor general on the part of the state as
Cont. the defendant in his proper person and the defendant being arraigned upon his
erraignment plead guilty as charged in the bill of indectment. It is therefore
considered by the court that the defendant make his peace with the state by the
payment of six and one fourth cents and that the plaintiff recover of the deO
fendant her cost by her about her suit in this behalf expended and the defendant
ordered in custody and etc. until his fine and cost aforesaid are paid or securit
given, and John T. Porter comes into court and acknowledges himself beound as the
security of the said Lewis T. Jones for the payment of the fine and cost aforesaid and the defendant is discharged from further recognizance.

P401   The State   )
        vs.   )   An assault and bettery
        John Hardwick)

        This day came as well the solicitor general on the part of the state as
the defendant in his proper person and the defendant being arraigned upon his
arraignment plead guilty as charged in the bill of indictment. It is therefore
considered by the court that the defendant make his peace with the state by the
payment of fifty cents fine and that the plaintiff recover of the defendant her
cost by her about his prosecution in this behalf expended and the defendant being
ordered into custody until fine and cost aforesaid are paid or security given.
Alfred Murray and William Arnold came into court and acknowledged themselves
securities for the payment of said fine and cost.

        The State   )
        vs   )   An affray
        Enoch Happy   )

        This day came as well the solicitor general on the part of the state as
the defendant in his proper person and the defendant being arraigned upon his
arraignment plead not guilty but for his trial put himself upon God and his
country and thereupon came a jury of good and lawful men, to wit, Mathias Deberry
, Hapel Hewett, John H. Ball, Thomas Laremour, John C. Stockton, John R. Collier,
Samuel Cholson, Henry Booth Drury Better, Beno B. Smith, William Atkins and James
Cord who being elected, tried and sworn well and truly to try the issue joined
upon their oaths do say the defendant is guilty as charged in the bill of indictment, It is therefore considered by the court that they defendant make his
peace with the state by the payment of five dollars fine and that the plaintiff
recover of the defendant her cost by her about her suit in this behalf expended
and the defendant be taken etc.

P402   The State   )
        vs.   )   Mart.
        Enoch Happy   )

        On motion of counsel for the state the defendant is ruled to give security
for the fine and cost of a suit this day determined against until paid or remain
in custody etc. and thereupon came Andreon Bruce into open court and acknowledged
himself secuity for the fine and costs of said suit together with the cost of
this motion.

        The State   )
        vs.   )   A & B
        William Thompson)

        This day came as well the solicitor general on the part of the state as the
defendant in his proper person and the defendant being arraigned upon his arraignment plead guilty to the charge brought against him. It is therefore considered

402
ont.

by the Court that the defendant make his peace with the state by the payment of one dollar fine and that that the plaintiffrecover of the defendant her fine together with her cost by her about her suit in this behalf expended and the defendant be taken etc. and on motion of the counsel for the state the defendant in this case is ruled to give security for the fine and cost aforesaid until paid or remain in custody and thereupon came John Reaves into open court and acknowledged himself bound as the security of the defendant for the fine and cost aforesaid together with the cost of this motion.

The Grand Jury this day returns into court the following bill of indictment, to wit, one against John Fussel for an assault and battery and one against Frederick Swandies for retailing spirituous liquors indorsed by the foreman of the Grand Jury true bill, and two presentments against John Ridings and one against William Laurince for retailing spiritous liquors indorsed by the Grand Jury True bills

The State   )
vs.   )   Retailing spirituous Liquors
John Ridens   )

This day came as well the solicitor general on the part of the state as the defendant in proper person and the defendant being arraigned upon his arraignment plead guilty to the charge here brought against him. It is therefore considered by the court that the defendant make his peace with the state by the payment of one dollar fine and that the plaintiff recover of the defendant her fine aforesaid together with her cost by her about her suit in this behalf expended and the defendant be taken etc.

The State   )
vs.   )   Retailing Spirituours Liquors
William Laremour   )

This day came as well the solicitor general on the part of the state as the defendant in his proper person and the defendant being arraigned upon his arraignment plead guilty to the charge here brought against him. It is therefore considered by the court that the defendant make his peace with the state by the payment of one dollar fine and that the plaintiff recover of the defendant her fine aforesaid together with her cost by her about her prosecution in this behalf expended.

The State   )
vs.   )   Retailing Spirituous Liquors
Frederick Swandeer   )

This day came as well the solicitor general on the part of the state as the defendant in his proper person and the defendant being arraigned upon his arraignment plead guilty to the charge here brought against him. It is therefore considered by the court that the defendant make his peace with the state by the payment of six and one-fourth cents and that the plaintiff recover of the defendant her fine fine aforesaid together with her cost by her about her suit in this behalf expended.

P40%
Cont.

An indenture of Bargain and Sale from the Board of Commissioners of the
Town of Jackson to James Brown and James K Polk for lots No 7, 27 and 29 as disignated in plan of said town was this day produced in open court and the execution duly acknowledged by Herndon Heralson, Chairman of the Board of said
Commissioners and ordered to be certified.

A bill of sale from Benjamin W. Medeares and Josiah Stephens to John C.
Gillespie for a negro girl was this day produced in open court and acknowledged
by the said Josiah Stephens, the Acknowledgment of the other maker having
been taken on a former day of. It is ordered to be certified.

A deed of trust from Benjamin Hancock to Charles Roady was this day produced in open court and the execution thereof duly proven by Joshua Haskill and
Turner Sullivan, subscribing witnesses, and ordered to be certified.

A bill of sale from Anthony F Gray B. S to Robert Murray was this day produced in open court and acknowledged by the said Anthony F. Gray and ordered
to be certified.

The persons appointed to settle with the administrator of estate of
Josiah Hayley deceased this day returned into court their report which w as
ordered to be recorded.

William E. Butler
vs
Robert G. Greer, Deft.

P404
Cont.

This day came into court Lewis C. Render and by virtue of a power of attorney from the said defendant, which is admitted to be the act and deed of said defendant, the said Lewis C. Fender confesses judgment in the name of and in behalf of the said defendant in favor of said plaintiff in a writing obligatory wxecuted by said defendant to the said plaintiff for the sum of five hundred dollars and fifty cents interest and cost of suit. It is therefore considered by the

P405
court that the plaintiff recover of the Dft. the said sum of five hundred and and forty seven dollars fifty cents, the debt and interest aforesaid on the confessed judgment aforesaid together with her cost of suit in this behalf expended.
Court them adjourned until tomorrow morning nine o'clock.

H. Haralson   JP.
B. G. Stewart   JP.
David Jarrett   JP.

Saturday morning 2nd. day of October 1824
Court met agreeable to adjournment present, the Worshipful Herndon Haralson B. G. Stewart and David Jarrett Administration of all and singular the goods and chattels of Martin Davis deceased is this day granted to Margaret Davis William Arnold and Robt. H. Wynne who thereupon qualified into bond with James Trousdale H. Haralson, David Jarrett, and George L. Wynne their securities in the penalty of two thousand dollars conditioned for the due administration of the estate of said decendent. It is therefore ordered that letters of administration issue accordingly.
Otdered by the court that forferture in the cases of the state vw. Robert G. Jones and Jarret M. Jelks be set aside.

Commissioners aetc.   )
vs.   )   In debt
Hick and Horton v   )

P406
This day came the parties aforesaid by their attorneys and the plaintiff dismisses their suit and the defendant assums the payment of the cost. It is therefore considered by the court that the plaintiff recover of the defendant the cost by them about their suit in this behalf expended and the defendant in mercy etc.

The administration of the estate of Joseph Tedford, deceased this day returned an inventory of the amount of sales of said estate.

Robert Stothart   )
vs.   )   Certiorari
Samuel H. Swann   )
This day came the parties aforessid by their attorneys and the plaintiff by his attorney moved the court to dismiss the certeorari which is done accordingly. It is therefore considered by the court that the pleintiff recover of the defendant the sum of thirtynine dollars and thirty nine cents the amount of the judgment rendered before the justice of the peace with twelve and one hai$ per cent interest on the same from the twelth of Febuary 1824 at the time of rendering of the judgment below together with his cost by him about his suit in this behalf expended and the defendant in mercy etc.

Wilson and Stewart   )
vs.   )   On motion to dismiss certiorari
Drury Bettis   )
This day came the plaintiff by their attorneys and moved the court to dismiss the certiorari which is done accordingly. It is therefore considered by the court that the plaintiff recover of the defendant drury bettis and Wiley Roy his security the sum of seventeen dollars and 41 cents with twelve and half per

P405 cent interest from the 2nd. January 1824 the time of rendering the judgment below
Cont.together with his cost by him about his suit in this behalf expended.

Joseph Spruce)
vs.) Certiorari
John Fair)

    The plaintiff by his attorney moved thecourt to dismiss the certiorari here-
in which was done accordingly. It is therefore considered by the court that the
plaintiff recover against the defendant John Fair and John F. Brown his security
the sum of twenty-four dollars and ninety cents the amount of the judgment rendered before the justice of the peace with twelve and one half per cent interest fro m
the 28th February 1824 together with the cost of this suit by him in this behalf
expended and be in mercy etc.

Mose F. Roberts)
vs.) In debt.
David Jarrett)

    The plaintiff by his attorney prayed an appeal from a judgment rendered
herein on a former day of court and thereupon which was granted him and entered
into bond with William Arnold in the sum of one hundred dollars.

William Guy)
vs.) In debt
Samuel H. Shannon)

    The plaintiff by his attorney prayed an appeal from a judgment rendered here
in on a former day of court and thereupon David Thomas, and S. A. Warner entered
into bond in the penal sum of two hundred dollars, conditioned for the prosecution
of said appeal.

    A deed of Bargain and Sale from Edward Farris to Dunguid Miums was this
day proven by the oath of B. G. Stewart a subscribing witness.

    A deed of conveyance from Robert L. Cobb to Nathan Boon for 150 acres of
land was produced in open court and the execution of the same was duly acknowledged by the said Robert L. Cobb act and deed and ordered to be certified.

Wilson and Stewart)
vs.) Certiorari
Thomas Elliott)

    This day came the plaintiff and moved the court to dismiss the certiorari
which was done accordingly. It is therefore considered by the court that the
plaintiff recover of the defendant Thomas Elliott and David Jarrett his security
the sum of twenty dollars and two cents with lawf l interest and the behalf expended and the defendant in mercy etc.

    Ordered that the following persons, to wit, William Deens, Philip Warlick,
Henry N. Coulter, John Murray, Burd Hill, Herbert Newson, Madison McLaurine,
Moses Oldham, John Weir, John Esters, William C. Mitchell Hendry D. Collins, John
Jackson, James McClery, Turner Tate, Henry Booth, John Spencer, Murdock Murchison,
Burd Smith, Hazael Hewett, Francis Taylor, Daniel Berrycraft, Thojas Coldwell
constitute the venire facias to attend as jurors at the next term of court and
that the sheriff summon them for that purpose and that William Weatherspoon and
John C. Gillespie be summoned as constables to attend on the court.

Wilson and Stewart)
vs.) Certiorari
John Stockton)

    This day came the plaintiff by his attorney and moved the court the dismiss

P408 the certiorari and after argument had thereon it seems to the court that the law
Cont.is for the defendant. It is therefore considered by the court that the ceriorai
be sustained and the cause set for trial.

P409   Danguid Minns this day came into open court and released Batholomew C. Stewart as administrator of the estate of Robert Edmonson, deceased, having received
all the papers and documents in his hands as administrator as aforesaid a report
of the settlement having alson been produced in open court and ordered to be recorded.

        John D. Shannon came into court and made oath of haveing attended and being
subpeenied to attend on the jury at the present term four days.

        Durguid Minns this day came into court and qualified as the administrator
of the estate of Robert Edmonson deceased.

        John R. Hyde this day came into court and entered into bond with William
Stoddert his security, for the purpose of keeping an ordinary who obtained an order
for the same at the last term of court but being omitted to be entered of record
the same is ordered to stand as if entered at the last term.

        A deed of mortgage from John D. Shannon to Thomas Shennon was this day pro-
duced in open court and proven by the oath of A. C. Nemons and Robert Wilson,
subscribing witnesses thereto and ordered to be certified.

P410 William Byler)
     vs.   )   Certiorari
John Tidwell)

        This day came the plaintiff by his attorney and moved the court to dismiss
the certiorari which was done. It is therefore considered by the court that the
plaintiff recover of the defendant sixteen dollars the amount of the judgment
rendered before the justice of the peace also his cost by him about his suit in
this behalf expended and the defendant in mercy etc.

        Drury Bettis Appeared in court and obtained a licinse to keep an ordinary
after having entered into bond in the penalty and condition prescribed by law with
Benjamin Gholson his security.

Paul Sherley   )
vs.   )   In debt
Ams Gibson, Adm etc.)

        This day came the defendant by her attorney and confesses judgment for the
sum one hundred twenty one dollars, the debt. It is therefore considered by the
court that the plaintiff recover of the defendant as administratrix the said
sum of one hundred and twenty one dollars the debt aforesaid together with his
cost by him about his suit in this behalf expended and the defendant in mercy etc.

P411   John Ridens came into court who obtained a license to keep an ordinary and
annooood entered into bond with Drury Bettis his security in the penalty and condition prescribed by law.

The State
vs.
Jacob Formault

        Jacob Formault who was on a warrent committed to the jail of this county
was this day brought into court and ordered to go hence and be discharged from
the said commitment.

The State   )
vs.   )   Affray
Enoch Happy)

        The defendant moved the court in metegation of the fine unposed on him on

P411   a former day of court and that the fine be one dollar instead of five.
Cont.   Court then adjourned until court in course

Sam. Taylor   JP.
W. B. Cross   JP.
James Trousdale   JP.

P412 Records of December Term 1824 Monday.
          At a court of pleas and quarter sessions begun and holden in and for the
County of Madison Monday 27th. day of December 1824.   Court met agreeable to ad-
journment.   Present the worshipful Herndon Haralson, William Draper, James Greer
Samuel S. Hunter, Green Hill William Atchison, Mark Christian, Samuel Taylor and
Guy Smith, gentlemen, justices.
          The resignation of Stephen Lacy as Coroner in and for the county of Madi-
son was this day handed in and received by the court.
          Ordered that the Clerk of this court post up at the court house doors
that an election for coroner to fill the place of Stephen Lacy will be held on
Tuesday the second day of this court and that the same day be set apart for trans
acting county business for the present term.
          A transfer of a plot and certificate from John Thomas to Henry Whitfield
for ---- acres was this day produced in open court and the execution of the same
was proven by the oath of John T. Bryon and ordered to be certified.
          A deed of trust from Edmond Jones to Samuel Dickens was this day produced
in open court and the execution of the same proven by the oath of John E. Jones.
          Ordered that the double tax on two lotts in the town of Jackson be remitted
for the year 1824. F by J. G. Cadwell.
          Aministration of the goods and chattels, rights and credits of James Priest
deceased, was this day granted to Nancy Priest, and Samuel H. Shannon who there
upon qualified as adm. and admr. and entered into bond in the penalty of one thou
sand six hundred dollars with Robert Wilson and Elijah Jones his securities.
It is therefore ordered that letters of Admr. issue accordingly.
P413   Ordered that David Sanders be overseer of the road from the bridge near
where the road crosses Johnsons Creek to section line dividing the 7 and 8 sectio
and work all the hands living equa-distant from any other road and crossing that
road at right angles.
          Ordered that the double taxes on 1500 acres of land in the name of William
Hill be remitted for the year 1824.
          Richard Mulden came into court and proved the killing of two wolves over
four months old in Madison County.
          Ordered that John McLennan's hands be attached to work on that part of the
road where Mr. Williams is overseer and that they be released from working on any
other road.
          Robert Lowery, Stephen Lacy, James McDoniel, John Minire, Jarret M Jelks,
   Jesse L. Kirk and John H. Hide and with their commissions from William Carroll,
Esq. Governor of the State of Tennessee appeared in open court and took the sever
oaths of qualification as justices of the peace in and for the county of Madison
and thereupon took their seats upon the bench.
          The resignation of John D. Shannon as constable was this day handed in re-
ceived by the court.
          On motion and petition filed, ordered that Benjamin H. Medaris be permitted
to alter road leading from Waddells bridge to Esquire Seats according to the pray
er of his petition soon as the same is opened and put in good order as the road.
          Ordered that David Shropshire Jailor of Madison County be allowed the sum o
sixty three dollars as per account filed and that the County trustee pay the same
out of any monies not otherwise appropreated.
P414   Ordered that Daniel Ross be overseer of the road from the county line to
Rosses old cart way and work all the hands here-to-fore allowed him and living
South of the river and East with Spencer Creek to the County line.

P414   Ordered that John M Johnson overseer of the roadwork from Ross's old cart
Cont. way to the low gap in the ridge and work all the hands South of the river from
Spencer's Creek to Dillards old place in addition to the hands heretofore
allowed him.

       Ordered that Elish Mathis overseer of the road work from the low gap in the
ridge to Chandlers Bridge and work all the hands Smith of the River from Dillards
old place to a point on said road apposite the fork of the river in addition to
those heretofore allowed him.

       Ordered that Henry Cassells be permitted to keep an ordinary in the County
of Madison who came into court and entered into bond with Jeremiah T. Rust
and Madison McLaurine with the penalty and condition prescribed by law.

       An indenture of sale from James Henderson and Deveraux Wynne to Vincent
Haralson for 40 acres of land was this day produced in open court and acknowledged
by them to be their act and deed and ordered to be certified for registration.

       An indenture of sale from Jordan Lambert to James M Key for fifty acres of
land was produced in open court and acknowledged by the said Jordan Lambert came
into court and after being examined privately and apart from her husband acknowledged her relinquishment of dower in and to said land and ordered to be so certified.

P415   Monday December 1824
       An inventory of the amount of sales of the estate of David Jackson, deceased
was this day returned into court with the allowance made by the commissioners to
the widow indorsed thereon.

The State   )
vs.   )
William Pace 2 cases   )

Same   )
vs.   )
James Dorris   )

Same   )
vs.   0
Benona Crawford   )

The Same   )
vs.   )
Jacob Formault   )

Same   )
vs.   )
William Deen   )

Same   )
vs.   )
John Fussel   )

Same   )
vs.   )
Charles Sevier   )

Same   )
vs.   )
Zebedee Lentry   )

       On motion it is ordered by the court that the cost in the aforesaid causes
be taxed to the county and that the county Trustee pay the same out of any moneys
not otherwise appropriated.

P418   Ordered that Philip Warlick be overseer of the road from Butlers Creek to
the creek below Warlick's Mill and work all the hands allowed Deveraux Wynne.

Ordered that the order made at the last term of court to view and mark a road
from the Poplar Corner ferry to intersect the East boundary line of Madison County
at or near where the Reynoldsbury road crosses the county line be renewed and that
the same shall be extended from said ferry to the West boundary line of said county
and that the jury heretofore appointed view the same and make report to the next
term.

Ordered that the order at the last term of Court appointing a jury of view
to mark and lay off a road from this place on a direction to Haywood County Court
House as far as the county line be renewed and that so soon as the same is marked
to be opened and cut out and that Lancaster Glover be overseer of the same from
Johnson's Mill to the County line and that Esquire Jarrett, Esquire Sounders be
appointed to divide the hands between the McGuire road and the present road.

Ordered that double taxes on 738¼ acres entered in the name of Mimrod Dodson
86 acres in the name of Larkin Carson 268½ in the name of William Stroud be remitte
for the year 1824.

Thomas Elliott this day resigned as constable in Caot Moores Company and on
motion it is ordered that the said Elliott shall put all the collection business
yet unfinished in his hands in the hands of Elijah Jones.

John H. Ball was this day duly and constitutionally elected coroner for the
county of Madison who thereupon took the several oaths of qualification and entered
into bond with Jesse L Kirk and George Todd his securities.

James F. Theobold was this day duly and constitutionally elected constable
in Captain Thomas Company who thereupon took the several oaths of qualification
and entered into bond with William Arnold and Wilson Hutchinson and Robert H.
Wynne his securities in the penalty and condition prescribed by law.

Administration of all and singular the goods and chattels, rights and credits
of Waid Jarret, deceased, was this day granted to David Jarrett who thereupon
qualified and entered into bond with Green Hill his security in the penalty of
three thousand dollars. It is therefore ordered that letters of Adm. issue accordingly.

David Jarrett was this day appointed guardian of Lavina Jarrett a minor
orphan of Waid Jarrett, deceased, who thereupon entered into bond with William
Arnold his security in the penalty of fifteen hundred dollars.

Ordered that Duncan McIver, Robert Hebett and Adam Brown be appointed to
settle with James McDaniel Guardian of the hairs of Robert Moore, deceased and make
report to the next term.

Ordered that the town commissioners be allowed one dollar per day for services rendered to wit Thomas Shannon 9 days John H. Hyde 15 days Daniel Horton
ten days James Trousdale eight days, William E. Butler six days H. Haralson fifteen
days, Vincent Haralson nine days, William Braden twelve days, Samuel Taylor fifteen
days, S. D. Hays eleven days William Harris, twelve days, B. G. Stewart, eleven
days, Adam Huntsman six days, Robert Hughes nine days as per bill filed.

P420   Josiah Pullen the executor of the last will and testament of Thomas Pullen
deceased this day produced in court and certified copy of said will together with
an inventory of the estate of said decedent which was ordered to be recorded and
it appearing to the satisfaction of the court that there is not sufficient personal
property to pay the debt and legacies mentioned in said will it is therefore ordered by the court that the negroes together with the other property be sold according to law.

Ordered that Samuel D. Waddill, Henry Cassels Senior, Jeremiah T. Rust,
David Jackson William Espy Owen Griffin, James Moore Micajah Midyett, Madison
McLaurine M. Deberry, Sugars McLemore and Alexander Patterson, them or any five
of them , be a jury of view to mark and lay off a road from such point of the road
leading from Jackson to Waddell's Bridge as they may think most suitable to the
county line on a direction to Gibson port and make report to next term.

P420   Ordered that Ethelridge Newsom be allowed the sum of fifty dollars for addi
Cont. ditional labor and expense in building a bridge over Forked Deer river and that
the County Trustee pay the same out of any monies not otherwise appropriated.

    Joseph Connor was this day duly an constitutionally elected constable in
Captain Moor's company.

    Ordered that the following persons, to wit, Lewis Griffin, William Harris
Thomas Harington, Charles Wortham, Exum Holland, Henry H. Horn, William King,
Moses Street, Collier A Steed, Daniel Bevel, John Gately, Richard Golden, Allen
Trousdale, Nathan Simpson Dawson Bond Robert Doak, John McClelland, Joseph Tar-
button Ezekial McCoy, Warham Easley, Abraham Shankle, John D. Shannon, Drury
Bettis, Jacob Bradbury, John A. Gibson and Alexander Greer, constitute the venir
men to serve at the next term of this court.

P421   Ordered that Joshua Weaver be exempt from paying double tax on 100 acres of
land 2 black polls and one white poll for the year 1824.

    An indenture of sale from William Jordon to John Harrison for 1/8 of an
acre of land was this day produced in open court and acknowledged by the said
William Jordan to be his act and deed and ordered to be certified for regestratioon

    An indenture of sale from the commissioners of the town of Jackson to
Michael Frey and David Binkley for lot no eleven in the plan of said town was this
day produced in open court and acknowledged by Herndon Haralson Chairman of the
board of said commissioners to be their act and deed and ordered to be certified
for registration.

    A power of attorney from Samuel H. Swan to William T. Brewer was this day
produced in open court and proved by the oath of Alexander B. Bradford and
William Arnold and ordered to be certified for registration.

    An indenture of sale from Thomas Shannon to William Jordan for 1/8 part of
an acre of ground was this day produced in open court and proven by the oath of
John Harrison and John Rudisell and ordered to be certified for registration.

    William Willburn this day appeared in open court and took the several oaths
of qualification as a justice of the peace for the county of Madison who thereupon took his seat upon the bench.

    Ordered that the order made at the last term to make an alteration in the
road passing the graveyard on the road leading from Jackson to John Swiss b e
renewed.

P422   The sheriff this day made return of the writ of venire facias to him direct-
ed from the last term of court with the following indorsement thereon, to wit,
I have summoned all the persons named in the within venire except John Weir
John Jackson, Henry Booth, Daniel Berycraft, Thomas Vinsant and Jesse M Hanna all
freeholders or householders and white males over twenty one years of age A. F.
Cray D. Shff. . In pursuance of which the following persons were then attending
Philip Warlick, Henry N. Coulter, Burd Hill Herbert Newsom, Madison Mc Laurine
Moses Oldham, Henry D. Collins, James McCreary Turner Tate, John Spencer, Murdock
Murchison, Burd Smith, Hazael Hewett, James Coldwell, and Greenup White and there-
upon the following persons to wit, Philip Warlick, Henry N Coulter Bard Hill,
    Herbert Newsom, Madison McLaurine, Henry D. Collins Turner Tate, John Spencer
Murdock Murchison, Burd Smith, Hazael Hewett, Greenup white and James Coldwell
were then and there empanelled, sworn and charged as a Grand Jury to inquire into
and for the body of the County of Madison with Philip Warlick their foreman who
thereupon ritered to consider presentments.

    James McClary and Moses Oldham were this day discharged as jurors at the
present term.

    Court then adjourned until tomorrow morning ten o'clock. John-

                                        John H. Hyde   JP.
                                        Guy Smith   JP.
                                        William Draper JP

P423 Wednesday 29th. December 1824

Court met agreeable to adjournment. Present, the worshipful John H. Hide, William Draper and Lemuel S. Hunter.

The administration of ascris G. Martin, deceased, this day returned into court an additional inventory of the estate of said decendant.

The administration of John Smith, deceased, this day returned into court an inventory of the amount of sales of the property of the decendant.

John T. Theobold was this day sworn to attend on the court and jury at the present term.

Ordered that Burrel Butter payonly three dollars instead of five the tax on one stud horse by him listed for the year 1824.

The report of a jury of view appointed to mark a road from this place to the house of Joshua Haskell was this day handed in and received by the court.

A receipt and bill of sale from Eldridge Newsom to Robert Murray was this day produced in open court and proven by the oath of Thomas Shannon a subscribing witness said to be executed by the said Newsom and ordered to be recorded.

P424   A receipt and bill of sale from Thomas I Smith Deputy Sheriff of Madison County to Alfred Murray for the purchase money of three negro slaves with an assignment of the same from said. Murray to Robert Murray indorsed thereon which was acknowledged on a former day of this court was this day produced in open court and certificate of the said sheriff indorsed thereon and by him acknowledged which is ordered to be recorded.

An indenture of sale from Robert Clanton to Obediah Dodson for seventy five acres of land was this day produced in open court and the execution of the same proven by the oath of John T. Bryan and Roderick McIver to be his act and deed and ordered to be certified for registration.

An indenture of sale from John Harris to James H. Wilson for 1/8 of an acre of ground was this day produced in open court and proven by the oath of Samuel D. Wilson and William Wilson and ordered to be certified for registration.

A bill of sale from Reuben Patterson to Elizabeth Parks with Thomas Parks assignment thereon was this day produced in open court and proven by the oath of Cader Colly one of the subscribing witnesses and ordered to be recorded.

An indenture of sale from the trusties of the university of North Carolina by their attorney in fact Samuel Dickens to Thomas Henderson for 228 acres of land was this day produced in open court and acknowledged by the said Samuel Dickens attorney aforesaid to be his act and deed and ordered to be certified for registration.

An indenture of sale from Thomas Hemderson to Richard Fenner for 228 acres of land was this day produced in open court and acknowledged by the said Thomas Henderson to be his act and deed and ordered to be certified for registration.

P425   An indenture of sale from Thomas Henderson to Richard Fenner for seven hundred and twenty six acres of land was this day produced in open court and the execution of the same acknowledged by the said Thomas Henderson to be his act and deed and ordered to be certified for registration.

A bill of sale from Joshua Haskill to Charles Ready was this day produced in open court and the Execution of the same proven by the oath of Stokely D Hays William E. Butler, subscribing witnesses there to and ordered to be recorded.

```
William C, Love    )
vs.                )    Sllander
Jonathan Huston    )
```

This day came the parties aforesaid by their attorneys and thereupon came a jury of good and lawful men, to sit, William Wilson, Wiley Ray, Samuel H Shannon, Charles Donley, William Burrow, John Barnhart, John Rayder, John Rhelps, Ruben P T. Stone, Thomas Hill, James Henderson and John T. Porter who being elected, tried and sworn well and truly to try the issues joined upon

their oaths do say that the defendant is guilty as charged in the declaration

P425 Mentioned and assess his damages reason thereof to seven hundred and ninety
Cont.nine dollars.

It is therefore considered by the court that the plaintiff recover of the de
fendant the damages aforesaid assessed together with his cost by him about his
suit in this behalf expended and the defendant in mercy etc.

John Rage)
vs.)   In case
John T. Porter)

This day came the parties aforesaid by their attorneys and thereupon came
a jury of good and lawful men, to wit, John Burrow, John Spencer, Joseph Spruce,
Jesse Tribble, Samuel H. Swan, William Hopper, Wm. Braden, Isaac Dillard
P426 John Dillard, James Johnson, Samuel Anderson and George Mizell who being elected
tried and sworn the truth to speak upon this issues joined upon their oaths do
say that the defendant did assume upon himself as the plaintiff in his declaration
hath alleged thereof against him and assess the plaintiff damages by reason thereof to one hundred and fifty nine dollars and nine cents. It is therefore considered by the court that the plaintiff recover of the defendant the damages aforesaid in form aforesaid by the jury aforesaid assessed together his cost by him
about his suit in that behalf expended and the defendant in mercy etc. and
the defendant prayed an appeal from said judgment to the next circuit court which
was granted him who entered into bond in the penalty of four hundred dollars with
Thomas I. Smith andBenjamin Gholson his securities.

An indenture of Sale from the commissioners of the Town of Jackson to Sarah
F. Gray for lotts No 37 and No. 82 in the plan of said town as this day produced
in open court and the execution of the same acknowledged by Herndon Haralson
Chairman of the board of said commissioners and ordered to be certified for registration.

Francis Herren)
vs.)   Case
Henry Pacie)

This day came the plaintiff by his attorney dismissed his suit herein and
confessed judgment for the cost of said suit. It is the defendant recover of
theplff. his cost by him about his suit in this behalf expended and the plaintiff
be in mercy etc.

Francis Herrin   )
vs.   ) Trespass V. A.
Malcolm Johnson, & Henning Pace, William and Alsy Pace)

This day came the parties aforesaid by their attorneys and the plff by
his attorneys dismiss his suit at his cost. It is therefore considered by the
court that the defts. recover of the plaintiff his cost by him about suit in
this behalf expended and the plaintiff in mercy etc.

P427 Henning Pace)
vs.)   A. and B.
Francis Herrin)

This day came the parties aforesaid by their attorneys and thereupon the
plaintiff dismisses his suit at his cost. It is therefore considered by the
court that the defendant recover of the plaintiff his cost by him about his suit
in this behalf expended and the plaintiff in mercy etc.

Henning Pace)
vs.) T V. A
Andrew and Frances Herron)

This day came the parties aforesaid by their attorneys and thereupon the

P427

Cont. plaintiff by his attorney dismisses his suit and confesses judgment for the cost of said suit herein expended. It is therefore considered by the court that the defendant recover of the plaintiff his cost by him about his suit in this behalf expended and the deft. in mercy etc.

Cyrus W. Bevard)
vs.) In debt
Adam R. Alexander)

This day came the plaintiff by his attorney and dismisses his suit at his cost. It is therefore considered by the court that the defendant recover of the plaintiff his cost by him about his suit in this behalf expended and the plff. in mercy etc.

William C. Leave)
vs.) In slander
Jonathan Huston)

This day came the plaintiff in open court and released six hundred and ninety nine dollars of the verdict in this case entered against said defendant.

P428   Court then adjourned until tomorrow morning nine o'clock.

          H. Haralson   JP.
          William Draper   JP.
          Sam Taylor   JP.
          Green Hill   JP.

Thursday morning 30th. December 1824

   Court met agreeable to adjournment. Present, the Worshipful William Draper, Green Hill and John H. Hide.

   Archibold W. Goodrich Appeared in open court and took the several oaths of qualification as practicing atty. in this county.

The State)
vs.) Gambling
William Curtis)

   The defendant in this case called out upon his recognisance. It is therefore ordered that sci fi issue against the security returnable here at the next term.

The State)
vs.) A & B
Williamson Curtis)

   The defendant in this case is called out upon his recognisance and it is ordered by the court that sci fa issue against the securities returnable here at next term of court.

The State)
vs.) Affray
William Braden)

   This day came the solicitor general on the part of the state as the defendant being arraigned upon his arraignment plead guilty. It is therefore considered by the court that the defendant make his peace with the state by the payment of two dollars fine together with her cost by her about her suit in this behalf expended and the defendant be in mercy etc.

429   Thursday December 30th 1824

B. G. Stewart and others, Commissioners
vs.

David and John P. Thomas   )   Debt

P429   This day came the parties by their attorneys and thereupon came a jury
Cont. of good and lawful men, to wit, Sanders, Carney Philip G. Tucker, Samuel H.
Swan, Henry D. Connolly, William Braden, John Barnhart, James Henderson, Ruben
P. T. Stone. Mathias Deberry, Thomas McReynolds, John D. Shannon, and Samuel
Anderson who being elected, tried and sworn to try the issues joined between
the parties on the several pleas of defts. upon their oaths do say We of the jury
find the issues in favor of the plaintiff and that the defendants have not paid
the debt of three hundred and fifty four dollars as the plaintiff by replying to
defendants several pleas in that behalf hath alleged and we assess the plaintiff
damages by reason thereof the Twenty four dollars. It is therefore considered
by the court that the plaintiff recover of the defendants the debt and damages in
form aforesaid by the jury aforesaid assessed together with their costs by them
about this suit expended and three hundred and thirteen dollars which is hereby transferred to Alexander B. Bradford, Appeal prayed and granted, B. G. Gholson
by atty. bond and security given.

        Homer Rainey)
vs.   )   Debt
Herndon Haralson)

        This day came the deft. by his atty. and introduced and offered to the court
his affidavit marked A and thereupon moved the court to be permitted to file
plea marked B. by way of amendment in this cause, which motion after argument
heard was overruled by the court and the deft. was excluded from filing his said
plea in this cause. To which opinion the court in overruling defendants application in this behalf, defendants by his counsel excepted and prayed that his
bill of exceptions might be signed, sealed and made a part of the road of the
cause which is done accordingly.

P430 Homer Rainey   )
vs.   )   Debt
Herndon Haralson)

        This day came the parties aforesaid by their attorneys, and thereupon came
a jury of good and lawful men to wit, Sanders Carney, Philip G. Tucker, Samuel
H. Swan, Henry C. Conolly, William Braden, John Barnhart, James Henderson Reuben
P. T. Stone, Mathias Deberry Thomas W. Reynolds, John D. Shannon and Samuel
Anderson, who elected tried and sworn, well and truly to try the issues joined
between the parties, upon their oaths do say they find the issues in favor of the
plaintiff and the defendant has not paid the balance of the devt of one hundred
and forty four dollars as in replying to deft's. plea in that behalf plaintiff
hath alleged and they assess the plaintiff damages by reason thereof to twelve
dollars and ninety six cents. It is therefore considered by the court that the
plaintiff recover of the defendant the balance of devt aforesaid with his damages
aforesaid by the jury aforesaid assessed together with his cost by him about
his suit in this behalf expended and the defendant in mercy etc. where upon the
deft. by his atty. prayed an appeal in the nature of a writ of error, to the
next Circuit court and entered into bond with William Harris, James Trousdale
and Benja. Gholson as his securities and the appeal is accordingly granted by the
court.

Josiah Pullen   )
vs.   )   Appeal
Bartholomew G. Stewart)

        This day came the defendant by his attorney and the plaintiff altho being
solemnly called came not. It is therefore considered by the court that the de--
fendant recover of the plaintiff his cost by him about his suit in this behalf
wxpended and the plaintiff for his false clamor be in mercy etc.

P431 Reuben P. T. Stone   )
      vs.   )   Case
      Benjamin Gholson   )

     This 689 cause continued on a affidavit of the defendant until next term of court

      George Yoke   )
      vs.   )   Debt
      William Arnold   )

     This day came the parties aforesaid by their attorneys and the deft because he cannot gainsay the plaintiffs cause of action hereof withdraws his pleas and confesses judgment for the sum of one hundred and eigh y four dollars debt and the further sum of sixty one dollars and 64 cents interest. It is therefore considered by the court that the plaintiff recover of the defendant aforesaid confessed together with his cost by him about his suit in this behalf expended and the defendant in mercy etc.

     Allen McVey   )
      vs.   )   In debt
      Samuel Woods   )

     This day came the parties aforesaid by their attorneys and the defendant withdraws his demurrer filed and pleads payment and thereupon came a jury of good and lawful men, to wit, Sanders Carney, Philip G. Tucker, Samuel H. Swan, William Braden, John Barnhart, James Henderson, Mathias Deberry Thomas McReynolds John D. Shannon, Henry G. Conolly, Samuel Anderson and John C. Stockton, who being elected tried and sworn the truth to speak upon the issue joined upon their oaths do say that the defendant has not paid the debt in the declaration mentioned of one hundred dollars and assess his damages by reason thereof to nine dollars. It is therefore considered by the court that the plaintiff recover of the defendant the debt and damages aforesaid by the jury aforesaid assessed together with his cost by him about his suit in this behalf expended and the defendant in mercy etc.

      Ephriam H. Foster   )
      vs.   )   In debt
      Deveraux Wynne and James Henderson   )

     This day came the parties aforesaid by their attorneys and thereupon came a jury of good and lawful men, to wit, Sanders Carney. Philip G. Tucker, Samuel H. Swan, William Braden John Barnhart, Mathias Deberry, Thomas McReynolds, John D. Shannon, Henry G. Conolly, Samuel Anderson, Robert Murray and John C. Stockton who being elected, tried and sworn to try the issues joined upon their oaths do say they find the issues in favor of the plaintiff, that the defendants have not paid the debt of one hundred and seventy four dollars as the plaintiff in replying to defendants pleas in that behalf hath alleged and assess the plaintiff d damages by reason of the detention thereof to sixteen dollars and eighty cents It is therefore considered by the court that the plaintiff recover of the defendant the debt and damage aforesaid in form aforesaid by the jury aforesaid assessed together with his cost by him about his suit in this behalf expended and the defendant in mercy etc.

      Joseph Anderson & James Knox   )
      vs.   )   Debt
      Samuel D. Wilson   )

     This day came the parties aforesaid by their attorneys and thereupon came a jury of good and lawful men, to wit, Sanders Corney, Philip G. Tucker, Samuel H. Swan William Braden, John Barnhart, James Henderson, Mathias Deberry, Thomas McReynolds, John D. Shannon, Samuel Anderson Robert Murray, John C. Stockton

P433 who being elected, tried and sworn the truth to speak upon the issues joined
and upon their oaths do say they find the issues in favor of the plaintiff and
the defendant hath not paid the balance of debt of fifteen hundred and ten dollars
as the plaintiff in replying to defendants plea in that behalf hath alleged and a
assess the plaintiff damages by reason of the detention thereof to one hundred
and thirty eight dollars. It is therefore considered by the court that the
plaintiff recover of the defendant the balance of debt aforesaid with the damages
aforesaid by the jury aforesaid assessed together with their cost by them about
their suit in this behalf expended and the defendant in mercy etc. from which
judgment to defendant prayed and appeal to the next term of Circuit Court and
entered bond with J. C. Wilson and William M. Wilson in the penalty of three
thousand dollars which is granted him.

Tiffany Wyman and Co.   )
vs.   )   In debt
John Hyde   )
          This day came the parties aforesaid by their attorneys and thereupon came
a jury of good and lawful men, to wit, Sanders Carney, Philip G. Tucker, Samuel
H. Swan, William Braden, John Barnhart, James Henderson, Mathias Deberry, Thomas
McReynolds, John D. Shannon, Samuel Anderson, Robert Murray and John Stockton,
who being elected, tried and sworn well and truly to try the issues joined upon
their oaths do say We of the jury do find for the plaintiff four hundred eighty
nine dollars the debt in the declaration mentioned and assess the plaintiff
damages by reason of the detention thereof to one hundred ninety nine dollars
and 24 cents. It is therefore considered by the court that the plaintiff recover
of the defendant the debt aforesaid together with the damages aforesaid by the
jury aforesaid assessed and also their cost by them about their suit in this
behalf expended and the def't in mercy etc.

P454 William Arnold   )
vs.   )   In debt
Turner Sullivan   )
          This day came the parties aforesaid by their attorneys and thereupon came
a jury of good and lawful men, to wit, the same jury as in the last above mentioned cause who being elected, tried and sworn, well and truly to try the issue
joined upon their oaths do say the defendant hath not paid the balance of debt
of one hundred dollars in the declaration mentioned and assess his damages by
reason of the detention thereof to five dollars and fifty cents. It is therefore
considered by the court that the plaintiff recover of the defendant the balance
of debt aforesaid with his damages aforesaid in form aforesaid assessed together
with the cost by him about his suit in this behalf expended and the defendant in
mercy etc.

John Spencer   )
vs.   )   Debt
Benjamin Gholson   )
          This day came the parties aforesaid by their attorneys and thereupon came
a jury of good and lawful men, to wit, Sanders Corney Philip G. Tucker, Samuel
H. Swan, William Braden, John Barnhart, James Henderson, Mathias Deberry, Thomas
McReynolds, John D. Shannon Samuel Anderson, Robert Murray, and John C Stockton
who being elected tried and sworn the truth to speak upon their issues joined
and upon their oaths do say that the deft. has not paid the debt of three hundred
and thirty eight dollars and ninety cents as the plaintiff in replying to the
defendant plea hath alleged and assess the plaintiff damages by reason of the
detention thereof to twenty dollars and three cents. It is therefore considered
by the court that the plaintiff recover of the defendant the debt and damages
aforesaid by the jury aforesaid in form aforesaid assessed together with his cost

P434 by him about his suit in this behalf expended and the defendant in mercy from
Cont. which judgment the defendant prays an appeal to the circuit court and entered
into bond with Thomas and Sam'l Shannon his securities in penalty of $700.00

'435 Joseph Linn and John Rutherford Trustees for the use of Ribert Murray)
vs.) Debt
Thomas Shannon)

This day came the parties aforesaid by their attorneys and thereupon
came a jury of good and lawful men, to wit, Sanders Carney, Philip C.Tucker,
Samuel H. Swan Henry G. Connelly, William Braden, John Barnhart, James Henderson,
Mathias Deberry, Thomas McReynolds, John D. Shannon, Samuel Anderson, and John
C. Stockton, who being elected tried and sworn well and truly to try the issues
joined upon their oaths do say that the defendant has not paid the debt of two
hundred and fourteen dollars 62½ cts. as the plaintiff in replying to defendants
plea hath alleged and assess the plaintiff damages by reason of the detention
thereof to eleven dollars and twenty eight cents. It is therefore considered
by the court that the plaintiff recover of the defendant his debt aforesaid with
his damages aforesaid in form aforesaid assessed together with his cost by him
about his suit in this behalf expended and the defendant in mercy etc. Appeal
prayed and granted and bond given etc.

Thomas L. D. Parks)
vs.) Debt
Thomas Harrington and William Wilson)

This day came the parties aforesaid by their attorneys and thereupon came
a jury of good and lawful men, to wit, Sanders Corney, Philip G. Tucker, Samuel
H. Swann, William Braden, John Barnhart, James Henderson, Mathias Deberry,
Thomas McReynolds, John D. Shannon, Samuel Anderson, Robert Murray and John C.
P436 Stockton, who being elected tried and sworn the truth to speak upon the issue
joined and upon their oaths do say that the defendants have not paid the debt of
one hundred and twenty dollars in the declaration mentioned as the plaintiff be
replying to Deft.'s plea in that behalf hath alleged and assess the plaintiff
damages by reason of the detention thereof to eight dollars and ninety-five cents.
It is therefore considered by the court that the plaintiff recover of the defendants the debt aforesaid with the damages aforesaid in form aforesaid by the jury
aforesaid assessed and the defendants in mercy etc.

John Linn and John Rutherford Trustees)
for the use of Robert Murray)
vs.) Debt
Aquila Davis)

This day came the parties aforesaid by their attorneys and thereupon came
a jury of good and lawful men to wit, Sanders, Carney, Philip G.Tucker, Samuel
H. Swan, William Braden, John Barnhart, James Henderson, Mathias Deberry Thomas
McReynolds, John D. Shannon Samuel Anderson, Henry D. Connolly, and John C.
Stockton, who being elected, tried and sworn well and truly to try the issue
joined upon their oaths do say that the defendant hath not paid the debt of one
hundred and thirty five dollars, the debt in the declaration mentioned and assess
their damages by reason of the detention thereof to six dollars and seventy-five
cents. It is therefore considered by the court that the plaintiff recover of the
defendant the debt aforesaid with the damages aforesaid in form aforesaid by the
jury aforesaid)assessed and the defendant in mercy etc.

)
Solomon Cotton
vs.   In debt
John B. Cross)

P437   This day came the parties aforesaid by their attorneys and thereupon came
a jury of good and lawful men, to wit, Sanders Carney, Philip G. Tucker, Samuel
H. Swan, William Braden, John Barnhart, James Henderson, Matthias Deberry, Thomas
McReynolds, John D. Shannon, Samuel Anderson, Robert Murray and John C. Stockton
who being elected tried and sworn the truth to speak upon the issues joined and
upon their oaths do say they find the issues in favor of the plaintiff and the
defendant hath not paid the debt of one hundred and ninety five dollars four
and half cent $192.04½ as the plaintiff in replying to the defendants plea in that
behalf hath alleged and assess the plaintiff damages by reason thereof to eleven
dollars and fifty cents. It is therefore considered by the court that the plaintiff recover of the defendant his debt aforesaid with his damages aforesaid by
the jury aforesaid assessed and the defendants in mercy etc. from which judgments
the defendant prayed and appeal to the next circuit court whihh is granted them
and entered into bond etc.

Robert Murray   )
vs.   )   Debt.
Benjamin Gholson   )

        This day came the parties aforesaid by their attorneys and thereupon came
a jury of good and lawful men, to wit, Sanders Corney, Philip G. Tucker, Samuel
H. Swan, William Braden, Henry C. Connolly William Braden, John Barnhart, James
Henderson, Mathias Deberry, Thomas McReynolds, John D. Shannon, Samuel Anderson
and John C. Stockton who being elected, tried and sworn the truth to speak upon
the issues joined upon their oaths do say that the defendant hath not paid the
balance of debt of two hundred and six dollars and two cents as the plaintiff in
replying to the defendants plea in that behalf hath alleged and assess the plaintiff damages by reason thereof to twelve dollars and seventy cents. It is there-
P438 fore considered by the court that the plaintiff recover of the defendant his
balance of debt aforesaid with his damages aforesaid in form aforesaid by the
jury aforesaid assessed together with his cost by him about his suit in this beha-
half expended and the defendant in mercy etc.

Marked out-
(James C. Roach)
vs.   )   In debt
Rovert H. Dyer)

        This day came the parties aforesaid by their attorneys and thereupon came a
jury of good and lawful men to wit Sanders Cassey , Philip G. Tucker, Samuel H.
Swan, William --------+Braden John Barnhart, James Henderson, Mathias Deberry
Thomas McReynolds John D. Shannon Samuel Anderson Robert Murray and John C.
Stockton who being elected, tried and sworn the truth to speak upon the issue.

William W. Woodfork   )
vs.   )   In debt
Robert Hughes and Herndon Haralson)

        This day came the parties aforesaid by their attorneys and thereupon came
a jury of good and lawful men, to wit, Sanders Carney, Philip G. Tucker, Samuel
H. Swan, William Braden John Barhhart, James Henderson, Matthias Deberry Thomas
McReynolds, John D. Shannon, Samuel Anderson, Robert Murray and aJohn C. Stockton
who being elected tried and sworn, well and truly to try the issue joined upon
P439their oaths do say that the defendants have not paid the devt of two hundred
and thirty five dollars as the plaintiff by replying to the defendants plea
in that behalf hath alleged and assess the plaintiff damages by reason of the
detention thereof to eighteen dollars and forty cents. It is therefore considered
by the court that the plaintiff recover of the defendant the debt aforesaid with
the damages aforesaid by the jury aforesaid assessed together with his cost by
him about his suit in this behalf expended and the defendant in mercy etc.

P439 Bartholomew G. Stewart, Joseph Linn, John Hardgraves,   )
Cont.Adam R.Alexander, and James Trousdale for the use of the)
board of commissioners for the Town of Jackson   )   Debt
vs.   )
Samuel Taylor, Carter C. Collier and S. D. Hays   )

     This day came the parties aforesaid by their attorneys and thereupon came a jury of good and lawful men, to wit, Sanders Carney, Philip G. Tucker, Samuel H. Swan, William Bradin John Barnhart, James Henderson Mathias Deberry Thomas McReynolds John D. Shannon Samuel Anderson, Robert Murray and John C. Stockton, who being elected, tried and sworn well and truly to try the issue joined upon their oaths do say the defendants have not paid the debt in the declaration mentioned of two hundred and fifty dollars as the plaintiff by replying to the defendants plea in that behalf hath alleged and assess the plaintiff damages by reason of the detention there of to twenty one dollars and twenty-five cents. It is therefore considered by the court that the plaintiffs do recover of the defendants the debt aforesaid with the damages aforesaid by the jury in form aforesaid assessed together with their costs by them about their suit in this behalf expended and the said defendants in mercy etc.

P440 The Same   )
vs.   )   In debt
William R. Hess, Nelson I Hess   )
and Herndon Haralson   )

     This day came the parties aforesaid by their attorneys and thereupon came a jury of good and lawful men, to wit, Sanders Carney Philip G. Tucker, Samuel H. Swam., William Braden John Barnhart, James Henderson, Mathias Deberry, Thomas McReynolds, John D. Shannon, Samuel Anderson, Robert Murray, and John C. Stockton who being elected, tried and sworn the truth to speak upon the issue joined upon their oaths do say that the defendants have not paid the debt of one hundred and sixty two dollars as the plaintiff in replying to the defendants plea in that behalf hath alleged and assess the plaintiff damages by reason of detention there of to thirteen dollars and seventy one cents. It is therefore considered b by the court that plaintiff recover of the defendant the debt aforesaid with the damages aforesaid by the jury aforesaid assessed and with the cost by them about their suit in this behalf expended and the defendants in mercy etc.

Same   )
vs.   ) Debt
Joseph F. Cloud, Anthony G. Gray William E. Butler)

Set aside and set for trial at next term.

P411 Same   )
vs.   )   Debt
William Arnold)

     This day came the parties aforesaid by their attorneys and thereupon came a jury of good and lawful men, to wit, Sanders Caney, Philip G. Tucker, Samuel H. Swan, William Braden, John Barnhart, James Henderson, Mathias Deberry, Thomas McReynolds, John D. Shannon, Samuel Anderson Robert Murray and John C. Stockton, who being elected tried and sworn well and truly to try the issue joine ed upon their oaths do say that the defendant hath not paid the debt of two hundred and one dollars as the plaintiff in replying to defendant plea in that behalf hath alleged and assess the plaintiff damages by reason of the detention
   there of to seventeen dollars and it is therefore considered by the court that the plaintiffs recover of the defendant their debt aforesaid with their damages aforesaid in form aforesaid assessed and their cost by them about their suit in

P411 this behalf expended and the defendant in mercy etc.
Cont.

Same	)	
vs.	)	Debt.
William Braden and	)	
Thomas Shannon	)	

This day came the parties aforesaid by their attorneys and thereupon came a jury of good and lawful men, to wit, Sanders Carney, Philip G. Tucker, Samuel H. Swan, Henry G. Connolly, John Barnhart, James Henderson Mathias Deberry, P442 Thomas McReynolds, John D. Shannon Samuel Anderson Murray and John C. Stockton who being elected tried and sworn well and truly to try the issue joined upon their oath do say that the defendants have not paid the balance of debt of one hundred and seventy six dollars as the plaintiff in replying to the defendant plea in that behalf hath alleged and assess the plaintiff damages byreason of the detention thereof to fourteen dollars and eight cents. It is therefore considered by the court that the plaintiff recover of the defendants the debt aforesaid together with the damages aforesaid by the jury aforesaid assessed also their cost by them about their suit in this behalf expended and the defendants in mercy etc.

Same	)	
vs.	)	Debt
John and Thomas Shannon	)	

This day came the parties aforesaid by their attorneys and thereupon came a jury of good and lawful men, to wit, Sanders Corney, Samuel H. Swan, William Braden, John Barnhart, James Henderson Mathias Deberry, Thomas McReynolds, Henry G. Cornelly, Samuel Anderson, Robert Murray, and John C. Stockton, who being elected tried and sworn well and truly to try the issue joined upon their oath do say that the defendants have not paid the debt of two hundred and one dollars as the plaintiff in replying to the defendants plea in that behalf hath alleged and assess the plaintiff damages by reason of the detention thereof to seventeen dollars and eight cents. It is therefore considered by the court that the plaintiff recover of the defendant the debt aforesaid with the damages aforesaid by the jury aforesaid assessed, together with their cost by them about their suit in this behalf expended and the defendant in mercy etc.

Jason H. Wilson	)	
vs.	)	Debt
John W. Cook	)	

This day came the parties aforesaid by their attorneys and thereupon came a jury of good and lawful men to wit, Sanders Carney, Philip G. Tucker, Samuel H. Swan, William Braden, John Barnhart, James Henderson, Mathias Deberry, Thomas McReynolds, John D. Shannon Samuel Anderson, Robert Murray and John C. Stockton who being elected tried and sworn the truth to speak upon the issues joined upon their oaths do say that the defendant hath not paid the balance of debtof two hundred and ninety dollars and forty six cents as the plaintiff in replying to the defendants plea on that behalf hath alleged and assess the plaintiff damages by reason of the detention thereof to five dollars and three cents. It is therefore considered by the court that the plaintiff recover of the defendant the debt aforesaid assessed and his cost by him about his suit in this behalf expended and the defendant in mercy etc.

John McNairy and Henry M Rutledge	)	
vs.	))	Debt
John T. Connelly		

P443   This day came the parties aforesaid by their attorneys and thereupon came
a jury of good and lawful men, to wit, Sanders Carney, Philip G. Tucker, Samuel
H. Swan, William Braden, John Barnhart, James Anderson, Mathias Deberry, Thomas
McReynolds, John D. Shannon, Samuel Anderson, Robert Murray and John Cl Stockton
who being elected, tried and sworn well and truly to try the issues joined upon
their oaths do say that the defendant hath not paid the debt of one hundreddollrs
as the plaintiff in replying to defendants plea hath alleged and assess the plaintiff damages by reason of the detention thereof to five dollars and fifty cents.
P444   It is therefore considered by the court that the plaintiff recover of the defendant their debt aforesaid with the damages aforesaid in form aforesaid assessed
and cost by them about their suit in that behalf expended and the defendant in
mercy etc.

John McNairy and Henry M Ruthledge   )
vs.   )   Debt.
Robert Hughes   )
        This day came the parties aforesaidby their attorneys and thereupon came
a jury of good and lawful men to wit Sanders Carney, Philip G. Tucker, Samuel H
Swan, William Braden, John Barnhart, James Henderson, Mathias Deberry, Thomas
McReynolds, John D. Shannon, Samuel Anderson, Robert Murray and John C. Stockton
who being elected tried and sworn the truth to speak upon their oaths do say that
the defendant hath not paid the balance of debt of ninety eight dollars in his
note filed and assess his damages by reason of the detention thereof to six dollar
and eighty six cents. It is therefore considered by the court that the plaintiff
recover of the defendant the balance of debt aforesaid with the damages aforesaid by the jury aforesaid assessed together with his cost by him about his suit
expended and the defendant in mercy etc.

James Stanley   )
vs.   )   Debt
John Spencer   )
        This day came the parties by their attorney and thereupon came a jury of
good and lawful men, to wit, Sanders Carney, Philip G. Tucker, Samuel H. Swan,
William Braden, John Barnhart, James Henderson, Mathias Deberry Thomas McReynolds,
John D. Shannon Samuel Anderson, Robert Murray and John C. Stockton, who being
elected tried and sworn well and truly to try the issue joined upon their oaths
do say that the defendant hath not paid the debt of eight handed and twenty-five
dollars as the plaintiff in replying to defendants plea in that behalf hath alleged and assess the plaintiff damages by reason of the detention thereof to
P445 to forty nine dollars and fifty cents. It is therefore considered by the court
that the plaintiff recover of the defendant the debt aforesaid with the damages
aforesaid in form aforesaid assessed together with his cost by him about his
suit in this behalf expended and the defendant in mercy etc.

Harris Bradford)
vs.   )   Debt
John Murray   )
        This day the parties aforesaid by their attorneys and thereupon came a jury
of good and lawful men to wit, Sanders Carney Philip G. Tucker Samuel H. Swan
William Braden, John Barnhart, James Henderson, Mathias Deberry, Thomas McReynolds
John D. Shannon, Samuel Anderson, Robert Murray and John C. Stockton who being
elected tried and sworn well and truly to try the issues joined upon their oaths
do say that the defendant hath not paid the debt of one hundred dollars as the
plaintiff in replying to deft's plea hath alleged and assess his damages by reason
of the detention thereof to ninety four dollars. It is therefore considered by
the court that the plaintiff recover of the defendant his debt aforesaid together

P446 with his damages aforesaid in form aforesaid assessed also his cost by him about
his suit in this behalf expended and the defendant in mercy etc.

Bryson B. Trousdale)
vs.) In debt
William Harris)

This day came the parties aforesaid by their attorneys and thereupon came
a jury of good and lawful men, to wit, Sanders Carney Philip G. Tucker, Samuel
H Swan, William Braden, John Barnhart, Mathias Deberry, James Henderson Thomas
McReynolds, John D. Shannon, Samuel Anderson, Robert Murray and John C. Stockton
who being elected tried and sworn the truth to speak upon the issue joined upon
their oaths do say that the defendant has not paid the debt of sixty dollars
as the plaintiff in replying to the defendants plea in that behalf hath alleged
and assess the plaintiff damages by reason of the detention thereof to two dollars
and seventy cents. It is therefore considered by the court that the plaintiff
recover of the defendant the debt aforesaid with the damages aforesaid in form
aforesaid assessed and also his cost by him about his suit in thsi behalf expended
and the deft. in mercy etc.

John McNairy and Henry M Rutledge Assignees
of William E. Butler)
vs.) Debt
James F. Theobold)

This day came the parties aforesaid by their attorneys and thereupon came
a jury of good and lawful men, to wit, Sanders Carney, Philip G. Tucker, Samuel
H. Swan, William Braden John Barnhart, James H. Henderson Mathias Deberry, Thomas
McReynolds, John D. Shannon, Samuel Anderson, Robert Murray and John C. Stockton
who being elected, tried and sworn the truth to speak upon the issues joined
on their oaths do say that the defendant hath not paid the debt in the declaration mentioned of sixtyfive dollars as the plaintiff in replying to defendants
plea hath alleged and assess his damages by reason of the detention thereof to
seven dollars and fifteen cents. It is therefore considered by the court that
the plaintiff recover of the defendant the debt aforesaid with the damages aforee
said by the jury aforesaid assessed together with his cost by him about his
suit in this behalf expended and the defendant in mercy etc.

Isaac Sitters and James W. Sitler)
vs.) Debt.
Benjamin Sholdson)

This day came the parties aforesaid by their attorneys and thereuponcame
a jury of good and lawful men, to wit, Sanders Carney, Philip G. Ticker, Sam'l.
H. Swan, William Braden, John Barnhart, James Henderson, Mathias Deberry, Thomas
McReynolds, John D. Shannon, Samuel Anderson, Robert Murray and John C. Stockton
who being elected tried and sworn well and truly to try the issues joined upon
their oaths do say that the defendant has not paid the debt of three hundred
and forty dollars and thirty one cents ans the plaintiff in replying to defendant
plea hath alleged and assess the plaintiff damages by reason of the detention
therefore considered by the court that the plaintiff recover of the defendant
the debt aforesaid with the damages aforesaid by the jury aforesaid assessed
together with his cost by him about his suit in this behalf expended and the
defendant in mercy etc, and the defendant prays an appeal in the nature of a
writ of error from said judgment entered into bondwith Thomas Shannon and John S.
Porter his securities, which was granted him to the next circuit court.

Matthew L. Dickenson of the Nashbille Bank
vs.
Benjamin Gholson) Debt.

P447   This day came the parties aforesaid by their attorneys and thereupon came
Cont. a jury of good and lawful men, to wit, Sanders Carney, Philip G. Tucker, Samuel
H. Swan, William Braden John Barnhart, James Henderson, Mathias Deberry Thomas
McReynolds, John D. Shannon Samuel Anderson Robert Murray and John C. Stickton,
P448 who being elected tried and sworn the truth to speak upon the issues joined upon
the issues joined upon their oaths do say that the defendant has not paid the balance
of debt of six hundred and thirty three dollars and thirty and a half cents and
assess the plff damages by reason of the detention thereof to nineteen dollars
forty nine and half cents. It is therefore considered by the court that the
plaintiff recover of the defendant the balance of debt aforesaid with the damages
aforesaid by the jury aforesaid assessed together with his cost by him about
his suit in this suit in this behalf expended and the defendant in mercy etc.
          An appeal prayed and granted in the nature of a writ of error to the next
circuit court entered into bond with Thomas Shannon and John T. Porter his securities, which was granted.

John Wilson   )
vs.   )   Debt
Samuel H. Swan   )

          This day came the parties aforesaid by their attornies and thereupon came
a jury of good and lawful men, to wit, Sanders Carney, Philip G. Tucker, Henry
G. Connelly, William Braden, John Barnhart, James Henderson, Matthias Deberry,
Thomas McReynolds, John D. Shannon Samuel Anderson Robert Murray and John C.
Stockton, who being elected tried and sworn, well and truly to try the issue joined upon their oaths do say that the defendant hath not paid the debt of two hundred twenty two dollars and seventy five cents as the plaintiff in replying to
the defendants plea in that behalf hath alleged and they further find the plea of
set off in favor of the plaintiff and do assess the plaintiff damages by reason
of the detention thereof to thirty-four dollars fifty cents. It is therefore
considered by the court that the plaintiff recover of the defendant the debt
aforesaid with the damages aforesaid by the jury aforesaid assessed together with
his cost by him about his suit in this behalf expended and the defendant in
mercy etc.

P449 Ezekiel B. McCoy   )
      vs.   )   Appeal
      William M. Wilson   )
          The plaintiff in this cause comes and dismisses his suit herein and confess-
es judgment for the cost herein. It is therefore considered by the court the
Defendant recover of the plaintiff his cost by him about his suit in this behalf
expended and the defendant in mercy etc.

James G. Haskill   )
vs.   )   Debt
Joshua Haskill   )
          This day came the plaintiff by his attorney and dismisses his suit herein
and confesses judgment for cost of suit. It is therefore considered by the court
that the defendant recover of the plaintiff his cost by him about his suit in
this behalf expended and the plaintiff in mercy etc.

William M Berryhill and William McKee)
vs.   )   Debt
Stockley D. Hays   )
          This day came the parties aforesaid by their attorneys and thereupon came a
jury of good and lawful men, to wit, Sanders Carney Philip G. Tucker, Samuel
H Swan, William Braden, John Barnhart, James Henderson, Mathias Deberry, Thomas

P449

ContMcReynolds, John D. Shannon, Samuel Anderson, Robert Murray and John C Stockton, who being elected tried and sworn, well and truly to try the issue joined upon thier oaths do say the defendant hath not paid the debt of two hundred and sixty eight dollars, sixty two hundred and sixty eight dollars, sixty two and three fourth cents in the declaration mentioned as the plaintiff by replying in that behalf hath alleged and do assess the plaintiff damages by reason of the deten-
P450 tion there of to forty one dollars and fifty cents. It is therefore considered by the court that the plaintiff recover of the defendant the debt aforesaid and the damages aforesaid by the jury aforesaid in form aforesaid assessed together with his costs by him about his suit in this behalf expended and the said de- fendant in mercy etc.

James C. Roach   )
vs.   )   Debt
Robert H. Dyer   )

        This day came the parties by attorneys and thereupon came a jury of good and lawful men, to wit, Sanders Carney, Philip G. Tucker, Samuel H. Swan, William Braden, John Barnhart, James Henderson, Mathias Deberry, Thomas McReynolds, John D. Shannon Samuel Anderson, Robert Murray and John C. Stockton who being elected, tried and sworn the truth to speak upon the premises do say that the plaintiff hath not paid the debt in the note of hands mentioned but he doth yet owe the sum of one hundred and forty one dollars debt and the further sum of fifteen dollars damages for the detention thereof. It is therefore considered by the court that the plff. recover of the defendant the debt aforesaid with the damages aforesaid by the jury aforesaid in form aforesaid assessed and also the cost by him about his suit in this behalf expended and the defendant in mercy etc

John McNairy and Henry M. Rutledge, Assignees   )
vs.   )
Wilson McReynolds, and Thomas I McReynolds   )

        This day came the parties aforesaid by their attorneys and thereupon came a jury of good and lawful men, to wit, Sanders Carney, Philip G. Tucker, Samuel
P451 H. Swan, William Braden, John Barnhart, James Henderson, Mathias Deberry, Thomas McReynolds, John D. Shannon, Samuel Anderson, Robert Murray and John C. Stockton who being elected, tried and sworn the truth to speak upon the issue joined upon their oaths do say that the defendants have not paid the balance of debt of nine- tyseven dollars and twenty nine cents as the plaintiff in replying to thedefend- ants plea in this behalf hath alleged and assess the plaintiff damages to two dollars and forty two cents. It is therefore considered by the court that the plaintiff recover of the defendant the balance of debt with the damages afore- said in form aforesaid by jury aforesaid assessed and the defendants in mercy etc. also their costs.

Bartholomew G. Stewart, Joseph Linn   )
Adam R. Alexander and James Trousdale Commissioners etc.)
vs.   )   Debt
Thomas I. Smith   )

        This day came the parties aforesaid by their attorneys and thereupon came a jury of good and lawful men, to wit, the same jury as in the last above case, who being elected, tried and sworn well and truly to try the issue joined upon their oaths do say that the defendant hath not paid the debt of one hundred and fifty one dollars as the plaintiff in replying to the defendants plea in that behalf hath alleged and assess the plaintiff damages by reason of the detention thereof to thirteen dollars and twenty three cents . It is therefore considered by the court that the plaintiff recover of the defendant the debt aforesaid with the damages aforesaid by the jury aforesaid assessed and the defendant in mercy etc.

2 Same)
vs.) Debt
William Arnold and S. D. Hays)

 This day came the parties aforesaid by their attorneys and thereupon came a jury of good and lawful men, to wit, the same jury as in case last aforesaid, who being elected tried and sworn well and truly to try the issue joined upon their oaths do say that the defendents have not paid the debt of two hundred dollars as the plaintiff in replying to the defendants plea in that behalf hath alleged and assess the plaintiff damages by reason of the detention thereof to seventeen dollars. It is therefore considered by the court that the plaintiff recover of the defendant the debt aforesaid with the damages aforesaid in form a foressaid by the jury aforesaid assessed and the defendants in mercy etc also their cost.

The same)
vs.) Debt
William R. Hess and S. D. Hays)

 This day came the parties by their attorneys and thereupon came a jury of good and lawful men, to wit, the same jury as in the above cause, who being elected tried and sworn will and truly to try the issue joined upon their oath do say that the defendents have not paid the debt of sixty dollars as the plaintiff in replying to the defendants plea in that behalf hath alleged and assess the plaintiff damages by reason of the detention thereof to five dollars and ten cents. It is therefore considered by the court that the plaintiff recover of the defendant their debt aforesaid with the damages aforesaid by the jury aforesaid assessed together with the cost by them about their suit in this behalf expended and the deft. in mercy etc.

53 Same)
vs.)
Thomas Shannon)

 This day came the parties aforesaid by their attorneys and thereupon came a jury of good and lawful men, towit, the same jury as in the last above case, who being elected, tried and sworn will and truly to try the issue joined upon their oaths do say that the defendant hath not paid the debt of two hundred and sixteen dollars as the plaintiff in meplying to defendants plea in that behalf hath alleged and assess the plaintiff damages by reason of the detention thereof to eighteen dollars and thirty six cents. It is therefore considered by the court that the plaintiff recover of the deft. the debt aforesaid with the damages aforesaid by the jury aforesaid assessed together with their cost by them about their suit in this behalf expended and the defendant in mercy etc.

The Same)
vs.) Debt
Stockely D. Hays)

 This day came the parties aforesaid by their attorneys and thereupon came a jury of good and lawful men, to wit, the same jury as in the last above miantion case who being elected tried and sworn, will and truly to try the issue joined upon their oaths do say that the defendant hath not paid the debt of two hundred and fifty one dollars as the plaintiff in replying to defendants plea in that behalf hath alleged and assess the plaintiff damames by reason of the detention thereof to twenty one dollars and thirty three cents. It is therefore considered by the court that the plaintiff recover of the defendant thelxr debt and damage aforesaid assessed and their cost by them about their suit in this behalf expended.

P454 Same   )
     vs.   )   Debt
Stokely D. Hays   )

This day came the parties aforesaid by their attorneys and thereupon came
a jury of good and lawful men, to wit, the same jury as in the last above mentioned case who being elected tried and sworn will and truly to try the issue joined
upon their oaths do say that the defendant hath not paid the debt of fifty one
dollars as the plaintiff in replying to defendants plea hath alleged and assess
the plaintiff damages by reason of the detention thereof to four dollars and
thirty three cents. It is therefore considered by the court that the plaintiff
recover of the defendant the debt aforesaid with the damage aforesaid by the jury
aforesaid in form aforesaid assessed together with their cost by them about
their suit in this behalf expended and the defendant in mercy etc.

Ordered that the order appointing commissions to settle with the trustee
and sheriff of this county be renewed as respects William Harris and Roderick
McIver and that James Henderson be appointed instead of Joseph Linn and thereupon
entered into bond as required by law and that they make report to the next term
of court.

Turner Sullivan   )
vs.   )   Debt
John F. Brown   )

This day came the parties aforesaid by their attorneys and thereupon
came a jury of good and lawful men, to wit, the same jury as in the case last above
mentioned who being elected tried and sworn the truth to speak upon the issue
joined between the parties, on their oath do say they find the issues in favor
of the plaintiff and that the defendant hath not paid the debt of one hundred
dollars as replying to deft's plea in that behalf, plaintiff hath alleged and they
assess the plaintiff damages by reason of the detention thereof to four dollars
P455 and seventy five cents. It is therefore considered by the court that the plaintiff
recover of the deft. and debt and damages in form aforesaid by the jury assessed
and also his cost in this behalf expended etc.

Court then adjourned until tomorrow morning 9 O'clock.
                                     H. Haralson   JP
                                     James Trousdale JP
                                     Jesse L. Kirk   JP.

Friday morning December 31st. Court met agreeable to adjournment. Present
the Worshipful Lemuel Hunter, Jesse L. Kirk, and James Trousdale William
Stoddert, Alexander B. Bradford and Daniel Horton, Plaintiffs
vs.   Motion to be discharged as security , Thomas Shannon Sheriff of Madison Carnel, Deft.

This day came the plaintiffs in their proper person, and thereupon produced into court a notice to the defendant, Thomas Shannon that the would apply
to this court at the present term to be released from further liability as the
security of the said defendant Thomas Shannon for the due performance of his
duties as sheriff of Madison County and the said Thomas Shannon thereupon came
into court and waived all exception to the said notice not being served in time
and consents that the application might be heard and considered by the county,
whereupon the said plaintiffs read their petition to the court, setting forth
that they went Thomas Shannon security for the due performance of his duties as
sheriff of Madison County at the court of pleas and quarter sessions Madison
County on the fourth Monday in December 1823 and representing further that they w
were in great danger of becoming liable on their bond to pay large sums of money
on account of the negligence in office of the said Thomas Shannon and thereupon

P456   the said Thomas Shannon agreed with the assent of the court that said securities William Stoddert, Alexander B. Bradford and Daniel Horton should be released and discharged from all further liability as security to said Thomas Shannon and it therefore accordingly ordered ajudged and decredd by the court that the said William Stoddert, Alexander B. Bradford and Daniel Horton be released and discharged from all further liability on their said bond as security for the said Thomas Shannon as aforesaid and thereupon the said Thomas Shannon offered to the court Benjamin, Gholson, John B. Cross, Wilson Hutchison and Thomas I. Smith as his securities for the due and faithful performance of his duties as Sheriff of Madison County who were received by the court and the Said Benj. Gholson, John B. Cross Wilson Hutchison and Thomas J. Smith together with the said Thomas Shannon accordingly entered into bond payable to the Governor of the State of Tennessee and his sucessors as the law directs which was duly acknowledged in open co court amd prdered tp be recprded/

Martin Lorance, Plaintiff
vs.   Motion against principal
Thomas Campbell, Deft.

    This day came the plaintiff by his attorney and the defendant though solemnly called came not, but made default, and thereupon the plaintiff by his attorney produced and filed in court in the state of Tennessee, said Thomas Campbell complanant against James Bratton Senr. James Brattan Jr. William Brattan, E. Howell and Robert Fleming defendants in equity from which transcript it appeared that the plaintiff was the security of defendant, Thomas Campbell in said case in equity and that judgment had been rendered in said Circuit Court of Carroll at the October term 1824 of said court against the said plaintiff Martin Lorance as security for the said Thomas Campbell for the sum of seven hundred and twenty dollars and thereupon the plaintiff by his attorney moved the court for judgment against the said Thomas Campbell for the said sum of seven hundred and twenty dollars and it appearing to the satisfaction of the court that the said Martin Lorance is liable and bound to pay the said sum of seven hundred and twenty dollars as security for the said Thomas Campbell. It is therefore considered by the court that the said Martin Lorance recover of the said Thomas Campbell the said sum of seven hundred and twenty dollars together with his cost by him in this behalf expended/

James Poor   )
vs.   )   Motion
James Trousdale and James Greer, Defendant   )

    This day came the plaintiff by his attorney and the defendants though solomnly called came not, but made default, and thereupon the plaintiff by his attorney produced in court a delivery bond executed by the said defendants in the penalty of one hundred and four dollars to said plaintiff conditioned that said defendant would deliver one bay mare and three head of cows to Anthony F. Gray, deputy sheriff at the Court house in the town of Jackson on the 28th. day of December 1824 the day of sale to satisfy an execution for forty six dollars 12 cents debt and five dollars 30 cents cost in favor of said plaintiff against the said James Trousdale, then the obligation to be void and it appearing to the satisfaction of the court and by return of said sheriff on the execution that the said defendahts failed to deliver and have the property aforessaid forth coming at the day of sale and that the said debt and costs remains unpaid on motion of plaintiff by his attorney. It is therefore considered by the court that the plaintiff recover of the defendants the said sum of one hundred and four dollars

P458 the penalty of said bond to be discharged by the payment of the aforesaid debt and costs with twelve and one half percent damages to the said plaintiff and double costs to the said A. F. Gray, deputy sheriff and the cost of this motion.

P458
Cont.

An indenture of sale from William E. Butler for himself and as attorney in face for aJohn McNairy and Henry M. Rutledge to Wiley Roy was this day produced in open court and acknowledged by the said William E. Butler for himself and as attorney in fact for John McNairy and Henry M. Rutledge to be their act and deed and ordered to be certified for registration.

An indenture of sale from Wiley Ray to John R. Collier was this day produced in open court and the execution thereof duly acknowledged by the said Wiley Ray to be his act and deed and ordered to be certified for registration.

A deed of mortgage from Thomas Williamson to Thomas Shannon was this day produced in open court and the execution and delivery of the same proven by the oath of Roderick McIver and William Stoddert subscribing witness thereto and ordered to be certified for registration.

The Grand Jury this day returned into court the following presentments one against James and John Fussel for an affray another against the same for an affray all signed by the said Grand Jury also an indictment against James Fussel for an assault and battery indorsed by the foremn of the Grand Jury "a true bill" and it is ordered thatcopias issued and etc.

P459
Joseph Moss   )
vs.   ) Order of sale
Herndon Haralson, Ryland Chandler Pitts Chandler and Vincent Haralson)

This day came the plaintiff by his attorney and produced into court an execution of Fi Fi, directed to the Sheriff of Madison County against said defendant at the instance of said plaintiff commanding the sheriff of Madison County to levy of the goods and chattels, lands and teniments of the said defendants the sum of one hundred and nine dollars 70 cents debt and interest and also nine dollars and 45½ cents costs of suit which the said plaintiff recovered of the said def'ts it the Court of Pleas and Quarter sessions at the September term last of said court on the 30th day of September which execution was issued 16th. December 1824 was returned by Thomas J. Smith, Deputy Sheriff with the following indorsement came to hand Dec. 18th. 1824 and levid on one negro woman by the name of Amy and one child named Charlotte the property of one of the defendants. Herndon Haralson, levied too late to well in time to make the debt and costs and thereupon the plaintiff by his attorney moved that an orderof sale of said negro woman Amy and child Charlotte levid on as aforesaid, should be issued, in pursuance of said execution and levy as aforesaid and the court being willing that what is right and just should be done.   It is therefore considered by the court that an order of sale issue from this court, directed to the sheriff of Madison county in this case in pursuance of the levy and execution as aforesaid to sell the property heretofore levied on.

Robert Gray   )
vs.   ) Certioari
Andrew Forbush)

This day came the parties aforesaid by their attorneys and the parties agree to dismiss their suit herein at the cost of the plaintiff the defendant paying the cost of the witness by him summoned. It is therefore considered by the court that the plaintiff recover of the defendant the cost aforesaid and that the defendant recover of the plaintiff the cost by him about his suit in this behalf expended and the parties in mercy etc.

Court then adjourned until tomorrow morning ten o'clock.q

H. Haralson   JP
James Trousdale JP
John H Hyde   JO
Jesse L. Kirk   JP

P460 Saturday 1st. January 1825

Court met agreeable to adjournment. Present the worshipful James Trousdale, Jesse L Kirk, John H Hide and Herndon Haralson.

Joseph Linn the administrator of the Estate of Joel Mading this day returned an inventory of the amount of sales of the dedendants which was ordered to be recorded.

James F. Theobold a constable sworn to attend on the vourt and jury proud four days.

P461   The Grand Jury this day returned into court the following presentments, to wit, one against Gutheridge Andrews for gaining one against William Johns for ga gaming and it is ordered that copies issued etc. and that the Grand Jury be discharged from further service at the present term.

An indenture of sale from William Reynolds to Herbert Newsom for thirty acres of land was this day produced in open court and acknowledged by the said William Reynolds to be his act and deed and ordered to be certified for registration.

A deed of mortgage from Herbert Newsom to William Reynolds was this day produced in open court and the execution acknowledged by the said Herbert Newsom to be his act and deed and ordered to be certified for registration.

A power of attorney from Adam Huntsman to Robert Murray was this day produced in open court and the execution of the same acknowledgeed by the said Huntsman and ordered to be certified etc.

A power of attorney from Joseph Linn to Robert Murray was this day produced in open court and the execution of the same acknowledged by the said Joseph linn to be his act and ordered to be certified.

Mr Weatherspoon proved five days attendance on the Grand Jury at the present term.

Court then adjourned until court in course.

                                        H. Haralson   JP.
                                        John H. Hyde   JP
                                        Sam Taylor   JP.

P462   Monday February 7th. 1825

At a Court of Pleas and Quarter Sessions began and held for the County of Madison in the state of Tennessee at the Court House in the Town of Jackson on Monday the 7th. day of February in the year of our Lord one thousand eight hundred and twenty five.

Present: the Worshipful Herndon Haralson William Draper, James McCutchen Bartholomew G. Stewart, Stephen Jarman, Lemuel Hunter, James McDaniel William Spencer, John Thomas, Mark Christian, Green Hill, William C. Love Jesse L Kirk and William E. Butler, Gentlemen, Justices.

A plot and certificate of Entry No 84 dated the 9th. day of December 1820 for three hundred and thirty four acres of land lying in the ninth surveyors district first range and tenth section entered in the name of Archebold Mahon was produced in open court and the transfer indorsed thereon was acknowledged by Thomas Shannon, Sheriff of Madison County and ordered to be certified.

Ordered that the following hands work on that part of the road that Herbert Newsom is overseer, to wit, Thomas Lofton, James Edwards, John Sandford, John Spencer, Eldridge Newsom, Abel Wells, W. Deal Vinson Cree A. S. Lackman Issac Moody , John Wright Senr. William Right John W. Right Allen McVey Reuben McVey Burd Hill John Burrow James Thomas Timothy Shaw William Butler, John Givens all the hands living within the bounds of said road.

On motion and petition filed ordered that the following persons to wit, William Draper, Gilbreath Nail, Lemuel S. Hunter, B. G. Stewart, Isaac Swan Joseph Eddings, George Shankle and John Estes them or any five of them be a jury to mark and lay off a road from about one mile South of where the Jackson

P463 road leading to Huntingdon crosses Spring Creek thence in a Southeastern direction to where the carrollville road leading to Jackson crosses the county line
and make report to the next term of court.

Monday February 7th. 1825

On motion and petition of John Brown, it is ordered by the court that he be
permitted to turn the road at or near the Northeast corner of his field and
running westwardly leaving the hollow below his field on the left and thence
intersecting the present road at the most cojvenient point so soon as this same
is opened and put in as good order as the present road.

Ordered that the order granting a jury of view to view a road of the 2nd.
class from the bridge at Shannon landing to the mouth of Clover Creek so far
as the South boundary line of Madison County be renewed and that Stephen Lacy Lar
kin Cason Joshua Weaver, Robert Clanton, Claibourn Chisum, Jacob Miller, Francis
Wallace, John D. McDaniel and Robert Howland them or any five of them be a jury
to mark and lay off the same and make report to the next term of court.

On motion and petition filed ordered that William Draper Isaac Swan, Henry
House. William Harris, John Shaw, Robert O'Neal and John Barnhart, them or any
five of them be a jury to view and mark a road of the third class from the county
line at or near Jerimiah Brooks on Cain Creek to some point of the Reynolds
Burg road between Alexander Greer and Champness Madings and make report to the
next term.

A deed of bargain and sale from William Blackemore to Philip R. Haley
for 58 acres of land was this day produced in open court and proven by the oath
Beryno Smith and Robert Grimmer and ordered to be certified for registration.

Ordered that James D. McCutchen be overseer of the road in the place of
Nathan Clark.

Ordered by the court, that there be a tax levid of 12½ cents on each 100
acres of land lying in the county of Madison for the year 1825 to be collected
and applied to the opening and improving the navigation of the river in the
Western District according to the act of Assembly in such case made and provided.

P464 Monday February 7th. 1825

Ordered that Owen Griffin be overseer of the road from the town of Jackson
to Nash's Bluff in the place of Benj. S. Brooks.

Ordered that George W. Taylor be appointed overseer of the road leading
from Jackson to Brownsville from the river to Johnson's Creek and work the follow
ing hands, Foster Golding and hands B. Stanley, Richard H. Burks, Edley Ewin,
James Cockrell and hands.

Ordered that Exum L Holland be permitted to turn the road leading from
Jackson to Harris Bluff so soon as the same is putin as good order as the
present road.

Ordered that the road leading from this place to the county line on a direction to Carrollville in Wayne County be established and that Newton Harris
be overseer of the same from a small branch East of Ezekiel B. McCoy and work the
following hands James Alexander, Henry N Coulter, James Tarbutton, Ebenezer
Haltom, Thomas Haltom, Moses Steed Calier Steed, John B. Manner, William Steel
and hands W. Haltom's hands, Jesse Jackson and all other hands living within said
bounds.

An inventory of the Estate also an inventory of the amount of sales of the
estate of James Priest, deceased was this day produced in court and ordered to be

recorded.

Ordered that the following taxes belevid and collected for the year 1825,

to wit, on each hundred acres of land 18¾ cents on each white poll 12½ cents on
each black poll 18¾ cents to be applied to the bridging the slews and repairing
that part of the road through the swamp crossing the river at the middle bridge
according to the act of assembly in such case made and provided.

P464   Adam Brown, Duncan McIver and Robert Hibbetts commissions appointed at the last
Cont.   term of this court to settle with James L. McDaniel Guardian of the heirs of Robert
        Moore deceased returned this day into open court a report of the same which was
        read by the court and ordered to be recorded.

P465   Monday 7th. February 1825
            Ordered by the court that John Estes be released from the payment of twenty
        five dollars half the appraised value of a stray horse by him taken up and that
        H. Haralson be released from the payment of three dollars and fifty cents half
        the valuation of a stray by him taken up also that Joshua Baker be released from
        the payment of four dollars half the appraised value of a stray by him taken
        up and that the county Trustee be allowed a credit in the settlement of his
        accounts for the same.
            Ordered that Micajah Midyett, Esquire, Daniel Tiffapan and John D. Shannon
        divide the hands and distance in the road leading from Jackson to Harris's Bluff
        between John T. Porters and William C. Mitchells overseers and furnish each over-
        seer with his distance and quota of hands.
            Ordered that the following persons be appointed to take the list of taxable
        for the year 1825 to wit.
            John H Hyde in the town company, James McCutchen in Justices com. William
        Spencer in Reaves company William Draper in Draper com., James Mc Daniel in
        Young's comp., R. Lowery in McLaurines com, Jarrett M Jelks in Smiths comr.,
        David Jarrett in Moor's comp., William Willbourn in Lacy's comp., The Sanders in
        Williamsons comp. John Thomas in Hills Comp., William Atchison, Freers Company
        and return the same to the next term of court.
            Ordered that the double taxes on the following tracts of land be remitted
        for the year 1824 to wit 274 acres 10th. district, age 309 Entry 959, 285½ acres
        10th. district range 5 sect. 8, Entry 480 listed in the name of John Wharton.
            A power of attorney from William Butler to Adam R. Alexander was this day
        produced in open court and the execution of the same duly acknowledged by the said
        William Butler to be his act and ordered to be certified.
P466.   Monday 7th. February 1825
            An indenture of sale from Robert H. Dyer John H. Hogg and William B. C.
        Killingsworth to Martin Wiggs for eighty and ¾ acres of land was this day proven
        by the oath of Elijah Baker and Dugold Gorgason and ordered to be certified for
        registration.
            An indenture of Bargain and sale from Herndon Haralson to Roderick McIver
        for sixty eight and one half acres of land was this day produced in open court
        and the execution of the same duly acknowledged by Herndon Haralson to be his
        act and ordered to be certified for registration.
            An indenture of bargain and sale from Samuel Dickens to Robert White for
        two hundred and twenty eight acres of land was this day produced in open court
        and the execution of the same proven by the oath of William Duty and Hiram Duty
        and ordered to be certified for registration.
            An indenture of Bargain and sale from Vencint Haralson to James Vaulx for
        fifty five acres of land was this day produced in open court and the execution of t
        the same duly acknowledged by the said vincent Haralson to be his act and ordered
        to be certified for registration.
            An indenture of bargain and sale from Thomas Hunt to Samuel Dickens for
        eleven hundred twenty six and ½ acres of land was this day produced in open court
        and the execution of same proven by the oath of Lucuis I. Polk and M. W Howard
        and ordered to be certified for registration.
            An indenture of bargain and sale from Thomas Hunt to Samuel Dickens for
        three thousand and two hundred and twenty nine acres of land was this day pro
        duced in open court and the execution of same proven by the oath of Lucius I. Polk
        and M. H. Howard and ordered to be certified for registration.
            An indenture of bargain and sale from William Polk to Thomas Hunt for three

P466thousand one hundred and ten acres of land was this day produced in open court and
Contthe execution of the same duly proven by the oath of M. H. Howard and Lucuis I.
Polk and ordered to be certified for registration.

P467 Monday February 7th. 1825

An indenture of bargain and sale from William B. Moore to Samuel Dickens
for one hundred and sixty acres of land was this day rpoduced in open court and
the execution of the same duly proven by the oath of Thomas Goodon and Lucius I
Polk and ordered to be certified for registration.

An indenture of sale from Samuel Dickens to Thomas Hunt for two thousand
two hundred sixty three and 4/6 acres of land was this day produced in open court
and the execution of the same acknowledged by Samuel Dickean and ordered to be
certified for registration.

A power of attorney from William P Anderson to Robert E. C. Dougherty was
this day produced in open court and the execution of the same proven by the oath
of Robert Hughes and ordered to be so certified.

A deed of bargain and sale from the commissioners of the Town of Jackson to
Daniel Horton for lott no nineteen was this day produced in open court and the
execution of the same proven by the oath of John Hardwick and Joseph F. Cloud and
ordered to be certified for registration

Court then adjourned until tomorrow morning nine o'clock.

David Jarrett   JP.
Stephen Lacy   JP.
J. B. Cross   JP.

Tuesday the 8th. day of February 1825

Court met agreeable to adjournment, present: the Worshipful John F. Cross
David Jarrett, Stephen Lacy, William Spencer, and James Trousdale, gentlemen,
justices.

An indenture of bargain and sale from William E. Butler and James Walker
to Peter R. Booker for seven hundred and fifty acres of land was this day produced
in open court and the said William E. Butler and James Walker acknowledged the same
to be their act and deed and ordered to be certified for registration

P468 Tuesday 8th. February 1825

An indenture of bargain and sale from William E. Butler and Peter R. Booker
to James Walker for nine hundred acres of land was this day produced in open
court and execution of the same duly acknowledged by William E. Butler on his part
to be his act and deed and ordered to be so certified.

An indenture of bargain and sale from John McNairy andWilliam E. Butler to
James Walker for six hundred and sixty four acres was this day produced in open
court and the execution of the same duly acknowledged by the said William E.
Butler for himself and as attorney in fact for John McNairy and ordered to be
certified for registration.

An indenture of bargain and sale from John McNairy Henry M. Rutledge and
William E. Butler of John F. Brown for 3 acres was this day produced in open court
and execution of the same acknowledged by the said William E. Butler for himself and as attorney in fact for John McNairy and Henry M. Rutledge to be his
act and deed and ordered to be certified for registration.

An indenture of sale from William E. Butler to Tobias Grider for ninety one
and half acres of land was this day produced in open court and the execution of
the same duly acknowledged by the said William Butler to be his act and deed and
ordered to be certified for registration.

An indenture of bargain and sale from Vincent Haralson to John Rayder
for forty acres of land was this day produced in open court and the execution of
the same duly acknowledged by the said vincent Haaralson to be his acr and deed
and ordered to be certified for registration.

P469   An indenture of bargain and sale from Vincent Haralson to Alexander Patton for part of lot No sixteen in the plan of the town of Jackson was this day produced in open court and the execution of the same duly proven by the oath of James Vaulx and Henry Strothers and ordered to be certified for registration.

      Tuesday the 8th. February 1825

      An indenture of bargain and sale from Lee Sullivan to Aquila Davis for twenty eight acres of land was this day produced in open court and the execution of the same proven by the oath of John T. Porter and Henry Strothers and ordered to be certified for registration.

      An indenture of bargain and sale Aquila Davis to Armour and Lake for 42 acres of land was this day produced in open court and the execution of the same duly proven by the oath of Alexander B. Bradford and William Harris and ordered to be certified for registration.

      An indenture of bargain and sale from John M. Patrick to John C. McLemore James Vaulx and James Carithers for two hundred and eighty acres of land was this day produced in open court and the execution of the same acknowledged by the said John M Patrick to be his act and deed and ordered to be certified for registration.

      A deed of gift from Thomas A. Dale to Elvina Darnall was this day produced in open court and the execution of the same proven by the oath of Duncan McIver snfS. Burrus subscribing witnesses thereto and ordered to be certified for registration.

      A deed of bargain and sale from the heirs of Philip Nebber deceased, to John P Landford was this day acknowledged by Stark Dupeny one of the heirs of the said Nebben to be his acr and deed for the purpose mentioned in said deed and on motion it was ordered that a dedimus potestatum issue to David Jarrett and William Spencer Esqrs. to take the examination of Sarah Dupeny wife of the said Stark Dupeny which was done accordingly and the said David Jarrett and William Spencer esqs. made return on the said dedimus that they had examined the said Sarah Dupeny privily and apart from her husband Stark Dupeny and she acknowledges that she freely and voluntarely and without pursuasion or threats of her husband relinquished her rights of dower in and to the premises mentioned in said deed all of which is ordered certified,

Reuben P. T. Stone	)	
vs.	)	Case
Benjamin Gholson and Bartholomew G. Stewart	)	

      This day came the parties aforesaid by their attorneys and thereupon the plaintiff dismisses his suit as to the defendant Bartholomew G. Stewart and the defendant Benjamin Gholson says he cannot gainsay the plaintiffs action against for the sum of one hundred and twenty three dollars. It is therefore considered by the court that the plaintiff recover of the defendant Gholson said sum of one hundred and twenty three dollars together with his cost by him about his suit in this behalf expended (except the attorneys tax fee) and the defendant in mercy and the plaintiff consents to stay execution six months in this case.

The State of Tennessee	)	
vs.	)	A & B
John Spencer	)	

      This day came as well the solicitor general on the part of the state as the defendant in his proper person and the defendant being arraigned upon his arraignment plead guilty as charged in the bill of indictment. It is therefore considered by the court that the defendant make his peace with the state by the payment of fifty cents cents fine and that the plaintiff recover of the defendant her fine aforesaid together with hercost by her about his suit in this brhalf expended and the defendant in mercy etc.

P471 Tuesday February 8th. 1825

The Sheriff this day made return of the writ of venire facias to him directed from the last term of court and with the following indorsement thereon, to wit, I have summoned all the persons named in the within veniri (except William Key, Daniel Bevel, Dawson Bond, Robert Doak and Jacob Bradbury) all of which are free holders and householders of my county February 8th. 1825. In pursuance of they were all attending except Drury Bettis and John A. Gibson Thomas Shannon Sheriff out of which the following persons, to wit, Alexander Greer, Exum Hollan, Lewis Griffin Henry H. Horn, Nathan Simpson, Collier A Steed, Allan Trousdale, John D. Shannon, John McColellan, George Shankle, Thomas Harington, Richard Golden, Wartham Easley, were then empanelled, sworn and charged as a Grand Jury with Alexander Greer their foreman to inquire into and for the boey of the county of Madison the thereupon retired to consider of presentments under the care of James F. Rheobold a constable to attend on the same.

Ordered that Minor Marsh be released from double taxes on twenty three acres of land for the year 1824.

Ordered that Francis Taylor be released of his fine as a delinquent juror at the last term of this court.

Ordered that John Gaitly be exempt from serving as a juror at the present term.

James F. Theobold and William Robinson were this day sworn to attend on the court and jury at the present term.

A deed of trust from William M Wilson to William Wilkerson was this day produced in open court and the execution of the same duly proven by the oath of Alexander B. Bradford and Robert Lake and ordered to be certified for registration.

P472   Tuesday February 8th. 1825

Francis Smith   )
vs.   )   Motion
William H. Doak, Constable and William Arnold,   )
A. R. Alexander Daniel, Horton, S. D. Hays and   )
Roderick McIver his securities   )

This day came the plaintiff and moved the court for cause to enter upon the docket andn ------ his motion for judgment against the defendent according to the acts of assembly in such case made and provided which was granted and the further consideration of the matter by and with the assent of the plaintiff and the defendants who appeared in court and agreed that the further consideration of the subjec matter of the aforesaid motion by prepared until a subsequent day of this term and no advantage to be taken by either side in consequence of said post ponement.

Francis Smith   )
11/27   )
William H. Doak constable and John T. Porter and)   Motion
Samuel H. Shannon, his securities   )

This day came the plaintiff and moved the court for leave to enter upon the docket and --------his motion for judgment against the defendants according to the acts of assembly in such case made and provided which was granted and the further consideration of the matter by and with the assent of the plaintiff and the defendants who appeared in court and agreed that the further consideration of the
P473 subject matter of the aforesaid motion be postponed and until a subsequent day of this term and no advantage be taken by either sidein consequence of said postponement.

Court then adjourned until tomorrow morning 9o'clock.

                              H. Haralson   JP.
                              John H Hyde   JP
                              Sam Taylor   JP.

P473 Wednesday Morning 9th. February 1825.
Cont.   Court met according to adjournment, present, the Worshipful Herndon Haralson,
John R. Hyde and Samuel Taylor, Gentlemen, justices.

Isaac Curry   )
vs.   )   Case
Benjamin Gholson   )

        This day came the parties aforesaid by their attorneys and thereupon came a
jury of good and lawful men, to wit, Moses Steed, William Harris, Ezekial B. Mc-
Coy, Charles Wortham, Samuel H. Swan, Samuel D. Wilson, Francis Taylor, Joseph
Carroll, Jesse Emory, William Johns, Enberry Tantrum, and Patrick M Duffy, who being
elected tried and sworn the truth to speak upon the issue joined upon their oaths
do say that the defendant did assum upon himself as the plaintiff in his
declaration hath alleged and assess the plaintiff damages by reason there of
two hundred dollars sixty two and one half cents.   It is therefore considered
by the court that the plaintiff recover of the defendant the damages aforesaid
in form a foresaid by the jury aforesaid assessed together with his cost by
him about his suit in this behalf expended and the defendant in mercy etc.

        On motion of the administrators of the Estate of Martin Davis, deceased
and it appearing to the satisfaction of the court that there is not sufficient
funds, purishable estate, in the hands of the administration to satisfy the
debt of the decedant, it is ordered that the administration proceed to sell
two negroes Ben and Mariah the property of said estate and apply the proceeds
to the payment of the debts of said decedant.

P474 Wednesday 9th. February 1825

William Guy   )
vs.   )   Debt no suit
S. D. Hays, James F. Theobold)
Samuel H. Shannon   )

        This day came the defts. by their attorneys and the plaintiff though
solemnly called, came not, but made default.   It is therefore considered by th e
court that the plaintiff be non suited and the defendant recover of the plaintiff be non suited and the defendant recover of the plaintiff their cost by t
them about their suit in this behalf expended and the plaintiff in mercy etc.

George W. Still   )
vs.   )   Covenant
John Barnhart &   )
Archibold S. Lackman   )

        This day came the plaintiff by his attorney and dismissed his suit here-
in and confessed judgment for the cost.   It is therefore considered by the
court that the defendant recover of the plaintiff their cost by them about
their suit in this behalf expended.

John H. Bills   )
vs.   )
John T. Porter & Aquila Davis and)   Appeal
Wilson Hutchison his securities   )

        This day came the parties aforesaid by their attorneys and thereupon
came a jury of good and lawful man, to wit, Joseph Barbutton, Stephen Lypert,
James Kincaid, John R. Collier, Charles Sevier, Robert Jones Allen McVey,
Thomas Wynne, John Rayder, Hugh Lacy, John Fussell and Aron Sanders, well
and truly to try the matters in dispute between the parties upon their oaths
    do find for the plaintiff and assess his damages by reason thereof to twenty-
one dollars.   It is therefore considered by the court that the plaintiff recover of the defendant and his securities the damages aforesaid with

P474 six per cent interest from the tenth of January 1824 the time of rendering
Cont. judgment before the justice of the peace also his cost by him about his suit
in this behalf expended and the defendant in mercy.

Henry Reagan   )
vs.   )   Appeal
John T. Porter and J. H. Wilson and Benjamin   )
Cholson, his securities   )

P475   This day came the parties aforesaid Wednesday 9th. February 1825 by their
attorneys and thereupon came a jury of good and lawful men, to wit, Joseph
Tarbutton Stephen Lypert, James Kincaid, John R. Collier Charles Sevier, Robert
Jones, Allen McVey, Thomas Whnne, John Rayder, Hugh Lacy, John Fussell and
Aron Sanders who being elected, tried and sworn will and truly to try the matter
in dispute between the parties upon their oaths do find in favor of the plaintiff and assess the plaintiff (torn out- and assess the plaintiff) damages
by reason thereof to nineteen dollars and forty cents. It is therefore considered by the court that the plaintiff recover of the defendant and his
securities aforesaid the damages aforesaid with six per cent interest from the
10th January 1824 the time of rendering judgment by the justices below also
his cost by him about his suit in this behalf expended and the defendant in
mercy etc.

John G. Porter)
vs.   )   Case
Joseph F. Cloud)
          This day came the parties aforesaid by their attorneys and thereupon
came a jury of good and lawful men, to wit, Joseph Tarbutton Stephen Lypert,
James Kincaid, John R. Collier, Charles Sevier, Robert Jones, Allen McVey,
Thomas Wynne, John Rayder, Hugh Lacy, John Fussell and Aaron Senders, who
being elected, tried and sworn will and truly to try the issue joined upon
their oaths do find for the plaintiff and assess his damages to six dollars.
It is therefore considered by the court that the plaintiff recover of the
 defendant his damages aforesaid together with his cost by him about his suit
in this behalf expended and the defendant in mercy etc.

Jordan G. Stokes   )
vs.   )   In case
John I Smith   )

Same   )
vs.   )   Covenant
Same   )
          This day came the parties aforesaid by their attorneys and agree by
consent of parties and with the assent of the court to have their cause transferred to the next circuit court for trial to be hear theron.
P476   Wednesday February 9th. 1825

William M Wilson)
vs.   )   Case
Robert H. Dyer   )
          By consent of the parties and with the assent of the court this cause
is transferred to the next term of the Circuit Court for trial to be had thereon

)
Samuel Thomas   Certiorari
vs.
Benjamin Gholson)

P478
Cont.   This day came the defendant by his attorney and the plaintiff the solemnly called came not but made default. It is therefore considered by the court that the plaintiff be non suited and the defendant recover of the plaintiff his cost by him about his suit in this behalf expended and the plaintiff for his false clamor in mercy etc.

J. M. Wilson & John Stewart   )
vs.   )   Certiorari
John Stockton   )

This day came the parties aforesaid by their attorneys and thereupon came a jury of good and lawful men, to wit, Joseph Tarbutton, Stephen Lypert, James Kincaid John R. Collier, Charles Sevier, Robert Jones, Allen McVey, Thomas Wynne, John Rayder, Hugh Lacy, John Fussell and Aaron Sanders who being elected tried and sworn to try the matter in dispute between the parties and not being able to agree in their virdict by consent of parties and with the assent of court they were discharged from rendering their verdict until tomorrow.

Alexander Patton)
vs.   )   Certiorari
John T. Porter   )

This day came the parties aforesaid by their attorneys and the defendant because he cannot gainsay the plaintiffs cause of action hereof against him comes into court and confesses judgment for the sum of fifty one dollars six and one fourth cents.

P477   Wednesday 9th. Feb. 1825
With six per cent enterest from the 23rd. day of July 1824, the time of rendering judgment before the justice of the peace and on motion of the plaintiff by his attorney, it is considered by the court that the plaintiff recover of the said defendant and Bruan his security the said sum of fifty one dollars and six per cent interest aforesaid together with his cost by him about his suit in this behalf expended and the parties agree to stay execution one month.

A transfer of
A platt and a certificate for one hundred seventy two acres of land was produced in open court and assignment thereof executed by B. Coleman, W. E. Butler and Alexander B. Bradford duly acknowledged by them and ordered to be certified.

A deed of mortgage from John Spencer to William Johnson was this day produced in opend ourt and the execution proven by the oath of Aaron H. Sanders and ordered to be certified for registration.

A deed of Bargain and sale from Evander McIver to Blackman Coleman for 640 acres of land was this day produced in open court and the execution thereof acknowledged by the said Evander McIver to be his act and deed and ordered to be certified for registration.

A deed of bargain and sale from Blackman Coleman to Evander McIver for two hundred acres of land was this day produced in open court and the execution of the same duly acknowledged by the said Blackman Coleman to be his act and deed and ordered to be certified for registration.

A Jury of view appointed at the last term of this court to view a road from near James Moore's to county line on a direction to Gibsonport, this day made report which was reviewed by the court and it is ordered that Sugars McLemore be appointed overseer of the same from James Moore's to the North fork of Forked Deer and work all the hands West of Cave Creek and North of the

P477 said McLemores, Micajah Midyett, Brooks Jarrett M Jelks and Patrick Duffy and
Cont. East of Deer Creek and North of the said Forked Deer river between Deer and
Cain Creek and that Samuel D. Waddill be overseer from the North fork to Gibson County line and work all the hands West of the Mouth of Turkey Creek
and South of Gibson County line and North of the river and East of the mouth
of Waddill's Creek to open and keep the said road in repair.

P478 Wednesday February 9th. 1825
          Administration of all and singular the goods and chattels, rights and
credits of John F. Wyatt, deceased, was this day granted to Austin A. King.
          Court then adjourned until tomorrow morning nine o'clock.

                                        H. Haralson   JP.
                                        John H. Hyde   JP.
                                        James Trousdale JP.

Thursday 10th. February 1825
          Court met according to adjournment, present, the Worshipful Herndon
Haralson, John H. Hyde and James Trousdale, gentlemen, justices .
          A power of attorney from John McIver to Evander McIver was this day pro-
duced in open court and the execution of the same duly rpoven by the oath of
James Carithers and B. Gillespie subscribing witnesses thereto to be the act
of said John McIver was this day produced in open court and the execution of
the same duly proven by the oath of James Carithers and B. Gillespie subscribing witnesses thereto to be the act of said John McIver and ordered to be certified for registration.
          An indenture of bargain and sale from William E . Butler for himself and
as attorney in fact for John McNairy and Henry M Rutledge to William Porter was
this day produced in open court and the execution of the same duly court and
  the execution of the same duly acknowledged by the said William E. Butler
 for himself and as atty aforesaid to be his act and deed and ordered to be
certified for registration.

The State   )
vs.   )   Assault
James Fusel   )
          This day came as well the solicitor general on the part of the state
as the defendant in his proper person and the defendant being arraigned upon
his arraignment plead guilty as charged in the bill of indictment. It is there
fore considered by the court that the defendant make his peace with the state
by the payment of one dollar fine and that the plaintiff recover of the defendant the fine aforesaid together with his cost by her about her suit in this
behalf expended and the deft. may betaken etc. S
State against James Fusell, Assault
          This day came as well the solicitor general on the part of the state as
the defendant in his proper person and the defendant being arraigned upon his
arraignment pled guilty as charged in the bill of indictment, It is therefore
considered by the court that the defendant make his peace with the state by
the payment of one dollar fine and that the plaintiff recover her fine aforesaid
together with her cost by her about her suit in this behalf expended.

P479 Thursday110th. February 1825

The State   )
vs.   )   Gambling
William Johns   )
          This day came as well the solicitor general on the part of thestate as
the defendant in his proper person and the defendant being arraigned upon his

P479 arraignment plead not guilty and thereupon came a jury of good and lawful men,
Contto wit, William Harris, William Boling, Chas. Bradon, Spencer Grant, Willie B.
Dyer, William C. Due, John C. Wilson, Francis Taylor, John Timms, James Kiper,
Charles Wortham, and Euberry Tantrums, who being eledted tried and sworn will
and truly to try rhw issue joined upon their oaths do say that the defendant
is guilty as charged in the bill of indictment. It is therefore considered
  by the court that the defendant make his peace with the state by the payment
of five dollars fine and that the plaintiff recover of the defendant the fine
  aforesaid together with her cost by her about her suit in this behalf expended and the defendant, in mercy etc.

The State vs.   )
vx.   )   Gambling
Cutheredge Anderson   )
        This day came as well the solicitor general on the part of the state
as the defendant in his proper person and the defendant being arraigned upon
his arraignment plead guilty as charged in the bill of indictment. It is
therefore considered by the court that the defendant make his peace with the
state by the payment of five dollars fine and that the plaintiff recover of the
defendant her fine aforesaid together with her cost by her about her suit in
this behalf expended and the defendant be taken etc.

The State   )
vs.   )   Assault
John Fussell   )
        This day came as well the solicitor on the part of the state as the de-
fendant in his proper person and the defendant being arraigned upon his arraignment plead not guilty as charged in the bill of indictment and for his trial
put himself upon his country and thereupon came a jury of good and lawful men,
to wit, Euverry Tantrum, Joseph Tarbutton, Stephhn Lypert, James Henderson,
Samuel H. Swan, Charles Matthews, John Knuckles, Newell Newsom, John Arnold,
John Harrison, Ruben P. T. Stone, and Moses Steed who being elected; tried and
sworn will and truly to try the issue joined.

P480 Thursday 10th. February 1825
upon their oaths do say the defendant is not guilty as charged in the bill
of indictment . It is therefore considered by the court that the deft. recover
of the plaintiff his cost by him about his suit in this behalf expended.

Samuel Bruff   )
vs.   )   Appeal
Lancaster Glover)
        This day came the defendant by his attorney and the plaintiff although bei
ing solemnly called, came not, but made default. It is therefore considered by
  the court that the plff. be non prossed and that the said defendant recover
of the plaintiff his cost by him about his suit in this behalf expended and the
plaintiff for his false clamor in mercy etc.

Daniel Johnson Adm etc.   )
vs.   )   Appeal
Eli Cockrane & John Arnold   )

Same   )
vs.   )   Appeal
John Arnold and Levi Cockrane)

P480   The death of Eli Cockrane ove of the defendants in above cause is here
Conttoday suggested to the court and the cause continued until the next term of court

George H. Watson   )
vs.   )   Case
Jobe Timms   )

        On opnsent of parties and with the assent of the court his cause is
continued until next term of court and on motion of the defendant by his attorney the plaintiff is required come in by the first day of the next term and
give additional security otherwise suit to be dismissed at his cost.

John C. Boyd   )
vs.   )   Case
Wilson Hutchison   )

        This day came the parties aforesaid by their attorneys and

P481   Thursday February 10th. 1825
and the defendant because he cannot gainsey the plaintiff s cause of action
hereof against him withdraws his pleas and confesses judgment for the sum of
one hundred and fifty dollars debt and the further sum of twenty seven dollars,
    intbrest. It is therefore considered by the court that the plaintiff recover
of the defendant the debt aforesaid together with the interest aforesaid in for
    aforesaid confessed and also the costs by him about his suit in this behalf
expended and the defendant in mercy etc.

George H. Watson   )
vs.   )   Case
Jabes Timms   )

        This day came the parties aforesaid by their attorneys and the plaintiff
because he is unwilling to prosecute his suit any farther dismisses the same and
thereupon came Foster Golden, John Timms and Allen McVey into court and confessed judgment together with the defendant for the cost of the suit herein. Iy is
therefore considered by the court that the plaintiff recover of the said defendant, Foster Golden, John Timms, and Allen McVey the cost aforesaid by him about
his suit in this behalf expended and the defendant in mercy etc.

J. H. Wilson and John Stewart   )
vs.   )   Certiorari
John C. Stockton   )

        This day came the parties aforesaid by their attorneys and thereupon came
the jury empanelled, sworn and charged in this case on yesterday and declared
they could not agree on their verdict and by consent of parties and with the
assent of the court Joseph Barbutton, one of the jurors in this is withdrawn an
and the rest of the jury are discharged from rendering their verdict in this cas
case and the cause continued until next term of court.

P482   Thursday 10th. February 1825
            Court then adjourned until tomorrow morning 9 o8clock.
                                    H. Haralson   Jr.
                                    John H Hyde   JP.
                                    Sam Taylor   JP.

                        Friday morning February 11th. 1825
        Court met according to adjournment. Present, the Worshipful Herndon
Haralson, John H. Hyde and Samuel Taylor, gentlemen, Justices of the peace.

P482 Francis Smith   )
Cont.vs.   )
    William H. Doak and William Arnold, Adam R.   )   Motion for a judgment
Alexander Daniel Horton, Stokely D. Hays and   )   for money collection
Roderic McIver his securities   )

      This day came the parties aforesaid by their attorneys and thereupon
the matters of law arising upon the plaintiffs motion herein came on and was
argued and the court being sufficiently addressed thereon are of opinion that
said motion be overruled. It is therefore considered by the court that the defendant go thereof hence without day and recover of the plaintiff their costs
by them about their defence in this behalf expended and the plaintiff for his
false clamor be in mercy etc.

      A bill of sale from Archibold Chaffin to Edward H. Chaffin was this day
produced in open court and the exedution of the same duly acknowledged by the
said Archibold Chaffin to be his act and ordered to be certified for registration.

      The Grand Jury this day returned into court an indictment against William
Higgins for gambling indorsed by the foreman of the Grand Jury a true bill.

P483   Friday February 11th. 1825
      Court then adjourned until tomorrow morning nine o'clock.

                       H. Haralson   JP.
                       James Trousdale   JP.
                       M. Midyett   JP.

              Saturday morning February 12th. 1825
      Court met according to adjournment Present, the Worshipful H. Haralson
James Trousdale and Micajah Midyett, Gentlemen, Justices

Edward G. Clouston   )
vs.   )   Motion for judgment for
John D. Shannon, Constable Thomas Shannon and   )   money collection
William Arnold, his securities   )

      This day came the parties aforesaid by their attorneys and thereupon on
motion of the plaintiff by his attorneys and it appearing to the satisfaction
of the court by the confession of the parties that the defendant have had due
notice of said motion and that there is yet in the hands of the said John
Shannon seventy eight dollars monies by him collected as constable for the said
plaintiff on the 4th. day of August 1824. It is therefore considerd by the
court that the plaintiff recover of thesaid John D. Shannon and Thomas Shannon
and William Arnold his securities the debt aforesaid with twelve and one half
per cent interest from the said 4th. day of August 1824 and also his cost by
him about his motion in this behalf expended and the defendant in mercy etc.

Joel Fenson   )
vs.   )   Debt
Jason H. Wilson   )

      This day came the parties aforesaid by their attorneys and thereupon came
a jury of good and lawful men, to wit, Ezekiel B. McCoy, Joseph Tarbutton,
William Harris, Charles Wortham, Charles Matthews Philip G. Tucker, Absolom
Massey, Jordon G. Stokes, Jesse Brown, William Tees, Thomas Norvill and Eli
Chandler, who being elected, tried and sworn, will and truly to try the issues
joined do say they find the issues in favor of the plaintiff that the defendant

P484 hath not paid the debt of one hundred and twenty five dollars in the declaration mentioned and assess the plaintiff damages by reason of the detention thereof to thirteen dollars twelve and half cents. It is therefore considered by the court that the plaintiff recover of the defendant the debt and damages aforesaid by the jury aforesaid in form aforesaid assessed together with his cost by him about his suit in this behalf expended and the defendant in mercy etc.

Harrel Fitzhue)
vs.) Debt
Willie H. Dyer &)
Joel Dyer)

This day came the parties aforesaid vy their attorneys and the defendants cause of action hereof against them withdraw their pleas and confess judgment for the sum of one hundred and then dollars, the balance of debt in the declaration and the further sum of seven dollars and fifteen cents interest. It is therefore considered by the court that the plaintiff recover of the defendant the balance of debt aforesaid with the interest aforesaid in form aforesaid by them confessed also the cost by him about his suit in this behalf expended and the defendants in mercy etc.

Samuel Dickens)
vs.) Assumsit
Benjamin Gholson)

This day came the parties aforesaid by their attorneys and thereupon came a jury of good and lawful men, to wit, Ezekiel B. McCoy, Joseph Tarbutton, Charles Matthews, Charles Wortham, Philip G. Tucker, Absolom Massey, Jordan G. Stokes, William Toes William Adkins, Thomas Norvill, and Eli Chandler, who being elected tried and sworn the truth to speak upon the issue joined returned into court and declared that they could not agree in their verdict, thereupon by consent and with the assent of the court a juror is with drawn and the rest of the jury are discharged from rendering their verdict and the cause continued until the next term of this court for trial.

P485   Saturday February 12th. 1835
Austin A. King to whom an order of administration on a former day of the present court on all and singular the goods and chattels rights and credits of John F. Wyatt, deceased, this day came into open court, took the oath of administration and entered into bond in the penalty of eight hundred dollars with John F. Brown his security with the penalty prescribed by law. It is therefore ordered that letters of administration issue accordingly.

Ordered that the early part of Monday next be set apart for transacting county business.

An indenture of bargain and sale from Thomas Shannon to Absolom Massey for a lot of ground in the town of Jackson was this day produced in open court and the execution of samd duly acknowledged by the said Thomas Shannon to be his act and deed and ordered to be certified for registration.

A bill of sale from Robert H. Wynne and William Arnold the Administrators of Martin Davis, deceased to Samuel Dickens was this day produced in open court and the execution of the same acknowledged by the said Robert H. Wynne and William Arnold Admr' as aforesaid and ordered to be certified for registration.

An inventory of the property of Martin Davis, deceased, was this day returned into court and ordered to be recorded.

Lancaster Glover) Appeal
vs.
Samuel Bruxsion of)the plaintiff by his attorney the non prosse entered on this

P485 case on a former day of this term is ordered to be set aside and thereupon the
Cont.plaintiff by his attorney and the defendant being solemnly called came not but
made default.   It is therefore considered by the court that the plff. recover
of the defendant $150 the balance of his debt, his cost by him about his suit
in this behalf expended and the defendant in mercy etc.

P486

Saturday 12th. February 1825
Court then adjourned until Monday morning 10 o'clock

William Draper   JP
M Midyett   JP.
Wm. Spencer   JP.

Monday morning 14th February 1825
Court met according to adjournment, present the Worshipful Herndon Haral-
son, Jarrett M Jelks, Micajah Midyett, William Spencer, William Draper, William
E. Butler, Lemuel S. Hunter, Samuel Taylor and John H. Hyde.

Ordered that William G. King be appointed overseer of the road in the place
of Esquire Jelks work all the hands living from the section line to the North
fork and within Range said road passer through to keep up that part of the road
lying within said range.

Ordered that the precinct election be established at the house of Joshua
Weaver's in this county.

Ordered that Robert Murray be overseer of the road from town to the creek
below Herndon Harelson's in the place of Moses Starns and work all the hands subject to the order appointing said Starns overseer.

Ordered that the county tax on land and polls be equal to the state tax
for the present year and that 12½ cents be levied on each 100 acres of land and
12½ cents on all taxable polls for the purpose of paying jurors.

Ordered that Samuel Taylor, Ezekiel B. McCoy John H. Hydes John H. Ball
and Samuel H. Shannin and Charles Sevier be a jury of view to view a road commencing at the Southeast corner of Stephen Lyperts lott and intersecting the
road leading out by M. Todds and such point as they think best leaving Doct.
Royals on the left and make report to the next term.

Ordered that the old jail be offered for sale on Tuesday the 8th. day of
the present term on a credit of six month.

P487   Monday 14th. February 1825
On motion and petition filed ordered that Adam Huntsman and Roderick Mc-
Iver have leave to build a mill on Butlers Creed near where the Lexington road
 crosses the same and that all orders heretofore granted to build mill or mills
on said creek be rescinded.

Ordered that Thomas Shannon Sheriff be allowed the sum of sixty seven dollar
as Jailor's fees and that the same stand of record as if entered at the last
term of court being then allowed and not entered on record.

)
James H. Wilson & John Stewart   Debt
vs.
)
James The Buddyn & Robert Hurtyas aforesaid by their attorneys and thereupon came
a jury of good and lawful men, to wit, Alexander Greer, Exum Holland, Lewis
Griffin, Henry H. Horn, Collier A. Steed, Allen Trousdale, John McClelland,
George Shankel, Thomas Barrington, Richard Golden, Warham Easley, and John
Fussell, who being elected tried and sworn, well and truly to try the issues
joined upon their oaths do say they find the issues as between the plff. & Deft.
James T. Pullen in favor of the plaintiff and that he has not paid the debt of one
hundred thirty five dollars and they assess his damage thereof to nine dollars
as to the issue joined between the Plff. and the oather defendant Dyer they find

P487 the issue in favor of defendant Dyer.
cont.   It is therefore considered by the court Plff. recover of Deft. Pullen the
debt and damage aforesaid in form assessed and his cost and that the other deft.
Dyer recover of Plff. his cost in this behalf expended.

Edmond Rivers   )
vs.   )   Appeal
Thomas Shannon   )
          This day came the parties aforesaid by their attorneys and thereupon came
a jury of good and lawful men, to wit, Ezekiel B. McCoy Joseph Tarbutton,
William Harris, Moses Steed, Charles Mathews, George Todd, Benjamin S. Brooks,
William C. Due, Gabriel Davy, John Bayder, George Berry, William Berry who being
elected, tried and sworn well and truly to try the matter in dispute between the
parties upon their oaths do say they find for the plaintiff and assess his damages to fifty three dollars and thirty four cents, It is therefore considered
by the court that the plaintiff recover of the defendant the said sum of fifty
three dollars and 34 cents in form aforesaid by the jury aforesaid assessed together with his cost by him about his suit in this behalf expended and the defendant prayed an appeal from the judgment rendered herein to the next term of
the circuit court and entered into bond with Lemuel S. Hunter his security in
the penalty and condition prescribed by law which is received and granted by the
court.

John Montgomery   )
vs.   )   Appeal
(marked out John G. Carithers))
Robert Murrey   )
          This day came the defendant by his attorney and the plaintiff though solemn-
ly called came not but made default. It is therefore considered by the court
that the plaintiff be non prossed and that deft. recover of him his costs bout
his suit in this behalf expended etc.

Rice Williams & Moses H. Parr)
vs.   )   Covenant
James H. Wilson   )
          This day came the parties by their attorneys and thereupon came a jury of
good and lawful men, to wit, Alexander Greer, Exum Holland, Lewis Griffin, Henry
H. Horn, Collier A. Steed, Allen Trousdale, George Shankle, Thomas Herrington
John McClelland, Richard Golden, Warham Easley, and John Fussell, who being
elected, tried and sworn, well and truly to try the issue joined upon their
oaths do say they find the issue in favor of the plaintiff and they assess the
plaintiff damages be reason of the non performance of defendants covenant in this
behald, to one hundred and fifty six dollars. It is therefore considered by
the court that the plaintiff recover of the defendant the damages aforesaid by
the jury aforesaid in form aforesaid assessed together with his cost by him
about his suit in this behalf expended and the defendant in mercy etc. from which
judgment the defendant prayed an appeal and entered into bond with Jason H.
Wilson and Samuel D. Wilson his securities in the penalty of $312.

P489   Monday February 14th. 1825

Thomas C. Haskins)
vs.   )   Certiorari
John Darnall   )
          This day came the parties aforesaid by their attorneys and thereupon came
a jury of good and lawful men, to wit, Alexander Greer, Axum Holland, Lewis

9 Griffin, Henry H Horn, Collier A. Steed, Allen Trousdale, John McClelland,
t. George Shankle, Thomas Herring, Richard Golden, Warham Easley, and John Fussell
who being elected, tried and sworn to will and truly try the matters in dispute
between the parties, upon their oaths do say they find for the pleintiff and
assess the plaintiff damages by reason thereof to fifty one dollars sixty two
and half cents. It is therefore considered by the court that the plaintiff recover of the defendant and Wilson Hutchins and John B. Cross the damages aforesaid with twelve and one half per cent interest from the 22nd. day of September
1823 the time of rendering judgment before the Justice of the peace and also his
costby him about his suit in this behalf expended and the defendant in mercy etc.

George Sanders   )
vs.   )   Appeal
Jordan G. Stokes   )
        This day came the defendant by his attorney and the plaintiff though solemn-
ly called came not but made default. It is therefore considered by the court
that the plaintiff be non prossed and that the defendant recover of the plaintiff his cost by him about his suit in this behalf expanded and the plaintiff for
his false clamor in mercy etc.

Bedford S. Wynne   )
vs.   )   On si fa
Simon Johns Heirs   )
        This day came the parties aforesaid by their attorneys and the plaintiff
dismisses their suit and confess judgment for the cost.
                    Monday 14th. February 1825
O It is therefore considered by the court that the defendant recover of the plaintiff their cost by them about their suit in this behalf expended and plaintiff in
mercy etc.

Robert Bedford and Robert H. Wynne)
vs.   )   on sa fa
Simon Johnson's Heirs   )
        This day came the parties aforesaid by their attorney and thereupon the
plaintiff dismisses their suit herein and confess judgment for the cost. It is
therefore considered by the court that the defendant recover of the plaintiff
their cost by them about their suit in this behalf expended and the plaintiff
in mercy etc.

James H. Wilson and John Stewart)
vs.   )   Certiorari
John Hardwick   )
        This day came the parties aforesaid by their attorneys and the defendant
withdraws his motion for a trial in this case and confesses judgment for the cost.
It is therefore considered by the court that the plaintiff recover of the defendant and securities his cost by him about his suit in this behalf expended and
the defendant in mercy etc.

George L Miler & Andrew Hynes
vs.   )
Joel Dyer   )   Debt
        This day came the parties aforesaid by their attorneys and thereupon came
a jury of good and lawful men, to wit, Alexander Greer, Axum Holland, Lewis
Griffin, Henry H. Horn, Collier A. Steed, Allen Trousdale, John McClelland,
George Shankle, Thomas Harrington, Richard Golden, Varham Easley and John Fusell

P490 who being elected, tried and sworn will and truly to try the issues joined upon
Cont. their oaths do say they find the issues in favor of the plaintiff and that the
defendant hath not paid the debt of two hundred and fourteen dollars and seventy
four cents as the plaintiff in replying to defendant plea in that behalf hath
alleged and they do further find that the defendant hath no set off and assess
the plaintiff damages by reason of the detention thereof to sixty four dollars
and twenty cents. It is therefore considered by the court that the plaintiff
recover of the defendant the debt aforesaid with the damages aforesaid by the
jury aforesaid with the damages aforesaid by the jury aforesaid in form aforesaid by the jury aforesaid in form aforesaid assessed together with their cost
by them about their suit in this behalf expended and the defendant in mercy etc.

Stephen Cantrell)
vs.   )   Debt
Turner Sullivan)

        This day came the parties aforesaid by their attorneys and thereupon came
a jury of good and lawful men, to wit, Alexander Greer, Axum Holland, Lewis
Griffin, Henry H. Horn, Collier A Steed, Allen Trousdale, John McClelland,
George Shankle, Thomas Harrington, Richard Golden, Warham Easley, and John
Fussell, who being elected tried and sworn the truth to speak upon the issue
joined upon their oaths do say they find the issue in favor of the plaintiff and
that the defendant hath not paid the debt of one hundred and thirty dollars in
the declaration mentioned and assess the plaintiff damages by reason of the detention thereof to five dollars and eighty five cents. It is therefore considered by the court that the plaintiff recover of the defendant the debt aforesaid
together with the damages aforesaid by the jury aforesaid assessed also his cost
by him about his suit in this behalf expended and the defendant in mercy etc.

Stephen Cantrell)
vs.   )   Debt
Henry D. Collier)

        This day came the parties aforesaid by their attorneys and thereupon came
a jury of good and lawful men, to wit, Alexander Greer, Axum Holland Lewis Griffi
Henry H. Horn, Collier A. Steed, Allen Trousdale, John McClelland, George Shankle
Thomas Harrington, Richard Golden, Warham Easley, and John Fussell who being
elected, tried and sworn, will and truly to try the issues joined do upon their
oaths do say they find the issue in favor of the plaintiff and the defendant hath
not paid the remaining debt of two hundred and forty dollars and forty cents
as the (marked out plaintiff on replying to) defendant in his plea in that behalf hath alleged and assess the plaintiff damages by reason of the detention
thereof to nineteen dollars and seventy cents. It is therefore considered by
the court that the plaintiff recover of the defendant the remaining debt aforesai
with the damages aforesaid by the jury aforesaid in form aforesaid assessed together with his cost by him about his suit in this behalf expended and the defend
ant in mercy etc.

George L Viles and Andrew Hynes)
vs.   )   Debt
John B. Cross   )

        This day came the parties aforesaid by their attorneys and thereupon came a
jury of good and lawful men, to wit, Alexander Greer, Axum Holland Lewis Griffin
Henry H. Horn, Collier A. Steed, Allen Trousdale, John McClelland George Shankle
Thomas Harington, Richard Golden, Warham Easley and John Fussell, joined upon
their oaths do say that defendant hath not paid the remaining debt of eighty five
dollars as the plaintiff in replying to defendants plea in that behalf hath
alleged and the defendant hath no set off and assess the plaintiff damages by

reason of the detention thereof to eighteen dollars and eighty five cents.
It is therefore considered by the court that the plaintiff recover of the defendant the balance of debt aforesaid together with his damages aforesaid in form aforesaid by the jury aforesaid assessed also their costs by them about their suit in this behalf expended and the defendants in mercy etc.

Stephen Cantrell)
vs.   )   Debt
Charles Brandon)

This day came the parties aforesaid by their attorneys and thereupon came a jury of good and lawful men, to wit, Alexander Greer, Axum Holland Lewis Griffin Henry H. Horn, Collier A. Stead, Allen Trousdale, John McClelland George Shankle, Thomas Harrington, Richard Golden, Warham Easley, and John Fussell who being elected, tried and sworn, will and truly to try the issue joined upon their oaths do say that the defendant hath not paid the remaining debt of one hundred dollars forty seven and one half cents as the defendant by his plea in that behalf hath alleged and assess the plaintiff damages by reason of the detention thereof to five dollars and seventy two cents.

It is therefore considered by the court that the plaintiff recover of the defendant the said remaining debt of one hundred dollars forty seven and one half cents with the damages aforesaid by the jury aforesaid in form aforesaid assessed together with his cost by him about his suit in this behalf expended and the defendant in mercy etc.

Samuel Crocket   )
vs.   )   Case
Coldwell C. Wilson)

By consent of parties this cause is continued until next term of court.

Henry Butler,   )
vs.   )   Debt
Benjamin Cholson)

This day came the parties aforesaid by their attorneys and thereupon came a jury of good and lawful men, to wit, Alexander Greer, Axum Holland Lewis Griffin, Henry H. Horn, Collier A. Stead, Allen Trousdale, John McClelland George Shankle, Thomas Harrington, Richard Golden, Warham Easley and John Fussell, who being elected, tried and sworn will and truly to try the issues joined upon their oaths do say they find the issues in favor of the plaintiff and that the defendant hath not paid the debt of two hundred and three dollars as the plaintiff in replying to defendants plea in that behalf hath alleged and assess the plaintiff damages by reason of the detention thereof to nine dollars. It is therefore considered by the court that the plaintiff recover of the defendant the debt aforesaid with the damages aforesaid by the jury aforesaid in form aforesaid assess together with his cost by him about his suit in this behalf expended and the defendant in mercy etc.

Robert Murray   )
vs.   )   Debt
Wilson Hutchinson)

This day came the parties aforesaid by their attorneys and thereupon came a jury of good and lawful men, to wit, Alexander Greer, Axum Holland Lewis Griffin, Henry Horn, Collier A. Steed, Allen Trousdale, John McClelland, George Shenkle Thomas Harrington, Richard Golden, Warham Easley and John Fussell who being elected tried and sworn will and truly try the issues joined upon their oaths do say that they fine the issues in favor the plaintiff and that the

P494 defendant hath not paid the debt of one hundred and seventy three dollars and
twenty one cents as the plaintiff replying to defendants pleas hath alleged
and assess the plaintiff damages be reason of the detention thereof to ten dollars. It is therefore considered by the court that the plaintiff recover of
the defendant the debt and damages aforesaid by the jury aforesaid in form aforesaid assessed and his cost by him about his suit in this behalf expended and
the defendant in mercy etc.

John Webb   )
vs.   )   Covenant
William Love   )
        This day came the parties aforesaid by their attorneys and thereupon came
a jury of good and lawful men, to wit, Alexander Greer, Axum Holland Lewis
Griffin, Henry H. Horn, Collier A. Steed, Allen Trousdale, Warham Easley and
John Fussell who being elected, tried and sworn, will and truly to try the issue
joined upon their oaths do say that they find the issue in favor of the plaintiff and assess the plaintiff damages by reason of the non performance of the
covenant to two hundred and forty six dillars, It is therefore considered by
the court that the plaintiff recover of the defendant the damages aforesaid
by the jury aforesaid assessed together with his cost byy him about his suit
in this behalf expended and the defendant in mercy etc.

Homer Rainey   )
vs.   )   Appeal
John Graves   )
        By consent of parties this cause is continued until the next term of court

Henry L. Douglass)
vs.   )   Debt
Richard A. Echols)
        This day came the parties aforesaid by their attorneys and thereupon
came a jury of good and lawful men, to wit, Alexander Greer, Axum Holland,
Lewis Griffin, Henry H. Horn, Collier A. Steed, Allen Trousdale, John McClelland
George Shankle Thomas Harrington, Richard Golden, Warham Easley andWilliam
Harris who being elected tried and sworn well and truly to try t e issue joined,
returned to consider of their verdict and returned again into court and not
being able to agree in their verdict by consent of parties and with the assent
of the court they are discharged from rendering their verdict herein until to-
morrow.
        Ordered that the sheriff summons the following persons to serve as jurors
at the next term of the circuit court, to wit, John Thomas Stephen Lacy, John
Mure Wm. Wilburn Jarret M. Jelks, Jesse . Kirk, Robert Lowery, Sugar McLemore
John H. Hyde, Robert H. Burks Jas McDaniels, Mark Matthias Deberry, John T.
Porter, George Hicks, Pitts Chandler Duncan McIver, Daniel Mading, George Todd
James Vaulx, A Willis, Thomas Lofton, Wm. C. Love Nathaniel Henderson John W.
Johnson and John McKennon and that he summon the following persons to serve
as jurors at the next county court.
Samuel H. Shannon, Will Espey, Robertson, Powell Harrison William Cartwright,
Lyons, Henry N. Coulter, James McCleary, Francis Taylor, John Hardgraves, John
Weir, Jas, Carithers, Hugh Lacy William Ruleman, William Doak Robert Glanton
Moses Oldham, Morris Hollum, Isiah Thompson Dex Wynne, William A. Edwards
Richard Sanders---- Herren Sam'l Anderson Thomas James and Sam'l Dickens.

        I Thomas Shannon sheriff and collector of the publick taxes for the county
of Madison do hereby report to court the following tracts of land as havingbeen

P495 given in for the taxes for the year 1824 that the taxes thereon remain due and unpaid and that the respective owners or claimants thereof have no goods or chattels within my county on which I can distrain for said taxes, to wit.

	Owners Name	NO. A.	En.	D.	R.	Sec.	WC.	Tax.	P. fee	Sh. fee	Clerkk
	John Brown, heirs	640	520	10	3.4	7.8		2.40	1.50	1.00	1.40
	Bowers and Watson	640	739	10	1	7		2.40	1.50	1.00	1.40
	Same	640	747	9	2	9		2.40	1.50	1.00	1.40
	Barncastle, Richard	182	969	10	1	9		16½	1.50	1.00	1.40
	Brown Nathaniel	274	1073	9	1	6		1.02½	1.50	1.00	1.40
	Cock, William Heirs of	640	68	9	2	7	SD	2.40	1.50	100	1.40
	Carpenter, Benjamin	75	158	10	1	10	Ld	.28	1.50	1.00	1.40
P496	Cock William Heirs of	640	--	9	2	7	LD	2.40	1.50	1.00	1.40
	Donel Andrew	640	958	10	3	8		2.40	1.50	1.00	1.40
	Same	640	--	10	-	-		2.40	1.50	1.00	1.40
	Dougherty George	230	306	10	1	9	LD	86	1.50	1.00	1.40
	Same	290	576	10	1	9	do	1.08¾	1.50	1.00	1.40
	Dun, John	1000	1138	10	2	7.8	SGD	3.75	1.50	1.00	1.40
	Donelson, Robert	1.33½	--	10	2	10		.50	1.50	1.00	1.40
	Edmondson Robt.Hs.of	640	--	9	2	8		2.40	1.50	1.00	1.40
	Same	169¾	--	9	1	11		63½	1.50	1.00	1.40
	Everett Matthew	640	--	9	2	9		2.40	1.50	1.00	1.40
	Ann Epps	40		~~110~~	1	9		15	1.50	1.00	1.40
	Freeman James	228	--	9	1	10		.85½	1.50	1.00	1.40
	Freeman & Bryan	228	412	10	3	6		.85½	1.50	1.00	1.40
	Harrington, Fairfax	640	1063	10	2	10.11		2.40	1.50	1.00	1.40
	Harden, William	172	---	10	1	9		.64½	1.50	1.00	1.40
	Huling F. W.	640		10	3	11		2.40	1.50	1.00	1.40
	Hyde Natwood	365		9	2	8		1.36¾	1.50	1.00	1.40
	Irwin Robert	2000	--	10	3	10		7.50	1.50	1.00	1.40
	Jones Andes	1000	--	-	-	-	CCreek	3.75	1.50	1.00	1.40
	Lock, Moses	1666	364	9	1	10		6.22½	1.50	1.00	1.40
	Mulherron James& Overton	784	621	10	3	7		2.89	1.50	1.00	1.40
	Mahan, Archibold	234	-	-	-	-	-	.87½	1.50	1.00	1.40
	McCaul, Akexander	320	-	9	2	8		1.20	1.50	1.00	1.40
	Same	200	-	9	1	-		.75	1.50	1.00	1.40
	Donley John	274	-	9	2	8		1.02½	1.50	1.00	1.40
	Nelson Robert	500		10	3	7		1.87½	1.50	1.00	1.40
	Robert Nelson	500	-	10	3	9		1.87½	1.50	1.00	1.40
	Norwood William	117	-	9	2	10		.42¾	1.50	1.00	1.40
	Nicholson O.P	400	561	-	3	10		1.50	1.50	1.00	1.40
	John Overton John	46½	798	10	1	10		.17¾	1.50	1.00	1.40
	Poston John H&E Nelson	267	73	10	45	10		1.00	1.50	1.00	1.40
	Folk Thomas	500	183	10	2	8		1.87½	1.50	1.00	1.40
	Swindle Isaac& A Stubblefield	72	914	10	4	4		27	1.50	1.00	1.40
	Skinner, Evans	193¾	337	9	1	9		72	1.50	1.00	1.40
	Smith Richard	1000	284	10	2	7		3.75	1.50	1.00	1.40
	Shuth Asa	186	575	-	2	10		.67½	1.50	1.00	1.40
P497	Sillivan, Lei 64 part of	480	232	10	2	9		1.80	1.50	1.00	1.40

P497 Owners Name	No. A.	En.	D.	R.	S.	Taxes	Tr. fee	Shf. fee	Clk.
Silliman Thos N.	100	--	10	2	10	.37½	1.50	1.00	1.40
Trotter, Richard	159	910	10	3	8	.57½	1.50	1.00	1.40
Tharp Wm. A	640	170	2	2	7.8	2.40	1.50	1.00	1.40
Weakly Robert	1875	--	10	4.5	10	703	1.50	1.00	1.40
Watson &Nergan	640	349	10	2.3	7	2.40	1.50	1.00	1.40
Same	640	749	10	2	7	2.40	1.50	1.00	1.40
Watson Richard C.	640	21	10	2	9	2.40	1.50	1.00	1.40
Webb Sandy Heirs of	640	--	-	2	7.8	2.40	1.50	1.00	1.40
Zenis Alben	454½	-	10	3	9	1.70	1.50	1.00	1.40
Bond John	640	-	10	-	-	2.40	1.50	1.00	1.40
Same part of 1000 entered in name									
G. D. Connolly	760	-	-	-	-	2.40	1.50	1.00	1.40

Thereupon it is considered by the court that Judgment be and the same is entered against the aforesaid tracts of land in the name of the State for the sum annexed to each being the amount of taxes, cost and charges due severally thereon for the year eighteen hundred and twenty four and it is ordered by the court that the said several tracts of land or so much thereof as shall be sufficient of each of them to satisfy the taxes, cost and charges annexed to them severally be sold as the law directs.

Ordered that the sheriff be released from the amount of taxes on lands reported for single taxes for the year 1823 as per list filed and also for double taxes reported for the same year as per list filed as not being able to sell the same for the taxes annexed them and that he be allowed a credit for the same in the settlement of his accounts with the state and county treasurer.

Court then adjourned until tomorrow morning nine o'clock.

William Draper   JP.
Wm. Spencer   JP.
John H. Hyde   JP.

P498   Tuesday February 15th. 1825

Court met according to adjournment, Present the worshipful John Hide, William Spencer, William Draper, and Lemuel S. Hunter, gentlemen justices.

Henry L. Douglas)
vs.   )   Debt
Richard A. Echols)

This day came the parties aforesaid by their attorneys and thereupon came the jury empanelled, tried and sworn in this cause on yesterday and declared they could not agree in their verdict and by consent of parties and with the assent of the court one of the jurors in this case is withdraws and the rest of the jurors are discharged from rendering their verdict and the cause continued until the next term of court.

A transfer of a plott and certificate from Herndon Haralson to James Vaulx was this day produced in open court and the execution of the same duly acknowledged by the said Herndon Haralson to be his act and ordered to be his act and ordered to be certified.

Joseph Herndon, Executor etc.)
vs.   )   Case
Benjamin Gholson   )

This day came the parties by their attorneys and thereupon came a jury of good and lawful men, to wit; Alexander Greer, Exum Holland, Lewis Griffin, Henry H. Horn Coller A. Steed, John McClelland, Allen Trousdale, George Shandle, Thomas Harington, Richard Golding, Warham Easley and William Harris, who being

P498 elected, tried and sworn will and truly to try the issue joined between the parties upon their oaths do say they find the issues in favor of the plaintiff and theyassess the plaintiff damages for the non performance of deft's promises in Plff's. declaration mentioned to one hundred fifty dollars and fifty cents. It is therefore considered by the court that the plff. recover of the defendant the damages by the jury in form aforesaid assessed together with his costs in this behalf expended and etc.

P499   Tuesday February 15th. 1825

Daniel Johnson, Administrator etc.)
vs.   )   Appeal
Eli Cochrane and John Arnold   )
        This day came the parties by their attorneys and thereupon the death of
Eli Cochrane one of the defts being suggested on the roll. It is ordered that the suit abote as to him whereupon the other defendant John Arnold by his attorne confessed judgment for twenty seven dollars fifty two cents with interest from the 9th. day of July 1824.
        It is therefore considered by the court that the plaintiff recover of the defendant together with William Arnold his security the debt and interest aforesaid confessed together with his cost in this behalf expended. Plaintiff by his attorney stays execution six months.

Daniel Johnson, Administrator,)
vs.   )   Appeal
John Arnold & Eli Cochran   )
        This day came the parties by their attorneys and thereupon the death of Eli Cochrane one of the defts being suggested on the roll. It is ordered that the suit abate as to him, whereupon the oather deft. John Arnold by his attorney confesses judgment for twenty six dollars and twenty six cents with interest from the 9th. day of July 1824. It is therefore considered by the court that the plaintiff recover of the defendant together with William Arnold his security the debt and interest aforesaid confessed together with his cost in this behalf expended and plff. by his attorney stays execution for six months.

Samuel A. Warner   )
vs.   )   Certiorari
Nelson I Hess   )
        This day came the parties aforesaid by their attorneys and thereupon came the jury of good and lawful men, to wit, Alexander Greer, Axum Holland, Lewis Griffin, Henry H. Horn Collier A. Steed, John McClelland George Shankle, Thomas Harrington, Richard Golden, Allen Trousdale, Warham Easley and William Harris who being elected, tried and sworn will and truly to try the matters of dispute between the parties upon their oaths do say they find for the plaintiff and assess the plaintiff damages to forty dollars. It is therefore considered by the court that the plaintiff recover of the said defendant, Hess and I. T. Pullen, R. H Dyer and William Harris his securities the damages aforesaid form aforesaid by the jury aforesaid assessed together with his cost by him about his suit in this behalf expended and the defendant in mercy etc. and execution staid 2 months.
        An indenture of bargain and sale from the Trustees of the University of North Carolina to Joshua Gazort for one hundred seventy four acres of land was this day produced in open court and the execution there of acknowledged by Samuel Dickens their attorney in fact to be his act and deed and ordered to be certified.

P500 B. G. Stewart and c Com r etc.)
vs.) Debt.
Joseph F. Cloud, Anthony F.)
Gray and William E. Butler)

This day came the parties aforesaid by their attorneys and thereupon the matters of law arising upon the plaintiff's demurer to the defendants plea here in came on to be argued and because it seems to the court that the law is for the plaintiff, it is considered that said demurrer be sustained and because the defendant say nothing further in bar of the plaintiff's action herein it is considered by the court that the plaintiffs recover of the defendant the sum of three hundred and seventy seven dollars the debt in the declaration mentioned also the sum of twenty five dollars and fifty cents the amount of interest accrueing on the same with their cost by them about their suit in this behalf expended and the defendant in mercy etc.

Board of Commissoners of the Town of Jackson)
vs.) Certiorari
William Braden and others)

P501 This day came the defendants aforesaid by their attorneys and the plaintiffs though solemnly called came not, but made default. It is therefore considered by the court that the defendants go thereof hence without day and recover of the plaintiff their cost by them about their defence in this behalf expended and the plaintiff for their false clamor may be in mercy etc.

Edmond Jones)
vs) Covenant
John Barnhart)

This cause is continued by consent of parties until the next term and leave is given to the parties to take depositions generally by giving 20 days notice of the time land place of taking the same.

William Curtis)
vs.) Case
James Foster)

Wiley B. Dyer)
vs.) Appeal
John Weir)

John D. Love)
vs.) Covenant
John Stobough & James McCutchen)

James T. Foster)
vs.) Appeal
William Higgins & A. D. Lawhorn)

By consent of parties the forgiving causes are continued until the next term of court.

Anthony Epperson)
vs.) Case
Samuel Dickins)

On affidavit of the plff this cause is continued until next term of court for trial.

Tuesday February 15th. 1825

P502 Nathias Deberry   )
     vs.   )
     Spencer Grant James Trousdale &   )   Appeal
     Herndon Haralson   )

       This day came the parties aforesaid by their attorneys and the case agreed
filed Marked "A" by consent of parties and with the assent of court this cause
is transferred to the circuit Court for (trial)

     Thomas Shannon   )
     vs.   )   Case
     John Rutherford   )

       By consent of parties and with the assent of the court this cause is con-
tinued until next term of court.
       Upon satisfactory proff made in open court that Joel H. D er is a man of
good moral character and more than twenty one years of age It is ordered that
the same be entered of record and certified accordingly he having resided in
the county of Madison for several years etc.
       An indenture of bargain and sale from Isaac Rutland to Elijah Jones for
fifty acres of land was this day produced in open court and the exechtion of the
same duly proven by the oath of H. C. Wiatt and Adam Brown and ordered to be certified for registration.
       An indenture of bargain and sale from Isaac Rutland th Adam Brown for two
hundred and thirty two and ¾ acres of land was this day produced in open court
and proven by the oath of H. C. Wiott and Elijah Jones and ordered to be certified for registration.

     Harrison Powell)
     vs.   )   Case
     Miles Fuller   )

       The plaintiff has leave to take deposition by giving the defendant 20 days
notice out of the state and ten days notice in the state.
       Asa B Midyett comes into court and records his stock mark as follows,
to wit, a crop in the right and acrop and spli in the left ear.

P503   Tuesday February 15th. 1825

     William Finney   )
     vs.   )   Debt
     Gibson and Arnold)

       This day came the parties by their attorneys and thereupon by consent it
is agreed that as regards Arnold one of the defts, this suit shall abote and
plaintiff has leave to amend and that the pleadings be made up and the case
tried at next term.

     Edward G. Clouston   )
     vs.   )   Motion
     John Shannon Constable &   )
     Thomas Shannon and William Arnold his securities.)

       This day came the defendant John D. Shannon and prayed an appeal from a
judgment rendered herein on a former day of the present term which is granted
him and entered into bond in the puralty of one hundred and fifty dollars with
Benjamin Gholson and Thomas I. Smith his secruities conditioned for the prosecution of his appeal.

     George L Miles, Andrew Hines)
     vs.   )   Debt
     Doel Dyer   )

       This day came the defendant by his attorney and prayed an appeal from

P503 a judgment rendered herein on a former day of the present term and intered into
bond in the penalty and with the condition prescribed by law and with Dhampness
Mading and Daniel Mading his securities for the prosecution of said appeal which
is granted him.

An transfer of a plot and certificate from Alexander B. Bradford and James
Carithers to Banks M Burrow, for forty acres of land was this day produced in
open court and the execution thereof acknowledged by the said Alexander B. Bradford and James Carithers and ordered to be certified accordingly.

A bill of sale from William Polk to Alexander Bostick was this day produced
in open court and the execution of the same duly proven by the oath of William
Stoddert and John T. Bryan to be the act and deed of the said William Pole and
ordered to be certified for registration .

Francis Smith vs.   )
William H. Doak and John T. Porter & Samuel H. Shannon) A motion for a judgment
his securities   ) for money collected.

This day came the parties aforesaid by their attorneys and thereupon the
matters of law arising from the plaintiffs motion herein came on and was argued
and the court being sufficiently advised thereon are ofopinion that the said
motion be overruled. It is therefore considered by the court thatthe defendants
go there of hence without day and recover of the plaintiff their cost by them
about their motion in this behalf expended and the plaintiff for his false clamor
in mercy etc.

Lancaster Glover)
vs.   )   On motion to set aside non suit in an appeal
Samuel Bruff   )

This day came the plaintiff by his attorney moved the court to set aside
the judgment by default taken in this case on a former day of the present term
which is accordingly done the deft agreeing to pay the cost of this term and the
cause is again set on the docket for atril. It is therefore considered by the
court that the plaintiff recover of the defendant the cost aforesaid by him
confessed and the plaintiff in mercy etc.

Court then adjourned until tomorrow morning ten o(clock.
                                        J B. Cross   JP
                                        M Midyett   JP
                                        John H Hyde   JP.

Wednesday morning 16th. February 1825
Court met according to adjournment, present theWorshipful J. H. Hyde, M.
Midyett and John B. Cross, gentlemen, justices.

P505   Wednesday February 16, 1825

Isaac Cury   )
vs.   )   Case
Benjamin Gholson)
This day came the defendant and prayed an appeal in the nature of a writ
of error from a judgment remdered herein on a former day of the present term to
the Circuit Court which is granted the defendant enterin into bond with John
Spencer and Thomas I. Smith his securities in the penalty of $400.00

)
Joseph Herndon, Esr etc.)   Case
vs.
BenjamThiÉhdayoname the defendant and prayed an appeal to the circuit court

P505
Cont.
from a judgment rendered herein on a former day of the present term, entered into bond with Duncan McIver and Thomas Shannon his securities in the penalty of three hundred twenty dollars which is granted him.

Henry Butler)
vs.) Debt
Benjamin Gholson)

    This day came the defendant and prayed an appeal from a judgment rendered herein on a former day of the present term to the next circuit Court entered into bond with Duncan McIver and Thomas Shannon his securities in the penalty of four hundred and twenty four dollars which granted.

Robert Murray)
vs.) Debt
Wilson Hutchison)

    This day came the defendant and prayed an appeal from a judgment rendered herein on a former day of the present term to the Circuit Court entered into bond with Thomas Shannon and Thomas I. Smith in the penalty of four hundred dollars which is granted.

Ruben McVey)
vs.) Certiorari
Cathrelee Cochrane)

    On motion of the plaintiff by his attorney leave is given to amend his warrent which id done accordingly to which opinion of the court in granting the amendment the defendant excepts and files his bill of exceptions marked (A) signed and sealed by the court

P506
Wednesday February 16th. 1825

George L Miles and Andrew Hines)
vs.) Debt
John B. Cross)

    This day came the defendant and prayed an appeal from a judgment rendered herein on a former day of the present term to the next term of the Circuit Court and offered alfred murray, R. H Wynne, and M McLaurine as his securities in the penalty of two hundred and seven dollars which securities were recived and the appeal granted.

    A bill of sale from Thomas I Smith, Deputy Sheriff of Thomas Shannon to B. G. Stewart for a negro boy named Casey was this day produced in open court and acknowledged by the said Thomas I Smith to be his act and ordered to be certified for registration.

Francis Smith)
vs.) On motion
William H. Doak & John T. Porter &)
Samuel H. Shannon, his securities)

    This day came the plaintiff by his attorney and tender his bill of exception to the court in overruling his mition on yesterday which by consent of the parties and of the court is received and signed and made a part of the record in as good and ample a manner as if tendered at the right time.

    Ordered that Joseph F. Cloud have a license to keep an ordinary in the town of Jackson on his giving bond and security as required by law which is entered into accordingly with Wilson Hutchison and Robert W. Wynne his securities
Court then adjourned until court in course

                    J. B. Cross JP.
                    B. G. Stewart JP.
                    John H. Hyde JP.

P507

Monday May Term 1825

At a court of pleas and quarter sessions began and holden in and for the county of Madison at the court house of said County in the town of Jackson before Herndon Haralson, Duncan McIver, James McCutchen, William Willbourn, James McDonald, Robert Lowry, William Draper, Mark Christian, Lemuel S. Hunter and Jarrett M. Delke, Esquires Justices of the Peace of said county and other their fellow justices of the peace of said county on the first Monday in May, being the second day of said Month in the year of our Lord one thousand eight hundred twenty five. Present the said justices of the peace, presiding Roderick McIver Clerk of said Court and Thomas Shannon Sheriff.

Ordered that Saturday next be set apart for thansacting county business and that the dlerk post the same at the court house door.

Ordered that William Birdson Micajah Midyett and Mathew Deberry be appointed to let the building of a bridge across the North fork of Forked Deer river where the main road leading from this places to Gibson Port crosses the same and that the sum of two hundred dollars be appropriated towards the complition of the bridge to be paid out of any monies in the county treasury not otherwise appropriated so soon as the same is completed-- provided the same cannot be done for up.

Ordered that William Willburn and Wm. Draper, Esqs settle with the Executor of the estate of William I. Hale, deceased and make report immediately which was done accordingly and ordered to be recorded.

8 Asa Weaver proves the killing of wolf in this county over four months old.

On motion and petition filed ordered that William L Flowers, Ruben P. T. Stone, William Right James Newsom and John Right be a jury to mark and lay off a road from Newsom and Knockly Mill to intersect the Hardeman County Road where the present road intersects and make report to the next term.

P507

Monday the Second of May 1825

Ordered that John Rayder be overseer of the road from town to the creek immediately East of Alexander Greer's and Work the hands heretofore allowed James Vauls.

On motion and petition of John T. Bryan, it is ordered that he be allowed permission to build a mill on big Black Creek on his own land in Range three and secion seven of the 10th. Surveyors district.

The petition of Thomas Smith and James Childres to build a mill on the middle fork of Forked Deer river on the lands of said Thomas Smith is this day granted them.

Ordered that John McClish be overseer of the road leading from Jackson to Haywood from Johnson's Creek to Range 2 and work all the hands living on Cedar Dreek agreeably to the division made by Esquire Sanders and Esquire Jarrett and that John Wharton be overseer of Range two to the county line and work all the hands on Cypress Creek indlucing Glover and Graves and all other hands equidistant from any other road.

Ordered that all the hands living equidistant from that part of the road on which Robert Clanton is overseer be attached to his list of hands.

Ordered that Ann Epps be permitted to turn the road around the East Corner of her farm instead of running as layed off by the jury of view.

Report of the Jury of view viewing a road from Shannon's landing to the county lind toward the mouth of Clever creek is received by the court and ordered tha̶t̶ ̶W̶i̶l̶l̶b̶u̶r̶n̶ ̶S̶h̶i̶n̶a̶ ̶b̶e̶ ̶o̶v̶e̶r̶s̶e̶e̶n̶d̶ ̶f̶r̶o̶m̶ ̶J̶o̶h̶n̶s̶o̶n̶ ̶C̶r̶e̶e̶k̶ ̶t̶o̶ ̶t̶h̶e̶n̶c̶e̶ ̶C̶a̶p̶t̶ ̶m̶i̶l̶l̶ ̶D̶r̶a̶p̶e̶d̶ Joshua Weaver overseer from thence to where the same entersects the Polk Ferry road and each to work all the hands living equidistant from any other road.

Monday May 21.1825

PAGE 243 MISSING

P510
Cont.
A deed from William Shepheard to John Reyder for 39 acres of land was this day produced in open court and acknowledged by the said William Shepherd to be his act and deed and ordered to be registered.

A deed of bargain and sale from Vincent Haralson to William Shepherd for 39 acres of land was this day produced in open court and acknowledged by the said Vincent Haralson to be his act and deed and ordered to be registered.

P511
A deed of bargain and sale from James Coldwell to Gabriel Anderson for 69 acres of land was this day produced in open court and the execution of same acknowledged by the said James Coldwell to be his act and deed and ordered to be registered.

A deed of bargain and sale from Vincent Haralson to Gabriel Anderson was this day produced in open court and acknowledged by the said Vincent Haralson to be his act and deed.

A deed of Bargain and sale from William Spencer to William Harris for 60 acres of land was this day produced in open court and acknowledged by the said William Spencer to be his act and deed and ordered to be registered.

P512   MONDAY MAY 2nd. 1825

Alexander Patton   )
vs.   )   On a Ca Sa
Clark Spencer   )

The sheriff this day produced in open court the body of the said defendant in pursuance of the act of assembly entitled an act for relief of insolvent debtors with respect to the imprisonment of their persons passed Oct. the 20th. 1824 and thereupon on motion and petition of the defendant and it appearing to the court that a writ of capias ad satis facumdun had issued to take the body of deft. from the circuit court of Madison County at the instance of the plaintiff which writ had been executed on the body of defendant who had given bond with sufficient security for his appearance at the present term of this court and the defendant having taken the oath of insolvency agreeably to law it is therefore ordered and adjudged by the court that said defendant be herein discharged from further imprisonment in this case.

The last will and testament of Thomas Byrn was this day produced in open court and proven by the oath of Shadrock Moseley and Benjamin Draper subscribing witnesses thereto and ordered to be recorded.

Homer Rainey   )
vs.   )   Appeal
John Graves   )

This day came the parties aforesaid by their attorneys and the defendant says he cannot gainsay the plff's action thereof against him for the sum of forty six dollars and forty five cents. It is therefore considered by the court that the plaintiff recover of the defendant and on motion of James Cockrill his security in the appeal the said forty six dollars and forty five cents together with his cost by him about his suit in this behalf expended and the defendant in mercy etc. and the plaintiff agrees to stay execution on this judgment until 25th. day of December next.

Court then adjourned until tomorrow morning nine o'clock.

                              H. Haralson   JP.
                              M. Christian   JP.
                              Sam Taylor   JP.

Tuesday May 3rd. 1825
Court met according to adjournment, present, the Worshipful Herndon Haralson John H. Hyde, Mark Christian and Samuel Taylor, gentlemen, justices, Roderick McIver Clerk and Thomas Shannon, Sheriff.

P51?   The sheriff this day returned the writ of veniri directed from the last
Cont.term of this court who made the following indosement thereon, to wit, I have
summoned all the persons named in the within veniri except William A. Edwards,
John Herrin, Richard Sanders, and James A. Lyons, who were not found all of
which are freeholders or house holders of my county and over twenty one years
of age signed Thomas Shannon Shff. In pursuance of which the following
persons were then attending to wit, John Hardgraves, William Cartwright, Moses
Oldham, Thomas James, William Espey, William Ruleman, Charles Robertson, William
Doak, Aseriah Thompson, James Carithers, Deveraux Wynne, Harrison Powell, and
Samuel H. Shannon and thereupon the above named persons were then drawn, sworn
and charged as a Grand Jury with John Hardgraves their foreman to inquire into
and for the bod of the county of Madison who thereupon retired to consider of
presentments under the case of Elijah Jones and officer sworn to attend on them.

$14.   Tuesday 3rd. day of May 1825
      Ordered that Francis Taylor, Moses Oldham, Henry N Coulter and James
Caruthers be fined each the sum of #2.50 each as delinquent jurors at the present term until they come in and show sufficient cause by the next term of court
for the remittance of said fine.

William M. Wilson   )
vs.   )   Case
Robert H. Dyer   )
      This day came the parties aforesaid by their attorneys and thereupon came
a jury of good and lawful men, to wit, John Hardgraves, Samuel H. Shannon,
William Espey, Gavriel Anderson, Deveraux Wunne, William Doak, Charles Robert,
Thomas James, Harrison Powell, William Ruleman, William Cartwright, James
Carithers, who being elected, tried and sworn will and truly to try the issue
joined upon their oaths do say they find the sissue in favor of the plaintiff
and assess the plaintiff damages by reason thereof to two hundred and eighty
dollars. It is therefore considered by the court that the plaintiff recover of
the defendant the damages aforesaid by the jury aforesaid assessed together
with his cost by him about his suit in this behalf expended and the plaintiff
agrees to stay execution in this case three months.

Henry Ll Douglass   )
vs.   )   Debt
Richard A. Echols.   )

Samuel Crocket   )
vs.   )   Case
Caldwell G. Wilson   )
      By consent of parties the foregiving causes are continued until the next
term.
P515   Tuesday 3rd. day of May 1825

Edmond Jones)
vs.   )   Dovenant
John Barnhart)
      The parties havelief to take deposetions generally by giving twenty days
notice in the state and forty days out of the state of the time and place of
taking the same to be read in evidence herein at the next term of court until
which term this cause is continued.

William Curtice   )
vs.   )   nCase
James S. Foster   )
      This dause is continued until the next term of this court as of an affidavit
of the plaintiff.

P515   Anthony Epperson)
Cont.   vs.   )   Case
        Samuel Dickens   )

        This cause is continued, as of an affidavit of the defendant until the
next term of court.

        Enoch Murphy   )
        vs.   )   Debt
        William R. Hess and R. H. Dyer)

        This day came the parties aforesaid by their attorneys and thereupon
came a jury of good and lawful men, to wit, Gabriel Anderson Thomas Wynne,
Moses Sterns, William Johns, Miles Fuller, Robert Webb Hendley Webb, James
McCarroll, Turner Tate Gutheridge Anderson, James H. Wilson, and Burwell Butler, who being elected tried and sworn, will and truly to try the issue joined
upon their oaths do say that they find the issues in favor of the plaintiff
and the defendant has not paid the debt of one hundred dollars as in replying
to defendants plea in that behalf hath alleged and they assess the plaintiff
damages by reason of the detention thereof to four dollars. It is therefore
considered by the court that the plaintiff recover of the deft the degt and
damage in form aforesaid by the jury assessed and also his cost in this behalf
expended etc.

P516   Tuesday May 3rd. 1825
        William Pillow)
        vs.   )   Debt
        James Brown   )

        This day came the parties aforesaid by their attorneys and thereupon came
a jury of good and lawful men, to wit, Gabriel Anderson, Thomas Wynne, Moses
Sterns, William Johns, Miles Fuller, Robart Webb, Hendley Webb, James McCarroll
Turner Tate, Gutheridge Andres, James H. Wilson and Burwell Butler, who being
elected, tried and sworn will and truly to try the issues joined upon their
oaths do say they find the issues in favor of the plaintiff and that the defendant hath not paid the remaining debt of four hundred and fifty dollars as the
plaintiff in replying to defendants plea in that behalf hath alleged and assess
the plaintiff damages be reason of the detention thereof to eight dollars.
It is therefore considered b the court that the plaintiff recover of the defendant the balance of debt aforesaid together with his damages aforesaid in
form aforesaid by the jury assessed and also his cost by him about his suit
in this behalf expended and the defendant in mercy etc.

        Thomas A. Thompson   )
        vs.   )   Debt.
        Thomas Byrn and Isaack Swan   )

        This day came the plaintiff by his attorneys and Thomas Byrn one of the
defendants came not and the said plaintiff suggests to the court that since
the last term of this court the said defendant departed this life and the same
is not denied and thereupon day is given by the court here until the next term
for the proper parties to appear according to the act of assembly in such case
made and provided.

        Samuel S. Hunter   )
        vs.   )   Debt
        Thomas Harrington and William Wilson)

        This day came the parties aforesaid by their attorneys and thereupon came
a jury of good and lawful men, to wit, Gabriel Anderson, Thomas Wynne, Moses
Starns, William Johns, Miles Fuller, Robert Webb, Hendley Webb, James McCarroll

P516
Cont. Turner Tate, Guthridge Andrews, Jas. H. Wilson and Burwell Butler who being elected, tried ans sworn will and truly to try the issue joined find the issue in favor of the pltff. and that the defendant hath not paid the remaining debt of one hundred and seventeen dollars as the plaintiff in and seventeen dollars as the plaintiff in replying to defendants plea in that behalf hath alledged and assess the plaintiff damages by reason of the detention thereof to one dollar and eighty cents. It is therefore considered by the court that the plaintiff recover of the defendants this balance of debt aforesaid with the damages aforesaid by the jury aforesaid assessed together with his cost by him about his suit in this behalf expended and the defendant in mercy.

P517   Tuesday May 3rd. 1825

William E. Butler, Assignee etc.)
vs.   )   In debt
John and William Arnold   )
This day came the parties aforesaid by their attorneys and thereupon came a jury of good and lawful men, to wit, Gabriel Anderson, Thomas Wynne, Moses Sterns, William Johns, Miles Fuller, Robert Webb, Hendley, Webb, James McCarroll, Turner Tat4, Guthridge Andrews, James H. Wilson and Burrel Butler who being elected tried and sworn will and truly to try the issues joined upon their oath do say they find the issues in favor of the plaintiff and that the defendant hath not paid the debt of four hundred and twenty five dollars as the plaintiff in replying to the defendants plea in that behalf hath alledged and assess the plff. damages by reason of the detention thereof to six dollars and twenty five cents. It is therefore considered by the court that the plff. recover of said def't. the debt aforesaid with the damages aforesaid by the jury aforesaid assessed together with his cost by him about his suit in this behalf expended and the deft. in mercy etc.

William E. Butler, Assign etc.   )
vs.   )   In debt
James V. Theobold and Robt. H Wynne)
This day came the parties aforesaid by their attorneys and thereupon came a jury of good and lawful men, to wit, Gabriel Anderson, Thomas Wynne, Moses Starns, William Johns, Miles Fuller, Robert Webb, Hendly Webb, James McCarroll Turner Tate, Gathridge Andrews, James H. Wilson, and Burnwell Butler, who being elected tried and sworn will and truly to try the issue joined upon their oaths do say they find the issue in favor of the plff. and that the defendant hath not paid the debt of one hundred and thirty four dollars as the plaintiff in replying to defendants plea in that behalf hath alleged and assess the plaintiff damages by reason of the dentention thereof to three dollars and sixteen cents. It is therefore considered by the court that the plaintiff recover of the defendant the debt and damages aforesaid by the jury aforesaid assessed together with his cost by him about his suit in this behalf expended and the defendant in mercy etc.

William Hopper   )
vs.   )   Debt
Benjamin Gholson)
This day came the parties aforesaid by their attorneys and thereupon came a jury of good and lawful men, to wit, Gabriel Anderson, Thomas Wynne, Moses
P518 Starns, William Johns, Miles Fuller, Robert Webb, Hendley Webb James McCarroll, Turner Tate Guthridge Andrews, James H. Wilson and Burwell, Butler, who being elected, tried and sworn, will and truly to try the issue joined upon their oaths do say they find the issue in favor of the plaintiff and that the defendant

P518 hath not paid the debt of one hundred and eighteen dollars as the plaintiff in
Cont. replying to deft's plea in that behalf hath alleged and assess the plaintiff
damages by reason of the detention thereof to two dollars. It is therefore
considered by the court that the plaintiff recover of the defendant the debt
and damages aforesaid in form aforesaid by the Jury assessed together with his
cost by him about his suit in this behalf expended and the defendant in mercy etc.

Edwards Bradbury)
vs.   )   Appeal
William McCaslin)

By consent of the parties by their attorneys all matters in difference be
tween them in this suit is referred to the final determination of Adam Brown,
Thomas Gordon, Greenup White, and Francis Taylor whose award thereupon when made
and returned to the next term of this court is to be made the judgment of the cour
and the same is ordered accordingly.

Ordered that John Barnhart and William Right be fined the sum of two dollars
each for non attendance as tallisman jurors having been summoned by the sheriff as
such.

A deed of bargain and sale from the board of commissioners for the town of
Jackson to William Espy was this day produced in open court and the execution of
the same acknowledged by Herndon Haralson as chairman of said board and ordered t
be registered.

A deed of bargain and sale from William Thetford to Samuel Dickens for
160 acres of land was this day produced in open court and proven by the oath of
Thomas James, The probate of the other witness having been heretofore taken and
ordered to be registered.

A deed of bargain and sale from David Jarrett and James Brown to William R.
Seat was this day produced in open court and acknowledged by the said David
Jarrett and James Brown to be their act and deed and ordered to be registered.

A transfer of a plot and certificate of Survey for 115 acres of land from
George W. Polland to Josh a Weaver was this day produced in open court and the
transfer thereon proven to be made by the said George W. Polland by the oaths of
Robert Clanton and Martin Houston and ordered to be certified accordingly.

A deed of trust from Absolem Maple to Robert Lake for was this day produced
in open court and the execution of the same proven by the oath of H. Strother and
W. M. Neill and ordered to be registered.

P519   Tuesday May 3rd. 1825
A deed of bargain and sale from Stephen Lypert to John Cartwright for three
and a quarter acres of ground in the town of Jackson was this day produced in
open court and the execution of the same proven by the oaths of Robert Hughes
and William Stoddert and ordered to be registered.

A deed of bargain and sale from John I. Smith and Bird B. Smith to James
Carithers for one hundred and forty acres of land was this day produced in open
court and proven by the oath of John F. Brown and filed for further probate.

Court then adjourned until tomorrow morning nine o'clock.
                                    H. Haralson   JP.
                                    Duncan McIver   JP.
                                    Sam Taylor   JP.

Wednesday morning 9o'clock.
Court met according to adjournment , present, the worshipful Herndon Harals
Duncan McIver, and Samuel Taylor, Gentlemen, Justices Roderick McIver Clerk
and Thomas Shannon Sheriff.

John Reid Esquire this day appeared in open court and took the several
oaths of qualification as practicing attorney in this court.

P519 Marked out--
Cont.Harris Bradford)
    vs.)   On motion
    John Murrey)

Henry G. Connolly &)
Wiley B. Dyer)
    vs.)   Appeal
    John Weir)

    This cause is continued as of an affidavit of deft's until next term of
court.

Anthony Epperson)
    vs.)   Case
Samuel Dickens)

    By consent of parties this cause is continued as of an affidavit of the
defendant until the next term of court.

John D. Love)
    vs.)   Covenant
John Stobough &)
James McCutchen)

    This day came the parties aforesaid by their attorneys and thereupon
came a jury of good and lawful men, to wit, Gabriel Anderson, Jordan G. Stokes
John C. Wilson, Jesse D. Russell, Samiel Bruff James D. Haynes, James H.
Wilson, Jason H. Wilson William Wilson, Miles Fuller, John Rutherford and
Benjamin Gholson who being elected tried and sworn will and truly to try the
issue joined upon their oaths do say they find the issue in favor of the plaintiff and assess the plaintiff damages by reason of the breach of covenant in
the declaration mentioned. One hundred and twenty four dollars and twenty cents
It is therefore considered by the court that the plaintiff recover of the defendant the damages aforesaid by the jury aforesaid assessed together with his
cost by him about his suit in this behalf expended and the defendant in mercy
etc.

Ruben McVey)
    vs.)   Certiorari
Cathaline Cochrane)

Samuel Crocket)
    vs.)   Case
Caldwell G. Wilson)

William Finney)
    vs.)   Debt
Gibson & Arnold)

    The forgiving cause an continued by consent of parties until next termf
of court.

P521   Wednesday 4th. May 1825

James S. Foster)
    vs.)   Appeal
William Higgins)
A. D. Lawhorn)

    This cause is continued until the next term of court as of an affidavit of
the defendants.

P521 Roderick McIver)
Cont.vs.)   I. T.
Amos Warner)

     By consent of parties this cause is continued until the next term of court

Walter Tedford   )
vs.   )   Covenant In debt.
Greenup White & Bartholomew G. Stewart)

     This day came the parties aforesaid by their attorneys and thereupon came
a jury of good and lawful men, to wit, Gabriel Anderson, Jordon G. Stokes
John C. Wilson, Jesse D. Russell, Samuel Briefly James D. Haynes, James H.
Wilson, Jason H. Wilson William Wilson, Miles Fuller, John Rutherford and Benjamin Gholson who being elected tried and sworn well and truly to try the issues
joined upon their oaths do say they find the issues in favor of the plaintiffs
and assess the plaintiff damages by reason of the breech of covenant in the declaration mentioned to one hundred ninety three dollars. It is therefore considered by the court that the plaintiff recover of the defendant the damages
aforesaid by the jury in form aforesaid assessed together with his cost by
him about his suit in this behalf expended and the defendants in mercy etc.

George L. Miles & Andrew Hines)
vs.   )   In debt
Douglass Ferguson   )

     This day came the parties aforesaid by their attorneys and thereupon
came a jury of good and lawful men, to wit, Gabriel Anderson, Jordon G. Stokes,
John C. Wilson, Jesse D. Russell, Samuel Bruff, James D. Haynes, James H. Wilson
Jason H. Wilson William Wilson, Miles Fuller, John Rutherford and Benjamin
Gholson who being elected tried and sworn will and truly to try the issues
joined upon their oaths do say they find the issues in favor of the plaintiff
and that the defendant hath not paid the debt of one hundred and five dollars
and fifty nine cents as in pleading he hath alleged and assess the plaintiff
damages by reason thereof to thirty one dollars and fifty cents. It is there-
P522 fore considered by the court that the plaintiff recover of the defendant the
debt aforesaid with the damages aforesaid by the jury in form aforesaid assessed
together with the costs by them about their suit in this behalf expended and the
defendant in mercy etc.

John Stewart)
vs.   )   Certiorari
John Stockton)

     This day came the parties aforesaid by their attorneys and the defendant
says because he cannot gainsay the plaintiffs cause of action thereof against
him confess for the sum of fifty two dollars and fifty cents. It is therefore
considered by the court that the plaintiff recover of the defendant and his
securities in the certiorari John T. Porter and Daniel C. Stockton the said
sum of fifty two dollars and fifty cents together with their cost by them
about their suit in this behalf expended and the plaintiff agrees, to execution
in this case until the first day of January next.

Lancaster Glover)
vs.   0   Appeal
Samuel Bruff   )

P522   This clause is continued until the next term as of an affidavit of the plff. and
Cont. the parties have leave to take depositions generally by giving ten days notice
       in the county and twenty days notice out of the county.

       A deed of bargain and Sale from John Catron as administrator of John
       Childress,deceased, to Roderick McIver for sixty four acres of land was this
       day produced in open court and the execution of the same proven b, the oath
       John H. Hyde a subscribing witness thereto and continued for further probate.

       A deed of bargain and sale from John Brown Executor of Willie Cherry,
       deceased to Daniel Cherry for 200 acres of land was this day produced in open
       and the execution of the same proven by the oaths of John F. Brown and C. D.
       McLean and ordered to be certified.

       Court then adjourned until tomorrow morning nine o'clock.

                                          H. Haralson   JP.
                                          Lim'l S. Hunter JP.
                                          John H. Hyde   JP.

P523   Thursday Morning 5th. May 1825
       Court met according to adjournment. Present, the Worshipful Herndon
Haralson, Lemuel S. Hunter and John H Hyde, Esquires, Justices, sitting, Roderick
McIver, Clerk and Thomas Shannon, Sheriff.
       A receipt from John Hardgraves to Thomas Lofton for the payment of monies
due to him on a note executed by the said Lofton to John Hardgraves was this day
produced in open court and acknowledged by the said Hardgraves and ordered to be rese
corded.

Solomon Roswell   )
vs.   )   Debt
James Trousdale, Lucius Trousdale   )
David Jarrett and Madison McLaurine)
       This day came the parties aforesaid by their attorneys and the defendants
say they cannot gainsay the plaintiffs cause of action thereof against them for
the sum of eight hundred dollars debt and the further sum of sixteen dollarsinterest
as specified on bond. It is therefore considered by the court that the plaintiff
recover of the defendant the said sum of eight hundred and sixteen dollars, the debt
and interest aforesaid as specified on bond together with his cost by him about
his suit in this behalf expended and the defendant in mercy etc. and the plff. agrees
to stay executedn nine months

Solomon Roswell   )
vs.   )   Debt
James Trousdale, Lucius Trousdale   )
and Madison McLaurine   )
       This day came the parties aforesaid by their attorneys and the defendant
say they cannot gainsay the plaintiffs cause of action thereof against them for the
sum of one hundred and fifty seven dollars debt and the further sum of nine dollars
and forty two cents interest as specified in bond. It is therefore soncidered by the
court that the plaintiff recover of the defendants the said sum of one hundred and
sixty six dollars and forty two cents the debt and inter4st aforesaid as specified
together with his cost by him about his suit in this behalf expended and defts. in
mercy etc. and the plaintiff agrees to stay execution herein nine months.

P524

                       Thursday May5, 1825

Samuel Dickens
vs.
Benjamin Gholson   Case

P524   This day came the parties aforesaid by their attorneys and thereupon came
Cont. a jury of good and lawful men, to wit, William Spencer, John Ridens, James
Kiser, Samuel Bruff, Miles Fuller, Lewis Griffin John Bradbury, John McFarland, William Burrow, Benjamin Linn, James Newsom, and Robert H. Hibbett, who
being elected, tried and sworn will and truly to try the issue joined upon
their oaths do say they find the issue in favor of the plaintiff and the defendant did assume upon himself in manner and form as the plaintiff in declaring in that behalf hath alleged and assess the plaintiff damages by reason of
the non performance and of the assumsit in the declaration mentioned to four
hundred and forty one dollars and forty five cents,. It is therefore considered by the court that the plaintiff recover of the defendant the damages aforesaid by the jury aforesaid assessed together with his cost by him about his
suit in this behalf expended and the defendant in mercy etc.

Harrison Powell   )
vs.   )   Case
Miles Fuller   )

     This day came the parties aforesaid by their attorneys and thereon came a
jury of good and lawful men, to wit, William Spencer, Gabriel Anderson, John
Ridins, James Kiser, John Bradbury John McFarland, Benjamin Linn, James Newsom,
Samuel Bruff, Robert H. Hebbett, Valentine Sevier and John Harrison who being
elected tried and sworn will and truly to try the issues joined returned into
court and declared they could not agree in their verdict and by consent of
parties and with the assent of the court William Spencer one of the jurors in
this case is withdrawn and the rest of the jury from rendering their verdict
and the cause transferred to the next term of the circuit court.

P525   Thursday May 5, 1825

     A deed of bargain and sale from Joel Dyer to James Fentress, Benjamin
Reynolds William Martin and Robert Jetton commissioners appointed to fix on the
perminant seat of justice in Dyer county was this day produced in open court
and the execution of the same proven by the oath of Moses Woodfin a subscribing
witness and filed for further probate.
     A deed of bargain and sale from Obediah Dodson and Susanah Dodson his
wife to Thomas Stamps was this day produced in open court and acknowledged by
the said Obediah Dodson to be his act and deed for the purposes therein mentioned
and the said Susan Dodson being examined by the court seperately and apart from
his husband the said Obediah Dodson acknowledged that she freely and bolunteirly
and without the threat and pursuasion of her said husband relinguish her
right of down in and to the premises in the said deed mentioned which is ordered
to be certified.
     A deed of bargain and sale from Susannah Dodson to Caleb Baker was this da
produced in open court and acknowledged by the said Susannah Dodson to be her
act and deed for the purpose therein mentioned and ordered to be certified.
     Court then adjourneduntil tomorrow morning nine o'clock.

                              Lemuel S. Hunter   JP.
                              H. Haralson   JP.
                              James Trousdale   JP.

326   Friday 6th. May 1825
     Court met according to adjournment, Present, the worshipful Herndon Haral-
son, Lemuel S. Hunter and James Trousdale, Esquires, justices of the peace, Rode
erick McIver clerk and Thomas Shannon Shff.

P526   A deed of bargain and sale from James freeman to James Fentress, Benjamin
Reynolds Robert Jetton and William Martin as commissioners to fix on the permine
ant seat of justices in the county of shelby was this day produced in open court
and the execution of the same duly proven by the oaths of Jesse Brown and Joel
Bugg subscribing witnesses thereto and ordered to be certified for registration

William E. Butler, Assignee etc.   )
vs.   )   In debt
James F. Theobold & Rovert Wynne   )

       This day came the parties aforesaid by their attorneys and thereupon the
siad defendant prayed an appeal to the circuit court of this county from a
judgment rendered herein against them on a former day of this court and
offered Wilson Hitchison and Benjamin Gholson securities in the appeal which was
received and the bond executed by them and the appeal granted.

       Walter Thedford   )
       vs.   )   On dovenant
       Greenup Thite and Bartholomew G. Stewart)

       This day came the parties aforesaid by their attorneys and the defendant
prayed for and obtained an appeal from a judgment rendered therein against him
to the circuit court and entered into bond with Robert H. Wynne their security
in the appeal.

       William E. Butler, Assignee etc.   )
       vs   )   In debt
       John and William Arnold   )

       This day came the parties by their attorney and the defendant prayed an
appeal from a judgment rendered herein to the circuit court which granted
them having entered into bond with alfred Murray their security in the appeal

P527   Friday May 6, 1825

       A deed of bargain and sale from the commissioners for the town of Jackson
to Alexander B. Bradford for one half of lot No. 6 in the plan of said town was
this day produced in open court and the execution of the same acknowledged by
Stokely D Hays chairman of the board of dommissioners for the town of Jackson an
ordered to be certified for registration.

       A deed of bargain and sale from the board of commissioners for the town
of Jackson for lot No. 45 in the plan of said town to William L Flowers was
this day produced in open court and the execution of same acknowledged by
Stokely D. Hays chairman of said board and ordered to be certified for
registration.

Mathias Deberry   )
vs.   )   In debt
John Darnall and John Rayden   )
       This day came the parties aforesaid by their attorneys and thereupon came

e jury to wit, Samuel H. Swan, Samuel Bruff, Gabriel Anderson, Burd Hill,
John Rutherford, James Kiser, Valentine Sevier, Benjamin Gholson, Benjamin Linn
Daniel Horton, Ruben P. T. Stone and Jefferson Caruthers who being elected tried
and sworn, will and truly to try the issues joined retired to consider their
verdict and returned into court and declared they could not agree in their verdict and thereupon by consent of the parties

P527 and with the assent of the court a juror is withdrawn and the rest of the jury
Cont. from rendering their verdict in this case and the cause transferred to the circuit court for trial to be had thereon.

Robert Hughes, Esquire, was this day appointed a commissioner (in the place of R. McIver resigned) to settle with the clerk, sheriff and county trustee and with William Banes and James Henderson, heretofore appointed to make report to the next term of court, the said Hughes having entered into bond etc.

P528   Friday May 6, 1825

A deed of trust from Joseph Royal to Mathias Deberry was this day produced in open court and proven by the oath of Martin Cartmill and filed for further probate.

John Murrey   )
vs.   )   On motion
Thomas C. Porter)

This day came the plaintiff by his attorney and the defendant tho solemnly called came not, but made default and the plaintiff moved the court for a judgment against deft. or the security of the defendant and thereupon came a jury of good and lawful men, to wit, Mathias Deberry, John D. Shannon William Espy, Isaac Delaney, Jason R. Wilson James H. Wilson, Harrison Powell, Jesse S. Harris, Benjamin Carney, John Royder, Thomas L Wynne and George Todd who being elected tried and sworn the truth to speak upon their oaths do say that the plaintiff was the security of the defendant in a note dated 22nd. day of December 1819, executed by the said defendant and the plaintiff to Harris Bradford, as herein the said Harris Bradford recovered a Judgment against the plaintiff at the Jan. term of this court for the sum of one hundred and ninety four dollars debt and damages and the further sum of nine dollars and t4n cents cost of suit. It is therefore considered by the court that the plaintiff recover of the defendant the debt and damages aforesaid with the cost aforesaid by the jury aforesaid assessed and also his cost by him about his motion in this cost by him about his motion in this behalf expended and the defendant in mercy etc.

Francis Herrin,   )
vs.   )   T. V. A.
William Pace, Henning Pace   )
Alsey Pace and Malcolm Johnson   )

This day came the parties by their attorneys and it appearing to the satisfaction of the court that the said defendants recovered of the plaintiff the sum of fifty dollars seventy seven and half cents cost of suit at the December term of this court wherein by the agreement of the parties the plaintiff should have had judgment against the defendant for the said sum of fifty dollars and 77½ cents as cost of suit. It is therefore considered by the court that the plaintiff by and with the assent of the parties recover of the defendant the said sum of fifty dollars 77½ cents as cost of suit and that the same stand entired of record as if it had been entered at the proper term and also the cost of this motion and the defendants in mercy etc.

Robert H. Dyer)
vs.   )   Certiorari
John F. Brown)

This day came the parties aforesaid by their attorneys and thereupon the matters of law arising upon the plaintiffs notion came on and was argued and the court being sufficiently advised thereon, it is considered that the certiorari granted herein be dismissed and the supercedias discharged and it is further considered by the court that the plaintiff recover of the defendant and on motion of Jeremiah Brown his security for the certiorari the sum of forty five dollars and twenty six cents with twelve and one half per cent enterest thereon from

P529 the 28th. of March 1825 the date of rendering judgment by the justice below up to
the present time and also his cost by him about his suit in this behalf expended
and the defendants in mercy etc.

Samuel D. Wilson Trustee of Madison County) Motion for
vs.) a judgment
Thomas Shannon, Sheriff and Samuel Shannon Herndon Haralson) for the amt.
Samuel Taylor, Benjamin Gholson Guy Smith his securities in a bond) of taxes un-
for the collection of the County revenues for the year 1823) paid for the
) year 1823

This day came the parties aforesaid by their attorneys and the motion
aforesaid by their attorneys and the motion aforesaid having been continued by
consent of the parties from Tuesday last to this day now upon taking up the same
on motion and assent of the defendant it is ordered that said motion be contunued
until the next term. And on motion of the deft. Thomas Shannon, Sheriff by his
attorney it is ordered and allowed by the court that the said plaintiff be allowed
further time of six months from 1st. Jany. last to collect the county and state
tax on reported land for the year 1824 for the sum of ---- for the state and the
sum of ---- due the county on said report.

P530   Friday May 6th. 1825
Court then adjourned until tomorrow morning nine o'clock.

                                      J. B. Cross   JP.
                                      William Draper JP.
                                      Duncan McIver JP.

          Saturday Morning 7th. May 1825
     Court met according to adjournment, present, the Worshipful Duncan McIver
John B. Cross and William Draper, Esquires Justices of the Peace, Roderick
McIver Clerk and thomas Shannon Shff.
     A power of attorney from Samuel H. Swan to William L. Brown was this day
produced in open court and acknowledged by the said Samuel H. Swan to be his act
and deed and ordered to be certified.
     A deed of bargain and sale from Herndon Haralson to Jacob Pirkins for lott
No. 36 in plan of the town of Jackson was this day produced in open court and the
execution of the same acknowledged by the said Herndon Haralson to be his act
and deed and ordered to be certified for registration.
     A deed of bargain and sale from John Montgomery to James Montgomery for sixty
acres of land was this day produced in open court and the execution of the same
duly acknowledged by the said John Montgomery to be his act and deed and ordered
that it be certified for registration.
     Ordered that the jury heretofore appointed, to wit, William Swan, William
Draper, Henry House, William Harris, John Shaw, Rovert 'Neal and John Barnhart
them or any five of them be hereby appointed to mark and lay off a road of the
third class from the county line at or near Jearniah Brooks on Cain Creek to some
point of the Reynoldsbury road between Alexander Creers and Champness Mading so
as to avoid the necessity of building bridges and make report etc.

531   Saturday 7th. May 1825
     A deed of bargain and sale from John Catron to Roderick McIver for 64
acres of land was this day produced in open court and the execution of the same
proven by the oath of Alexander Greer the probate of the other being taken on a
former day of court and ordered to be certified for registration.

P531   Ordered that the hands of Mr Boles and West Fentress be work on the road
on which Lewis Coorpender is overseer of.

        A transfer of a plot and certificate of Survey from Burd Hill to Samuel B.
Martin for 50 acres was this day produced in open court and the execution of the
same acknowledged by the said Burd Hill and ordered to be certified.

Soloman Roswell   )
vs.   )   Original Attachment
Richard Sanders   )

        This day came the plaintiff by his attorney and the defendant being attached
by his property and solemnly called to come into court replevy his said property
and plead to issue came not but made default, It is therefore considered by the
court that the plaintiff recover of the defendant his damages in this case sustained by the breach of said covenant mentioned but because there damages are unknown
it is ordered that a jury come here at the next term of this court to inquire of
such damages etc. until which term this cause is continued.

        The resignation of Micajah Midyett as a Justice of the Peace was this day
handed in and received by the court.

P532 Benjamin Gholson   )
vs.   )   Attachment
Richard Sanders   )

        This day came the plaintiff by his attorney and the defendant being attached
by his property and solemnly called to come into court and replevy and plead to
issue, came not, but made default. It is therefore considered by the court that
the plaintiff recover of the defendant ninety six dollars and ninety five cents,
the debt in the declaration mentioned and also his cost by him about his suit in
this behalf expended and that an order of sale issue to the sheriff commanding
him to sell the property attached or so much thereof as shall be sufficient to
satisfy said debt and cost etc.

        The report of the Jury of view appointed on a former day of court to mark
and lay off a road on make such alteration in the road from near William Penn's
to Jackson was this day handed in and received by the court and it is ordered
that James Trousdale Esquire be overseer of the road in the place of William Penn
and Jonathan Walsh be continued overseer and have all the hands heretofore allotted
him and that Jesse M Hannah be appointed overseer in the room of Samuel D. Wilson
have all the hands of formerly alloted said Wilson.

        Ordered that the folloowing persons, to wit, Daniel Mading, Alfred Sharp
George Todd, Watt Epps, Peter McCollom, Western Harris, Samuel Dickens, John Mc-
Farland Richard Thompkins Joseph Dillard, Thomas Byod, Iredell Williams, William
Wilson, James Rohers, William Dean William Weaver, William Spencer Benjamin Booth
John Graves, Michael Clark, Newton Harris, John Hutchison, Thomas Vincent, Henry N
Coulter, Ebenezer Haltom, andDavid Sanders be and they are hereby appointed jurors
to the next term of the county court and that the writ of veniri facias issue to
he sheriff accordingly.

        Ordered that the following persons, to wit, David Jarrett, J. W. Fort, Thomas
Crutcher, David Sanders, Stephen Lacy, Green Hill and Theophilis Sanders to a jury
of view to mark and lay off a road from the North West corner of Col Williams
out fence to the mill of said Williamson and make report accordingly.

33

William Pillow
vs.

James Brown   )   Debt

P533
Cont.
    This day came the deft by his atty. and prayed an appeal to the next Circuit Court of Madison County and entered into bond with John R. Collier conditioned as the law directs which appeal is granted by the court.

    Ordered that the sheriff proved to sell the Old court house to the highest bidder on the Saturday next after the rise of the next circuit court on a credit of three months.

John B. Cross)
vs.)   On motion
John Darnall)

    On motion of the plaintiff by his attorney and it appearing to the satisfaction of the court that Thomas C. Haskins as plaintiff recovred a judgment against the said John Darnall and John B. Cross and Wilson Hutchison his securities in the certiorari dismissed at the last term of this court and it appearing to the satisfaction of the court that the said John B. Cross has paid the sum of thirty three dollars and 37½ cents as one of the securities of the said Darnall. It is therefore considered by the court that the said John B. Cross recover of the said John Darnall the said sum of $33 & 37½ cents and also his cost by him about his motion in this behalf expended and the defendant in mercy etc.

    On motion and petition filed ordered that Hugh R. Lacy be permitted to build a mill on his own land in Range 2 sect. eight and on Johnson Creek.

    Andrew Turner was this day duly and constitutionally elected constable in Captain Williamsons company who thereupon entered into bond with David Jarrett and John Minire his securities and took the several oaths prescribed by the constitution and laws of the state.

P534
                           Saturday 7th. May 1825

    Ordered that the different magistrates appointed to take on the list of taxables for the present year be required to select from their respective companies all the compotent jurors within the same and make report to the next term and on application that the clerk furnish each magistrate with a copy of the order and provide 2 boxes for holding the names.

    Ordered that Esquire Welks take the list of taxables in Capt Thomas I Smith company and make return of the same to the next term of court.

    Ordered that the following persons be appointed judges to superintend the election in their several precents, to wit, Jackson, Samuel Shannon, Wyatt Epps, Martin Cartmill, Frank Taylors, Thomas Gordon, James McCleary Andrew Stewart, Weaver's John Thomas William Willburn Theophilis Sanders, Poplar Corner, Guy Smith, John McClemon & Bignal Crook Mount Pinson, Thomas Reeves, McMcKinney and Nathaniel Henderson and that the sheriff furnishe them with a copy of this order.

    A deed of bargain and sale from Alexander B. Bradford to Henry Booth for one hundred and fifty acres was this day produced in open court and the execution of the same acknowledged by the said Alexander B. Bradford and ordered to be certified for registration.

    Court then adjourned until court in cause.
                      H. Harelson   JP.
                      J. B. Cross   JP.
                      James L McDonald JP.
                      John Thomas   JP.

P535
                        Monday August Term 1825
    At a court of Pleas and Quarter Sessions began and held in and for the County of Madison at the court house in said county in the town of Jackson before Bartholomew G. Stewart, James L. McDonald, John Thomas James Trousdale, Mark Christian, William Draper, John R. Hyde, Rovert Lowry, William Atchison, Green Hill and Lemuel S. Hunter, Esquires, justices of the peace of said county on the

P535 first Monday in August being the first day of said month in the year of our Lord
Cont. one thousand eight hundred and twenty five, present, the said justices of the
peace presiding, Roderick McIver clerk of said court and Thomas Shannon Sheriff.

Ordered that Monday next be set apart for transacting county business and
that the same be posted up at the court house door.

An indenture of bargain and sale from Benjamin Gholson to Mathias Deberry
for three hundred and ninety & ¾ acres of land was this day produced in open court
and the execution of the same proven by the oath of William Stoddert and Roderick
McIver subscribing witnesses and ordered to be registered.

Court then adjourned until nine o'clock tomorrow morning to meet at Doctor
Mallory Room over the store house of Horton & Elrod.

James Trousdale   JP.

M Christian   JP.

Robert Lowry   JP.

P536   Tuesday 2nd. day of August 1825
Court met according to adjournment, Present, the Worshipful James Trousdale
Mark Christian, William Atchison, Robert Lowry, Herndon Harelson, John H. Hyde,
and William Willburn Esquires, Justices of the Peace in and for the county
of Madison and State of Tennessee with Roderick McIver Clerk and Thomas Shannon,
Sheriff.

The sheriff made return of the writ of venire focias to him directed from
the last term of this court with the following return made thereon, to wit,
Came to hand the same day issued and executed except Iredell Williams, James
Bogers and Newton Harris not found, all of whom are free holders or householders
of my county and lawful age in pursuance the following persons were then attending
to wit, Samuel Dickens, Daniel Mading, Michael Clark, Henry N. Coulter, Richard
Tomlinson, William Weaver, Thomas Boyt, John Graves, Peter McCollom, William
Spencer, Western Harris, Benjamin Booth, Alfred Sharp, Thomas Vincent, William
Dean, George Todd and Ebenezer Haltom, and on motion and sufficient cause shown
to the court, Samuel Dickins and Daniel Mading were discharged from further attendance at the present term and Michael Clark discharged until Tuesday next, out
of the remaining number then attending the following persons were then sworn and
charged as a grand jury to inquire into and for the body of the county of Madison
to wit, Henry N. Coulter, Richard Tomlinson, William Weaver, Thomas Boyt, John
Graves, Peter McCollom, William Spencer, Western Harris, Benjamin Booth, Alfred
Sharp, Thomas Vincent, William Dean, George Todd and with Henry N. Coulter their
foreman who thereupon retired to consider of presentments.

On motion David Estes is discharged as a juror until Tuesday next.
John Mc Farland, Evenezer Haltom, Josiah Dilliard and William Wilson were
this day sworn as petit jurors for the term.

Ordered that a precingue election be held at the house of Henry Cassels
on the North fork of Forked Deer river in Madison Co. and that the sheriff
summons Samuel D. Waddell William Knight and Joseph Ainsworth as judges at the ensuing election for Governor member of congress and members of the legislature.

P537   Tuesday Aug. 2nd. 1936
Ordered that the sheriff summon the following to wit, John Hardgraves,
Benjamin W. H. Mederis, Willis, Nichols, Samuel D. Weddill Francis Taylor, Madison
McLaurine, Sugars McLemore, William C. Love Micajah Midyett, James Stalkeep,
Joseph Answerth, Thomas Lacy, David Jarrett, Martin Lorance, Jonathan Walsh Wil-
liam Draper, William Steel, Exekiel B. McCoy, Thomas Henderson John McKinney,
William McClelland, Gilbreath Naill, Stewart Breganes, John Thomas, John D.
Shannon, and Wilie Harris as jurors to serve at the next circuit court holden for
Madison County.

Ordered that the sheriff summon Burwell Butler, John Clark, John Weir,

P537 William Freer, James Tapley, David Jackson, Elish Halefield, John Rosbury, John
Cont. Dunlapk Abner Musgrave, George Grey, Philip Warlick, James Henderson, Joshua
Weaver, Robert Clanton, Henry Marsh, Harrison, Powell, John F. Draper, Joseph
Edwards John Estes, Milton Young Lemuel Hutchins, Isiah Midyett Hazael Hewitt,
Bird Hill and Mathias Deberry to serve as jurors at our next county court held for
Madison County on the first Monday in November next.

An indenture of bargain and sale from Samuel Dickens as attorney in fact
for the Trustees of the University of North Carolina to Jacob H. Port for two
hundred ninety six & 9/10 acres of land was this day produced in open court and
the execution of the same acknowledged by the said Samuel Dickens, to be his act
and deed and ordered to be registered.

An indenture of bargain and sale from Samuel Dickens and atty in fact for
the trustee of the University of North Carolina to James Coldwell for two hundred
and seventy five acres of land was this day produced in open court and acknowledged by the said Samuel Dickens to be his act and deed and ordered to be registered.

Ordered that the following persons be appointed judges of the election to
attend at the several precincts in this county, to wit, Mark Christian, James
Trousdale and Stephen Lacy esc. at Jackson, Thomas Gordon, James McCleary and
Andrew Stewart at Taylors John Thomas, Wm Willburn and Theophilis Sanders at
Weavers Guy Smith John McClelland and Bignal Crook at Poplar Corner, Thomas Reaves
John McKinney and Nathiel Henderson at Mount Pinson and that the sheriff summon
them for that purpose.

Court then adjourned until tomorrow morning 10 O'clock.

J. B. Cross   JP.
H. Haralson   JP.
A. R. Alexander JP.

P538   Wednesday 3rd. August 1825
Court met according to adjournment, Present, Herndon Haralson, John B.
Cross and Adam R. Alexander, Esqr. Justices of the court of Pleas and Quarter
Sessions for Madison County with Roderick McIver clerk and Thomas Shannon, Sheriff
Court then adjourned until tomorrow morning eight o'clock.

John H. Hyde   JP.
J. B. Cross   JP.
Sam Taylor   JP.

Thursday morning August 4th. 1825
Court met according to adjournment, Present John H. Hyde John B. Cross
and Sam Taylor Esquires Justices of the court of pleas and quarter sessions for
Madison County with Roderick McIver Clerk and Thomas Shannon, Sheriff Court then
adjourned until tomorrow morning eight o'clock.

John H. Hyde,   JP.
M Christian   JP.

Friday morning Aug. 6, 1825. Court met according to adjournment. Present-
John H Hyde, and Mark Christian Justices of the court of pleas and quarter session
for Madison County with Roderick McIver Clerk and Thomas Shannon Sheriff.
Court then adjourned until tomorrow morning 10 o'clock.
B. G. Stewart   JP.
Sam Taylor   JP.

Saturday morning Aug 7th. 1825
Court met according to adjournment. Present B, G. Stewart and Samuel Taylor

P538
Cont. Esquires, Justices of the Court of Pleas and Quarter Sessions for Madison County
        Court then adjourned until Monday morning nine o'clock to meet at the
Court house.

                                                H. Haralson   JP.
                                                Wm. Draper   JP.
                                                Robert Lowry   JP.

P539   Monday morning Aug. 8th. 1825
        Court met according to adjournment Present. the Worshipful Herndon Haral-
son Lemuel S. Hunter, William El Butler, William Draper, Green Hill, Robert Lowry
Jesse L Kirk, William Willburn, Minairi Thomas Gordon and Adam R. Alexander, Esqu
ires Justices of the Court of Pleas and Quarter Sessions for Madison County with
Roderick McIver, Clerk, and Thomas Shannon Sheriff.
        Ordered that the hands of Lewis Bond be added to the list of hands allowed
Green Hill, Esquire, as overseer of the road.
        The report of the Jury of view, viewing a road from at or near Col. Thomas
Williamson's from at-er-nearthe mill of said Williamson was this day handed in
and received and ordered that the said Williamson be overseer of said road and th
he be allowed the following hands to cut out and open said road, John Minair
James D. Williamson, William Polk and Bennet Bridges.
        Ordered that David Shepshire Jailor, be allowed the sum of seventy six doll
and twenty five cents and jailor fees and that the county trustee pay the same
after deducting from that sum twenty dollars and twenty five cents the amount of
a note given by said Shepshire to Thomas Shannon Shff . for the old jail out of
any monies not otherwise appropriated.
        Ordered that Thomas Gordon Esq. having proven in open court the killing of
one wolf in the county of Madison over the age of 4 months be allowed a certificate therefore.
        Ordered that Bassell Davis be overseer of the McGuires Ferry Road in the
place of Benjamin Booth from the bridge to Johnson Creek and work all the hands
as far South as Sedon Harris's indluding said Harris and sons and as far West as
Races Creek so as not to enterfere with the hands of any other road.
        Ordered that William Ruleman be overseer of the road from Jones Creek to
McIvers branch and work all the said hands West of said branch so as not interfer
with hands of any other road.
        Ordered that Joseph Shelby be overseer of the Mount Pinson road from Chandl
new bridge on the middle fork of the river to the deep gap and work the follow-
ing hands, to wit, Thomas Carlton and James Matthews, Thos. Shelby's hands, Robert Phelps, William C. Love's hands, William Higgins, Adon Williams and Leonard
Lawhorn, William Toe's hands, minor and Elish Marsh and hands. --Scarborough,
P540 John and Sterling Talley, John Crain and hands, James Tarbutton, James Alexander,
Jesse Wilkon---Parks, Henry N. Coulter, and William W. Berry to keep the same in
repair.
        On motion and petition filed ordered that Jacob Fort, John Andrews, Alfred
Simpson, Lewis Bond, Andrew Hammil and Theophiles Sanders be a jury to view and
mark a road commencing where the road lately marked out by the county court of
Haywood intersects the county line, thence to the McGuire road the nearest and
best way and make report to the next term of court.
        On motion and petition filed ordered that the following persons, towit,
John Arnold Thomas Lofton, William Wright, Herbert Newsom, and Philip Moody be a
jury of view to mark and lay off a road from the road near Major John Arnold by t
way of the Loftons then by the way of Newsoms Mill and intersect the Mount Pinson
road at or near that place and make report to the next term of court.
        Ordered that Thomas Haley be appointed overseer in the place of Henry Butle
from Meridian Creek to the county line and work all the hands above Thomas Mill a

P540 the hands on Clover Creek above Esqr. Dillard.

Ordered that the hands of William Henry and Bassil Davis build a bridge across Johnson's Creek where the McGuire Ferry road crosses the same and open the road through the bottom of said Henry & Davis be appointed overseers of the same.

Upon Satisfactory proof made in open court that R. C. Pruitt is a man of good moral character and more than twenty one years of age it is ordered that the same be entered of record and certified accordingly.

The resignations of Thomas Gordon and Adam R. Alexander Esquires as justices of the peace were this day handed in and received by the court.

Ordered that Larkin Carson and John Gilliam be over seers of the road from Johnsons Creek to the county line, Larkin Carson on the East End and John Gilliam on the West End and work all the hands not subject to work on any other road that they agree to the distance and hands.

P541   Monday Aug. 8th. 1825

Ordered that John McClelland Thomas I Smith Micajah Midyett freeholders in the county of madison lay off to Mes. Hannah Dyer a sufficient portion of the present crop stock and provisions for her support one year and make rs ort to the next term of court.

On motion and petition filed ordered that Reuben Golden have leave to build a mill on Bear Creek being the owner of the land on both sides of the stream.

Ordered that John Mitchell be overseer of the road from Menddian Creek to the Fowler Ferry road and work the following hands William Dean, Moody Mitchell and hands Jacob Hill, Samuel B. Martin and William Harvell.

Ordered that John R. Collier be overseer of the road from Butlers Creek to town and work the hands of R. Chandler, Parks Chandler, Moses Starns,———Reeves, A. L. Martin and hands A. B. Bradford and hands H. Haralson's hands, William Harris hands, Robert Hughes and hands and all the hands living West of said creek South of said road and North of the road crossing at he upper bridges.

William Stotts proves by the oath of Nathen Thomas the killing of one wolf in Madison County under the age of four months.

Administration of all the goods and chattels, right and credits of Joel Dyer, deceased is this day granted to Daniel Meding who thereupon took the oath of an administrator and entered into bond with Champness Meding his security in the penalty of one thousand dollars.

Ransom H. Byrn this day came into open court and took upon himself the execution of the last will and testament of Thomas Byrn deceased, which was produced in open court and proven as the last term of court and thereupon took the oath of an executor and entered into bond with Joseph Cock his security in the penalty of two thousand dollars.

Monday August 8, 1825

A deed of trust from Joel Dyer to Daniel Meding for the use of Sarah J. Dyer was this day produced in open court and the execution of the same together with the interlineations thereon to be made before signing was proven by the oaths of Henry L. Gray and Lewis Boling subscribinh witnesses thereto and ordered to be registered.

An indenture of bargain and sale from Vincent Haralson to Robert Burne for fifty eight and one half acres of land was this day produced in open court acknowledged by the said Vincent Haralson to be his act and deed and ordered to be certified for registration.

A deed of conveyance from James Coldwell to Robert Bunne for forty one and one half acres of land was this day produced in open court and acknowledged by the said James Caldwell to be his act and deed and ordered to be certified

for registration.

P542   A deed of conveyance from Vincent Haralson to Robert Murray for one third part of lot No. 16 in the town of Jackson was this day produced in open court and the execution thereof duly proven by the oath of Herndon Haralson and William Arnold and ordered to be certified for registration.

A deed of bargain and sale from Herbert Newsom to John Nuckles for eighty two acres of land was this day produced in open court and the execution thereof duly proven by the oath of Andrew L. Martin and filed for further probate.

A deed of conveyance from Lee Sullivan to Alexander Braden for six hundred forty acres of land was this day produced in open court and the execution thereof duly proven by the oath of Robert Hughes and John T. Bryon and ordered to be certified for registration.

P543   Monday Aug. 8th. 1825

A deed of conveyance from Robert Murray to James Lee and John Lee for one third part of lot No. 16 in the town of Jackson was this day produced in open court and the execution thereof duly proven by the oath to James Tisdale and John H. Hyde and ordered to be certified.

A deed of conveyance from Lawrence McGuire, William H. Henderson, Charles White, N. T. Perkins and Thomas G. Nixon commissioners for the town of Brownsville to Joseph H. Talbot for lots No. 15, 25, 53 & 105 as designated in the plan of said town was this day produced in open court and the exection thereof duly proven by the oath of Thomas L. Smith & David Shopshire and ordered to be so certified.

A deed of conveyance from the President an Trustes of the University of North Carolina by their attorney in fact Samuel Dickins to Vincent Haralson for acres of land was this day produced in open court and the execution thereof duly proven by the oath of James Caldwell and Andrew L. Martin and ordered to be certified for registration.

A deed of trust from Benjamin Gholson to Joseph H. Talbot was this day produced in open court and duly proven by the oath of William F. Cheter and James Kiser and ordered to be certified.

P544   Monday 8th. August 1825

Robert Lawry this day returns an additional tax list for t e present year which is received and ordered to be recorded.

This day came personally Joseph Cook into open court and made oath that he was in fear of death or some bodily hurt to be done or to be procured to be done to him by Robert Hardwick of the state of Tennessee in the county of Madison and that he does not require surity of the peace against him out of malice or for mean vexation but for the cause aforesaid whereupon a capias instenter was ordered and directed to be issued against the body of the said Robert Hardwick which was done accordingly which capias was returned into open court executed and the said Robert Hardwick came into open court and offered Charles D. McLean, John D. Shannon and Robert H. Wynne as his securities for the peace whereupon the said Robert Hardwick Charles D. McLean, John D. Shannon and Robert Hardwic H Wynne severally acknowledged themselves bound and to one the State of Tennessee the sum of one hundred dollars to be levied for their goods and chattel lands and tenaments but to be void on condition that the said Robert Hardwick keep the peace towards all good citizens of the state of Tennessee and particular towards the person of the said Joseph Cook for and during the term of twelve months and one day from and after this day.

Court then adjourned until tomorrow morning ten o'clock.

                                        H. Haralson JP.
                                        Lim S. Hunter   JP.
                                        John H Hyde   JP.

                Tuesday 9th. day of August 1825
Court met according to adjournment H. Haralson, Lemuel S. Hunter and John H. Hyde, Esquires, Justices of the court of Pleas and Quarter sessions for Madison County and others their fellow justices of the peace for said county

P545   with Roderick McIver Clerk and Samuel Shannon, Sheriff.
                    Tuesday Aug. 9th. 1825

Henry L. Douglass   )
vs.   )   Debt
Richard A. Echols   )

        This cause is continued as of an affidavit of the plaintiff until the
next term of court.

Edmond Jones   )
vs.   )   Covenant
John Barnhart   )

        The parties in this case have leave to take deposition generally by giving
20 days notice of the tim and place of taking the same and the cause continued
until the next term of court.

William Curtice   )
vs.   )   Case
James Foster   )

        This day came the parties aforesaid by their attorneys and the parties
each paying half the cost. It is therefore considered by this court that the
plaintiff recover of the defendant one half the cost in this case and that the
defendant recover of the plaintiff one half the cost and that the defendant and
plff. be in mercy etc.

Henry G. Connolly Wiley B. Dyer   )
vs.   )   Appeal
John Weir   )

        This day came the parties aforesaid by their attorneys and thereupon came
a jury of good and lawful men, to wit, John McFarland Ebenezer Haltom, Josiah
Dillard, William W lson John T. Hutchison, MichaelClark, William C. Mitchell
John Spencer, William Childress, George Goodloe, James Wynne, and William C.
Due who being elected tried and sworn will and truly to try the matters of dispute between the parties upon their oaths do say they find for the plaintiffs
and assess their damages to twelve dollars. It is therefore considered by the
court that the plff. recover of the defendant the damages aforesaid together
with their cost by them about their suit in this behalf expanded & the defendant
in mercy etc.

P546   Tuesday Aug. 9th. 1825
Anthony Epperson   )
vs.   )   Case
Samuel Dickens   )

        This day came the parties aforesaid by their attorneys and the plaintiff
dismisses his suit and confesses judgment for the costs. It is therefore considered by the court that the defendant recover of the plaintiff his cost by
him about his suit in this behalf expended and the plaintiff for his false clamor
in mercy etc.

Reuben McVey   )
vs.   )   Certiorari
Cathalene Cochrane)

        This cause is continued by consent of the parties until the next term of
court.

Samuel Crocket   )
vs.   )   Case
Caldwell G. Wilson)

        This day came the parties aforesaid by their attorneys and thereupon came

P546 a jury of good and lawful men, to wit, John McFarland, Ebenezer Haltom, Josiah
Dillard, William Wilson, John T. Hutchison, Michael Clar, William C. Mitchell,
John Spencer, William Childress, George Goodloe James Wynne, andWilliam C. Due
who being elected, tried and sworn will and truly to try the issue joined between the parties find the issue in favor of the plaintiff and assess the plaintiff damages to ninety one dollars and eleven cents. It is therefore considered
by the court that the plaintiff recover of the defendant the damages aforesaid
by the defendant the damages aforesaid by the jury aforesaid assessed together
with his cost by him about his suit in this behalf expended and the defendant
in mercy etc.

Thomas Shannon   )
vs.   )   Case
John Rutherford   )

William Finney   )
vs.   )   Debt
Gibson Admr. etc.)

        By consent of the parties and with the assent of the court the foregoing
causes are continued until the next term of court for trial.

P547   Tuesday August 9th. 1825

James S. Foster   )
vs.   )   Appeal
William Higgins & A. D. Lawhorn   )
        This day came the parties aforesaid by their attorney and thereupon came
a jury of good and lawful men, to wit, John McFarland, Ebenezer Haltom, Josiah
Dillard William Wilson, JohnT. Hutchison, Michael, Clark, John Spencer William
C. Mitchell. William Childress George Goodloe, James Wynne, and William C. Dew
who being elected, tried and sworn will and truly to try the matters of dispute
between the parties upon their oaths do say they assess the plaintiff damages
to thirty one dollars twelve and a half cents. It is therefore considered by
the court that the plaintiff recover of the defendant the damages aforesaid by
the jury aforesaid assessed together with his cost by him about his suit in this
behalf expended and the defendant in mercy etc. Whereupon a rule was given the
defendant to show cause why they should have a new trial.

Roderick McIver for the use of the State of Tennessee   )
vs.   )   2 Tams
Aemos Warner   )
        This day came the parties aforesaid by their attorneys and the defendant
because he cannot gainsay the plaintiffs cause of action comes into court and
confessed judgment for the sum of fifty dollars. It is therefore considered
by the court that the plaintiff recover of the defendant the said sum of fifty
dollars together with his cost by him about his suit in this behalf expended
and the plaintiff agrees to stay execution herein six months.

Lancaster Glover   )
vs.   )   Appeal
Samuel Bruff   )
        This day came the parties aforesaid by their attorneys and thereupon came
a jury of good and lawful men, to wit, Johm McFarland Ebenezer Haltom, Josiah
Dillard, William Wilson, John G. Hutchison, Michael Clark, John Spencer, William
Childress, George Goodloe, James Wynne John Rutherford, and Elijah Baker, who
being elected tried and sworn will and truly to try the matters of dispute between the parties assess for the plaintiff and assess his damages to nine dollars
and fifty cents. It is therefore considered by the court that the plaintiff

P547recover of defendant the damages aforesaid by the jury aforesaid assessed together with his cost by him about his suit in this behalf expended and the deft in mercy etc.

P548   Tuesday Aug. 9th. 1825

Samuel Gholson)
vs,   )   Certiorari
Isaac Delaney)

Edward Bradbury)
vs.   )   Appeal
William McCaslin)

Archebold S. Lackman)
vs.   )   Case
Benjamin Gholson   )

(John C. McLemore)
(Error vs.   )   Debt
(Samuel D. Weddell)

Elijah Bigelow   )
vs.   )   Debt
John R.Collier & Nathaniel Henderson)
        By the consent of parties and with the assent of the court the foregoing causes are continued until the next term of court.

Joseph & Robert Wood   )
vs.   )   Debt
Benjamin Gholson & Benjamin Deckerd)

The Same)
vs.   )   Debt
The same)
        On affidavit of Benjamin Gholson one of the defendants-- the above causes are continued until the next term of court for trial.

William Johns   )
vs.   )   Debt
Benjamin Gholson)
        On affidavit of the defendant this cause is continued until next term of court.

Charles Carson)
vs.   )   Certiorari
Francis Taylor)
        On affidavit of the defendant this cause is continued until next term of court.
        Francis Taylor was this day released of his fine imposed as a delinquent juror.

P.549 James Vaulx & John C McLemore)
vs.   )   Dertiorari
John B. Cross   )
        This day came the parties by their attorney and thereupon came a jury of good and lawful men, to wit, John McFarland, Ebenezer Haltom. Josiah Dillerd

P.549 William Wilson, John T. Hutchison, Michael Clark, John Spencer William Childress
George Goodloe, James Wynne John Rutherford andElijah Baker who being elected
tried and sworn will and truly to try the matters in dispute between the parties
upon their oaths do say they find for the plaintiff and assess their damages
to seventy nine dollars and ninety two cents. It is therefore considered by the
court that the plaintiff recover of the defendant the damages aforesaid by the
jury aforesaid assessed together with their costs by them about their suit in
this behalf expended and the defendant in mercy etc.

Solomon Russwell)
vs.   )   Attachment, Covenant, writ of inquiry of damages.
Richard Sanders)

    This day came the parties aforesaid by their attorneys and thereupon came
a jury, to wit, John McFarland Ebenezer Haltom Josiah Dillard, William Wilson
John T. Hutchison, Michael Clark, John Spencer, William Childress, George Goodloe
James Wynne, John Rutherford and Elijah Baker who being elected, tried and
sworn, will and truly to inquire of the damages in this case sustained, do
say that they do upon their oaths assess the plaintiff damages to three hundred
and twenty six dollars and ninety three cents by reason of the breech of covenant
assigned in said plaintiffs declaration. It is therefore considered by the court
that the plaintiff recover of the defendant the damages aforesaid in form assessed by the jury aforesaid together with his cost by him about his suit in this
behalf expended and that an order of sale of the property attached issue accordingly etc.

P550   Tuesday Aug. 9th. 1825

Robert H. Wynne& William Arnold Assignee etc.)
for the use of William E. Butler   )
vs.   )   Debt.
Isaac Swan   )

    This day came the plaintiff by their attorneys and the defendant though
solmnly called came not but made default. It is therefore considered by the
court that the plaintiff recover of the defendant his debt of three hundred and
twenty dollars and eleven dollars and 20 cents together with his cost in this
behalf expended etc.

James H. Wilson Jason H. Wilson   )
John Carson   )
vs.   )   Debt
John T. Brown   )

    This day came the parties aforesaid by their attorneys and thereupon came
a jury of good and lawful men, to wit, John McFarland, Ebenezer Haltom, Josiah
Dillard William Wilson, John T. Hutchison, Michael Clark, John Spencer,
William Childress, George Goolce, James Wynne, John Rutherford and Elijah Baker,
who being elect d tried and sworn will and truly to try the issues joined in
favor of the plaintiff and that the deft. hath no set off as in replying to
defendant plea in that behalf hath alledged and that the defendant hath not paid
the debt of one hundred and twelve dollars and fifty cents and assess the plaintiff damages to three dollars and thirty six cents. It is therefore considered
by the court that the plaintiff recover of the defendant the debt aforesaid
with the damages aforesaid in form aforesaid by the jury aforesaid assessed together with his cost by him about his suit in this behalf expended and the deft.
in mercy etc.

P551   Tuesday Aug. 9th. 1825

    John T. Porter   )
    vs.   )   Case
    R. E. C. Dougherty   )

        The parties have leave to take deposition generally by giving twenty days
notice of the time and place of taking the same and the cause in continued until
next term of court for trial to be had thereon.

    William Polk   )
    vs.   )   Debt
    Aquila Davis   )

        This day came the parties aforesaid by their attorneys and thereupon
came a jury of good and lawful men, to wit, John McFarland, Ebenezer Halton,
Josiah Dillard, William Wilson, John T. Hutchison, Michael Clark, John Spencer
William Childress, George Goodloe, James Wynne, John Rutherford and Elijah
Baker wjo being elected tried and sworn will and truly to try the issues joined
upon their oaths do say the find the issues joined in favor of the plaintiff,
that the defendant hath not paid the debt of three hundred and fifty two dollars
as the plaintiff in replying to defendants plea in that behalf hath alleged
and assess the plaintiff damages to $25.00 and that the defendant hath no set
off. It is therefore considered by the court that the plff. recover of the defendant the debt aforesaid with the damages aforesaid by the jury aforesaid in
form aforesaid assessed and also his cost by him about his suit in this behalf
expended and defendant in mercy etc.

    James H. Wilson   )
    vs.   )   Case
    Rice Williams   )

        This day came the deft. by his attorney into open court and the plaintiff
though solmnly called to prosecute in this behalf came not but made default.
It is therefore considered by the court that the plaintiff be non suited and
that the plaintiff be a defendant recover of the plaintiff his cost by him
about his suit in this behalf expended and that the plff. for his false
clamor be in mercy etc.

P552   Tuesday August 9th. 1825

    The State   )
    vs.   )   Affray
    William Allman & Asa Midyett)

        This day came as well the solicitor general on the part of the state as
the defendants in their proper persons and the defendants came into court and
plead guilty to the charges herein brought against them. It is therefore considered by the court that the defendant make their peace with the state by the
payment of five dollars fine each and that the plaintiff recover of the defendant her fine aforesaid together with her cost by her about her suit in this
behalf expended and that the defendant be taken etc.

        An indenture of sale from John Rayder to George Goodloe for thirty nine
acres of land was this day produced in open court and the execution of the same
proven by the oaths of Robert Hughes and John T. Bryan and ordered to be certified for registration.

        An indenture of bargain and sale from John McNairy, Henry M Rutledge and
William E. Butler to Wilson O McRenolds for a lot of ground was this day produced in open court and the execution of the same acknowledged by W. E. Butler
for himself as attorney in fact for the said McNairy & Rutledge to be his act
and deed and ordered to be registered.

        A bill of sale from Thomas Shannon, Sheriff to CharlesR. Abott for a negro
woman named Phillis was this day produced in open court and the execution of the

P.552same acknowledged by the said Thomas Shannon Shff. to be his act and deed and
    ordered to be registered.
          Court then adjourned until tomorrow morning ten o'clock.
                       H. Haralson   JP.
                       L. S. Hunter JP.
                       James L McDonald JP.

P553
                       Wednesday August 10, 1825
        Court met according to adjournment, present, Herndon Haralson, Samuel
S. Hunter and James L. McDonald Esquires and others their fellow Justices of the
Peace in and for the county of Madison withRoderick McIver Clerk and Thomas
Shannon, Shff.

Lancaster Glover)
vs.   )   Appeal
Samuel Bruff.   )
        This day came the defendant into open court and prayed an appeal from
a judgment rendered herein to the next term of the circuit court which was granted him and thereupon entered into bond with Alexander B. Bradford and Joel H.
Dyer his securities in the penalty of fifty dollars.
        An indenture of bargain and sale from the heirs of Isaac Price to William
Price for 1000 acres of land was this day produced in open court and the execution of the same proven by the oath of Austin A. King and James Brown subscribing
witnesses thereto and ordered to be certified.
        A power of attorney from William McWilson and Samuel D. Wilson to Andrew
L. Martin was this day produced in open court and the execution of the same
proven by the oath of William H. Hicks and subscribing witness thereto and ordered to be registered.

State   )
vs.   )   A & B
William Witherspoon)
        Ordered by the court that the solicitor general file a bill of indictment
ex office in above case.

Alexander B. Bradford)
vs.   )   Debt
John Murray   )

Joseph L. Davy   )
vs.   )   Debt
John & Wilson Hutchison)
        By consent of parties the foregoing causes are continued.

John & Wilson Hutchison
vs.
John Murray
        This cause is continued as of an affidavit of pltff.
                   Wednesda 10th. August 1825
P554

George W. Still   )   In covenant
John Barnhart & Archibold S. Lackman)

        This day comes the parties aforesaid by their attorneys and thereupon
came a jury of good and lawful men, to wit, John McFarland, Ebenezer Haltom,
William Wilson, John T. Hutchison, John Spencer, James Wynne, George Goodloe,
John D. Shannon, John Rutherford, Rutherford Robison, John Murray, and Henry
James who being elected, tried and sworn, will and truly to try the issues joined

P554 upon their oaths do say they find the issues in favor of the plaintiff and assess
the plaintiff damages by reason of the defendants non performance of the covenant in plaintiffs declaration mentioned to six hundred and thirty three dollars
and thirty seven and one half cents. It is therefore considered by the court th
that the plaintiff recover of the defendant the damages aforesaid by the jury
aforesaid in manner and form aforesaid assessed together with his cost by him
about his suit in this behalf expended and the defendant in mercy etc.

John Nickoll   )
vs.   )   In covenant.
James H. Wilson, Samuel D. Wilson & Jason H. Wilson.   )

        This day came the parties aforesaid by their attorneys and thereupon came
a jury of good and lawful men, to wit, John McFarland, Ebenezer Halton, Josiah
Dillard, William Wilson, John T. Hutchison, John Spencer, James Wynne George
Goodloe, John D. Shannon Rutherford Robison John Barnhart, and George L. Wynne
who being elected tried and sworn will and truly to try the issues joined between the parties upon their oaths do say they find the issues in favor of the
plaintiff and assess the plaintiff damages by reason of defendants non performance of the covenant in plaintiffs declaration mentioned to twenty five hundred
and fifty dollars, and twenty four cents. It is therefore considered by the
court that the plaintiff recover of the defendant the damages aforesaid by the
jury aforesaid in form aforesaid assessed together with his cost by him about
his suit in this behalf expended and the defendants in mercy etc.

James H. Wilson etc.)
vs.   )   Case
John Murrey   )

        This cause is continued as of an affidavit of the plaintiff until the next
term of court.

P555   Wednesday Aug. 10th. 1825

Thomas Hatton, Administrator of the   )
Estate of Thomas Andrews ,deceased   )
vs.   )   In debt
William C. Love   )

        This day came the parties aforesaid by their attorneys and thereupon came
a jury of good and lawful men, to wit, John McFarland Ebenezer Halton, Josiah
Dillard, William Wilson, John T. Hutchison, John Spencer, George Goodlow John
D. Shannon, Rutherford Robison John Rutherford, John Murrey and Henry James
who being elected, tried and sworn will and truly to try tye issues joined upon
their oaths do say that the defendant hath not paid the remaining debt of six
hundred and five dollars as the plaintiff in replying to defendants plea in
that behalf hath alleged and assess the plaintiff damages by reason thereof
to twenty one dollars, It is therefore considered by the court that the plaintiff
recover of the defendant the remaining debt aforesaid with the damages aforesaid in form aforesaid by the jury aforesaid assessed together with his cost
by him about his suit in this behalf expended and the defendant in mercy etc.

John C. McLemore   )
vs.   )   Indebt
Samuel D. Waddill   )

        This day came the parties aforesaid by their attorneys and thereupon came
a jury of good and lawful men, to wit, John McFarland, Ebenezer Halton. Josiah
Dillard, William Wilson John T. Hutchison, John Spencer, George Goodloe, John
D. Shannon Rutherford Robison, John Rutherford, John Murrey and Henry James

P555 who being elected tried and sworn will and truly to try the issues joined on
their oaths do say they find the issues in favor of the and that the defendant
hath no set off and that he hath not paid the debt of one hundred and forty
eight dollars and dixty cents in the plaintiff declaration mentioned and assess
the plaintiff damages by reason of the detention thereof to five dollars eighty
seven and a half cents . It is therefore considered by the court that the plaintiff recover of the defendant the debt aforesaid with the damages aforesaid by
the jury aforesaid in form aforesaid assessed to gether with his cost by him
about his suit in this behalf expended and the plf. agrees to stay execution
in thi case three months.

P.556   Wednesday 10th. August 1825

John Nicholl   )
vs.   )   In covenant
James H. Wilso, Samuel D. Wilson &   )
Jason H. Wilson   )
          This day came the parties and thereupon the defendants b their attorney
prayed an appeal in the nature of a writ of error to the next circuit court and
produced in open court and power of attorney with the proper certificate of probate from William M. Wilson and Samuel D. Wilson, to Andrew L. Martin and auth-
orizing said Martin to sign their names and affix their seals as security for the
plaintiff s and thereupon entired into bond in open court with the said William
M Wilen and Samuel D. Wilson & John C. Wilson as their securities for the prosecution of said appe l which appeal is granted them accordingly.

Nicholas Willbourn   )
vs.   )   Certiorari
John F. Brown   )
          This day came the defendant by his attorney and the plaintiff though solmn-
ly called came not but made default. It is therefore considered by the court
that the defendant recover of the plaintiff his cost by him about his suit in
this behalf expended and the plaintiff for his false clamor in mercy etcl.

Richard Lyon   )
vs.   )   Certiorari
George W. Curtis   )
          This day came the defendant by his attorney and the plaintiff though
solemnly called came not but made default. It is there considered by thecourt
that the defendant recover of the pla ntiff his cost by him about his suit in this
behalf expended and the plaintiff for his false clamor in mercy etc.

Mathias Deberry   )
vs.   )   Appeal
Jesse L. Harris   )
          This day came the parties aforesaid by their attorney and thereupon came a
jury of good and lawful men, to wit, John McFarland, Ebenezer, Haltom, Josiah
Dillard, William Wilson, John T. Hutchison, John Spencer Wynne George goodloe
John D. Shannon, Henry James, Rutherford Robison nd Charles Brandon, who being
elected tried and sworn will and truly to try the matters in dispute between the
partied upon their oaths do say they find for the plaintiff and assess the plaintiff to three dollars and twelve and halfcents. It is therefore considered by
the court that the plaintiff recover of the defendant and his securities his
damages aforesaid in form aforesaid b the jury aforesaid assessed together with
his cost by him about his suit in this behalf expended and the defendant in mercy.

Wednesday 10th. August 1825

P557 David Jarrett   )
      vs.   )   Debt
      Daniel Ross.   )

The defendant by his attorney comes and dismisses his suit herein at his cost. It is therefore considered by the court that the plaintiff recover of the defendant his cost by him about his suit in this behalf and the defendant in mercy etc.

The Grand Juty impanelled, sworn and charges to inquire in and for the body of the county of Madison this day returns into court the following bills, to wit, a prosentment against John Arnold, and Roderick McIver for an effray one against John Arnold Robert D. Fletcher for an effray one against Jesse Russel and William Nesbett for an effray one against John D. Shannon and Benjamin Mayor for an effray one against William Weatherspoon for assault and battery upon which bills it is ordered by the court that capisses issue commanding etc.

The sheriff failing to come into court and give bond and security as required by the law for the collection of the taxes for the present year and after proclaimation being made at the court house door to have the appointment to come and make it known for all those who wished, Jesse M Hannah was thereupon appointed by the court to collect the taxes for the present year and thereupon came into court and entered into bond with bartholomew G. Stewart, Elijah Jones and Richard Tomlinson his securities in the penalty of five thousand five hundred and fifty six dollars conditioned for the collection and payment of the taxes f for said year.

John B. Raser   )
vs.   )   Case
Jesse Taylor & Christopher Williams   )

The plaintiff has leave to take the deposition of George Shafer and others in the State of Mississippi by giving the opposit party thirty days notice of the term and place of taking the same.

Court then adjourned until tomowwor morning ten o'clock.

                        H. Haralson   J".
                        James L McDonald   JP.
                        Jesse L Kirk   JP.

P558   Thursday August 11, 1825
Court met according to adjournment, present Herndon Haralson, James L McDonald and Jesse L Kirk Esquires, Justices of the Peace and others their fellow justices of Madison County with Roderick McIver Clerk andThomas Shannon Shff.

The State   )
vs.   )   Affray
John Arnold   )
R. McIver   )

This day came as well the solicitor general on the partof the state as the defendants in their proper persons and the defendant plead guilty to the charge here brought against them . It is therefore considered by the court that the defendants eached be fined five dollars and that the plaintiff recover of the defendants her fine aforesaid together with her cost by her about her suit in this behalf expended.

State   )
vs.   )
John Arnold)   Affray

P558   This day come as well the solicitor general on the part of the state
as the defendant in his proper person and the defendant plead guilty to the
charge brought against him. It is therefore considered by the court that the
defendant be find one dollar and that the plaintiff recover of the defendant
her fine aforesaid together with her cost by her about her suit in this behalf
expended.

The State   )
vs.   )   A & B
William Henry   )

        This day came as well the solicitor general on the part of the state as
the defendant in his proper person and the defendant being arraigned upon his
arraigned upon his arraignment plead not guilty to the charge here brought
against his country and thereupon came a jury of good and lawful men, to wit,
John McFarland Ebenezer Haltom, William Wilson, Josiah Dillard, John T. Hutchison Allen C. Mumma, John Spencer John Barnhart, James Brown, John D. Shennon.
Reuben P. T.Stone and Charles Donley who being elected tried and sworn the
truth to speak upon the issue joined do say We of the jury find the defendant
is --guilty as charged in the bill of indictment. It is therefore considered
by the court that the defendant make his peace with the state by the payment
of ten dollars fine and that he plaintiff recover of the defendant her fine
aforesaid together with her cost by her about her suit in this behalf expended.
                    Thursday 11th. August 1825

James S. Foster   )
vs.   )   Appeal
William Higgins & A. D. Lawhorn   )

     This day came the defendants by their attorney and withdrew their motion
by-their-attorneyfor a new trial in this case.

Henry M Clay   )
vs.   )   Debt
Jesse Taylor & Christopher Williams   )

John B. Raser   )
vs.   )   Debt
Jesse Taylor & Christopher Williams   )

     The parties in the foregoing causes have leave to take depositions in
the state of Mississippi by giving the opposite party thirty days notice of
the time and place of taking the same to be read in evidence at the next term
of this court.

The State   )
vs.   )   A & B
William Weatherspoon)

     This day came as well the solicitor general on the part of the state as
rhe defendant in his proper person and the defendant being arraigned upon his
arraignment plead guilty as charged in the bill of indictment. It is therefore
considered by the court that the defendant make his peace with the state by the
payment of five dollars five and that the plaintiff recover of the defendant
her fine aforesaid together with her cost by her about her suit in this behalf
expended and the defendant be taken etc.

Same   )
)
vs.   )   A & B
Same   )

P559   This day came as well the solicitor general on the part of the state as the defendant in his proper person and the defendant being arraigned upon his arraignment plead guilty as charged in the bill of indictment. It is therefore considered by the court that the Plff. recover of the defendant twenty five cents fine together with her cost by her about her suit in this behalf expended and the defendant be taken etc.

P560 The State   )
    vs.   )   Affray
    William Nesbit)

    This day came as well the solicitor on the part of the state as the defendant in his proper person and the defendant being arraigned upon his arraignment plead guilty to the charge here brought against him. It is therefore considered by the court that the defendant be fined one dollar and that the plaintiff recover of the defendant her fine aforesaid together with her cost by her about her suit in this behalf expended and the defendant be taken etc.

    The Grand Jury this day returned into court an indictment against William Henry for an assault and battery also a presentment against Daniel Carr and Allen F. Williams for an affray.

    The State   )
    vs.   )   Affray
    James Fussell)

    This day came as well the solicitor general on the part of the state as the defendant in his proper person and the defendant being arraigned upon his arraignment plead guilty to the charge here brought against him as charged in the bill of indictment. It is therefore considered by the court that the defendant make his peace with the state by the payment of one dollar fine and that the plaintiff recover of the defendant her fine aforesaid with her cost by her about her suit in this behalf expended and defendant be taken etc.

    An indenture of bargain and sale from Henry M. Rutledge and William E. Butler to Benjamin Gholson for a lot of ground in the town of Jackson was this day produced in open court and the execution of the same duly acknowledged by W. E. Butler ordered to be certified for registration.

    Trustee of Madison County)
    vs   )   Motion
    Thomas Shannon & others   )

    On affidavit of the deft. it is ordered that this case be continued till next term of the court.

P561 Joseph Cox
    vs.
    Austin King William Arnold & John T. Brown

    This day came the parties by their attorneys and thereupon the defendants because they cannot gainsay the plaintiffs action in this behalf withdrew their plea and confess judgment in proper person for the sum of three hundred and fifty one dollars and cost of suit. It is therefore considered by the court that the plaintiff recover of the defendants the said sum of three hundred fifty one dollars and his costs in this behalf expended and that defendant be in mercy etc. appeal to the next circuit court prayed by defendants by their attorney who thereupon entered into bond with Robert H. Wynne their security for the prosecution of the same which is granted them accordingly.

P561 William Polk)
   vs.   )   Covenant
Aquila Davis)

    This day came the parties and thereupon the defendant by his attorney
prayed an appeal to the next circuit court and thereupon in open court entered
into bond with Robert H. Wynne and Adam R. Alexander his securities for the
prosecution of the same which appeal is granted him accordingly.

Mathias Deberry)
   vs.   )   Motion for alias fi fa
Washington J.Dewitt)

    Upon affidavit of Joseph H. Talbot attorney for the plaintiff and it appear-
ing to the satisfaction of the court that the fi fa heretofore issued to
Henry County was miscarried and never came to hands of the sheriff of Henry county it is therefore ordered by the court that the plaintiff have leave to send
out an alias fi fa.

    Court then adjourned until court in cause.
                 James L. McDonald JP.
                 Jesse L. Kirk   JP.
                 J. M. Jelks,   JP.

P562   Monday Nov. 7, 1825
    At a court of pleas and quarter sessions began and held in and for the
county of Madison at the court house of said county in the town of Jackson
before Herndon Haralson, William B. Butler, William Atchison James Creer,
Robert Lowery James L. McDonald Jarret M Jelks, David Jarrett, James McCutchen
William Wellburn, Stephen Lacy Lemuel S. Hunter Esquires, Justices of the Peace
for said county on the first Monday November being the seventh day of said
month in the year of our Lord one thousand eighty hundred and twenty five,
present, said Justices of the peace presiding, Roderick McIver, Clerk of said
court and Thomas Shannon Sheriff.

    Daniel Madding the administrator of the estate of Joel Dyer, deceased,
this day returned an enventory of the estate of said decedent together with
an inventory of the amount of sales which is ordered to be recorded.

    Administration of all and singular the goods and chattels , rights and
credits of John R. Collier is this day granted to Elizabeth A. Collier and
Wyett Epps who thereupon took the oath of administratrix and administrator and
entered into bond with Mathias Deberry and Andrew L. Martin their securities
for the due performance of said administration in the penalty of four thousand
dollars whereupon it is ordered by the court that they have atters. of administration accordingly.

    The last will and testament of William Matlock was this day produced
in open court and proven by the oaths of Richard Coop and Jasper Needham
subscribing witnesses to be the last will and testament of thedecedent where
upon came Jonathan Walsh into open court and took upon himself the burthen and
execution of said will until such time as the person named in said will shall
come forward and administrators who thereupon entered into bond with James
Green and Joseph Cox as his security in the penalty of seven hundred dollars..
It is therefore ordered by the court that letters of administration be granted
him with the will annexed.

    Administration of all and singular the goods and chattels, rights and
credits of Robert Granham dec. is this day granted to Stephen Jarmen he having
qualified as administrator and entered into bond in the penalty of sour hundred
dollars with James Creer and John Gartely his securities and it is therefore
ordered that letters of administration issue accordingly.

    A sealed packet containing the last will and testament of Thomas William-
son, deceased was this day produced in open court by David Lane a subscribing
witness to said will and testament who made oath that the same was sealed up

P562and put into his possession and that the same had not been broken open nor
undergone any alteration from the time of sealing the same and thereupon the
said David Lane and Thomas Stallings made oath that said will was signed,
sealed and delivered in their presence as the last will and testament of the
decedant. Whereupon James Williamson and William H. Moore the executors named
in the said will came into open court and took upon themselves the burthen
execution of said will having entered into bond with David Jarrett and James
McCutchen, their securities, and qualified as executor to the said will. It is
ordered that letters testamentory issue accordingly.

P563

Monday November 11, 1825

Drury Bettis having this day applied to court for a license keep an ordinary in this county. It is ordered by the court that he be allowed them
accordingly having entered into bond with John Ridens and Robert H. Wunne
his securities so soon as the taxes and costs are paid.

John Ridens having this day applied to court for a license to keep an
ordinary in Madison County, ti is ordered by the court that he be allowed
them accordingly on payment of the taxes and cost of the same having entered
into bond with drury Bettis andRobert H. Wynne his securities.

Bennet Maxey and John Jackson were this day duly and constitutionally
elected constable in and for the county of Madison Bennet Maxey in Captain
Justices Company and John Jackson in Captain Thomas Smiths company who thereupon came into court and entered into bonds, the said Bennet Maxey with mark
Christian and Mathias Deberry his securities and the said John Jackson with
Robert Lowry and Joshua Cozart his securities in the penalty and with the conditions prescribed by law.

Ordered that John Givens be overseer of the road in the place of Robert
Clanton from Roddy's causeway as far as the said clanton worked and worked
the hands allowed the said Clanton.

On motion and petition filed order4ed that Daniel Ross Nathaniel Henderson
William Williamson Henry Marsh, Daniel Harkins Jr. Thomas Henderson John Mc-
Kinney and John M Johnson or any five of them be a gury of view to mark and
lay off a road from at or near Mr. Nell's when there is a road opened by
ordered of Henderson County Court by the way of Mount Pinson to intersect
the Fowler ferry road leading from Jackson South of the widow Hayles and that
so soon as the road is spaced that the same shall be opened and that John Reid
be overseer of the Meridian line in cutting out said road and that John M
Johnson be overseer from the county line of Henderson to the river and work the
following hands, to wit, Thos. Henderson John Yount, Daniel Harkins, Sr. Daniel
Harkins Jr. John M. Johnson Nathaniel Henderson, Stark Dupey's David Parker,
G. Goodman, Thomas Reaves, Danl. Ross, Wisdom and Sterling Tallys to open the
same. On motion and petition filed ordered that Seymour Spencer Herbert Newsom John Right Robt Duncan, Zachariah Hardridg, Hugh McNight, William McMillan
and James McNight or any five of them be a jury of view to mark a Road from
Butlers Bridge by Newsoms Mill to intersect the road marked off from McNairy
court house toward Jackson at the most suitable point and make report to the
next term of court.

P564

November Monday 7th. 1825

On motion and petition f iled ordered that Charles Robison be overseer of
the road marked out from Jackson toward Brownsville on that part of the road
lying between Jackson and Davis ferry and work the hands of Samuel Ceruthers
said Robisons hands, Leven Benton and hands, James Brown and Hands Lake &
Annour Hands, and that the same road be continued from the river to Johnson
Creek where GeorgeW. Taylor by a former order of court was appointed overseer
and that said Ta lor be allowed the following hands, to wit, Mathias Boon and
hands Davis Robertson and hands, Foster Golden and hands a nd including the

P564hands in the following bounds, running a line from Goldens to the Widow Stanleys
and the road to the river and widow Stanleys hands, Richard H. Burk and hands
and the hands between a line from said Burks to Taylor and the road then North
to the river.

On motion and petition filed it is ordered that Archibold Reid by permitted to alter the road passing through his farm so as to avoid dividing and
direction toward Carrollville so as to shun his farm.

On motion and petition filed it is ordered that John Thomas Jesse Springer
Capt. Savage, William Willbourn, Giles Hudspeth, and John Stockton be jury of view
to mark a road from said Willburns to the South boundary of Madison and make
report to the next term of court!

Ordered that Beverly D. Acree be appointed overseer of the road in place
of John Weir and work the hands allowed said Weir.

Ordered that John Huddleston be appointed overseer of the road from
the East bank of Jones Creek to Ezekiel B. McCoys and work all the hands East
of the creek South of the road and west of said McCoys indluding said McCoys
hands to keep the same in repair.

On motion and petition filed ordered that Joel Massey, William Kendrick
James Alexander Jr. James Alexander Senior and John Guthrie be a jury of
view to mark and lay off a road from some distance on the present road East
of the Bridge on the middlw fork of the river and Pitts Chandler's running
Eastwardly so as to intersect the road leading from Jackson through the Southern
part of Henderson County toward Wayne and make report etc. and that the petitions
lay out the same.

A jury appointed at the last term to view a road from Maj. Arnolds to
intersect the Mount Pinson road this day made report which was receibed by
the court and AdamBarnhart overseer from Arnolds to Newsoms Mill to work the
follosing hands, James A Edwards, John Sandford, Wm. Spencer Sen'r. John Spencer
Jr. Hiram Spencer, Eldridge Newsom, Newit ewsom James M. Newsom, Herbert
Newsom, Vincent Greer, Stokely D. Hays, Reuben McVey, John Arnold, Wm. Rigjt
John W. Wright, John Right, King Carter, John Hobbs, John Mitchell, James
McNight, Wm. Dean. John Thomas Sen. John Thomas Jr. and Thomas Lofton in open-
ing said road and that Pleasant C. Dyol.

P565   Monday Nov. 7, 1825
be overseer from Meridian Creek to Jesse Browns and work all the hands West
of Cobbin branch and that William McMillan, be overseer from Cabbin Branch to
the McNairy County line and work all the hands East of the Cabbin branch on
the South of the river in cuttin out said road.

On motion and petition filed ordered that John Givins William Willburn,
Robert Clanton, Moses Wilson and William Hail be permitted to make an alteration in road from about ½ mile South of the forks of the road leading towards
the mouth of Clover Creek and the road leading by said Clantons to where the
So. boundary of Entry of 274 acres of land entered in the name of the President
and Trustee crosses said road.

The commissions heretofore appointed by the court to contract for the
building of a bridge across the North fork of Forked Deer river this day reported to court that they contracted with Isaac Hopkins for the sum of two
hundred dollars and that the said Hopkins has completed the same according to
contract which was received by the court and the said sum of money to be paid
out of any monies in the treasury not otherwised disposed of.

Ordered that Jerimiah T. Rust be overseer of the road in the place of
Samuel D. Waddell from the North fork of Forked Deer river to the Gibson County
line and work all the hands West of the mouth of Turkey Creek South of Gibson
County line and North of the river and East of the mouth of Waddell's Creek
to keep the same in repair.

Ordered that the double taxes on all taxable property and polls in Madison County be remitted on the payment of the single taxes and cost.

P565   Ordered that William Atchison be released from payment of the taxes on 89 acres of land for the present year.

      Ordered that William Thetford be released from paying tax 160 acres of land as charged to him for the present year.

      Ordered that Baptist McNab be released from the taxes on 90 acres of land as charged for the present years taxes.

      Ordered that Alexander McCaba be released from the taxes on 520 acres of land as having been twice listed for the present year.

      Ordered that William Nash be released from taxes on 500 acres part of 750 acres, as having been given in and paid by Deloach for the present year.

P565   Monday November 7th. 1825

      Ordered that Abel Willis, Duncan McIver, andRobert H. Hibbits or any two of them be appointed to settle with James L McDanald Guardian for the heirs of Robert Moore, deceased for the present year and all arrearages that remain unsettled and make report to the next court.

      Ordered that James L. McDonald, Robert H. Hebbits and William Draper be appointed to settle with Duncan Mc Iver, Administrator of the estate of William Griffith, deceased, and make report to the next term of court.

      An indenture of bargain and sale from Duncan McIver to Wilham Seely for three hundred acres of land was this day produced in open court and the execution of the same proven by the oath of James L McDon old and Thomas N. Giles and ordered to be certified for registration.

      A deed of trust from Micajah Turner to Richard H. Burke was this day produced in open court nd acknowledged by the said Turner to be his act and deed and ordered to be so certified.

      An indenture of bargain and sale from H. M. Rutledge andWilliam E. Butler to John Barnhart for one acre and a quarter of ground in the town of Jackson was this day produced in open court and acknowledged b the said William E. Butler for himself and as atty in fact for Henry M Rutledge to be his act and deed and ordered to be certified for registration.

      An indenture of sale from James Brown to Mathias Deberry for eighty acres of land was this day produced in open court and the execution of the same by the oath Thomas Shannon and by having proved the handwriting of Samuel Taylor deceased a subscribing witness thereto to be the ac deed of said James Brown and ordered to be certified for registration.

      A deed of trust from Edmond Jones to Samuel Dickesn was this day produced in open court with the schedules thereto annexed and proven by the oath of Albert A Hale a subscribing witness thereto the probate of John C. Jones being heretofore taken it is ordered to be certified for registration.

      An indenture of sale fromThomas Brown to James Montgomery for fifty acres of land was produced in open court and proven by the oath of John C. Gillespie a subscribing witness and filed for further probate.

      A bill of sale from Jason H. Wilson to Lewis Needham was proven in open court by the oath of Bartho omew O. Stewart and ordered to be registered.

      An indenture of sale from Lemuel S. Hunter to Thomas Harrington William Wilson and Young E. Wilson was this day produced in open court and the execution of the same acknowledged by the said Lemuel S. Hunter to be his act and deed and ordered to be registered.

P566   Monday Nov. 7th. 1825

      An indenture of sale from William E. Butler to John Mitchell for seventy acres of land was this day produced in open court and the execution of the same acknowledged by the said William E. Butler to be his act and deed and ordered to be certified for registration.

      A transfer of a plot and certificate of surving from Jacob Miller to James Wallin for fift y acres of land was this d y produced in open court and the transfer thereon proven by the oath of James Andrews and James D. Williamson

P566 on and ordered to be so certified.

A plot and a certificate of survey for 266 acres with a transfer of the same indorsed thereon from Burd Hill and Thomas Lofton to Williamson B. Lofton was this day produced in court and the transfer acknowledged by the said Burd Hill and Thomas Lofton and ordered to be so certified.

Ordered that Alexander B. Bradford solicitor be allowed the sum of fifty dollars for exofficio services for the present year.

Ordered that Thomas Shannon Sheriff be allowed fifty dollars for ex-officio service for the present year.

Ordered that Roderick McIver Clerk be allowed the sum of forty dollars for ex-officio services for the present year.

Ordered that Roderick McIver be appointed over seer of the road from the line of the corporation to the bridge and the creek below Herndon Haralson and work all the hands heretofore allowed John R. Collier.

John McGill comes into open court and makes oath of killing a wolf in Madison County over four months old.

William Atchison proves the killing of a wolf in Madison County over four months old which ordered to be certified.

Ordered that William Kendrick be appointed overseer of Roses road in the place of John M Johnson and work the former hands.

Ordered that James Alexander Senr. be released from the taces in 140 acres of land for the year 1825.

P567   Monday November 7th. 1825

This day came into court Wilson O McReynolds and applied to have William F. Step aged about sixteen years and John Step aged about fourteen year two orphan boys bound to him to learn the art and mystery of the house carpenters business and it is accordingly done and thereupon came the said Wilson O McReynolds into open court with   his securities and give bond conditioned as the law directs to Herndon Haralson Chairman of said court for the fathful performance of his suty to school educate and learn said apprentices the art and mystery of a carpenter etc.

Court then adjourned until tomorrow morning 9 o'clock.

                                    H. Haralson   JP.
                                    William Draper   JP.
                                    James L McDonold   JP.

www.ingramcontent.com/pod-product-compliance
Lightning Source LLC
Chambersburg PA
CBHW081428270326

41932CB00019B/3131

* 9 7 8 0 7 8 8 4 9 0 7 9 8 *